Becoming a
Family Counselor

Becoming a
Family Counselor

A Bridge to Family Therapy Theory and Practice

Thomas W. Blume

WILEY

JOHN WILEY & SONS, INC.

Published by John Wiley & Sons, Inc., Hoboken, New Jersey.
Published simultaneously in Canada.

For general information on our other products and services please contact our Customer Care Department within the United States at (800) 762-2974, outside the United States at (317) 572-3993 or fax (317) 572-4002.

Wiley also publishes its books in a variety of electronic formats. Some content that appears in print may not be available in electronic books. For more information about Wiley products, visit our web site at www.wiley.com.

Library of Congress Cataloging-in-Publication Data:
Blume, Thomas W.
   Becoming a family counselor : a bridge to family therapy theory and practice
/ by Thomas W. Blume.
         p.   cm.
   Includes bibliographical references.
   ISBN-13: 978-0-471-22138-8 (cloth)
   ISBN-10: 0-471-22138-4 (cloth)
   1. Family psychotherapy.   2. Family counseling.   3. Family counselors.   I. Title.
   RC488.5.B58   2006
   616.89'156—dc22
                                                      2005019109

Printed in the United States of America.

10 9 8 7 6 5 4 3 2 1

Chapter 3

The Field Matures   73

Chapter 4_____
Behavior: Learning, Habits, and Reinforcement   **109**

Chapter 5

Organization: Planning, Decision Making, and Action   **141**

Chapter 6

Narrative: Language, Culture, and Identity   **179**

Chapter 10_____

The Ethical Family Counselor   **297**

Chapter 11

Future Directions for Family Counseling

Over the past 25 years, I have seen tremendous change in the family therapy field and have found my own perspective changing as well. I remember teaching about social constructionist understandings of families in the early 1990s when I was not clear in my own mind what these new theories meant, and I went through a period when I found much of the literature confusing. This book grew out of my experience teaching introductory courses in couple and family counseling and supervising individually trained counselors as they incorporated family work into their agencies and practices.

I wrote this book for three reasons: First, professors, students, and mid-career professionals need an introductory text that clearly and accurately reflects the family therapy literature in its postmodern era—the years since approximately 1980. Second, the field needs a text that reaches beyond the family therapy literature to incorporate research and theory from related academic disciplines such as social and developmental psychology, family studies, and sociology. Finally, introductory texts have become so complex, drawing on over 50 years of literature, that students may be overwhelmed. Having chosen to study family therapy because of its overall goals and systemic principles, students founder on the shoals of their introductory textbooks. The message many students take away from their readings is, "It's impossible to know what you're doing if you work with families." I have tried to present a more encouraging picture, working toward goals of integration and clarity in choosing and presenting material.

I deliberately rejected the idea that this should be a comprehensive reference book. Instead, I have limited my citations, focusing on representative works that will give the introductory reader a sense of how the literature fits together. I also rejected the goal of organizing the material according to the conventional "Major Models of Family Therapy" format. The complexity of the most widely accepted models, with their overlapping and competing concepts, is confusing for a reader who is new to the field. To simplify the presentation and clarify the issues, I have imposed on the family therapy literature my own template—a taxonomy of theoretical and practical options, organized by the acronym BONES, that focuses on a small number of recurring themes that appear repeatedly in classic and contemporary models.

Part I of the book is an overview of family counseling. Chapter 1 provides an orientation to the field, including a partial transcript of a session that illustrates the complexity and the underlying organization of family-level intervention. Family work is presented as both connected to and distinct from approaches that focus on the individual. Professional identity issues are identified for those who plan to become specialized as family therapists or counselors. Chapters 2 and 3 offer an integrated historical view of family therapy, including summaries of several well-known approaches. Chapter 2 introduces a social constructionist perspective and applies that perspective to the social and professional context of family intervention. Examples represent the theorists and practitioners who created the new professional field of family therapy in the middle of the twentieth century. Chapter 3 examines developments in the field after

1980, with an emphasis on the contributors who introduced feminist and postmodernist perspectives.

Part II of the book presents a more detailed analysis of family-level issues and family-level intervention. Chapters 4 through 8 highlight the various ways in which different theorists and practitioners have integrated the five themes identified in my taxonomy: Behavior, Organization, Narrative, Emotion, and Spirituality (BONES). Each of these chapters begins with a case study, followed by an integrative review of theoretical and research literature, and ends with the implications of the chapter theme for engaging with couples and families, assessing their needs, designing and implementing an intervention program, and evaluating outcomes.

In Chapter 4, relationships are seen as contexts created by the learned behaviors of individuals. Behavioral (B) understandings are shown to have broad relevance and power for addressing issues related to couples' and families' acquisition and transmission of skills, knowledge, and behavior patterns. In Chapter 5, organizational (O) patterns are emphasized. The reader is offered multiple ways of understanding, recognizing, supporting, and altering patterns in couple and family relationships. In Chapter 6, the concept of narrative (N) is used as a window into sociocultural and cognitive views of meaning-making in relationships. Readers are offered a variety of language-based techniques for engaging with couples and families and helping them to change. In Chapter 7, emotion (E)—a theme missing from many family therapy models—is explored from multiple perspectives. Relational interventions focus on emo-tional contact and emotional competence. Finally, in Chapter 8, the recently rediscovered theme of spirituality (S) is presented as possibly the oldest professional orientation to couple and family work and as one that is applicable to many kinds of relationship issues.

Part III addresses the implications of a family perspective for the student or mid-career professional. Chapter 9 addresses the personal challenges of family work, using an in-depth case study to demonstrate emotional and intellectual challenges. Chapter 10 examines issues of ethical practice when practitioners and clients are viewed in systemic and relational context. And Chapter 11 offers reflections that may help the reader to stay in touch with what will happen in the future of family counseling.

The book is organized to emphasize integration and is designed to facilitate learning through application. Boxes explore issues in greater depth, and every chapter offers suggested individual and group activities as well as selected readings for further study. Transcripts and summaries of fictionalized cases are used to bring abstract concepts into greater focus, and the connection between theorizing and acting is highlighted throughout. Readers are encouraged to find their own connections to the material and to identify theories and practices that seem compatible with their professional and personal identities. Ethics codes are included for the American Association for Marriage and Family Therapy, the American Counseling Association, and the International Association for Marriage and Family Counseling.

My experience in the family counseling field dates from 1978–1979 when, as a graduate student, I was given the opportunity to be the director of the Second Family Therapy Network Symposium in College Park, Maryland. In those days, it was possible to have a personal family therapy library that included nearly all the works in print. I was fortunate to have as my teacher and guide the visionary Charles H. Simpkinson, who had such a library—and who knew many of the authors personally. From Chuck I gained an appreciation of the field as a work in progress—a shared struggle against the problems that had stymied generations of helpers. During that period I was also challenged by the experience of working with Richard Simon, whose passion for new ideas was an inspiration. I have also been fortunate, in my years as a doctoral student at Texas Tech University and more recently in professional organizations, to study and collaborate with many others whose names have become well known in the field. I am especially grateful to Harv Joanning, whose openness to new ideas and dedication to inquiry brought me in contact with innovators in the field, and Brad Keeney, who challenged my understandings and connected me with postmodern thought.

I have learned not only from academic studies, however, and I owe thanks for many of my personal and professional understandings to my wife and frequent collaborator, Libby Balter Blume. My three sons, Nathan, Sean, and Wesley, have been collaborators in a different way, directly and indirectly challenging my assumptions about parenting. I was also fortunate to have had the experience of growing up in a rather large extended family; living close to two sets of grandparents; and observing the joys, pains, and dramas that unfolded across the generations.

I was fortunate to spend several years teaching young children, and they taught me that the individual is an illusion—we are all part of something larger than ourselves. As a beginning family therapist, I was privileged to work with Emily Brown, who modeled professional dedication, excellence, and teamwork. I have been inspired by many wise and challenging professors. I want to particularly acknowledge Russ Crane, Judith Fischer, Steve Jorgensen, Greg Lehne, Ted Sarbin, Gwen Sorrell, Ruth Uhlmann, and Janet Weaver. I am deeply indebted for the feedback from colleagues and students who read draft chapters of the book, especially Dan Austin, Chuck Cole, Ross Flynn, Barbara Gambino, Melissa Elliott Griffith, Cora Haskins, and Hillary Jennings. Nell McKay was an invaluable source of support, handling many production details, and along with Pat Faircloth performed critical research tasks. I also want to acknowledge the hundreds of students and clients—and their families—who have enriched my understandings of human relationships.

Finally, I want to thank Oakland University, who supported this project with a sabbatical leave and administrative assistance, and Tracy Belmont, my Wiley editor, without whose optimism and support this book would not have come into existance. This has been a team effort, but in the end, I am solely responsible for errors and omissions.

INTRODUCTION

Orientation to Couple and Family Counseling

Before we begin to examine the process of becoming a couple and family counselor, I would like to clarify what that means. This is similar to something I do with couples and families—as we begin to work together, I often interrupt the flow of conversation to compare our interpretations of a word or verify that we are talking about the same thing.

I'm going to start with an assertion of fact: The words *couple, family,* and *counseling* have meanings for you. I can't be sure what your meanings are, although I know that for many people the word *family* invokes stereotyped images of households, each consisting of two biological parents and their children. *Counseling* invokes, for many people, stereotypes of a professional sitting in an office participating in thoughtful, empathic one-on-one conversations. And the word *couple* is notable because of what it is not—counseling and therapy literature usually refers to helping *marriages,* not couples. By the end of this book, each of these words will have some added meanings. The phrase *couple and family counselor* describes a wide range of possibilities that we will explore.

Just as with a family who comes to me for help, I can't guarantee that we will immediately "be on the same page" regarding the topics we discuss. As I hear a family's story, I gradually replace my initial impressions—often based on stereotypes—with more realistic images of the unique, fascinating, and challenging relational world that particular family inhabits. I'd like you to take a similar approach to learning about the unique, fascinating, and challenging relational world of the couple and family counselor.

People often seem to learn best from stories. In Chapter 1, I'll tell stories about family counselors as individuals. In Chapter 2, I'll tell stories about family counselors as a group; how they came together, how the group formed its identity, and who the celebrities were during those exciting years. Chapter 3 continues the story to the present day as the group has found its identity threatened by internal differences and is resolving the problem by learning to live together and integrate perspectives. Once we have skimmed the field in this way, we'll be ready to examine it in more depth—the goal of Part II.

Couple and Family Counselors: Individual Portraits

A varied group with a shared commitment and some shared skills and understandings.

Objectives

In this chapter, you learn to:

1. Distinguish family counseling from other forms of helping.
2. Recognize the complexity of couple and family interaction.
3. Appreciate the contribution of basic counseling skills in effective family work.
4. Recognize the need for specialized family counseling skills.
5. Make sense of credentialing options for couple and family counselors.

1

Chapter

Introduction

This book is designed for people who seek to (1) help couples and families with their relationships; (2) help individuals with educational, emotional, behavioral, health, career, or other issues that are somehow interconnected with their relationships; and in some cases (3) change something about society that is interconnected with relationships. The statement, "I am a family counselor" is a statement that involves elements of competence, identity, and choice. There are many different things that might be meant by such a statement, so we need to define and contextualize our terms and examine the options you'll have if you choose to cross the bridge into this territory.

Some Definitional Issues

One of the core concepts that will be stressed throughout this book is the power of language—the ability of interconnected patterns of words and stories (*discourses*) to shape human realities. What am I hoping to accomplish with my word choices? Let's look at some examples:

Couple versus Marriage
There are many issues that any two people living together might have to resolve. They may attempt to share economic and other household responsibilities in an equal manner, or they may organize responsibilities by role ("The dishes are your job, I only do outside tasks."). They may or may not share responsibilities for child rearing (taking care of a roommate's child is not an unusual arrangement). The thing that seems to set some friendship or living-together arrangements apart from others is the degree of commitment that is involved in being defined as a couple—whether married or not. Implied in the word (couple) is an expectation that two people are no longer making decisions as individuals, that they are somehow influencing each other's choices and will be held responsible for each other's behavior. This intensity of interdependence, more

than legal status or the presence or absence of sexual activity, seems to make these relationships special and call for their special treatment. Whether or not a couple lives together, it often makes sense to provide help to them as a unit rather than individually.

Counseling versus Therapy

The distinction between counseling and therapy is not clear, but the connotations of these two words may influence the attitudes of helpers and their clients. The word therapy seems most often to be connected with services that are given to someone who is sick or injured, or who has a dysfunction or deficiency of some kind: physical therapy, chemotherapy, radiation therapy, estrogen replacement therapy. It would be inconceivable that a head of state would introduce someone as "one of my most trusted therapists." "One of my most trusted counselors," on the other hand, is a comprehensible introduction. A counselor is someone who offers expertise and support to those whose functioning is good but not all it could be: investment counselor, career counselor, nutritional counselor. The term implies respect, caring, and competence.

A colleague once remarked that people in his community seemed to prefer saying that they were getting counseling instead of therapy, and as a result many clinics called themselves "counseling centers" regardless of the professional identities of their staff. In the case of work with families, however, the "therapy" word seems to have become popular along with another term, "mental health," and both words imply that people seek help because they are "ill." This connotation is problematic. Most people can use help in their lives at particular times; they are not mentally ill, but they are suffering. What professionals and volunteers do, in their efforts to help people, seems to have less to do with titles than with attitudes and beliefs toward helping. For me, the preference for the word *counseling* is less about the economics and politics of the service delivery system than it is about what I want to say about the work I do. I used to think I was "fixing" families, and I now see myself as collaborating with them to provide whatever help I can offer.

Cultures of Helping

I wrote this book with a broad audience in mind. Therefore, readers may have a variety of terms to describe the people with whom they work—they may be patients, parishioners, prisoners, or pupils. I will be using the word *client* which, although it doesn't communicate all the nuances of a counseling relationship, is widely accepted and has special associations that I find helpful in the practice of couple and family counseling.

The first association has to do with a *contractual relationship*. A client, whether the setting is the advertising industry or the practice of law, is a person who hires a professional to perform complex services that must conform to both the client's expressed wishes, the professional's best judgment, and the ethical standards of the profession. The term *consumer* is less appropriate because it derives from an economic setting in which people are continuously shopping and there is no commitment involved. The other association has to do with the idea of a *group identity*. A client can be a group of people or a legal entity (such as the state of Massachusetts). The medical metaphor of patient, in which services are delivered patient by patient, is inappropriate when a professional sees the problem and the need for change as shared by the group.

A Day in the Practice of a Couple and Family Counselor

It's a typical day in the office of Sheila Nakamoto, family counselor. She has a variety of active cases: people who come in as frequently as twice a week or as rarely as once every 3 months. Today she has seen two couples; one pair are contemplating a commitment ceremony and the other pair are contemplating divorce. She has met with two troubled adolescents and their parents; the first, a 17-year-old boy, was referred because he made suicide threats, and the second, an angry 13-year-old girl, had stayed out all night several times in the previous month. She has worked with a divorced dad who is planning how to introduce his 4-year-old son to his new love, and she's seen an adult sibling group who are working on their relationships following the recent deaths of both parents. It's been a challenging day, one that has kept her on her toes, but the day isn't over yet. She still has to conduct a first session with Sarah Baxter and her family. We'll use this case to get a feel for Ms. Nakamoto's work.

Ms. Nakamoto considers herself a family counselor (or family therapist) because her practice has two special characteristics. First, she often works with people who come in identifying their problem as a relationship problem: family planning, sexual difficulties, couple conflict over retirement plans, discipline, sibling conflict, and parental concern over a young adult's lifestyle are issues that may present themselves. But there's a second reason: even when she receives calls from people who aren't identifying their concerns in relationship terms, she chooses to understand their issues in a relationship context. In many cases, she will organize sessions with all of the parties she believes are part of the interaction, but family counseling is not defined as much by who is in the room as by "who is in the counselor's head." Family therapy with one person has a long and proud history.[1]

The Baxter/Klein family are fictional. I created them, just as a screenwriter or novelist might, out of bits and pieces of my clinical experience. In this case, though, the goal is not entertainment but illustration. I wanted to create a family scenario that showed the complexity of the issues a family counselor faces when one individual's problems—Sarah's depression and school failure—are viewed in context.

The Baxter/Klein Case

Nineteen-year-old Sarah Baxter came home last weekend in the middle of her second year at Midwestern State University, suffering from a recent onset of depression and refusing to take the medication prescribed at her student health center.

Ms. Nakamoto typically asks for several family members to be present for a first meeting. She likes to see how people interact, and she wants to set the expectation right away that most problems will be seen as somehow belonging to the group rather than an individual. Because she asked on the phone, "who else in the family should be part of our work?" rather than the more customary "who else lives in the home?" she found out about Sarah's grandmother who was her primary caretaker in the preschool years, when her parents divorced and who continued to provide a second, after-school, and vacation home after her mother remarried. So the first session will be attended by Sarah; her mother, Sally Klein, a 38-year-old part-time secretary from a White Baptist family; her stepfather, Ben Klein, a 42-year-old Jewish warehouse manager; and Sally's divorced mother, Dolores Simpson, 63, who recently retired from a nursing career. Sarah's older sisters Kelly and Melissa won't be there; Kelly, 21, is at school in another state, and Melissa, a 25-year-old mortgage broker, said she couldn't get time off from her job. Sarah's father and stepmother will be brought in for a separate session. They could have been invited this time, but Ms. Nakamoto chose initially to focus on the mother's side of the family.

Stakeholders and Expectations

Ms. Nakamoto is asking herself in anticipation of the session, "What do these people want from me?" Actually, a more accurate question might be, "What different things will the different people in the room want from me?" or even "Who are the stakeholders in this counseling process and how can I address all of their concerns?" Multiple stakeholders are always involved, even if a counselor has only one person in the room, and Ms. Nakamoto wants to be aware of—but not be controlled by—their different goals.

She knows that one of the stakeholders in this case is the University—Sarah was a referral from the campus Counseling Center. Another is Midwestern Mutual, the health insurance company that will be asked to pay for the counseling. A third is the family's extended family and immediate community—their friends and neighbors, religious group(s), and others who have supported them through their family life. The state is

---

[1] See, for example, Szapocznik, Foote, Perez-Vidal, Hervis, and Kurtines (1989).

a stakeholder as well. It issues licenses to helping professionals because the community wants to reduce the toll of emotional and behavioral problems and increase the happiness and productivity of all its citizens. All of these stakeholders are likely to agree that Sarah's well-being is the primary concern, even though they may also have some special goals.[2]

But in addition to these "outsiders," all the individuals in the family may be expected to have their own agendas, based to a great extent on their different positions in the world, and their special goals are going to influence the process. Let's listen in to some of their preadmission thoughts:

SARAH: *I hope that this counselor isn't like some of the nontalking, robotic note takers I had to go see when I was in high school.* I'm not the one with the problem here. *I just got tired of being in school when I don't know what I want to do, and my stupid stepfather wouldn't let me drop out as long as I was getting up and going to class every day. My parents are the ones who need help!* All Mom has done since I went away to school is call me three times a day to tell me how much she misses me. If she's that lonely, she should leave Ben and go back to school herself—*I know she wanted to be a math teacher, and she'd be good at it.* He wouldn't even miss her. I bet he wouldn't notice she was gone till he ran out of bottled water and granola bars.

BEN: *I hope this counselor can drum some sense into Sarah.* That kid has never had the drive of her sisters. *I don't know how she thinks she's ever going to be able to make it in the world, unless she thinks she'll find some hardworking guy like her mother did who'll support her. Things have gone straight downhill in Sarah's life* since Sally cut back to part time. *I don't know what happened to Sally, she seemed to be such a level-headed person and then she snapped or something when Sarah started high school.* At least if Sarah stays home Sally will have something to do so she's not depressed.

SALLY: *I hope that this new counselor can finally get to the root of whatever's been troubling Sarah.* She's always been too sensitive for the real world, and I had to quit work when she was in high school just to help her manage her life. She reminds me of myself, *looking for someone to lean on all the time. I'm really worried about Ben—he really doesn't understand Sarah, and I think he'd leave me if Sarah stayed at home till she's 28 like the neighbors' daughter. Actually, he's been so preoccupied for the past couple of years* I really am worried about our marriage; *maybe this is a place we can talk about that once Sarah is straightened out.*

DOLORES: *I just wish Sally hadn't remarried so fast and had found someone who really appreciated her children.* Ben's been a good provider, but he has about as much sensitivity as a lug wrench. If Sarah hadn't had me to help out, I don't know how she would have made it this far. I'm going to see if she can move in with me; *I think that Sally and Ben are headed for divorce, and the last thing Sarah needs is dealing with them yelling at each other and keeping her awake at night.*

I have highlighted some thoughts that foreshadow ways in which family members will attempt to influence the counseling process. On one hand, Sarah, her mom, and Dolores are on the same track, in a way, blaming the problem on Ben and how things have changed since he joined the family. Ben and Sarah, on the other hand, agree that Sally is going through a hard time. However, each of them blames Sally's problems on the other one. Like many young adults, Sarah is worried about her parents. She can see that her mother is "stuck in the past," and she's hoping to give her a boost to move on with her life. And Ben, a typical stepfather, has dedicated himself to being the disciplinarian in the family. Sally, for her part, illustrates a common response among parents whose children have problems in school. Since Sarah entered high school, Sally has identified with her problem child and she is having a hard time separating their identities and needs. Dolores, like many grandparents, has times when she is critical of both parents and thinks she could do better.

---

[2] Later in the book, we address special kinds of cases where the legal system, managed-care system, and other stakeholders are more active in directing the goals of counseling.

Working with Multiple Clients

This session has the potential of being a frustrating hour or hour and a half, and thoughts of sessions such as this could keep some people from choosing to be family counselors. Only part of the story will come out in the first session, and what is said may be more opinion than fact. The choices the counselor makes during this first session—the questions she asks and the ways in which she responds to what people say—will shape the process, and she'll want to be *intentional* about those choices. Fortunately, because Ms. Nakamoto is an experienced practitioner with a wealth of specialized training, she isn't anxious about the various twists and turns the case may take. She knows many ways of working with a family and she's pretty sure she can get things back on track if there's a temporary setback.

Focus

Even in an individual counseling session there are choices to make. If seen by herself, Sarah might bring up her feelings about Ben, her concerns about her mother, her sense of being ignored or compared with her sisters, and dozens of other topics. A single interviewee normally presents so much information in one hour that it can't all be explored at once and some things have to be deferred. Some counseling approaches (e.g., person-centered) emphasize trusting the process and believing that anything of importance will come up again and again until it's dealt with. Other approaches (e.g., cognitive and behavioral) emphasize choosing the issues that will be addressed and keeping the process focused on those that seem to have the greatest potential for change. Many individually oriented counselors would be fearful that the "truth" will not be revealed unless Sarah has the opportunity to talk in a private session.

With multiple individuals, interviewing them one at a time could eventually bring out all the elements of a complex story. But there's a risk—a virtual likelihood, in fact—that they wouldn't sit passively for the six or eight sessions that it might take to get around to all the stories. Therefore, the family counselor generally starts to work with the family before all the

perspectives have been explored in depth, making theory-informed guesses about what is happening in the couple or family and what they need to do to improve their relationships.

In the Baxter/Klein family's case, Ms. Nakamoto quickly put together several theory-informed guesses:

- The *stepfamily formation process* has been incomplete and Sally and Ben's relationship needs more attention (Whiteside, 1989).
- There is a set of interlocking *relationship triangles*—we may think of them as shifting coalitions—that make family members feel pushed and pulled by each other (Kerr & Bowen, 1988).
- There are conflicts over childrearing strategies, because Sally and Ben have *different parenting orientations* (Haley, 1976), and Dolores is likely to have opinions as well.
- Sarah is the last child left at home, and therefore her imminent departure—what is sometimes called the *empty nest syndrome*—might represent a spiritual crisis for a family whose primary reason for existance came from the daily activities of parenting (Frankl, 1984).
- Gender is somehow implicated in these relationships. With a boy, the family would have been less likely to show a *centripetal pattern* (Beavers and Hampson, 2003) that pulls young adults back rather than encouraging them to leave.

I think of these as different paths or threads that a counselor could follow. The further Ms. Nakamoto goes down any one of these paths, the harder it will be to go back and explore another one. In the first session, she will try to explore a little bit of each one, thus keeping her options open.

Directive Style

In the hour and a half that she has set aside for this first session, Ms. Nakamoto will act differently from the passive, empathic stereotype of a counselor. She is likely to tell the family who she wants to hear from and to whom that person should speak. She may put words into people's mouths, and she may ask them to repeat themselves or to rephrase something. She believes that her effectiveness depends on building a sense that her office is a place where it is safe to acknowledge reality, even when the reality is scary and confusing. To that end, she'll try to show herself as strong, sensitive, and resilient. The session opens:

SHEILA:[3] *Ben, you were the one who called me, would you mind saying* what you see happening *that* you felt *needed my help?*

Even though Ben has been given permission to go first, this does not imply that his version of the story has any greater validity than any other and the idea of multiple perspectives is clear from the outset.

BEN: *I was sitting down to lunch with my wife the other day, and we were interrupted with a phone call from this counselor, I think her name was Dr. West, telling us that Sarah was at the University clinic. Things have been rocky the whole year and a half Sarah's been away at school. Her mother's moping around, the house is a mess, I have to come home after a hard day at work and wait for dinner because Sally's been on the phone with Sarah, and I don't think that Sally's handholding is helping. They talk about her assignments, they talk about the boys Sarah's met, they even decide together what movies Sarah will go to see with a date.*

Ben is responding to part of what was asked. He's saying what he saw happening, but the story is starting to look like it could take a while to get to the crucial question—why is the family coming for help NOW?

SHEILA: *Excuse me for interrupting, but I think I'm getting more information than I can handle right now. You said the University counselor called, and I think you were about to tell me what the reason was?*

---

[3] When a transcript appears in this book, I will often use first names so as to more clearly identify the person to whom I am referring. In practice, the use of first names, titles, and family names must be carefully considered as part of sensitivity to race, class, gender, and culture.

Right away the rules are being clarified—"I am in charge, and I will try to help you tell the story so that you make your point."

SALLY: *He always does that, I can't ever get him to make a point.*

Sheila ignores this comment as a potential distraction, filing the information away without letting it interrupt the flow. If the whole session starts to involve this kind of bickering, she'll jump in.

SARAH: *Mom, Stop it!*

Another potential distraction.

BEN: *As I was saying, they called and said that Sarah was sedated and resting in the infirmary, and we should come and get her. Her roommate called in the dorm officials because she wasn't going to classes, wasn't eating or getting dressed, and hadn't turned in any of the assignments for the semester. I couldn't believe it! She had just been on the phone with her mother the previous day, and she pretended everything was all right! It's this kind of sneaky, dishonest stuff that used to get her into trouble in high school, and her mother is just greasing the wheels for her to flunk out and flip hamburgers the rest of her life. I can see why she's depressed—she knows she's going to spend her life in a trailer park, married to some mechanic, and her sisters have their pick of medical schools and law schools!*

This goes on a little longer than is really good for Sarah, but Sheila is pretty sure it's nothing Sarah hasn't heard before. She let Ben reach a natural stopping point because she wants to create an expectation that she will be balanced and fair in hearing all sides.

SHEILA: *So it sounds like you agree that she was acting like a depressed person, and you think that it was okay that the school called you, and you are worried too. But you want me to understand that you feel this is part of a larger pattern, not just a thing that happened out of the blue.*

Family counselors quite often take a statement and emphasize its positive, caring aspects. We'll discuss the rationale behind this kind of intervention, "positive connotation," later in the book. This response serves double duty, as it is also an "active listening" response that invites Ben to either verify that he has been heard accurately or else expand on and clarify his remarks.

BEN: *Actually, I'm not so sure. I think that maybe she's not really in trouble, you know, emotionally, but she just got caught letting things slip and she staged this whole thing so she could get sympathy instead of punishment. I know, she's Miss Innocent, she looks like she's some kind of victim, but let me tell you, I've seen how she wraps her mother around her little finger and she always gets whatever she wants.*

Ben focuses his attention on the invitation to describe how this fits his view of "a larger pattern."

SHEILA: *Is this something you've said to Sarah, or is she just hearing it for the first time?*

Rather than focus on the truth or error in what's just been said, Sheila responds to this remark as communication among family members. Whether Ben reports that he's said it over and over or he says this is the first time, Sheila is going to turn this into a conversation between Ben and Sarah about their stressful relationship. The session continues with information gathering, both from the stories told by the individuals and from the observed interactions that Sheila encourages.

Awareness of Being "Inducted" into the Family

Not only is this kind of session complex in terms of facts, allegations, and interpretations, it is also an emotional experience for the counselor. Even reading this brief exchange may have been enough for you to start taking sides and making judgments about the story. To some extent, you have already become part of the family system; you've learned some of their language and their folklore, you've been invited to take sides in their arguments, and different family members are already starting to claim you as their ally. You may have had the same kind of experience with couples or families you've visited or met for recreation; within a few minutes you became a part of their ongoing drama.

What's important to recognize is that the successful family counselor is not so much a person who knows how to avoid emotional complexities as one who has learned to recognize that the emotions belong to the couple or family. Knowing that the Klein's relationship problems were well established before they arrived in her office, Ms. Nakamoto will not feel that she has to resolve things in one session. Let's go back and hear how she ends the session:

SHEILA: *I really want to commend you all on how brave you've been to come in here and let me see so much of your pain and anxiety. I can see that there's a lot of love and commitment, and yet I can see that things probably haven't gone as well as you had hoped, Ben and Sally, when you began thinking of combining your lives. Sarah, I'm wondering if you might feel as confused as I did hearing all the different descriptions of you. Maybe they're all true to some extent, and then you have some work to do to make all the pieces fit together. Being a college sophomore is a thrilling and scary position to be in; everyone has such hopes for you, and maybe sometimes you wonder if you've somehow fooled them and you're not really so great. Dolores, you've been such an active part of Sally's family, I am impressed with how well you've all worked together.*

Now, as you can see I don't have everything all figured out yet, and I'm sure I'll still be sorting things out for a couple more sessions, but I think I already know enough to be of some help. I think that we all agree that the top priority is restoring Sarah to functioning at her best. Sarah, the semester at this point might be a challenging little bit of white water that offers a great opportunity for you to show yourself how well you can cope—or it might be a whirlpool that's going to suck you down further. I hesitate to recommend either staying home or going back, having just met you all, but I think either way has its risks and its advantages.

How about going home and between now and next Wednesday I'd like each of you put together two lists, reasons you think, Sarah, you should go back to finish this semester, and reasons you think not. We'll use those lists next week to go to the next step.

There are a number of interventions embedded in this closing message, and I won't try to highlight them all here. You may find that you can recognize some of them after you've read through the rest of the book.

What I want to call attention to at this point is Sheila's attempt to maintain a position of openness vis-à-vis the different positions in the family while also making a strong statement that she's on Sarah's side. This is often a challenge with young people because they usually aren't the ones paying the bills and therefore the parents or grandparents feel entitled to be given a pat on the back.

Knowing that Sarah is likely to feel embarrassed and fearful, Sheila has been careful to repeatedly shift from talking about Sarah to talking to her—this is an intentional move, part of expressing caring and demonstrating an alliance.

Sheila assumes that the time between this session and the next can be used as part of the counseling, and therefore she ends by telling the family how they can best use that time.

Developing the Skills of the Family Counselor

In an ideal world, every troubled family would be seen by an experienced, highly trained family counselor such as Ms. Nakamoto—someone who has studied many approaches to family counseling and who has a wide range of options for handling every problem. But the demand for family services exceeds the supply of such qualified practitioners. Nearly every clinic now gets calls asking for couple and family therapy, and interns often find that sites expect them to be prepared for family sessions. Every beginning counselor should be ready to find a qualified supervisor; get help selecting some readings for self-study or enroll in specialized classes; and begin learning how to address emotional and behavioral problems in a couple or family context as well as to directly intervene in disturbed relationships. Rather than focus only on the expertise required to be an advanced family counselor, I intend to help every reader to evaluate his or her existing strengths and learn how those strengths can be applied in the context of family therapy. Therefore, we need to start with a discussion of basic competence in counseling.

Counseling Competence— Common Factors

One of the most exciting counseling trends in recent years has been a reemphasis on *common factors* that underlie many different ways of being a helper. This is similar to the investigation that Carl Rogers (1957) was engaged in 50 years ago, relying on existentialist philosophy and the methods of science to create a theory about what aspects of a helping relationship were essential and which were optional. In more recent investigations of this kind, as we will see, leadership is coming from multiple groups of authors with different scholarly orientations and research methods but a shared commitment to finding the common factors that unite effective counseling efforts.

Person-Centered Approaches

There is considerable overlap between the "person-centered" work of Carl Rogers and the writings of existentialist authors such as Martin Buber (1958) and Rollo May (1969) as they describe human relationships. Relationships, say the existentialists, have the potential to bring out the best in people—to challenge and support them in ways that help them move past their limitations. For Rogers (1957), a primary question had to do with the qualities of a helping relationship. His access to university counseling centers allowed him to study counseling relationships using audio recordings; over the years, he continually revised a list of qualities that seemed to be present in cases that had positive outcomes and he described a step-by-step process in which the client came to view both the self and the problem in different terms. Rogers eventually extended his studies into the domain of personal relationships, asserting that a couple could work toward a goal of creating a relational space that encouraged personal growth in the same ways as professional counseling relationships (Rogers, 1972). More recently, Gaylin (2001) and M. Snyder (2002) have taken the person-centered tradition back into the family counseling room to provide guidelines and challenges for practitioners. The characteristics discussed next are most often cited as associated with positive outcomes from counseling.

A Helping Relational Environment

Individual counselors are generally trained to create a relationship in which clients feel invited to open up, discover themselves, and become more like their ideal selves. One of the clearest messages in such a relationship is, "You don't need to keep experiencing the disappointment and frustration you have been living with; you are better than this." Such a relational environment communicates hope and acceptance in equal measure; people feel permission to either remain the same or change.

It is hard to extend this relationship to more than one person, however. Even when individuals feel support and acceptance from the counselor, they do not necessarily experience the same safety from one another. For couple and family members it is unrealistic—at least, at the beginning—to think that all members will feel equally safe and supported in the counseling process. But in families, just as in counseling groups, it is possible to create a network of equally supportive relationships—to get the support from each other, not from the counselor. In such a counseling environment, a special rule applies—"You will not be punished for what you do or say here."

Rather than attempt to give each individual an equally supportive relationship with the counselor, Gaylin suggests that the family counselor direct attention to the group instead of the individuals. A counselor can enter the room with the couple or family so that they are engaged as a whole—perceived, accepted, and challenged together. This approach exhibits respect not only for the individual members but for the family culture. The counselor is a learner rather than an expert.

Client Incongruence

Rogers believed that a helping encounter required client readiness, defined as a state of incongruence—an incompatibility between self-perception and experience. His image of a good counseling relationship was one in which the client was safe to search feelings, thoughts, memories, dreams, and the relationship with the counselor for clues as to what needed to be resolved. The counselor did not attempt to reduce or eliminate incongruence by avoiding painful realities, but rather acknowledged and reflected the challenges expressed in the client's story.

In the case of couple and family counseling, it is not only individual incongruities that are problematic; the group as a whole may be feeling an incompatibility between their ideals and their experience. Just as with individuals, couple and family clients may not initially recognize the incongruences or they may recognize and attempt to keep them hidden because of fear or embarrassment. And some family counseling clients seem to hold back because they fear that counseling will make problems worse rather than better. Their efforts to hide problems are driven by panic, fear, and misunderstanding, rather than by a desire to avoid change.

Couple and family counseling offers the professional a unique opportunity for gathering information about what needs to be changed, as well as strengths that might not be mentioned in an individual session. Interviewed together, family members bring information to the front that might have taken months to discover without the additional voices in the room. Given an accepting attitude, one disclosure seems to lead to another and the counselor does not have to wait for the real issues to emerge.

Counselor Congruence

Relationships that help people grow also seem to be ones in which people are honest with themselves and others. Helpers who relate in an honest and direct manner model this behavior for everyone in the room. They attempt to be honestly aware of inner conflicts, to recognize anxiety, and to vigorously confront prejudices and misunderstandings that interfere with relationship.

But such congruence is challenged when one enters a relational system—counselors become *inducted* into the preexisting patterns of interaction. This is one of the reasons that the family counseling field pioneered the use of audio and video recording as well as live supervision; systems are extremely powerful. Sometimes it is only after the session is over, looking at a videotape, that a counselor is able to discover how incongruent he or she became. Stepping into a relational system where conflict is denied, where the family belief system "Mommy and Daddy have always loved each other" is learned from birth, a sensitive and responsive counselor is in danger of joining the avoidant pattern. By remaining congruent, though, the helper will speak and act in ways that may contradict some clients' expectations. This expanding of behavioral options is an important lesson for clients who have held themselves to rigid and ineffective performances of what they believed was the "correct" role for a husband or wife or parent. Furthermore, as Carl Whitaker was fond of demonstrating (e.g., Napier & Whitaker, 1978), a congruent helper can earn the trust of multiple family members through speaking the words that have been forbidden.

Accurate Empathy

Relationships that encourage people's movement toward their best selves also seem to be ones in which participants feel understood for their uniqueness. People generally respond to an empathic listener by exposing more of their unique thoughts and feelings. This opening up is something people can feel and observe in themselves; they may comment on the difference between their behavior in the counseling office and their behavior elsewhere. The reason that the word "accurate" appears in this description is that even when helpers attempt to empathize their attempts can fail—the helper has responded to a generic client rather than the one in the office. Being told

that a client's mother died, a counselor might respond, "You must miss her terribly." That might be accurate for some clients, but for others it denies their strained relationships.

Gaylin (2001) notes that accurate empathy is often difficult to create for more than one person at a time. The counselor might have an easier time being empathic with some family members than others, and those who do not feel understood are often in a position to block any further counseling efforts. Therefore, the family counselor must attempt to deliver *balanced empathy*. Through efforts to reach out to some and hold back from others, the counselor should try to avoid "playing favorites." This is an especially hard task with couples, who often seem to compete for acceptance and understanding.

In the end, people want empathy not from the counselor, but from their loved ones. Herein lies a danger for the counselor. The counselor's sensitivity and professional knowledge can lead to an experience of empathy that surpasses what is felt at home. A woman might say, "You've only known me for a few minutes, and you already understand me better than my husband." In such a case, the husband may perceive the counselor as a threat. Therefore, in couple counseling and in work with families of adolescents, an effective counselor will try to increase participants' accurate empathy for each other.

Let's imagine an intake session with the family of Dave, an adolescent who expressed some suicidal thoughts in a school assignment. If the counselor, Frank, were meeting with the boy alone, his primary goal might be to gain access to the boy's cognitive and emotional state. In this family session, however, Frank can explore a wider field, including other family members' emotional expressions, and he may feel a desire to both assess and teach:

FRANK: *Dave, I can imagine a lot of different thoughts and feelings a person might be having after wrecking his grandmother's car, especially when it's only a month after getting your driver's license. Do you think that you've succeeded in getting those thoughts and feelings across to your mother and your grandmother?*

Rather than assuming that he knows Dave's responses, Frank is making allowances for confusion and inviting Dave to express whatever he's thinking and feeling. Note that the emphasis isn't on Dave's being understood by the counselor, but on his being understood by his family. Therefore, Frank is cautioning the family that they shouldn't assume what Dave's thoughts and feelings are.

GRANDMOTHER: *There's nothing he can say that will make up for the damage. I'll be without a car now, because it wasn't worth the repair costs and I can't afford a new one.*

Dave's grandmother registers her concern that his feelings aren't the only ones that are important—his actions have had an impact on others.

FRANK: *I'm sorry to hear that! This is a real crisis, then, and maybe everyone has thoughts and feelings they'd like to share? Dave, would you mind if I check that out?*

Frank accepts this input, reflects what he believes to be a statement for the group, and creates an opening for information that would challenge those assumptions. Notice that he's pointed out that he is still focused on Dave, even as he checks in with others and highlights the idea that people can have different responses.

Unconditional Positive Regard

Finally, effective helping relationships seem to be ones in which the helper communicates a genuine caring for the client(s). This caring helps to offset the inevitable point when one or more couple or family members will be shown to have acted in ways that were ineffective, hurtful, and often inconsistent with their values and goals. Rogers' (1957) concept of unconditional positive regard was an attempt to express a kind of caring that was unconnected with the client's behavior. This was consistent with Rogers' theory. He believed that people became estranged from themselves, behaving in ways that were so focused on external evaluation that they had lost the ability to be their own sources of evaluation. The helping relationship was designed to shift the attention away from ex-

ternal judgments and into the client's values, goals, and self-perceptions.

Applied at the couple and family level, this caring is directed not so much at the individual as at the relationship system. It is the relationship that has become distorted by efforts to match external definitions of acceptable behavior, and it is the relationship that must reject external evaluation and search within. Unfortunately, one of the most widely used terms in describing families with problems—the popularized and overused *dysfunctional family*—sounds as if it judges the family and finds it without merit. Counselors who seek to communicate a positive view of a relationship system may find themselves often searching for words because their language is impoverished in relationship-oriented concepts.

The Contemporary Search for Common Factors

The search for the active ingredients of counseling dates to long before Rogers, however, and continues through the present (e.g., Lambert, 1992). One of the most visible compilations of such work is by Hubble, Duncan, and Miller, whose edited volume *The Heart and Soul of Change: What Works in Therapy* (1999) brought together various researchers and theorists to reflect on the common elements that appear throughout various approaches to counseling or therapy.

Individual Counseling Relationships

Hubble and his co-authors base their work on Lambert's (1992) reviews of research on sources of change in psychotherapy. Lambert sorted research findings into four categories: Extratherapeutic factors, Common factors, Expectancy or placebo factors, and Techniques. The first of these categories will not be examined here, except to acknowledge that Lambert found evidence linking 40% of all therapeutic change to factors such as client strengths and chance events—beyond the control of the professional. Placebo and expectancy factors (beliefs that counseling would work) were considered by Lambert to be responsible for another 15%, and he estimated that 15% of therapeutic effectiveness was the result of the unique contributions of specific counseling models, theories, techniques, or approaches. This fits with a long research tradition that has found differences among counseling approaches to be only marginally significant. Luborsky, Singer, and Luborsky (1975) were among the first to suggest that similar outcomes might result from actions and attitudes that were common to all the different therapeutic approaches.

Hubble and his colleagues (1999) focus most of their attention on the estimated 30% of change that can be attributed to common factors—of which the relationship with the counselor is the most significant. In a detailed examination of the relationship factors that seem to be so powerful, Bachelor and Horvath's (1999) chapter in the Hubble, Duncan, and Miller book shows that research on the interaction between counselors and clients has become increasingly sophisticated. In earlier studies, Luborsky et al. (1975) identified two factors in the *therapeutic alliance:* mutual liking, and collaboration or shared responsibility. Later researchers added factors such as empathy, reciprocal understanding, respect, and undistorted perceptions, and found their relative importance to change over time. The clients' positive evaluation of the alliance in the early stages of counseling was most critical.

Both the counselor and client contribute to variations in the importance of different factors. Bachelor and Horvath (1999) cite one empathy study in which 44% of the clients valued a cognitive type of empathetic response, whereas another 30% preferred a more affective type of communication, and others saw empathy in terms of information sharing or nurturance. No single kind of empathic response, it seems, can be guaranteed to work with all clients. Effective counselors, according to Bachelor and Horvath, encourage communication about positive and negative perceptions of counseling. Clients, however, must be equally committed to the relationship. In the mutuality of such a relationship, both client and counselor are likely to be influenced by each other.

Motivation and Hope

In another chapter of the Hubble, Duncan, and Miller book, Prochaska (1999) reports on a research program showing that change processes have many common elements, regardless of whether or not they involve professional help. He and his colleagues have demonstrated that change, in medical as well as emotional/behavioral problems, involves progress through six predictable stages: Precontemplation, Contemplation, Preparation, Action, Maintenance, and Termination. The most effective helping approaches have been found to be those that matched clients' needs, helping with movement into the next stage (see Figure 1.1). For people to move from Precontemplation to Action, they must become more convinced of the possible benefits of changing and they must also become less fearful of the possible costs.

Prochaska's work has special significance for the family counselor. In the typical first session with a couple or family, it is clear that not all members are equally ready for change. For example, one partner has initiated the counseling and the other is coming to save face or to provide support. In cases involving adolescents, counseling is usually initiated by a parent and the adolescent has little choice about participating. Special attention must be given to participants who are still in the Precontemplation and Contemplation stages, using strategies that increase awareness of inter-

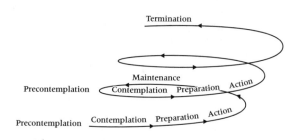

Figure 1.1

Prochaska Stages of Change

Source: From *Systems of Psychotherapy: A Transtheoretical Analysis,* fifth edition, p. 523, by J. O. Prochaska and J. C. Norcross, 2003, Pacific Grove, CA: Brooks-Cole. Reprinted with permission.

personal problems and offer visions of a future relational environment in which they will receive support and affirmation without sacrificing their most valued goals.

Couple and Family
Counseling Relationships

In the same volume, Sprenkle, Blow, and Dickey (1999) summarize discussions in the MFT literature relating to common factors. They report that few authors have explicitly set out to link basic counseling concepts with couple and family work. They do report, however, a number of robust research findings that support an emphasis on a strong counselor-client relationship. Alexander, Barton, Schiavo, and Parsons (1977), for example, are cited for their findings that "relationship skills (warmth, affect-behavior integration, humor) accounted for 44.6% of outcome variance in a study of systems-behavioral intervention with families of delinquents" (Sprenkle et al., p. 335). They also point to a widely discussed Stolk and Perlesz (1990) study that found clients in a training clinic to be more satisfied with the first-year students than with the second-year students. That study is often cited as demonstrating that a focus on specific intervention skills can displace students' focus on counseling relationships. And they report Kuehl, Newfield, and Joanning's (1990) ethnographic data showing that therapist "caring" was seen by clients as essential in their success. At the same time, they call attention to a general lack of specificity in defining the qualities of a good therapeutic alliance when couples and families are involved.

Sprenkle and his co-authors identify three common factors unique to work that is done in the context of couples and families:

1. *Relational conceptualization:* Couple and family approaches are distinctive for their linking of human problems to relationships. This level of conceptualization allows the family practitioner to analyze complex situations and identify resources that may be enlisted in the pursuit of change. A relational conceptualization of problems also reduces the tendency to blame individuals for their suffering.

2. *Expanded direct treatment system:* Viewing problems as located in relational systems, the couple and family practitioner is prepared to focus on the people and institutions that have contributed to problem development and continuation.

3. *Expanded therapeutic alliance:* This focus on a multiperson treatment system requires that the family practitioner be adept at simultaneously forming and sustaining therapeutic alliances with more than one person.

In conclusion, a strong and well-documented body of literature demonstrates that a few basic principles, rigorously applied, can make a tremendous difference in the lives of those clients, patients, or parishioners who come to us for help. The fact that the principles are few in number and can be described simply should not be taken to mean, however, that it is easy to live up to these simple principles. For most people who want to be effective counselors, an extended training program is necessary to disrupt familiar patterns of culturally accepted social interaction and to refine these simple skills to the point where they work together.

The Special Identity of the Family Counselor

Suppose you decide that your counseling efforts will include working with couples and families. You may already be committed to being excellent in all the common factors of counseling that have just been described, and this decision will probably involve new learning about families and specialized theories and skills. But I propose that it may go even further—it may challenge your identity.

Identity Processes

Identity is a term you'll be encountering frequently in this book; it is a theme in many conversations about couple and family relationships. Along with the related concept of *self,* the concept of identity has special meaning in the

European-Western intellectual tradition that can be traced to the philosophical teachings of ancient Greece (Fishbane, 2001; Gergen, 1994). This tradition has glorified the strong (generally male) hero figure who sacrificed personal relationships for the pursuit of "greater" concerns such as war, geographical exploration, poetry, painting, medicine, business, and politics. Stories of great explorers, surgeons, artists, and business leaders have been told in terms of their individual characteristics—their identities. Teamwork and mutual influence are included in only a few exceptional stories (the Wright Brothers, the Curies, the Roosevelts). Even the stories of powerful ruling families are broken down into stories of individuals.

Erik Erikson, in his theory of psychosocial development, captured the central principles of this culturally embedded view. Mature individuals, according to this theory, were ones who had developed their emotional autonomy and self-knowledge so that they could get their human needs met without compromising their goals, beliefs, or principles. Even though a person might live well into adulthood without establishing an identity, Erikson viewed adolescence as a pivotal period for making identity choices through the processes of exploration and commitment. You couldn't, he said, make a true commitment without having explored your options. Those who committed too readily or submitted to influence were likely to be uncomfortable with their lives.

But identity also can be seen relationally, as something that is *negotiated with others* (Fishbane, 2001; Gergen, 1994) rather than as an individual product. This relational view of identity is more consistent with non-Western cultural traditions, seeing human behavior as a collaboration rather than a competition among people. We'll examine this second conceptualization of *social identity* in Chapter 6, viewing people in the context of their relationship systems. At this stage, however, we're considering issues of professional identity: how you and others describe the things that define you in your profession. From this relational view of identity, it's not enough that a person wants to claim a new identity, he or she has to be able to achieve validation of that claim from sig-

nificant others. How can "family counselor" become a credible, integral part of your identity?

Shared Interests and Goals

Long before there were professional couple and family counselors, diverse cultures included roles for people who helped others with their relationships. The professionalization of these functions can be viewed as both a helpful and a dangerous trend. The existence of credentials and training involves a shift toward greater sophistication and accountability, in many cases, but it can also represent a loss of cultural history and connectedness.

Matchmakers
One of the ways a helper has entered into the family arena is as a *matchmaker*—a professional or nonprofessional who brokers marriage and other couple relationships. One may be appointed or recruited for this work, and may be paid or not. The matchmaker may perform some kind of *commitment ritual* for the families and the community or give this task to a political, legal, or religious leader. Such an endorsement by the community, in theory at least, guarantees the new couple that they will have support when they experience difficulties.

Community and Religious Leaders
In some societies, the person who helps with personal relationship difficulties is the same person who helps with community disputes—acting as an *advisor, mediator, or arbitrator* who either helps achieve mutually satisfactory solutions or else imposes community norms. Individuals who provide this kind of assistance may also be responsible for transmitting and enforcing the spiritual and legal traditions of the community. Being concerned with people's spirits seems to involve a spiritual or religious advisor in the individual's human relationships; one of the most visible roots of the family counseling profession is in religious communities.

Direct Service Providers
With or without formal education, other people volunteer in their communities to assist families who are struggling with poverty, social isolation,

disability, or illness. These helpers provide direct assistance—washing clothes, preparing food, repairing windows, driving to medical appointments—and they work more indirectly by helping people identify sources of help. Volunteers visit people in their homes, and they work in community settings such as storefronts, where walk-in services attract those who might not have planned to get help. Religious institutions are frequently the sites for food and clothing banks as well as free clinics serving walk-in patients.

Mental Health Professionals

Beginning in the early twentieth century, a new professional orientation began to manifest itself in the United States. Contributors were variously identified with the disciplines of psychiatry, gynecology, clinical psychology, social psychology, social work, communication studies, and anthropology. Participants used a variety of terms to describe what they were doing, but there was a general consensus that (1) personal relationships were an essential part of human life and (2) there might be a connection between individual-level problems and family functioning. This emerging new *paradigm* (Kuhn, 1970) is documented in a handful of books and journal articles.

Every voice was welcomed in the attempt to put this vague set of ideas into language that did not distort the discussion. As Paul Rosenblatt documented much later in *Metaphors of Family Systems Theory* (1994), the language of professionals can carry meanings that were not intended. Developed for their precision and their metaphorical impact when describing individual-level phenomena, the familiar words of psychoanalysis and behaviorism were found to be limiting when used to describe relationships. The languages of family scholarship, at the same time, grounded in the larger-group disciplines of sociology and anthropology, were not well adapted to describe the combination of group and individual phenomena found in families. The situation called for creativity and courage.

Family Counselors and Therapists

By the 1950s, the emerging group of "family therapists" found a welcome in organizations such as the American Association for Orthopsychiatry

and the National Council on Family Relations. Isolated scholars and practitioners who had been rejected for their radical ideas also began to find peer support through local networking, and international contributors came to assume central positions in the emerging dialogue.

Gurman and Kniskern's *Handbook of Family Therapy* (1981), an edited volume showcasing many of the new field's key theories, represented a milestone in the development of family work. A new language based on systems was beginning to dominate the writings and clinical conversations of family counselors. Many family counselors expected that all differences in theory would be resolved, leading to a single universal family approach. Instead, competitiveness and fragmentation became the norm for the emerging field.

In the past 20 years, however, the idea of a single all-encompassing theory has lost its appeal. With a broad range of family approaches available, family counselors (and family scholars) have found increasing acceptance in seminaries, and in schools of medicine, nursing, and education, as well as in the mental health disciplines of psychiatry, psychology, social work, and addiction treatment. The idea of family level practice continues to face opposition, but it makes sense to consumers as well as professionals. It is an exciting time to be part of the movement.

Shared Perspective

The core assumptions that provide the "glue" for this movement are simple and powerful, but they are distinctive from previously dominant beliefs that the individual is the center of human society:

- *Belief in the priority of relationships:* It may seem hard to deny that relationships are significant in human well-being and achievement. Nevertheless, many people act as if all except the most superficial business and professional relationships are pathological and unnecessary. For example, the male-dominated professions of psychology and psychiatry have appeared, at times, to value family primarily as an economic and biological necessity. Those who valued relationships found allies in social work and home economics. These professions were founded by women and had their roots in community-level knowledge of people's interconnectedness and emotional dependence on each other. Family counselors see relationships at the center of all human activity.

- *Belief in the power of relationships:* Once relationships are seen as central in human life, it seems apparent that troubled relationships should be part of the process of helping troubled individuals. People who feel misunderstood and rejected by the ones they love, who feel blamed for others' choices and problems are often profoundly affected by such a negative emotional experience (Goldner, 1989). Whereas relationships can negatively influence their members, of course, relationships can also powerfully affect moods and behavior in a healthy way. Counseling relationships as well as purely personal relationships demonstrate on a daily basis that caring, concern, and respect bring out the best in people. Family counselors share a belief that human life will be improved to the extent that every individual has the opportunity to be loved and valued in close relationships.

- *Belief in the potential for change in relationships:* If relationships could not be changed, then the professional's ability to help a troubled individual would be limited. Many mental health professionals seem to believe that their only option consists of helping people to live with negative, frustrating, emotionally draining relationships. But family counselors are committed to the idea of change, even if people's previous efforts at making changes have not been successful. When people's relationships seem "stuck," it is possible that they have inadvertently blocked change by trying too hard.

- *Belief in the limits of intervention at the level of the individual:* Finally, family counselors believe that helpers cannot rely on individual-level approaches alone. Even in the case of seemingly individual problems such as broken bones, learning disorders, and tooth decay, colleagues in other fields are starting

to believe that efforts can be improved by being aware of context—even if they only have direct contact with one family member. We explore, throughout the rest of this book, some of the theories that describe the family's contribution to change. We will find a general agreement on the idea of family level intervention.

Shared Expertise

The beliefs I just described would not have been enough to build a professional community if family counselors didn't also demonstrate effectiveness. Having a commitment to families and a belief in family strengths is not enough to qualify a person to claim the identity of family counselor—the client, the community, and the professional peer group have to be able to trust that the professional knows how to help relationships. As I discussed earlier, common factors exhibited by all effective helpers provide the core for family counseling. What distinguishes the couple and family counselor, however, is the existence of special competencies that make those common factors work to their best advantage when working with a relationship system.

Scholars have attempted to define the essential skills of the field (Piercy, Laird, & Mohammed, 1983; Pinsof, 1979). Because there are many different ways of being helpful with families, however, there is not a universal set of attributes and behaviors that characterize all couple and family counselors. We return later to the challenge of evaluating and certifying competence and expertise; for the moment I want to merely create a sketch of the various identifying features we would observe if we create a detailed portrait of this varied group. To illustrate the variety of characteristics we will be seeing, Table 1.1 presents examples from different lists of the specialized knowledge and skills possessed by couple and family counselors.

These lists were created for different purposes, by authors who were referring to theory-driven or empirically determined definitions of

Table 1.1   **Specialized Knowledge and Skills**

Minuchin & Fishman (1981)*	Tomm (1988)*	Patterson, Williams, Grauf-Grounds, & Chamow (1998)*
Spontaneity	Lineal questions: Problem explanation, problem definition	Initial hypothesizing
Joining		Developing a connection
Planning	Strategic questions: Leading, confrontation	Defining client expectations for therapy
Reframing	Circular questions: Behavioral effect, difference	Building motivation
Enactment		Examining history of problems and previous/current treatment
Intensity	Reflexive questions: Hypothetical future, observer perspective	
Restructuring		Creating a therapeutic triangle
Boundaries		
Unbalancing		

*Selected and adapted from the authors' work.

what a family counselor should do. Because the words used have special meanings—we can say that they are *codes* that hold meanings that may not be apparent to the reader—I will summarize just a few themes that can be recognized in the various definitions of competence.

Conceptual and Perceptual Skills

Some kind of formal or informal theory can be seen in the work of every competent family counselor. As illustrated in the Baxter/Klein case earlier in this chapter, relationship counseling involves making sense of partial and conflicting information. Depending on the counselor's understanding of the situation, a variety of interventions might be helpful. In some cases, referral to a specialized resource—such as a rape crisis center or a psychiatrist—is needed.

Theories have been described as being like maps, in that they provide their users with some ability to navigate a complex new territory before they have gotten to know it in detail. The specialized theories used in couple and family counseling have been developed in response to relationship complexity and they highlight different combinations of issues—we might think of them as landmarks, streets, subways, lakes—that underlie people's requests for counseling.

Some of the most popular family counseling theories have themselves been complex (e.g., Beavers & Hampson, 2003; M. Bowen, 1978; Minuchin, 1974). Practitioners who are expert in such complex frameworks have demonstrated their ability to describe many-layered processes that offered multiple opportunities for assessment and helpful interaction with couples and families. In the study of family counseling, it is common for beginners to get the impression that they must match that level of understanding and conceptual fluency. Continuing the map analogy, these approaches are like carrying a book of maps that will allow you to identify every street and every stream. The availability of all that knowledge is comforting, but in a way it creates a sense of dependency and anxiety—you may be reluctant to let go and explore. One of my motivations in writing this book has come from watching students become overwhelmed by multiple, competing, complex theories to the point where they seemingly lost their ability to explore and discover on their own.

I interpret the common factors literature to mean that a relatively simple theory may be as useful a guide for action as a complex theory. One of the most important functions of a theory is that it lets you ignore some of what is happening around you—you've made choices about what is important to pay attention to, and you can let the rest of it go. In a room with several people gesturing, talking, crying, or sitting in stony silence, it's very reassuring to know that you don't have to absorb all that information.

Therefore, in this book we'll not only look at some complex theories but also explore ways in which many of the simplest theories can be useful with couples and families. Carrying the map analogy further, we'll remain aware of the limitations of every map and not assume that "because a street is not on the map, it doesn't exist." In addressing relationship system issues, some theoretical maps don't clearly include significant landmarks such as death and dying; poverty and malnutrition; cultural patterns of understanding and relating; alcoholism or other addictive problems; family violence; slavery and forced relocation; infertility, miscarriages, and stillbirths; sexuality and sexual orientation; chronic illness and disability; gender, race, age, and class as patterns of injustice; and sexual abuse of children and elders. Every family counselor faces a lifelong challenge to continually expand and enrich his or her understandings and awareness of undiscovered relationship realities.

Cognitive Flexibility. In pursuit of that goal, one of the most important conceptual skills for the family counselor is *cognitive flexibility*—the ability to repeatedly and smoothly shift frames of reference. There have been many times when I was challenged to think in two different ways to communicate with individuals or coalitions who were experiencing problems with each other. In one case I needed to view the world both as an engineering problem, full of facts and intervening variables and tolerances and failure rates, and as an emotional network in which everyone was mysteriously but powerfully connected through feelings of closeness and distance, comfort and fear, pride and shame. With another family I had to see the guiding principles of life as discipline, respect, obedience, and obligation but also see the basic life principles as freedom, choice, adaptation, and creativity. To the extent I was able to

enter such different worlds of discourse, I could help clients to better integrate and coordinate their lives.

Pattern Recognition. Another conceptual skill that is helpful to the family counselor is the ability to find patterns in the observed and experienced world. George Kelly (1963), one of the founders of cognitive therapy, assumed that many people's problems in living resulted from difficulty organizing experiences into categories and patterns. Every minute of their lives represented something new, never encountered before, and therefore mysterious and unmanageable. A family session can feel this way, with the counselor overwhelmed by behavior and statements that make no sense at all. The competent family counselor finds ways to organize events into sequences, intergenerational repetitions, communication errors, gender stereotypes, or other kinds of categories.

Interpersonal Skills

Effectively engaging a group of people, especially a group whose preexisting patterns of interaction may interfere with productive discussions, requires specialized interpersonal skills that are not needed by professionals who practice with individuals. Group counseling skills are often a better reference point; the group counselor faces a similar challenge, trying to stop being the pathway through which all communication passes. The simplest form of interaction—and the one that clients seem to expect—sees the professional as the hub, participating in multiple one-to-one conversations (Figure 1.2). But family and group counselors often try instead to encourage and facilitate direct, meaningful interactions among their clients.

Multiple Attending. Couple and family counselors have found that some skills of individual counseling, as described under Common Factors, aren't especially helpful with more than one person. For example, most people respond well when they feel attention and focus from another. Such *attending* is a key skill for individual counselors; it is

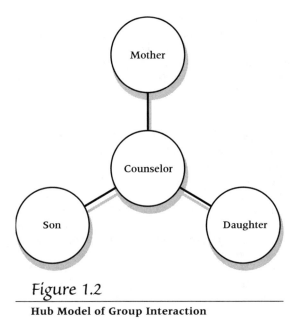

Figure 1.2

Hub Model of Group Interaction

cess in which people take turns having one-on-one conversations with the counselor and people may become inattentive or disruptive when they are not the object of focus.

When the goal is to facilitate interactions, the counselor may find it helpful to sit in a more neutral position and respond with more speculative and doubtful, or even directive comments such as "I think I understand your perspective" or "I'm not sure she realized what you were asking for. Turn to her and tell her now." Attending not only to the speaker but also to the "audience" who are waiting to describe a different experience, the family counselor may make eye contact with nonspeakers and even use facial expressions and gestures that reassure them that they are going to get their turn. Depending on the level of conflict and the maturity and emotional stability of each participant, the counselor may find it necessary to occasionally interrupt a speaker in order to verbally reassure the "audience" or address their disruptions, and then reestablish the attention on the speaker.

assumed to help the client to become aware of feelings and thoughts, and to make connections between events that previously seemed unconnected. Unfortunately, this experience of calm, focused attention is something that is hard to create for more than one person at a time. Further, such a focus may conflict with other goals such as deconstructing multiple perspectives; structuring decision making; providing much-needed information on a developmental stage of childhood; or encouraging and facilitating a dialogue among the participants. A passive, receptive posture does not allow the counselor to interrupt or break eye contact, and these are essential skills for the group and family counselor.

The attending skills shown by the couple and family counselor may be varied but will typically include subtle verbal and nonverbal behaviors that are more commonly studied in group process. With an individual, the counselor attempts to sit facing that person, offer as little disruption as possible, and reassure the speaker that his or her statements are being heard accurately without judgment. Used in a group, couple, or family situation, this same posture tends to create a pro-

Even the most experienced, qualified couple and family counselor finds it hard to adequately attend to all that goes on in a multiple-person session, and therefore audio and video recordings are helpful in providing an opportunity to return to a session and find missed information. In many training and practice settings, recordings are supplemented by either a co-therapist in the room or a consulting team who are viewing through a one-way mirror or on a video link. These additional observers can, with prior arrangement, interrupt to call the counselor's attention to a missed comment or gesture. With a backup observer system, the counselor is freed from anxiety about observing every glance and responding to every muttered comment.

Engaging. In most cases, when a couple or family group arrive in a counselor's office, the issues include emotions. While some clinical theorists (e.g., Beck, Rush, Shaw, & Emery, 1979; Bowen, 1978) have suggested that a distant, rational observation of emotion is possible, contemporary emotion scholars (e.g., Turner, 2000) view human emotion as a system of automatic, unconscious reciprocal interactions and suggest that it is impossible for a person to remain "outside" or "apart from" an emotional experience. Stepping into a room with two or more members of a relational system is not only a challenge of shifting attention and respecting multiple perspectives, it is an emotional experience for the counselor.

Many of the founding theorists and practitioners of family counseling came from the mental health community, trained in being careful and remote, and were White, privileged men—not known for their range of emotional sensitivity or expression. Some of the early family therapy history may be read as an attempt to make couple and family sessions "safe" by keeping conversations on rational subjects and limiting the open expression of emotion. This history is all the more fascinating when we look at the early years of family therapy, as we will in the next chapter, and see a strong presence of emotionally dynamic, expressive individuals who did not shy away from their own feelings or those of the clients. But these role models—Ackerman, Satir, Whitaker—were hard for many people to emulate and the less emotionally demanding approaches came to dominate.

Yet, emotion continued to show up in the consulting room. No theory or technique can prevent a couple and family counselor from feeling pulled into bonding with children and adolescents or feeling shock and grief when helping a couple prepare for the husband's imminent death from emphysema. When a new couple arrive in the counselor's office, in most cases each partner is trying to be liked. The experienced couple counselor is able to recognize the agenda and let both partners know that they are in an emotionally safe place—the counselor isn't going to fall in love with either of them. Parents and adolescents come into the counselor's office portraying each other as insane, incompetent, hate-filled, and cruel. The experienced family counselor is able to provide a corrective emotional experience in which no one wins the prize for best-loved family member.

Co-counselors, video recordings, and consulting teams are effective strategies for helping to develop this area of competence as well. A co-counselor or a consulting team can point out the times when the counselor seems to be favoring one sister over another or smiling at the apparent lies of an attractive young man. With experience, the counselor can—with help from consultants—learn to directly confront apparent lies and not only resist seductions but help a client to quit behaving seductively.

Cooperative Decision Making. When people are confused, mistrustful, hurt, anxious, and seemingly locked in sequences of mutually destructive behavior, listening to them and engaging with their daily life issues can be tremendously helpful. In many cases couples and families seem to spontaneously generate new patterns of interaction, apparently responding to the experience of validation and permission that comes from being with an authentic, caring person who is not overwhelmed by their lives. People seem to learn at a deeper level, and to make more lasting changes, when they discover their own new ways of doing things rather than being taught. Some things like learning to ride a bicycle (or counseling?) can't be taught so much as they have to be learned through trial and error.

Many relationships, however, by the time they arrive in the counselor's office are in a state of chaos that seems to demand immediate relief. For example, many couples come for counseling only after separating and filing for divorce, looking for signs of hope before a 90-day waiting period is over. Parents may come to the office with an adolescent son or daughter who has just been released from a hospital following a suicide attempt. These situations and many others cannot wait for a major system change. Furthermore, as Pinsof (1995) observes, the institutions and clients who pay for counseling services have an expectation that change will happen as quickly as possible. When a simple planning session will resolve a dilemma, a general relationship focus may be helpful but it may not be justified. At these times, it is possible for a helper to try to increase the options that people consider in looking for solutions—to serve as an expert on either the content of their struggles (e.g., birth control options, planning for guardianship of a relative with dementia) or the process of decision making.

Once again we confront the history of family counseling. Those who helped to create the movement and who sought training in the first few decades were, for the most part, mental health practitioners who saw problems as arising from an internal source and who expected to find "systems" to be complicated and challenging. Something as seemingly simple and direct as planning and decision making didn't fit their theories of problem formation and change. They assumed that people who came for help had already tried direct problem solving and had failed in that endeavor because of some deeper relationship problem. When an author refers to something as "just counseling, not really therapy" the statement generally reflects this bias.

Fortunately this bias has lost some of its power over the past few decades. One of the reasons is the demonstrated success of what are now referred to as *psychoeducational* methods (Goldberg-Arnold, Fristad, & Gavazzi, 1999) with families challenged by chronic physical or mental illness, developmental disabilities, trauma, and injury, as well as those who are struggling to cope with external problems such as natural disasters or plant closings. An additional reason is the success of research-based work on conflict processes and problem solving (e.g., Fisher & Ury, 1981). There is a strong body of research (Swanson, 1993) showing that peoples' effectiveness as couples, families, and teams in the workplace is increased when they have better information for making decisions and they are assisted with the intellectually challenging and emotionally draining process of resolving differences and making joint commitments. Taken together, these developments fit with an increasing emphasis on building family strengths and resiliency (A. C. Johnson, 1995; Walsh, 1998) rather than assuming that families are suffering from problems that need to be fixed.

Family counselors find that often there are no trusted advisors, extended family members, or friends with whom decisions can be discussed. Decision making in such a state of isolation—for example, the decision to take a chance on conceiving a child—may turn on issues of power and opportunity rather than on carefully considered review of alternatives. Family interaction can become a paralyzing process in which long-standing differences are continually recycled into new versions of the same struggle, such as a clash between rigid order and chaotic spontaneity or an oscillation between contrasting discipline strategies of harsh control and permissive inattention. A skilled helper, in such a situation, can encourage a process of cooperative problem solving in which different perspectives are honored, information is carefully processed, every reasonable alternative has a chance to be evaluated, each decision is addressed as part of a relationship history, and follow-up discussions are scheduled to review the effectiveness of the decision.

Paradoxically, the information revolution in many parts of the world (including the widespread availability of personal computers and Internet access), may have increased couples' and families' need for assistance in locating and making sense of information. There are many valuable resources online and in bookstores, but at the same time many web sites and published materials are outdated or inaccurate. A skilled family counselor, under these circumstances, can use homework assignments and even guided searches in sessions to help couples and families develop better skills at using information.

Facilitating problem solving is one of the most important ways in which a helping professional can have a rapid, dramatic, and lasting impact on a relationship system. Just as people come to counselors when they are confused and seeking help with life's challenges, couples and families should feel that they do not have to wait for a disaster to seek the assistance of a couple or family counselor.

Personal Challenges of Family Counseling

Most family counselors agree that choosing to work with couples and families is a life-altering choice. Family counseling is extremely personal work that can be hard to leave at the office, intense in both its emotional rewards and its emotional challenges. In addition to fine-tuning their cognitive and interactional skills, professionals must confront echoes of their own family of origin and current relationship experiences; manage the anxiety of not knowing a solution to a problem; and handle the responsibility of knowing that whatever they do is likely to have an effect of some kind.

Throughout this book you will be invited to examine your personal style and your family/relationship history to assess strengths and identify issues that are likely to arise in the counseling process.

Confronting Echoes of Our Own Families

In the relatively intimate setting of a couple or family counseling session it is not uncommon for a counselor to experience thoughts and feelings that don't seem to fit the situation. Listening to a husband describing his anguish at having to give up an extramarital relationship, I may feel outrage that he is defending this behavior. Or in the same situation, I may join him in his anger at an unjust world that requires people to deny their feelings. Neither response is appropriate if I want to be a helper instead of a helpless reactor caught up in the family's emotional field.

Such feelings may be echoes of our own family relationships—from our families of origin or even from our current couple and parental relationships. Adlerian family counselors (e.g., Carlson & Sperry, 2000) believe that people learn essential relationship understandings at an early age. Gender, birth order, and parents' ways of handling discipline are among the factors that might have shaped a counselor's responses to anger or tension in others. Even after years of professional training, a client might invoke a response that belonged to the counselor's relationship with her mother.

Likewise, the object relations perspective (D. E. Scharff & Scharff, 1987) tells us that intense experiences (early experiences, especially) are retained in *object relations schemata* that become activated in similar settings. To the extent that a counselor is out of touch with such memories, a sudden feeling of fear or anger in a session may be interpreted as a valid response to the people in the room. And Bandura and Walters' (1963) social learning theory suggests that people learn not only from their own experiences but also from observing the experiences of others. Therefore, I could have learned a fear of confrontation by seeing my mother's discomfort in similar situations.

Exercises. This danger of carrying personal history into other people's family sessions has led to a tradition of having family counselors-in-training complete various self-discovery exercises that help the family counselor to be protected against these jarring experiences. One approach, illustrated in Box 1.1, uses family sculpting exercises in which the students' vari-

---

BOX 1.1

Family Reconstruction

Every family is unique, and yet there are many commonalities. A professional who has worked with the family of a suicidal college student—or the family of a child tennis prodigy—can be more helpful to future clients whose lives include those same themes. This principle has been used in training family counselors, assuming that any group of trainees includes people who have experienced a variety of special couple and family experiences.

One of the ways of making use of these varied and powerful family histories is to reenact or *recon-struct* (Bardill, 1976; Satir & Bitter, 2000) these relationships in the present. Students take turns involving their classmates in dramatic reenactments or other action techniques. Ten minutes spent playing the role of a classmate's dying father or her twin sister can powerfully expand your understanding of a life position quite different from your own. Sharing these new discoveries in a group discussion provides a rich source of new ideas about relationships.

ous relationship constellations are reproduced (Bardill, 1976; Satir & Bitter, 2000). A second (see Family Mapping at the end of the chapter) involves gathering and analyzing students' families of origin information. These exercises are often personally challenging; relationships are emotionally charged, and we often rediscover painful truths about ourselves and our loved ones as we take a new look at our relationship histories. The goal is that these discoveries will happen when the others in the room are fellow professionals, rather than when clients are looking for help.

Diverse Credentials

We are now ready to come back to the issue of evaluating and certifying a person's competence as a family counselor. This can be a complicated topic, because there are multiple ways to gain credentials and the credentials have different impacts. But this kind of complexity should appeal to a family counselor because it is complicated and multidimensional.

Professional Organizations

There are at least two contrasting views of how a group of qualified individuals can be created and maintained. In European history, these two views describe the *professions* and the *guilds*. Professions were collaborations between the universities who defined a knowledge base and professional societies that emphasized either extensive training or testing as criteria for membership. Having studied under qualified teachers and passed the examinations for entry into the society, the professional was left to self-regulate based on *ethical principles* and *knowledge of the field*. The learned doctors of medicine, law, and religion defended their exclusive right to determine what was appropriate conduct, and furthermore they resisted the idea of regulating the practices of their members. In medicine, there was no agreement about the causes of disease or about effective practice; every physician was expected to be a scholar-practitioner who contributed discoveries to the field.

This tradition stood in contrast to the guilds of the time, whose continuous monitoring of their members served to assure customers that their *work* met high standards. Creative deviations from accepted practice were only acceptable to the extent that they passed peer review. Both traditions addressed the community's need for a way to identify those who were worthy of public trust. Both traditions emphasized the idea that the community was being served not only by the individual but by the group who endorsed that individual.

Over the centuries, the concept of profession has been broadened to include more groups that claim specialized knowledge and therefore the right to control the education and credentialing of their members. Contemporary professions continue to set and enforce their own stringent education and testing requirements for entrance, and their peer credentialing is often given extra weight by a license or certificate issued by the state. At the same time, the professions have become more guild-like, as professionals themselves, licensing boards, and other groups—consumer organizations, for example—have called for increased monitoring and disciplining activity once an individual is credentialed. Ethical principles have been translated into Ethics Codes, violations of which may result in expulsion from a professional association, loss of a license, and prohibition from further practice.

Organizations for Couple and Family Counselors.
In the early years of exploration in couple and family counseling, most of the pioneers were active in social work, psychology, counseling, or psychiatry. Their interest in working with families was not uniformly supported by their peers and was considered, in some cases, to be unethical conduct. They needed an organization that more closely matched their shared identity. In the late 1970s, the American Association of Marriage Counselors (AAMC), its membership swelling with newly trained family professionals, reorganized and changed its name to the American Association for Marriage and Family Therapy (AAMFT). This organization began to define a new profession that would

self-regulate and would seek official recognition and licensing for its members. AAMFT has grown over the years to be the most widely recognized family therapy association in the United States. The organization offers various levels of membership, depending on education, testing, and experience.

Other family practitioners have continued to identify as counselors, nurses, psychiatrists, psychologists, addiction counselors, and social workers, choosing to work toward mainstream acceptance of work with couples and families. These efforts have been successful, as family approaches are visible in the literature of each field. Over time, each of the various professions has developed its own internal or affiliated subgroup for family specialists. The International Association for Marriage and Family Counselors (IAMFC) is one of the latter groups. A subgroup of the American Counseling Association, IAMFC has no requirements for general membership but offers a specialty certification for people who seek to strengthen a family-oriented identity.

In addition to professional organizations who perform some credentialing and monitoring functions, many other organizations address the need for intellectual sharing and collaborative activity in a field that is still developing. In the early years when the traditional mental health fields were resistant to family approaches, many professionals found a receptive climate in the American Orthopsychiatric Association or in the National Council on Family Relations—groups that continue to serve family professionals. Family Process, publisher of the journal of the same name, was formed in the early 1960s; out of that group was formed the American Family Therapy Academy (AFTA). AFTA continues as a small group with membership limited to advanced practitioners and educators. Many professionals in the United States also belong to the International Family Therapy Association (IFTA), which publishes the *Journal of Family Psychotherapy,* welcomes members at any educational level, and moves its annual congress to different parts of the world in an attempt to create linkages and encourage growth of the field.

Consumer Groups.   There is no active consumer organization for couple and family counseling clients; groups equivalent to the Alliance for the Mentally Ill either have not formed or have not survived. A unique professional/consumer alliance, however, has developed over the past several years. The Coalition for Marriage, Family, and Couples Education sponsors a comprehensive web site and an annual Smart Marriages conference promoting themes of family wellness, family strengths, and preventive intervention. Many of the best-recognized names in the field typically appear on the program, and this organization shows signs of becoming a significant force in defining the future of family counseling.

Licensing—A Separate Profession?

Opinions differ as to whether or not there should be a separate couple and family therapy profession with a body of knowledge and a set of ethical principles that make it unique. I will examine this situation as a systemic conflict; this exercise will give us a chance to practice skills of cognitive flexibility, attempting to understand two different ways of interpreting the same set of events.

Specialty.   The practice of couple and family counseling may be viewed, from one side, as similar to a medical specialty. Let's take pediatrics as an example. Pediatricians know some things that their colleagues in other specialties don't know, and therefore they have the ability and the responsibility to set standards for use of the professional title and access to positions where their expertise is required. Yet some of this specialized knowledge is shared with the general practitioner of medicine, and every physician is able to gain access to specialized pediatric information. Pediatrics exists, then, as an enhanced, regulated level of specialized practice along with dermatology, psychiatry, and other specialties that take parts of general practice and advance them to a higher level. The profession of medicine internally monitors the activities of its members to ensure that they don't make claims for expertise that they don't have.

If this view is applied to the field of couple and family counseling, then we see various groups that might claim this specialty. During the early years of family therapy experimentation, most of the founding generation were professionals in medicine, nursing, social work, counseling, and psychology. Despite some initial resistance, over the past 40 years each of these professions has developed its own books, journals, and organizations or societies that provide training, credentialing, and peer review of people who counsel families. As respect for family practice has grown within each of these professions, there has been increasing emphasis on requiring education and supervised experience before one can claim to be a specialist. Ethics codes universally forbid making false claims about one's credentials, even though most other professional groups are not as active as medicine in monitoring their members' activities.

This is similar to the position of the American Counseling Association (ACA)[4] regarding couple and family counselors. The American Counseling Association views couple and family counseling as a specialty area within counseling, not unlike group counseling or counseling with children and adolescents. For those who want to explore issues related to their specialty practice, an ACA-sponsored group, the International Association of Marriage and Family Counselors, sponsors events at the ACA annual conference and publishes a journal, *The Family Journal: Counseling and Therapy for Couples and Families,* in which issues of best practice and professional ethics are explored and debated. The group's leadership has the authority to articulate the ethical standards for the specialty and to coordinate with accreditation groups regarding training and credentialing. Within the ACA, introductory coursework in couple and family counseling is expected to be part of every counselor's preparation, and counseling departments in universities are encouraged to offer special-

ized training as well; the Council for Accreditation of Counseling and Related Educational Programs provides accreditation for specialty programs. Just as pediatrics may be part of a physician's general practice, couple and family counseling is not restricted to individuals holding special credentials, but instead counselors are encouraged to evaluate their own work and seek advanced training, supervision, and credentialing appropriate to their own practices. Psychologists, social workers, psychiatrists, and psychiatric nurses take similar positions.

New Profession. The situation may be viewed, from the other side, as similar to an alternative approach to medicine. We'll take osteopathy as an example. Osteopathic medicine developed in the United States as a distinctive approach to illness and wellness. The basis for their separation from the traditional practice of medicine was ideological; osteopaths didn't merely do things differently from conventional doctors, they rejected many conventional assumptions about disease and cure and they shared a belief in healing systems that conventional doctors viewed with suspicion.

For decades, the split between osteopaths and conventional physicians was so great that the two groups were not permitted to practice together either in private clinics or in hospitals. Both groups seemed to believe that the split was necessary in order to establish (from the osteopathic side) or maintain (from the conventional medicine side) standards of practice that excluded various techniques that each group considered harmful to patients. The past 20 years have seen greater integration, though. At this time, combined MD/DO practices are increasingly common, and hospital privileges are open to both groups regardless of the professional affiliations of the hospital. Separate educational systems continue, but at this time faculty in a school of medicine or osteopathy may come from either background. Each group continues to make and implement its own decisions about training, credentialing, and disciplining its members.

If this view is applied to the field of couple and family counseling, the osteopathic position

---

[4] Similar positions have been taken in other professional groups.

is similar to the position of the American Association for Marriage and Family Therapy.[5] The organization began to claim the existence of a new profession when it established its own professional journal, the *Journal of Marital and Family Therapy*, in 1962 and began to hold an annual conference during the 1970s with the goal of exploring and debating issues of best practice and professional ethics. Since its founding, AAMFT insisted that members document specialized knowledge and specialized experience; various levels of membership were created for students and interested professionals. By the late 1970s, AAMFT Clinical Membership began to assume the status of a national credential; Clinical Membership required screening of qualifications and could be withdrawn for ethics violations. Over time the standards were made more rigorous and specific, a cadre of carefully screened supervisors was established, and the group worked with state-level organizations to either create or rewrite laws so that certificates and licenses in Marriage and Family Therapy were limited to individuals whose preparation included training and supervision similar to that of AAMFT Clinical Members.

The basis for this separation was ideological; marriage and family therapists didn't merely do things differently from conventional counselors and therapists, they did things differently because they rejected many conventional assumptions about human problems and change processes and they believed in practices that mainstream mental health professionals viewed with disdain. This was not a totally separatist position; separate facilities were not necessary, providing the climate was supportive of those applying a family orientation. At the same time, specialized facilities were desirable because counseling and therapy offices often didn't accommodate families well and furthermore some of the training methods favored by MFTs—

videotaping and observing couple and family sessions—were considered unethical by the mainstream and were difficult to implement without structural and technological modifications of offices.

Over the 50-year history of this separatist effort, AAMFT, its professional conferences and journal, and its sponsored legislative efforts have been quite successful, creating opportunities for training and practice with a primary focus on relationship systems. Marriage and family therapists have gained recognition from many insurance companies, U.S. government programs, and state legislatures. At the same time, some of these successes have been achieved by de-emphasizing marriage and family therapists' beliefs and their preference for working with relationship systems instead of individuals. MFTs who have worked within mixed-orientation settings report that they perceive pressure to practice like conventional counselors or therapists despite their special credentials.

Licensing Laws. As of 2003, specialized licenses or certificates for couple and family counseling exist throughout most of the United States. The specific expectations vary widely, but all require at least a master's degree with specific family related content and clinical experience. As many of these licensing laws are relatively new, however, public and professional awareness is limited and discrimination in employment and payment is common. The legislators and licensing board members who create these credentials have considerable influence on the shape of the profession. Some laws have been inclusive, as in the case of Michigan's 1979 law that allowed any psychologist, social worker, or pastoral counselor to become a Certified Marriage Counselor without specialized training of any kind.[6] Such laws can weaken public perception of expertise, as the community is exposed to certified individuals who lack the ability to deliver specialized services. A growing trend toward more restrictive

---

[5] See Chapter 3 for a more detailed history. The organization and its journal had different names at the time of their founding.

[6] Later amended to match national standards.

laws, requiring not only specialized education but also an extended period of supervised clinical experience and a national licensing examination, severely limits the number of people who may claim the title but it is hoped that this smaller number of licensed individuals will gain credibility through their proven ability to meet community needs.

Market Forces

Over the past 15 years, the helping professions in the United States, as well the careers of individual professionals, have increasingly come under the control of the insurance industry and various government-sponsored payment systems. These groups, in a movement called *managed care,* have established their own credentialing systems, relying to some extent on professional memberships, certifications, or licensure but adding requirements for specialized training, more courses and longer periods of training status and advanced supervision, and adherence to their rules for practice. Their preference for brief, cost-effective service is clear, and they use various techniques to limit the length of service.

Individuals whose professional memberships or license do not match what is preferred by the group, or whose training does not match the group's additional standards, are excluded from a *preferred provider panel.* Psychologists and psychiatrists have nearly universal access, and other professional groups including professional counselors and marriage and family therapists are treated inconsistently. There are no universal standards, although legislation has forced equal treatment of all licensed professionals in some states. Excluded professionals may be denied payment or they may be offered substantially reduced fees. Furthermore, in most cases these reimbursement systems are designed with the individual as the unit of service, making couple and family work difficult to plan and document within their procedures despite the fact that other systems value couple and family interventions as cost-effective. In medical reimbursement systems, preventive care is often not paid for, and therefore assistance is limited to families with at least one individual with a mental or other medical disorder. These groups, then, not only exercise control over who may practice in a mental health profession but they also limit what these professionals may do. Practicing outside these reimbursement systems is an option, but that choice often leads to reduced income.

The Preparation and Credentialing System—Options

As these various efforts interact, with their different goals and methods, there seems to be considerable confusion among professionals and clients. In much the same way that beginning counselors have a hard time accepting the idea that experts disagree on how to help clients, it is hard to accept the idea that there is not a single answer about what is an adequate level of preparation for working with couples and families. For many practitioners, couple and family work will be something that is done only under rare circumstances. Such a professional, having completed a basic course in family work, would be advised to locate a specialized family supervisor to provide support for those rare cases. Other counselors will see couple and family work as a frequent option in their practices; they would be advised to find specialized coursework, in addition to specialized supervision, so they can move toward a reasonable level of comfort with their family cases. For the counselor who wants to be seen in the community as the person to whom couple and family cases should be referred, there is no doubt that specialized practice requires advanced education and credentialing of some kind.

At one time, there were few qualified faculty available to teach advanced coursework in couple and family counseling, and therefore advanced training was generally found in free-standing institutes. At this point, most universities have, among their faculty, qualified family specialists, and advanced coursework is becoming more and more available. Readers are encouraged to explore the options that fit with their circumstances, recognizing that continuing professional education is necessary regardless of how many courses are taken in the near future.

Choices

Just as the concept of identity is a central theme in this book, so are the concepts of opportunity, choice, and decision making. Once again, we have the opportunity to begin exploring a relationship issue that has applications in counseling couples and families.

Within relationships, opportunities arise through planning or happenstance: a child graduates from high school, there is a sale on lawn furniture, or a warning from the doctor raises questions about lifestyle issues. To take advantage of these opportunities, someone must exercise choice. In many cases, the choice can't really be made alone, and often people's choices interact to constrain one another as well as build on one another. In our professional lives, counseling professionals exercise choice as well. In the preceding pages, I have offered an overview of the kinds of choices you may be faced with as you consider becoming a family counselor; the actual choices will depend to a great extent on the particular opportunities that come your way.

Right now, however, you have the choice of how you'll make use of this book and the course (if any) in which you are enrolled. You may set goals for yourself that will demand different kinds and amounts of work, with the resources that are provided at the end of each chapter along with other resources that you find online, in libraries, in your community, in internship and work settings, and even among your friends and relatives. I like to think of the choices as dividing themselves essentially into three categories:

1. Go all the way to making Couple and Family Counselor your professional identity.

2. Become more aware of family perspectives, feeling reasonably sure that you will work with couple and family issues occasionally.

3. Become sufficiently aware that you can refer appropriate cases to someone who specializes in couples and families.

Even if you choose not to specialize in couple and family counseling, you may find yourself engaging in some family-related helping activities (see Box 1.2), either as a volunteer or as a paid professional.

BOX 1.2

Family Counseling: Specialized Activities

Given their commitment to couple and family life and their specialized skills, what can we expect to see family counselors doing in the community? Some will be sitting in offices, seeing client couples and families for 45- to 50-minute sessions in conversations that closely resemble office practice with individuals. The neighboring offices might not even notice the difference between such a practice and an individual-oriented counseling practice.

But that is not the only option; the possibilities are almost endless. Here are a few things that are being done in different places by family specialists, using their background in different ways:

- Bring multiple couples or families together in groups.

- Monitor e-mails between divorced parents.

- Consult with schools, clergy, or employers of clients.

- Travel to a family business workplace for consultations.

- Provide home-based services, on call night and day.

- Hold day-long sessions with out-of-town visitors.

- Attend family reunions, funerals, or weddings.

- Work as a group of counselors on the same case.

- Help a family to plan rituals.

Being a couple and family counselor is about values, sensitivities, and concerns as much as it is about activities. A family counselor is one who hears the voices of family members in every conversation, regardless of who is speaking. Possibly this is not, in fact, a choice. Once you hear those voices, it is hard to tune them out.

Suggested Individual and Group Activities

Your understanding of concepts and issues presented in this chapter may be enhanced by the following activities:

- *Look in Yellow Pages, local newspapers, and Internet directories for couple and family counselors.* Who are the family counseling practitioners that serve your community? Look in the Yellow Pages and on the Web, using search terms such as "marriage counseling," "family counseling," and "family therapy." What does this search tell you about community needs, accessibility, credentialing, and orientations?

- *Family mapping.* Later in this book, you will be introduced to the standardized symbols and the rule system used in *genograms*—visual maps of family relationships that are often used with families in counseling. Possibly you have already been exposed to genograms.

The standardized symbols have been developed to facilitate sharing information about frequently seen family configurations, and they may not capture the way you have experienced your family. Kaslow (1995) suggests "projective genogramming," setting aside the rules and discovering your own way of visually representing your relationship systems.

Using only the most basic structural conventions—each person must have a symbol, and relationships must be indicated by lines—draw your family and label the people and the relationships. Once you have completed your family drawing, sit down with a fellow student and describe your diagrams to each other. What were you emphasizing? Did your diagram make sense to your partner? Did his or her questions make you aware of things you had left out?

Suggested Readings

Baptiste, D. A. (2002). *Clinical epiphanies in marital and family therapy: A practitioner's casebook of therapeutic insights, perceptions, and breakthroughs.* New York: Haworth.

Lewis, J. M. (1979). *How's your family? A guide to identifying your family's strengths and weaknesses.* New York: Brunner/Mazel.

Napier, A. Y., & Whitaker, C. A. (1978). *The family crucible.* New York: Harper & Row.

Nichols, M. P. (1999). *Inside family therapy: A case study in family healing.* Boston: Allyn & Bacon.

Retelling the Story: Couple and Family Counseling in the Early Years

Growing out of diverse professional orientations and practice traditions, this new field experienced rapid growth and intense competition.

Objectives

In this chapter, you learn to:

1. Understand the multiple contexts that have shaped couple and family counseling.
2. Distinguish between a story and the way it's been told.
3. Analyze family approaches in terms of their goals and assumptions.
4. Appreciate the variety of early family counseling efforts.
5. Recognize names, places, and ideas that dominated marriage and family therapy during its growth years.

2

Chapter

Stories are central to family counseling. People come in with stories and counselors try to connect with them through those stories. We listen for what people's family stories tell us, not only about the events that apparently occurred, but also for what they tell us about the storytellers (see Buttny, 1993) and about the family (including their community and their culture, broadly defined). As John Byng-Hall (1979) said about the myths that are told over and over in families, there's a carefully hidden message in some stories. A careful listener can often detect coded messages such as: "Never trust strangers," "If you're patient and good, you'll be rewarded," "A good life is a life lived in nature," or "No matter how hard we try, people like us always lose." Therefore, we listen for ways in which people's stories may keep them stuck.

Many of us grew up hearing about events that happened before we were born, learning who we are by learning about our families and cultures, absorbing messages from family stories. Students—and professionals who are in a period of transition—return, in a way, to this position in their adopted "family" of professionals. They listen to stories of their chosen profession in two ways: to learn both about the factual history and to learn about the culture of this profession. For the purposes of this chapter, the literature of the family therapy field is examined as a collection of stories.

The story of family therapy (how it came into existence, its struggles for acceptance) is fascinating. As a graduate student in 1976, I felt like one of the early settlers in a new territory.[1] Thirty years later, the story seems to be changing. Some U.S. authors (e.g., Beels, 2002; Hoffman, 2002)

---

[1] This exciting period of time for newcomers to the field is portrayed eloquently by Peter Fraenkel (2005).

are suggesting that the story was distorted, overlooking many contributors. Authors such as Kaslow (2000) and Ng (2005) have begun the process of providing their U.S. colleagues with reviews of the field's history in other countries. According to these authors and others, there are still exciting things going on in family counseling—there's still a movement; it's just a different movement. At the same time, other authors (e.g., Minuchin, 1998; M. P. Nichols & Schwartz, 2004) say that the excitement of the developing field is over and what we're left with is confusion, disappointment, and skepticism. In this chapter, and the one that follows, I try to organize these competing voices so that you can search for a story that makes sense to you.

The Context of This Telling

If there's one thing that family counselors and therapists seem to agree on, it's that context is important. When a family's relationships are not working as they should, the family professional looks at the contexts in which they are attempting to create or maintain the relationships. This contextual view of human existence is what people generally mean when they say "systemic"—everything is part of something else, and objects can't be separated from their larger systems. For our present task, though, I prefer to use words that are less precise than "objects" and "systems."[2] The contexts we are talking about are extremely subtle and they overlap and merge in nonphysical ways.

I am going to focus on the story of family counseling or therapy as a social and political movement: how it came into existence, and the internal and external struggles that shaped its development. Before we start examining this story in its various contexts, it may be helpful to take a detour and briefly introduce some of the current social and intellectual contexts that are influencing my way of telling the story. These contexts are important not only be-

cause they may help to explain how I interpret the story but also because they become, as we move into recent events, part of the story.

Postmodernism

In the past 15 to 20 years, the concept of *postmodernism* has become widespread among scholars of many disciplines. The term may be somewhat confusing when it is encountered because it is used for two different concepts.

Historical Postmodernism

In the less common usage, postmodern refers to a historical period that is being shaped by the communications media, the political and economic developments, and the transportation systems of the late twentieth and early twenty-first centuries. Postmodern realities, from this perspective (see, e.g., Dickens & Fontana, 1994) are ones that reflect a world in which people are living without many of the barriers—time and distance, political and currency limitations on travel, language differences—that formerly kept people apart. People are increasingly confronting both their differences from one another and their essential sharing of the human condition. At the same time, information technologies have separated people from their own direct experience. In postmodern culture, mental health professionals and social scientists expect to see new kinds of personal and social problems. Toward the end of this book, we spend time exploring some of the implications of this social change but for now we set this use aside.

Intellectual Postmodernism

In this chapter, we're talking about postmodernism as an intellectual movement. Used this way, *postmodern* describes an attitude or set of scholarly expectations that critically examine the history of *modernism*. That definition, in turn, requires thinking of the term *modern* differently from its popular usage of "up-to-date." The modern period in Western society began with the rise of industry in the early nineteenth century and reached its peak in the 1950s and 1960s. That era was organized around a belief that human problems were solvable through research and scien-

---

[2] These words reflect the dominance of the physical and biological sciences in academic circles, even when scholars are describing language and culture.

tifically based rational intervention. Interpretations of art, music, and human relationships during this period were dominated by language and images that came from the physical and biological sciences—language and images of certainty, precision, and objectivity. The mental health field was created during the modern era, based on the metaphor of modern medicine: People's problems were inside them and these problems (diseases) could be classified, diagnosed, and cured by applying appropriate treatments. Family therapy, another modern invention, defined problems as inside the family and applied treatments to the family.

Postmodernism, in contrast, embraces uncertainty and complexity and considers assertions of fact to be only the observers' subjective perceptions. In the human service fields, postmodernist authors have rejected ideas of scientific certainty and have chosen to see human problems as complex interactions that involve language as well as behavior and emotions.

Cultural and Political Awareness

Postmodernists tend to focus on linguistically shared (cultural) understandings of human experience. Michel Foucault (1979), one of the central figures in postmodernist scholarship, conducted historical research on understandings of concepts such as sexuality, insanity, and punishment. In his books, he demonstrated that each of these concepts is a cultural artifact that can be tracked from its early usage, developing over time as it was named, validated through usage, and eventually used as an accepted principle for understanding human behavior. Foucault's analysis showed that the language practices of labeling, categorizing, and describing problems increased the dominant social group's ability to suppress dissent and achieve a high degree of conformity. Foucault, a gay man, was especially sensitive to the processes through which social groups attempted to control their members. His work has become essential reading for feminists and others who

are concerned with social inequalities and injustice.

The term *discourse* is an essential part of this kind of analysis, referring to an interactive language process in which events come to have shared meaning. In its simplest form, a discourse may be created by one person applying a label to an experience and one or more others verifying or joining in the labeling. This kind of *discursive replication* takes place constantly within groups of people who share language, beliefs, and cultural backgrounds. An exchange such as A: "These kids today," B: "Yeah, we couldn't have gotten away with some of this stuff," involves not so much sharing of information as sharing of a perspective or a *position* (Davies & Harre, 1990). Foucault, in his documentation of language used to describe the mentally ill, criminals, and sexual minorities, showed that professional and academic conversations often sound very much like the conversations of ordinary people. In the case of professionals, just as in everyday speech, the positioning of the *other* is an essential part of establishing a sense of shared experience: A: "Addicts give me the creeps." B: "I hear there's nothing you can do, they all relapse." These professionals, though trained to be empathic and to see every person as unique, are engaging in negative stereotyping—the same kind of process that characterizes the discourse of hate groups. This social process of *othering* (categorizing people so that they are different, somehow other than one's own kind) distances people and makes it difficult to understand their feelings and their motivations.

In a discursive world, the professional and political leaders who shape a discourse have an unequal *influence* over the way things are described and, as a result, over options that are considered and decisions that are being made. People who are able to influence events in their favor are referred to as having *power*, although the word brings with it some unintended meanings. A more obscure term favored by scholars who refer to the social process of influence is *hegemony*—a social rather than a physical process (remember the physical metaphor?), and it is understood to work in subtle and insidious ways.

A light bulb doesn't anticipate the current that is applied to turn it on, but a person who anticipates influence sometimes acts on that expected influence without a word being spoken or a gesture being delivered. In fact, as Foucault argued, the recipient of influence often takes on the rule-enforcing function; those in charge do not have to actively enforce their rules because the enforcement will be done by others who want their approval.

There is a final word, then, that needs to be included in this discussion: *Privilege* is the intangible possession of those who benefit from hegemony. In Foucault's histories, the sane, the heterosexual, and the law-abiding seem comfortable with whatever is done to those who are insane, homosexual, or criminal because they know it won't happen to them. Helping to enforce the rules that control the undesirables is a way of proving you're okay. In the work of feminists, especially feminists of color, the operation of privilege has been shown to be central to many, if not all, human organizations (see, for example, bell hooks, 2000). Rather than deny privilege or seek its eradication, a postmodern perspective seeks to recognize it and to use it to help overcome injustice.

Social Constructionism and Narrative

Berger and Luckmann's (1966) book *The Social Construction of Reality* was not a big seller, and it had little immediate impact outside academic sociology. However, this was one of the first English-language works in the new intellectual movement of *social constructionism* (Gergen, 1994). Social constructionism, in turn, has profound implications for counseling in general and for couple and family counseling, in particular.

Within the social constructionist tradition, the idea of *narrative* has come to be widely used when referring to certain kinds of discourse that have special meaning for couple and family counseling. Storytelling, or putting experiences into some kind of meaningful form so that they can be shared with others, is an essential part of human interaction. Narratives not only incorporate choices of language to describe events and perceptions (e.g., "she was screaming and looking like she wanted to kill me") but also order events in a way that implies purpose and movement (e.g., "once he saw me heading for the door, he decided to tell me about his affair"). A well-constructed narrative, exemplified by fictional narratives such as *Moby Dick* or *Peter Pan*, seems to pull the listener or reader into the drama. At the same time, it *privileges* a particular way of seeing the events; as this version is repeated, it comes to be more accepted than other ways of seeing the same events.

Familiar narrative structures—sequences and terms that seem to recur across many stories in a cultural tradition—may be referred to as *narrative themes*. Themes provide a sense of familiarity; novelists, playwrights, filmmakers, and television writers keep repeating such themes as an unlikely romance, a ship's crew lost at sea, or twins separated at birth. In much the same way, people's shared experiences tend to be familiar in form as they are retold; the audience participates in the telling by anticipating what comes next.

We may say, then, that narratives people create about their experiences—through their telling—*construct*, or create the experience. The prevailing narrative themes of a culture transmit and perpetuate its values and its definitions of reality. When shared experience has been put into narrative form and repeated many times, it is difficult for participants to "step outside the narrative" and reconstruct their experience to match different perceptions of the events.

The Dominant Marriage and Family Therapy Story

Later in this book, we take these ideas and apply them in work with families. For the moment, we examine the story of family therapy. The popular story of family therapy is a compelling tale, especially because it includes three narrative themes that are nearly universal in contemporary Western culture: the healer, the discoverer, and the hero.

The Healer

A recurring theme in religious stories, family stories, moral lessons, and popular fiction is the healer. Whether a saint, a doctor, or a loving relative, she or he is described as caring more about others than about the self. Recipients of this person's healing efforts are invariably described as improved by the encounter. Great healers make a difference when lesser healers have failed, and the greatest healers take no credit for themselves, for example, Mother Teresa, Albert Schweitzer, and Jonas Salk.

In *Power in the Helping Professions*, Adolph Guggenbuhl-Craig (1986) cautions about the dangers that such a narrative poses for helpers. People may be drawn to the counseling professions as a remedy for their sense of powerlessness; even if their own lives are out of control, helping others may redeem them. Entering a helping interaction with a need to change others, the *wounded healer* runs the risk of denying others' reality after they refuse help or otherwise fail to fit into the story.

Healer Stories: Miraculous Cures

The family therapy stories that drew the greatest public attention to the emerging movement were stories of the amazing achievements of people such as Nathan Ackerman, Virginia Satir, Don Jackson, Carl Whitaker, and Salvador Minuchin. These individuals, who all worked in extremely active ways with families, were reputed to accomplish change in cases that had resisted years, even generations of intervention by others. Their legendary status was increased by the creativity they shared. Despite their efforts to train others, no one ever duplicated their methods or results.

Many of the pioneers of family therapy worked with families of patients diagnosed with schizophrenia—considered essentially incurable in the psychiatric institutions of the time. After watching patients deteriorate on release to their families, these professionals began to intervene directly with family members. Family interven-

tions were effective in reducing symptoms and keeping patients out of the hospital in a time when effective medications had not yet been developed. This success led some theorists in the 1960s to believe that schizophrenia was caused by relational disturbances. Gregory Bateson and his research team in Palo Alto (Bateson, Jackson, Haley, & Weakland, 1963) investigated possible connections between confused communication and disordered thinking. Their studies, which included family interviews and family interventions, were best known for their *double-bind hypothesis*.[3] Murray Bowen (1966, 1978) presented an equally compelling argument that four generations of increasingly disordered family processes were required to produce a schizophrenic.

Family healers also became known for their effectiveness with adolescent delinquents (Minuchin, Montalvo, Guerney, Rosman, & Schumer, 1967) and with patients suffering from anorexia nervosa (Minuchin, Rosman, & Baker, 1978). A few family sessions achieved change in cases that had been failures in other treatment regimens. Here, too, the success of family therapy led to conclusions that family problems had caused the disorder. People in families characterized by emotional confusion, impossible-to-satisfy expectations, and pervasive anxiety tended to display many kinds of problems that disappeared when family relationships improved.

The Hero

A particularly compelling theme in the United States, where the family therapy story took shape, is the theme of the hero—a mythical form that was popular in ancient Greece and is essentially the same story that is told of the American West. An individual, typically a boy or young man, starts off with unlimited potential but no resources, accepts a mission of great importance,

---

[3] The double bind was described as a contradictory set of demands such that an individual who satisfied one was automatically violating the other (see Chapter 5 for more detail). The double-bind hypothesis stated that people in such situations might become insane rather than face the impossibility of pleasing others.

and eventually succeeds after numerous trials of his courage and stamina.

One fictional example of such stories is *The Neverending Story* (Ende, 1983). It has all the required elements: The young hero faces a long series of obstacles and yet he keeps going because the fate of the world is in his hands. He is at the center of a battle with the forces of evil, and, with him as their standard-bearer, the forces of good are able to win. Such stories are reassuring to those who can identify with the hero. The danger of this narrative form, however, is that it tends to glorify a single perspective and cast all opponents or competitors as evil.

Hero Stories: Intellectual and Political Battles

Some of the early family therapists were fond of portraying their work consistently with the hero narrative theme. Jay Haley and Salvador Minuchin fit the image as they were both creative, energetic, optimistic, and hard-working. Haley was probably the most obviously heroic of the group, with his unconventional credentials—his only advanced degree was a master's degree in communication—and his habit of openly challenging the people he saw as the enemy. But Minuchin was, in a way, a more compelling heroic figure. An immigrant who grew up as a Jewish settler in Argentina, he was a champion of the poor and underserved. Both Haley and Minuchin developed intensely loyal groups of collaborators and students.

In the hero narrative, some characters play the part of the enemy. Heroic versions of the family therapy story seem to include two sets of enemies. In the early stories, the ones that served to unite the field through the early 1970s, the enemy was the mental health establishment. Brave family therapists sought to rescue patients from abuse at the hands of misguided people working in self-serving institutions. The passion of this position can be seen in Haley's (1963) fictitious memo from a mental hospital, instructing the staff that treatment consisted of keeping the patient in a one-down position until the patient had learned to defeat all the therapist's strategies.

By 1979, the individual-oriented, passive, traditional mental health system was not the most dangerous enemy. That enemy had become weakened by a generation of battles with various challengers. The message of family therapy, along with various other messages of revolution in the mental health world (e.g., Gestalt, Rational Emotive Therapy, Transactional Analysis), had reached the public. The new enemy was apparent converts who claimed to be family therapists but who used theories of problem formation and change that did not focus on systemic processes. Haley characterized this movement as "How to continue doing what you've always done but call it family therapy" (personal communication, 1979).

The Discoverer

A third narrative theme, strongly identified with European and U.S. history, is that of the discoverer. In this tradition, the young are valued not so much for their strong bodies as for their vision—their pursuit of goals that no one else understands. For the discoverer, the obstacles are wrong turns, fatigue, limited resources, and lost confidence. The enemies, we may say, are ignorance and doubt.

Discoverers succeed if they reach a destination never before reported in their home culture and return to their people with exciting stories and documentation of their travels. Success comes not from divine intervention but from intellectual power—the ability to envision that not yet seen—and a combination of courage and hard work. This narrative theme can be problematic as it tends to equate the unpopular and misunderstood with the good, and to represent tradition as misguided and weak.

Discoverer Stories: Vision, Journeying Together

The discovery theme in family therapy was epitomized by researchers and authors such as Murray Bowen, Gregory Bateson, and Nathan Ackerman who shared new ideas about human problems in a handful of books and journal articles in the

1950s and 1960s. Sailing on uncharted waters, leaving behind the familiar coastlines of their analytic training, these adventurers used innovative methods—film, transcriptions of audio recordings, hospitalization of whole families—to test and modify their tentative formulations about how people interact. Clinical interventions seemed, at times, to be experiments that were more focused on generating knowledge than on alleviating suffering. Together, these scholars saw themselves as documenting a new story of human life. The story was told primarily among the community of insiders—the emerging group of family therapists—and its inaccessibility was one of its charms. For the discoverer, once the masses find your exotic destination, you are indistinguishable from a tourist.

The first family therapy textbooks didn't appear until the early 1970s. In one, Vincent Foley (1974) explains the need for integrating the various works in the field and clearly identifies himself as not one of the discoverers but rather one who has heard their stories and is passing them on. Foley gained his perspective by surveying professors who taught family therapy, seeking their nominations of the most frequently taught family therapy authors and innovators. By 1978, however, family therapy was in the public eye. *The New Yorker* published a lengthy story on Salvador Minuchin (Malcolm, 1978). From that point on, exotic terms such as system, rubber fence, and schizmogenesis were no longer proof of insider knowledge, as they were finding their way into textbooks and popular magazines, and the discovery theme was less applicable.

An Alternative Story, Phase I: The Discovery Years

In his foreword to one of the classic textbooks of the field, Salvador Minuchin—a central character in many versions of the dominant story—describes the history of family therapy this way: "Born in the late 1950s, family therapy seemed to spring fully formed out of the heads of a group of

seminal thinkers and practitioners" (Minuchin, 2004). This portrayal is typical of statements found in many of the classic works in the field (e.g., Satir, 1964/1967).

But the story commits a couple of narrative errors. The focus on the springing forth of a "fully formed" movement in the 1950s denies many gradual, incremental changes that had been moving for decades in the direction of conceptualizing and engaging the couple or family as a unit rather than as a group of multiple research subject or clients. Furthermore, by locating the activity inside the "heads" of individuals, this story denies the systemic understanding that is the hallmark of the family therapy movement. Yes, there was a group of seminal thinkers and practitioners, but they functioned as a system. Their interactions—direct and indirect—inspired, informed, challenged, and corrected their individual efforts. The product is something that might better be credited to the group process than to the individual group members.

Gradual, Incremental Change

The movement to provide professional help to couples and families dates back to the early nineteenth century and the beginning of the industrial revolution. Economic and political reorganization of industrialized society created rapid social change in many parts of the world. Whereas the European and American social systems of the seventeenth and eighteenth centuries moved children seamlessly into the workforce through apprenticeships, agricultural jobs, and servant positions (Aries, 1962), the growth of factory production and mechanized farming eliminated many traditional opportunities for youth. Children were readily employable in the factories, though, and newly fashionable *nuclear families* consisting of two parents and their children began moving to urban areas where jobs were plentiful. Child labor laws soon followed, however, and the new urban areas were teeming with unskilled, restless young people who had no *extended family* to provide stability. These new "delinquent youth" created panic in their communities, and adults mobilized in attempts to control this new social problem (Schneider, 1992). There were two approaches to this new social phenomenon: focusing on the environment or focusing on the youth themselves.

Social Orientation

The theorists, researchers, and practitioners in the first camp viewed families in all of their forms as positive resources for social survival and betterment. These social reformers—often inspired by religious teachings—portrayed history as stories of families who always cared for each other and lived as emotional and economic units. Nomadic families, in their view, always moved together and shared members' varied talents in surviving; agricultural families always shared land and pooled their labor to produce food. A family, according to the religious idealists, shared a spiritual life through ritual, prayer, and the disciplines of their tradition.[4]

It was in such a climate that the social sciences began to evolve. The new sciences of anthropology, sociology, economics, and communication studied "the family" as a group—its challenges and its variations—with the goal of improving human life. Social scholars such as Parsons and Bales (1955) concluded that changing social patterns had led to a loss of the traditional *functions* of the community. The most critical lost function was that of socializing children to become responsible and productive members of society. In the industrial society, a nuclear family had been left to meet all of its own needs, and additional resources were needed to preserve and strengthen these weakened families.

The interventions that grew out of this social orientation were sometimes respectful and supportive, sometimes arrogant and disruptive, but they shared a belief that a healthy community was made up not of individuals but of family groupings. Community resources were mobilized, often by religious groups, to provide economic and other support for those families that were perceived as weakened or functioning poorly. Programs included in-home and center-based help with issues of parenting, family resource management, nutrition, family planning, couple communication, and couple sexuality. By the middle of the twentieth century, many kinds of family counseling were being done by professionals and by trained volunteers in settlement houses, religious institutions, social service agencies, and hospitals (Beels, 2002; Broderick & Schrader, 1991).

Individual Orientation

In the second camp, the family as a group was suspect. The Enlightenment preceded the Industrial Revolution and was a time when scholars in European culture glorified the individual, the "self" who was personally responsible for his or her actions and whose moral decisions were of great importance for society. With the individual as the locus of action, educational and religious institutions in the eighteenth and nineteenth centuries had attempted to create model citizens. Social control efforts had begun to shift from laws, rules, walls, and gates to internal control based on ideals and values. Those who transgressed were seen as spiritually weakened or as sick, not living up to their potential as essentially good and valuable citizens. Religious leaders blamed social problems on the moral breakdown of society, and evangelical religious movements announced their goal of saving the souls of the poor, the emotionally troubled, and those in prison.

It was in this climate that Freud and his contemporaries began to work. Focusing more on the problems of the wealthy than those of the poor, the psychoanalytic movement regarded family as a negative force. This view had some merit; bourgeois families in the major cities, trying to copy the ruling classes but lacking their economic resources, had created lifestyle patterns that led to intense dependencies and high levels of anxiety in their small family groups (Aries, 1962). Freud and other psychoanalysts believed that medical as well as emotional problems resulted from

---

[4] Aries (1962) has said that these images described only the wealthy and warned that the self-sufficient family is a recent ideal promoted by the upper classes in Europe and those who emulated them.

unchecked emotional forces in the emotional pressure cooker of the nuclear family.

Mothers were central in the psychoanalysts' criticism of the behavioral and emotional core of the family—they exercised tremendous power to control children through their intimate involvement in children's early experiences (see Box 2.1). Analysts encouraged adult patients to pull away from their parents, and they believed that an emotionally disturbed child would be helped by providing a "healthier" relationship—one that was free of judgment and dependency—in the treatment room. In many cases, children were temporarily removed from their parental homes to reduce the family's negative influence.

When doubts about the effectiveness of both the spiritual and psychoanalytic agendas were expressed in the middle of the twentieth century, the alternative was the new perspective of behaviorism. Behavioral teachings addressed emotional and behavioral problems by focusing on the individual; the theory explained that the individual had developed these problems in a social environment, but it was easier to change the individual's learned response patterns than to attempt environmental change.

Integration
By the 1950s, when the family therapy movement began to take shape, there was considerable frustration in both the social and individual orientations and the United States seemed to be divided according to geography. In the eastern part of the country the more individual view dominated, whereas professionals in the western states emphasized the social group more strongly. Within each of the two orientations, a variety of research and practice efforts developed. What we see in this early stage of the family therapy literature, even more than the diversity of theories, is the obvious respect and care that is shown in the writings of these early explorers. Rather than making grand claims for the significance of their work, they were excited to be doing things that they considered important and they were pleased to have the opportunity to share their work.

Professional Groups and Collaboration

The professionals who contributed theories and strategies to the family therapy movement came from varied backgrounds, each of which added its own flavor to the mixture.

Social Workers
Social work in the United States dates back to at least 1877. The model was borrowed from work done in Great Britain, a secularization of parish visits by ministers and deacons (Broderick & Schrader, 1991). A primary concern of this movement was families' economic well-being, therefore direct financial aid was often a focus of

---

BOX 2.1

Mothers in the 1950s

The mid-twentieth century was a period in which motherhood had tremendous symbolic importance in the United States. On one hand, women were being portrayed as saintly, innocent, pure, and angelic. In Hollywood films, for example, Doris Day and similar bland heroines replaced stars who had been sexually aggressive and emotionally complex. On the other hand, though, authors such as Philip Wylie (1942) were citing Freud as their authority, accusing American society of denying women's sexuality and thereby distorting family relationships. While mothers of successful sons were revered (for the most part, women had little access to roles in which they themselves could achieve), more often mothers were blamed for emotionally crippling their sons.

assistance efforts.[5] As social work developed into a professional field, its writings showed increasing sophistication. Economic differences were recognized as multidimensional and class differences were shown to reflect orientation to different group norms. In helping to create the movement that became family therapy, social work contributed not only a model of analysis and intervention but also a massive research program. Mary Richmond's (1917) book, *Social Diagnosis,* exemplified the scientific and scholarly activity of early social workers. Drawing on medical and social case records of juvenile delinquents, Richmond provided solid documentation that families' circumstances were deeply implicated in their patterns of interaction and their varying levels of coping.

As the field developed, social workers not only focused on parent-child problems but also identified couple relationships as central to people's lives. At the fiftieth anniversary celebration of Family Social Casework in America in 1928, Richmond presented a paper on marriage counseling, and in 1943 the Family Service Associations of America published what is credited with being "the first volume entirely devoted to marriage counseling" (Broderick & Schrader, 1991).

Home Economists and Family Sociologists

Another group of concerned citizens responded to the needs of these same families—whose lives were dominated by dislocation, poverty, and limited access to social resources—by creating settlement houses. These home economists provided classes in which women gained access to sound research-based information designed to help them to manage their limited resources and use sound nutritional principles to improve their families' health. As experts on both the positive and troubling aspects of couple and family relationships, home economists took action when they saw opportunities to apply their knowledge. One opportunity came in the form of college and uni-

versity courses in marriage and family living. College students were an accessible population, and researchers studying family life attributed considerable power to the couple relationship—often formed during the college years. Courses were heavily focused on mate selection processes, along with the same issues that were addressed in community settings—parenting, sexuality, nutrition, economic planning—and delivered as a mixture of didactic content and personal exploration assignments.

Mental Hospitals

The nineteenth century focus on deviants and criminals led to sanitariums and asylums where emotionally disturbed individuals could be protected from the demands of normal life and could receive treatment for their disorders. Treatment models were based on many different understandings of mental illness, ranging from psychoanalytic assumptions about internal conflict to existentialist assumptions about retreat from responsibility.

Psychiatrists directed treatment in these facilities, but the majority of patient contacts were with other kinds of staff members including psychologists and social workers. Extended returns home were not uncommon for private patients, and treatment teams in the private facilities spent considerable time working with patients' families trying to reduce stress and create a nonjudgmental home environment.

Child Guidance Clinics

According to Aries (1962), childhood was first defined as a distinct life stage during the Enlightenment period; prior to that time children were not viewed as significantly different from adults. Protection of children was not deemed necessary, and there were no societal rules that restricted a child's access to adult opportunities, responsibilities, and risks.

The modern period created images of the child as a special kind of person, innocent and without malice. No human could live up to that unrealistic image, so many children were considered defective when compared to such an ideal. The idealization of children did, however, motivate people to dedicate resources to their well-

---

[5] Beels, writing from a feminist-informed postmodernist perspective, expresses concern that the real agenda of these paternalistic efforts was to help the poor to look like the middle class.

being and therefore during the nineteenth and early twentieth centuries child welfare agencies and child guidance centers came into existence. Similar to mental hospitals, child guidance clinics typically were staffed with psychiatrists and psychologists who diagnosed and treated children, supported by others—mostly social workers—who worked with the families but who did not provide therapy or counseling.

Marriage Counselors

The twentieth century saw the emergence of marital counseling—often with an emphasis on sexual functioning. The sexual liberation movement, inspired by psychoanalytic theory, led to a new science of human sexuality. By 1942, marriage counseling had become a professional specialty crossing many disciplinary boundaries, and the American Association of Marriage Counselors involved prominent researchers and counseling professionals such as Kinsey, Masters, and Johnson. A strong medical presence in the group attempted to keep marriage *counseling*—essentially a lay activity—separate from any kind of *therapy*, which during those years was practiced only by psychiatrists and other physicians.

The New Family Therapy Movement

Building on social change, scientifically gathered data, emerging theories, and established intervention models, during the 1950s a new movement began to coalesce. Virginia Satir summarized that period as follows: First, clinicians shared an observation that successful treatment of individuals sometimes led to a deterioration in other family members. Next, they began examining family groups in their clinics, and then "once therapists started to see the whole family together, other aspects of family life which produced symptoms were revealed, aspects which had been largely overlooked" (1964/1967, p. 3).

The early stirrings of this new movement appeared in many places. Off in the world of pure science, Bateson (1951), von Bertalanffy (1967), and Wiener (1961) were exploring ideas about human systems and mental health. In psychiatry and psychology, Ackerman, Bell, Bowen, Bowlby, Satir, and Whitaker were conducting unconventional kinds of interventions with patients and their families. These innovators learned about each other's work through the American Association for Orthopsychiatry, whose conferences welcomed family therapy presentations and whose journal published occasional family therapy papers. The earliest overviews of the movement did not appear until the early 1960s. I use three documents to assemble a representative picture of that period.

The first is the founding issue of the journal *Family Process*, published in 1962 with Jay Haley as its editor. The new journal not only published conventional articles, as would be expected of a professional medium, but also included a newsletter-like section where discoveries and questions were shared (see Box 2.2). The second is the 1965 book, *Intensive Family Therapy*, edited by Ivan Boszormenyi-Nagy and James L. Framo. This book is almost exclusively a product of the eastern United States, where family therapy approaches had more of a psychodynamic flavor. Several of the authors in that book assumed a central role in the next 20 years of family therapy; a search of family therapy textbooks will find almost universal mention of contributors Nathan Ackerman, Ivan Boszormenyi-Nagy, Murrray Bowen, James Framo, Carl Whitaker, and Lyman Wynne. But others who were represented in this collection—Richard Felder, Raymond Fogelson, Paul Franklin, David Rubenstein, Harold Searles, Anthony Wallace—did not become prominent in the emerging field, and their names are not as well known (see Table 2.1 on p. 45).

The third document is titled *The Field of Family Therapy*, a summary prepared by a committee of the Group for the Advancement of Psychiatry (GAP; 1970). The report, including a ranking based on mental health practitioners' nominations for significant contributions to family therapy, provides a picture of the diversity in the field. The authors organized it to highlight the distribution of work across the various disciplines and different parts of the United States,

BOX 2.2

Family Affairs from Family Process Volume 1

The aim of this column is to report on ongoing research work in the area of the family and small group process. It is hoped that brief information given here about research design and theoretical views will stimulate correspondence between interested parties. We are asking the cooperation of our readers in reporting on their projects and in writing us about their opinion of other projects or of work they feel needs doing.

Doctor Henry Grunebaum from the Massachusetts Mental Health Center writes us that his group is interested in conjoint family treatment of patients with psychoses and a followup study of these treated cases is planned. In addition, Dr. Grunebaum reports, Boston Psychopathic Hospital has been admitting the children of psychotically disturbed women so that an unusual opportunity is afforded to study mother-child relationships.

Doctor Nathan Ackerman reports that The Family Institute of New York City is planning a Research Conference on "The Science of the Family" to be held at Arden House in 1962. The Family Institute is busily engaged in professional training and has been working with seven service organizations in Westchester County including psychiatrists and pediatricians in the same communities. The first of a series of composite films on conjoint family psychotherapy is now completed and is being distributed on a rental basis to accredited professional training centers. This training is made available through the auspices of The Family Institute and the Jewish Family Service.

Doctor Theodore Lidz reports that he and his associates at Yale are continuing to analyze their data on 17 families with schizophrenic patients. Three articles are being submitted for publication shortly: one, a study of the siblings of schizophrenic patients; two, the comparison of the parent-child relationships of male and female schizophrenic patients; and three, a sociologically oriented paper on the alienation of the families of the schizophrenic patients prepared with the assistance of Doctor Ezra Vogel. They report that they are currently attempting to replicate McConaghey's consistent finding of a thought disorder in one parent of schizophrenic patients on the Lovabond version of the Rappaport Sorting Test. David Rosenthal at NIMH is working on a similar project and exchanging views with the Yale Group.

Doctor Ivan Boszormenyi-Nagy from the Eastern Pennsylvania Psychiatric Institute tells us that their family therapy project in schizophrenia has been running four years. The clinical material is derived from a 20 bed ward of selected young female schizophrenic patients. The patients are involved in individual psychotherapy, in therapeutic community, and daily group meetings. In addition, there are family meetings, and to date ten families have been seen almost three years.

Source: Extracts from "Family Affairs," Don Jackson's column in the first issue of *Family Process,* 1962, p. 53.

---

and their format allowed even the most obscure article to receive some notice.

As we look back at the names in the GAP rankings (Table 2.2 on p. 46), some would be expected—Virginia Satir and Nathan Ackerman were ranked at the top. In a mental health climate where the typical practitioner was attempting either to be silent (analytic) or scientifically detached (behavioral), both Satir and Ackerman attracted attention with their dramatic, confrontational, active styles.

But in hindsight, it is surprising how few of the survey respondents mentioned Haley, Bowen, and Minuchin, who would also lead major movements by the end of the 1970s.

Theoretical Underpinnings
Just as many practice traditions converged in the 1950s, several intellectual traditions can be seen in these early efforts. These perspectives may be best understood as theory-building efforts that

Table 2.1   **Contents from Intensive Family Therapy**

1. *A Review of Concepts in the Study and Treatment of Families of Schizophrenics.* Gerald H. Zuk and David Rubinstein
2. *A Theory of Relationships: Experience and Transaction.* Ivan Boszormenyi-Nagy
3. *Intensive Family Therapy as a Process.* Ivan Boszormenyi-Nagy
4. *Rationale and Techniques of Intensive Family Therapy.* James L. Framo
5. *Family Psychotherapy with Schizophrenia in the Hospital and in Private Practice.* Murray Bowen
6. *Family Dynamics and the Reversability of Delusional Formation: A Case Study in Family Therapy.* Nathan W. Ackerman and Paul F. Franklin
7. *Some Indications and Contraindications for Exploratory Family Therapy.* Lyman C. Wynne
8. *Countertransference in the Family Treatment of Schizophrenia.* Carl A. Whitaker, Richard E. Felder, and John Warkentin
9. *Mystification, Confusion, and Conflict.* Ronald D. Laing
10. *The Identity Struggle.* Anthony F. C. Wallace and Raymond D. Fogelson
11. *Systematic Research on Family Dynamics.* James L. Framo
12. *The Contributions of Family Treatment to the Psychotherapy of Schizophrenia.* Harold F. Searles

reflected the different worldviews, social locations, and personal experiences of various researchers, teachers, and practitioners. A few theoretical elements appear repeatedly in the original conceptions underlying each of these perspectives, while at the same time each perspective has evolved over time.

Anthropology and Sociology. Within the various academic traditions, the most relevant area of scholarship for family counselors would focus on human interactions. In the early part of the twentieth century, there were two such disciplines—anthropology and sociology.

Anthropology, the older of the two disciplines, grew out of the European fascination with the varieties of human social behavior. Some anthropologists were involved in historical studies of lost cultures, but the majority were fo-

cused on unique living cultures—often those regarded as at risk of disappearing. Researchers typically spent extended periods immersed in the culture they were studying, focusing much of their attention on the language and other symbols through which the culture was maintained. It was common for an anthropologist to recruit one or more informants from within the culture, individuals who would be interviewed at length. Informants were encouraged to share their cultural myths and stories, explain the rules and practices of their communities, and teach the visitors the skills required for functioning in their cultures.

Among the most visible anthropologists studying families were Margaret Mead, whose work challenged Western assumptions about sexuality and gender, and her ex-husband Gregory Bateson, who became a powerful influence in the family therapy movement of the 1950s. Bateson had a long-standing interest in cultural patterns of insanity before he turned his attention to schizophrenia in modern societies. In one example, he theorized that a ritual called *Naven*, in which participants exhibited behavior that violated cultural norms, served a covert function by reducing tensions among the Iatmul people of New Guinea.

Anthropology's focus was directed toward the special case—the special culture, and special individuals in that culture—while sociology's focus was more directed toward the general case. Sociologists used methods that aggregated the experiences of individuals and families into large samples and their theories were theories of group tendencies. Early sociologists, strongly influenced by Marxist theory, were especially concerned with economic forces and social structures and the ways in which people were socialized to fit into their prescribed positions in society. In family sociology, mate selection was a popular subject for study not only because of its relevance but also because the phenomenon showed individuals making choices that clearly expressed societal values. Sociological concepts of social exchange, reciprocity, role performance, and conflict have been influential in shaping the goals and techniques of family therapy.

Table 2.2   **GAP Report Table**

		By Area			By Professional Affiliation			
Theorist	**Total**	**Calif.**	**West**	**East**	**Psychiatrists**	**Psychologists**	**Social Workers**	**Others**
Satir	54	32 / 59%	13 / 24%	9 / 17%	15 / 27%	8 / 14%	25 / 48%	6 / 11%
Ackerman	52	14 / 27%	15 / 29%	23 / 44%	16 / 31%	7 / 13%	25 / 48%	4 / 8%
Jackson	51	27 / 53%	6 / 12%	18 / 35%	21 / 41%	10 / 20%	15 / 29%	5 / 10%
Haley	32	13 / 41%	8 / 25%	11 / 34%	11 / 34%	7 / 22%	9 / 28%	5 / 16%
Bowen	24	2 / 8%	4 / 17%	18 / 75%	8 / 33%	4 / 17%	9 / 38%	3 / 12%
Wynne	19	4 / 21%	5 / 16%	10 / 53%	13 / 69%	1 / 5%	4 / 21%	1 / 5%
Bateson	17	5 / 29%	4 / 23%	6 / 35%	7 / 41%	3 / 18%	6 / 35%	1 / 6%
Bell	15	7	5	3	5	3	5	2
Boszormenyi-Nagy	9	2	1	6	2	2	4	1
Sullivan	6	3	1	2	2	3	1	
Lidz et al.	6	2	2	2	4	1	1	
Brody	5	1	2	2	2	1	1	1
Spiegel	5			5	3		1	1
Whitaker	5		1	4	2		3	
Kempler	4	4					4	
Paul	4	1	1	2	2	1	1	
MacGregor	3	1	1	1	2			1
Minuchin	3	1		2			1	1
Scheflen	3	1		2		1	1	1
Singer	3	3			3			
Szurek	3	3			2			1

*Percentages are indicated separately by area and professional affiliation only for theorists most frequently mentioned.
Source: From *The Field of Family Therapy,* by the Group for the Advancement of Psychiatry, 1970, New York: Author. Reprinted with permission.

Existential Philosophy and Humanistic Psychology. Many of the twentieth century's best-known figures in the counseling and psychotherapy field were strongly influenced by existentialist beliefs about the human condition and the nature of mental health. Existentialists interpreted mental illness as a failure to cope with reality; as a result, they encouraged people to become more authen-tic—more aware of their experiences, their moods, and their thoughts.

Humanistic psychology, based on existentialist thought, became popular in the post-World War II period when the United States and Europe were burying their dead, rebuilding their cities and their countryside, returning their factories to the production of civilian goods, and spending time with their families. The new movement addressed mental health problems as failures to be authentic, but with a new twist. Humanistic approaches defined the fully functioning person as one who was engaged in relationships. The demand for authentic relationships continues to be a driving force in the field of family counseling.

Communications. Any observer of humans must notice that verbal and noverbal communication is a constant part of our interactions. Communication itself is a rather broad term, however; the branch of communication that had such an influence on the early development of family counseling was focused on interpersonal communication through speech and nonverbal processes.

One of the most significant contributions from communication scholars is the idea that people *send* confusing messages that are hard for recipients to *decode*. Study of nonverbal communication, facilitated by film, was an important part of the research that documented this phenomenon. This awareness led to a family counseling focus not only on clarifying primary (explicit) messages but also on discovering and articulating secondary (often, conflicting and less acceptable) messages. The concept of *communication problems* became a central element in the public's image of family counseling, and many families today begin the first session by saying, "We have trouble communicating."

Behavioral Psychology. Possibly the most radical influence in the human sciences of the late nineteenth and early twentieth centuries came from the behaviorists. This movement sought to create a research-based science that described humans and other animals without any assumptions about consciousness (Wozniak, 1994). In Pavlov's experiments with dogs and Thorndike's experiments with cats, the new science explored questions of how animals acquire new skills; it was a small and predictable leap from experimenting on animals to experimenting on humans.

Behavioral theories and their clinical applications became extremely popular beginning in the 1920s, as shown by the popularity of John Watson's (1928) *Psychological care of infant and child.*

Under behavioral control, said Watson, a child would be a happy, satisfied, productive member of society. A generation of children was brought up under behavioral regimes that discouraged holding and comforting babies because such handling would reinforce crying and selfishness. Direct applications of conditioning theories to couple and family intervention did not occur until the 1970s, but behavioral approaches quickly became part of the mainstream of family work.

Developmental Psychology and Physiology. The same valuing of science that produced behaviorism extended to another approach with family problems, the child study movement. Around the turn of the century, child study centers were established at major universities and in major cities around the United States. These centers, exemplified by the Yale Child Study Center established by Arnold Gesell, conducted a variety of research programs that led to a "mapping" of normal infant, child, and adolescent development. The findings of Gesell's research program were published in a series of parenting books that educated parents about their children's developmental needs—books that continued to be republished into the 1980s.

In contrast with the behaviorists' belief that a child's personal characteristics could be altered without limit, the new science of human development—grounded in a naturalistic philosophical base established by Jean Jacques Rousseau—fostered a belief that every child's development proceeded according to a plan that allowed for little modification without injuring the child. The focus of parenting, then, was not to reshape children but rather to provide appropriate, challenging, supportive environments in which the natural processes of development could reach their optimal outcomes. Parents were encouraged to listen to their children, to observe them, and to anticipate their needs so as to make the best use of every opportunity for development.

Psychoanalytic Theory. Overriding all of these traditions, however, the first two-thirds of the twentieth century seem to have been dominated by Sigmund Freud and the people he either trained or inspired. Dr. Benjamin Spock's (1945) *The Common Sense Book of Baby and Child Care* serves as an example of this influence. This popular parenting book (which is still for sale in an updated edition) presented the post-World War II generation of U.S. parents with ideas that seemed radical at the time: Babies were not selfish or spoiled if they cried; rather, they were needy and vulnerable and a loving parent should respond with holding, feeding, and other attention.

Such ideas, while they had parallels in many cultures throughout the world, contrasted sharply with the child-rearing principles of the previous generation of U.S. parents: feed at scheduled times, don't hold babies or they become selfish, train them to live the way you want them to live when they're adults. The basic idea that humans have physical drives and emotional needs eventually gained acceptance in many fields; family counselors generally share some such belief, approaching couple and family interactions with a goal of helping each member to become more self-aware by expressing his or her inner experience.

Individual Psychology (Adler). If Freud and his loyalists had a significant influence on the first two-thirds of the twentieth century, so did a variety of movements that opposed Freudian ideas. Especially influential in early family counseling efforts was Alfred Adler's *Individual Psychology* (Hoffman, 1994). Adler, like Freud, viewed individuals as having been strongly influenced by family experiences in early development. In Adler's view, though, the most powerful experience was a natural human tendency to feel small and insignificant. This feeling could grow—depending on environmental influences—into weakness and self-denial or into overcompensation and bullying. Like Freud's work, Adler's work was widely disseminated by others. Rudolph Dreikurs' (1976) popular book based on Adlerian ideas, *Children: The Challenge,* has influenced generations of counselors, educators, and parents in the United States.

In contrast with Freud, Adler's theory was essentially optimistic and emphasized the continuing process of reshaping people's lives through reviewing and modifying early influences. Partners in couple relationships could challenge each other to become more like their ideal selves, and parents could give their children emotional support, while communicating that no individual is the center of the world. Applied in family counseling, Adlerian ideas contributed to a general attitude of respect and support that fit well with many other perspectives.

Early Models—The Leading Citizens in a Frontier Town

Literature from the 1960s and early 1970s shows a widespread family therapy community populated by many individuals who made original contributions and many others who worked hard to document the emerging paradigm. I think of it as a frontier town, a place where adventurers and ambitious business people set up tents and hastily constructed buildings to serve a steady stream of seekers who rode into town. The richness of this diverse community is striking; theorists and researchers represented a wide range of disciplines, even one author—Jay Haley—who did not have any formal training in the mental health field. The law enforcement in this frontier town, such as it was, consisted of the editors and publishers who selected some workers to stay and encouraged others to move on.

My goal for this book is to avoid overwhelming you with details of all the complex differences in the family therapy literature, and at this point that goal presents a challenge. Every one of the key contributors to the family therapy movement was a person of great personal wisdom and power, a person who deserves considerable attention. Therefore, rather than try to tell the story of every leading citizen, I have chosen three whose extensive writings and filmed sessions, plus descriptions in other authors' literature, make it possible to reconstruct their work.

Ackerman

One of the most visible and memorable figures in early family therapy was Nathan Ackerman. Ackerman, a psychoanalytically trained psychiatrist, expressed doubts about the idea that pathology occurred in a single person. He wrote in 1958, "Psychiatric illness as a single or isolated instance in family life hardly occurs. Almost always other members of the family are also ill. The sick behaviors of these family members are often closely interwoven, and mutually reinforcing" (quoted in Bloch & Simon, 1982, p. 236). For Ackerman, treating families as units of pathology didn't require a new theory because Freud had explained pathological interaction and mutual influence. Even as Ackerman pioneered the treatment of families, he insisted that he was updating and not replacing psychoanalytic theory with ideas such as child influences on parents, processes of social interaction, and the functioning of the family as a whole (Ackerman, 1958).

A case study from the mid-1960s illustrates the kind of dynamic, active, engaging style that made Ackerman a legend (Ackerman & Franklin, 1965). In this session, as in nearly every filmed session showing Ackerman interacting with families, Ackerman was not the primary therapist; he was the case supervisor and the director of a research project. With this 16-year-old girl, Helen, and her parents, who have been in therapy together for a year, Ackerman returns to one of the unresolved themes of the therapy: Helen's discomfort with a distant and unemotional relationship with her father:

DR. A.: *What you are really saying . . . when he comes home from the office and you want to know what should you ask him . . . you're really saying what kind of a man is he? Aren't you?*

HELEN: *Yes. I can't ask him how he gets along with his assistants, how he gets along with his nurses, how he gets along with teeth.*

DR. A.: *Well, take a look at him. What do you really want to know about Daddy?*

HELEN: *(hesitantly) Well . . . I want to know what kind of a person he really is, outside of his dentistry, outside of any business matters.*

Ackerman moves quickly, then, and in a few short interchanges he is saying,

DR. A.: *Your daughter has to remind you that you have a throb in your veins, that you're not just a mechanical man.*

HELEN: *A robot.*

FATHER: *Especially now that spring is here.*

HELEN: *What has spring got to do with it? You're the same way whether it's September or December, or whether it's May. (Mother breaks in laughing.)*

DR. A.: *Well, what he's saying is that he's capable of a heart flutter in springtime.*

FATHER: *That's right.*

DR. A.: *Are you in love this spring?*

FATHER: *(exaggeratedly) Oh, sure. (He and mother laugh.)*

HELEN: *Are you in love?*

FATHER: *Of course; all the sap starts flowing. (Mother continues to laugh. Father joins in.)*

And not long after that,

DR. A.: *Helen looked at you and said that if she were to judge by surface impressions, you would seem to be an utterly inanimate, unfeeling, mechanical man, a robot. You say no. Comes springtime, you fall in love all over again.*

HELEN: *And then every winter, he goes back. You know.*

DR. A.: *Helen looks at you and says you hide from her. Your manliness. . . . (Helen breaks in. It isn't clear.) (to Helen) Do you want to talk? (to father) She wants to see you.*

These brief extracts show Ackerman breaking ranks with psychoanalytic tradition, not only by bringing family members into the same room, but also by using a combination of lightheartedness and pointed challenges, alternately joining with the adolescent and then with her parents, stepping away from the safety of professional language by playing with themes of sexuality and emergence into adulthood as he helps them renegotiate their relationships.

Satir

Virginia Satir's name may be the one most often associated with the idea of family therapy. In the 1940s, working as a teacher, she had visited homes and worked with her students' families on issues of motivation and decision making. She returned to full-time graduate study after 6 years in the classroom, she explained, to better learn how to help people. However, it was not her graduate social work training that defined her work. In later reflections (Satir & Bitter, 2000), she saw her innovations as a rejection of the social worker role and a return to her natural ways of working with people: direct, caring, and determined. Her style was, like Ackerman's, an active one. She interrupted, she told people what to say, and she told them clearly what she was seeing.

Satir moved from Chicago to California in 1959 to help Don Jackson found the Family Therapy Training Center at the Mental Research Institute. An experienced therapist and teacher, she had been teaching family work to psychiatric residents, and *Conjoint Family Therapy* (1967) was a direct outgrowth of that training—she said it was essentially an expansion of her lecture notes. A dense book for 208 pages, it contained a graduate curriculum in family developmental issues emphasizing the development of a strong emotional system; family communication, with an emphasis on accurate understanding and congruence; and family diagnosis, viewing any symptom as the result of a blocked developmental process. What is more, it presented sample therapeutic dialogue and a step-by-step outline for conducting the early phase of family intervention (Figure 2.1).

Satir, like many of the pioneers of the 1950s and 1960s, expected that the reader would be shocked and even offended by the basic idea of bringing couples and families into an office together. She worked hard at articulating the rationale for her work. One of the most dramatic of those efforts was her participation as one of the featured family therapists in Jay Haley and Lynn Hoffman's *Techniques of Family Therapy.* Satir, like the other participants in their project, was interviewed as the authors reviewed the audiotape of one of her family therapy sessions. The following session (reprinted from Haley & Hoffman, 1967, pp. 99–128) involved the family of Gary, a 17-year-old boy who had been hospitalized after a crisis during a European vacation.

Satir was aware of making choices in the session and she had strong beliefs about what was helpful. This is the intake session, and Satir has just welcomed the family—Gary, his parents, his older and younger sisters, and his brother, the youngest—to her office:

SATIR: *I wonder what, as you're all sitting here, as you're thinking about it, what is it that you expect? (Pause) As you came here?*
GARY: *I didn't think about it. I knew I was going to come down here. But I, ah, I was kind of dubious of, that it would do any good. To be frank.*
SATIR: *Well, we have your contribution. Everybody else has ideas, 'cause you're all here.*

Satir explained to Haley and Hoffman that she liked to take charge with a question, and she had directed the question to the group because she wanted to make it clear that all were obligated to participate. She would eventually go around the family and insist on hearing from every member. At the moment, though, Gary was not finished speaking:

GARY: *Funny, today I had this, this, this, ah, now at the time we had this ward meeting up at the hospital, and I'm immediately controlling it, unfortunately.*
SATIR: *You were doing what? I didn't hear.*
GARY: *Controlling the meeting. Because this, I sit there and try to draw people out.*
SATIR: *I see.*
GARY: *'Cause this doctor . . .*
SATIR: *Well, that will be my job here. (female laughter)*
GARY: *That's right.*

Satir explained to Haley and Hoffman that she was assuming Gary was speaking indirectly about his perception that he had to manage his family, and she was informing him that he could turn that job over to her. Note the metaphorical quality of this communication.

Later in the session, Satir had gathered several statements supporting her belief that there was a problem around the theme of handling differences or disagreements in the family, and she began to escalate the issue. Like the salesperson who asks whether the customer wants the 6-month plan or the 2-year plan, she did not offer the option of saying that these disagreements didn't occur:

SATIR: *All right. Then, you see, if we start putting our thinking caps on, then we can begin to remember that this is not a family of angels, but a family of*

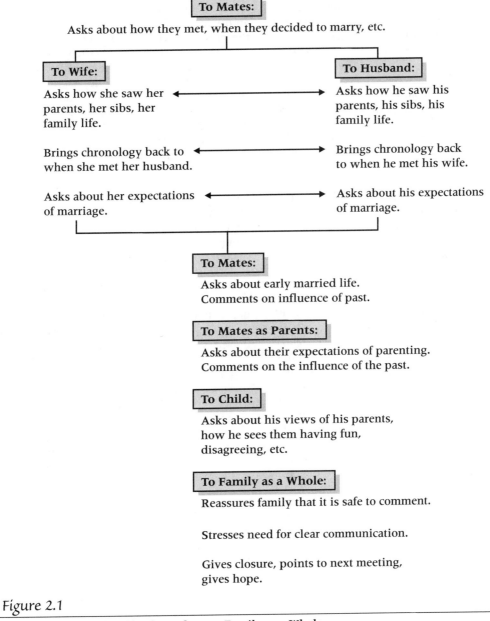

Therapist asks about the problem

To Mates:

Asks about how they met, when they decided to marry, etc.

To Wife:

Asks how she saw her parents, her sibs, her family life.   ←——————→   **To Husband:** Asks how he saw his parents, his sibs, his family life.

Brings chronology back to when she met her husband.   ←——————→   Brings chronology back to when he met his wife.

Asks about her expectations of marriage.   ←——————→   Asks about his expectations of marriage.

To Mates:

Asks about early married life.
Comments on influence of past.

To Mates as Parents:

Asks about their expectations of parenting.
Comments on the influence of the past.

To Child:

Asks about his views of his parents, how he sees them having fun, disagreeing, etc.

To Family as a Whole:

Reassures family that it is safe to comment.

Stresses need for clear communication.

Gives closure, points to next meeting, gives hope.

Figure 2.1

Main Flow of Family-Life Chronology to Family as a Whole

Source: From *Conjoint Family Therapy* (p. 135), by V. Satir, 1967, Palo Alto, CA: Science and Behavior Books. Reprinted with permission.

people in which people are going to be disapproving and disappointing as well as loving. Now, Mother, tell me—what do you think happens when Dad disapproves of something you do, and he doesn't tell you about it?

MOTHER: *I suppose I freeze up and I get quiet and . . .*

GARY: *Hmmm.*

MOTHER: *. . . and resentful. I don't think he ever . . .*

FATHER: *I think you'll have to get the question rephrased again. I slipped a little bit, just exactly what you said.*

SATIR: *That is, when your wife knows that you disapprove of something, but you haven't said that you disapprove of it, but she knows it. Then what does she do?*

MOTHER: *I think that's what I do (Loud laugh by Gary, humming sound from Tim)*

GARY: *Ha, ha—we've got a game!*

MOTHER: *I would hurt him with my silence.*

SATIR: *You would hurt him with a silence.*

In response to the interviewers' questions, Satir explained that she interpreted the "game" comment to mean, "Games like this go on in our house." She said that her substitution of "a silence" for "my silence" was intended to recognize that the tactic was something that was not the mother's alone, but was something everyone had available. The interviewers were surprised at the mother's frankness, and Satir explained that it was common as people "put something together. If I had asked her this question at the outset, she wouldn't have been able to answer this way."

This annotated transcript shows an extremely skillful observer of people and user of language. Satir is politically aware and doesn't deny the parents their higher status, yet she insists on recognizing their fallible personhood. She diagnoses the family problem in the first few minutes of the session, and even in the intake session she begins to alter one of the family's most sensitive patterns of interaction.

Bell

For a third representative of the pioneer generation I can think of no one whose work offered a greater contrast in assumptions and styles, when compared with Ackerman and Satir, than psychologist and former clergyman John Elderkin Bell. Bell was one of the first therapists to attempt therapy with family members together in an office,[6] having expressed his frustration with the prevailing child guidance center approaches in the 1950s. Unlike Ackerman and Satir, he maintained an attitude of exploration and scientific detachment when he reported on his sessions (an attitude that also showed up in his interactions with families). In fact, Bell's writings were so cautious that a reader of his 1975 book would get the impression that family therapy was still a rare, experimental activity at that time.

Despite his caution, though, Bell had, in the 1960s, developed a well-conceptualized approach that was distinctive for its respectful attitude toward children. Working from a background in group therapy, Bell discouraged parents from speaking in the first few sessions. Children in Bell's sessions were encouraged to ask for modifications in family routines and rules, and parents were encouraged to take those requests seriously. Bell believed that focusing on the children's requests helped to increase the children's motivation to work with the therapist.

The following exchanges, drawn from recordings made in 1955 when Bell visited Scotland, show Bell operating in a very different manner from both Ackerman and Satir. His comments range from extended lectures when he's with the parents to brief, noninvasive comments during the family's conversations. Nine-year-old Jean is the *identified patient*,[7] referred for behavior that would probably earn her a diagnosis of Attention-

---

[6] This is one of family therapy's best-loved anecdotes. J. E. Bell (1975) said he got the idea from hearing John Bowlby describe seeing family members together, but later found out that he had misunderstood. Bowlby and his colleagues in England were merely holding information sessions with families.

[7] This term was adopted in the early years of the family therapy movement as a way of communicating the belief that the actual patient was the family system, despite the fact that one member had been identified as the object of concern.

Deficit/Hyperactivity Disorder (ADHD), under current criteria: "She wants to talk all the time. She's irresponsible. She has so much that she wants to talk about, to speak about, that she must get it all out. . . . She doesn't have staying power . . ." (p. 24). Jean has been seen extensively in individual therapy, with little effect.

BELL: *Jean may eventually be able to tell us what are the problems that make her act as she does. Of course this maybe isn't up on the top of her mind. It may be buried down, and we may have to work for a while in order to really find out what the difficulties are. But at the beginning, I would like to give her a chance, especially, to talk and to tell us what she feels might be wrong with the family. But I also want Sandy in on it, because I don't want him to feel that this is just for Jean alone, but that he is also a part of the family.*

FATHER: *Yes.*

BELL: *And we'll see what Jean has to tell us. Now, if she's like the other youngsters that I've known in this situation, she'll begin to complain about all sorts of little rules and regulations and things like that about the family life. This is sort of the way the youngsters test out how freely they can talk about things.*

He began, in the second session, what he referred to as the *child-centered phase* of family treatment. We don't have an extended transcript of this phase, only a few scattered sentences, but the structure is clear: Bell was restraining the parents and attempting to—in effect—conduct a child session with the parents in the room:

BELL: *Do you feel, in a way then, Jean, that you're in the worst position in the family?*

JEAN: *Yes, well since I'm the, what's the word, the youngest in the family, it doesn't feel very, it feels very, it feels very strange to me, for everyone seems to be doing. To tell me what to be doing instead of telling everybody else what to do.*

BELL: *Yes, yes. And that's something that the youngest in the family usually feels, because there are just so many older people around to boss, and not very many who listen.*

By the fourth session, Bell said, the process shifted to the *parent-child interaction phase.* A series of simple, direct child requests had been heard and had led to some changes in the family rules, and Jean began to talk about being confused by her own temper outbursts. At this point Bell stopped restraining the parents, believing that he had empowered the children enough to guarantee that they would express themselves openly, and an exchange began in which the mother attempted to enforce her rules about wearing a coat while playing outside.

Bell was concerned that his handling of several key comments by mother or daughter seemed to be allowing their anxiety to be getting too great for productive conversation, and in fact both the mother and daughter were talking about how they'd prefer to discuss their feelings in separate therapy sessions. He offered that option with someone else as the therapist, but restated his goal of opening up family communication. The session moved into a new level after the mother tried to coax Jean into talking about a "secret" that she had referred to, one that the mother seemed to know about.

It was two more sessions before Jean let her mother tell the story for her—a story of various lies Jean had told. Bell considered this to be a pivotal session, as he viewed the mother-daughter secret as blocking the father and brother out of their relationship, as a kind of resistance to the desired climate of openness in family treatment.

Not long afterward, in a discussion of Jean's behavior at dinnertime, Bell said, "I know you hate it, I know it is painful and uncomfortable. But on the other hand there is something about it that suggests there are good reasons why you have not taken a firm enough stand to stop it."

From that point on, Bell said, the therapy moved into a phase of *father-mother interaction,* focusing on the parents' marital relationship. Challenged to address their differences, the parents came back to therapy in a few weeks having worked out a new set of rules about mealtime and about times when they disagreed. Bell saw this as the time to move into a phase of *sibling interaction.* During that brief phase, Sandy and Jean addressed their misunderstandings and frustrations and committed to a more mutually supportive relationship.

Reviewing the process at the conclusion of therapy, the father expressed some confusion about what had changed: ". . . we've never had anything, any definite opinions from you yet, and yet there has been a great difference." The family concluded that the structured time to hear from each other in the presence of a neutral party had been helpful, and they planned ways to continue a more consistent and open pattern of communicating among themselves.

An Alternative Story, Phase II: The Consolidation Years (1970–1979), a Search for Consensus

By 1970 pressure was mounting for someone to define this new movement in the social and behavioral sciences. The term *family therapy* seemed to have widespread support and now served as a shorthand term that was not too specifically aligned with any theory and implied many things:

- Human problems often seem to make better sense when viewed in relationship contexts.
- Just as individual behavior can be seen as conforming to patterns, groups of individuals seem to reenact sequences that involve behavior and related emotions.
- The relationship context of a behavior or emotion sometimes seems to involve people who are not physically present and who may no longer be alive.

The new movement was still known to only a handful of insiders; newcomers to the field in the early 1970s had a hard time finding readings and training in family therapy even though they had heard rumors of its existence. The relatively new journals *Family Process* (1962) and *Journal of Marriage and Family Counseling* (1965), had limited circulation. There were only a few books that ex-plicitly addressed family therapy theories and methods, and the few research and training centers were rather small and known only to the already initiated. How did this relatively obscure new field, with its small group of hard-core adherents, grow into a movement that eventually influenced every branch of the human services and mental health systems?

Social Change

The rapid change during the 1970s cannot be understood properly without appreciating the social context. The United States had been in a period of rapid postwar change during the 1940s, 1950s, and 1960s—a time of increased childbearing referred to as the "baby boom," a building boom in real estate, and growth in higher education paid for by the GI bill. These changes reached a crisis point by 1964 when the baby boom reached young adulthood. A generation who had been brought up with privilege and high hopes, on one hand, and fear of nuclear war, on the other, was confronted with an economic downturn and rapidly growing casualties in Vietnam. At the same time, the older generation—adults during World War II and the Korean War—were struggling with a rising divorce rate, increasingly open racial tensions, and their own fear of nuclear annihilation. Birth control was revolutionized by oral contraceptives (Box 2.3) and a sexual revolution was becoming visible on college campuses (B. Bailey, 1999) and in the suburbs (see Updike, 1960). Meanwhile the youth counterculture, identified as the hippie movement, had spread from a few campus communities to become a nearly universal presence, exemplified by the Woodstock concert of 1970.

In a few short years, the peaceful 1950s had disappeared into memory and society was in disarray. Such times have always been good for the human services and mental health fields: Federal funding of graduate mental health training and community mental health centers was growing, mental hospitals and drug treatment centers were expanding, high schools were hiring guidance counselors in record numbers, and nearly every family seemed to be experiencing a drug problem

---

BOX 2.3

College Life before Oral Contraceptives

Distribution of oral contraceptives in the United States began in the early 1960s, and many authors have linked that change in contraception to a *sexual revolution* that changed many aspects of society (see B. Bailey, 1999). It may be hard for those born after 1970 to imagine the America of 1960. College dormitories were not only universally segregated by sex (not merely on separate floors, but in separate buildings), but women's dorms were also locked at a curfew time. Women's curfews were as early as 9 or 10 P.M. on school nights, and only women over the age of 21 had building keys. A woman who failed to return to the dorm by curfew was subject to disciplinary action and could also be denied access. Administrators acknowledged the difference in men's freedom to study and to be involved in off-campus activities, but the inequity was considered necessary because they considered unsupervised women to be a problem for themselves and for society.

---

or a divorce. Yet, long-term outpatient psychotherapy and hospitalization, mainstays of the mental health field, were being challenged not only for being expensive and slow but also for having failed to succeed with severe problems such as schizophrenia and anorexia nervosa. The media were looking for alternatives, clients were looking for alternatives, and many practitioners were dissatisfied with the results of their work.

Systems Fervor

Some of the most successful treatment models, in this climate of competition for credibility and attention, shared the new family systems perspective. This family systems conceptualization aided the spread of family-oriented counseling, partially because of its scientific-sounding, readily understood metaphors: terms such as *levels, boundaries, feedback loops, rules,* and *control systems.* Systems-based models had created, by the mid-1970s, a dramatic break with the individual-level theory base of earlier approaches.

General System Theory

General System Theory (GST) started as a rather nonspecific statement that biological systems had to be understood in terms of their wholeness. Biologist Ludwig von Bertalanffy was motivated by his discomfort with the prevailing scientific tradition, founded on the ideas of René Descartes, in which complex phenomena were studied by reducing them to their smallest parts and examining the parts (this is referred to as reductionism, or Cartesian science). In "The History and Development of General System Theory" (1975), published after von Bertalanffy's death, he recalled the tentative nature of his systemic theorizing in the 1930s and his perception that the intellectual climate at that time was initially not supportive of systemic ideas. Through the 1940s von Bertalanffy's attention was focused on mathematical modeling of systems, using simultaneous equations, and on theorizing about open systems. He became convinced that a systems theory would have applications outside biology, and in 1950 released his first statement of General Systems Theory. While GST was often understood to mean "everything connects with everything else," the goals of von Bertalanffy and others may be better understood from the research program of the Society for General System Research, which was published in 1954 and quoted by von Bertalanffy (1975):

Major functions are to: (1) investigate the isomorphy of concepts, laws, and models in various fields, and to help in useful transfers from one field to another; (2) encourage the development of adequate theoretical models in the fields which lack them; (3) minimize the duplication of theoretical effort in different fields; (4) promote the unity of science through improving communication among specialists. (p. 155)

GST's proponents, then, believed that they were creating a new language for science, a language that moved beyond the distracting specifics of astronomy, biology, and psychology to express universal rules about the way the universe was organized. Complexity, in this new conceptual model, was not a threat; the more complex the system, the more dramatic the results would be when science eventually proved that organizational principles could be identified. Concepts such as wholeness, system levels, system goals, open and closed systems, rules, and equifinality were empirically—often mathematically—validated and were shown to have application across many sciences.

During the 1950s and 1960s von Bertalanffy and other systems theorists began to explicitly look at the implications of a systemic orientation for problems related to mental health and social functioning (Buckley, 1967; von Bertalanffy, 1967). Human behavior systems were wonderfully complex and offered the ultimate challenge. At the same time, many social and behavioral scientists welcomed a new tool that might help them to achieve a greater understanding. The mavericks who were attracted to couple and family counseling were likely to be attracted to this new scientific paradigm as well. By 1970 the term *family systems* started to appear in the titles of family therapy articles, and within 10 years the language of systems had begun to dominate the field. We will return to a detailed examination of systems theory later, in Chapter 5.

Cybernetics

Von Bertalanffy's work was closely paralleled by Norbert Wiener's (1961) work in physics—using Thomas Kuhn's (1970) term, a new scientific *paradigm* was beginning to emerge as the limitations of the Cartesian paradigm became more obvious. Wiener, a scientist engaged in weapon develop-ment, observed the parallels between the control processes in physical systems and the organizational patterns in human relationship systems. He labeled his new science *cybernetics,* and began to explore the ways in which the newly developed concept of feedback applied to such human phenomena as mental illness.

Feedback, as Wiener and his colleagues were using the term, was a system of error correction through which an electronic control system could use information from its own performance to correct itself. This electronic system was merely attempting to match the performance or feedback through which living systems accomplished much the same thing. Some years later, biologist Humberto Maturana would become famous for his experiments in which he simulated the function of a frog's vision system, computing time, speed, and distance to extend the tongue on time so that it would intersect with a fly's trajectory. Computer technology was, through its attempts to simulate living processes, learning about those control processes.

The concept of cybernetics was soon applied to describe control processes in family systems. Error correction, in this case, involved family and community attempts to keep various kinds of actions within system-specific limits. A certain amount of youthful rebellion, for example, might be encouraged, but at the same time there were limits and excessive rebellion would activate some kind of a compensatory mechanism. A feedback process that led to more acceptable levels of the rebellious behavior would be described as a *negative feedback loop* while a process that led to increasing rebellion would be described as a *positive feedback loop.*

Advanced Models—Captains of Industry

As I try to reconstruct the field of family therapy in the 1970s and early 1980s, the lead characters resemble descriptions of Andrew Mellon and the industrial giants of the nineteenth century and early twentieth century in the United States. They were successful and privileged, and many had gained their positions of power and privilege in part because their personal characteristics—drive and ability—enabled them to work their way up from humble beginnings. It is also worth noting that nearly all were white males, and their access to opportunities was also a factor in their success. In the case of the giants of the new family therapy field, all had some special combination of effectiveness both in the counseling room and in communicating with others about their work. The consumers of family therapy literature and training in this period were seeking clear, usable approaches to use with families. A 1984 survey by Quinn and Davidson (Table 2.3) shows how the rankings had changed since the GAP report.

Of the 426 Texas family therapists who responded to the Quinn and Davidson survey, over half reported that they used, at least part of the time, six popular models to shape their understandings of couple and family issues and guide their interventions. The survey's authors expressed some concerns regarding the 85% who reported using predominantly one approach termed "communications." The authors concluded that the term was so broad that it included a variety of work that would have been more appropriately placed in one of the other five categories. My focus is therefore on the remaining models: strategic, structural, experiential, behavioral, and intergenerational, in order of this prevalence. Approaches used by less than half of the respondents have been left out. Table 2.4 summarizes these five traditions.

Strategic

Growing out of the Mental Research Institute in Palo Alto, the approaches labeled "strategic"

Table 2.3 **Popularity of Models**

Model	Reported Clinical Use (N = 396)		Order of Most Frequently Used Orientations (Percentages in Parentheses)			Rank Representing Prevalence of First Choices Selected (N = 380)	
	N	%	First	Second	Third	%	Rank
Communication (Satir, Couples Communication Program)	331	85.1	98 (29.6)	90 (27.2)	54 (16.3)	25.8	1
Strategic (Haley, Mental Research Institute)	263	66.4	54 (20.5)	53 (20.2)	56 (21.3)	14.2	2
Structural (Minuchin)	246	62.1	36 (14.6)	38 (15.4)	61 (24.8)	9.5	4
Experiential (Whitaker)	240	60.1	46 (19.2)	57 (23.8)	55 (22.9)	12.1	3
Behavioral (Patterson, Stuart)	218	55.1	26 (11.9)	36 (16.5)	51 (23.4)	6.8	7
Intergenerational (Bowen, Framo, Boszormenyi-Nagy)	206	52.0	30 (14.6)	44 (21.4)	44 (21.4)	7.9	6
Psychodynamic (Meisssner, Dicks, Kernberg)	127	32.0	35 (27.6)	24 (18.9)	16 (12.6)	9.2	5
Other*	104	26.2					
Functional (Alexander)	43	10.8	1 (2.3)	7 (16.3)	7 (16.3)	2.6	8

*Composition of this category is described in text.
Source: From "Prevalence of Family Therapy Models: A Research Note," by W. H. Quinn and B. Davidson, 1984, *Journal of Marital and Family Therapy, 10,* pp. 393–398. Reprinted with permission.

Table 2.4 **Dominant Perspectives in the 1970s**

	Strategic	Structural	Experiential	Behavioral	Intergenerational
Representative centers	Mental Research Institute Haley-Madanes Institute Institute for Family Studies (Milan) Ackerman Institute	Philadelphia Child Guidance Center	Big Sur University of Wisconsin	University of Oregon University of Washington	Georgetown Family Center Eastern Pennsylvania Psychiatric Institute
Representative names	Don Jackson Janet Beavin Paul Watzlawick Jay Haley Cloe Madanes Mara Selvini Palazzoli Peggy Papp	Salvador Minuchin Bernice Rosman Braulio Montalvo Harry Aponte	Virginia Satir Carl Whitaker	Richard Stuart Robert Weiss Nathan Azrin Neil Jacobson Gayla Margolin	Murray Bowen Ivan Boszormenyi-Nagy Geraldine Spark James Framo
Sample assumptions about problems	Communication occurs at multiple levels, leading to confusion Problems result from attempts to solve problems Every symptom is part of some kind of triangle	Systems need to change over time Structural imbalances and coalitions create problems Internal and external system boundaries are important	Interactions are shaped by symbolic traces of other experiences People need validation Problems result from a failure to connect with self and others	Problems result from learning Negative behavior that is reinforced is likely to continue Punishment leads to a coercive cycle in families	Problems are passed on from one generation to the next Families are emotional systems Symptoms result from emotional imbalances in families

Sample assumptions about change	People rebel against authority People feel incapable of making change Disrupting a stuck system releases change	Helpers must find the system level where the problem resides Family members can learn new patterns of interaction	People's faulty assumptions need to be challenged Direct confrontation and intense feeling are healing experiences	Family members can reinforce desired behavior Reciprocal reinforcement creates a positive climate for change	Intervention involves the extended family People need to learn how to safely handle their complex feelings in relationships
Sample techniques	Paradox Reframing Letters	Joining Enactments Arranging a crisis	Sculpting Holding Play	Specific goals Behavior counting	Coaching Adult sibling sessions
Time frame	Brief	Brief to Medium	Medium	Medium	Longer

59

appeared in many forms. Their core was a very simple idea, as stated by Jay Haley:

> *Therapy can be called strategic if the clinician initiates what happens during therapy and designs a particular approach for each problem. When a therapist and a person with a problem encounter each other, the action that takes place is determined by both of them, but in strategic therapy the initiative is largely taken by the therapist. He must identify solvable problems, set goals, design interventions to achieve those goals, examine the responses he receives to correct his approach, and ultimately examine the outcome of his therapy to see if it has been effective. (1973b, p. 17)*

Strategic approaches grew out of a few basic assumptions, many based on systems and communications theories:

- Relationships are organized and predictable. They operate according to systemic *rules*.
- Relationship systems resist change. A tendency for *homeostasis* returns a system to its familiar patterns if it is disrupted by therapeutic or natural forces.
- All behavior is communication and incorporates *feedback* from other communication.
- When people are presented with a *double bind* (a communication that sets up two contradictory expectations) there is no way to comply with both parts and therefore they are likely to reject both alternatives. Symptomatic behavior may be a way to refuse to comply with either command.
- Direct guidance for family relationships is ineffective; people have already received good advice from others, and it has not usually been followed.
- Most people rebel against authority, and they will rebel against anyone who gives them advice; therefore, whatever the professional tells them to do, they will do the opposite.
- Systems tend to reorganize themselves into new forms if their unhealthy patterns are somehow disrupted.

Haley was a driving force in the development of this tradition, but Haley was not the originator of all of these ideas. Many of them were derived from the work of Phoenix-based psychiatrist and hypnotherapist Milton Erickson, who developed and first applied the concepts of *therapeutic paradox* in his work. First as a researcher, later as a budding therapist, Haley became an expert in Erickson's work (see Haley, 1973b). I return to Haley and his colleagues, but, first, I would like to introduce other significant strategists and describe their contributions.

Mental Research Institute. The Mental Research Institute or MRI in Palo Alto was founded in 1958 by Don D. Jackson, MD, a member of the legendary Bateson research team. Jackson, who hired Virginia Satir as director of training of MRI, was a creative and dynamic presence in the room with families (an archive of research films has been maintained) and he took readily to Erickson's theories and techniques. With a staff that eventually included Janet Beavin Bavelas, Jay Haley, and Paul Watzlawick, MRI became the center of communication-based and systems-influenced therapies. When Jackson died unexpectedly in 1968, the systemic communication theories underlying the MRI approach had just been articulated in the 1967 publication of Watzlawick, Beavin, and Jackson's *Pragmatics of Human Communication; A Study of Interactional Patterns, Pathologies, and Paradoxes.*

By 1974, in *Change: Principles of Problem Formation and Problem Resolution,* the MRI brief therapy team of Watzlawick, Weakland, and Fisch more clearly articulated a strategic approach including key elements that would be common to many of the other strategic approaches—understanding the problem in context and disrupting the homeostasis that maintained the problem. What made the MRI approach unique was its focus on previous efforts to change. As the MRI gospel was often paraphrased, "The problem results from the family's attempts to solve a problem."

The MRI approach characterized the family as:

- Caring and motivated rather than resistant
- Having already tried to make changes related to some problem that they perceived
- Having made things worse, rather than better, through these efforts at change
- Unaware that their "solutions" had become new "problems"

The MRI approach during the 1970s, then, was a systemic, brief therapy approach that involved reconstructing the history of the problem through two steps:

1. Interview clients and inventory everything they have tried so far.
2. Tell them to stop all of their attempted solutions.

Such paradoxical ideas as telling the clients that "you may not be able to handle the change" (*restraining change*) were useful in getting people to stop their current efforts. The restraining message provided them with a reasonably clear direction—keep doing what they had been doing. This strategy minimized subtle accommodations that kept discomfort and frustration within manageable limits. Therefore, frustration would build, eventually disrupting the systemic pattern that—according to the theory—was somehow helping to maintain the problem. Once the disruption was accomplished, the therapy was ended, usually in eight sessions or less. The theory suggested that people would not need the help of a professional once they had stopped the self-maintaining problem behavior (Watzlawick et al., 1967).

Milan/Ackerman Institute in New York/Galveston. In Milan, Italy, beginning in 1967, Mara Selvini-Palazzoli and her colleagues developed their own strategic approach based on *Pragmatics of Human Communication*. The Milan-based group worked with multigenerational families and many of their referrals came from practitioners or treatment facilities in rural communities. The families, many of them obsessed with the responsibility of caring for schizophrenic adult children, had difficulty with frequent visits, which led to a pattern of

meeting on a monthly rather than a weekly basis. Therefore, the Milan team evolved an approach that compressed as much disruption as possible into each intervention. The interventions focused on multiple and contradictory messages, *positive connotation* (an Ericksonian intervention, praising people for their creativity in developing their problems), and restraining change. Sessions typically ended with a prescription of actions that should be performed until the next session, and might also include a message to the family from the treatment team (two therapists in the room with the family and two observing from the next room). These prescriptions and messages were designed to unbalance the family.

One of their typical interventions consisted of a letter that was carefully composed by the team. The family was told to read the letter together in a particular way—rituals were also a Milan specialty—several times a week for the next month. The following example, a letter to 6-year-old Bruno, demonstrates positive connotation and a paradoxical prescription. Bruno's mother and father were assigned to take turns reading the letter in the absence of the extended family, and discussion of the letter was forbidden:

Now Bruno, I understand why you are acting crazy: to help Daddy. You've decided that he is weak and that by himself he isn't strong enough to control Mommy. So you do everything you can to keep Mommy busy and pinned down, and Chicco [3-year-old brother] helps you with his tantrums. Since you're taking care of the job of controlling Mommy, Daddy has more time for his work, and can take it easy. (Selvini-Palazzoli, Boscolo, Cecchin, & Prata, 1978, p. 128)

This example shows the provocative tone that made the Milan work legendary. The Milan work drew adherents, however, because of its documented effectiveness. Lynn Hoffman, in *Family Therapy: An Intimate History* (2002) recalls her first experience with the legendary "Milan Team" when Selvini-Palazzoli and colleagues visited New York's Ackerman Institute in 1978. Rather than a group of imposing professionals, Hoffman met a group of rather ordinary people who refused to act like authority figures. The Milan effect, it seemed, came partially from the fact that these experts were so unpredictable. Their interventions often complimented people on having found creative ways of resolving family conflicts or managing losses, and they rarely offered solutions. Over the next few years, the Ackerman Institute became home to a brief therapy project modeled after the Milan group.

The uniqueness of each Milan-style intervention, so effective with clients and so popular in therapeutically sophisticated New York, tended to limit its marketability elsewhere in the United States. The counselor in the market for family approaches wanted to know what to do. Therefore, the Milan visitors met rather cautious responses once they ventured beyond New York City, with one exception: the Galveston Family Institute, founded by Harry Goolishian and co-led during the late 1970s by Harlene Anderson. Harry, like the Ackerman faculty, had been part of the psychodynamic and the strategic movements, and his restless spirit was captured by the alternative energy of this new work. Galveston, Ackerman, and Milan teams worked closely together in the early 1980s.

Haley/Madanes. Jay Haley, one of the original staff members of the Bateson project in 1953, produced work at a voluminous rate through the 1960s and early 1970s—he was the director of research of the Philadelphia Child Guidance Center at the time he edited *Changing Families* in 1971. I have chosen to focus on the approach Haley and Cloe Madanes developed as a team following a 1976 move to Washington, D.C. (they had collaborated with Salvador Minuchin in Philadelphia). In a new setting, the Family Therapy Institute of Washington, D.C., they created an intimate environment where cases typically were served by treatment teams involving a trainee in the room with a family, supported by a consultation team that interrupted sessions for discussions about the case or called in suggestions by telephone.

Haley and Madanes in the late 1970s were distinctive for:

- An awareness of developmental issues
- An absolute commitment to solving the family's presenting problem

- An explicit focus on professional power
- A triadic view of family processes
- Intentional use of metaphor

Milton Erickson sprinkled his work with stories of "when I was a boy" and he believed that problems were often best understood in terms of a client's stage of life or a family's developmental challenges (Haley, 1973b). In *Leaving Home* (revised in 1997), Haley reflects Erickson as he also offered a sensitive, focused picture of the developmental challenges in the lives of families with adolescent sons and daughters. Madanes, in *Strategic Family Therapy* (1981), showed extraordinary sensitivity to the relationships between parents and children—and a spirit of playfulness that was rare in the field.

Haley and Madanes were focused on winning in a struggle against the client's symptoms, by using a variety of techniques. In a technique that demonstrated Haley's belief in exercising professional power with clients, a couple had to agree to a negative consequence that would be applied if they didn't comply with the therapist's directives. The consequence was to be so offensive that they would push past their relationship fears. In another power-based strategic technique, developed by one of Haley's students (Price, 1996), the adolescent identified patient was warned that failure to stop the symptomatic behavior would result in a terrible unknown consequence. Haley took the position that the family therapist's job was to make change happen when people thought they were incapable of change (Haley, 1976).

Madanes and Haley's model for conceptualizing and disrupting a family problem often focused on the problem as part of a relationship triangle. For example, see Figure 2.2, depicting Frank and Suzanne, dealing with Frank's alcohol problem.

In this conceptualization, Drinking is a character that has special power in the family so long as Frank and Suzanne cannot successfully join forces against it. In the therapy process, the therapist would direct Frank and Suzanne in changing their interactions so as to increase their mutual support, develop a working coalition to increase their power, and defeat the problem. Typically, ac-

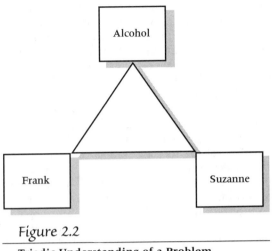

Figure 2.2

Triadic Understanding of a Problem

cording to Haley and Madanes, such a productive coalition was hard to achieve because people feared something about change or some family member actually was in a secret alliance with the problem. They encouraged the use of strategic interventions, not only to directly implement change but also to uncover such covert alliances.

Possibly the most dramatic of Haley and Madanes' contributions during this period was their explicit work with metaphor. Problems, they said, were analogic communication—communication through analogy. A symptom might be metaphorically telling about a problem experienced by a family member, or it might be communicating about the relationship. In *Strategic Family Therapy* (1981), Madanes used this metaphorical understanding to direct interventions in a series of powerful case studies.

Structural

Salvador Minuchin was probably the most successful of the new breed of family therapists. With a background working with underprivileged families at Wiltwyck School in New York and having worked as a young psychiatrist in Israel, he was well prepared professionally. He demonstrated skills with a wide range of clients, but showed a special sensitivity to the complexities of family life. His theoretical model made sense of

the exciting new language of systems, he could describe his techniques and train others to use them, and he used the new medium of videotape to document his work.

The Philadelphia Child Guidance Center, an urban clinic serving the most needy of the city's population, had existed for years before Minuchin arrived in 1965 as its new director. Minuchin was joined over the years by names that appear repeatedly in the family therapy literature: Braulio Montalvo, Bernice Rosman, Bernard Guerney, Jay Haley, Harry Aponte, Lynn Hoffman, Cloe Madanes, Marianne Walters, Thomas Todd, Jay Lappin, Charles Fishman, and many others. Minuchin and his coworkers combined clinical experimentation, creativity, and scholarship to produce a comprehensive, effective, and replicable approach to family counseling. The complex approach that became known as "Structural" Family Therapy showed many influences:

- The conceptualization of individuals in families, developing their own identities and influencing each other's identities, was essentially psychodynamic.
- The understanding of contemporary families, as places where people had to work through conflicts that belonged to the society as a whole, was sociological.
- The view of families needing to change with the needs of their family members was based in theories and research on human development.
- The understanding of systems processes—both the development of problems and the reorganization of the family to produce change—came from General Systems Theory.
- The interactional style—engaging and directing the family as a person with sensitivity and emotion—showed the influence of Satir and Ackerman, the most widely recognized pioneers in the field.

Practitioners of Structural Family Therapy were noted for their ability to produce observable change, especially with families (such as those including psychosomatic members) who had puzzled and frustrated therapists using more traditional orientations. The techniques used were dramatically different from what mental health practitioners were accustomed to seeing.

- Rather than maintaining a professional distance, structural family therapists were taught to develop relationships by *joining* the family.
- Rather than talking about what the family was doing at home, structural family therapists were taught to produce *enactments* and work with interactions in the session.
- Rather than wait for the family to change, structural family therapists were taught to induce a crisis.

Minuchin used a developmental understanding along with the language and the imagery of systems theory to make sense of dysfunctional family processes. Family systems were seen as made up of nested *subsystems* (e.g., a parental subsystem and a child subsystem). It was possible, then, to focus intervention on the system level—the *therapeutic system*—at which the problem was most readily changed. Every system operated according to a principle of *wholeness,* meaning that partial information on the system might not make sense and a true picture of the family interactions could only be obtained by seeing the whole family.

Every subsystem, as well as every larger system, had *boundaries,* metaphorical cell walls that were more or less permeable to information, emotion, and physical action. A family might need to modify boundaries to accommodate the developmental needs of the members or the characteristics of their environment. The external boundary, for example, might need to be closed in a family with out-of-control children, whereas the external boundary might need to be opened for a family with their first child entering school. If a parent was crossing the internal boundary between the adult and child subsystems, creating a *cross-generational coalition,* the parental subsystem boundary might need to be strengthened.

Where some other authors addressed children as merely "symptom bearers" whose issues were indicators of a family level dysfunction, the structural approach emphasized the need for families to adapt over time to meet the needs of the adults and children alike. The developmental theme is central in Minuchin's *Families and Family Therapy* (1974), which features a chapter-long interview with a young couple chronicling their courtship, wedding, and early marriage through the birth of their first child.

The Philadelphia Child Guidance Center made extensive use of video recording and one-way viewing rooms with teams of observers. Members of the training staff sat in teams: They critiqued the work of each therapist and identified the key points of effective intervention and opportunities for improvement. Not only was this an effective training device, it was also popular with the community. The faculty's direct involvement in treatment teams reassured clients that their case was getting attention from experts.

Experiential

The label used in Quinn and Davidson's survey for this set of approaches is only one possible term. Another, more descriptive term is *symbolic-experiential,* a composite that implies there is not a single way of defining this work. The two words say important things. First, humans share a *symbolic* world, in which their symbols—including words—are extremely powerful. Therefore, effectiveness in working with human problems, especially at a family level where symbols are readily observable, is increased if we are skilled at accessing and manipulating those symbols for their helping potential. Second, many human problems seem to result from a failure to live in the *experiential* present. Emotional connection, decisive action, and joy in living are reduced when people fail to experience what is around them. The helper's role, then, may be one of putting the symbolic world into perspective and opening up the unprocessed world of current experience.

The tradition is one that owes much to the humanistic movement in individual counseling, which means that we can expect to find elements of existential theory mixed with various assumptions about human potential, self-knowledge and self-acceptance, human connectedness, and spirituality. In the 1970s two branches could be seen on this tree: Virginia Satir and Carl Whitaker. Each of these family therapists operated from a unique mix of theory, intuition, and skill.

Satir. We examined Virginia Satir's early work in this chapter already. In the early 1960s, she was a seasoned practitioner whose work was mature and highly evolved. Not long after the release of her classic *Conjoint Family Therapy* (1967) Satir left the Mental Research Institute and began spending much of her time at Big Sur, a California retreat center. There she continued to evolve professionally, expanding her work in many directions.

Satir's book *Peoplemaking* (1972) was an effort to reach beyond the limited market of professionals and put a self-help resource into the hands of every reader. In *Peoplemaking,* she simplified her message from the complex model she had presented in 1964, focusing on self-esteem maintenance in families and on teaching people to recognize what she had identified as four destructive communication styles: blaming, placating, computing, and distracting (see Box 2.4). Her message of validation as the central process of relationships came to be distilled into something like self-esteem, except a family level phenomenon—not "self" at all. She said that healthy families had a reservoir of good feeling about every member that she referred to as "pot" (the term came from a metaphor of a cooking pot into which everyone contributed ingredients and all were free to serve themselves). High-pot families were ones in which everyone thrived, and low-pot families were ones in which only a few had enough to survive. Emotional openness and congruent communication were the ingredients that went into the pot, feeding everyone. Touch, laughter, and tears were the techniques of this experiential work.

Peoplemaking (1972) was followed by *Changing with Families: A Book about Further Education for Being Human* (Bandler, Grinder, & Satir, 1976), co-authored with the originators of Neurolinguistic Programming (NLP), Richard Bandler and John Grinder. This more scholarly work provided details of the linguistic assumptions that had appeared in *Peoplemaking* and in Satir's clinical work. *Changing with Families* is one of the clearest, most concise books in the field, consistent with its authors' goal: "We want to emphasize that the model for family therapy which we present here is designed to create experience. . . . Our model, essentially, is a way of helping people-helpers to tune themselves into the ongoing processes for growth of the families with whom they are working" (p. 4). The reader is provided with extensive transcripts in which the multiple levels of speaker intent and listener understanding are analyzed and the process of clear, nondirective communication is gradually defined.

During the 1970s, Satir also became more explicitly spiritual in her work, embracing new colleagues—healers, mystics—from outside the human services and mental health fields. From this networking grew her Avanta Network, founded in 1977, which survives to this day as Avanta, The Virginia Satir Network and can be found at www.avanta.net. She became involved in issues of world peace as well as personal growth.

Satir's influence in the 1970s was becoming more diffused, rather than more focused. She had established herself as a leader and remained one of the most recognizable names in the field. Since her 1967 book she had moved further and further away from theory, and she was best known among family counselors for her active, engaging posture. Satir popularized the techniques of sculpting—posing people as sculptures to help them communicate the emotional messages that often were distorted in words. She challenged counselors to get out of their seats, engage people in meaningful encounters, and help them find new ways to be supportive to each other.

Whitaker. Carl Whitaker, like Satir, was difficult to categorize. Even before the advent of family approaches, Whitaker had been a controversial figure in the mental health field. Despite somewhat conventional psychiatric training during World War II, by the late 1940s he had created a psychiatry department at Emory University that was known for practices such as "bottle feeding, physical rocking of patients, and other aids which stimulate in both therapist and patient the requisite affect for infantile satisfaction of the patient" (Simon, 1992, p. 101). Whitaker was drawn to the work of the family therapy pioneers

BOX 2.4

Satir's Four Communication Styles

Illustration: Blaming, Placating, Computing, and Distracting

Virginia Satir identified four problematic communication styles that tended to occur in couple and family interactions. These styles can be present without destroying relationships, when they appear from time to time and when people have multiple styles available. When they become rigidly identified with particular individuals, however, they prevent people from communicating effectively. These styles involve *double-level messages*, messages in which "your voice is saying one thing, and the rest of you is saying something else" (1972, p. 60). With these styles, problems do not get solved and emotional connections wither. Satir often portrayed these styles in physical caricatures such as the illustration below. Let's imagine these styles as they might appear when a group of adult brothers—Adam, Ben, Casper, and Don—get together immediately following the death of their mother.

Placating is a style that denies personal power by elevating the other. The placater is concerned only with others—their preferences, their comfort, their goals, and their satisfaction. Adam, the placater in this group, will be obsessively focused on everyone else's feelings of loss and he will apologize for everything he says and does.

Blaming is a style that denies power by taking a victim role. Others are characterized only in terms of their misdeeds and their imagined hostility. Ben, the blamer in this group, will criticize his siblings for hastening Mom's death or for keeping him from being present at her death. (Adam makes a great target for any blame.)

Computing is a style that denies everything except information and logical decisions. Others are characterized as overemotional and incompetent, and the computer is constantly teaching—or withdrawing into contemplation. Casper, the computer in this group, will oscillate between lecturing about stages of grief and discussing funeral plans in detail.

Distracting is a style of total confusion. Neither self nor others are seen in any depth as the distracter shifts focus from present to past, reality to fantasy, and physical to mental concerns. Don, the distractor in the group, will talk about the last few movies he's seen, sports trivia, entertainment trivia, his brothers' children, his own career, and plans for dinner.

Each of these patterns might be observed in any family. When they become fixed and inflexible, as in the case of these four brothers, meaningful conversations cannot take place.

Source of illustration: Peoplemaking, by V. Satir, 1972, Palo Alto, CA: Science and Behavior Books. Reprinted with permission.

and quickly established himself as a risk taker, a believer in disrupting family rigidity through whatever means were necessary.

Whitaker's strength lay in his ability to disrupt the story people were accustomed to telling—the one that helped them to stay stuck in their problems—and open up a conversation about truths they had never acknowledged. Consistent with the label, "experiential," he specialized in putting people in situations they had never faced before. He used himself as a tool in this effort, gently mocking himself as a farm boy who was uncomfortable with being considered an expert. He challenged family rules of every kind, inviting family members to disclose the secret coalitions and disagreements that they kept hidden from themselves and others. *The Family Crucible* (Napier & Whitaker, 1978) portrayed his dramatic, irreverent, and sometimes shocking approach at the same time it demonstrated the effectiveness of his gentle, humorous interactions with families.

Whitaker's work was strongly intergenerational; particularly in couple work, he expressed a belief that people tended to replicate the families of their childhood. He often used cross-generational interactions in his office and stories of family history to make sense of current experience, but he denied having a theory beyond believing that he needed as many people as possible participating in the change process. He seemed sometimes to be a reluctant leader in the field; he published little and did not build large institutes or organizations. But he was a leader nonetheless, and he was a powerful force in the family therapy movement of the 1970s and 1980s. He preached a message of encountering people, leaving behind the safety of theories and assumptions and instead learning directly from each family about their world.

Behavioral

The better-established actors in the strategic, structural, and experiential traditions were joined, in the 1970s, by a group who quietly organized their entrance and in less than 10 years took center stage. Like the structural and strategic groups, the behaviorists focused on cases where others were

being unsuccessful, and they established a strong record of producing results. Furthermore, behaviorism was committed to a tradition of testing work as it developed: The nature of behavioral interventions lent itself to collecting extremely persuasive outcome data. By the early 1980s there had been many contributors to the behavioral couple and family therapy literature, but the leadership was concentrated in the hands of a few. These behavioral leaders were, notably, in diverse academic positions (though generally clustered in the western United States) as opposed to the private institutes and psychiatry departments that had been the home of other family movements.

Patterson. Gerald Patterson has been active in applying behavioral principles to all aspects of couple and family life, but he is notable in this group for his focus on parent-child relationships and child behavior problems. Building his approach on principles of operant conditioning, Patterson developed a family counseling process that simultaneously trained parents in the principles of reinforcement and worked through the parents to accomplish behavior changes in a target child. His popular book *Families: Applications of Social Learning to Family Life* (1971) was itself a demonstration of behavioral principles. Written for family members to share, and using a programmed instruction format to guarantee maximum retention of information, the book was designed to help children and parents to communicate about family issues by using a common language.

Stuart. Richard Stuart was a pioneer of behavioral couple therapy. A rigorous scholar as well as practitioner, he addressed couple issues as a complex set of intersecting behavioral processes, while acknowledging developmental processes in couple relationships. Stuart is best known for his core concern with increasing the positive reinforcement value of a couple relationship. Arguing against popular notions of caring, in which acts of thoughtfulness and kindness must be true expressions of positive feelings, he theorized that positive feelings result from caring acts. Stuart used behavioral methods to help partners increase their reciprocal pleasing behaviors.

Azrin.   Nathan Azrin, who like Stuart focused on couple relationships, developed a research and intervention program focused on the concept of reciprocity. His approach to couples involved teaching explicit negotiation skills through which partners could equalize their satisfactions and mutually work toward an increase in the reward value of their relationship.

Jacobson and Margolin.   Neil Jacobson and Gayla Margolin are the latecomers to this list, but in the early 1980s their work began to dominate the behavioral couple literature because of its clarity and its incorporation of a broader definition of behaviorism. Their inclusion of cognitive elements helped to make behavioral couple therapy accessible to practitioners who had rejected the "black box" approach.

Intergenerational

Ranked sixth by the respondents to Quinn and Davidson's 1984 survey, the intergenerational tradition nevertheless held a strong position in the couple and family counseling field. Whereas structural and strategic family therapists emphasized the speed and efficiency of their work, multigenerational family therapists expressed a fear of superficial change and emphasized the long-lasting and efficient changes that could be achieved by using the family in the office as agents of change in their larger families.

The intergenerational movement, like the strategic movement, grew out of research and intervention with families involving schizophrenic members. As with the strategic therapies, there was not a single dominant voice in the intergenerational tradition, but in this case the field was smaller. In the 1970s there were three main research and training efforts whose work showed traces of the psychoanalytic movement so pervasive in the 1940s and 1950s.

Bowen.   I was living in Washington, DC, when I first heard about family therapy in the mid-1970s. For the most part, people in the mental health community there either had some family therapy training or didn't know about the new field at all. Those who had been trained seemed to be loyal to one tradition or another, and I found that there were many Bowen-trained people in my social world. As soon as I went to the library and found Bowen's work, I was hooked. He wrote about his own family, and it seemed just like my family! He became my hero.

Murray Bowen was a hero for the whole movement during the early days of family therapy—in more ways than one. In the 1950s, at the same time Bateson was focusing his research team's activity on the family communication patterns of schizophrenics, Bowen was challenging the psychiatric establishment by treating schizophrenics with a radical new approach that involved hospitalizing the whole family for observation and intervention. With this rich background of observational and clinical data (he referred, in 1966, to having "12 years and over 10,000 hours of family psychotherapy") combined with his psychoanalytic background, he was uniquely positioned to redefine Freudian theory for family practitioners. But he also assumed heroic status when, in a legendary conference presentation, he talked about his interactions with his own family as an example of challenging family patterns.

For most readers, Bowen's Family Systems Theory (Bowen, 1978) succeeded in leaving its Freudian roots far behind. The multiple concepts in Bowen theory are a study in themselves, and a detailed presentation of the theory is not possible in the space available here. I identify, however, a few concepts that seem to have been most influential in the popularity of the theory.

The central concept of *differentiation of self* is generally viewed as the single most memorable aspect of Bowen's approach. Echoing earlier formulations by Jung, Adler, and others, Bowen suggested that problems of all kinds—including schizophrenia—were more likely in families where individuals were not allowed to express their own thoughts and feelings. In such a family, he said, instead of separate selves there was an *undifferentiated family ego mass*, a confused interactional pattern in which the only acceptable response to another's discomfort was to join in the discomfort. Bowen predicted that people would normally end up with partners who were no more differentiated than they were, and therefore there would be little change from generation to generation.

When two people shared a low level of differentiation, their relationship could take many forms, but all of the alternatives would have destructive elements. Most commonly, they would handle their mutual vulnerability through one of two processes. The first and most damaging he called a *cutoff*—a more or less permanent suspension of contact with another family member that prevented the resolution of any problems. The second, more workable pattern involved bringing in a third person or object to make a *triangle*. This triangling, he said, was the core of the *intergenerational transmission process,* a pattern in which the most vulnerable of a couple's children would become the scapegoat for the family's pathology.

Bowen pioneered the use of a *"genogram"* (Figure 2.3), a visual map that facilitated tracking intergenerational patterns and identifying triangles or other problem relationships.

The Bowen approach seemed to many observers to not be family therapy at all. By the time he published *Family Therapy in Clinical Practice* (Bowen, 1978), Bowen had adopted a pattern he said he learned from his experience training psychiatry residents. He often worked with whomever he identified as the most motivated member of the family, assuming that the rest of the family members would slow down the work. With this client, then, he would engage in a long-term process of challenging expected behavior patterns in the extended family. The therapist acted as a coach, helping the client

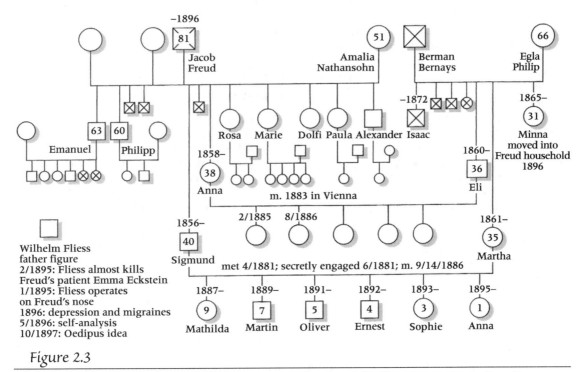

Figure 2.3

Sample Genogram—Freud's Family in 1896: Parenthood and the Next Generation in Freud's Immediate Household

Source: From *Genograms: Assessment and Intervention,* by M. McGoldrick, R. Gerson, and S. Shellenberger, 1999, New York: Norton. Reprinted with permission.

to identify cutoffs or other sensitive relationships and conducting various kinds of experiments—homework, sometimes requiring weeks or months to complete.

Boszormenyi-Nagy. Holding a less complicated view and espousing a less clear-cut pattern of intervention, Ivan Boszormenyi-Nagy started from the same point of believing that problems in a current generation were somehow related to processes that extended back beyond that generation. According to Boszormenyi-Nagy, whose work would eventually be called "Contextual" Family Therapy, families became dysfunctional because there was something unresolved in the extended family. In modern societies with their economic and geographic mobility, the unresolved issue was most likely to be an ethical obligation he referred to as *loyalty*. His book, *Invisible Loyalties* (Boszormenyi-Nagy & Spark, 1973), was popular for its strong ethical position and its sensitivity to emotional currents in families.

Families with loyalty problems, according to Boszormenyi-Nagy, were ones in which members of a younger generation or siblings had benefited unfairly from the sacrifices of other family members. This was a theory of its time and place; in the industrial age, family economic well-being had become unbalanced and fragmented. The United States, with economic and social discourses prioritizing success over relationships, was home to many families within which privilege and wealth were unfairly distributed. According to Boszormenyi-Nagy, problems came from failing to acknowledge and act on intrafamily obligations. Change, in this model, came from reconnecting across generations and across the artificial boundaries of households to reunite with family and restore the appropriate level of interdependence, concern, and mutuality.

Framo. James Framo, of the three theorists included in this group, was for many years harder to categorize. It wasn't until the 1970s that he started to use the term *object relations* to describe his work, and at that point the picture of his professional career came into focus. It is this late 1970s/early 1980s version of Framo that we examine.

Framo's version of Object Relations Theory (we explore other views of object relations in Chapter 7) interpreted current relationship patterns as significantly influenced by lifelong learning from the *Family of Origin* (FOO). Because he considered this process and its effects to be ongoing and lasting, Framo gave the childhood family (whether or not they were still living) special status within people's relationship networks. One might pull away from parents and siblings, but one could never eliminate the traces of the family. Framo believed that every couple could benefit from spending time with their sibling groups and/or parents, recalling and reprocessing their experiences and their ways of making sense of those experiences. Framo's, like Nagy's, was a gentle sort of family therapy, not driven by theory as much as a natural outgrowth of a human connection with the people who came into his office.

Change, But Not Too Much Change

Reviewing the dominant models from this period, we can see a theme emerging. The most popular approaches were those that promised to eliminate problems by taking the emphasis off the identified patient and changing the family system. Change was, according to the systemic concept of homeostasis, difficult to accomplish. Family therapists had to use extremely powerful methods—and nearly any extreme method was justified—if they wanted to help people disengage from negative emotional and behavioral patterns.

However, in the waning years of a historical period when popular culture glorified recreational drug use and sexual experimentation, change was suspect. Families might be convinced to change, but only if it was in the direction of more conventionality. The most popular approaches were not those of Satir, Ackerman, and Bell, powerful leaders who aligned themselves with children and challenged parental authority. That 1950s notion had been tried, and it had been discarded. The dominant approaches of the 1970s were ones that blamed problems on weak family bonds and emphasized the need to restore the nuclear family.

Suggested Individual and Group Activities

Your understanding of concepts and issues presented in this chapter may be enhanced by the following activities:

- *Your genogram.* If you haven't already begun a formal genogram for your own family, go to http://www.multiculturalfamily.org for instructions and begin (at least 3 generations are recommended). If you have begun a genogram, return to the project and continue filling in missing pieces. This is an endless process—there are always questions one has not yet been able to answer. Many people like to use software that helps with symbols and facilitates sharing information with conventional genealogy chart programs.

- *Triangles.* Recall a time when a problem occurred in one of your relationships (or in a popular film), and try to identify triangles that may have contributed to its occurrence.

- *Systemic analysis, MRI style.* Pick the same problem (or another one) and find a way to make sense of the problem as resulting from the attempt to solve another problem.

Suggested Readings

Hoffman, L. (1981). *Foundations of family therapy: A framework for systems change.* New York: Basic Books.

Hoffman, L. (2002). *Family therapy: An intimate history.* New York: Norton.

Satir, V. (1967). *Conjoint family therapy.* Palo Alto, CA: Science and Behavior Books.

The Field Matures

No longer a new and uncharted field, family counseling begins to consolidate discoveries and celebrate diversity.

Objectives

In this chapter, you learn to:

1. Recognize differences between modern and postmodern assumptions.
2. Observe the constantly changing nature of couple and family relationships.
3. Describe the multiple forces that shape contemporary service delivery.
4. Understand the changing discourses of couple and family counseling.
5. Appreciate the new integrative spirit in the field.

3

Chapter

By the late 1970s and early 1980s, it seemed that those who were trying to grow family therapy had met many of their goals. The first introductory textbooks had started to appear (e.g., Foley, 1974; I. Goldenberg & H. Goldenberg, 1980), providing an overview of the field. Systemic diagnosis and intervention were becoming commonplace ideas, even if sometimes misunderstood. And many states were beginning to regulate the practice of marriage and family counseling (W. C. Nichols, 1992). Moving away from its status as a fringe topic in mainstream journals, family therapy now had at least four dedicated journals. Training centers had grown and proliferated; every major city, it seemed, had a family therapy institute. In universities, family therapy courses (and entire programs) were starting to appear in departments such as social work, human development and family studies, and family medicine. Family therapy had arrived as a major participant in human-service theory and delivery systems.

This consensus was short-lived. The previous decades had centered on a teacher/disciple or a coach/player pattern that raised the leaders as it subordinated their followers and marginalized those whose perspectives were outside the mainstream. In retrospect, such a relationship pattern should have been familiar to systems-oriented family therapists. It had been described by Bateson (1972) as a *complementary* pattern (increasing difference), which often led to a breakdown of a relationship system unless it was balanced by *symmetrical* (equalizing) tendencies. And such a system breakdown did take place: As Nichols and Schwartz (2004) wrote, "Somewhere in the mid 1980s a reaction set in" (p. 44). Describing the changes in the 1980s is a challenge. It reminds me of taking children to a family reunion and trying to explain relationships: "Uncle Jim and Uncle Frank used to be really close, until Jim married Frank's former girl friend and since then they don't talk to each other."

Many interpretations of the next few years are possible. Changes may have occurred because the new field hadn't really found its voice but, instead, was attempting to fit new ideas into old containers. Lynn Hoffman (2002) speculates that family therapy authors created confusion as they sometimes used old language to express new ideas. A storyteller might portray the 1980s in terms of a as a newly popular concept at that time: a midlife crisis (Sheehy, 1976). Like individuals' midlife crises, this period of distress left the field stronger, while also making it more sensitive to its own processes and its relations with others.

For many people in the field, the first signs of a shift appeared in the journal *Family Process* in the early 1980s. Words began to appear that did not have a long history in the family therapy field: *ecosystemic epistemology, second-order cybernetics, constructivism, feminism, postmodernism.* By the end of the 1980s the field would be once again in a period of exploration, gathering its intellectual inspiration from many traditions. The major training centers, with their emphasis on dominant family therapy models, would dwindle in size and influence. As a result, students coming into the field would find the situation to be confusing. Overwhelmed with a staggering number of theories, discouraged by the critical attacks directed by one theorist against another, many professionals would turn their attention away from family counseling as an arena of study and practice.

A new wind began to blow through the field by the mid-1990s, however, leaving a mood characterized by many things. One was a return of mutual tolerance and support among leaders of the field; authors who had emphasized their differences instead emphasized their commonalities. A second was the return of an optimistic attitude toward families; the newer theories suggested that people were resilient, unlikely to be damaged by a counselor's choice of interventions. An-

other was the increasingly pragmatic nature of the innovative work that was being published and offered in workshops. Finally, a strong movement for integration encouraged creative efforts by beginners and experienced counselors alike.

In this chapter, we make sense of this period by examining the social context before looking at internal processes in the field: personnel changes, organizational maturation, and intellectual movements. I intend to show that this large, diverse system—the network of authors, teachers, supervisors, and practitioners who identify with the terms *couple and family*—has overcome hard times and is moving into a vigorous, productive future.

Societal Change

The social changes of the 1970s—open discussion of sexuality, changing roles and structures in families, increasing career options for women, liberalization of divorce processes—created a society in which the issues facing family therapists were different from those of 30 years before. Where the authors of the 1950s and 1960s had generally described working with rigidly organized nuclear families in which male dominance was assumed to be the norm, the family therapist of the 1980s saw new trends. These changes in the social climate sometimes challenged the relevance of mainstream approaches, stimulating reexamination of their assumptions and increasing the attention that was given to alternatives.

Sexuality in the United States

The sexual revolution that began in the mid-1960s was fueled by many forces including new birth control technology, but the most dramatic changes did not become apparent until the 1970s. College campuses withdrew from their efforts to restrict students' sexual behavior. Middle-class couples not only began to rent motel rooms without pretense of marriage but also openly cohabited without marriage (Bumpass, Sweet, & Cherlin, 1991). Both men and women began having their first sexual experiences earlier, and rates

BOX 3.1

Alternative Lifestyles in the 1970s

Some time in the mid-1960s a new social movement began to be visible in the United States. Often subsumed under the label "hippie," this cultural phenomenon included many elements that attracted attention from the media—particularly experimentation with drugs, sexual options, and eccentric styles of dress. For many participants in the hippie movement, these aspects of their lives were part of something larger. Inspired by an earlier generation of "beat" poets and musicians, but more committed to changing their society, the hippies saw themselves as engaged in a revolution. They rejected their parents' value systems and the trappings of secure middle-class existence at the same time that they rejected war, environmentally destructive behavior, and racial and economic exploitation. Sex was a powerful symbol and represented freedom from all social constraints.

For some in the hippie era, a tie-dyed T-shirt and bell-bottom denim pants were the limits of their rebellion. They continued to go to school, work at traditional jobs, live in dorms or apartments, and seek relationship happiness in monogamous dating and marriage. In cities and university communities, as well as in many rural areas, though, another phenomenon was visible—communal living in large houses, on farms, or in camping areas. Communes ran the gamut from some that were asexual and apolitical to others that constituted serious social experiments. Some people pursued a goal of nonpossessive sexuality, sharing beds and partners just as they shared food and clothing, while others sought to expand the notion of commitment by entering into group marriages. Many communal groups were bound together by political goals; living together was a natural extension of their commitment to environmental activism, and they kept their sexual lives separate from their communal investment of time and resources. Essentially, this era saw the same variety of social visions and experimental lifestyles that had been seen in prior utopian movements. It ended as abruptly as it began, with a cultural shift toward conservative lifestyles in the late 1970s.

---

of extramarital affairs increased. Marriage became less mandatory, as people postponed or rejected marriage without giving up on sexual fulfillment, and those who married did so later (see Box 3.1).

Not only did Americans in the 1970s drift away from the marriage patterns of their elders, but many of them also rejected these traditions in more dramatic ways. For example, suburban couples were rumored to have had "key parties" at which car and house keys were drawn randomly to see who slept together that night. Group marriage was not unheard of, with three or more people announcing that they were all part of a single marriage and they were sexually available to each other. *Open marriage* was offered as an ideal; its proponents suggested that marriage was strengthened by adding the energy outsiders brought into the marital bed.

Same-sex relationships moved out of the shadows in this climate of new openness about sex. Lesbian, gay, bisexual, and transgender (LGBT) activists organized marches and successfully challenged the designation of homosexuality as a mental disorder. By 1973, the first openly lesbian candidate was elected to public office in Ann Arbor, Michigan, and by 1986 an openly lesbian couple in California was permitted to adopt a child. The new recognition of same-sex couples led to their inclusion in major studies of couple relationships and sexual behavior (e.g., Blumstein & Schwartz, 1985).[1]

---

[1] As this book is being written, a new chapter is being written for LGBT relationships. Same-sex couples are being married in some parts of the United States and Canada, precipitating a new wave of repressive legislation.

The sexual revolution was not without its casualties, however. By the early 1980s a herpes epidemic had been discovered, apparently the product of a generation in which oral contraceptives and implanted devices had replaced condoms. The trend toward casual sex began to reverse as a new concern with sexual history became part of dating. HIV/AIDS appeared on the scene soon afterward, further inhibiting the mood of experimentation that had been sweeping the United States and drawing attention to unprotected sex that had become common in many communities. The control of sexually transmitted diseases (STDs) has become a higher public health priority, and a conversation about STDs has become a regular part of couple and family counseling.

A Changing Family Landscape

The revolutionary spirit of the 1960s and 1970s encouraged a reconsideration of all institutions, and family life was a popular target for reformers. Many challenges to traditional roles and traditions were driven by gender ideology: But family patterns have also been challenged since the 1970s by changing patterns of divorce and remarriage, economic change, lengthening life spans, and new technology. Judith Stacey (1996) coined the term *postmodern family* (see Box 3.2) in an at-

---

BOX 3.2

Postmodern Families and Couples

People are basically the same creatures we were 100 years ago—we eat, sleep, work, fall in love—but contemporary relationships face special challenges. Life in the past few decades has been described as *postmodern*. This term tells us that (1) the modern era has ended; and (2) there is some consistency to the era we're in: It has a name.

In the United States and increasing numbers of other countries, it seems that many people are immersed in a fast-paced existence, driven by competition and anxiety. Closeness and intimacy have little time to develop when life is lived on a schedule. At the same time, consumerist values have emphasized freedom of choice. As a fast-food chain has often reminded us, "You can have it your way." Whether at home or away, postmodern adults and children are wired to separate entertainment devices. They have learned to block the distracting influence of real people in their environment and their closest relationships may be online. In the marketplace of choices, friends and loved ones seem to have become optional accessories.

The postmodern era is not only about private communication, however. Baudrillard (1975) alleges that increasingly sophisticated mass media have altered people's relationship with reality. Images of murders, fires, earthquakes, tsunamis, wars, and famines are sent from around the world by satellite, and in a *mediated world* (Grodin & Lindhof, 1996) these images are mixed with fictional disaster stories that are increasingly realistic. Images of suffering are juxtaposed with advertising images of parties, cruises, and glamorous cars and clothes. It is hard to be unaware of human diversity and especially of human suffering, but it is also hard to take them seriously. When images can be manipulated so easily, seeing is no longer believing.

In this postmodern world, it seems that couples and families are experiencing new kinds of relationship dysfunction. Kenneth Gergen (1991) said that we are flooded with sophisticated and competing identity messages that are hard to integrate into coherent personal and relationship narratives. Intimacy—the experience of letting one person matter more than others—may seem like a threat to sanity. Relationship counseling for postmodern couples and families is still being defined, but it seems to involve helping people restore balance in their lives and connect with real people instead of simulations.

tempt to organize these experiences for a public conversation.

Gender

American feminism was forged in the experiences of prior generations as pioneer women discovered their abilities to lead wagon trains, the suffrage activists of the nineteenth and early twentieth centuries overcame opposition to women's voting, and women of the World War II generation stepped into men's jobs in the factories as well as in the military. But the contemporary feminist movement can be traced to the pivotal writings of Germaine Greer and others who, in the early 1960s, began to question family patterns that relegated women to the kitchen and the nursery while their husbands, fathers, and sons achieved dominance through the status and wealth they got from labor-force participation. This message was especially meaningful to the generation of women who are eloquently portrayed in *The Women's Room* (French, 1988), a novel describing one woman's gradual evolution from depressed housewife to university professor. The newspaper *Off Our Backs* went to press in 1970, and *Ms.* magazine became an overnight success after it began in 1973. An informal feminist movement was creating social unrest and inspiring individual women to change their lives through a group technique known as "consciousness raising."

In 1979, when I began working with couples and families, many of my first appointments involved capable, frustrated women who were being told by their husbands, "You are not allowed to go to school or work. If you insist on having a job, we're getting a divorce." However, the picture would soon change. Inspired by feminist authors and political leaders, a younger generation of women were growing up in the 1970s and 1980s with expectations of equality and opportunity. Couple and family relationships were changing, and these changes were showing up in the offices of family counselors. Many couples showed signs of stresses related to ambiguous gender expectations; without a script telling them what to do, they were forced to make decisions about issues that were not optional for prior generations.

Career Options

The women's movement in the United States precipitated dramatic changes in society as a whole, but none was as pivotal as increasing the career options facing girls and women. In the 1950s and 1960s, it was still common to joke about women going to college for only one reason—to find a husband who would support them. Women who did enter the paid labor force were often ridiculed and subjected to sexual harassment, paid less, given stereotyped tasks that involved little responsibility, and denied promotions. As late as 1970 a female doctoral student in sociology wrote of being criticized for wasting resources that should be used for men who would be serious about their careers (Fox, 1970).

By the late 1970s, the picture had changed. Women had increased access to paid work, and their labor force participation gave them an economic independence that threatened male dominance. Women led a trend toward later marriage and later childbearing, exercising their ability to choose career satisfaction over relationship satisfaction. In 1980, a series of White House conferences on families was held, and participants expressed concern with making workplaces more family friendly—making both men and women workers more available to attend to family needs. But these changes did not occur in many workplaces, and women's success in the employment market left many homes seeking a new kind of organization. Men did not immediately step into taking on their share of errands, cleaning, or even the care of children and elderly family members. The depressed housewives of the 1960s had been replaced by angry husbands and unsupervised children of the 1980s. In the following 20 years, the number of unsupervised children and adolescents would become a concern in many communities.

Divorce, Remarriage, and Stepfamilies

Divorce reforms in the 1970s eliminated barriers that had kept generations of people in marriages that were emotionally and physically destructive. Even before changes in the legal climate, divorce rates began escalating at the end of World War II. Nevada became a "divorce factory" as it placed few restrictions on applicants for divorce. By contrast, in some other states, divorce could only be obtained by proving that adultery had occurred, and such proof required costly legal and investigative services. Reformers cited the hypocrisy of a system that allowed the wealthy to end their marriages while the majority of people lived in marriages that had already ended emotionally, and they suggested that the emotional and health costs of unwanted marriage were unjustified. By 1985, every state had incorporated "no-fault divorce" rules that did not require either partner to prove the other unfit. There was a rapid upsurge of divorces, but the divorce rate leveled off in 1980; since that time U.S. divorce rates have slowly declined.

With current divorce estimated to be between 40% and 50%, half of new marriages now involve at least one previously married partner and the stepfamily has become the norm in the United States (see Box 3.3). Stepfamilies have unique organizational and emotional characteristics that are more complicated than the stereotyped family that was portrayed in many classic family therapy texts. In a household where loyalties are not consistent and jealousy and misun-

derstanding are common, negotiation and parenting skills are challenged. And the typical stepparent tries to do the impossible—to become an important person in the lives of children who just experienced a loss and aren't about to get attached now that they know what it feels like to be disappointed.

Single Parent Families

The trends just described all contributed to a growth in single parent families. Single dads as well as single moms became more numerous as a result of the escalation in divorce rates, but there was an additional increase in the rate of never-married single mothers. Increasing numbers of pregnant women now remain single where they might have married in a prior generation—bowing to social pressure or seeking the economic security of a male partner. Economic realities have changed, with many single women earning salaries in the same range as those that support male-headed households. Furthermore, the social stigma of single motherhood has lessened considerably, and single parenthood has gained in respectability (C. Anderson, 2003). In a legendary conflict between conservative U.S. Vice

---

BOX 3.3

The Ubiquitous Stepfamily

Stepfamilies are not a new phenomenon. Cinderella's fictional stepmother dates back to a time when life was brief for both women and men; the stepparent of those times was replacing one who had died. Only with the high divorce rates of the past 50 years has divorce become more common than widowhood as a reason for remarriage and creation of a stepfamily.

Images of stepfamilies are often negative (see Bernstein, 1999, for a history). Activists have sought to remove the negative connotation of "stepfather" or "stepmother" at the same time that many professionals—like Emily and John Visher (1996), after creating their own stepfam-

ily—have started support groups and written encouraging guides to stepfamily life.

In the past 30 years, researchers (e.g., Whiteside, 1989) have provided rich descriptions and theoretical analyses that portray stepfamilies as strong, vital, and healthy environments. School systems and other social institutions have slowly adapted to the reality that many children have more than one home address. In the contemporary United States, nearly every child over the age of 3 knows that some children live with two biological parents but there are many other family forms as well.

President Dan Quayle and TV actress/producer Candice Bergen, Bergen was accused of glamorizing and promoting single motherhood when her character chose not to marry the father of her child. Changing rules for eligibility and access to reproductive technology, along with revised adoption rules, have made it possible for women to have children without involving a partner of any kind.

These decades of change have led to an increase in studies that explore the full range of positive and negative qualities that have been attributed to the single parent family. Single moms call attention to the clear values they are able to establish, with no competing voice from an adult partner, and the efficiency of their decision making. Many of the advantages of the two-parent household—primarily having to do with the availability of more adults to share the responsibility for caregiving and supervision—seem to be shared by any household with two or more adults.

Multigenerational Families

At the same time that the nuclear family ideal was losing its dominance, changes occurred that led to increasing numbers of multigenerational families. Immigration brought large numbers of refugees from Europe, South America, Africa, and Asia: Many of these refugees found the nuclear family model to be either unworkable or undesirable. Furthermore, steel mills and other factories shut down across the United States and a large segment of the labor force moved from middle-class status to living on part-time work or working at low wages. These workers found the multigenerational household attractive for economic reasons. The shift from an industrial to a service economy led to new incentives for families to stay together: For the family who cleaned offices, just as on the farm, more hands increased the productivity of the family unit.

The 1970s and 1980s were an especially challenging time in the U.S. economy, as many cities lost industrial employment and families were required to either relocate or accept reduced living circumstances. In addition to these stresses on families, the college graduates of 1980 faced a job market that was flooded by the baby-boomer generation. A new family form became more widespread as children began to remain in their parents' homes as young adults and the "crowded nest" family became an increasingly common pattern. In these families, the problem was not so much the abuse of authority as it was an absence of clear expectations. Despite the economic advantages of a multigenerational household, many parents continue to express discomfort with the ambiguous and contradictory expectations of being roommates with their children.

Technology and Families

Families in the 1970s and 1980s did not yet experience many of the technological challenges that have arrived in homes during the past few years, but there were nevertheless ways in which technology was changing the issues that faced family counselors. One change came from the proliferation of television sets and, eventually, video games: Family members were spending less time interacting with each other. The new American family had a TV set for each member. The content of television was also becoming more culturally diverse as satellite transmission was making it possible to beam live pictures from around the world (this would prove problematic for countries who imported violence and sex from the United States).

Families in the 1980s also found their homes invaded by media that challenged their values in new ways. Cable television and rental videotapes bypassed the film rating process: Even though children could not go to a theater and watch explicit sexual material, they could (and did) watch it at home. The family boundary was being breached. Within a few years, personal computer use had developed to the point that online communities were forming. A sophisticated user could use a home computer to trade pornographic pictures and engage in sexual conversations with online "cybersex" partners. Children and adults alike began to take advantage of this additional opening in the family boundary. Today, unsupervised adolescents on the Internet are a great concern not only because of their vulnerability to exploitation but also because online chats and games have an addictive quality that interferes with studies and active life-styles. (In Chapter 11, we continue to explore the interactions between relationships and technology.)

Changing Grandparenthood

The nuclear family ideal of the 1950s and 1960s was achieved in part by rejecting the tradition of family members providing physical care for aging parents. Young couples of those decades were able to relocate in search of jobs because the older generation, with modern nutrition and medicine, typically lived until the grandchildren were adolescents or young adults before they became dependent on family or others. This trend toward longer lives and healthier grandparents did not stop, and, by the 1980s, a new kind of family conflict was starting to appear in counselors' offices. When children and adolescents were in conflicts with their parents, those conflicts were starting to include active, resourceful grandparents who were allied with the grandchildren. This trend has been exacerbated in the past 10 years by technology: From the privacy of their bedrooms, children use cell phones and e-mail to call in their grandparents as allies. It's almost as if some of the characteristics of a multigenerational household are being restored, because separate residences don't keep people apart.

Grandparents have been getting recognition for other new roles in families, as society sees more middle-class, mainstream grandparents stepping into the position of primary caregiver. This is a trend that takes many forms, and therefore it's hard to generalize about grandparent-led families. Some involve substance-abusing parents, while others involve parents who are deployed in military action. But the commonalities include ambiguity, conflicts over values and priorities, challenges around access to resources, and issues of aging and well-being. Even though grandparents are living longer, they are in a period of life when they are more likely to be struggling with serious illness, disability, and demanding programs of medical treatment.

Changes inside the Field

This social inventory suggests that professionals in the 1980s were being asked to work under changing conditions. They were facing new problems and, because the families were changing, their old strategies were working less often. This need for different viewpoints was timely, and it fit well with one of the trends we see in the 1980s—the increasing contribution of ideas and techniques from an international family therapy movement.

There were also changes within the community of family therapists/counselors. Change at the level of leadership is easy to assess because the leaders recorded their ideas in articles and on videotapes, but an accurate picture of change in regular practices is harder to achieve. Anecdotal evidence suggests that family practitioners are still catching up with the changing demands, new ideas, and institutional changes of the past 25 years.

Personnel Changes

One kind of unbalancing took place through the deaths and retirements of early leaders in the field,[2] and the emergence of new visionaries who brought different intellectual, cultural, and personal histories to this work. These changes in the personnel of the field operated in a way that any student of systems could have predicted; the emerging field was no longer the same system, and therefore it behaved in ways that could not be predicted with knowledge of the subsystems alone. The passionate, charismatic leadership of the 1970s began to be replaced by a new generation of leaders in the 1980s—not the high-energy entrepreneurs of the first generation but instead a group of more conservative, careful people who sought to preserve and extend the various traditions. The following are a few key changes.

---

[2] The earlier deaths of Nathan Ackerman and Don Jackson were significant, but the consensus-building fervor of the 1970s seems to have minimized the disruptions of these losses.

Departures

As the 1980s began most of the founding generation were still alive, and most of them were in the same settings where they had done their most significant work. Many had been in mid-life when the movement was young. The next 20 years would see retirements and deaths of people whose passion, vision, and warmth had carried the new field through its early struggles.

Bowen/Georgetown Family Center. During the years that Murray Bowen (d. 1990) directed the Georgetown Family Center, Michael Kerr served in various roles for 20 years. During those years Dr. Kerr became more and more the spokesperson for Bowen Family Theory; in 1988 *Family Evaluation* (Kerr & Bowen) was published, and Kerr's authorial voice could already be detected. At this time, Georgetown Family Center continues to operate under Kerr's leadership. Once a whirlwind of innovation, the center—now renamed the Bowen Center—has become focused on teaching and extending Bowen Family Systems Theory.

Minuchin/Philadelphia Child Guidance Center. Salvador Minuchin stepped down from the position of Family Therapy Training Center director in 1975 to explore writing and other activities, bringing in Charles Fishman as a coauthor and giving the direction of the Center to Harry Aponte. Minuchin's influence on the field was not immediately diminished by this move. Structural Family Therapy continued to develop and he continued to be identified as its creator. However, he gradually turned his attention away from the structural tradition he had created, focusing on other work. Fishman and Rosman's 1986 volume *Evolving Models for Family Change: A Volume in Honor of Salvador Minuchin* commemorated his retirement from the Center.

Bateson. Gregory Bateson (d. 1980), had been one of the intellectual leaders of family therapy even before the field existed, and he maintained a central role until his death through his relationships with individuals, his extensive speaking/training schedule, and his writings. It seemed as if his death brought renewed interest in his work. Keeney, Dell, and others in the 1980s made Bateson's ideas even more popular than they had been in his lifetime.

Satir. Virginia Satir's death (1988), for different reasons, did not create a leadership gap in the family counseling field because she had already turned her attention elsewhere, as I described in Chapter 2. Frank Pittman (1989) was one of many who expressed sadness upon her death: He remembered that her personal intensity and intimate way of working had contributed to her marginalization in the field's competition for dominance. Satir's death was a wake-up call. For women in particular, her memory served as a challenge to return to the radical spirit that had initially shaken up the psychiatric establishment and made room for the growth of family therapy.

Whitaker. Carl Whitaker retired as a professor in 1982 but remained active as a clinician, speaker, and trainer up until the time of his death in 1995, never abandoning his determination to surprise himself and others with his wit and insight. One of his last projects (Whitaker & Bumberry, 1988) was a book, *Dancing with the Family: A Symbolic-Experiential Approach,* and accompanying videotape in which his challenging style can be seen at its best.

Arrivals

But there were also significant additions to the roster—people and institutions whose presence was becoming more visible and who would give leadership to what was coming. The following examples demonstrate the increasingly academic tone of the field during the 1980s and 1990s.

Gurman. Alan Gurman, in the 1980s, began to assume a key role as an editor of marriage and family therapy publications. His growing prominence in the field showed how far family therapy had come; not an innovator but rather a researcher and a compiler of others' work, Gurman rigorously sought balance in the field by showing its diversity. The comprehensive *Handbook of*

Family Therapy (Gurman & Kniskern, 1981) was only the first in a series of handbooks that have provided an overview of current trends.

Sprenkle. Douglas Sprenkle, whose publications in the field now include over 80 refereed journal articles and six books, was a graduate student in the 1970s who quickly became a key faculty member and chair of Purdue University's MFT program—where he remains today. As an advocate of applied research and former editor of the *Journal of Marriage and Family Therapy,* he has played a key role in defining the field as its theories and practices evolved.

McGoldrick. Monica McGoldrick, author or editor of 11 books and 32 articles or book chapters, became affiliated with the new family therapy movement in the early 1970s. By 1980 she was Betty Carter's co-author on *The Family Life Cycle: A Framework for Family Therapy,* now in its 3rd Edition (Carter & McGoldrick, 2004). Director of the Multicultural Family Institute in New Jersey, she is widely recognized as a genogram expert as well as a scholar and activist for issues including ethnicity and culture, gender, and loss.

Carlson. Jon Carlson, a professor of counseling at Governors State University who came to family work with an Adlerian background, has been a prolific author and editor on couple and family topics including intimacy, dysfunctional couples, and adolescence. In addition to publishing 30 books, 120 journal articles, and a popular series of videotapes, in 1992 he founded *The Family Journal*—which continues, under new editorial leadership, to be a primary source of information for couple and family counselors.

Organizational Maturation

As change happened at a local level in the various clinics, institutes, and university departments where family counseling was being created and taught, there were corresponding changes at organizational levels that contributed to a growing crisis and new climate for innovation.

National organizations struggled to define the emerging field in the United States. The American Association for Marriage and Family Therapy focused on the goal of promoting specialized training and achieving uniform standards and licensure for MFTs in every state. Alternatively, the newly formed American Family Therapy Academy, including many of the founders of the field—Bowen, Framo, and Boszormenyi-Nagy—as members, became more of an arena for intellectual debate. Throughout the upheavals of the 1980s and 1990s both groups would provide opportunities for the exchange of ideas and even heated debate in their journals. In addition, the American Psychological Association, the National Council on Family Relations, and the American Counseling Association created new divisions to facilitate the sharing of theories and research related to family work, and the International Family Therapy Association began to sponsor conferences. Finally, the proliferation of journals during the 1970s and 1980s can also be seen as contributing to ending the period of consensus. By 1990, when the *Journal of Couples Therapy* was founded, the field was represented by at least eight refereed publications that were devoted exclusively to the topic of couple and family counseling. Diverse voices were being heard, and family issues were being discussed around the world.

The Managed Care Revolution

The 1990s saw the proliferation of a new relationship between practitioners and funding sources. Managed care was an innovation designed to limit what were perceived as out-of-control expenditures for mental health services; it achieved that goal by making it harder to be reimbursed for counseling services and by explicitly calling for shorter-term approaches. Over time, an additional demand for "empirically validated approaches" has become common as well. This preference for briefer approaches, especially ones that lend themselves to being clearly delivered in a manner that can be replicated and measured, has now shaped the behavior and the interests of a generation of practitioners.

Technology and Professional Communication

Finally, as we look at changes over the past 25 years we can't ignore the influence of printing and communication technology on the ways in which professionals exchange ideas with one another. In the 1950s, 1960s, and 1970s print journals remained pretty much the same. They were cumbersome mechanisms for distributing information, requiring the professional services of typesetters and press operators. Photocopiers were both rare and hard to use, so students and professionals had to go to libraries to read the journals. Newsletters, the rapidly produced mass-market alternative to journals, were often hard to read because of the poor quality of reproduction. In quick succession came high-quality, low-cost copiers; desktop computers with the ability to compose and print camera-ready text; fax machines; and Internet databases from which entire journal collections can be downloaded to a local printer. And with these changes came increased sharing of information in all forms including online newsletters, interactive conversations with authors, online courses complete with video clips, and creative web sites with competitive placement on search engines.

The net result of these changes was a democratization of ideas, a weakening of institutional power, and a shift in the locus of decision making. In the 1960s the editors of a few books and journals decided what knowledge would be most useful for the would-be family counselor. In the present-day marketplace of ideas, there often is no editor deciding what is worth reading. The text a professional is reading online may be a part of a dissertation, a page from the encyclopedia, or a high school term paper. The consumer of ideas, just as the consumer of other products, must learn to distinguish glitter from quality, but there is a potential for a bright and creative person to reach a worldwide audience without sponsors, degrees, or professional credentials.

The 1980s: A Midlife Crisis

Many authors (e.g., Nichols & Schwartz, 2004) have pointed out the confusion that overtook the field of family therapy in the 1980s. For some observers, that confusion has not ended. Having lost the certainty that they perceived in the dominant perspectives in the 1970s, critics fear that the field has become incomprehensible or, worse, irrelevant. Looking back, the period of the 1980s seems instead to be a time when the field experienced a crisis which required letting go of its youth. Old truths were questioned, new language was introduced, and words were stripped of familiar meanings. The writing of that period is openly conflictual, and it is tempting to ignore everything published between roughly 1979 and 1992. But that crisis is an important part of where the field is today, and I will attempt to provide a brief guide to the drama of the times, its major themes, and some of the contributors whose work was most influential during that period.

Feminist Challenges

During the 1970s, intellectual movements and societal forces around the world were being increasingly shaped by feminist discourse—conversations initiated by women and organized around themes that women brought to the forefront. Women organized to overcome patriarchy at the societal level, and they supported each other in their fight for equality of opportunity and freedom from violence in their homes. Unfortunately, the individual woman who lived with a man, especially if they were married, found it hard to put these principles into operation. This was an opportunity for family therapists to make a difference.

Rachel Hare-Mustin (1978, 1980) was among the first to apply feminist concepts to the special world of family counseling, calling attention to a systematic male bias in the theory and practice of family therapy. For example, Structural Family Therapy's assumptions about healthy family structure seemed to imply that households without men were inherently problematic. Family therapists, said Hare-Mustin, were trained to treat men gently in their initial engagement with couples and families, yet their theories treated gender as irrelevant. Male privilege was unspoken, unmentionable, and unchallenged, while girls and women were encouraged to fulfill their traditional roles as caretakers. As a result, the net effect of family therapy's involvement was to stabilize the status quo and defend patriarchy. To the extent that family counseling theories emphasized the goal of stabilizing and preserving families, family counseling discouraged people from addressing patterns that included spousal violence and sexual abuse of girls.

Hare-Mustin's work was paralleled by efforts of others—including Marianne Walters, Betty Carter, Peggy Papp, and Olga Silverstein—who organized themselves in the late 1970s as the Women's Project in Family Therapy. In their work with families, as well as their writing and their conference presentations for fellow professionals, these authors called attention to gendered experiences and raised important questions about the ways in which gendered patterns worked to the disadvantage of both males and females. Marianne Walters left Philadelphia Child Guidance Center to establish her own training center in Washington, DC—after Betty Carter's center in New York, the second MFT training center led by a woman.

Within this new tradition, two major themes emerged. First, feminist family therapists were committed to changing the lives of *marginalized people*. The metaphor being used here refers to the "margins" of society—a location away from the center of action that limits access to resources and participation in political and economic activity. Women, from this perspective, were marginalized by the industrial revolution. In an economy that paid by the hour and paid some people more than others, contributions such as child rearing and caretaking for elders seemed to have no value. And men, who typically went out into the community for work, had identities that were not dependent on their partners and children. Feminist family therapists focused on the many kinds of value that people had—not only their community

status or their income but also their interpersonal value to each other, their human potential. And this theme quickly resonated with professionals working with clients who were marginalized not by their sex but by race, educational level, language, religion, and other factors. Feminists provided leadership for a new generation of more socially responsible family therapists.

Feminist family therapists also called attention to the existence of *power* in social systems. This observation was not news to all professionals. After all, Jay Haley's writings (e.g., 1986) claimed that family relationships and counseling was always a struggle over power, and family sociologists had examined power in families (e.g., Cromwell & Olson, 1975). Even so, many family therapists were shocked by this message. Gregory Bateson had famously claimed that power was a myth, an "epistemological error" (Bateson, 1972) that became real only if people believed in it. His ecosystemic perspective denied power as an explanatory principle; those who believed in their own power, he said, would feel defective when that power didn't work and would abuse themselves and others in pursuit of success. However, Bateson was unable to make power disappear by denying its existence, and feminist authors brought the field's attention to the considerable disparities in physical and economic power that existed in couples and families. Spousal violence and economic control, for the most part benefiting men at the expense of women and children, were labeled and made a focus of intervention. As with marginalization, the feminist challenge was quickly carried forward to provide impetus for a revived social justice orientation in family counseling.[3]

Emerging Postmodernism

Another unbalancing influence came from an intellectual movement that was just beginning to gain recognition in the United States, a broadly defined movement that has many names for its subdivisions—*postmodernism, poststructuralism,*

---

[3] See Chapter 10 for more detailed implications of feminist challenges.

narrative, and *social construction* are a few common labels. While he did not use any of these terms, Fritjof Capra (1982) wrote one of the first American books to challenge the intellectual traditions of *positivist* science—a science based on the assumption that rigorously examining phenomena would yield clear answers and expand knowledge. Capra, who acknowledged Gregory Bateson as a major influence, started with theoretical and research advances of quantum physicists and tied these advances to what he predicted would be a massive reorganization of society. Physical realities, the physicists discovered, are illusions—solid matter is not solid and reality is influenced by measuring it. Bateson had been saying similar things about social phenomena—they cannot be observed without altering their forms. Capra asserted that such a view of the world, similar to the beliefs of many ancient religions, was beginning to coalesce into a trend. Citing Thomas Kuhn (1970), Capra predicted a *paradigm shift*—the replacement of familiar ways of thinking with new ways that would only gradually become clear. (Twenty years later, it appears that Capra may have been right.)

The view Capra described stood in contrast with what he said was the dominant Western perspective—a rationalist, scientific movement dating back to the late 1700s. That movement, based on ideas of Isaac Newton and René Descartes, had declared that mind was separate from the physical world; that all things, mental and physical, were knowable; and the new procedures of scientific inquiry would eventually lead to the eradication of physical disease, social unrest, poverty, emotional distress, and destructive relationships. At its peak, this *modernist* movement had reached into all aspects of contemporary life through its structural metaphors—the language of Newtonian physics (forces, pressures, elements, mechanisms) was the language through which relationships, emotions, and the arts were understood.

Capra was by no means the creator of this new movement. Similar revolutionary ideas were being expressed in many academic fields. Jacques Derrida (1998) rejected the structuralist approach to studying literature, claiming that different readers actually weren't reading the same book because they all added their own assumptions to the words on the pages. Michel Foucault (1980) was documenting the social process through which societies created artificial categories to control their outcasts. And a young family therapist named Bradford Keeney (1979) was challenging the validity of psychiatric diagnoses. These *postmodern* and *poststructuralist* ideas, including questions about the nature of reality and assumptions about the power of language, challenged many popular theories and practices.

Two of the most influential figures in carrying this new movement to family counselors were Humberto Maturana and Francisco Varela (1992). Varela's cognitive background and Maturana's biological orientation produced a compelling message: Humans were language-dependent, and human systems were language systems. Each family or other social group had its own self replicating, systemic pattern of language and interaction—described by their concept of *autopoesis,*—and those patterns limited the options available to the system. Language, in this formulation, gained a new importance, and repeating language patterns deserved the kind of respect given to repeating behavior patterns. Only by attending to a system could one understand how it worked, and change was not something accomplished by direct planning. A counselor could help to create the conditions for change by introducing discrepant feedback (*perturbation*), but there was no way to predict how or when the system might reorganize. This message about the limits of science, and the need for a less power-oriented approach to families, would be interpreted differently by audiences.

The Epistemology Debates

Throughout the 1980s, there were two overlapping discussions of epistemology going on at the same time, and Maturana and Varela were significant figures in both debates. *Epistemology,* the branch of science and philosophy to which Jean Piaget owed his allegiance, is the study of how people come to know about themselves and their environments. Family therapy was torn between the traditionally opposite camps, the objectivists and the constructivists.

Objectivism has been the dominant philosophy of science for generations. The objectivist view of the world sees it as containing real objects and phenomena; knowledge is achieved as people examine the real world, then share their observations and validate each other's discoveries. Constructivists, alternatively, have assumed that each person has to make sense of reality and people's realities differ. As a philosophical stance that doubts any assertions about objective reality and focuses on the individual's ways of constructing a mental and linguistic reality, constructivism has been part of the mental health field since the time of George Kelly (1963). Strategic family therapy approaches, with their tradition of "reframing" behavior, incorporated constructivist ideas.

Two new constructivist movements were formed in the 1980s. The first was a partial incorporation of constructivist assumptions, exploring the idea that families—not just individuals—could develop unique constructions of the world. David Reiss's book *The Family's Construction of Reality* (1981) introduced many readers to the concept of the *family paradigm,* a hypothetical family-level set of beliefs and assumptions that tended to organize the system's responses. This theory, backed by extremely well-organized research, made sense to many professionals who started attending to indications of a family's way of making sense. Applied to family therapy through the work of Constantine (1986), the family paradigm approach captured the imagination of many practitioners.

But the same period also saw the development of *radical constructivism* (von Glasersfeld, 1984; Varela, 1984), a biologically oriented movement challenging assumptions that humans can trust their perceptions of reality. An implication of this position, for those working with couples and families, addressed the serious challenge people face at attempting to coordinate their separate, flawed constructions of shared experiences. If reality was not truly known, it was inappropriate for a professional to take an expert position in relation to a client; instead, the professional

should act as a consultant with the client in a process of jointly discovering the client's reality. The abstractions of constructivism, supported by scientific discoveries of brain science, challenged family therapists to abandon some of their assumptions that they could identify systems and feedback loops—or even say what was and wasn't a family.

The constructivist challenge overlapped with another epistemological issue. One of the most-often cited works in the revolution of the early 1980s was Paul Dell's *Family Process* article, "Beyond Homeostasis: Toward a Concept of Coherence" (1982a). Dell, who has described himself as a former strategic family therapist who "read *Pragmatics of Human Communication* cover to cover three or four times before I finished graduate school" (Dell, 1982b, p. 407), acknowledged many new influences—Bateson, Maturana, Keeney—in his reconceptualization of systems thinking. Homeostasis did not help in explaining change, he said, it explained instead why change shouldn't happen. His proposed concept of *coherence* rather than homeostasis described transactions at multiple system levels—an ecosystemic perspective. Questioning the systemic nature of early works by Bateson, Jackson, Haley, and Weakland, Dell said that a more systemic epistemology would require professionals to abandon notions of causality and control.

Many of these points were based on the work of Brad Keeney, whose visibility began when he was still a staff member at the Menninger Foundation and a doctoral student at Purdue. Keeney, who had studied Bateson's work and who had spent time with Bateson shortly before his death, published a series of papers (Keeney, 1979, 1982; Keeney & Ross, 1983; Keeney & Sprenkle, 1982) that challenged accepted practice, building on the concepts of *ecosystemic assessment* and *ecosystemic epistemology.* Keeney introduced the idea of an "aesthetic" approach to families in contrast to the "pragmatic" approach of Watzlawick et al. (1967). In his classic *Aesthetics of Change* (Keeney, 1982), he promoted the idea of respecting a system and subtly altering its recurring feedback patterns to precipitate a crisis that would allow change to happen.

The epistemological changes identified by Dell and Keeney spread rapidly through the field. Some of the changes of this period are captured in *Family Therapy: An Intimate History*, an autobiographical work by Lynn Hoffman (2002). Hoffman, who like Dell identifies herself as having worked for years in a strategic mode, wrote a series of papers beginning in 1983 documenting her rejection of her earlier work and her movement toward a postmodern perspective. Hoffman's writings from this period were challenging and sometimes confusing. Like many others, she was trying to distance herself from ideas that seemed to conflict with her newfound fascination with language processes and evolutionary change. She continued to evolve as a voice for the new approaches, largely through collaborations with others who were on similar paths. Her work with Tom Andersen, originator of the reflecting team (Andersen, 1987, 1991) appears to have been especially meaningful (see Chapter 6). At this time, she remains an advocate for a perspective that eschews certainty and manipulation, maintains an openness to spontaneous change, values relationships over techniques, and focuses on the power of narrative and discourse in people's lives.

In Galveston, Texas, Harry Goolishian and Harlene Anderson epitomized the radical rejection of tradition. Goolishian and Anderson, who had been strongly strategic in their orientation, amazed and confused many when they demonstrated and taught new ways of working with families in the mid-1980s. These approaches were remarkable for their lack of manipulation or professional posturing. Lynn Hoffman (2002) recalled observing the demonstrations of this new work and thinking that it looked like a casual conversation. But Goolishian and Anderson gradually articulated the core concepts and key behavioral elements of their new collaborative language systems (CLS) approach—listen, use the clients' own language, accept them, and respect their desire to change (H. Anderson & Goolishian, 1988; H. Anderson, Goolishian, & Winderman, 1986).

Dell's homeostasis article (1982a) appeared, along with the Keeney and Sprenkle piece, in a 1982 issue of *Family Process* including several works challenging the field's certainty about theory and methods. With the family therapy mainstream under attack, defenders quickly organized and a debate during the next several years left many observers confused. Typical was an article by Coyne, Denner, and Ransom (1982), staff members at the Mental Research Institute, who appeared to feel personally attacked. After all, Dell and his associates had rejected *Pragmatics of Human Communication* (Watzlawick et al., 1967) along with the core concept of homeostasis. Quoting George Orwell to support their argument, Coyne and his colleagues characterized the new work as propaganda. They suggested that the challengers had created a caricature of the MRI work: "Has anyone met a therapist who uses 'homeostasis' in such a pseudoexplanatory, reified manner?" (Coyne et al., 1982, p. 392). And they summarized the papers as having "ignored or rejected" "the standards of intellectual discourse" (p. 393).

The argument continued through at least 1986, when Shields wrote that "The new epistemologies are, in fact, weak theories" (p. 360). The heat of the struggle had dissipated, however, and the central figures in the debate had moved on to other issues. Commentators (e.g., Auerswald, 1987) seemed to agree that Bateson probably used the word epistemology in confusing ways, and they excused those who followed his lead. But the conversation had clearly changed the nature of family therapy discourse, calling attention to families' own attempts to make sense of their experiences.

Cybernetics and Second-Order Cybernetics

Not long after the writings about ecosystemic epistemology appeared, Keeney and Ross (1983) presented a completely different set of issues. Again citing Bateson, they expressed concerns that brief family therapists were (1) focused on change to the exclusion of stability in clinical families, and (2) insufficiently aware of the systemic nature of their interaction with those families. They said that a simple cybernetics—formulate a plan, implement the plan, observe the feedback, revise the plan, and implement the revised plan—denied the family's active participation in the process. A troubled family, they said, "comes to therapy, in most cases, with a request to alter the way it changes in order to stabilize itself" (p. 379). They proposed a less directive, *second-order cybernetics* stance—a more respectful posture, one that served primarily to introduce randomness into the system rather than demand specific changes. Their intervention model involved extremely tentative kinds of interventions, avoiding directives and depending on the delivery of information. The process of moving toward a successful outcome, in this model, required that the therapist "shift from being an observer of families to an observer of one's observing families" (p. 381).

The Keeney and Ross (1983) article did not provoke the kind of outcry that had occured in 1982. But Lynn Hoffman (1985) received more attention when she explored a similar theme a few years later. Hoffman, citing Bateson for her inspiration, presented an article on second-order practice in which she linked her work to that of the popular Milan team. Others made the same connection: Golann (1988) wrote, "The early Milan approach described by Selvini-Palazzoli and her associates may be seen as a beginning of a second-order model because it placed greater emphasis on therapist neutrality, circularity, and positive connotation" (p. 53). This second-order cybernetic[4] discus-sion seemed to resonate with many professionals in the field but nevertheless created new controversy.

This time, critics did not focus on either the language or the ways in which these new ideas seemed to be criticizing accepted practice. There were few rebuttals from the old guard being ac-

cused of being simplistic and insensitive in their first-order approaches. Instead, critics took issue with the second-order claims of having become less hierarchical and less intrusive. Golann said that the introduction of new information, if done with the intention of altering a family, was possibly more troubling than direct influence because it was "a therapeutic wolf clad as a second-order sheep" (1988, p. 56). The field was on a path toward something new, but it didn't exactly trust those leading the way.

An article by Brent Atkinson and Anthony Heath (1990) suggests that the conversation over second-order approaches had not ended. They acknowledged that "Any conscious, consistent attempt to minimize or maximize a particular variable, action, experience, or pattern may lead to higher-order systemic problems" (p. 147), and concluded "perhaps the most important thing that humans can do in this age is to learn a way of experiencing a shift in personal epistemology, or way of experiencing the world" (p. 149).

By the time Atkinson and Heath wrote these words, innovations in practice had moved far ahead of what was envisioned in 1985. Tom Andersen's (1987, 1991) use of reflecting teams, for example, was creating a less hierarchical experience in which professionals were able to use both their expert and personal wisdom. And the Galveston team of Harlene Anderson and Harry Goolishian had begun to implement their "therapeutic conversation" approach. In fact, Atkinson and Heath's article was answered by Anderson and Goolishian in an article (1990) where they first presented the concept of problem "dis-solving" through narratives and stories.

From Constructivism and Cybernetics to Social Construction. H. Anderson and Goolishian (1990) proposed to end the use of the term "cybernetic," troubled by its mechanical metaphor. They said, ". . . we have found ourselves moving away from the patterns of cybernetic theory to what we call a 'postcybernetic' interest in human meaning, narrative, and story" (p. 161). The language of cybernetics had caused problems, they said: "Issues of reframing, positive connotation, therapeutic strategies, and the confrontation of narra-

---

[4] In a confusing parallel use of terms, Maruyama (1963) had used the term "second-order cybernetics" with a different meaning. It appears that some authors who used the term in the 1980s were unaware of this problem.

tives in order to deconstruct old narratives or to provide new narrative possibilities, are all examples of rhetoric as opposed to the dialogue that we believe is essential to a therapeutic conversation" (p. 161). Anderson and Goolishian were speaking for another new wave of family work that "leans heavily on the premise that human action takes place in a reality that is created through social construction" (p. 161).

Social construction, as distinguished from constructivism, was a sociology term coined by Berger and Luckmann (1966), who described the gradual process through which interacting groups start with a shared observation, label it, and through use of the label gradually reify and institutionalize the "thing" that did not exist until it was labeled. Viewed from this perspective a person's perceptual/conceptual world was not constructed by the individual, but rather the process of constructing reality was something that was done in interaction with others. It had taken approximately 20 years for Berger and Luckmann's idea to reach the level of the family practitioner.

Goolishian and Anderson were not alone in rejecting the cybernetic metaphor and finding an alternative language for working with social construction. Other pioneers included Michael White and David Epston in Australia and New Zealand, who were achieving the same change in their language and their interactions with clients. White (1986, p. 169), in a transitional article, cited Bateson as his source for a cybernetic view of a world in which "events take their course because they are restrained from taking alternative courses." But his reading of Bateson emphasized the idea that "In this world, recipients respond to, or act in relation to, a perceived difference or distinction. Distinctions are critical, as they provide the source of all new responses" (p. 170). He said, "The therapist contributes to the family's perception of . . . contrasts by working to develop double or multiple descriptions of certain events, standing these descriptions side by side for family members and then inviting them to draw distinctions between these descriptions. This provides news of *'difference which makes a difference' "* (p. 172).[5]

---
[5] A quote from Bateson.

The 1990s and beyond: Reexamining Values and Settling Down

Like the life crises that clients bring into our offices, this group identity crisis did not get resolved all at once. Instead, throughout the 1990s, the field seemed to gradually accommodate to the challenges of the prior decade. For some who found themselves on the front edge of a new movement, support was newly available from an international community of postmodernist philosophers, linguists, and other scholars. For other family therapists and counselors, the disruptions did not make much of a difference. For example, on the behavioral side of the field issues of power and collaboration were not irrelevant, but the language of Bateson and Maturana was not a part of their discourse. For still others, the 1990s would be a time for reexamining core values, taking stock, and making some changes. While some practitioners who identified themselves as strategic or structural did not find the criticisms to be credible, others took the criticisms as a call for redefining their work.

For many, the different intersecting ideas of the 1980s provided an opportunity to find a more comfortable, authentic version of themselves. These self-transformers, along with the newcomers to the field who had not yet found an identity, formed a strong coalition that shared the general postmodern/poststructural vision enough to tolerate differences in terminology. The field as a whole came to realize that intense differences were reducing credibility and integrative efforts therefore increased.

In the following pages, we look at some different kinds of experience in the newly matured field of couple and family counseling.

Life Goes On

Many of the movements during the 1980s and 1990s were essentially continuations of work that was relatively untouched by the social and intellectual trends I have just described. These movements include Behavioral Couple and Family Therapy, Medical Family Therapy, and Object Relations Family Therapy.

Additionally, the strategic and structural traditions continued to hold to many of their most cherished ways of working, at the same time that they accepted some of the challenges.

Behavioral and Cognitive-Behavioral Approaches

Before 1980, behavioral couple and family counseling was a small but growing specialty gaining considerable attention because of its ability to produce positive outcome studies. These trends continued well into the 1990s. Not only did basic behavioral approaches such as social-skills training receive strong research support, but those approaches were also supplemented by new work that challenged the boundaries of the behavioral camp. Cognitive-behavioral approaches were gaining ground in the individual counseling arena and cognitive-behavioral strategies proved effective with couples and families as well.

One of the significant contributions was Robin and Foster's Behavioral-Family Systems Approach for working with adolescents (1989). Their approach, focused on training families in problem-solving techniques to reduce conflict, depended heavily on structured assessment. The book offers an Issues Checklist, written in accessible language, including 44 "things that sometimes get talked about at home." Having identified frequently talked-about issues, adolescents and parents rate them on "how hot are the discussions for each topic?" They also provide a Conflict Behavior Questionnaire with separate versions that ask about parent and adolescent perceptions of 75 different possible interactions. Their structured approach moves from an engagement/assessment phase through a skill-building phase, leading to intense conflict resolution and disengagement.

In the arena of couples counseling, the behavioral studies of Weiss, Jacobson, and others in the 1970s had gained their credibility from the idea of corrective feedback—procedures were field-tested and refined. Holtzworth-Munroe and Jacobson (1991) put it this way: "What distinguishes BMT from other approaches to treating couples is its commitment to empirical investigation as the optimal road to development." It was extremely distressing to these researchers when their own outcome studies began to cast doubt on their methods. Jacobson and Christensen (1996), in *Acceptance and Change in Couple Therapy*, documented the troubling results. Studies featuring each of the core components—behavior exchange and communication/problem-solving training—produced statistically significant improvements, and in combination the techniques, performed even better. When results were reexamined some years later, however, the investigators looked more closely at the numbers. About a third of couples showed no change during treatment and of the successes, approximately a third relapsed within 2 years.

Jacobson and Christensen (1996), therefore, reexamined traditional BMT, concluding that it relied on accommodation and collaboration—easier for some couples to achieve than for others. The less successful couples, they hypothesized, were not adept at meeting halfway but responded to the "force-feeding" of the program by temporarily acting more cooperative and eventually returning to their negative, competitive ways. They finally decided that stable relationships needed a balance of change-oriented strategies for handling the things that could be modified, along with improved abilities to "work things out despite . . . differences and problems" (p. 11).

In their improved version of behavioral couple work, which Christensen and Jacobson (1996)[6] referred to as Integrative Behavioral Couple Therapy (IBCT), considerable attention was given to the goal of helping couples to achieve intimacy; become more accepting of each other's different ways of doing things; and commit themselves to change only in selected areas.

---

[6] In the midst of testing this new approach, Neil Jacobson died in 1999.

Medical Family Therapy

Medical family therapy (or family systems medicine), a movement that began in the 1980s, quickly became an established field with its own journal (*Families, Systems, and Health*) and organization (the Collaborative Family Healthcare Association). The movement has been strongly associated with the Chicago Center for Family Health and the Department of Psychiatry at the University of Rochester, New York. The medical community has been extremely supportive of this new specialty, as family dynamics are extremely powerful in healing processes and coping as well as behavioral compliance with a treatment plan (Rolland, 1994). Several specialized graduate programs exist at this time.

Object Relations Family Therapy

Another quiet innovation from the 1980s was the increasing application of object relations ideas in family work. Whereas James Framo acknowledged an object relations perspective, he also had been one of the family therapy pioneers who essentially rejected their psychodynamic backgrounds when the new movement started; therefore, Framo's work was independent of trends in the object relations community.

Object relations family practitioners of the 1980s and 1990s were more explicitly tied to the theory and to the traditions of psychodynamic practice. The team of Jill Savege Scharff and David E. Scharff (1987) from Washington, DC—one of the most established centers of psychoanalytic training in the United States—has played an important role articulating the relevance of object relations phenomena for practice with families. At the core of Object Relations Theory is the assumption that early emotional experiences combine with later experiences to shape an individual's relational patterns such as trusting, holding back, punishing, or rewarding. Object relations family therapists search for events and relationships that helped establish negative patterns at the same time that they focus on changing current relationships so that positive interactive cycles can develop.

Biogenetic Emphases

Former collaborators David Reiss and Peter Steinglass are among those who have investigated the ways in which multigenerational and individual-level biology fit into family systemic patterns. As editor of *Family Process* in 1991, Steinglass appealed to the field to pay attention to new findings on behavioral genetics with implications for biological difference so significant that "two siblings sitting in the same family therapy session will in fact be participating in two different environmental contexts" (p. 267). He called for renewed attention to the idea of temperament and other ways of conceptualizing individual differences.

That journal issue included a ground-breaking article by genetic researchers Dunn and Plomin (1991) in which the concept of *nonshared environment* was explored. Rather than operating directly to create the range of individual differences in a family, they argued, subtle genetic differences seem to lead to interactions that amplify those small differences. Over the following decade, Reiss led a research team that tested this assumption (Reiss, Plomin, Neiderhiser, & Hetherington, 2000). Studying two-parent birth families and stepfamilies, they were able to demonstrate that children in the same family are parented differently. Despite the power of these research findings, however, it remains to be seen how the biogenetic theme will influence practitioners.

Reconnections with Feelings

Following the deaths of Virginia Satir and Carl Whitaker, there was a brief period when it appeared that emotion was moving even further toward the margins of family counseling. The dominant voices in the field appeared to be focused on issues of behavior and language, and emotional issues were too ambiguous to fit into these conversations. New leaders have emerged—some of them newcomers, others familiar but often overlooked—to return this aspect of human experience to intervention with families.

The past 20 years have been a fertile time for biological and ethnographic research that seems to agree on the essential nature of emotion in human lives. In this new climate, a variety of theories have been applied to make sense of the intense love, anger, depression, and anxiety that are observed in clinical couples and families. In Chapter 7 we will focus on the work of Leslie Greenberg and Susan Johnson, whose contributions together and individually (e.g., Johnson & Greenberg, 1994, 1995) enriched the field's theoretical understandings and provided techniques that provide a balance of comforting structure and disruptive power.

Reconnections with Spirituality
The spiritual dimension of family work was relatively neglected among the first generation developers. Probably the only figure in the 1970s whose work had a noticeably spiritual tone was Satir, although religious institutions had a long history of being concerned with relationships and the marriage enrichment movement—dating from the early 1960s—had been spiritually influenced. Kelly's (1992) review of journal articles concluded that only 1% of the family therapy literature addressed religion in a positive way.

The early 1990s saw many contributions that changed this picture. Burton (1992); Gutsche (1994); Prest and Keller (1993); and Stander, Piercy, MacKinnon, and Helmeke (1994) all surveyed the field and called for more attention to spirituality. Even though spiritual issues continued to be challenging to articulate and uncomfortable for some practitioners to address, they were no longer overlooked and even came to be a major theme in some people's work.

Strategic and Structural Developments
The events of the 1980s left their marks on authors, trainers, and practitioners who identified themselves as strategic and/or structural. The decade had begun with some efforts at merging the two powerful and competing perspectives, which had so much common heritage. The two literatures were quite compatible, each having its strengths and its limitations. By the end of the 1980s, neither perspective had the kind of loyal and adversarial following that had made integration impossible. Stanton and Todd's (1982;

Stanton, 1991) integrated structural/strategic approach, which once seemed bold, now found ready acceptance.

On the strategic side, the leaders of the field worked hard to ride the wave and support colleagues and trainees as their work came under attack. The *Journal of Strategic and Systemic Therapies* (JSST), known for attempts to stretch the field with diverse and challenging voices, published its tenth anniversary issue in 1991. The senior coeditor and publisher, Don Efron, commented on the "flow of thought from the hard core Strategists of the early 80s to the Softer but Wiser therapists of today" (p. 104). He invited authors from the first issue to reflect on their earlier work and also included articles on the current state of the field. The various authors acknowledged tremendous change in the language they were using and in their stance regarding the people they worked with; only Steve deShazer expressed a belief that he had remained more or less consistent during the decade.

In 1992 the *Journal of Marital and Family Therapy* published a special issue with a series of papers on the topic, "Strategic-Systemic Therapy—Erosion or Evolution?" Among the contributions, the outgrowths of a conference panel discussion 2 years before, was a plea from Don Efron (1992) acknowledging that "there are attacks" and "images from the past have come to haunt us . . . our popular impression still seems to be of scheming therapists developing clever little interventions to defeat resistance while ignoring deeper issues" (p. 3). He closed with words of encouragement, saying "The strategic-systemic coalition has been, and is continuing to be, a unique method capable of providing immense assistance to families" (p. 3).

As the 1990s progressed, even some traditional strategic therapists showed a softer, less-controlling side of themselves. In the newly renamed *Journal of Systemic Therapies*, a 1993 special edition on strategic humanism included an article by Cloe Madanes rejecting the stereotype of strategists as devious and manipulative and stating that "strategic therapy is a conservative approach, characterized by the belief that humanism is the starting point" (p. 69). Topics addressed in the same issue included relationship-building with clients (Belson, 1993) and various interventions that emphasized skill building, negotiation, and play.

The MRI approach in the 1990s, according to Weakland, Johnson, and Morrissette (1995), continued to adhere to the basic assumptions set forth in *Pragmatics of Human Communication* and other classics. Wendel Ray, current director of the Mental Research Institute and director of the Don D. Jackson Archive, said in a 2002 interview "I think the problem is that we've somehow disconnected ourselves from our theory. We disconnected ourselves from the interactionally oriented philosophy/theory that constitutes the matrix out of which all these ideas came. . . . We are so caught up in learning about new, and new is good, that we forget that there is a background" (Malinen, 2002).

Transformations

Several contemporary movements had their roots in the 1980s, when their creators took new inspiration from the intellectual upheaval of the times and transformed work that had begun with different assumptions.

The Solution-Focused Movement

Through the decade of the 1980s, when many other new ideas were proposed and then rejected, Solution-Focused Brief Therapy (SFBT) was flourishing. Its primary authors Steve deShazer and Insoo Kim Berg avoided the waves of controversy that swept the field, apparently because of their rather simple and elegant way of putting ideas into clinical practice. In 2003 the newly formed Solution-Focused Brief Therapy Association held its first conference, and all indications suggest further growth.

SFBT thinking generally derives from the MRI assumption that client problems result from ineffective attempts to solve other problems. Clients are not assumed to be incompetent, but rather are seen as having gotten stuck in a pattern that keeps them from accessing their own strengths. deShazer, trained in the MRI approach but a student of postmodern ideas, and Berg,

with additional perspectives from her Korean cultural background, transformed the MRI message into a teachable, powerful, collaborative, and culturally sensitive approach.[7]

The basic assumption of solution-focused work is that clients respond to a hopeful stance that accentuates their positive qualities. Solution-oriented authors note the tendency for a first interview to have a tone of negativity as professionals seek problem stories and then try to make the problem stories as detailed as possible. A solution-oriented practitioner is more likely to focus on times when the problem did *not* appear—*exceptions*. Solution-oriented practitioners try not to define the client in terms of the problem; instead, they seek in their early contacts with clients to promote thinking about desired outcomes: "If you weren't having this problem, how would your relationship look?"

Once a preferred future is described, the SFBT process involves specifying desired outcomes, "scaling" those outcomes, identifying steps that will help move toward them, and crediting clients with effective performance. The scaling is an important step—no one ever starts from zero progress toward an outcome, and the sense of having already made some progress is an important motivational piece. The greatest power of the approach may come from the counselor's success in convincing the clients that they are already doing some of what is needed and to take credit for their actions. Hoyt (2002) provides a list of agency (efficacy) questions, including the following:

- How did you do that?
- How did you get that to happen?
- What was each of you doing differently when you were doing better (or when there wasn't a problem, or when the exception happened)?
- How did each of you decide to do that?

Solution-focused work is extremely popular with agencies as well as clients, because case documentation provides evidence of progress, and

---

[7] Steve deShazer died in 2005.

the approach has been used with quite a variety of populations. At the same time, it has not been without its detractors. Friedman (1993), for example, noting that a reader of the SFBT literature might get the impression that the techniques always work, called for a greater focus on the need for basic counseling skills.

Social Constructionist Approaches

By the end of the 1980s, as the debates over epistemology, constructivism, cybernetics, and second-order practice were subsiding, there was a consistent winner in every debate: social construction. Sometimes it was named, sometimes it was implied, but there was general support for the idea that people's relationships, including the interactions between helpers and the couples and families they served, were organized by some kind of social construction process. This clinical discovery was clearly related to discussions that had been taking place in allied fields (e.g., Berger & Luckmann, 1966; Sarbin, 1986), and family practitioners who led the integration of social constructionist ideas acknowledged their debt to a generation of philosophers, linguists, sociologists, anthropologists, and psychologists.

The following examples illustrate applications of social construction; Chapter 6 examines these ideas and applications in more depth.

Reflecting Teams. Tom Andersen credits his major discovery to accident rather than planning. As a family therapist accustomed to using a consulting team behind a one-way mirror, but encouraged by colleagues from Milan to be creative in his work, he decided in 1985 to reverse the lighting and let the family see and hear the team talking about them. The results were so impressive that he began to use this modified team structure. Andersen was part of an international group of family therapists, including faculty from the Ackerman Institute, so it was not long before he was invited to show his work in the United States. Lynn Hoffman wrote of her first experiences of being a team member for Andersen's demonstration in Brattleboro, Vermont:

. . . the shock of no protection took my breath away. Suddenly it was clear to me what a conspiracy of silence our profession rests on. I found I began to shun not just clinical words but clinical thoughts, and psychological language, which came so easily during backstage exchanges between colleagues, now began to seem like a form of hate speech. (2002, p. 150)

The reflecting team structure had the effect of leveling the hierarchy. Professionals were encouraged to speak honestly and directly about their responses to clients, and many found that their language and attitudes were profoundly altered by this shift. Hoffman noted that reflecting team conversations were less about the problem and more about the helping relationship—including the decision to seek help. In a new context, it was expected that the story would come out differently. These ideas were influenced by many others, including Goolishian and Anderson.

Collaborative Language Systems. Harlene Anderson's career as a family therapist began as a staff member with the legendary Timberlawn project. It was there that she came to be a close colleague with Harry Goolishian, and when he organized the Houston/Galveston Center for Family Therapy, Anderson became a key member of the faculty. Over the next 2 decades she would be Goolishian's close collaborator in training and publication until his death in 1991. In 1997 she published *Conversation, Language, and Possibilities: A Postmodern Approach to Therapy,* which still stands as the most complete statement of what has come to be called the collaborative language systems (CLS) approach.

One of the key distinctions in this new approach was the switch to "problem determined systems" rather than families as the treatment unit. Anderson et al. (1986) proposed that every problem situation is defined as a problem by a social group who share that definition. The family is an arbitrary choice of the location for intervention, as there are extrafamilial influences such as courts, schools, and neighbors that have also contributed to the process. What is important, they said, is identifying *all* the individuals and institutions that have contributed to defining something as a problem—the "problem determined system."

Refusing to focus on the behavioral patterns that have been labeled as problematic, Anderson et al. (1986) talked about the "languaging of the problem." From their perspective, the language pattern was the easier one to disrupt. The interactive style they developed to accomplish this disruption was one in which the professional takes a "not knowing" stance. When people find that all of their familiar terminology and their key assumptions have to be explained, they typically respond by reexamining their story and somehow arriving at new conclusions.

Narrative.   Probably the most popular way of applying social constructionist ideas, though, is through the use of a narrative metaphor. From this perspective, people's lives are seen as stories that are simultaneously enacted and recorded. As no person can either enact or tell a story with complete independence, narrative work is essentially social constructionist in its core assumptions. At the same time, the introduction of the narrative metaphor emphasizes the local level where discourses are reproduced, thereby providing considerable opportunity for a client to enter into the process of social construction. Every telling of a story, from this perspective, is a new telling and therefore the "restorying" of an interaction changes that interaction.

Like many other leaders in narrative/social constructionist counseling, Michael White, from Australia, was originally trained in more traditional strategic approaches. In the mid-1980s he began to experiment with the revolutionary technique of *externalizing conversations;* with anthropologist David Epston, his close colleague from New Zealand, he published *Narrative Means to Therapeutic Ends* in 1990. More than just an articulation of the creative ways in which White and Epston worked with clients, this book was an eloquent introduction to postmodernist thought—especially the work of Michel Foucault. Given Foucault's interest in mental pa-

tients, prisoners, sexual minorities, and others who are subjugated by society, it should not be a surprise that White and Epston have become known for the social justice orientation in their work. In recent years, influenced by their work with the native populations of Australia, New Zealand, and North America, they have become increasingly focused on the spiritual component of narratives. White and Epston's orientation has proved useful with a variety of client groups and problems, and each of them has done dramatic and effective work at larger system levels (see Epston's "Anti-Anorexia League" archives on the web site www.narrativeapproaches.com) as well as at the family and individual levels.

Here is a snippet of conversation from a session with Michael White in 1993. In this conference presentation, he was one of three people who took turns interviewing the same couple. (This format recalls the legendary "Gloria" films of 1964.) The session has been examined extensively by Kogan and Gale (1997); the transcript, taken from their article, is coded according to rules of Conversation Analysis (CA)—a system for enhancing transcribed speech so that it reflects the hesitancies and imprecision of the speaker. Coding indicates pauses (e.g., .5 indicates a half-second pause), repeated and half-spoken words, lengthened words (e.g., o::r), overtalking by the partner (e.g., "yeh" in the middle of Jane's talking) and phonetic spelling. It shows White performing a function Kogan and Gale call *reciprocal editing,* ". . . a mutual process whereby the attributions evolving between all participants are open and fluid. In this session, it begins with the therapist offering a shift in meaning in response to a client account" (Kogan & Gale, 1997, p. 113). We pick up the conversation just before the therapeutic shift:

JANE: *And I have to say that um (.) that I would always I had to um be in control of everything (.) I had to be in control of (.5) of him (yeh) of our relationship I thought I I thought if I could keep it all under control (.) um for some reason I would be a hap happier and my contribution is to let go and t'own up and to take his advice.*

MICHAEL: *When you say in control you mean like sort of take responsibility for (1.0) for most things o::r or feel that you are responsible for lots of things is that what you mean by in control o::r do you mean something else?*

JANE: *(3.0) um yes I probably had to take responsibility (.) (yeh) for everything (.) (okay, yeh) mhm (yeh).*

In this seemingly easy, but carefully crafted word substitution White shifts the dominant story of Jane's controlling into a new story of her taking responsibility. Through a series of such subtle challenges, in this session the volunteer couple appears to discover and implement several new ways of describing themselves and their relationship. Some other specific techniques of narrative counseling are explained in Chapter 6.

The Critics

Despite the enthusiasm with which social constructionist approaches have been greeted, there remain those who have doubts. One of the most vocal has been Salvador Minuchin, who wondered in the *Journal of Marital and Family Therapy* (1998) "Where is the family in Narrative Family Therapy?" (see Box 3.4).

Minuchin, of course, is one of the people who had most directly challenged orthodox mental health practice by putting family members in a room together and having them talk about their problems—attempting to reproduce the conversations and emotional confrontations that happened at home. Minuchin's argument questioned how the new approaches addressed relationships.

Probably the strongest statement in his article said that many social constructionists "jump over the family as an intermediate construct and

---

BOX 3.4

Where Is the Family in Narrative Family Therapy?

Salvador Minuchin (1998) wrote a controversial article titled "Where Is the Family in Narrative Family Therapy?" in which he explained that he was responding to conference and training sessions where Gene Combs, Charles Waldegrave, Michael White, and Karl Tomm had demonstrated their work. Reviewing the postmodern and social constructionist literature, he expressed appreciation for the increasing attention to power, context, and culture in people's lives but at the same time worried that these contemporary approaches were missing out on other issues. He asked, "How would this theory explain bonding?" and "How does it explain the way conflict between parents affects their children's views of themselves?" He concluded that the newer approaches were not focusing on the family—"that prominent, intermediate locus of context and

culture within which people live . . ." (p. 403). His challenge led to a series of articles in the *Journal of Marital and Family Therapy* exchanging opinions with the authors he had observed and others such as Harlene Anderson and Carlos Sluzki.

Minuchin showed respect for positive aspects of the emerging trend, but also expressed dismay that the new group of authors seemed to have misread his classic writings—in which he thought culture and context were central. The feeling was mutual: His colleagues shared the experience of thinking that their work was being misread.

As Kuhn (1970) described, in this debate scholars from different paradigms were using different language, and therefore it was difficult to reconcile the arguments. The debate remained unresolved.

deal directly with people in the larger culture" (p. 399). Another of his criticisms related to the technique of interviewing one family member in the other's presence. This kind of conversation, he said, prevented "observing the way in which family members affect each other in their transactions" (p. 399). Minuchin seemed concerned that people were misunderstanding his work and therefore losing traditions that might have been helpful to the families. At the same time, he seemed troubled by the apparent inconsistency within this new movement.

Demonstrating that the age of postmodernism and social constructionism is not without its debates, various authors responded to Minuchin's comments. Both sides made excellent points. Minuchin cited his own work to show that he had not been as culturally inflexible as alleged, and the social constructionists explained the relational aspects of a process that Minuchin considered individual.

Culture

Culture is a word with strong meanings in its anthropological roots, but it has lost precision as it has entered common speech. Until recently, writings about culture in couple and family relationships tended (1) to classify people into cultural groups that were assumed to be homogeneous, and (2) to imply that a helper could, based on such a classification, know how culture functioned in a particular relationship. Even when such a presentation was handled with sensitivity, it often left the reader frustrated when a particular family didn't match the literature. With the emergence of narrative and social constructionist understandings, culture as a way of understanding human relationships has become a more powerful theme.

Culture is both a source of meanings, guidelines, and strategies for living and a product of people's daily lives. That is, culture is constantly being regenerated and transmitted through its enactment. Cultural strengths, such as respect for the environment, are kept alive through enactment, and so are problematic cultural traditions, such as subordination of women or infanticide.

When a culture loses its rituals, lifestyles, and language, as has happened with many cultural traditions, the culture may be portrayed in art but it will never again have its power. One of the challenges in contemporary societies, with multiple cultures living in close proximity, involves finding ways to simultaneously honor cultural traditions that disagree on rules for living.

The literature on cultural issues has changed, in the past 20 years, not only because of newer theories but also because of increasing visibility for authors who represent culturally diverse perspectives (e.g., Arnold, 2002; Berg & Jaya, 1993; Falicov, 1999). Multiple viewpoints are contributing to an understanding of the complexity of culture and its significance in people's lives. Rather than culture being a fixed characteristic possessed only by minority groups, culture is being recognized in fluid, overlapping streams of discourse that cannot be reduced to labels and groups.

Race, Class, Gender, and Sexual Orientation

A smaller movement—tentative still, but visible—involves turning the field's attention back to social justice. Facundo (1990) discusses the likelihood of overdiagnosing or underdiagnosing low income or poor clients—blaming the victim. He presents a powerful case study in which cultural values and discussions of the family's economic struggles helped a family to challenge a psychiatric diagnosis, expect more from each other, work harder to support each other, and eventually bring adults and children to higher levels of functioning. As Inclan and Ferran (1990) indicate, a systemic understanding requires that counselors neither ignore economic issues nor assume that the only realities that matter are economic ones.

Boyd-Franklin (1993) describes the complexity of the overlaps among race, class, gender, and family structure, and suggests that counselors need to not only engage poor minority families in conversations about their collective experience of disempowerment but also to help them take action to become more empowered. Pinderhughes (1990), discussing both the need for and the dangers presented by African American families' efforts to achieve and maintain middle-class status, calls for a focus on educating family members about the sociopolitical realities they face at the same time that we provide meaningful help in dealing with larger system problems. Along with Kliman (1998) and Hardy (1989), she reminds professionals that the helper's own race and class may distort relationships with clients, and calls for efforts toward greater self-awareness.

Sexual orientation is another social justice concern that has been central in the changes of the past 25 years. In 1980, there were few professional writings on gay, lesbian, bisexual, and transgendered people's relationships. Scholars in the last 25 years have published extensively on special relational issues of sexual minorities, however (e.g., Clark & Serovich, 1997; Laird & Green, 1996), and family counselors are becoming aware that large numbers of people have been excluded from discussions of "family."

Integrationist Moves

As all of these changes have been taking place, a more subtle shift has been gaining momentum—a more positive view of theoretical integration (Lebow, 1997). We briefly looked at some of the work of integrationist researchers in Chapter 1, but the focus was on counseling basics—issues such as establishing an alliance with clients. Within couple and family counseling, other conversations have been taking place that seek to preserve the variety of theories and methods in the field but to somehow free practitioners to create their own combinations.

These conversations typically contrast integration with eclecticism, which refers to practicing in a way that uses a variety of approaches depending on circumstances. Even though Arnold Lazarus (e.g., Lazarus, Beutler, & Norcross, 1992) has made articulate arguments for *technical eclecticism,* a high level of practice in which the professional has a wide variety of skills available, critics argue that such practice can present clients with a fragmented experience and unintegrated techniques may reduce each other's effects. Integrationists say the combining of ideas and techniques

from different sources is a complex but manageable goal that can be achieved only by careful, thoughtful planning.

Three different integrative strategies can be identified. The first is *metatheorizing,* examining how theories are constructed and how people make choices between theories. Metatheoretical work is challenging and rare. The second involves *transtheoretical analysis*—identifying the threads of internally consistent conceptualization that repeat themselves in various models. Finally, an integrationist may create an *integrated model* that can be applied to many cases. This kind of integration is present throughout the history of counseling theories and can be seen in virtually all of the well-known approaches to individual and family counseling.

Metatheorizing.   Possibly the challenge of metatheorizing has never been described better than it was by Howard Liddle (1982), who said, "The contemporary clinician faces a complex and highly politicized realm when attempting to learn about the family therapy field" (p. 244). (Note that he was speaking over 20 years ago!) He expressed concern that people might maintain an eclectic stance to avoid the crisis of choosing among approaches that all claimed superiority, especially if no one could provide research findings that supported those claims. Liddle's solution to that crisis was to step back from the competing models to examine theory and the process of theorizing. He was especially critical of efforts to combine all theories into bigger and better models that include everything. He explained: "From this unfortunate view, the secret to a great recipe would consist of combining a large number of ingredients. As great chefs would tell us, however, the key lies not in the number but in the combination itself; and further, the process of integrating ingredients takes great skill and experience" (p. 245).

Liddle opposed such an inclusive goal, based on two arguments. The first argument focused on the clinician: "just as gourmet chefs could not, at the beginning phases of their careers, skillfully mix just the right amount of herbs and spices, the average clinician cannot be expected initially to perform at a similarly expert and sophisticated level." The second argument questioned the approaches themselves: . . . "even if we would assume that most cooks could, with work and proper training, become experts of international cuisine, the evolutionary level of the ingredients themselves (the techniques of the schools of therapy) must be brought into question" (p. 246).

Liddle's (1982) proposed solution was a periodic "epistemological declaration." This would be *our own idiosyncratic statement of what we know and how we know it, what and how we think, and what and how we make the clinical decisions we do"* (italics in the original). This checkup would focus on issues of definition, goals, therapist behavior, dysfunction/normative behavior, and evaluation. He concluded that ". . . effective communication with and between others regarding models of therapy can be maximized by first determining our own epistemological underpinnings (again, a process of listening to oneself)." Patterson (1997) called for the same kind of self-assessment, but in his formulation it was possible to apply different premises to different cases. The key was to first classify the overall approach that determined the goals for the case; once the goals were clear, decisions about ways of meeting those goals would be simplified.

Lebow (1997) focused less on the informal process of achieving a personal integration and more on the formal creation of integrative models. A long-time advocate of integration, he expressed delight in the amount and the quality of integrative work that has occurred. Furthermore, he noted, people have been combining approaches that had at one time or another been considered incompatible.

In this primer for the designer of integrative approaches, Lebow stressed the need for not only bringing together raw materials from different theoretical perspectives—theories, strategies, and interventions—but also creating some kind of theory that "transcends" their separate contributions. Differences could not be ignored, but instead would need to be addressed in discussions of how the ideas work with one another— an interaction he referred to as a dialectic between concepts. When the possible interactions were considered, it might be necessary to select some parts and exclude others that would

not have fit. He provided multiple examples of integrative efforts that had been field-tested and had proved effective with particular populations, concluding that no single model could address every problem and no set of decision rules would ever eliminate the need for clinical judgment in applications.

Transtheoretical Efforts. Barnhill (1979) created one of the first explicit transtheoretical integrations in family therapy. He expressed concern that the field wasn't clearly focused on goals in working with families, and proposed a multidimensional construct of "healthy family functioning" that included eight dimensions: Individuation, mutuality, flexibility, stability, clear perception, clear communication, clear role reciprocity, and clear generational boundaries. These dimensions functioned as a "family health cycle" and therefore each area of functioning was dependent on the other areas. Each of the prevailing approaches to family therapy addressed one or more of these dimensions, according to Barnhill (see Figure 3.1). Their primary difference was their emphasis, and nearly every approach would eventually lead to working on multiple dimensions. He was, of course, writing during the peak years of competition among models, so he was cautious in his suggestion that "family therapists should perhaps be trained in a variety of schools or styles of family therapy so that they can intervene at any point in the family health cycle" (p. 98). Unfortunately, Barnhill's contribution was largely overlooked for many years.

Sprenkle et al. (1999) reviewed relevant literature looking for common change processes that have been described as specifically operating in couple and family counseling. They found that Garfield's (1992) integrative categories of reattribution, reinforcement, desensitization, and information and skills training have all been documented in various models of family work. Reattribution appears to be a key ingredient, with many approaches focusing on the need to replace negative meanings with more optimistic and less blaming ways of understanding relationships. Reinforcement has special meaning in work with couples and families, as family counselors seem to

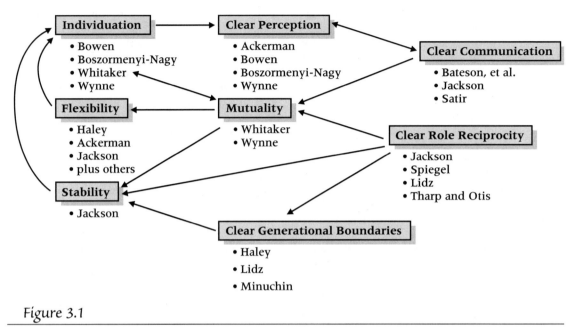

Figure 3.1

Barnhill's Integrative Map

Source: From "Healthy Family Systems," by L. R. Barnhill, 1979, *Family Coordinator, 28,* pp. 94–100. Reprinted with permission.

provide less reinforcement than individual counselors, but the counseling process directly affects the reinforcements that participants give each other. Desensitization, according to Sprenkle and his colleagues, has received little attention in couple and family counseling except for its specialized applications in sex therapy (see Chapter 4). Information and skills training is central to many approaches: The authors cited a classic study by Friedlander, Ellis, Raymond, Siegel, and Milford (1987) in which family therapy pioneers Minuchin and Whitaker were found to work primarily through information, interpretation, and guidance. Overall, Sprenkle and his colleagues concluded that the common pathways running through couple and family counseling are behavioral, cognitive, and emotional. They suggested that most approaches have tended to "gradually evolve in ways that emphasize the common path-

ways initially downplayed or neglected in their theoretical base" (p. 351).

In this book, I organize the theories and methods of the field according to my own transtheoretical scheme, a taxonomy of family therapy theories and methods. Like taxonomies in the biological sciences, this one is designed to impose an organizational structure on data that might otherwise be overwhelming to a new student. The examination of theoretical "family resemblances" is intended to clarify the essential assumptions underlying techniques—assumptions that are essential for maximum impact.

I propose that these assumptions, in the field of family counseling, fit into five themes or dimensions. The five dimensions—Behavior, Organization, Narrative, Emotion, and Spirituality or BONES—are labeled according to their most important central understandings of relationship

Table 3.1   **The BONES of the Family: Five Themes for Assessment and Intervention**

Couple and family relationships can be understood in multiple ways. This book presents the options as classified into five themes with many sub-themes. The following listing of sub-themes is a partial list, organized to illustrate the complexity of each theme.

Theme				
Behavior	**Organization**	**Narrative**	**Emotion**	**Spirituality**
Skills	Structure and function	Identity	Connection	Ethnosensitivity
External knowledge	Conflict	Externalizing	Internal experiencing	Beliefs/themes
Internal knowledge	Development	Complexity	Emotional expression	Instrumental practices
Cued responses	Intergenerational patterns	Dominant and alternative discourses	Empathy	Metaphysics
Contingent responding	Communication	Hypnosis	Emotion management	
Social learning	Systemic patterns			
	Evolution of systems			

processes, but the themes (Table 3.1) are theoretically derived and often overlap to some extent. Chapters 4 through 8 describe these dimensions in detail, offering research and theory summaries as well as descriptions of relevant methods. In Chapter 9, I illustrate the five themes in action.

Integrated Models. Nearly every model of psychotherapy and counseling involves some degree of theoretical integration. Pure theories are focused on description, whereas the models used by practitioners offer structures for decision making and action that typically include three pieces. A clinical theory explains how people are supposed to function effectively; how problems occur; and how to help other people make changes. Rather than being more integrative than their predecessors, contemporary authors may seem more integrative because they are more explicit in their borrowings and open about the ways in which their ideas intersect with others.

William Pinsof's (1995) work, presented in his book *Integrative Problem-Centered Therapy: A Synthesis of family, Individual, and Biological Therapies* is an example of such an integration. His decision model (Figure 3.2) assumes that the alliance with clients has been the first priority in establishing a counseling relationship. He then leads the practitioner through assessing a variety of possible influences on the development and maintenance of a problem cycle before designing and implementing a strategy for breaking the cycle. Outcomes are continually assessed, and cases are assigned to one of three statuses. The first concludes that the problem is resolved, and no further intervention is needed. The second concludes that a new strategy is needed—even though the strategy was properly implemented, it was inappropriate. The third concludes that the strategy was sound, but hasn't been implemented properly. Both the second and third options require returning to the assessment process so that the new or revised problem-solving process is

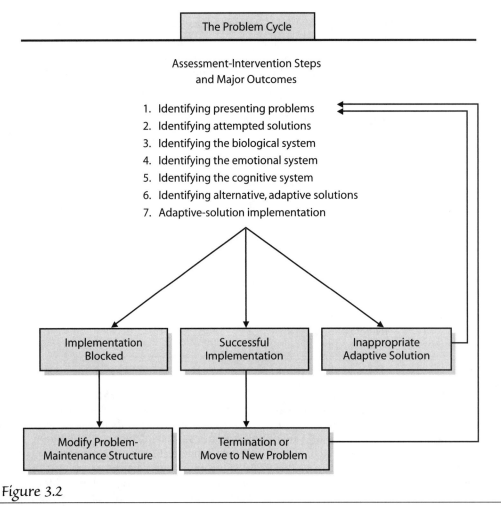

The Problem Cycle

Assessment-Intervention Steps
and Major Outcomes

1. Identifying presenting problems
2. Identifying attempted solutions
3. Identifying the biological system
4. Identifying the emotional system
5. Identifying the cognitive system
6. Identifying alternative, adaptive solutions
7. Adaptive-solution implementation

| Implementation Blocked | Successful Implementation | Inappropriate Adaptive Solution |

| Modify Problem-Maintenance Structure | Termination or Move to New Problem |

Figure 3.2

Pinsof Decision Model

Source: From *Integrative Problem-Centered Therapy: A Synthesis of Family, Individual, and Biological Therapies,* by
W. M. Pinsof, 1995, New York: Basic Books. Reprinted with permission.

appropriate for the individuals, their situation, and their specific relationship. Incorporated in this model are assumptions from many sources, and Pinsof's references allow the reader to locate those sources for further information.

As an integrative model for family work, the multisystemic therapy (MST) model is significant because of its extensive documentation and field testing with a variety of specific populations (Sheidow, Henggeler, & Schoenwald, 2003). Starting from a core set of systemic assumptions derived from GST and Urie Bronfenbrenner's ecosystemic model, MST describes ways in which different factors at various system levels are implicated in the development and maintenance of problems. The MST analytical process involves a recursive cycle of identifying misalignments, developing and testing hypotheses about needed changes, and assessing progress toward overarching goals. Within this planning and monitoring structure, clinicians are encouraged to develop specific interventions to meet defined problems.

Growth and Increasing Diversity

This chapter has surveyed a period in which the United States experienced dramatic social change and the new profession of family therapy struggled with questions of stability and change. Service delivery systems, theories, and client populations have evolved tremendously. The family professional now works with diverse families and helps those families to make sense of a changing world, and professionals have become sensitive to client issues once overlooked. Fortunately, the contemporary helper has access to high-quality research and a wide range of theories and techniques. Having skimmed some of the most influential theories and techniques in the first part of this book, we will now take a much more careful, thorough look at the knowledge and skill base available for family-level intervention.

Suggested Individual and Group Activities

Your understanding of concepts and issues presented in this chapter may be enhanced by the following activities:

- *Current events.* Search for current news stories on changing motherhood, fatherhood, and sexuality. Do the authors identify trends? Do their analyses attempt to shape the trends they are observing?
- *Historical informants.* Interview people who (1) began dating or (2) became new parents in three different periods such as 1950, 1970, and 1990. How did their experiences differ?
- *Textbook and journal analysis.* Find scholarly documents from the period 1980 to 1990 in different fields including the arts and the social sciences. What evidence do you find for a paradigm shift?

Suggested Readings

Capra, F. (1982). *The turning point: Science, society, and the rising culture.* New York: Bantam Books.

Hare-Mustin, R. T. (1994). Discourses in the mirrored room: A postmodern analysis of therapy. *Family Process, 33,* 19–35.

Kuhn, T. S. (1970). *The structure of scientific revolutions* (2nd ed.). Chicago: University of Chicago Press.

Family Therapy in Its Midlife: Five Themes

I suggested in the previous chapter that we are in a new developmental period of family counseling, no longer dominated by idealistic visionaries in conflict but instead open to contributions from a large pool of realistic, mastery-level practitioners in collaboration. The collaborative attitude, flexibility, openness to change, and desire for integration we now see in family counseling are characteristics associated with maturity.

In using the developmental metaphor of maturity, I am calling up an image of the mature practitioner, performer, or craftsperson—the person who is comfortable with the basics of his or her craft and who has the flexibility to mix traditional and new ideas in a constantly changing flow of expert work. In family counseling, this flexibility and competence are needed in contemporary practice because families who have come for help in recent years differ in many ways from those seen by family counselors of the past. Family therapy continues to need updated concepts and techniques.

Mastery-Level Performance and Integration

An expert practitioner integrates decision making and action into a seamless whole. Carl Whitaker (personal communication), in his later years, insisted that he worked without a theory. Harlene Anderson (1997) and Lynn Hoffman (2002) likewise have idealized the goal of acting and speaking without conscious deliberation. How is this achieved by an individual? Can a whole professional group act this way?

The secret of such expert performance lies in integration of action and decision. The beginner, whether in a craft such as weaving or a professional field such as law or family counseling, tends to see each action and decision separately. At a more advanced skill level, the weaver, the lawyer, or the family counselor organizes decisions into sequences and patterns that reduce anxiety and provide fairly consistent outcomes. At the expert level, a person implements but also alters these sequences and patterns without feeling a loss of direction.

If we apply this model to group functioning, we may see a similar developmental pattern. As a group of beginners, the field of family counseling was initially focused on each action and each decision as if they were separate: Should we see the parent(s) and the child together for the first session, or should we see a parent alone before bringing in the child? As it reached a more advanced level, the maturing field organized such decisions into sequences and patterns (e.g., Strategic Family Therapy or Structural Family Therapy) that minimized the need for making hundreds of small decisions. I contend that the field has now developed the ability to repeat those sequences and patterns but is also able, through integrative and metatheoretical efforts, to abandon rigid sequences and patterns without experiencing loss of direction.

If integration is the goal, how can we put together the variety of work that's been done over 50 years of innovation and refinement? I believe that a review of family counseling and family therapy literature shows consensus on five common themes that may be observed in successful family intervention; the next five chapters explore the field as viewed from these five perspectives. Rather than being mutually exclusive, these five general themes can be addressed in combination; in fact, they can be recognized in various configurations in many of the best-known approaches. The chapters in this section follow the mnemonic device B-O-N-E-S; I refer to this organizing system or *taxonomy* as "the bones of the family." Each chapter includes learning experiences for the reader to explore these themes in his or her relationship history and clinical experience.

Themes, Not Originators or Models

The material in the following chapters is organized differently from the preceding section,

which organized the history of family counseling according to author (the person who wrote about a unique way of addressing couple and family issues) or model/approach (a package of ideas and techniques).

In earlier chapters, I featured key authors as well as many of the most influential models or approaches from each historical period. That traditional presentation had advantages, in that there is a common language shared by family counselors and a key word such as "intergenerational" summarizes large amounts of information and speeds up communication. In the early days of family counseling this kind of shorthand worked well because a newcomer could quickly learn the small number of key authors and major approaches.

In the past 20 years, however, many authors have entered the field and the literature has become much more complex (May, 2003). The 17 major models of family therapy identified by the Association of Marital and Family Therapy Regulatory Boards, who administer the national MFT licensing examination, represent only a small percentage of the distinct approaches that are in current use. The rapid increase in information is one of the reasons I developed the BONES taxonomy.

But there is a more important reason for developing a taxonomy based on common themes. Many approaches in the literature are creative efforts that bring together existing ideas and techniques, combining them to utilize the unique sensitivities and knowledge areas of their creators. This is the contribution of an innovator such as Satir, Jacobson, de Shazer, or Johnson.[1] Following the lead of Liddle (1982), I compare this creativity in family counseling to what happens when a great chef prepares a dish that astounds and delights those who taste it. In most cases, the ingredients used in world-class restaurants are essentially the same as those used in neighborhood restaurants and school cafeterias, but they are handled and combined with great sensitivity and skill. When a chef shares a recipe it allows others to achieve approximately the same results.

---

[1] When I refer to an originator such as Susan Johnson, I understand that the work actually is the result of many collaborations and therefore incorporates *many* unique sensitivities and bodies of knowledge.

The problem with the recipes shared by Satir, Jacobson, deShazer, and Johnson is that the user may be confused about the ingredients, especially when terms such as *communication, behavior, solutions,* and *emotion* have so many meanings.

This widespread confusion has led me to develop a taxonomy that seeks to clearly differentiate among similar-sounding concepts and techniques. This system is used in the following chapters to examine the essential themes that keep appearing in different forms throughout the history of family counseling. In many cases, I may upset readers as I separate concepts and techniques that generally appear in combination or combine works that others have found incompatible. My revised presentations are intended to reduce the reader's confusion, however, by specifying similarities and differences whenever possible.

Theory and Research

Human beings are often described as *theorizing* about their experience. That is, they condense their shared experience into organized language patterns highlighting aspects that seem especially relevant (Kelly, 1963). People who spend their time together watching football games or growing roses are likely, over time, to find or develop theories that help them interpret and predict what happens on the football field or in their rose gardens.

This theoretical activity seems to be a uniquely human ability that allows us to manage complex experiences by simplifying them. After all, even one minute of raw, unprocessed reality has in it thousands of sensations, reflections, and actions. Any attempt to communicate an experience can't help but omit something, and good communicators focus on the parts that they consider most important. We've all known people whose stories were cluttered with distracting details: "Then I got dressed. I chose the shirt with the orange stitching and pearl snaps, I think I bought that one when I was in Houston, because I was worried about buttons if they had to bandage my hand." Simplicity is not a flaw in a theory—every good theory desig-

nates things you can afford to ignore. Behavioral theorists, for example, may have chosen to ignore narrative, emotion, and spirituality, while theorists examining spirituality may have chosen to ignore the interpersonal context.

Family counseling theories typically incorporate three interrelated sets of observations, which describe and explain (1) an optimally functioning relationship, (2) a relationship that is troubled in some way, and (3) processes that help people or relationships move from being troubled toward a state of optimal functioning.

Family scholars and counselors have created a rich history of different theories about relationships and human functioning, but the couple and family counseling literature does not seem to reflect this richness. A few rigorous clinical scholars have documented their theoretical roots (e.g., Minuchin, 1974; Schnarch, 1991), but many popular authors have held theory discussions to a minimum and moved directly to action. Jay Haley (1976) described this choice in his statement: "This book is designed for therapists and should not be misunderstood as an attempt to map how society and the human family are in actuality or how they should be if all were well. What is offered are simplistic formulations of social situations that can help a therapist recognize typical interchanges and determine what to do" (p. 7).

When a theory has been shared and repeated many times, we can assume it has meaning for some people. I take the position in the following chapters that the introductory family counseling student should be familiar with the mainstream theories of family counseling. I summarize what I see as the theoretical building blocks or ingredients that make up different approaches to family counseling, and I provide reading suggestions for the student who wants more theoretical depth.

Just as there is a rich literature of couple and family theory, there is also a wealth of couple and family research findings, which often serves to validate the theories in the field but sometimes leads theorists to reconsider their assumptions (e.g., Gottman, 1994). Here, too, I summarize some works that I consider helpful or challenging. However, these research findings provide subtle information that cannot be adequately compressed into a textbook such as this one and I strongly encourage the reader to read the key works identified in these chapters and to stay abreast of current research.

Interconnectedness in Relationship Processes

One of the reasons that family counselors have moved toward theoretical integration is that relationship processes are interconnected. Intervention in any part of a system seems to have impact on other parts, and therefore the following five chapters are of equal value: A family counselor can't choose incorrectly from among the five themes: Behavior, Organization, Narrative, Emotion, and Spirituality. Not only are they all valid and well tested over time, they are integrated in people's lives so that any theme, when used as a starting place, eventually brings about changes in the others.

Behavior: Learning, Habits, and Reinforcement

The problems presented by a couple or family are associated with learned behaviors and understandings.

Objectives

In this chapter, you learn to:

1. Identify behavioral aspects of relationship processes.
2. Differentiate among multiple traditions that describe behavior in relationships.
3. Use theory and research to distinguish between positive and problematic behavior patterns.
4. Describe and explain commonly accepted behavioral interventions.
5. Select, plan, and implement behavioral couple and family interventions appropriate to treatment goals.

4

Chapter

The first theme in the BONES taxonomy describes human behavior as environmentally determined and learned. This chapter views human relationships not only as environments that have shaped and maintained current behavior but also as powerful learning situations where people can change undesirable or unsuccessful aspects of their behavior.

This optimistic, pragmatic perspective is applied to a broad range of issues that clients bring into counseling: Learning principles can be used to explain nearly all behavior. Not only is this perspective broadly useful, it also has the advantage of being theoretically simple. Working from a behavioral perspective doesn't require a lifetime of study, and many of the core concepts can be taught to children. Gerald Patterson demonstrates how teachable this kind of material can be in *Families: Applications of Social Learning to Family Life* (G. Patterson, 1971). It is written in a simple

style, using a programmed instruction format, and each chapter ends with a review so that the reader learns key ideas such as change, learning, problem, reinforcement, and consistency. Patterson recommends that all members of a family read the book so that they better understand what they are trying to do together. He explains his goals in the introduction:

People can use the principles of social learning theory to cope with everyday problems of family behavior management. How do you teach an 18-month-old child to eat something besides dessert? How do you teach a 6-year-old child to go to bed when you ask him to? How do you teach a mother to stop nagging and scolding all the time? How do you train a father to come out from behind his newspaper? How do you negotiate with an adolescent about the use of the family car? How do you teach yourself and your spouse to stop fighting with each other? All of these problems require that we understand how to change the behavior of another person, and how to change our own behavior. (p. 2)

I once overheard a behavioral psychologist saying, after he sat through a family systems lecture, "I just don't see the need for all these other theories. It's all just reciprocal reinforcement." In a way, he was right. Family members do provide reinforcements to each other. You may find that once you start to see the world in terms of reinforcement and antecedent stimuli, the stimulus-response sequence seems to explain all human behavior. Learning theory, applied in a careful and sensitive manner, is an extremely versatile starting position for a family counselor. However, learning is only one lens for seeing phenomena: Chapters 5 through 8 offer alternative ways of describing relationship processes.

In presenting the Behavior theme in couple and family counseling, I try to give equal coverage to—and distinguish among—three closely linked phenomena:

1. *Learning theories* focusing on the acquisition and maintenance of behavior
2. Specific *behavioral/learning elements* that appear in a variety of approaches to couples and families, even when the authors do not identify them
3. Approaches to prevention and intervention that use the label "behavioral"

A Case Illustration: The Tommasini Family

The intake session of the Tommasini family was like many first sessions with families in which the identified patient is an adolescent. Dr. Rodriguez opened with a statement about seeing problems from a family perspective, about the special challenge of keeping family relationships together when young people are focused on leaving home, and about her goal of making sense of problems by hearing everyone's perspectives. The parents, however, had already decided what the problem was and they were there to describe it.

Angelo and Gina had assembled and organized evidence intended to prove, beyond a reasonable doubt, that their 16-year-old daughter Paulette was disturbed and it wasn't their fault. She was the third of three daughters, and both her sisters had done beautifully in school, relationships, and home life . . . it was clear that these people knew how to bring up perfect children. The oldest, Julia, was newly graduated from a nearby state university and was about to get married. The second daughter, Tina, was also away from home, going to a college out of state. And then there was Paulette. She was a junior at a suburban high school, the kind of school where 95% of the graduates were going to college, and she was getting Cs and Ds. Yes, she had a hard time with school, she had been diagnosed with a learning disability in elementary school, but they had enrolled her in tutoring and study classes, everything a good student would want. The fact that she was not keeping up with the rest of the students was proof of her willfulness and self-destructiveness. Worst of all, she said she didn't care; she didn't want to go to college anyway!

Gina, Angelo, and Paulette were the only ones in attendance at the first session. Angelo, who had set up the session, seemed to want to do all the talking. He had clearly given much thought to the problems they were having. He explained that Paulette seemed angry at her mother, she had probably been emotionally unstable since childhood, and she was doing this to ruin her mother's life. He further explained that Gina had never been a strong woman and this was destroying her. Paulette was jealous of her sisters—the two of them got along so well together and she'd always been the outcast—and since she couldn't compete she was doing the only thing she could do to get attention. Finally, he admitted thinking that maybe Paulette was really suicidal, and this behavior was a cry for help. It was the last idea that led Angelo to call

Dr. Rodriguez, because his other ideas had led to power struggles. Now, he was starting to think that Paulette was chronically depressed and needed medication. The psychiatrist couldn't see her for 6 weeks, though, and the school counselor had suggested family counseling.

At this point, Gina started talking, too. It wasn't easy for Dr. Rodriguez to get a simple, direct report about what was happening. When the parents weren't blaming Paulette, they were blaming each other: "He's too tied up in his job," "She's never liked Paulette as much as her other daughters," "If she weren't at work when Paulette comes home from school, then Paulette would do her homework when she's awake," and so on. They were several minutes into the session before Dr. Rodriguez was able to interrupt the story and ask for specifics about what they hoped to change in counseling. Specifically, over the next 10 minutes, she heard about the following behavioral problems with Paulette:

- She didn't stay on task when studying.
- She often didn't turn in homework when she had done it.
- She waited until the last minute to do assignments.
- She lied to her parents about having homework to do, and she lied about doing it.
- She expressed a negative attitude toward education.

Then Dr. Rodriguez went over the list to verify that she and the family were in agreement; these were some clearly identifiable problems that would allow her and the family to determine if there was progress or change. As Dr. Rodriguez asked the family members for their input, she was also able to conduct her own assessment regarding some relationship issues. It appeared to her, given the way that the parents had presented the situation, that the family was unrealistic in its expectations of high school students and did not seem very effective in solving problems. She still needed at least two additional sources of information to properly create a treatment contract with the family.

First, she needed to hear from Paulette, and, second, she needed to facilitate more interaction so she could observe how the family communication process functioned.

She invited Paulette to contribute, because her parents had done most of the talking, and prefaced that request with a reminder that she needed everyone's opinions. Like many adolescents who have been clearly labeled as the problem, Paulette seemed reluctant to say anything. Dr. Rodriguez went further, emphasizing the goal of having a good family and said that there must be some things Paulette would like to see changed. She said that Paulette's concerns would be judged by the same standard applied to the parents' goals: They would have to be things that could be described clearly so that the counselor and the family would know whether the behavior changed. Paulette was able to voice two complaints:

1. She wanted to stay out past her current curfew of 10 P.M. on weekends, 9 P.M. on school nights.
2. She wanted her parents to support her career goal of attending art school and becoming an artist.

Time was running out for the first session. Dr. Rodriguez could see that assessing family problem-solving skills was going to require more time. But she could get their impressions, so she addressed a question to the family in two parts: (1) Are all of these complaints new, or are they things that people have talked about before, and (2) if they have been talked about before, what has happened when you have tried to talk about them?

As the counselor expected, everyone agreed that the entire list of complaints from both sides had been aired many times and that whoever was complaining usually abandoned the process because of either "yelling" (on the parents' part) or "sulking" (on Paulette's part).

By the end of the first session, Dr. Rodriguez was able to propose an initial treatment contract:

1. The primary goal of treatment would be "increasing Paulette's success behaviors."[1] Dr. Rodriguez and the family would continue to explore what that success should look like and develop a list of specific expectations, but Paulette should expect that she would have to complete all homework, stay on good terms with her teachers, and, until such time as she proved it wasn't needed, her parents would provide help in meeting school requirements.

2. Related to the primary goal, Dr. Rodriguez would be looking for contextual factors that seemed to be part of the targeted behavior patterns. If she found anything that seemed to be closely connected to those patterned behaviors, it would be a likely candidate for change.

3. A third goal would be "a family life that makes everyone want to be there." The family would be asked to develop specific ideas as to what this meant. Everyone should expect that there would be negotiations on all the rules and expectations of family life.

Reassured that their primary concern was being taken seriously, the parents relaxed and agreed that some things might be negotiable. As often happens, Paulette agreed to work with this program because she heard the message that the agenda was not totally focused on pleasing her parents.

Over 6 months, the counseling process focused on many behavioral elements, including the following:

- *Improving basic communication skills:* Family members learned to verify that they were understanding each other and to modify their communication when they were experiencing misunderstanding.

- *Improving assertiveness skills:* Both Gina and Paulette became more effective in identifying and pursuing goals that they felt strongly about.

- *Improving problem solving and contracting skills.* The family learned a step-by-step process through which concerns were identified, options were considered, reciprocal changes were negotiated, and changes were implemented.

- *Improving skills of emotional expression:* Emotions in the Tommasino family had been either suppressed or else expressed in destructive ways. New skills enabled family members to safely express a wide range of feelings, and to provide Paulette with a rationale for family rules.

- *Improving parenting skills:* The parents learned to work together as a team, valuing their different styles rather than opposing each other.

- *Improving self-management skills:* Paulette learned new strategies for managing study tasks, and the family learned to provide a better study environment.

- *Adding to knowledge:* The parents increased their understandings of normal adolescent development, learning disabilities, and careers in the arts.

- *Breaking negative response cycles:* All family members, including the couple in their marital interactions, developed techniques for breaking their habits of treating each other badly.

- *Increasing positive family interactions:* Even though the larger family of Paulette's childhood had been held up as the perfect image of family fun, this new, smaller family group learned to enjoy their time together.

Varying the format with different family members for some sessions, Dr. Rodriguez provided training in relationship skills and coached participants to work toward getting positive responses from each other: First, inside the sessions, later with homework assignments. She was able

---

[1] Paulette's mood swings and self-destructive behavior pattern fit the criteria for a *DSM-IV* diagnosis of Adjustment Disorder with Mixed Disturbance of Emotions and Conduct, but Dr. Rodriguez preferred to work from a strength-based, nonpathologizing perspective. As I discuss in Chapter 9, in most cases at least one family member—the Identified Patient—is eligible for third party payment of counseling fees.

to arrange sessions with Paulette and each of her older sisters; from those sessions Paulette learned that life had not been so easy for her sisters during the times that had been portrayed so positively—one had struggled with alcoholism—and Paulette was able to develop a more adult relationship with each sister. With new problem solving and other communication skills, the family gradually renegotiated many of their expectations.

Within 6 months, Paulette's grades were Bs, which was good for a student with a learning disability and limited academic interest. She completed and turned in assignments, and her teachers had positive comments about her attitude. The family had explored art schools and had agreed to a summer internship at a craft center. Curfews were renegotiated as part of a total package of family expectations, and Paulette was given a pool of 30 "late minutes" each month, which could be saved up if they weren't used.

Finally, because Angelo and Gina were increasingly being left alone with each other and would soon be living as a childless couple, Dr. Rodriguez set up a few couple sessions and began helping them to renegotiate what they wanted from each other.

Theory and Research

At its core, the behavioral perspective is based on the assumption that it is possible to influence the contextual and learned components of human behavior. Parents exhibit such a belief when they talk about how they are attempting to instill values or get a child to stop biting fingernails. A woman exhibits such a belief when she expresses frustration that her male partner hasn't stopped leaving the toilet seat up. Her partner may exhibit an equally strong belief if he expresses a fear of becoming "a trained seal" if he is attentive and considerate. Schools, games, gang life, couple sexuality, and the flow of traffic on streets all operate on the assumption that people will learn and use new information and skills if they are properly taught.

Context

Behavior is contextual. This generalization is especially true when the idea of context is broadened to include unseen aspects of context such as family expectations, economic stresses, and marital conflict. To the extent that the family as a context for behavior is understood through *behavioral analysis* (Kanfer & Saslow, 1965), professionals can help a family to become a context in which the functioning of all family members is optimized (Falloon, 1991).

Katie, age 5, seemed to validate this theory from the moment she arrived in Marilyn Owens' office. Katie was suffering from ADHD, her mother said. She was driving her mother crazy with her out-of-control behavior and the small neighborhood preschool insisted that she get some kind of treatment or she would have to leave. But the child in the office did not display any disordered behavior! She walked into the room, immediately selected a set of multicolored blocks off the shelf, and spent the entire session creating a complex building (and she put the blocks away when she finished). In the intake session, a few details of Katie's daily life were shared. She was living with her divorced mother, who drove her to school in the morning. From school, she went to her grandmother's house, where she spent the afternoon and ate dinner. Mom arrived around 6:30, drove her home, and they spent the evening together. After discussing the basic idea of creating a calming, consistent environment for Katie, Marilyn asked to have Grandma present for the next session, so a more complete picture could be accomplished.

The grandmother's contribution to the behavioral analysis was dramatic. As the person who picked Katie up each day and received the teacher's reports on classroom behavior, she was extremely well informed on the problem history. She said, "If I had to live with her mother I'd be bouncing off the walls, too. The child gets up about 15 minutes before she has to leave for school, by the time they leave the apartment they're running late, Katie eats breakfast in the car, and I think she sometimes gets dropped off on the sidewalk instead of being walked into the school. If there's anybody in this family who has

ADHD it's my daughter!" Mom agreed that the picture was not inaccurate. She was chronically out of control and always late. Katie did, she admitted, arrive at school in a state of tension, sometimes with her shoes untied.

Marilyn saw the situation as ideal for simple changes. With her coaching, the mother-grandmother team worked together to analyze the situation and develop plans. Mom started setting her alarm an hour earlier, waking Katie earlier, laying out her own clothes and Katie's clothes the night before, the two of them started having breakfast at home before they drove to the school, and she walked Katie into the classroom early enough to briefly speak with the teacher.

As a result, the teacher no longer approached Grandma with a list of complaints each day, Grandma and Katie had wonderful afternoons and then went to the apartment to have dinner and wait for Mom. Six weeks after arriving in Marilyn's office, the family had its final session. With a changed context, Katie had left the chaotic behavior behind.

Teaching and Learning

Humans, with our highly developed neocortex, have a special ability to change the behavior typical of our species. We transmit from one generation to the next the lessons learned and new solutions developed. Maturana and Varela (1980, 1992) said that the ability to share learnings through language is a species-specific biological characteristic of humans. A human skill such as predicting the weather or turning plants into clothing is a biological parallel with the ability of an octopus to change its color to blend into its surroundings.

The emergence of these human teaching and learning abilities is shrouded in prehistory. In various places around the world written languages emerged at different times. Songs, rituals, and legends may have been shared widely among a society, while more closely guarded secrets would have been shared only among elite groups of magicians, priests, healers, or political leaders.[2]

---

[2] See Auel (1984) *The Clan of the Cave Bear* for an fictional portrayal of a prehistoric society in competition with its less-advanced neighbors.

Where religious or cultural teachings were recorded on paper, civilizations had an advantage over their neighbors whose traditions were oral—libraries could hold far more information than could be remembered by one individual or group of individuals. However, there was still a need for teachers, sages, oracles, and troubadours—not everyone had access to the books. Universities and then public schools made learning available to larger segments of humanity, and eventually electronic media allowed instantaneous access to information sources all over the world. Technology continues to modify the knowledge transmission process.

Philosophy and Methods of Education

This historical progression brings us into a recent period in which we have records of people's awareness of the teaching and learning process. Philosophers are especially concerned with the process of transmitting beliefs and understandings (poets may be equally concerned, but they do not discuss the process as openly). Plato, describing Socrates, demonstrated a powerful approach to education: Involve the learner as a seeker of answers. In the Socratic model of education, the student's goal was to impress the teacher. The teacher's praise and respect, rather than the learning itself, were the sources of motivation for the learner.

Jean-Jacques Rousseau is credited with leading a newer teacher/learner tradition, beginning in the 1750s in France. Rousseau rejected the hierarchical relationships that Socrates symbolized; in the new society that Rousseau imagined, all people were equal, and learning occurred through experience rather than through guidance from a teacher. This "discovery" approach to learning was updated in the twentieth century by John Dewey and Carl Rogers, among others, and its effects can be seen in contemporary higher education as well as in nursery schools. Clinical education—the combination of real challenges and guidance from instructors—has spread from medicine into business, engineering, and teaching. In this model of education, the learner is assumed to not only gain knowledge from the activity, but to also gain self-confidence from the achievement of learning. Motivation comes not from external reward but from internal satisfaction.

Another teaching revolution occurred through the discoveries of behavioral researchers, who questioned the efficiency of both Socratic teaching and discovery learning. The scientific study of teaching/learning processes was applied to specific learning tasks where efficiency and accuracy were especially important. This revolution has had impact on classroom practices at all levels of education.

Nonverbal Learning

Human learning works pretty much the same as learning in other species; this assumption has been widespread since Pavlov. Repetition seems to be a key element; salience, or importance of the information, seems to be another; and a guide or teacher is a third. On a recent excursion to Manhattan with my golden retriever, it only took two or three trips to the pet-friendly park, seven blocks from the hotel, for my dog to remember the way. She was motivated and she had a teacher. More complex learning incorporates multiple small learnings. Olympic-level performance on a skateboard involves knowing how to steer, jump, land, and handle irregular surfaces, but for a beginner staying upright is a challenge.

Skills of human relating—how to initiate an interaction, how to manage eye contact, how to pace and coordinate activities—are generally not taught in school or in other organized settings. Most people achieve this learning informally in play and shared living experiences, and the person who does not learn the basic skills of human interaction is frequently called names. But to some extent "geeks" or "nerds" are merely a result of the increasing isolation created by contemporary lifestyles and careers (Riesman, 1950/2001). Without much social experience (repetition), unclear about the value of the learning (motivation), and not having adult teachers who have the skills themselves, some children grow up with a limited ability to initiate and maintain relationships. Couple and family counselors sometimes teach

skills that clients could have learned in early childhood.

Relationship Knowledge

I am starting from the assumption that there is valuable knowledge that previous generations—and contemporary scholars—can contribute to people's ability to have successful and satisfying couple and family lives, and yet many people find themselves poorly prepared to function. Alice Rossi's classic sociological analysis, *Transition to Parenthood* (1968), pointed out that modern cultures provide very little preparation for becoming parents. Others have documented adolescents' limited interpersonal problem-solving skills (Selman & Demorest, 1984) and knowledge of sexuality (Gray, House, & Eicken, 1996). Many professionals believe that postmodern couples and family groups are becoming increasingly isolated and often miss information that would help them with their relationships.

At the same time that we acknowledge that some people lack information, we must also admit that information can have negative effects. For example, Freud—who worked in the context of systematic repression of sexuality and emotion in nineteenth century Vienna—taught that repression creates mental illness. This teaching became widely accepted, contributing to an opposite societal problem with unregulated pursuit of sensation. Similarly, many people have been taught that anger is a toxin that will destroy the body if it's not released through angry outbursts. This teaching, a distortion of beliefs that may have had some basis in clinical research, has contributed to a glorification of angry behavior. When experts presume to give people information, we should be careful about the information we provide.

Core Behavioral Principles

Until researchers demonstrated that human learning was predictable and responsive to careful intervention, discussions of learning were based on opinion and anecdote. A skilled orator, armed with appropriate quotations from Plato or Aristotle, was likely to be considered an expert on education.

Pavlov's dog experiments around the turn of the twentieth century, which showed that a carefully executed training process could produce a new response pattern, were planned as an exploration of digestive processes. But the research also demonstrated that animal behavior could be manipulated, and it was but a short jump from that discovery to the hypothesis that similar training procedures might work with people. It was nearly 50 years later, following years of dramatic research and theory-building by B. F. Skinner (1953) and others, before the scientific study of behavior began to be translated into counseling for individuals with emotional and behavioral problems (Plaud & Eifert, 1998). During the 1960s and 1970s applications of *behavior modification,* as the approach was known, became widespread in classrooms and clinics.

Behavioral perspectives were not widely applied with families until researchers began to study *social learning,* the process of people teaching and influencing each other (Bandura & Walters, 1963). Social learning theory postulates that people acquire both prosocial behaviors and problem behaviors through the processes of modeling and social reinforcement. Tests of the theory, both in the laboratory and in the clinic, have demonstrated that social influences are powerful and complex enough to cause simplistic behavior modification procedures to fail; careful analysis is required to identify the environmental influences that support a problem behavior. Research continues on behavioral aspects of couple and family processes, with increasing attention to emotional and cognitive elements of learning and behavior.

After a century of behavioral research, the helping professions can rely on several key principles that are essentially beyond dispute; they appear repeatedly in the applications we discuss next. The behaviorally oriented practitioner is trained to be an empiricist, driven not so much by theory as by the scientific method of hypothesizing, testing hypotheses, and refining the hypotheses based on "hard data." Therefore, effective and ethical practice requires that behavioral techniques are not delivered by rote, but instead are utilized in a careful program that continually assesses results and adapts as needed. Just as any other counseling approach, behavioral practice

functions best when delivered within a positive helping relationship.

Acquiring or Strengthening Behavior

Behaviorists prefer to focus on desired behavior rather than on problem behaviors. The following concepts describe the process of promoting appropriate, satisfying behaviors and replacing problem behaviors with prosocial behaviors (Azrin, Naster, & Jones, 1973; G. R. Patterson, 1975; Robin & Foster, 1989; Webster-Stratton & Herbert, 1994).

A *baseline* is a quantitative assessment of a target behavior before starting a program intended to alter behavior. Baselines are generally expressed in terms of a *rate,* the frequency of the behavior in a given time period.

A *stimulus* is an environmental situation or event that precedes or coexists with a behavior. Random, low-intensity stimuli are less likely to create learning than stimuli that are repeated or very intense.

A *response* is a unit of behavior. Every behavior is a response to stimuli, even if the stimuli are not identified.

An *antecedent stimulus,* often referred to as a *cue,* is one that occurs before the response. The kind of learning studied by Pavlov, known as classical conditioning, occurs when an antecedent stimulus and a response become associated through repetition. This conditioning is most often an accidental occurrence; the sound of a person's voice is followed by pleasant experiences, and after a while a conditioned response of a positive mood change begins to occur based on voice alone (this is a behavioral explanation of "falling in love").

A *reinforcer,* often referred to as a *contingency,* is a stimulus that occurs following the behavior. *Positive reinforcement* (sometimes referred to as reward) is the basic tool of social learning: People tend to repeat experiences that are clearly and consistently associated with something pleasant (a positive reinforcer). Reinforcement is dependent on many factors, but frequency and consistency seem to be essential. Most children and adults are reinforced positively by attention and praise.

Negative reinforcement is an alternative way to increase or *strengthen* a behavior. A negative reinforcer is a consistent negative stimulus (such as whining or disruptive behavior) that is stopped when the desired behavior is performed (children condition parents, too!). This process may appear similar to punishment, but the two ideas are based on different assumptions and have different outcomes.

Differential attention refers to the idea that any special attention may reinforce a problem behavior. Criticism, complaints, and insults may be intended as negative reinforcers, but for some people negative attention is better than no attention. Therefore, it is generally better to focus on increasing positive behaviors and ignore negative behaviors.

Shaping refers to gradual learning of complex behavior sequences. Such learning may require a long practicing period before desired behaviors are good enough to match expectations. In the shaping process, the complex learning is supported by reinforcing *successive approximations* of the desired outcome. A child's making of her bed would be taught by praising any effort at the beginning, gradually praising only her best efforts until standards were met.

Observational learning occurs when behavior is seen as connected with higher status or rewards that are received by others. Many relationship behaviors are learned this way, observing adult family members during childhood. Status differences in those years make adult behavior especially influential. Observational learning during adulthood is more likely to focus on peer and media influences (e.g., men in all-male job settings often learn to address wives and children in abusive and insulting ways).

Response chains are behavioral sequences in which one behavior becomes a cue for another behavior. Smoking, for example, can be associated through repetition with eating.

Cognitive mediation is a behavioral principle that was discovered when behavioral research was extended to humans. For humans, thought is not only a behavior but also a stimulus and becomes part of the environment for other behaviors.

Response generalization. Conditioning is not always a precise process, and therefore responses often appear in reaction to something similar to the conditioned stimulus.

Reducing or Eliminating Behavior

Along with the process of strengthening desired behaviors, a reciprocal process can reduce or eliminate undesired behaviors. This process has been studied extensively.

Extinction is the weakening and eventual disappearance of a conditioned response. When the conditions—cues or consequences—associated with a behavior are no longer present, it becomes extinct more or less rapidly (Skinner, 1953). In practice, it may be difficult to weaken a response because behaviors are often cued and reinforced in multiple ways. The removal of one reinforcement (Mom's attention) still leaves other reinforcements (watching my brother cry) in place.

Reciprocal inhibition is the reduction of one behavior by conditioning a new behavior that conflicts. An older sibling who is taught to hold and comfort a baby, for example, may stop teasing and provoking the baby. Some counselors (e.g., Gladding & Henderson, 2000) may rely on this same process when they encourage humor as a substitute for anger; it is difficult to maintain rage while smiling.

Time out, explains Gerald Patterson (1975), is time out *from reinforcements* (whatever those reinforcements are), and it is used most effectively with very young children because they have few ways of finding alternative reinforcements. Time out is a mild intervention, one that works only gradually and requires consistency, but it is much less destructive than hitting and yelling.

Limit-setting is a rather vague term that may describe many things. In the present discussion, I am referring to actually preventing or blocking a behavior (and any reinforcement that comes from the behavior). This is not punishment that follows the behavior, it is gentle intervention designed to ensure that the behavior doesn't occur. Over time, conditioned response patterns can then disappear, replaced by positive ones.

Natural consequences are the opposite of limit-setting. When a behavior will, without any intervention, lead to a negative outcome, then allowing that outcome to occur helps to weaken the behavior. Many people are confused about this principle. If the consequence is perceived as manipulation, it may contribute to a coercive cycle (see later). Canceling a family trip to the zoo because Samuel didn't get out of bed in time might be a natural consequence; canceling the trip because Samuel didn't eat all his breakfast seems to be manipulation. Telling a child "this was the natural consequence of your action" is neither necessary nor convincing, especially if the consequence was actually created for the purpose of punishing the child.

Reciprocity

Azrin et al. (1973) were among the first to point out that couple and family relationships consist of mutual, reciprocal reinforcement. They suggested that marital partners should use the "reinforce the reinforcer" strategy for improving their relationships, diagramming it as shown in Figure 4.1.

Marital discord, according to Azrin et al. (1973), may result from imbalance or inadequacy in either the delivery or the recognition of reinforcers.

A key feature of the Azrin approach was *contracting*. Azrin and colleagues promoted relationship contracts with clear expectations for desired behaviors and clear consequences when the expectations were or were not met. Relationships could be changed by *negotiating* new contracts that promoted desired behaviors and discouraged problem behaviors.

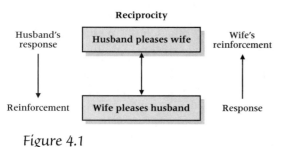

Figure 4.1

Azrin Figure

Source: From "Reciprocity Counseling: A Rapid Learning-Based Procedure for Marital Counseling," by N. H. Azrin, B. J. Naster, & R. Jones, 1973, *Behavioral Research and Therapy, 11*, pp. 365–382. Reprinted with permission.

Negativity

Gerald Patterson (1982) described a frequently observed *coercive family process* in which family members attempt to control each other's behavior with punishment. In this pattern, A punishes B for the behavior that B is using to punish A. This process tends to escalate over time, as neither A nor B will be successful and each will feel that more severe punishment is necessary. The pattern is often heard in the presenting stories told by couples and families in counseling.

Patterson's concern with punishment fits into a long-standing concern among behaviorists. Skinner (1953) was evangelical about his view that punishment is a negative influence in social groups. He argued that just as positive behavior could be learned, negative behavior could also be learned. His research demonstrated, he said, that positive reinforcement—properly administered—was sufficient to keep people behaving in ways that served the group. *Walden Two* (Skinner, 1976), his futuristic novel, described a society where all social needs were met through a social contract that required all community members to share in the burdens as well as the benefits of their life together. Garbage collection and earning money for community needs were equally necessary and individuals willingly contributed their time in all the ways necessary to make the community a success.

In a similar way, according to Patterson, the coercive cycle can be broken by increasing the positive reward value of a relationship, focusing on getting more of what people want instead of stopping the things they don't want.

Self-Management

One of the best-kept secrets of behavioral theory is the idea that individuals can influence their own behavior using behavioral principles. Skinner demonstrated this principle in his own life (Bjork, 1993), arranging reinforcements in such a way that the desired behaviors were strengthened and undesired behaviors were extinguished. Cognitive self-management is another option. This approach depends on cue control, on the individual's ability to insert a new thought into an otherwise predictable sequence. Anger can be reduced by choosing to think in ways that don't fit an angry response.

The Process of Counseling with Couples and Families

In each of the five chapters in this section, we follow a similar outline as we talk about intervention. First, I describe and explain the unique process of counseling from the perspective of the chapter. The presentation is more or less chronological, starting with early contacts with clients and progressing toward a point when intervention may be considered complete. After presenting the options, I briefly summarize the strengths and concerns that might lead a professional to either choose or avoid the approach.

Engaging: Becoming Empiricists Together

Many behaviorally oriented professionals prefer to have clients complete questionnaires before the first session. This is consistent with the value placed on assessing clients' perceptions of their relationships and the behavioral principle of establishing baselines before intervening. An inappropriate case can then be addressed in a different way or referred to someone who works differently.

The professional wants to ensure that the whole counseling experience sends a message of simple, straightforward scientific objectivity. Most behavioral family counselors prefer to see everyone together at the beginning of the process so that interactions can be observed. Introductions, questioning style, and even seating arrangements emphasize the priority of achieving and maintaining an objective stance. It may be helpful to explain this objectivity because it can be somewhat impersonal and may seem uncaring. So the first few words spoken in the opening session orient the clients: Here's who I am, here's how I work, here's what I will expect from each of you. When younger children are involved, the counselor may want to take extra time to give older family members a chance to "translate" the orientation.

Couple or family members are invited to be co-investigators in a project that will:

- Gather information from multiple sources, reducing subjectivity.
- Identify presenting problems in behaviorally specific terms.
- Identify desired outcomes in behaviorally specific terms.
- Select behaviors for intervention and prioritize them.
- Establish baseline rates for the target behaviors.
- Intervene to increase desired behaviors and reduce problem behaviors.
- Monitor change and alter interventions as needed.
- Continuously review goals and recognize achievements.
- "Graduate" clients when they seem to maintain changes.[3]

Presented in this way, the process offers reassurance to each participant that he or she will be heard, the process will continue until changes are accomplished, and goals and methods will be discussed in a straightforward, open, direct manner. When relationships have been confusing and emotionally draining, such a presentation can have a calming effect.

Strengthening Positive Expectations

In the opening example of this chapter, Angelo was an observant and optimistic client; he knew what irritated him, and he was convinced that he could get it stopped. However, many times a couple or family counselor is confronted with a situation like this one:

SHARON: *Well, I don't really see that there's anything he could do that would make me feel that old feeling again. It's just lost. We don't have a marriage*

---

[3] The maintenance of behavior change has been a problem with some kinds of behavioral intervention.

any more, we are just roommates, and I'm tired of living that way.

COUNSELOR: *Bernie, can you help out here? Can you remember specific complaints that Sharon's made, maybe ones she can't remember? It would be a big help if someone could find an identifiable problem.*

BERNIE: *You know, she's always mad about something, I stopped paying attention a long time ago. I don't have a problem. I think it's the way a marriage is supposed to be, she has her life and I have mine. But specific complaints? She gives me dirty looks sometimes, like when she picks up empty cans from the coffee table, I think that's the biggest one—she doesn't think I'm neat enough, and I don't think anybody could please her.*

SHARON: *It's not even just the filth and the chaos—dirty underwear on the floor, ashes in the sink—he never pays attention to me, we don't like any of the same things, he doesn't respect my opinions, sex when we had it last was like I wasn't there, I think he was fantasizing about someone else. I want out.*

COUNSELOR: *Okay, I asked for specifics and you came up with some. It sounds like you're in a phase now, though, when you really don't think you can expect any change and you'd rather end the relationship than continue to be frustrated.*

Both partners' negative expectations and apparent lack of motivation are serious barriers to the kind of active involvement that would produce change. It is at times like this that behavioral counselors draw upon the traditions of their field and intervene so that people are less focused on the negative aspects of the relationship and more closely in touch with their positive history together. The intervention goes like this:

COUNSELOR: *Bernie and Sharon, it sounds like things have gotten pretty tense and frustrating. But I assume that when you first got together it was different, or you probably wouldn't have had anything to do with each other. How was it you first met?*

SHARON: *He was my older brother's best friend in high school. I couldn't stand him at the time, but then both of them went away to college and I didn't see him for a couple of years, and when I ran into him at the mall I couldn't believe it! He was really good*

looking and he was so nice, not like the boys I had been dating, he knew how to talk to girls . . .

This is often the way the story changes. The counselor can see postures change, smiles emerge, and bodies turn toward one another as the couple return to the "good old days." They remember times when they were positively reinforcing each other and they couldn't get enough of each other's company. Because this line of questioning is so helpful in creating a *positive set,* an attitude of positive expectations, it is recommended as an early part of the couple interview (Jacobson & Margolin, 1979). The positive set can be further increased between sessions by using an intervention such as "surprise your partner," a variation on Stuart's *caring days* intervention (see Box 4.1).

Assessing System Characteristics, Strengths, and Needs

Behaviorally oriented counselors have many of the same assessment concerns as any other family counselor. They need to know, in essence, what brought people into their office and what will constitute a successful outcome for counseling. One of the things an assessment process can do is to help clients sort out their own confusions about these two questions. Some issues may, in effect, be red herrings that serve to distract from other issues that might be more productive; thus, choice and sequencing of treatment focus may be critical. Behavioral couple and family interventions generally start by assessing the state of the relationship. For example, Stuart (1980) explained that sexual complaints and relationship complaints seemed to overlap, but he believed that it was not wise to focus directly on sexual issues until the counselor had verified that the couple had effective communication and a working alliance.

Observational Assessment

Every couple and family counselor conducts some kind of assessment, whether it is formal or informal. This process assessment begins with the first contact in which the counselor notes who initi-

BOX 4.1

Surprise Your Partner

Behavioral therapists in the 1970s generally worked from a core belief that positive reinforcement increases the likelihood that a behavior will be repeated. This belief, applied to intimate relationships, led to a hypothesis that *mutual positive reinforcement* by partners would be likely to result in escalating levels of good feelings and generosity on both sides. Each person would feel reinforced for being nice and would, as a result, be even nicer. Therapeutic strategies based on this belief proved extremely effective, particularly with couples that seemed to lack hope.

Positive reinforcement is defined by the recipient, not by the giver, and therefore Azrin (e.g., Azrin et al., 1973) and others developed techniques for helping partners learn more about each others' preferences so that they could provide meaningful reinforcements. Stuart (1980) added the idea of concentrating positive behaviors into *caring days*—one or the other partner would focus extra energy on pleasing actions. An effective version of this strategy adds the element of surprise. The directive given to the couple is:

> During the next week, I would like each of you to pick a day when you will make special efforts

to make the other one feel loved and appreciated by doing things the other will like. But you must keep this plan a secret, and even on the day you've picked you should not announce what is happening but wait for your partner to notice. Next week, when we meet again, I'll ask about these experiences to see how successful you were in giving each other the experience of special attention.

Several options are possible. In the ideal case, both perform well as givers of special attention and both are aware of the gestures that were directed toward them. In many cases, however, one or both return to say, "I don't think she remembered—I didn't notice anything," or "I could see him trying, but everything he did was wrong. I hate roses, and he bought me a dozen of them." In such cases, the assignment has succeeded in producing change. It has helped the partners learn how to give in meaningful ways—and to notice each other's efforts. With repetition, the assignment leads to greater success and increasing relational satisfaction.

---

ated the contact, how the request was defined, and how much urgency was communicated. In a telephone call, and even more clearly in the office, the counselor learns through the clients' responses to questions: Do they seem willing to let the counselor take charge and define the process? Do they stay on task? Do they work together?

A behavioral approach values objectivity. To add rigor to the process assessment, the professional may structure the observations and pay attention to such questions as:

- Do there seem to be gaps in information?
- Does communication seem to be ineffective?

- Are there problem behavior sequences that might be altered?
- Are there unintended reinforcements for problem behaviors?

This kind of informal assessment may meet a counselor's needs for treatment planning and discharge planning, but many times a more detailed, standardized process is useful and the counselor may want to have observational data structured and quantified (Bagarozzi, 1996; Webster-Stratton & Herbert, 1994). Several authors have created checklists or observational rating scales that assist in organizing this observational assessment,

BOX 4.2

Measuring Personal Space

Crane and Griffin (1983), noting that many couples seemed to suffer from differences in preferred physical distance, created a simple, easily implemented assessment procedure. Partners are asked to stand and approach each other in the center of the room until they feel that they have reached a comfortable distance. In the typical case, one partner continues to approach after the other has started to back away—showing that

their "settings" are different. A simple tape measure is used to measure the near and far distances at which the two feel uncomfortable and seek to make adjustments.

The procedure is effective at focusing participants' attention on this common interpersonal pattern, and discussion of the pursuer-distancer roles seen in this exercise often leads to discussing parallels in other interactions.

and the most effective tools not only provide data but train the observer to become better at discriminating phenomena. A simple example of this kind is Crane and Griffin's (1983) use of personal space as an indicator of marital quality (see Box 4.2). In its pure form, this technique structures an assessment process and provides quantitative data that can be charted from intake through the end of the counseling process. Even when used informally, assessment of personal space improves sensitivity to client behavior and makes the counselor more capable of using postural information in assessing every clinical encounter.

Self-Report Instruments

The pioneers of behavioral couple and family counseling brought with them a tradition of written records, including daily counts or measurements, as an essential part of any rigorous, self-correcting program of change. This assessment tradition, so different from the conversation-based assessment methods used by other family counselors, provided the pioneers in behavioral counseling with comfortable and effective tools that seemed to help couples and families to be more specific in their complaints, their expectations, and their recognition of change.

The value of specificity was recently challenged by Jacobson and Christensen (1996), however, and the informed counselor will want to understand

both its strengths and its potential risks. To summarize the Jacobson and Christensen position, couples and families trained to be more specific in their complaints and their expectations may become less willing to compromise and accept something less preferred. The fact that checklists and other questionnaires provide structure for intervention should not be sufficient reason for their use. Like any other professional decision, the decision to formally collect client self-report data is complex.

Over the past 30 years, counselors and researcher have created a variety of instruments with different purposes. The best of them are easy to administer, provide a wealth of information for planning and monitoring the process of counseling, and generate positive comments from clients who enjoy the focused time they spend filling out the scales (see Table 4.1 for a partial list). From rather simple scales that emphasized classifying and counting behaviors, behavioral family counselors have extended the paper-and-pencil method to a wide range of self-report instruments that explore clients' definitions of their issues. Measures of peoples' perceptions, operating within the theoretically and technically integrative cognitive-behavioral tradition, risk introducing greater subjectivity but seem to be worth the risk because they provide a condensed version of the relationship history including a clinically rich mixture of culture and

Table 4.1   **Behavioral Assessments**

Webster-Stratton and Herbert (1994) list the following instruments used in their parenting program:

Type of Instrument	Name of Instrument	Description
Parent rating	Child Behavior Checklist	Assesses 20 social competence items and 118 behavioral problems.
Parent rating	Eyberg Child Behavior Inventory	Assesses total number of problem behaviors and their intensity.
Teacher rating	Behar Preschool Questionnaire	Yields Total Behavior Problem Scale and three subcale scores.
Teacher rating	Teacher Report form of the Child Behavior Checklist	Provides a different list of items observable in a school setting.
Teacher rating	Teacher Rating Scale of the Perceived Social Competence Scale for Young Children	Assesses teacher perceptions of four domains of social competence.
Teacher rating	Teacher Child Adaptive Behavior Inventory	Assesses four domains of problem-related behavior and coping.
Teacher rating	Teacher Assessment of Social Behavior	Rates four behavioral dimensions.
Child self-rating	Perceived Competence Scale for Young Children	Pictorial scale, yields scores on General Competence and Social Acceptance.
Child performance task	Child Social Problem-Solving Test-Revised	Asks child to describe what a character in a story might do, then classifies the solutions.
Child performance task	Child's Attributions	Asks child to provide explanations of a story character's behavior.
Child self-rating	Loneliness and Social Dissatisfaction Questionnaire	Children rate themselves on 26 items, producing a single loneliness score.
Mother observation	Parent Daily Report	Monitors 19 negative and 19 prosocial behaviors every 24 hours.
Mother interview	Mother Daily Discipline Interview	Gathers details of each day's problems and how parent handled them.
Video observation of parent-child interaction	Dyadic Parent-Child Interactive Coding System	Coders rate a daily 30-minute videotape on 29 behavior categories.
Video observation of peer interaction	Peer Problem-Solving-Interaction Communication-Affect Rating-Engagement Coding System	Coders rate a 15-minute play episode on 40 behavioral categories.
Mother and father self-report	Marital Adjustment Test	Rates relationship quality/satisfaction.

(continued)

Table 4.1   *(Continued)*

Type of Instrument	Name of Instrument	Description
Mother and father self-report	Beck Depression Inventory	Measures severity of depression and specific symptoms.
Mother and father self-report	Brief Anger-Aggression Questionnaire	Assesses level of anger.
Mother and father self-report	Family APGAR	Assesses family members' satisfaction with 5 components of family functioning.
Mother and father self-report	Family Crisis-Oriented Personal Scales	Measures family problem-solving attitudes and behaviors
Video observation of parent interaction	Problem-Solving-Interaction Communication-Affect Rating-Engagement Coding System	Coders rate a 15-minute discussion for positive and negative communication characteristics
Mother and father self-report	Life Experience Survey	Assesses positive and negative life experiences over the past year.
Mother and father self-report	Parenting Stress Index	Assesses stress in 7 dimensions of the parent-child relationship.

expectations, communication errors, attributions, and other relationship elements.

Self-Observation

Webster-Stratton and Herbert (1994), working with families of conduct-disordered children, note that "A particular difficulty for therapy arises when parents are unable or reluctant to see any connection between their own actions and those of their child or between their own personality and that of their child" (p. 98). They use what they refer to as *connecting questions* to facilitate parents' reflection on these possibilities. A few of the questions they list are:

- *Do you see anything of yourself (your partner) in your child (his behavior/attitudes/personality)?*
- *Do you remember being anything like your child at his or her age (in behavior/attitudes/personality)?*
- *In what ways do you believe that your influence has made its mark on your child (positive influences' negative influences)? (p. 98)*

Collaborative Learning

Skills and knowledge are often viewed as totally separate. One learns *about* conflict as a process in family life (knowledge), and one learns *how to manage* conflict (skills). The distinction can be useful as a way of highlighting the options a family counselor may exercise; for example, assigning readings (knowledge), organizing couple groups (knowledge and skills), giving homework exercises (skills), or asking for in-office enactments (skills). The distinction is somewhat artificial, of course, as skill is required to find out about a partner's feelings, memories, and intentions.

Relationship success in families and couples requires *collaborative* learning. As people become more involved in each other's lives, they are continually learning how to be more successful in the process of learning with each other, about each other, and about themselves from each other. Some of the family topics that challenge mutual understanding include:

Careers.   The work people do has varying impact on their lives. For some people, a job is merely a place they spend 8 hours each day and they keep that part of life in a separate compartment emotionally and behaviorally from their relationships. But other people's work life intrudes into personal life: Managers, machine operators, police officers, tax preparers, waiters, and retail clerks can all find themselves in complex emotional interactions that leave them tense and distracted when they come home. These careers also impose schedules on family life as April 15 approaches or the plant adds an afternoon shift. When family life and career come into conflict, it is hard to make changes in either place. A police family may demand a move from patrol to desk duty, and the officer may agree that the move is necessary, but the move may take several years to accomplish. In an ideal world, career choices are made with informed consent from everyone (including children) impacted by the choices—and a family counselor can be helpful.

Sexual Responses and Preferences. Discomfort with talking about sex seems to be widespread among both clients and helpers. When I first began counseling couples, I used to ask, "Are there any sexual concerns that I should be aware of?" Few of my clients reported sexual problems; but that finding did not match what I was reading about population norms. I eventually realized that my tentative questioning style fit too well with the clients' own discomfort, and I began to structure my assessment differently. At first, I tried a problem-solving approach; if people could say what they wanted from each other, I could help them negotiate for what they wanted. This might be similar to asking, "Do you like your eggs fried or scrambled?" but instead it would be, "Do you prefer to be on top or on the bottom?" I found that people didn't exactly have answers to these questions. I concluded that sexuality is not only a matter of choice, it is a complex interaction that incorporates feelings, identities, and contexts (Blume, 1998, 2002). When I could help couples overcome their reluctance to discuss sex, they found that the conversation was reinforcing—it created a new sense of intimacy while it facilitated positive and lasting changes in their sexual interactions.

Recreation. Committed relationships frequently put personal preferences in opposition; an out-door person and a movie buff may frustrate each other, and a runner and a swimmer may feel put upon if they are asked to join in each other's activities. The solution for a couple does not have to be one of sharing all activities, despite popular relationship advice. Cuber and Haroff's (1965) classic study of marriages suggests that people can be happy with many shared activities or they can be happy with quite separate lives, but they must work out plans that fit their preferences.

Family Planning. Of all the issues that seem to be ignored in early relationship conversations, one of the most important has to do with plans for parenthood or nonparenthood. The nonparenthood option, being viewed somewhat negatively in the majority culture, is an especially difficult position to discuss. Conversations about fertility may be even more challenging, and many couples find that their options are limited when they decide they want a child. Counselors can be especially helpful in facilitating such a conversation.

Mood Management. Not everyone is going to live like the Brady Bunch, smiling all the time and always upbeat. Moods are part of life, and relationships seem to work more smoothly when people can work through their expectations and their abilities to meet those expectations. A partner who wants to be ignored when she is tense and anxious about an upcoming exam, for example, may not have communicated that desire and may instead receive solicitous attention. In counseling sessions together, the mismatch can be identified and resolved.

Interpersonal Distance. People may also have different preferences for closeness. When differences exist, relationships seem to benefit from direct and clear communication about the times when they need time alone or need more physical or emotional support. Preferences of this kind are often unspoken and may actually lie outside the partner's awareness. In conversation, it is likely that they will not be brought up. Questionnaires can be very helpful in organizing the process of examining one's preferences and making requests.

EXAMPLE: If you want your partner to "work late" *much less,* then you would circle *–3.* If you want your partner to "be more affectionate: *more,* then you would circle *+2.* If "be more affectionate" is a major item in your relationship, you would put an *X* in the last column.

I want my partner to:	–3 Much Less	–2 Less	–1 Somewhat Less	0 No Change Wanted	+1 Somewhat More	+2 More	+3 Much More	Major Item
. . . Work late.	[–3]	–2	–1	0	+1	+2	+3	
. . . Be more affectionate.	–3	–2	–1	0	+1	[+2]	+3	X

Figure 4.2

Sample Question from ACQ

Source: From "Comprehensive Areas of Change Questionnaire" (p. 122), by D. E. Mead and G. M. Vatcher, in *Handbook of Family Measurement Techniques,* volume 3, B. F. Perlmutter, J. Touliatos, and G. W. Holden (Eds.), 2001, Thousand Oaks, CA: Sage. Reprinted with permission.

The Areas of Change Questionnaire (Mead & Vatcher, 2001) exemplifies the behavioral value for accurately describing behavior and the belief that intervention should be guided by establishing baseline problem levels and then measuring ongoing change. Figure 4.2 shows a sample item. It provides a behavioral description and scores the behavior as something the respondent wants more of, wants less of, or accepts at its current level. Once the instrument is scored, couple partners' profiles can be compared to help a couple in setting goals and priorities.

Intervening: External Knowledge

The assessment process often leads to the conclusion that a couple's or family's relationship problems result from a lack of information; some people have been cut off from wisdom and experience they should have gained from their elders and others have found their sources inadequate to their needs. Parents of a hearing-impaired toddler, for example, or a couple considering adoption may find their experience to be unique among their family and friends. Clear, authoritative information, delivered by a professional rather than by a friend or family member who might be biased, is frequently all that is needed for people to manage new situations.

Some get such information from reading; we might say that librarians and the authors of mar-riage manuals and parenting books were doing couple and family counseling long before the American Association of Marriage Counselors formed in 1942. With television and now the World Wide Web, information has become available to many people who do not have access to a comprehensive library. At the same time, these popular information sources may not really be authoritative, and professionals should be prepared to help people locate and choose appropriate sources of needed information.

Reading, on the web or in print, does not meet everyone's information needs, however. Materials may be at too advanced a reading level, or vision problems and learning disabilities may prevent people from using print sources. Reading is also a solitary learning process; different readers may learn radically different lessons from the same text, so there is often a need for teaching. People get valuable relationship information from pediatricians, OB-GYN specialists, urologists, and other medical personnel in addition to counselors. They learn about children and parenting from teachers, about their aging relatives from nursing home staff and home caregivers, and about death from clergy and funeral directors. Religious settings, community centers, schools, and clinics provide people with choices for relationship-oriented classes. Referring clients to an appropriate professional or to a community course is often the most responsible way to handle information needs.

Relationship Knowledge

Over the past 50 years, scholars have developed a rich body of research concerning effective relationships and how they are formed and maintained (e.g., Stahmann & Heibert's, 1997 *Premarital and Remarital Counseling: A Professional's Handbook*). Multicouple or multifamily group sessions are often a useful way to help couples and families learn about commonly experienced issues. For example, early relationship needs for boundary formation have been documented and have been explained in easily understood theories. In my counseling of new couples, I find that normalizing this challenge helps them to discuss their loyalty conflicts as friends and family members compete for attention. For the counselor who wants current scholarship related to relationships, a variety of professional organizations and journals exist.

Couples have been shown to benefit greatly from relationship classes (Halford & Moore, 2002). In some classes, couples are essentially given a full curriculum in couple and family counseling and taught to anticipate the normal challenges in the course of a couple relationship. Other classes feature a core theory that is expected to reduce problems and increase relationship success; theories vary, so a family counselor is advised to be familiar with the options available in the community. Relationship courses are often a mixture of voluntary students, either individually or as couples, and those who have been advised to take a class. In the state of Michigan, a bill requiring a marriage class before getting a marriage license has been introduced in the legislature several times, and many religious communities require a marriage preparation class. Couples can voluntarily enroll in relationship enhancement courses either in their early time together or later when they are experiencing difficulties.

Because of the intense competition in popular relationship literature and the powerful effect of trendy books, it is helpful if family counselors are familiar with the books that clients have been reading. With such knowledge, the counselor can speak directly to the limitations of a particular theory or relationship movement. Books and other materials that oversimplify complex issues can exacerbate problems.

Parenting Knowledge

Another body of scholarship addresses human development topics and the process of parenting. Some of this work is intended for professionals in fields such as education, nursing, and counseling, but there are many popular titles directed at parents and would-be parents. There are no clear instructions for bringing about a happy and successful life for a child, but generations of parents have sought guidance in making the difficult decisions they face. The family counselor should have one or two familiar parenting books to recommend and discuss as the need arises.

Parenting can be a frightening responsibility, and every day can offer dozens of opportunities to make a difference for better or worse. When more than one person is actively involved in parenting, these daily decisions are opportunities for conflict and, if a child is not thriving—physically, emotionally, socially, scholastically—opportunities for blame. The list of possible parenting decisions in Box 4.3 illustrates the complexity of the issues.

In attempting to resolve such questions, parents typically rely on family traditions, try to recall memories of their own childhood experiences, ask others what they are doing with their children, and seek expert information and advice. Some reject the advice of their own parents or siblings and in stressful circumstances—new stepfamily situations or during the preparation for a first child—partners may mistrust each other's judgments and reject each other's viewpoints. At these times, the family counselor wants to be informed, to share information effectively, and to help people to resolve their differences in light of new information.

The informed counselor needs ways of staying up-to-date with human development theories and research—or referring families to sources of such information—regarding topics such as prenatal nutrition, separation issues with a toddler, or transition from elementary to middle school. The web site http://www.cyfernet.org is an excellent example of the resources available to practitioners as well as parents. In the community,

---

BOX 4.3

Parenting Decisions

Management of differences is difficult when strong feelings are involved, and parenting decisions often bring people's value differences to the forefront. The need to make decisions about parenting can start long before birth, with decisions about prenatal care, nutrition, and lifestyle change. Pregnant women are encouraged to abstain from smoking and to seriously limit their alcohol intake, and they are also urged to avoid exposure to toxic cleaning solvents and many communicable diseases. Planning for living arrangements with a baby is best done before the baby is delivered, and many first-time parents find that their spare time is filled working through their differences about

redecorating or remodeling to create a child-friendly environment.

The birth process itself is another topic that calls for resolving possible differences based on beliefs about safety, support, and emotion, and some couples' plans are revised right up until the moment of birth. The process does not get easier once a baby has input as well; different viewpoints usually exist on the classic debate about letting an infant cry versus trying to prevent crying. Education, choice of friends, nutrition, and sleeping and waking hours are all issues that require decisions. Clearly, families that have decision-making problems experience frequent discomfort and may have a hard time taking action of any kind.

---

high-quality parenting classes may be offered by hospitals, social service agencies, U.S. Agricultural Extension offices, and schools. In the counselor's office, teaching may be more effective if the counselor assigns readings, videotapes, television series, and web-based teaching material. Such assignments are especially helpful in stepfamily and new parent situations where one partner has far more knowledge than the other.

Knowledge of Aging, Death, and Dying

Family counseling cannot ignore the end of the life span, even though counselors more frequently work with couples and families in midlife. Given the increased life span of people in many parts of the world, couple relationships are lasting as long as 60 or 70 years; therefore, a young couple can expect that half of their relationship history will occur after the age of 50. Also, illness and accidental death are not unheard of in younger families and every family counselor should be informed on the processes of aging and on issues of grief and loss. People are often

helped by having conceptual tools for making sense of their experiences, and, just as in parenting issues, the family with aging members often seeks information to help with major decisions.

Compared with couple formation and parenting, the end of the life span is less represented in both professional literature and books, videos, or other media that would be available for clients to read. Hargrave and Hanna (1997) provide an overview of aging and families that can be helpful in getting oriented to the literature and the issues.

Knowledge of Systems

Another body of information comes from philosophers, sociologists and psychologists, religious leaders, family scholars, and family counselors who have studied family well-being, health, effectiveness, and optimal functioning. Froma Walsh, in her book *Strengthening Family Resilience* (1998), provides a balanced overview of this literature, but the counselor who would be an effective advisor to families is likely to make the study of couples and families an ongoing project.

Intervening: Internal Knowledge (Self and Other)

If it is important to have knowledge about people in general, how they form relationships and what their needs are, it is at least as important to know about the particular individuals in the couple and/or family. People are not interchangeable, and knowing about divorce and remarriage is not enough preparation to help a mother and her 7-year-old son renegotiate their relationships as they move into a small apartment, learn to depend totally on each other, and then try to fit into yet another family formation with a father and his 12-year-old daughter and 14-year-old son. People in relationships need intimate knowledge of their own and each other's learning histories and their response patterns, and counseling can help them to develop this knowledge.

Moods and Temperament

Human emotion is a central issue in relationships (see Chapter 7). Couple relationships, parent-child relationships, and extended family relationships are all influenced by emotional states and moods. Especially in relationships of individuals with mood disorders, communication of positive emotions can be disrupted. In the case of depression, others may feel blamed for a depressed mood or they may become critical of the depressed individual (Gollan, Friedman, & Miller, 2002). Such extremes may require specialized counseling techniques, as family members in these relationships are likely to need skills and knowledge related to the particular emotional confusion they face. Webster-Stratton and Herbert (1994) discuss the implications of temperament in the parenting of children who are eventually diagnosed with conduct disorder.

Normal mood changes, including those experienced by many women in the course of their menstrual cycles, are also sometimes confusing both for the person experiencing the mood and for others. Counseling can help individuals find effective ways to share mood changes with others. At the same time, partners or family members can learn to minimize upsetting and confusing interactions.

Beliefs, Attitudes, and Discourses

Beliefs are also a central theme in relationships; we return to this theme in other chapters, viewing beliefs as products of relationship experience (Chapter 5), as assimilation of socially transmitted meanings (Chapter 6), and as essential ingredients in a healthy spirituality (Chapter 8). But when viewed as a learning phenomenon, the most striking component of relationship beliefs and attitudes is the extent to which they can change, confusing self and others. Many couple relationships fail because of attitudes or beliefs that were not apparent at an earlier stage. For example, I have worked with several couples whose priorities for retirement were radically different; over their years together they had developed very different ideas about critical issues such as aging, finances, caretaking, and recreation.

Couple and family counselors can facilitate conversations in which people try to put their attitudes and beliefs into words. As clients succeed in identifying points of confusion or actual differences, they can work together to find ways to accommodate each other and make plans on how to handle the incompatibilities. In some cases, such as an early relationship couple considering commitment, clients may decide that their beliefs and attitudes are so different that they are unlikely to meet their personal goals if they stay together.

Conditioned Responses

People's patterned, conditioned responses may be confusing, like moods, and they may become manifest only under certain circumstances. What is certain is that they will be different—no two people respond the same way to all situations, and these responses are often surprising. The new partner who has never seen a loved one in the presence of her parents may be amazed at her "uncharacteristic" shy or aggressive behavior. An adult son, after 30 years of observing his father, may still be amazed at his dad's different speech patterns and posture when visiting the grandparents.

There is no way for a couple and family counselor to create or to even anticipate all the situations in which clients learn new things about each other. But structured tasks designed around some common, predictable events and conflicts can be helpful in learning about one another. Gerstein (1999) offers a selection of activities for families that are designed to facilitate this kind of interpersonal learning.

Intervening: Teaching Relationship Skills

I began this chapter with a discussion of learning. Many times, couples and families who come for counseling need little more than new or improved skills. Many of these skill areas fall into the general category of communication, and family counselors have seen some of these skill deficits so often that the problems are documented and validated skill-training programs are available. In U.S. society, where people have been inundated by articles and books criticizing their ways of communicating with each other, "We don't communicate" is one of the first statements that new clients often make.

However, the word "communication" is too broad to guide the choice of a behavioral approach to couples and families. I try to get a more specific statement by offering alternatives: "When you say there's a communication problem, do you mean that you are silent when you are together, or could it be instead that the things people are saying aren't really addressing the important issues?" In the end, there appear to be several major categories of "communication problems" that can be addressed with a skill-based intervention.

Basic Communication

Many ways of improving communication in relationships are extremely simple and some of the most useful communication training programs use a simple model to help people evaluate their own behavior and make changes. Floyd, Markman, Kelly, Blumberg, and Stanley (1995), for example, in their Prevention and Relationship Enhancement Program (PREP), begin by teaching the *speaker-listener model*. According to this description of communication, a speaker has a message he or she is trying to impart and the listener is attempting to receive that message. When the message received does not seem to match what the sender intended, then communication is considered flawed. The training, which includes both didactic and experiential components, teaches couples to recognize and overcome miscommunication and revise the process so that "intent equals impact."

Gottman and his colleagues (e.g., Gottman, Coan, Carrere, & Swanson, 1998) have challenged this basic-skills approach, pointing out their research showing that people do not simply communicate facts but instead communicate emotions. One danger in training partners to listen is that an "accurately" reflected message may escalate negative emotions. If a woman responds to he partner's negativity by saying, "I hear you saying that you hate me and you wish we had never met," the response may (1) communicate a rational, distancing attitude that is not what was intended and (2) emphasize and even escalate negative affect. Gottman promotes de-escalating responses, even when they may not seem to achieve the goal of transmitting information.

Another criticism of basic-skills approaches notes that communication is shaped by issues of gender and power. Philpot and Brooks (1995) describe training efforts focusing on gender-related communications problems. Along with Real (2002) and Tannen (1991), these authors suggest that problems with gendered communication patterns can be resolved through a focus on differences in verbal and nonverbal expression. They particularly recommend that partners be helped to accept the uncertainty of communication and be trained in empathic skills to avoid misinterpreting each others' communication attempts. We will return to these and other communication issues in Chapter 5.

Conflict Management and Problem Solving

A key relationship skill, according to many family scholars and clinicians (e.g., Gottman, 1994; Guerin, Fay, Burden, & Kautto, 1987; Robin & Foster, 1989), involves handling conflict. In every couple and family relationship, there are times when differences in values and preferences are difficult to resolve. These are often decision-making opportunities, times when participants are facing the consequences of their different views. At these times, people have opportunities to work toward shared solutions—not only for a present conflict but also for their larger relationship issues.

This conflict management process is so important because it has a destructive effect when handled badly. Gottman and his research team (e.g., Gottman & Krokoff, 1979) identified four patterns of negative conflict behavior in couples—criticism, defensiveness, withdrawal, and contempt—that predict divorce and violence. Krishnakumar and Buehler (2000) have documented the extent to which interparental conflict contributes to impaired parenting. In cases of parents' extreme conflict behavior, according to Cummings and Davis (1994), continued exposure leads to emotional and behavioral problems in children. In Chapter 5, we return to conflict as an organizational issue; for the moment, we are concerned with skills.

Nearly all behavioral approaches to relationships include training in the skills of conflict management or problem solving or both. In conflict resolution approaches such as the one that formed the basis for traditional behavioral couple therapy (Jacobson & Margolin, 1979), couples were taught to follow a clear process that emphasized cooperation and minimized competitiveness.

Fisher and Brown (1988) offered a more complex understanding, suggesting that such a cooperative approach is easier to establish and maintain when negotiators focus on issues rather than outcomes: what they refer to as *interest-based* versus *position-based* negotiation. Starting with a position, "This is what I want," seems to elicit an oppositional response. If one partner demands an earlier mealtime, the other demands that the mealtime be even later. Instead, starting with "We seem to have a problem agreeing on when to eat" accomplishes two things. First, it often leads to the partners beginning with an agreement, "Yes, we are having a problem with that," and seeking a mutual definition of the problem. Such an issue-focused beginning results in a list of several issues that can then be addressed separately. More important is the sense that the partners are standing together against

Table 4.2 Collaborative Problem Solving

Identify issues, not preferred outcomes.

Subdivide issues wherever possible, take one at a time.

Explore alternatives.

Examine alternatives.

Develop and bargain to achieve a plan that has mutual support.

Develop an implementation plan.

Document decisions.

Review the process and decisions, and repeat when needed.

(Each step in this sequence is critical to the success of the overall process.)

the problem rather than standing on two sides battling each other. Table 4.2 illustrates a structured, interest-based problem-solving sequence that often helps people to resolve conflicts.

The work with the strongest research base is John Gottman's. His varied research career, including studies of children's conflicts, has more recently involved video studies of couples during extended stays in his laboratory. He says that positive outcomes in heterosexual couple conflicts depend on a "soft start-up" rather than a verbal attack on the partner, and they involve a search for mutually acceptable solutions. Gottman's work has begun to broaden in recent years. He not only describes effective and ineffective problem solving but also now suggests that trying to solve problems is often unrealistic; many problems are not solvable. Instead, people with successful relationships seem to have sustained their positive feelings for each other despite conflict and to *dialogue with each other* about their unresolved problems rather than insist on solving them.

Brent Atkinson (2005) has extended the work of Gottman and others in his conflict management model. He applies the principle of soft startup (he refers to it as a "prerequisite for relationship success"), but places equal emphasis on three other prerequisites: accepting influence, effective repair, and a complex he refers to as "respecting your partner's dreams, holding on to your own." Particularly important in his formulation is a process of repair, which he considers essential because partners are imperfect and don't always handle earlier steps perfectly. Atkinson's integrative approach mixes a behavioral focus on the learning of habits—he assigns homework and provides workbooks—with elements of meaning-making, acceptance, and emotion management.

Assertiveness

Assertiveness is closely related to conflict as an element of relationship functioning. Assertive behaviors—identifying and articulating one's observations, understandings, and expectations—do not lead to domination and exploitation of others. Instead, dominant and exploitive behavior is more likely when assertiveness failures lead to feelings of frustration, anger, and fear. Lack of assertiveness has often been addressed as a women's issue, as it is highly correlated with women's victimization by larger partners and stronger adolescent children. Unassertive males may experience many of the same outcomes, especially in relationships with male partners whose dominance is culturally supported. Assertive behaviors, as distinguished from both ineffective requests and aggressive demands, are relatively easy to teach in a group format.

Assertiveness training is often provided to only one family member with the understanding that relationship change will result from that individual's increased ability to resist influence attempts. Gordon and Waldo (1984) conducted research that supports this assumption, finding that both assertiveness trainees and their partners who had not gone through the training reported greater relationship satisfaction following 14 to 25 sessions in a group format. Shoemaker and Paulson (1976), working with a child guidance center population, described a group assertion-training program for mothers. In their group, as in many assertiveness training programs, participants were taught the principles of assertion and then helped to develop their self-observation skills and to substitute effective assertions for the ineffective prior behaviors of withdrawal or aggression.

On the other hand, a unilateral change in relationship behavior is often unsuccessful or could lead to violence. Ronfeldt, Kimerling, and Arias (1998) found that men reported more partner violence when they expressed dissatisfaction with the power dynamics in their dating relationships. A potentially more effective approach prepares partners or family members for the likelihood that increased assertiveness can be expected.

Sexuality

Sexual interaction is another core relationship skill that has been clearly addressed in the behavioral literature, with great success. Prior to the 1950s sexual problems were addressed—if at all—through a combination of education and psychodynamic treatment. Professionals assumed that an individual who knew anatomy and sexual techniques, given a good emotional connection with a partner, would have no sexual problems. William Masters and Virginia Johnson (1966), with their careful laboratory studies of sexual responses and later with their well-documented treatment program, changed that view in a decade.

Masters and Johnson treated sexuality as a behavioral realm that could be studied like any other, by systematic observation. Despite the media attention created by their procedures—having 700 men and women engage in masturbation and intercourse in their laboratory, connecting the subjects to instruments so that their sexual responses could be measured with instruments—Masters and Johnson earned tremendous respect both with their peers and with the lay public. Their careful descriptions of the male and female sexual response cycles, published in *Human Sexual Response* (1966) became the basis for a new science. Their clinic, opened in 1970, became world famous, and the Masters and Johnson tradition continues in multiple locations despite Dr. Johnson's retirement and the recent death of Dr. Masters.

Masters and Johnson believed that people learned sexual response patterns through social learning and other conditioning processes. Praise and attention reinforced behavior positively, and escape from an anxious or frustrating experience served as negative reinforcement. Rapid ejaculation was seen as a conditioned response for men whose early sexual experiences had involved masturbation and a goal of achieving orgasm as quickly as possible. Erectile dysfunction was an example of negative reinforcement; anxiety about premature ejaculation was relieved when a man's erection subsided or wouldn't occur at all. Vaginismus resulted from a fear-driven muscle-tensing response that produced pain, thereby reinforcing the fear and the tensing of muscles.

These explanations were supported by the results of behaviorally based treatment programs, often involving homework assignments requiring mutual exploration of bodily sensation and avoidance of intercourse. Couples were encouraged to learn not from books but from each other, developing a shared understanding of the ways in which their sexual responses fit together. Over the past 30 years, these ideas have been applied to a variety of problems and extended by many authors.

Parenting

A final category of relationship skill includes interactional styles and specific techniques that parents can use in their efforts to bring up strong, sensitive, capable children and adolescents. Intervention in parenting skills need not wait until birth; infant mental health programs have developed procedures for screening prospective parents and working intensively with those who seem overwhelmed or unaware. Infants in such programs are healthier, more securely attached, and demonstrate more rapid language development (Bristor, Wilson, & Helfer, 1985).

Parent-child communication is a specialized field that builds on the basic principles that would be applied in any relationship arena but addresses the unique dynamics introduced by developmental variations, power differentials, generational differences in language and values, and emotional overlays that interfere with speaking and being heard. Because of the developmental, cultural, and content complexities involved in critical parent-child discussions of topics such as bullying, sexuality, and drug use parent-training programs have been created to provide information and opportunities for skill development. An excellent example is the Can We Talk? program (http://www.neahin.org/canwetalk), sponsored by the National Education Association.

Webster-Stratton and Herbert (1994) specialize in the skills parents need for working with "problem" children whose behavior fits diagnostic criteria for *conduct disorder*. They begin with an assumption that the parents are accustomed to being blamed. Rather than describing their program as correcting parenting errors, their "collaborative process" addresses parents as competent problem solvers. They teach parents to assess a situation, apply specific research-tested techniques to fit a particular need, and combine the behavioral basics with a program of self-care techniques that focus on the skills of parental coping.

Webster-Stratton and Herbert's (1994) approach starts with teaching a sensitive and complex understanding of behavioral principles and techniques. Many elements of their approach (e.g., positive reinforcement, negative reinforcement, differential attention) have been described in other parenting materials. However, these behavioral techniques may face some parental opposition (see Box 4.4).

Intervening: Cue Focus

If behaviors are linked to cues in the environment, then a family should have special power for change because the family members control so many cues. They might be able to choose the community in which they live; the language used in the home; the daily schedule; decoration, use, and arrangement of rooms; choices of leisure activities; exposure to positive and negative models; diet; spiritual practices; and many other aspects of the family environment. These freedoms are dependent on many factors, however, and many minority families face economic limitations and other forms of discrimination that limit their options.

Even when a family has options, altering their choices requires that partners and/or family members be committed to change and that they work together. Early behavioral family therapists found that carefully negotiated changes were frequently ineffective because the family members did not work together well enough to implement them (Falloon, 1991). Therefore, cue control techniques may be best kept in reserve until some simpler relationship changes have started to work.

BOX 4.4

Uncomfortable with Behavioral Interventions?

The view many people have of behaviorism is negative—behaviorists are seen as cold and scientific, not as warm and caring. According to some critics, behavioral methods are unfair because they are so powerful. Children should not be coerced, say these critics, they should be allowed to find their own way. Responsibility is learned by making decisions, not by being programmed to respond in socially approved ways.

Behavioral methods are not the only way of achieving success as a parent. Where effective alternatives exist, children and families thrive. The model of parenting that Baumrind (1991) has labeled *authoritative,* for example, is one that requires no allegiance to behavioral theory: Parents simply exercise a moderate degree of direct control—locking up the liquor, setting and enforcing a curfew—and explain their rules as being motivated by love. Compliance is assumed to result not from reinforcement or the blocking of cues but from restricted options, loyalty, understanding, and self-respect.

When parents fail to make authoritative parenting work, however, they may fall back on unscientific techniques of punishment and bribery instead. Punishment and bribery are no less coercive than behaviorism and no less unfair. Instead of cue control and contingency management, parents alternate between buying new video games and grounding their children for weeks at a time. Family counselors under these circumstances may want to help parents reconsider the potential value of behaviorism.

Cuing the Desired Behavior

Whenever possible, the changes desired in a family should be positive and involve movement toward what is desired rather than movement away from something negative. The process that naturally leads to conditioned responses can be used intentionally to build associations between desired behavior and any antecedent stimulus.

Sexual responses, a major area of concern in couple relationships, are a perfect area for building associations. Clothing and cosmetics manufacturers have known this for generations; visual, olfactory, tactile, and auditory stimuli are easily organized so that an eventual state of arousal will be richly associated with antecedents. When such associations are effectively used, a couple can prepare for lovemaking by spending hours in preparation. They can take a swim or have a romantic meal together, spend time talking and verbally stroking each other, bathe and dress to make themselves most arousing for each other, and eventually arrive at touching each other when they are so aroused that every touch has special effects.

Many other interaction states can be set up in similar ways by creating a sequence that is associated with the desired outcome. Preparation for mealtime can enhance appetite and promote interaction at the table. Preparation for shared prayer or meditation, at home or in a place of worship, can help family members focus and set aside the distractions of work, sports, and friendships. A supportive context for school and home study can support curiosity, positive attitudes toward learning, and dependable handling of responsibilities.

Identifying and Altering a Conditioned Response

Weakening a problem behavior, from the cue control perspective, requires careful behavioral analysis. The problem behavior has to be located in clock time, social context, and space. The counselor may ask for a time and space analysis: "Please walk me through the time right before Angela leaves for school. Who is in which rooms? What is happening there? If someone else comes into the room, does that change what is happening?" Often a problem behavior occurs because the environment is not set up for appropriate behavior and somehow sends a mixed signal. Studying, for example, may be hard to do in a room that has been associated with play and activity, and a television set in the dining area does not promote interaction. Family problem solving and planning can inform environmental changes that work in seemingly miraculous ways to eliminate problems.

Weakening Response Chains I: Introducing New Behaviors into the Sequence

When an environmental cue cannot be removed or eliminated, it is sometimes possible to reduce its effect by imposing a new step between the conditioned stimulus and the response. Punching holes in walls, for example, is usually not something that a person does throughout the day; it is something that occurs in specific social situations. A careful history helps link the behavior with antecedent stimuli, and this knowledge can help reengineer the encounter for the future.

George, a 35-year-old man, had engaged in hole-punching a few times, much to the distress of his young children and his smaller, less powerful wife, Vickie. Careful questioning produced the response chain shown in Table 4.3.

At each of these steps, there were opportunities to alter the response chain by introducing a behavior that made the next step less likely. Success was measured not by waiting to see whether he punched another hole in the wall, but by judging whether the withdraw/demand/anger cycle was interrupted.

Early in the process, George had the option of changing his commuting pattern so that he reduced, rather than increased, his levels of stress and tension. He had the option of challenging his self-pitying thoughts, which appeared to be part of the chain leading to his outbursts. He agreed to work on a program to make these changes. Other family members contributed to changing the sequence as well. In this case, a family problem-solving session led to an experiment: Vickie set a timer when George walked in the house, and until the timer went off the children were expected to stay out of the living room and the bedroom. The timer setting started at 10 minutes; depending on how the experiment went, the time

Table 4.3   **Cued Response Chain**

Event	Response Chain
The computer at work crashed and lost his files, resulting in a lost contract.	Initial cue—experience of failure and frustration
He threatened to have the computer technician fired.	His cued response—verbal aggression
The computer technician quit.	Effect of his response on the environment, creating new cues
His coworkers teased him for his impulsive behavior.	New cue—experience of humiliation and rejection
He left work early to drive home.	His cued response—withdraw to a safe place, tense and distracted
He forgot to fill the tank and ran out of gasoline.	Effect of his response on the environment, creating new cues
After walking a long distance to buy gasoline, he drove aggressively and became more tense. He arrived home to find the driveway blocked by a neighbor's car.	Another experience of failure and frustration
	His cued response—physical aggression

could be lengthened or shortened, and other changes could be made as well.

The experiment was successful. The combined effect of a changed way in driving home, along with clear limits that the children could follow, enabled everyone to work together toward a joyous reunion once the timer rang. The children were less anxious, George was less rejecting, and Vickie was able to shift her attention to other matters because she had another active parent sharing the responsibility for the household.

Weakening Response Chains II: Systematic Desensitization

In a similar case, the process I just described did not work because the mother, Sandra, an emergency room nurse, was so agitated when she walked in the door that she seemed to take an hour to calm down and the household couldn't stay quiet for an hour. The behavioral technique of systematic desensitization was added to the chain-breaking program. In its classic form, this is an individual-level counseling process, in which one individual works with the counselor to gradually reduce the intensity or duration or frequency of a conditioned response. Using techniques that have been widely described in the individual counseling literature (Wolpe, 1970), Sandra started calming herself on the drive home, pulling off the road until she felt calm and only driving until the tension returned and then repeating the calming process. When she was able to arrive in the driveway in a calmer state, she began to use the time in the driveway to calm herself before entering the house.

When systematic desensitization is used in a family setting, people can work together to improve the process. In the classical process, the client is asked to imagine the anxiety-provoking situation. Throughout the drive home and in the driveway Sandra was able to do this as well. But in the family enhanced process, she was able to continue the training once she entered the house; she was able to withdraw when she felt tense and take as long as needed to calm herself. All family members participated in planning and implementing the changes and assessing change.

Intervening: Contingency Focus

The previous group of intervention strategies focused on the association between responses and their antecedent stimuli. The contingency management approach, popularly known as *behavior modification,* is even more widely known and represents the mainstream of behavioral intervention.

Improving Reciprocity

Starting from the assumption that reinforcement for positive behavior will yield more positive behavior, Azrin and colleagues (1973), Stuart (1980), and others trained partners to reciprocally reinforce each other's desirable relationship behaviors. Such reciprocity-focused programs for couples start by identifying the behaviors that are of greatest interest to the partners and work toward increasing those behaviors.

When attempting to intervene in this way, the counselor wants to ensure that a relationship partner is a good observer and doesn't overlook events that are inconsistent with preconceptions. (Trial lawyers know that witnesses may remember a poorly dressed bystander as a robber when the actual robber was dressed in new, stylish clothes.) At the couple level, this means that Sam may respond to his partner's complaints, and after weeks of new behavior—compliments, reduced complaining—go by, the partner continues to say "Sam will never change." Stuart's (1980) concept of *caring days* addressed this perceptual distortion by contracting for the specific days when caring gestures would be demonstrated. Knowing that Thursday was the day, a partner would be more likely to notice things that happened on Thursday.

Reducing Unintentional Reinforcements

A contingency focus also calls attention to the possibility that a partner or a parent may be providing positive reinforcement for an undesired behavior. This idea appears frequently in the parenting literature, especially with regard to attention. In a sibling group, parent attention is often spread rather thin. A parent who is working one or two jobs and caring for three children cannot provide all of them with attention in equal amounts. If a child's behavior and/or emotional responses attract extra parental attention, learning theories suggest that the child is likely to continue in the same pattern. Paradoxically, taking a child to see a counselor may work as a reinforcement, making it less likely that the child will abandon the "successful" behavior. Family counseling cannot eliminate this possible effect, but it has the advantage of giving less attention to the identified patient.

Authentic Assessment

In many cases, the most effective contingency management option available in a relationship system is one of strengthening desired behavior. This is the classic behavior modification approach, in its typical form applied with a child. The child's current behavior is assessed (establishing a baseline) and then the child is offered positive reinforcements for desired behavior.

If 10-year-old Kadisha's mother wants her to stop teasing her younger sister, she can threaten and bribe the older girl in an attempt to stop the problem behavior, but this attention to the negative behavior is counterproductive. Instead, a behaviorally sophisticated mother identifies an alternative behavior that is incompatible with continued teasing. For example, she might ask Kadisha to be responsible for teaching her sister how to braid her hair. She could be given structure to help her meet this expectation; for example, she could be offered specific reinforcements if she spends 15 minutes twice a day in teaching and practicing together. To the extent that Kadisha succeeds in helping her sister to become more mature and happy, she earns specific reinforcements as well as the generalized reinforcement of her mother's attention.

Many parents need careful instruction if they are going to be effective in using behavioral principles with their children. Gerald Patterson's (1971) *Families: Applications of Social Learning to Family Life* is an excellent resource, written at a level that can be shared with older children. Patterson makes the point that everyone in the family can use positive behavioral principles with each other, rather than ineffective and damaging methods of punishment.

The following guidelines seem to increase the effectiveness of a behavior-strengthening program:

- Behavioral expectations must be specific—not just "act nice" but "stand facing your grandparents, make eye contact, and say hello."
- Reinforcement must be consistent, at least during the initial phase of a program. Parents who fail to consistently notice and reinforce desired behavior find that their behavioral programs don't work.
- Reinforcers are unique to the individual. One child may work for an extended bedtime once a week, while another may work for a favorite meal or a visit to the mall. If it doesn't affect behavior, it's not a reinforcer.
- Even though the expectations may be specific, the principle of shaping suggests that it may be effective to start by reinforcing a reasonable attempt, then gradually raise the standards for reinforcement.
- With a younger child, reinforcement should be tangible—a hug, a cookie—and should occur quickly following the desired behavior. An older, more emotionally, and cognitively sophisticated child can accept symbolic reinforcers. In a typical point system, 5 or 10 earned points brings a low-value reinforcer and points accumulate toward a major reinforcer.
- The number of behavioral goals should be matched to the child's age. A young child can only handle one "program" at a time and the parent has to clearly prioritize which goal will be addressed first. With an older child, it may be possible to earn points in multiple ways and they add together.

Assessing Effectiveness

In a way, the goal of every client is to get away from the counselor as quickly as possible. Not only is counseling a financial and time stressor for most people, but the family's relationship with the counselor can easily turn into one of dependency. The counselor, likewise, does not want to expend resources beyond the time when they are needed. Assessment can help determine when it is safe to end or at least suspend the process.

Authentic Assessment

If assessment has been continued throughout the intervention process, and the assessment accurately reflects the status of the behaviors being addressed, then discussions of goals, risks, and discomfort should be relatively clear and open. In many cases, clients will feel more comfortable discontinuing as soon as their goals have been met, and a good behavioral program includes ways of documenting that the process has been successful.

Empowering the Recipient

Most clients will not want to leave until some kind of "certified problem-free" status is achieved. Part of the reason has to do with diminished agency. When changes occur quickly as part of a weekly counseling process, the couple or family may come to worry that they cannot manage their lives without the counselor. Some counselors gradually taper the process from weekly to twice monthly, every 3 weeks, and monthly. By the time the clients have been away from the counselor for a month, they generally see themselves handling the stresses of daily life without help.

Closure

Any solution to an existing problem may be temporary, because new circumstances are likely to demand new accommodations, but the typical couple or family completes a behavioral counseling process fairly quickly and moves on. Because behavioral approaches communicate a positive message about families and focus on current issues rather than "causal factors," people are generally not embarrassed about coming back for one or more sessions when they recognize that things aren't going well. This request is more likely if the counselor normalizes the need for continuing support and helps the clients to anticipate that they are likely to experience disruptions or new needs to renegotiate their reinforcements.

Cautions, Concerns, and New Directions

Despite its advantages, this teaching and learning perspective has its limitations and can actually support negative patterns in families. Earlier, I recalled hearing a behaviorist express doubts about the need for other theories. I also recall—with a shudder—hearing another self-proclaimed behaviorist dismiss the need for learning how to live with others' cultures, limitations, or preferences. He said, "Now that the technology exists for changing human behavior, we no longer have to put up with behavior we don't want." Dogmatic, arrogant views such as this have led to negative views of behaviorism, and amateur behaviorists can be dangerous. The literature on child abuse and neglect includes many stories in which the perpetrators were "just trying to teach" one lesson or another.

It is important that you be aware that some behavioral beliefs can be used in ways that are destructive. When you find clients or professionals expressing behavioral beliefs in these ways, you may be challenged to either try to teach them more positive versions of behaviorism or else offer them alternative perspectives that move them away from the dangers of their rigid beliefs. It is with such a helpful intent that I provide the following critiques.

Modernism, Positivism, and the Myth of Human Perfection

A belief in the perfectibility of human nature— what many people mean when they use the term "humanism"—has motivated generations of leaders to work toward the elimination of crime, poverty, exploitation, and disease. The metaphors of the industrial age—finding and combining sources of power, using physical principles to multiply force and increase leverage, lubricating and replacing parts to increase the efficiency of a machine—served to give social reformers greater hope that eventually societies could be engineered to run as smoothly as a high-speed printing press or a factory full of mechanical looms. Watson's and Skinner's behaviorism fit perfectly into this tradition; they promised that applied behavior analysis would eventually allow humans to live in a utopia where happy workers lived in harmony.

The past 100 years have seen a gradual erosion of the dream of social engineering. Within the behavioral community, researchers and clinicians have begun to look at their beliefs and methods with an eye to their limitations. Christensen, Jacobson, and Babcock (1995) announced a radical rethinking of the goals and methods of behavioral couple therapy. In this newer approach, the emphasis moved away from change and shifted to accepting a partner's differences (see Chapter 7). They explained that the changes were based on research evidence that (1) efforts focused on skill development and behavior change did not always produce change or improved relationship satisfaction, (2) many gains achieved in behavioral couple therapy seemed to disappear within 2 years, and (3) the change-oriented procedures seemed to encourage an emotional climate of criticism, intolerance, and anger.

Hierarchy, Power, and Abuse

One of the greatest concerns regarding behavioral approaches, ironically, comes from their effectiveness. Behavioral techniques used in service of dominance, control, exploitation, or abuse can have disastrous consequences. During the consciousness-raising movement in the United States (Shreve, 1990), many middle-class and upper-class women discovered a profound unhappiness and lack of identity as they performed tasks and played roles for which they were conditioned and for which they continued to be reinforced. They had not realized the extent to which their families, their schools, and their communities had shaped their behavior.

The ability to reward and punish is unequally distributed in nearly every social group; the people who have greater access to the rewards and the means of punishment (privilege) have a greater ability to see their goals met and their preferences honored. Part of the power that belongs to the more privileged members of a couple

or family is the ability to get institutions and professionals involved in furthering their ends. Family counseling often is initiated by a family member who is trying to repair a crumbling system of dominance and control, and the family counselor must carefully assess the needs of the group before accepting goals that are articulated by one or two members.

Suggested Individual and Group Activities

Your understanding of concepts and issues presented in this chapter may be enhanced by the following activities:

- *Search for reinforcers.* Interview friends and family members to learn about what they consider to be your reinforcement preferences—what alters your behavior? Is it attention, touch, praise?
- *Environmental scan.* Imagine that you are trying to help an extraterrestrial visitor to unobtrusively attend a gathering of your family. What are the specialized skills and understandings that will be necessary for this guest to fit in?
- *Learning history.* Recall a time when you decided to change something about yourself. Were there others who influenced that decision? How did you go about eliminating old behaviors and acquiring new behaviors?

Suggested Readings

Gottman, J. M., Driver, J., & Tabares, A. (2002). Building the sound marital house: An empirically derived couple therapy. In A. S. Gurman & N. S. Jacobson (Eds.), *Clinical handbook of couple therapy* (3rd ed., pp. 373–399). New York: Guilford.

Patterson, G. R. (1976). *Living with children: New methods for parents and teachers.* Champaign, IL: Research Press.

Skinner, B. F. (1971). *Beyond freedom and dignity.* New York: Vintage.

Organization: Planning, Decision Making, and Action

The problems presented by a couple or family are part of an organized family level process or system.

Objectives

In this chapter, you learn to:

1. Recognize and identify organized patterns in couple and family relationships.
2. Distinguish between adaptive and maladaptive relationship patterns, based on theory and research.
3. Explain commonly accepted organizational interventions.
4. Select from a broad range of interventions to help people reorganize their relationships.

5

chapter

The second dimension of the BONES model, Organization, incorporates many theories that share a central concept: People are seen as interacting in ways that are *organized* by patterns. Like the behavioral perspective, the organizational perspective honors and anticipates change. If a problem pattern can be recognized, it can be changed. In contrast with the behavioral perspective, an organizational view does not interpret these patterns as individual learning histories. They are seen as group-level phenomena—organizational needs, organizational history, and organizational structure. Although the theories in this chapter are often referred to by the umbrella phrase "seeing families as systems," the perspective does not require a formal systems theory. It merely assumes that humans are best understood in groups—together in a single moment or over generations, in a household or across thousands of miles.

You may already be asking, "Why do we need organizational theories? Wasn't behaviorism a theory that focused on interaction?" You are correct to some extent. This is only one of many overlaps observed as I force our complex field into a simple model. To the reader's question, I have two answers.

1. First, behavioral viewpoints and organizational viewpoints are different at a basic level. The Behavioral theme describes relationships as changing because individuals learn new skills and habits, acquire knowledge, and develop new concepts. The Organizational theme makes the relationship itself a character in the story. The relationship has needs or goals, and it designates individual members to perform roles.

2. Second, all the themes we look at have rather ragged boundaries. They are what some mathematicians refer to as "fuzzy sets," as it

is not possible to identify a theory with one theme and state that it doesn't belong with any of the others. The themes described in the BONES model fit together differently, depending on each theory; one possible combination is illustrated in Figure 5.1. Some theories or practices are very strongly associated with one theme and unrelated to other themes, while other theories and practices apparently overlap with one or two BONES dimensions. I have tried to provide a guide to the connections.

When organizational ideas began to emerge in the helping professions, they were praised for their ability to end discussions of "who is suffering more" and inspire a collaborative approach to change. *The dysfunctional family,* a term coined by Virginia Satir (1964/1967), was an organizational description with which Satir hoped to shift the blame away from individuals—in this case the mothers of schizophrenics—and onto the interactions of the whole family (Hoffman, 2002). Early family therapists created the term *identified patient* to imply that a problem existed not inside one individual but in the whole group. Current organizational theory and practice continue to aspire to these same goals. In the hands of a skilled practitioner, an organizational perspective does more than merely shift the problem away from scapegoated individuals: It inspires hope, focuses attention on areas of needed change, and then facilitates change.

A Case Illustration: The Carpenter-Flores Family

Sheila Carpenter and Maria Flores arrived in Wally Green's office, asking for help with their couple relationship. Sheila explained that they had been a couple for about 5 years, ever since Sheila's divorce. During those years, they had always found some time during the week to be together, but that was difficult because Sheila's law practice kept her busy 50 hours a week or more. Their time together, mostly weekends, had been spent at Sheila's house because she was the primary parent for her twin daughters, Jennifer and Jessica, age 15. Maria had a son of her own, Patrick, 17, but Patrick lived in a small town 200 miles away and he didn't visit often. When Patrick spent half the summer with his mom the couple saw very little of each other.

Wally interrupted with a concern that he was already getting a one-sided view of things because Maria had remained silent so far. However, Maria said she wasn't much of a talker and Sheila was the one who had asked for the session, so Wally agreed to a temporary one-sided perspective.

Sheila resumed her story. She said, "I'm finding it increasingly hard to be around Maria and the girls at the same time. In the early years of the relationship, we all played together. We camped, went to the mall for fun, and went to movies as a family. Maria was wonderful because of her relationship with the twins. But over the years things have changed. The four of us never do anything together anymore, and when we do spend time together, Maria does nothing but criticize. I feel that Maria is driving the girls away, and I'm afraid I'll sacrifice my girls to please her. They never seem to spend time at home anymore, and when

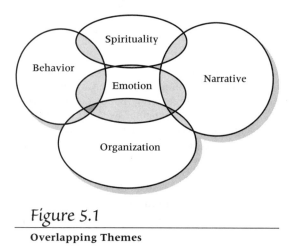

Figure 5.1

Overlapping Themes

they are home they lock themselves in their room. I think they're afraid of her, she gets so angry."

Maria seemed anxious to enter into the conversation at this point, so Wally suggested that it was time to switch perspectives. Maria said, "Their room! That pigsty! After all the work we did to finish the upstairs for them, and they've totally trashed it. The reason they stay in there is that there are rules in the rest of the house! If it weren't for me there wouldn't be any adult influence on those girls at all, with Sheila all wrapped up in her work. I'm sick of being the grownup! She's afraid I'm driving the girls away? If it weren't for me they would never have a meal at home. Dump me? Please! I'm sick of this!"

Sheila, in turn, began to list Maria's failings. She didn't think Maria was very serious about her art restoration business; the shop was mostly a place to hide because Maria liked paintings more than people. She said that Maria was not only critical with the girls, she griped about everyone and was such a judgmental person her own son didn't want to be around her either. Maria then countered with further criticisms of Sheila: She was so permissive she'd already bought each of the girls a car, even though they still had their learner's permits. The session had quickly turned into a mutual blaming session. Wally stepped in:

"I can see how much you both care," Wally said, "and it's easy to see what has kept you together despite the challenges you've faced. I hear a lot of disappointment that things aren't as good as they used to be, and I hear a lot of fear about where things may be headed. It sounds like the old days were great, and something's changed. Are you both with me so far?" He got nods from them both. "I think I may be able to help because the situation you've described so far makes sense to me. Hardly anyone has the same relationship with a 15-year-old that they had with the same child at 10, and there have been a lot of changes in the past 5 years. And then you add in the stepfamily piece, I know, it's not official but you're living that way, and you've gotten trapped in a bad movie. I think you're probably all wonderful people, but you just don't know how to get along and you're worried about the children. Right?"

Wally's summary seemed to calm them down somewhat; they stopped competing over who was the worst partner and began to talk about their shared anxieties about the twins. Sheila was worried about alcohol and other drug use and all the other ways in which adolescents could get into trouble. She knew she wasn't around much to supervise and she wanted Maria to move in and become the parent-in-charge, but things had gotten to such a state that Maria seemed to inspire rebellion more than she did obedience. Furthermore, she was afraid that the girls were feeling uncomfortable about their mom's sexual identity, a topic that had only become apparent since Maria had been around. Maria expressed much the same list of anxieties, adding her experiences with Patrick. Patrick had been a model child until about 15, when he started hanging around with a friend who had a car. The cars gave them the ability to go the city, and he was only 16 when he was arrested with a group of friends shoplifting. Since then she had felt that she had to keep him under constant surveillance when he was at her house, and she was sure that Jennifer and Jessica were getting into trouble behind Sheila's back.

Wally had enough information by the end of the first session to believe that he had identified some relationship-level issues. He was confident that the following issues, if addressed, would free the family as a unit to further evolve so that the needs of all members were met:

- The family (as a group) was going through an adolescent transition that would involve changes in all their relationships.
- The parents were influenced by the myth of "adolescent storm and stress," which was leading to negative expectations for the twins.
- Discussions of sex and sexual orientation, a universal issue for adolescents, had been avoided.
- Maria's presence as an "outsider" challenged the definition of the family. She was competing with the girls for Sheila's time and affection, but her position was unclear. With no sign of commitment, the twins had been waiting for Maria to disappear.

- Sheila and Maria, too, were struggling with the definition of their relationship.
- Jessica and Jennifer were only 3 years away from adult privileges including the right to move out on their own, and therefore all parties might be "holding their breath until it's over."
- Patrick's role in the family was unclear, but it was likely that there would be new issues if he started being treated as a third child in the family.

With the first session drawing to a close, Wally had a few immediate goals. He wanted to give the couple some feedback on what he had heard, assign a homework exercise that would either validate or challenge his impressions, and unbalance the family as a unit, with the hope that the unbalancing would facilitate change.

He started by describing the triangle that he observed, and he talked about the "easy way out" if Maria would go away and leave the children to have Mom all to themselves. He thought the situation was likely to become better if the parents could work as a team, but felt somewhat handicapped by not having met Jennifer and Jessica. Therefore, his preference would be that the next session include the girls.

This suggestion brought Sheila and Maria together in challenging his plan. This was about the two of them as a couple, and they didn't want to give the children a chance to get between them. They asked, couldn't they try for a few weeks as just the two of them?

The situation was now one that many family counselors would consider ideal. The problems with the children were being viewed as a product of the couple relationship and the couple wanted to meet without the children. Because the couple relationship was, in Wally's view, the source of the problems, he agreed. He asked that the children be invited to send their comments in writing if they wanted to have input into the family decisions, and he gave the parents two business cards to pass on. For them as a couple, he asked that each of them take notes during the week so that they would be prepared to talk

about the times when they could see the triangle operating.[1]

Consistent with Wally's theory, Maria and Sheila came in the following week disappointed that the triangle hadn't been visible all week.[2] They had been watching, and they were concerned that they might be overlooking important events. They had other things to talk about, though. There had been a school event, a "lock-down party" at which the children were carefully supervised and out of the house, and the evening gave the couple an opportunity to talk about what was happening and what they wanted. Sheila had admitted for the first time that she felt like a failure as a parent and she needed Maria's help. This represented a significant shift in the relationship balance; Maria was getting credit for her present and future efforts.

Wally concluded that the focus on the couple relationship was working and suggested that further work with the girls be postponed and continue the couple-level sessions. Changes that appeared over the next few months included the following:

- Maria and Sheila made plans and took steps to define themselves more clearly as a couple. They began to make plans for Maria to move into Sheila's house. Because of potential discrimination they still felt a need to be cautious, but they had concluded that family members and coworkers—as well as the twins and Patrick—needed to understand their relationship.
- The couple explored differences in child-rearing beliefs that had made it hard for them to work as a team and explored ways of using their different perspectives instead of denying them. (Jennifer and Jessica sent messages of relief that things were clearer.) Rules became more consistent, as the parents stopped undermining each other.
- Maria and Sheila also reevaluated the developmental needs of the twins, concluding that it was time for the girls to have separate

---

[1] This *restraining tactic* is explained in the chapter.
[2] Wally's restraining tactic had triggered changes.

rooms and to be treated more as individuals. Jessica had begun to take school much more seriously and studying had become difficult for her when Jennifer spent much less time on her work.

- The family started talking more about their long-term plans, including college and career choices.
- Jennifer and Jessica were invited to discuss their parents' sexual orientation and to discuss their own sexual concerns.
- Sheila began to step out of her familiar position as the "pivot" in the family and communication began to flow directly between Maria and the girls.
- Over the December holidays, Patrick was invited for a week when he was brought up to date on current changes in his mother's life, given some time with Sheila and the girls, and invited to a session with Wally. He expressed some apprehensiveness at first, but was reassured when he found that he had a room in the "new house" and summer plans were going ahead as usual.

Wally's matter-of-fact style and evenhanded approach when talking about issues of money, sex, discipline, and household management remained consistent, but he began to work himself out of the couple's major discussions saying, "I think you can work this out without me." Approximately 6 months after they started, Sheila and Maria agreed that they had met their goals and wanted to stop counseling if they had the option of coming back. Wally agreed. He had not yet met Jennifer and Jessica, but their problems seemed to have disappeared.

Theory and Research

The central concept that distinguishes the Organizational perspective is the idea that human thoughts, emotions, and behavior are organized; they don't occur independently or randomly but instead are patterned in relation to social, temporal, and physical contexts. You may demonstrate

an organizational belief when deciding whether to go to the bank early in the morning: A time when few people are there, but these few may be depositing cash receipts from businesses, thus taking more time. You may think in an organizational way when invited to have pizza with a new acquaintance and his 4-year-old daughter. You don't know much about the daughter, but you know some things about 4-year-olds, so you decide against wearing a new white suit. Such understanding of social patterns is often implicit and unrecognized, except to the extent that some people are credited with "common sense."

In their attempts to understand how human relationships are organized, social scientists have proposed and tested a number of theories. We see in this chapter how these theories have been used in designing interventions for couples and families. First, we examine some organizational theories in their "pure" forms to see how they can help a counselor understand the complexity and interrelatedness of family processes.

Functionalism and the Structural Metaphor

As we have noted, the organizing metaphor of the late nineteenth and early twentieth centuries was physical science—physics, chemistry, geology, and biology. All phenomena were described using the new structural language. First in medicine, later in the social sciences, scholars followed the Cartesian approach of dividing a phenomenon into its essential parts and studying the parts. They also formed and tested hypotheses about how the parts fit together to determine their functions. At the beginning of the twentieth century, architect Louis Sullivan declared "form follows function" and that principle shaped the sociological theory of William Talcott Parsons (1951).

Family Functions
Applied to family life, this pattern of thinking—*functionalism*—popularized a view of social groups as made up of structural units referred to as *roles*. Role, for Parsons and other functionalists, had a special meaning—roles were sets of interlocking

expectations for behavior. Smooth and effective social functioning was assured so long as people performed their roles with commitment and skill. Individual and group problems in modern societies were understood as resulting from *role conflict* (situations where satisfying one set of role demands would cause an individual to violate another set) and *role ambiguity* (situations in which participants did not have a clear understanding of what was expected). This view had significant impact on individual as well as family intervention; counselors learned to help people recognize and negotiate the expectations they face at home, at work, and in their communities.

The functionalist tradition also asserted that roles had to be appropriate—the roles ensured that the social unit survived—and much of Parsons' work focused on the *essential functions* of human societies (see Table 5.1 for examples). Functionalist scholars of the mid-twentieth century believed that families had, in modern times, become overburdened because families were now performing functions that once had been performed by the larger community. This trend was predicted to continue because of family mobility. Either families were going to have to improve their ability to perform these functions—change their roles—or else society would have to organize new "mechanisms" to perform them.

Parsons and his colleagues divided family life into *instrumental* and *expressive* roles and made the now-controversial statement that society would function best if instrumental roles were performed by men and expressive roles were performed by women (Parsons & Bales, 1955). This set of assumptions became a central target for feminist challenges. Feminist family therapists (e.g., Hare-Mustin, 1978), following in the footsteps of scholars such as Margaret Mead (1935/2001), asserted that both women and men were limited if they were confined to the behavior appropriate for their group without consideration of their individuality and their circumstances.

Other, less controversial functionalist assumptions survived and continue to shape family counseling. Most people agree that any society needs its members, especially its most vulnerable members, to be fed, clothed against climatic extremes, sheltered, and protected from aggression. Most people would also agree that decisions must be made, reproduction must be assured, young people must be socialized, conflict must be managed, and sexuality must be incorporated in forms that serve the needs of the group and individuals. Either the family must have the capability and the willingness to meet these needs, or the functions have to be turned over to the larger group.

A counselor becomes a functionalist when he or she examines a couple or family to determine whether individual and family needs are being met. In contemporary family life, such an analysis often points to children's needs for nurturance, guidance, and supervision after school.

Conflict

Conflict management is one of many functions identified by family sociologists (Sprey, 1969, 1971). Peoples' different perceptions, understandings, and goals lead to situations in which agreement is difficult or impossible. According to

Table 5.1   **Functions of Families**

Group Needs	Related Activities
Survival of individuals	Protecting members from predators and enemies and the elements, caring for the sick and injured, hunting, gathering, producing, and/or distributing the essentials of life
Continuance of group	Reproducing, recruiting
Socialization of new members	Creating bonds, teaching essential knowledge, expectations, and skills
Order	Coordinating sexuality and other activities, enforcing rules
Meaning	Preserving and sharing stories, memories, traditions

Sprey (1971), "The family process *per se* is conceived of as a continuous confrontation between participants with conflicting though not necessarily opposing interests in their shared fate" (p. 722). Before Sprey, sociologist George Simmel (1955) said that conflict was not only inevitable, it contributed to the life of a group because without conflict—the disruption of ongoing patterns—no adaptive changes could occur. As Weingarten and Leas (1987) said more recently, "the very differences that interest two people in each other in the first place often become the forces that drive them apart. The ability to confront, to reconcile, and to accept differences must be developed for relationships to be arenas of growth rather than of stagnation or oppression" (p. 408).

This perspective, accepting and valuing conflict rather than opposing it, led to a science of conflict processes—studying effective and ineffective management of conflict. Morton Deutsch (1969) demonstrated that conflicts tend to follow self-maintaining patterns of either escalation—*destructive conflict*—or reduction—*productive conflict*. Research methods in this area differ, but the findings are consistent. Conflict processes vary according to expectations, perceptions of issues and resources, perceptions of self and other, and use of either competitive or cooperative tactics; the processes can be altered by a variety of interventions (Deutsch, 1973; Fisher & Brown, 1988; Fisher & Ury, 1981).

Much of the family counselor's work may be seen as focused on attitudes and expectations; when people approach a particular conflict with an expectation of solving the problem cooperatively, they are less likely to use aggressive tactics (see Box 5.1). Weingarten and Leas (1987) organized their view of couple conflict according to 5 levels of conflict. At lower levels, couples were seen as focused on an all-or-nothing view of their problems and sometimes seemed bent on eliminating each other; a counselor was seen as a rescuer, intruder, ally, or judge but both partners were convinced that one person would win and the other would lose. At the highest levels, partners actively sought a way to resolve the conflict in a positive manner (what Fisher & Ury, in *Getting to Yes*, 1981, called a "win-win" solution), and the counselor was seen as a consultant or advisor. At the lowest levels (they used the word "war"), Weingarten and Leas recommended working separately until a nonaggression pact could be

BOX 5.1

Ravich Train Game

Robert Ravich (1969) studied positive and negative management of conflict using a creative strategy that not only yielded meaningful data but also provided a dramatic illustration of negative conflict processes—therefore it offered potential for counseling couples. He positioned pairs of research subjects—including married couples—on opposite sides of a model railroad table. On that table, two trains ran on circular tracks that were joined in the middle (a figure-eight pattern). Each participant had control of one train. The instructions were simple—each participant earned points for completing the circle with his or her train, and points at the end of the exercise translated into rewards of some kind. There was one challenge: The partner's train could be blocking the shared part of the track at the time when it was needed. If people cooperated, both could maximize their scores.

In a remarkable percentage of cases, subjects in the Ravich (1969) research did not achieve the high scores that were theoretically possible because they lost track of their goals. Instead of trying to complete the circle, they adopted the goal of blocking each other. It appeared that the shift occurred as soon as a blockage occurred. Rather than interpret the other's actions as a simple error, participants tended to interpret them as intentional and hostile. They responded in kind, leading to reciprocal frustration and increasing hostility.

worked out. In between these extremes, partners could discuss conflicts in the presence of the counselor but they needed support, teaching, and restraining as they struggled over real and symbolic issues.

Zuk's (1988) approach to conflict processes was quite different, focused not on conflict and its resolution but rather on its aftermath. He identified four stages in a *conflict cycle:* (1) active dispute; (2) blaming; (3) shame, guilt, or denial; and (4) reparation, reconciliation, or retribution. What differentiated between successful families and families who were caught in ongoing patterns of distress was the blaming that led to shame and guilt, which might be resolved in the final stage. Bowen (2002) and Framo, Weber, and Levine (2003) contributed ideas about how blaming can be prevented or its effects can be weakened: They called for dialogue in which people increase their interpersonal understanding; accept shared/partial responsibility, when appropriate; and give up a search for right and wrong in favor of a connection.

Models of Healthy Family Structure and Function

Among the most popular descriptions of family needs is the circumplex model (Olson & Gorall, 2003). This theoretically derived model, which has been operationalized in a series of self-report and therapist rating scales for assessing particular families (described in this chapter), is represented in a visual image that portrays family units as varying on two structural dimensions that predict family functionality—flexibility and cohesion. Figure 5.2 shows how a hypothetical family might vary over time on these two dimensions. Note that extremes on either dimension are generally considered problematic, while variation in the midrange is normal and functional.

The circumplex model provides a way of depicting family level characteristics that make intuitive sense to many practitioners and families. In the popular culture, both flexibility and closeness are sometimes represented as if more is better. This visual model can challenge such understandings and facilitate conversations to create an agenda for intervention. According to this theoretical model, a moderately adaptable family is

one that shows some flexibility in response to changed procedures, rules, expectations, and interactions. A moderately cohesive family is one that shows some tendency to do things together, values each other's companionship, and depends on each other for emotional support. Extremely high and extremely low levels on either dimension are considered indicative of problems.

A second visual model that has been readily accepted by practitioners and clients, the Beavers/Timberlawn model (Beavers & Hampson, 2003) likewise represents family functioning as healthier to the extent that extremes are avoided. The diagram (Figure 5.3) shows optimal functioning toward the right side along with descriptive terms characterizing the ideal family in which connection and independence are balanced. Toward the left side, some families can be seen as dysfunctional because they are extremely *centrifugal*—losing their members through poor supervision or ejecting them by creating a hostile environment. Others are dysfunctional for the opposite reason (*centripetal*)—using control and emotional sabotage to prevent their members from leaving.

Development

The concept of development is a familiar metaphor. Whether the reference is to infants, athletic teams, diseases, or photography, the idea of development communicates that something changes over time and knowing what something looks like at one point in time doesn't predict what it will look like at another point.

In couples and families, many developmental processes can be readily observed. People are born and grow older, eventually dying; the life span generally includes periods of power and weakness; and the changes of one individual can enhance or destabilize the life of the group or various members. The family of a child who becomes a successful high school athlete is transformed into a combination training facility, booster club, and agent's office, while the family of a child with spina bifida is transformed into a nursing/rehabilitation facility. In addition, relationships develop; as they move toward commitment, partners get to know each other and

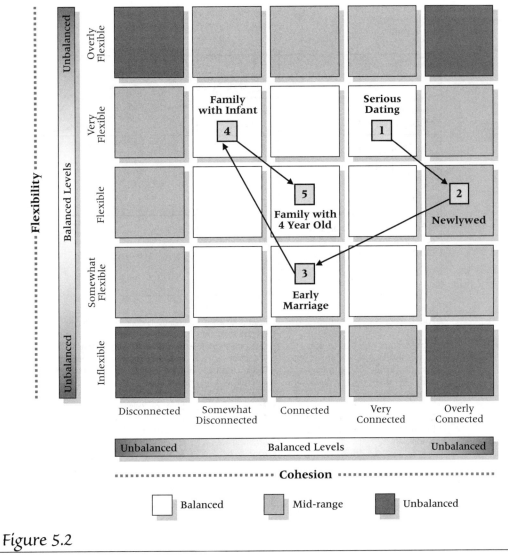

Figure 5.2

Circumplex Model

Source: From "Circumplex Model of Marital and Family Systems" (p. 525), by D. H. Olson and D. M. Gorall, in *Normal Family Processes,* third edition, F. Walsh (Ed.), 2003, New York: Guilford Press. Reprinted with permission.

accommodate each other's preferences and needs (Cate, Huston, & Nesselroade, 1986). Later-life families learn to keep family connections alive despite distance, economic and lifestyle differences, and political conflicts (Framo et al., 2003).

Duvall (1957), writing when the nuclear family was the norm, provided family scholars with a developmental framework organized around the assumption that every family went through a period of child rearing. According to her *developmental crisis* concept, family problems were often the result of a current or recent change in family organization such as birth, enrollment in school, or high school graduation. A

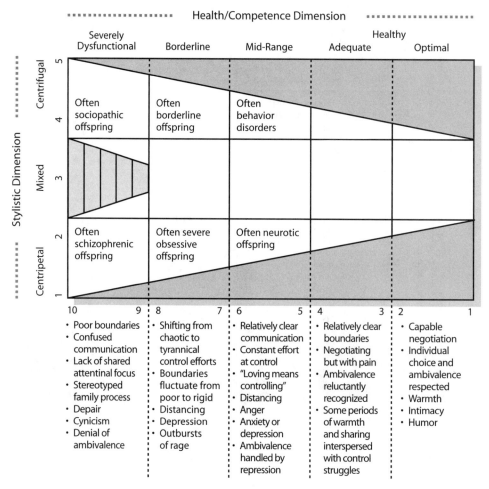

Figure 5.3

Beavers/Timberlawn Model

Source: From "Measuring Competence: The Beavers Systems Model" (pp. 549–580), by W. R. Beavers and R. B. Hampson, in *Normal Family Processes,* third edition, F. Walsh (Ed.), 2003, New York: Guilford Press. Reprinted with permission.

family needed to resolve the crisis of each developmental stage to successfully handle subsequent developmental challenges.

More recently, the developmental approach to family problems has more often been described in terms of the *family life cycle* model (Carter & McGoldrick, 2004; Combrinck-Graham, 1985; Gerson, 1995), based on Duvall's work but with a change in language. Families are

assumed to face *developmental tasks* rather than developmental crises. J. M. White (1991) has updated Duvall's original model to address diverse family forms and abandoned the attempt to predict stages. Families are portrayed in White's theory as experiencing distress during times of *transition* when one stage and its organizational patterns come to an end and a new stage calls for some kind of reorganization. Stages may be defined by changes in factors not mentioned in the family life cycle model, such as household composition, health status of one or more members, and employment and/or residence. One family might go through 11 or 12 stages in the time another spends in a stable period when nothing seems to be changing. Periods of dysfunction are normalized by this theory—families will become less effective between stages, but adaptive skills, awareness, commitment, and a period of adjustment will return them to effectiveness.

Adolescence, a Family Developmental Stage

The period of adolescence is a social phenomenon. It does not exist in some societies and its forms vary considerably across families, economic strata, and communities. Its beginning is defined, in some cases, by physical maturation—puberty is often associated with adolescence. But the social experience of adolescence is more about expectations than it is about physical reality. In many contemporary societies, the social experience of adolescence has gradually extended itself to begin well before puberty; 10-year-olds dress, talk, and behave as members of the adolescent peer group. And adolescence does not end, as Erik Erikson is alleged to have said, until one stops acting like an adolescent.[3] In the meantime, families are influenced by the presence of one or more members who are part of the adolescent culture—offering opportunities for sexual activity, gambling, and substance use.

Transitions into adolescence and, on the other end, from adolescence into early adulthood are family-level transitions. The young person and the family must renegotiate who they are with each other—renegotiate their identities (Box 5.2). They may change what they call each other, where and how they spend time together, and what they expect in terms of respect, affection, and involvement in decision making. These negotiations often involve conflicts and call upon the family to use effective conflict management strategies. In the majority of cases these negotiations take place without

significant disruption, challenging popular assumptions of adolescent turmoil and emotional distress.

Developmental Domains

Developmental change can be seen in many different domains or areas of activity; family developmental literature describes changes in careers (Moen, Kim, & Hofmeister, 2001), gender (Blume & Blume, 2003), sexual orientation (Morrow, 1999), school functioning (Wendt & Ellenwood, 1994), and family economics (Burggraf, 1997). Relationships have tremendous impact on their members' decisions, feelings, thoughts, and behavior. In some families, children are expected to provide physical and economic support for elders, which may conflict with other priorities. There are families and cultures in which heterosexuality is expected and acknowledging differences would be an offense—even if Uncle Jack appears to be in a committed relationship with another man. Some families expect children to learn relationship skills from school and television, while others teach them from the preschool years.

Development is not all about influences and expectations, as families also differ in their readiness, their ability, and their preparation to address issues such as school attendance or learning to drive. Driving, for the family with an adolescent, is a major turning point; Parents become less tied to the child, and the child becomes less dependent. Families may talk about this event for years in advance, as they seek to build knowledge and values consistent with safe and responsible driving—or they may depend on school and friends to provide this socialization. Sex is talked about in some families and in others is treated as if it doesn't exist. The same is true of alcohol and other drug use.

Development is also about accommodation and adaptation. Career fields change, and parents who expected their children to work at the local factory may lose that option when the factory closes. Gender options changed tremendously over the past 70 years, and a three-generation gathering may include family members who fit perfectly into their own generations but cannot comprehend each other's ways of *doing gender* (Blume & Blume, 2003; West & Zimmerman,

---

[3] In the contemporary United States and some other countries, adolescence is often followed by a new stage known as Emerging Adulthood (Arnett, 2004).

BOX 5.2

Renegotiating Family Identities during the Adolescent Years

Lamont was the ideal youngest child. In contrast with his older sisters, he was content to go shopping with his mother and grandmother and accompany them to church. Six feet tall at the age of 14, he was built like a man but still acted like a boy. Then he entered high school, and things changes.

The first sign of the change was that one day Lamont didn't come home at his usual time. Instead, he called to say that he had to work with classmates on a school project. He arrived at his grandmother's house late for dinner, ate quickly, and then went back to his friend's house. After a series of phone calls, he came home well after his old 9:00 school day curfew. The changes kept coming during the next few months—his clothes, his hair style, his language, his posture all began to conform to his new hip-hop image. "What happened to my little boy," his mother asked, and Lamont said, "He died of boredom."

Lamont wasn't the only one who was going to change. His sister who went to the same high school was instructed on how to dress and on where she was allowed to park her unfashionable car. Lamont asked about moving to a house with a basement so he could have a place to have friends over. Mom was lectured about smoking, and Grandma was ordered to stop being so "touchy-feely." Lamont even challenged Mom about her new boyfriend.

The family began to push back—Lamont had to keep his feet off the furniture, and he had to clean up his language when he was at home. He had to be respectful to his sister at school, and one of his new friends was declared off limits after some money disappeared from the house. When Lamont was eligible for driver's education, the balance of power temporarily shifted—to get his mother's signature, he had to bring his grades up and spend more time helping around the house.

Over the next few years, the negotiations continued. Each side had a stake in keeping the family together, and everybody made accommodations. Lamont's high school graduation and acceptance to college was a group achievement.

1987). Career changes, which have become increasingly common, often require higher education or training; therefore, many families find themselves changing their child care/parenting plans as well as their economic expectations. Working with couples and families, then, calls for specialized knowledge in many domains.

Events

A developmental look at couples and families notes the pivotal times when relationships are transformed. The transition to parenthood is one of those points. Alice Rossi (1968), in a family sociology classic, explained why this change is so significant for parents in the United States and other industrialized societies. Rossi observed that the role of parent seems to be mandated—it is ex-

pected that everyone will assume it, and rejecting the role attracts attention. Many people do not assume the role voluntarily—the timing, if not the choice to become a parent at all, is not intentional. And then this new role is irrevocable—it is very hard to back out of being a parent and no change in legal status eliminates the knowledge of the child's existence. But most of all, parents in this culture are not prepared for the task. Most new parents have had little contact with children (even fewer have had prior experience with newborn babies); the transition is sudden, and there are few guidelines. Rossi's analysis still seems relevant after 35 years.

Every phase of children's lives then has its own quality, and parents can find their lives changing dramatically with events such as the entrance into school (including preschool), the movement into high school, and the launching of young adults into independent living status. (The last is not so much an event as a series of events. See Johnson & Wilkinson, 1995.) The family's relationship to the world changes—more involved with others when the child enters school, involved with a powerful and sometimes frightening peer group in high school, and left in isolation as the child learns to survive without parental interference. A case example shows the intensity of one of these changes:

> *Bob and Sue Levin were clearly upset when they called for the counseling appointment. Their 3-year-old daughter Shayna had been playing at a neighbor's house when she was approached by a 5-year-old boy who exposed his erect penis and tried to initiate sex play. She didn't tell her parents right away, but after a few sleepless nights she told them she was confused and afraid. The neighbors, asked about the incident, viewed it as a harmless instance of sexual curiosity, but the Levins were afraid that Shayna was the target of a predator. They were not only fearful, they felt guilty; financial pressures and career demands had led them to work at home and not provide the kind of supervision needed by a young child.*
>
> *The counselor did not work directly with Shayna; instead, in 5 sessions she and the parents developed and implemented a plan for home intervention. They reviewed parenting expectations and set up new procedures to guarantee that Shayna was properly supervised. The parents also involved Shayna in designing and building a "dream chaser" that would keep bad dreams away, and the plan worked. Shayna slept better. It also seemed that the project helped Bob and Sue as much as it helped Shayna; the three of them were now a bit older and wiser, they knew that the world was not entirely safe, but they saw that the incident represented a triumph of their family. They had been tested, and they had stuck together.*

Adulthood offers family developmental challenges independent of child rearing. Sibling relationships are hard to maintain, no matter how close brothers and sisters may have been in childhood and adolescence (Schulman, 1999), and those relationships are threatened when a new person is brought into the family as a partner or spouse. Not only does this new family member (formally recognized or not) change interactions with his or her presence—making jokes, complaining about health problems, talking about topics that don't fit the family pattern—he or she eventually contributes to identity changes in the sibling. Weddings, from the family counselor's perspective, can serve an important role by marking this change in relationships and helping to build linkages between the new and the old relationship systems.

Retirement is another pivotal event and status change. Many people are surprised by the realities of retirement, even if they have given considerable attention to planning. For retirees in couple or family relationships, new realities create conflict with routines that have been stable for decades. And there are symbolic as well as practical aspects to the change. Not only does the new retiree have to deal with lost relationships, unstructured time, and an ambiguous status, retirement is one of the closing chapters in a life story. Physical and mental effects of aging add their own complications (Van Amberg, Barber, & Zimmerman, 1996).

The counselor who wants to help families through such events needs to be extremely sensitive to developmental processes and the uniqueness of each situation—abilities, vulnerabilities, social support, potentials for coping as well as potentials for cognitive error, misjudgment, and feelings of rejection and failure. As Jencius and Rotter (1998) found in a study of bedtime rituals, effective parenting solutions have much in common because of the developmental context but they are all different because of the special qualities of a family.

Processes

However, development is not just major events and crises. Developmental scholars have described change processes that alter what people need from each other and what they have to offer. Some changes are biological in nature; the growth and development of the human body—brain tissue, muscle, organs, and bone—is well documented. Biological change brings changes in relationships. For example, child relationship patterns for some divorced mothers change when physical discipline and dominance will not work for a 110-pound mother and adolescents who tower over her. Later in the life span, parent-child relationships often are defined by the declining physical capacity of the parent and the need for the adult child to become a caregiver.

Other changes are more *psychosocial*, borrowing a term from Erik Erikson (1964), with both internal and external components. Couple relationships go through exploratory times, when people are getting to know each other, and as they approach commitment they often show shifting priorities. Families and friends may be distressed by this process, feeling that they are being pushed out by the new love interest. Another psychosocial shift is observed when families include children who are going through the years of middle childhood and adolescence. They often discover that their time together is becoming fragmented

because of outside demands, and the family has to become more intentional about finding opportunities to be together. Stepfamilies often face both of these developmental processes at the same time, presenting some special challenges (see Box 5.3). A developmentally sophisticated family counselor can help to normalize people's relational experiences as well as contribute to their effective responding.

Even a family's financial life can be seen as a process. Over time, it is typical for adults to struggle financially in their twenties and thirties; they typically are facing educational expenses and a need to equip themselves with the material goods that are expected in their peer group—clothing, furniture, recreational and entertainment equipment, tools, and so on. The financial challenges of young adulthood are increased if they become parents. Prenatal care and childbirth, pediatric care, clothing for a growing child, toys, education, and other costs can be extremely stressful. As shown in Figure 5.4, a nuclear family household can be seen as starting with low levels of resources and high levels of financial demands.

BOX 5.3

Stepfamilies

One of the most dramatic changes in U.S. society in the past few decades has involved rapid growth in the number of stepfamilies. With a high divorce rate and greater public acceptance of divorced individuals, half of all U.S. marriages are remarriages for one or both partners. Many of these people are parents, and stepfamilies are now the most common form of household in this country.

Every marriage brings together people who might otherwise not have chosen to be related to each other—the in-laws. But the stepfamily is particularly intense in this regard because the in-laws are going to be intimately involved in each other's lives. Resources are often stretched, and

stepsiblings may end up sharing rooms or wearing each other's hand-me-down clothes. Older stepsiblings often become caregivers for younger ones, and stepsiblings of the same age often feel that they are in competition for attention and approval. Most "blended families" learn to live together, but others struggle for years. Scholars who have studied the stepfamily phenomenon (e.g., Whiteside, 1989) say that much of the problem results from applying nuclear family standards of cohesiveness. The stepfamily may be a special kind of group that functions best when some members are allowed to remain somewhat distant from each other.

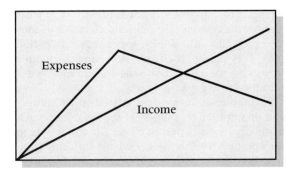

Figure 5.4

Family Finance Graph

In the Nuclear Family pattern, the typical American adult begins earning money when expenses are low. Creating an independent household requires spending at levels that exceed income, creating debt.
Eventually many people achieve a status in which income rises and expenses decline, producing wealth.

Over time, the discrepancy between income and demands generally reverses itself as adults become more adept in their areas of business or craft or they are promoted in their jobs and increase their earnings, while children gradually move away from financial dependence on their parents. Many couples in their fifties and sixties face the opposite of the situation they faced in their younger years.

Communication, Systems, and Structures

I observed earlier in this chapter that nineteenth century scientists typically described human lives using mechanical metaphors. This tradition was partially replaced, in the twentieth century, with electronic metaphors (encoding, overload) and metaphors derived from the emerging sciences of systems analysis (feedback, homeostasis) and communications. These models for understanding relationships overlap tremendously, as they share an image of invisible and powerful connections that have some scientifically verifiable existence. Gregory Bateson (1951) performed a key role in the application of these new metaphors for human

life, contributing his anthropological perspective and participating in interdisciplinary conferences where human problems were linked with emerging science.

Communication

The communication focus in couple and family counseling has deep roots in efforts to help couples and families in planning and problem solving, but the Bateson project (see Chapter 2) was pivotal in expanding the definition of communication. Studying families of schizophrenics, Bateson and his Palo Alto research team concluded that these families showed patterns of communication such as the *double bind* that were disabling one or more family members: denying their realities, limiting their choices without admitting the manipulation, and keeping them unsure about their relationships. Working with relational communication, as the Palo Alto group viewed it, was a life-or-death struggle to break patterns that were subtle and resistant to change.

It should not be surprising that theories of human systems have focused on communication processes, as communication seems to define humanness (Maturana & Varela, 1992; Turner, 2000). But the concept of communication is broad; engineers use communications language to describe systems that are purely mechanical as well. Within this broader perspective, communication has to do with any transmission of information; a bathroom scale can be said to communicate by pointing to a number. Computers communicate through streams of digital code, cats and dogs communicate using their ears and tails, and people communicate through a multitude of behaviors that carry meaning. Communication is not dependent on words; instead, words are merely a tool that provides some degree of efficiency and specificity, and the alternative of using sign language has become extremely sophisticated and powerful since its introduction over 200 years ago in France.

As Turner (2000) interprets evolutionary evidence, human sensory and neurological systems are particularly attuned to visual and tactile information about emotional state. This sensitivity to nonverbal information complicates human communication when words are transmitting one message and a contradictory message is being sent through vocal tone and timing, posture, gesture, and facial expression. People who are adept in fields that depend on interpersonal communication—sales, management, drama, and counseling—display exceptional abilities to work with nonverbal signals of agreement and disagreement, pleasure and distress, or connectedness and alienation. These communication skills are often learned and used without any active awareness.

Power and Influence.   Bateson (1972) suggested that there was a second message that lay "behind" any overt message that two humans exchanged—a message about their relationship. For example, a simple request such as "May I please have a drink of water?" communicated that the other person could deny the request and therefore defined the speaker as dependent. This focus on hierarchy in relationships, Bateson said, is shared by all mammals. The relationship information essentially constitutes an unacknowledged *analog* or *command* message that accompanies the *digital* or *report* message that is the apparent content of an interaction. Over thousands of years, humans have created cultural symbols to communicate subtle messages about relationships through clothing and other bodily adornments, size and arrangement of living spaces, and number and types of possessions. When a woman announces that she is afraid of her husband's anger, she may be responding to nonverbal and symbolic messages. His scowling expression, along with his hunting boots, deer trophies, and gun cabinet, offset any reassuring statements he may make about his peaceful intentions.

I mentioned that there is often an implied request or demand in messages (what Bateson called the command level). When a request or demand is presented in a clear way that accepts the other as a decision maker, the request may be rejected and the person who openly asked might feel foolish or helpless. Therefore, many people disguise their requests or present them in ways that create some pressure (e.g., "I am going to pass out if someone doesn't get me a drink.") While such communication often results in com-

pliance, the long-term result is often loss of trust and resistance to future requests. Families of adolescents and young adults, for example, may find that they have used physical and economic threats so often that the younger generation is determined to escape the family.

Many relationships suffer from such indirect and manipulative influence (power), but such patterns are also perceived in situations where they do not exist. A partner who is suffering from migraines or hearing loss can be accused of using the physical problem to avoid responsibilities. Analyzing a family's communication patterns is easier if people get opportunities, in the presence of the counselor, to display their familiar ways of interacting.

Nonverbal Communication.   Nonverbal communication is extremely powerful—according to Turner (2000), the human emotional system enables groups to coordinate their actions through silent and instantaneous signals. But many people are not very sensitive to either their own nonverbal messages or those of others. In the days of the Bateson project and studies of Don Jackson's therapy sessions with families, technology was limited; the only option was film with intense, unnatural lights. Videotape soon followed, and researchers joined pioneers Birdwhistell (1952) and Scheflen (1978) in using microanalytic techniques. These researchers showed that subtle changes in individual posture and facial expression were linked in the interactions of multiple participants. More recently, scholars have examined interactions of heterosexual couples (Gottman, 1994) and parents with infants (Fivaz-Depeursinge, 1991). This research has demonstrated that human nonverbal behavior is related to feelings and moods, desires and reactions, and that people can become more effective at attending to each other's nonverbal communications.

Culture and Gender in Communication.   Returning to the verbal realm, differences in communication style and content have been studied widely using multiple methods. Conversation analysis techniques have demonstrated that members of some cultures—and men in general—are more likely to engage in a style of *turn-taking* that includes multiple interruptions, finishing another person's sentences, *overtalking*, and raising the voice to gain entry into the flow of discussion. In contrast, other groups display more open negotiation of turn-taking or less obviously assertive ways of having one's viewpoint expressed. These communication habits work well when all discussants are operating by the same rules, but they conflict in many couples and families (e.g., see Tannen, 1985, 1991).

Other researchers have noted the tendency for women in Western cultures to be more emotionally expressive than men—a difference that does not seem to reflect a lesser degree of emotionality in men (Gottman, 1994; Kiecolt-Glaser, 1999). There are also cultural differences in nonverbal communication—interpersonal distance and eye contact, which interfere with relationships.

The communication perspective links emotional and behavioral symptoms to communication flaws, and the couple and family counselor is directed to perform a communication analysis. Because so much of communication happens outside awareness, it is assumed that clients cannot sort through what they are saying and doing without help. The following are some common communication problems that are observed in relationships.

Communication Flaws.   Many people suffer from poor communication because they are unaware that they are not saying what they thought they were saying—or the listener is hearing the words in a way that the speaker could not have anticipated. People are communicating, but their intended messages are somehow lost in the process. A man intends to express appreciation and love to his partner, but the partner reports, "He never appreciates what I do for him and he takes me for granted." A child complains that his mother is critical and demanding but his mother asks, "I don't know what's wrong with Jaime, I tell him constantly how good he looks, how polite he is, what a good job he does taking care of his little sister, how can he think I'm critical of him?"

One way of understanding these mismatches is a *sender-receiver model of communication.* This model grew out of the telegraph as a communication technology, a process that imposed a one-way flow of information and independence between sender and receiver. The sender, in this model, is assumed to have an internalized message unit that is waiting to be sent, and the receiver is assumed to have little or no idea what that message consists of. The sender *encodes* the message in some verbal or nonverbal form and sends the encoded message. The receiver does not have direct access to the pure message but instead receives it in its coded form and attempts to decode its meaning. Every receiver applies decoding rules learned throughout a lifetime of experiences. A member of a large family might have learned, for example, "When people tell you about someone else's criticism of you, it's really a sneaky way of criticizing."

The sender-receiver model has been effective in researching and working with many kinds of communication problems. Researchers have studied both naturally occurring and experimentally manipulated errors, showing how much confusion can result from words being used in different ways or words and gestures being interpreted differently. Counselors can train family members in *active listening* to gradually bring partners or family members closer together in their expectations and interpretations. Just as it does in the hands of a person-centered counselor, the technique of active listening increases communication accuracy because the listener continuously feeds back and confirms the messages that he or she has heard.

Indirect Communication.   Other authors (e.g., Epstein, Ryan, Bishop, Miller, & Keitner, 2003) have examined the idea that people somehow hide messages in a metaphoric or indirect form that protects the communicator from rejection if they go undetected. This idea is not new—it can be found in Freud's work—but Freud was less concerned with the process and more concerned with the content of the hidden message. If such a process takes place, it stands to reason that it would be most likely to occur with messages that have a high level of importance. Such messages might address sensitive topics such as "how I feel about Mom's new boyfriend," "I'm gay," or "I am afraid the dog died because I left her out for two hours on that hot day last week."

Indirect communication is not as easily described using the sender-receiver model. A better model for this work is based on the idea that communicators are co-creators of meaning. Maybe there isn't a clear message at all—just a range of possible messages. Rather than seek the correct answer people would need to explore all the possible meanings. From this perspective, a child who gets sick the day her mother goes into the hospital could be invited into a conversation with the question, "How could we interpret this?" and family members could speak about its meaning for them.

Double Binds.   Many times communication is deceptive or hard to decipher because the miscommunication involves an internal contradiction. A parent who says, "I want you to take school seriously," and who then expresses contempt for teachers, is creating a double bind; the child will offend the parent's expressed values if she obeys the direct request. Likewise the parent's instruction to the daughter to "be more independent" would create a double bind; if she performed an "independent" act it would be a violation of the instruction, because she did not do it independently. Bateson and his colleagues believed that double binds often serve an individual or relationship function—in this example, the child is likely to fail in school (and thereby remain dependent on the parent), but the open show of concern protects the parent from being blamed. In such cases, there is an unspoken rule against acknowledging the contradiction.

Frames and Punctuation.   People's communication problems often result from interpretive messages that are appended to their factual statements. If a wife merely reports that her husband slammed the door as they were leaving for a family trip, he might agree. His response could be different, however, if she presented the same information this way: "Harry is always so anxious about being late. One of the kids broke a shoelace while getting ready, and that put Harry into such a bad mood that he slammed the door as we were leav-

ing." The *frame* being presented is one of anxiety; the slamming of the door is interpreted as proof of Harry's emotional problem. Yet another frame might have used the same incident as proof that Harry was angry at his wife, that he was drunk, or that he was a careless person who didn't notice when he slammed doors. The incident was *punctuated* by starting with the broken shoelace, thereby supporting the frame. If the sequence had been extended to include prior events, it might have proved a better fit with a different interpretation. Harry might have broken a tooth at lunch that day, he might have heard the night before that his mother was dying, or he might have found out in the prior week that his employer was planning to lay off 40% of the people in his division.

Sex as Communication.   One of the most powerful arenas of nonverbal communication for many couples is their sexual relationship. Partners who are attentive and sensitive send strong messages of caring and validation by remembering each other's sensitivities and preferences; over time, such sexual communication can make the sexual bond one of the most reliable ways of achieving feelings of closeness. Conversely, a partner who consistently rejects the other's requests, or who repeatedly proposes an activity the other has disliked, can seem to be communicating unconcern or even hostility.

Systemic Models

The term *systems,* as used in common speech, has moved far beyond the limited and specific usage anticipated by von Bertalanffy and his colleagues in the Society for General System Research (see von Bertalanffy, 1975, for a review). Von Bertalanffy's revolutionary idea—that the world is organized into systems that must be understood in their own terms, not in terms of their parts—has become generally accepted. The vocabulary of systems theory has come into common usage, especially in the social, behavioral, and medical sciences, and the term "system" has begun to mean that it is hopeless to try to figure anything out since everything is interconnected. The "system" label seems to have given many people permission to abandon theory. However, even such general use of the system concept has proved useful.

For example, Satir's (1964/1967) approach to families was not an elaborate system model, but it was probably the one that was best known in the early 1970s. Satir believed in complex interactions, but she worked by focusing on specifics—particularly on family roles. She observed that family roles were reciprocal and interconnected and it was very difficult for a person to alter his or her roles without reciprocal changes from others. She taught clients to recognize and break free of four rigid communication roles (Box 2.4) that became destructive over time: placating, blaming, computing, and distracting (Satir, 1972). These four were contrasted with leveling, a more flexible style that demanded emotional integrity. Her student Sharon Wegscheider (1981) popularized a systemic role analysis of the alcoholic family, identifying the danger of fixed and self-destructive

BOX 5.4

Young Single Mother Families

The rates of adolescent pregnancy and parenthood in the United States have declined dramatically (Ventura, 2003) but continue to be higher than in many other countries. The ages and circumstances of young single mothers vary widely. The youngest, 11 or 12 years old, are clearly unable to support themselves and may have limited ability to provide appropriate parenting to a child. A 17-year-old new mother may have the ability to find work and may be competent as a caregiver—but the arrival of a child will have profound implications for her relationships and her career plans. Some young mothers are, as popular images would suggest, girls and women (both urban and rural) whose educational and career options seem limited because of their poor achievement record and an apparent lack of community or family support. Others have been planning to attend college and graduate school. Some are in transient relationships; others have been dating the same partner for several years. Some are repeating a family legacy with generations of history; they may have grandmothers only 25 or 30 years their senior. Others are only children of 50-year-old mothers who are professors, counselors, or business owners.

In many cases, the young mother turns over direct care of her infant to her mother; this is especially common in cultures where family relationships are considered more important than achievement and status. The grandmother may have limited financial resources or a demanding career, but she has a proven record as a caregiver, and she doesn't want to see her daughter drop out of school. When the new mother is ready to take full responsibility, often when the child is 4 or 5 years old, all parties expect that she can step into the full-time role of mother. In the meantime, she will have a limited role in her child's life. For the child, growing up with Grandma is a wonderful experience.

The situation seems ideal, except for two main kinds of problems. First, grandparents who are primary caregivers often report that they feel overwhelmed. Some have other responsibilities such as caring for aging parents, they may have medical conditions that limit their physical activity, they may find it necessary to defer life plans such as retirement or even marriage, and they may find that they are no longer welcome visiting their peers, whose homes are not child-proofed. But there is a second, more organizational problem that may arise when the young mother tries to step into the parenting role. She is not very convincing in this role and continues to be pushed aside as Grandma and the child(ren) continue their close involvement. Family counseling at this time may help the family to transform itself.

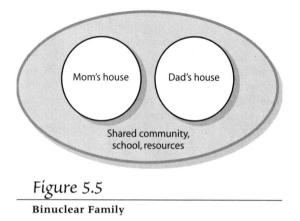

Figure 5.5

Binuclear Family

patterns that replicated themselves generation after generation. In both of these formulations, it is the system—not the individual—that must eventually change, even though a single client might carry much of the responsibility.

More recently, the use of the family system metaphor is illustrated in Constance Ahrons' descriptions of the interconnectedness of two post-divorce households. Ahrons (1994) used the metaphor of the *binuclear family system* (Figure 5.5) to convince divorced parents that their decisions, their lifestyles, and their relationships had real and significant impact on each other. Ahrons' creative use of systems language is interesting because it demonstrates that these words do not draw attention anymore and journal articles rarely debate the validity of a systemic perspective.

Even though these two examples were rather simple, systems theory has contributed an elaborated set of terms and concepts that continue to be used by counselors who view relationships systemically.[4] Simon (1995) cautions against too great a reliance on these concepts, however; they should be used to enhance one's perceptual awareness, but they have a potential to restrict it instead. The reality of a couple or family is always more complex than any set of abstract concepts can capture.

---

[4] Scott Johnson's (1993) structural analysis of Kafka's *The Metamorphosis* is an entertaining way to see some of these concepts applied.

Wholeness.   This is probably the single most universal systems concept—a system can be understood only by considering it as a whole. For the family counselor, this means that one will get a partial view by interviewing a family while one member is in the hospital or out of town. The concept of *emergence,* a related term, predicts that new characteristics emerge once an object/organism is functioning in its systemic context. A new system will come into existence when a family moves from one neighborhood to another.

Subsystems and System Levels.   Newcomers to systems concepts often ask, "How do you know you are observing all the pieces of the system?" The answer is, you always *are* observing all the pieces of a system, but the one you are observing (including an individual client) is always a part of larger systems and therefore its functioning may be altered when viewed in a larger context.

Families are made up of multiple *subsystems,* they are part of larger systems as well, and the systems overlap. In a large family, the males may operate as a subsystem, couples may operate as subsystems, and the over-50 members may operate as a subsystem (see Figure 5.6). When nested

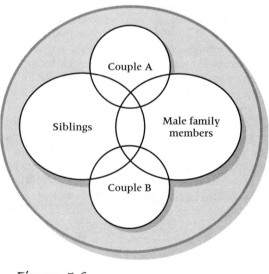

Figure 5.6

Systems and Subsystems

systems are described, the term *system levels* refers to more-inclusive or less-inclusive systems.

Boundaries. Systems and subsystems exchange information, goods, and energy (and, in human systems, emotions). Like the wall of a living cell, the *boundary* is the surface—metaphorical, not physical—where these exchanges take place. In a nuclear family, the walls, doors, and windows of the home are parts of the boundary, but there may be other critical elements as well—telephones and computers are key points of exchange.

Open and Closed Systems. Boundaries tend to be more or less open to the outside, but most experts agree that living systems are *open systems* and attempts to totally close their boundaries will result in *entropy*—a gradual loss of energy as a system dies from not being renewed.

Recalling the earlier discussion of family development, one of the ways in which families seem to change over time—with the addition and departure of members, along with children's growth from infancy into adulthood—is that family boundaries have to be more open or closed at different times. When young adults are seeking to find long-term partners, a family's boundary may open to a wide range of lifestyles, languages, cultures, and religions. Ten years earlier, the same family might have worked to achieve the opposite goal, trying to keep their sons and daughters away from people who would introduce them to new ideas, new behaviors, and new expectations.

Boundaries are not all external; internal boundaries of families are another major concern for the couple and family counselor. Interpersonal and subsystem boundaries can be so weak that family members become *enmeshed*—unable to separate their thoughts, experiences, and feelings. Even among siblings, boundaries can be too open; sibling and stepsibling incest are far more common than many people recognize.

Generational Boundaries. Most family counselors agree that children and adolescents benefit from having clearly delineated boundaries between generations. When adults do not fulfill their responsibility of being in charge, according to this

formulation, *parentified* children are likely to sacrifice their preparation for future responsibilities to protect younger or weaker siblings. This view is not universal, however; many cultures encourage exceptions to this rule. An oldest male child in a Latino family, for example, may be expected to socialize with other "men" and give orders to his siblings.

System Goals, Equifinality, and the Homeostasis Debate. Moving from the structure of a system to its functioning, systems theory asserts that every system has *goals* that determine its organization and its performance. Some organisms seem to be primarily committed to their own survival, but the drone honeybee is a clear exception—his survival is secondary to defending and nurturing the queen bee. In the human body, similarly, we might say that the liver's goal is to block toxins—even if its tissues are killed in the process—in service of a larger system goal. When a subsystem—a nuclear family, for instance—performs in ways that don't make sense, considering different system levels may be helpful. In many traditional cultures, for example, younger siblings are expected to sacrifice themselves and their children to ensure the success of their older siblings.

Systems theory further asserts that (1) a system will seek to achieve its goals by modifying various aspects of its organization and performance (*homeostasis*), and (2) systems typically have multiple ways to pursue the same goal (*equifinality*). In biological systems, these principles can be observed as, for example, the regular administration of a stimulant drug leads to compensatory responses in the nervous system that overcome the stimulation and return functioning to its preferred levels. The multiple compensatory mechanisms include physical alteration of the cell walls, changing their sensitivity to chemical stimulation, production of antagonistic chemicals that block stimulation, and production of other chemicals that elicit opposing responses.

In families, it has been alleged that problems come into existence because systems do not want to alter their organization and the symptoms somehow divert energy away from real change. A conflicted couple, fearful of divorce, might find it easier to stay together if one of them becomes depressed. Children's school problems and medical problems have often been cited as apparent homeostatic mechanisms, averting divorce by bringing parents together in a coalition united against a common enemy. Price (1988) accused the mental health field of stabilizing dysfunctional families by focusing on a child's symptoms but overlooking the underlying processes.

The assumption of homeostasis, applied to the functioning of couples and families, has been intensely debated. If a counselor (or teacher, judge, nutritionist, etc.) expects the relationship system to resist change, the professional may approach the couple or family in an adversarial manner. Many of the earliest systems-influenced family therapies were characterized by techniques that sought to disable the homeostatic "mechanism." Since the concept came under attack in the early 1980s (Dell, 1982a), most family counselors seem to reject homeostasis as an idea that produced more problems than it solved.

Change and Stability.   Change is generally the goal of people who seek counseling for themselves or others. That goal is ambiguous, though, because there seem to be two kinds of change in systems. *First-order change* is a transitory and adaptive response that allows a system to continue operating without its goals being challenged. The adaptive responses in the human nervous system, in the aforementioned example, were first-order changes. The nervous system did not modify its preferred settings, rather it tried to restore them. But family therapy researchers Watzlawick et al. (1967) identified another possibility: *second-order change,* which altered the goals of the system and made it hard to return to old patterns. A family that keeps trying new strategies to keep its children innocent and protect them from sexual material on television, even when they are in high school, may be demonstrating first-order change. When they conclude that their children are surrounded by sexual messages and they offer to talk to their high school students about those messages, they are demonstrating second-order change.

Change also is not universally desired. Resistance to change can be adaptive, as Peter Steinglass and his colleagues (Steinglass, Bennett, Wolin, & Reiss, 1987) demonstrated in their study of families who refused to adapt to alcoholism. Keeney (1982) was among the first voices in the family therapy field to emphasize that intervention should have the dual goals of stability *and* change. There is such a thing as a necessary amount of stability. Even if marital interactions and responsibilities are being renegotiated, someone still has to get up in the morning and drive children to school or let the dogs out.

Rules.   Watzlawick et al. (1967) used the mathematical term *rules* to describe the unspoken and sometimes unrecognized expectations that are built into a relationship system. A rule may demand that disagreements between adults be resolved without hitting or it may characterize people as losers and weaklings if they give up without a fight. Often, the rules that are most relevant in counseling can only be inferred. A rule against success, for example, might be inferred if several family members reject academic and economic opportunities; more successful members are excluded or criticized, and children are encouraged to plan for a future in which they are marginalized, unappreciated, and impoverished.

Elements, Sequences, and Patterns.   Inside a system, the interacting parts—referred to as *elements*—tend to repeat certain *sequences*. It is these *patterns* of interaction that make the system function in a relatively predictable way. Imagine that a counselor asks a question to one partner, that partner starts to respond, and the other partner immediately changes the subject. This sequence might occur from time to time in any relationship, but if it happens three times in 15 minutes it's a pattern. Family counselors seek to identify and change negative patterns, replacing destructive or ineffective sequences to free the family from their problems.

Sequences help to understand a relationship system and also help with making change. A trained couple and family counselor will notice that, for example, children in the Stuart family look at their mother for approval before answering the counselor's questions. Respecting these sequences is essential when the professional is trying to gain access and credibility. The counselor who encourages the Stuart children to "ask your Mom if you can talk now" may get a second opportunity to meet with the family, while one who ignores this sequence may wonder why the family did not come back. The details of relationship sequences are especially important in planning and implementing change.

Feedback Loops and Circularity.   System rules operate through *feedback loops*—the system senses or monitors the extent to which expectations are met and goals are achieved. A jealous partner may check cell phone memories, or a parent may watch the leftovers on dinner plates to monitor a daughter's eating patterns. The system alters its performance depending on the feedback. When an ex-husband's telephone number appears on a bill it may activate a new husband's worry/investigate/discover/withdraw sequence. His withdrawal activates the new wife's corresponding loneliness/anger/punishment sequence, and more telephone calls occur. These interlocking sequences demonstrate the principle of *circularity;* rather than having clear causes and effects, relationship patterns typically are organized so that any event may be seen as either a cause or an effect.

Hierarchy.   As systems are nested inside each other, there is an implied hierarchy of needs and resources; the lower-level system depends on the survival of the higher-level system (e.g., a family of bats depends on the environment to keep providing insects for food). Disturbing the hierarchy and giving priority to a subsystem can destroy the larger system; therefore, many family counselors have emphasized the need to preserve the privileges and authority of parents. Such a stance must be carefully examined in families where there is indication of parents abusing power. Likewise, it may not fit with families in which a rigid hierarchy is preventing adolescents from moving appropriately into young adulthood.

Triangles.   Another enduring systems concept is the idea that relationship *triangles*—subsystems involving three individuals or two individuals and some inanimate third entity such as work, alcohol (refer back to Figure 2.2 in Chapter 2), or politics—are potentially troublesome (see Bowen, 1978; Haley, 1976; Minuchin, 1974). Bowen has the most complete explanation of the phenomenon; he said that a two-person relationship is unstable because of emotionality and conflict. The tension is reduced by routing some of the emotion into a third person, a pet, or an inanimate object. Problems arise as one side of a triangle becomes progressively stronger and the others shift from positive to negative. The concept is quite teachable—when training programs use exercises to help new family counselors to think in triangles, their students report that they quickly begin to perceive triangles in their relationship systems at home, work, and school.

There are several developmental transitions when triangles are especially problematic. Pregnancy and childbirth often challenge family relationships: The new mother reports feeling as if she and the baby are tightly bonded and no one else understands them, and these feelings are intensified if others respond with criticism, rejection, or ridicule. But such feelings are likely for any primary caretaker of the infant. When a parent is too young to take full responsibility, mother and grandmother may take turns feeling like the outsider in the triangle (see Box 5.4). Stepfamilies are also especially prone to a triangling process as the new couple finds their primary relationship tested by children and adolescents who complain of lost attention and unfair and unequal treatment.

Coalitions.   Triangles are just one form of *coalition*, and a coalition is just an informal subsystem. Coalitions are not inherently positive or negative, they are omnipresent and they can work either for or against larger family goals. The presence of coalitions is significant for the family counselor because they affect the power dynamics in a family.

Coalitions are generally problematic to the extent that they remain hidden. A parental coalition is generally viewed as a positive family characteristic; parents (or a single parent and another parent figure) are expected to provide emotional support to each other as well as make decisions together. Alternatively, cross-generational coalitions are identified as a structural variation that may create problems: A grandparent can align with a group of children, for example, to share information and to join in plans to manipulate the parent(s). The coalition has access to information at multiple levels, and its members have multiple routes to influence decision processes. As a result, parental power is nullified and—in extreme cases—family decisions can end up in the hands of a 7-year-old.

Complementary and Symmetrical Systems

Bateson identified two opposing tendencies in social systems, each of which could result in an eventual breakdown of the system. Bateson did not suggest that these two tendencies could or should be eliminated from social groupings; instead, he cautioned against allowing either to become a rigid pattern. Allowed to coexist, the two patterns balance each other effectively.

In the *complementary* pattern, individuals or groups interacted in such a way that an increase in one party's aggression, emotional expression, or illness was met by the opposite response from the other party. This organization is often seen in long-term couple relationships. One person has become louder over time and the other has become quieter over time; one's physical fitness has improved as the other has become fatter. This solution often works for quite a while, as it minimizes competition and one party counterbalances the other's extremes. But the process, according to Bateson, has no built-in limits. Not only can it result in both sides experiencing negative consequences of escalating behavior, but it also results in increasing discomfort and alienation leading to dissolution of the system.

The alternative pattern is no less problematic. In a symmetrical system, one party's behavior is matched by the other's: Insults are traded for insults, inattention is met with inattention, and violence is met with violence. That also means that achievement is met with achievement, and many times symmetrical families are extremely high

functioning as a result. Competition to be the more rejecting, selfish, and adulterous member of a couple would of course lead to an end of a relationship. Other kinds of escalation can also create so much pressure that the system doesn't survive. I once interviewed a couple whose symmetrical relationship had become so dysfunctional that they argued intensely about which one of them was loved more by the family dog.

Cybernetics

As a parallel scholarly movement when general systems theory was being developed, cybernetics was less readily understood. The basic idea of systems—wholeness—and the language of systems theory were readily understood by most people. Cybernetics, alternatively, was a relatively obscure term and its implications were not as immediately obvious.

Cybernetics is the science of *control systems*, originally developed for electronic and mechanical applications. The metaphor that is generally used in explaining what is now called "simple cybernetics" or "first-order cybernetics" is the household thermostat; it exists to maintain a *preferred state* within preset limits, not too hot and not too cold. When the limits are exceeded, the control system activates some kind of device that heats or cools the air to return the temperature to the preferred state. In relationship systems, the preferred states being maintained have to do with a variety of dimensions that are valued by the system or one or more subsystems—closeness, for example, which is a chronic source of relationship dissatisfaction. When a couple's limits for closeness (too close or too distant) are reached, their relationship typically has mechanisms for correcting the problem. A small accident—getting burned on the stove or cut by a weeding tool—might elicit concern from the other, or the relationship might use more conventional mechanisms such as food, sex, or gifts. Angry outbursts, complaints, and unresponsiveness are a few reliable ways to achieve distance.

A family's control mechanisms come under scrutiny when they create problems. A malfunctioning control mechanism that continually escalates a variable is called a *positive feedback loop;* if it continually minimizes the variable it is a *negative* feedback loop.[5] According to cybernetic theory, if an adolescent daughter's abusive language is getting more troublesome for the family it may be because there is a positive feedback loop operating—somehow the normal settings are not operating the way they should and instead the normal restraining efforts make things worse.

Cybernetic analysis tends to focus on sequences. Nearly anything new that is introduced into a sequence might break the loop.[6] Asking the family to observe a sequence, for example, will change the sequence. This cybernetic perspective guides many of the interventions that might fit into the category "Paradoxical Directives" in this chapter.

Intergenerational Patterns

It is hard to see parents and children (or even three and four generations) together without noticing that resemblances go beyond the physical and include patterns of behavior and emotion. This observation is not a new one; literature, folk stories, and religious texts provide many instances of fortunate and unfortunate intergenerational patterns. What has come with formal scholarship is a variety of theories attempting to explain the influence of prior generations. Psychoanalytic theories have focused on the emotional component of such patterns, and behavioral theories have focused on the learning component. Anthropologists have created theories about cultural transmission of understandings and expectations, and sociologists have theorized about social structures. Alternative conceptual models include genetics, skill transmission, family paradigms, narratives, emotional climate, and differentiation of self. The following models are those most often used in clinical work with families.

Bowen Theory. Murray Bowen's (1978; Kerr & Bowen, 1988) Family Systems Theory was, along with Minuchin's Structural Family Therapy, one of the most complex and fully articulated theories created specifically for family intervention. Bowen's approach, an extension of psychoanalysis, was particularly noteworthy for its intergenerational emphasis. While Bowen might work with problems in a couple relationship or a parent-child relationship, his theory called for compiling a complete intergenerational history. Problems in families, according to Bowen, were primarily the result of insufficient *differentiation of self.* Differentiation was a property of the system, not of the individuals, something carried forward from the *family of origin.* Members of families low in differentiation were unduly influenced by each other's thoughts and feelings. Because of *reactivity* they lost the ability to make rational decisions, and their interactions became toxic in the *nuclear family emotional system.* Adulthood and a new *family of orientation* provided opportunities for people to work toward greater differentiation.

At this point Bowen's ideas might sound similar to the concept of enmeshment, mentioned earlier. Bowen was not so focused on overinvolvement; instead, he focused on the opposite alternative—when people resolve their discomfort through *emotional cutoff.* He found disrupted relationships, including decades of not speaking with siblings or parents, widespread among families.

Family disruptions from emotionality and reactivity, according to Bowen's theory, are caused to a great extent by the *family projection process* and the *intergenerational transmission process.* These concepts refer to different ways in which family stresses are transformed into individual and group pathology. In the family projection process, one or more children are selected for special attention, which evolves through three steps (Bowen Family Center, 2003):

1. The parent focuses on a child out of fear that something is wrong with the child.
2. The parent interprets the child's behavior as confirming the fear.
3. The parent treats the child as if something is really wrong with the child.

---

[5] These terms are sometimes confusing, because the thing that is being increased in a positive loop—anger, truancy, anorexia—may be something that is viewed as negative.

[6] Consider the parallel with behavior chains, described in Chapter 4.

As a result of this extra attention and the identification of the child as not being normal, the child is impaired in individual and relational functioning. In future generations, this more impaired family member tends to pass on the limited differentiation from childhood, partially because people tend to choose partners at their own level of differentiation. Every family develops branches that fall below the rest of the family in the intergenerational transmission process.

Object Relations.   From the object relations perspective, intergenerational families are systems of recurring perceptions and habits that are established in infancy.[7] In the early years, according to Bowlby (1988), infants and toddlers are powerfully affected by their interactions with their caregivers. Early learnings of acceptance and support or rejection and abandonment lead to further experiences, which become relationship patterns—withdrawal or demandingness—that reestablish themselves in adult relationships. To the extent that such relationship patterns remain unchallenged, parents then provide their children with the kind of parenting they received.

Like Bowen-influenced practitioners, object relations family counselors (e.g., Framo et al., 2003) assume that adults are affected by their early experiences but also that they can work toward new, more appropriate relationships. Much of this change takes place in current relationships: relationships with adult sexual/life partners, friendship and work relationships, and relationships with children. Framo emphasized choice. He believed in the value of even a single session in which the childhood family was reconvened to process old memories and perceptions, experiment with new behavior that was forbidden for a child, and reshape self-perceptions in light of reflected appraisals from siblings and parents whose own viewpoints had changed.

Intergenerational   Loyalties. Boszormenyi-Nagy and Spark (1973) blended existential philosophy, psychodynamic theory, and spirituality into a focus on the inevitable *debt* that every generation

owes to its parents and prior generations for bringing them into the world and providing them with the means to reach adulthood. Their orientation to family work, known as "contextual" therapy, focuses attention on actual and inferred intergenerational guilt. The contextual model does not suggest that there is an option of entering adulthood without such guilt, but rather that individuals—and entire generations in families—can become dysfunctional because they have not found ways to acknowledge the contributions of past generations.

Ecosystemic, Evolutionary, and Chaos Theories

Organizational principles operate not only at the level of the household and the intergenerational family but also at larger system levels. Havas and Bonnar (1999) provide a comprehensive picture of the extrafamilial factors that impinge on families with adolescents, and Piotrkowski and Hughes (1993) explore the interaction between home and work in the lives of dual-career couples. Systems theorists and clinicians alike have sought to conceptualize the family's interaction with larger systems.

Ecosystemic Epistemology

Bateson's multilevel understandings of human processes contributed many ideas to the movement that became family therapy, but his viewpoint always included the broader context. By 1979, in *Mind in Nature,* this perspective had become refined into a view of people in larger systems—*ecosystemic epistemology*—proposing that nature and humanity interacted in such subtle ways that it was impossible to ever know the entire reality of people's lives. This viewpoint led Bateson in the direction of a more spiritual relationship with all of life.

In recent years, the family counseling field has been increasingly influenced by another theorist who conceptualized families in an ecosystemic way—human development theorist Urie Bronfenbrenner (1979). Bronfenbrenner's analysis, more pragmatically focused than Bateson's, has been adopted by professionals who work in

---

[7] This theory is examined in more detail in Chapter 7.

community systems such as schools, hospitals, courts, and protective services. This approach distinguishes among issues that are most appropriately addressed at different levels and suggests that change is best accomplished by engaging representatives of those levels and encouraging a change in their ways of responding to a family (Robbins, Mayorga, & Szapocznik, 2003).

The Second Cybernetics

When systems thinking was still rather new, Maruyama (1963) challenged the cybernetic focus on deviation-amplifying positive feedback loops; he encouraged scientists to look for naturally occurring negative feedback processes. Less restraint of positive feedback at one system level would naturally lead to a *runaway* process that activated negative feedback at a higher system level—a *second cybernetics*. It was not until 1982 that this expanded understanding of cybernetics reached the level of family practice.

One implication of the second-order cybernetics perspective was an improved understanding of the professional as part of a new system—the therapy system. This idea was not new, as Minuchin (1974) had written about becoming an insider and working from inside the system. What the second-order perspective offered was the ability to recognize that the family without the professional and the family with the professional were different system levels. A professional who focused only on the family level was likely to create problems.

Evolutionary and Chaos Theories

Evolutionary theory has grown out of the investigations of many researchers. Studies of species and ecosystems (e.g., Wilson, 1988) suggest that *functional adaptations* are retained in the genetic makeup of species through selective reproduction, while *unsuccessful adaptations* die out in the gene pool. According to Wilson and others, contemporary humans have inherited genes that led to the survival of our ancestors. This aspect of evolutionary theory is explored in Chapter 7.

The evolutionary perspective is a theory of discontinuous change, proposing that adaptations do not appear through gradual refinement so much as through "quantum leaps" precipitated by crisis. Maturana and Varela (1992) expand on this idea in their concept of *autopoesis*. Living systems, they say, can reconfigure themselves, but the nature of that reconfiguration cannot be predicted. A human relationship system does not resist change so much as it just does not show that change until it occurs. For the professional, this principle cautions against pushing, pulling, and prodding a system. Nothing from the outside can cause change; it must come from within as a response to something that *perturbs* the system.

The most recent entry into studies of large-scale complexity is *Chaos Theory*. Originally a mathematical system, this theory was designed to explain apparently unpredictable ways in which changes occur in complex systems. Many people have heard of the idea that a butterfly's wings beating in one part of the world can create events elsewhere. As applied to couple and family work (e.g., Butz, Carlson, & Carlson, 1998; Weigel & Murray, 2000), Chaos Theory provides concepts that are more specific than those of Evolutionary Theory. First, Chaos Theory identifies *turning points* at which *phase shifts* occur. Only in hindsight is it possible to identify a turning point. The turning point might be the call from an emergency room saying that a drug-abusing daughter has been admitted in an incoherent state; however, the turning point might have occurred 3 years earlier when she was caught stealing pills from her grandmother's medicine cabinet. At the turning point, the system moves into a qualitatively different organization *attracted* toward some new kind of stability. The counselor cannot direct an outcome and cannot even create a crisis, but the counselor can contribute to the combination of forces that lead to the crisis. Out of the crisis, the family reorganizes.

The Process of Counseling with Couples and Families

The preceding discussion of organizational theory included references to many of the best-known and most popular models of working with couples and families. The structural, strategic, and intergenerational traditions, in particular, are readily accepted by many clients, have proved useable in many kinds of practice, and are easy to learn. Beyond its traditional models, the organizational perspective has also grown through the work of innovators whose integrated approaches owe much to the first generation of family therapists. Because of the complexity of the mainstream organizational approaches and newer organizational integrations, the contemporary practitioner can include—and integrate—almost every possible kind of relationship intervention (Lebow, 1997). Therefore, I limit this chapter to include only those counseling techniques that do not fit in another of the BONES themes. Figure 5.7 represents the Organizational theme as a conceptual center, surrounded by other themes that address parts of the organizing process. I provide suggestions when organizational issues are addressed by an intervention that is described in another chapter.

From Theory to Practice

As the traditional models have developed over the years, they may not appear the same as the

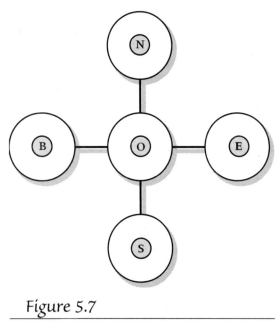

Figure 5.7
Organization as the Center

textbook versions or the classic family therapy literature. A reader comparing works from the 1970s with more recent writings will find declining emphasis on the models' differences and more on the values that they share. Simon (1995) addressed this concern in relation to the structural tradition, as did Friedman (1991) for the intergenerational, both commenting that their models were often applied in a rigid and mechanistic manner. These authors agreed that professionals need to rely on professional judgment and on their own unique gifts in making the personal connections that help people face anxiety and frustration in the process of making organizational change.

Changes in the traditional models may be illustrated by the historical conflict between strategic and structural work. It is hard now to imagine that combining those traditions was once considered unprofessional. Linda Stone Fish and Fred Piercy (1987) conducted a study of the core assumptions held by leaders in the two traditions; they concluded that the differences were so great that it was unwise for a beginner to attempt an integration. Almost 20 years later, the two models retain their separate identities in the literature, but there are few practitioners left who emphasize the difference—partially because other distinctions have become more useful.

Direct and Indirect Approaches
One distinction that continues to exist in current organizational work has to do with the directness of the intervention. Papp (1980) classified intervention options with families according to their assumptions about clients and their beliefs about transparency. Direct techniques were ones that openly informed clients about what was expected and assumed clients would comply. Many relational problems can be addressed in this way; people have not known what to do differently, or they have attempted changes and their attempts have failed because they were not implemented properly. Watzlawick (1982), despite his association with metaphor and paradox, acknowledged the utility of direct interventions:

... because many of our interventions are complex and unusual, it is important to state clearly that we ascribe no virtue to complexity or novelty for its own sake *(emphasis in original). If change can be brought about by simple and direct interventions, such as direct suggestions or requests for altered behavior, so much the better. (p. 128)*

Direct interventions include many, if not all, of those presented in the Behavioral chapter as well as many that will appear in remaining chapters.

The opposite kind of intervention, in Papp's (1980) formulation, is based on assumptions that individuals can behave differently but for some reason the system resists change efforts. When the counselor's view of the problem includes such assumptions, it is more logical to use indirect techniques that predict—and depend on—system resistance. Each of these options is explored in this chapter.

The Stance of the Counselor

The other contemporary distinction acknowledges two profoundly different stances or attitudes toward the counseling process.

The first is often referred to as a *first-order stance* (Simon, 1992). For the first-order professional, counseling is a hierarchical interaction that calls for expert knowledge and skillful intervention. The clients' contribution is limited, providing information about the problems that brought them for help. Counselors operating from this posture seem to view their work as a kind of engineering. The helping process is directed by professionals, who seek input from other professionals, while the clients are expected to comply with the experts' recommendations. As Jay Haley (e.g., 1963) has often noted, this stance fits well with the expectations of many clients. They feel powerless to make change in their lives, and they are looking for someone who will take charge and fix things.

The second posture is referred to as a *second-order stance*. In this stance, professionals (I move from the singular to plural here, because second-order work often includes teams with multiple voices) see themselves as standing inside a new, temporary system of mutual influence with the clients. Second-order professionals are assumed to have useful and valid ideas, even to have ex-

pertise in some areas, but they do not consider themselves experts on any particular family and they do not see themselves as experts on how change will occur. They offer to be consultants for the clients, but at the same time they do not want to be part of the problem-maintaining system. This stance can be confusing to clients who expect a first-order relationship, and it is probably most effective in the hands of professionals who inspire confidence even though they are refusing to be directive.

As you read about the following techniques and assumptions, you will find that some fit with both first- and second-order stances, while others are more clearly associated with one or the other. Simon (1995) challenges the assumption that the two stances are incompatible: What is important, he says, is that the professional is offering the kind of help that the clients are seeking.

Engaging: Contracting for Organizational Change

In contrast with the behavioral approach in Chapter 4, which promised careful, gradual, emotionally safe movement toward predetermined and precise changes, an organizational perspective makes few promises but offers the possibility of rapid, possibly chaotic change. (Risk-avoidant clients may choose to avoid this uncertainty.) The process usually moves directly from a phone call or Internet contact to a first appointment without paper-and-pencil assessment or precounseling orientations that might take away from the intensity of the need.

The counselor typically emphasizes two priorities early in the process: (1) establishing a working relationship with the couple or family and (2) developing a view of the problem in context. These two agenda items are often accomplished at the same time with a family intake.

Professionals differ on the question of demanding to see all family members at the first session. At one extreme are practitioners influenced by Bowen theory, who readily accept the situation in which only one family member is available. Their work focuses more on historical than immediate data, and one person can begin the process by filling in much of the family history. Bowen (1978) viewed this eventuality as positive and characterized the people actually in the office as the most motivated members in the family; he said it was just as well the others stayed away. At the other end of the spectrum, most structural and strategic practitioners prefer to have more people in the first session to provide more information on interactions. Haley (1976) and others have defined the issue as one of control; the professional should say who is involved and who is not. In the middle are authors such as Wachtel (1994), who encourages the counselor to consider on a session-by-session basis when it is most advantageous to invite parents, the symptomatic child, or parents and child(ren) together.

Establishing a Working Relationship

When members of a couple or family enter the counselor's office, what is immediately visible is their number—2, 3, 4, 5, or 15 of them—and their differences—big or little, dark or light, old or young, cocky or humble, noisy or silent. There have to be places to sit (I personally feel that laps are okay for the youngest), even if there may not be an opportunity in the first session to speak to them all individually. In Chapter 1, I suggested that the counselor should try to engage with all members early in the process, but engagement is not achieved only by having conversation time, it requires emotional contact with the group. And it requires choices. Jay Haley, in *Problem-Solving Therapy* (1976), provides a very detailed analysis of the choices a counselor may make in a first session—whom to talk to, what to ask, and how to respond. Haley's strategic model assumes that every session influences those that follow, so he tries to begin in a way that will not close off future options.

Minuchin (1974) taught the skills of *joining* as a critical task, saying "The therapist's data and his diagnoses are achieved experientially in the process of joining the family" (p. 89). He encouraged the counselor to adopt the family's symbols—their language, posture, even style of clothing—to communicate an intent to fit in as a "distant uncle." Videotapes show Minuchin walking into the room wearing a tie and then taking his tie off, apparently to match an adult male who is more casually dressed. He said:

> The family may assimilate the therapist's input to its previous transactional patterns without difficulty. This produces learning but not growth. The family may also respond by accommodating itself, either by expanding its transactional patterns or by activating alternative patterns. Finally, the family may respond to the therapist's input as if to a completely novel situation. The probe has become a restructuring intervention. If the family does not reject it, there will be an increase of stress in the system. The homeostasis of the family will be unbalanced, opening the way for transformation. (pp. 90–91)

Developing a Systemic View

A key element in effectively engaging with a couple or family, from an organizational perspective, is a kind of free-floating attention that helps keep the counselor from becoming too closely identified with any single person's perspective. Many first interviews start off in a way that suggests the first person to speak has a greater investment in the counseling process. It is tempting to think of that person as the one who must be heard or else there will be no second or third session. But such an alliance nearly always backfires. Independence of thought is a hard goal to meet, especially with couples, but it is essential to this perspective. With three people in an interaction, there often seems to be a pull to take sides. A wife asks, "I couldn't put up with a thing like that, could I?" No matter how much the counselor may agree, any side-taking at the beginning of the process interferes with *systemic empathy*. If an active listening response is used, it has to be modified: "If I'm hearing *your perspective* correctly, you're saying that your father just hates to see you have fun."

Hypothesizing

Before we get to a discussion of techniques, you need to understand dynamic assessment as a theorizing process. With so many ways of making sense of family interactions and so much information available, a professional can easily become overwhelmed. The counselor can't help but develop some initial "hunches" to try to see how the individuals fit together, how their actions and perceptions are linked into multiperson systems, sequences, or patterns.

The Milan Team of Selvini-Palazzoli, Boscolo, Cecchin, and Prata (1980) published a legendary paper *Hypothesizing-Circularity-Neutrality: Three Guidelines for the Conductor of the Session.* Their set of three simple principles, useful with many theoretical perspectives but driven by a second-order engine, began with hypothesizing: focusing attention by choosing to try out a theory. Wally, in the case that opened this chapter, acted on a hypothesis—one might even say, a hunch—that the family's problems were related to incomplete transitions and resulting confusion. That formulation helped him to seek and gather information that could either support or refute his hypothesis. His hypothesis seemed to be validated as he proceeded to gather information. Without a hypothesis, he might have had a hard time focusing on anything.

Conducting a Dynamic Assessment

Just as there is not a clear distinction between the processes of joining and developing a systemic view of a problem, these processes overlap with dynamic assessment. By dynamic, I refer to an *active* process of assessment, one that gains new information by using existing information to guide "probes" (Minuchin, 1974). An organizational perspective suggests that the best way to find out about the system is to activate it, set off its programmed responses, check its reflexes. The concept is essentially one of tampering with the way in which things organized themselves as the clients entered the room. A simple intervention might be to ask people to change places, using whatever excuse makes sense. Likewise, a counselor could designate a person to speak; interrupt a story and shift topics; or even step outside the room. Handled respectfully, such *perturbations* of a system provide

information about how it handles change. And any assessment process has the potential to perturb a system by introducing new ideas.

Global Ratings

The *Diagnostic and Statistical Manual of Mental Disorders-IV* (American Psychiatric Association, 1994) included, in an appendix, a new rating scale designed to represent the severity of relationship problems. This scale, the 100-point Global Assessment of Relational Functioning (GARF), parallels the individually focused Global Assessment of Functioning (GAF) that was an accepted and proven part of the *DSM*. Lyman Wynne, one of the authors of the measure, has written that the GARF "has the special merit of being practical—that is, suitable for routine and quick inclusion in clinical records—and is capable, the growing evidence indicates, of quite reliably making distinctions among the various levels of relational dysfunction and changes in level of dysfunction during the course of therapy" (1998, p. viii). Wynne's last point is a crucial one; using the GARF it is possible to not only identify problems but also recognize growth and change.

The basic scale asks the rater (the practitioner) to assign points based on the family's affective and instrumental functioning, with three areas of focus: problem solving, organization, and emotional climate. A research team engaged in validating the scale went on to develop other versions for client self-rating, described in Yingling, Miller, McDonald, and Galewaler (1998). For example, they created a categorical rating scale using illustrated stories that portray different levels of dysfunction: *The Three Bears, Little Red Riding Hood, Cinderella, Hansel and Gretel,* and *The Ugly Duckling.* Scores and ratings can be represented visually to provide feedback to clients.

Mappings

Given the complexity of family stories, it is not surprising that families themselves—and their stories, influenced by various professionals they have consulted—arrive in a counselor's office confused. That is one of the reasons they need a counselor. Parents, teachers, and tutors may have tried several solutions for a child's poor performance in math, and nothing has worked. At such times, it can be reassuring to have a visual aid to help keep track of key bits of information. Three visual assessment devices are used extensively with families, while dozens of others appear in books and journals. All of these techniques involve the couple or family in the creation and evaluation of their own assessment documents.

Genograms.   Starting from a simple genealogical tool, family therapists have created a very flexible and easily used visual system for tracking intergenerational information. McGoldrick, Gerson, and Shellenberger's (1999) state-of-the-art inventory of symbols and rules for genograms not only describes the processes of recording and interpreting family information but also provides samples featuring high-profile families (e.g., Freud's family, Figure 2.3). Genograming is not only a system for recording information, it is also a tool for keeping couples and families on track with a line of questioning. If the counselor's hypothesis relates to conflicting school achievement expectations, the genogram can be coded to show levels of education on both sides of a family—including cousins, half-sibs, and even neighbors—and the visual aid helps people remember to bring in missing information for the next session. With the aid of computer programs or low-tech solutions such as acetate overlays, a single copy of a family's genogram can be repeatedly annotated to show changes such as different household structures over time, allowing the tracking of many developmental issues.

Ecomaps.   Hartman's (1995) ecomapping technique is focused more on the contemporary context than on the intergenerational context. Symbols and spatial relationships on ecomaps help to show the various influences that may have contributed to problem formation or that may be part of a solution. This procedure, like the genogram, is valuable for its ability to record information for subsequent sessions, structure a conversation, and share information with family members who have missed sessions.

Time Lines.   A simple time line, as demonstrated by Stanton (1992), can be extremely useful in organizing chronological information, especially when the counselor is considering the possibility that seemingly unrelated events might somehow interact. Details of family history often are not readily available and must be added over time. The visual record permits keeping track of the missing data as well as testing the hypothesis.

Multidimensional Rating Scales

Various instruments have been created to assess clinically relevant aspects of a client couple or family. The following three instruments are examples of carefully validated, highly reliable measurement designed to determine a couple or family's level of need—the severity of their problems—and the specific areas needing focus.

Self-report instruments vary in their length and reading level; they have to be evaluated carefully for their fit with a setting and with the client population. Used properly, they can give the professional greater confidence in choosing areas of intervention. Their authority helps to convince clients and funding sources that family level intervention is necessary. And they provide the potential for assessing change.

Family Adaptability and Cohesion Evaluation Scale: FACES.   The circumplex model, described in this chapter, identifies family cohesion, flexibility, and communication as organizational issues deserving special attention. The widely used Family Adaptability and Cohesion Evaluation Scale (FACES), now in its fourth edition, FACES IV (Olson, Gorall, & Tiesel, 2002) operationalizes these concepts in a self-report rating instrument which has been enhanced to sample a wide range of functioning. As an alternative to the self-report instrument, the Clinical Rating Scale (CRS; Thomas & Olson, 1993) can be used by the professional to assess client needs and develop plans for appropriate intervention.

McMaster Clinical Rating Scale.   A more multidimensional approach to conceptualizing and assessing healthy family functioning, the McMaster Model of Family Functioning (MMFF) (Epstein, Ryan, Bishop, Miller, & Keitner, 2003) describes healthy families as manifesting effective functioning on six dimensions: problem solving, communication, roles, affective responsiveness, affective involvement, and behavioral control. The Family Assessment Device, based on this model, is a self-assessment rating scale that has been translated into 16 languages. For clinical use, however, a more useful measure may be the 7-item McMaster Clinical Rating Scale, with which a clinician can score families at the beginning and throughout intervention (Miller et al., 1994).

Marital Satisfaction Inventory. Researchers have created many different measures to assess couple relationship functioning. These instruments vary in their assumptions as well as their format, but the majority are focused on partners' subjective impressions of their relationship. Some of these self-report measures are relatively short, easily completed in a waiting room but providing little specific information, while others require more time to complete and provide more detailed information. The Marital Satisfaction Inventory-Revised (MSI-R) (D. K. Snyder & Aikman, 1999) is an example of the latter approach. Douglas Snyder and his associates have spent 25 years validating and refining the MSI-R, which assesses 12 dimensions of couple satisfaction:

1. Global distress
2. Affective communication
3. Problem-solving communication
4. Aggression
5. Time together
6. Disagreement about finances
7. Sexual dissatisfaction
8. Role orientation
9. Family history of distress
10. Dissatisfaction with children
11. Conflict over child rearing
12. Inconsistency

Couples' scores can be plotted against norms (computerized scoring is available) and

can be used for both planning and monitoring of intervention.

Enactments

Among Minuchin's contributions to the history of family therapy was his emphasis on *enactment*—the technique of having people reproduce, in a therapy session, the kinds of interactions they may be having elsewhere. Clients often begin counseling in a storytelling mode, assuming that the counselor wants to hear about "what has happened." While such an interview can be productive (in Chapter 6, we explore many ways in which people's stories can be the focus of intervention), such stories are nearly useless in letting the counselor know how people really interact. It can be helpful to ask, when a couple or family refers to getting stuck in their conversations about a difficult topic, "Could you have that conversation here, so I can hear how it goes?" The dynamics that can be observed in such a slice of real interaction provide a rich source of information.

A well-executed enactment requires more than merely asking people to talk. People often speak to the professional, not to each other, unless the professional is clear and direct about the expectations. Nichols and Fellenberg (2000) studied 21 video-recorded enactments and trained observers to identify specific techniques that contributed to positive or negative outcomes. The most effective enactments were carefully set up by recalling conversations that hadn't worked at home and then specifying a topic to be discussed. Successful therapists restrained themselves from speaking during the enactment, assumed a physical posture of noninvolvement, redirected participants back to each other if they tried to talk to the therapist, encouraged free and direct expression, and praised the participants. Effective enactments were followed by a critique of what had worked and not worked, along with encouragement of further dialogue.

Enactments are not limited to their function as an assessment process. As Simon (1995) explains, enactments provide opportunities for direct intervention, as we discuss later.

Circular Questioning

An equally dramatic technique—and one that also works as intervention, not only as assessment—was described by the Milan team in the 1980 paper mentioned earlier. *Circular questioning*, the second principle in that paper, refers to asking questions in such a way that answers provide multiple levels of information. Rather than ask a mother how she feels about her youngest daughter's imminent departure for college, the counselor can ask the daughter, "How do you think your mom feels about you leaving?" Likewise, a counselor might ask a father, "What do you think made your son so upset when his friends forgot to pick him up for the game?" These questions are not seeking facts—a more expedient way to get the "facts" about feelings, thoughts, and events might be to ask a different person in the session. These questions are useful because they stimulate discussion and they call for responses. Instead of leading to a dry interview pattern of question, answer, these questions bring forth interactions in the office.

Homework

A completely different approach to organizational assessment comes from the strategic therapy tradition. This perspective assumes that office-based assessment and intervention lack *ecological validity*; only in their real-life settings will people interact according to their established patterns. Because the system's responses to challenge will provide information about how the system functions, assessment and intervention tend to overlap in homework assignments beginning after the first session.

Haley (1976) proposed that a counselor end a first session with a paradoxical request that the couple or family avoid making any changes until a complete assessment could take place. Let's say that the professional might say, using a mock-behavioral approach, "Mrs. Gonzalez, I really won't know what to do until I have more information. I'd like you to go home this week and count how many times Juanita uses profanity. It's absolutely essential to start with a good baseline. Juanita, whatever you do, try not to be any more respectful to your mother this week so that she

can get an accurate count." If Juanita follows the directive and keeps her profanity at its current level, she provides useful information and she has also demonstrated something about her level of commitment—an issue that remains to be explored further. It is more likely, though, that she will rebel by stopping or reducing her use of profanity. That rebellion could be the beginning of a systemic reorganization. (This kind of assessment would be unethical if it involved illegal or dangerous behavior.)

A different kind of homework assignment might be used following an intake session in which a child's problems appeared to be part of a triangle with two parents. The parents could be instructed to change roles for the week, with the less involved parent taking over all decision making, direct care, and discipline responsibilities. Either response would be useful: If the parents succeeded in making the changes, the child would benefit from a reorganized family system. If they resisted, their failure to comply would provide a more complete picture of the issues in the family.

Organizing a Response Based on Assessment

Solid organizational information, together with a good organizational hypothesis, leads to an organizational intervention plan. In the Carpenter-Flores case, several assumptions about stepfamily issues and adolescent development were noted. Of all the organizational changes taking place, the one that seemed to be progressing least smoothly was the relationship between the parents. This assessment led to interventions focused on describing, then resolving their ambiguous status with each other and with the girls. The following examples show similar movement from an assessment phase into an intervention stage using different theories.

An Eco-Structural Home-School Analysis. Aponte (1976) described a case in which a child was in trouble at school—speaking abusively to his teacher, including the use of racial slurs. Aponte conducted the first interview at the school with the school personnel, family, and child present, hypothesizing that all were somehow contributing to the child's problem. In the interview,

Aponte and co-therapist Lynn Hoffman determined that the child was feeling alienated at school, abused by his siblings, the parents provided little guidance or support at home, and the school had a negative view of the child. The assessment led to a plan to rebuild parent-child relationships, stop sibling abuse, and create a new record of positive school performance.

Getting the Family Developmentally Unstuck. Quinn, Newfield, and Protinsky (1985) reported a case in which a 12-year-old girl had been stealing at home and in the community. While they observed that the parents' marital problems were likely to have contributed to the problem, the team's hypotheses also focused on the patient's fears about moving from the security of elementary school to middle school. They selected a goal of helping her to feel better about the upcoming change by planning a family ritual—a graduation celebration for family and friends—that not only helped her feel good about the change but also brought the parents together in sessions to plan and implement the celebration.

Intervening: Direct, Compliance-Based Change Techniques

Haley (1976) notes that many professionals have little or no training in how to formulate or deliver a directive, and their training may have made them uncomfortable making any kind of direct suggestion. He recommends practicing this essential skill—learning how to be specific and how to express clear expectations that directives will be followed.

Challenging Patterns in the Interview
Direct interventions often involve in-session behavior. This is especially true of subtle interactional problems. With a couple or larger family unit present in the office, the counselor can redirect or revise statements, alter seating positions and postures, and correct apparent errors in interpreting each other's behavior. Colapinto (1991) describes several areas of focus: changing family structure through enactment, homework (extending an enactment beyond the

boundaries of the session), boundary-making (a special form of enactment), working on complementarity (pointing out the ways in which subsystem members shape each other's behaviors and so on), intensity (a quality that attaches to interventions), unbalancing (to change the hierarchy), and crisis induction (creation of a situation that leaves the family no choice but to face an avoided conflict).

Challenging Patterns from a Distance
However, desired changes often relate to behavior that cannot be separated from its context. Changing the way a parent handles a young child's bedtime is something that can only be done at home, with the child, around bedtime (Jencius & Rotter, 1998). What can be done in sessions, if behavior changes are going to be implemented between sessions, is to develop an understanding of why the change is needed, specify the change, plan for the change, and then evaluate the experience afterward.

Blocking Previous Patterns, Sequences, and Attempted Solutions
Pinsof (1995) leads clients through an analysis of problem development, assuming that problems develop through an ineffective effort to manage normal relational needs. Having linked a problem to both the unmet need and to the ineffective efforts, he contracts with clients to disrupt the problem behavior and work on implementing adaptive strategies. He describes one case in which the parent had used rigid rules to attempt control over three children. Once this history was examined and the parent reduced the controlling tactics, a more supportive stance resulted in happier, more compliant children.

Directing Communication
People may be performing ineffectively in their family roles because they are unaware of a better way of doing things. Communication problems often fall into this category; a common intervention with couples is to ask partners to converse in a different way, hoping to disrupt old patterns of hearing what they expect to hear. Options have included having people talk while they sit back-to-back, having them converse by

telephone, and encouraging them to use structured listening techniques. With one couple, who had a long-time distressed marriage, this kind of intervention was almost miraculous. After an initial assessment phase, the counselor asked them to experiment with a new technique for listening. They returned hand in hand, both of them saying the same thing—"I just discovered what a fascinating, dynamic person I'm married to."

Taking Sides and Other Techniques of Alignment

Family relationships become distorted when people fall into patterns of speaking more to one person than another, even avoiding some family members because of apparent conflicts or hurt feelings. The counselor, recognizing such a configuration in the office, can openly announce the intention of breaking up a coalition and supporting the "victim." By openly siding with the outcast, moving people around and directing conversations in sessions, and asking them to spend time differently between sessions, the counselor can help them break destructive patterns and rediscover joy in their family.

Intervening: Paradoxical or Defiance-Based Change Techniques

The previous group of interventions assumed that clients are capable of making choices and cooperating with change processes. These assumptions are not shared by all professionals, and they may come into question with a particular couple or family. When it seems that being direct does not work, there are other alternatives. The following examples illustrate the range of possibilities.

Paradoxical Directives

Nearly everyone has heard of the idea of "reverse psychology," as it is often described. The idea of asking for the opposite of what is wanted did not originate with family therapists; the average parent discovers at some point that the 2-year-old is more likely to eat her cereal if she is told, "I've

decided you're getting too much cereal. From now on we're going to eat only bananas for breakfast." The Palo Alto group, notably Jackson and Haley, became fascinated with Milton Erickson's techniques of telling clients to do things that they insisted were involuntary—such things as vomiting when they were anxious. Erickson showed that clients would often rebel against his directives. Their "involuntary" behavior patterns ceased once they were required to repeat them.

Haley (1976) describes a therapist who applied this kind of paradoxical directive with a family including a 9-year-old boy whose constant masturbation—in public, "without pleasure"—was so severe that he wore holes in his clothes and he was excluded from activities he enjoyed. The problem seemed to be systemic, involving the boy's behavior and others' responses. The professional first secured permission from the boy's mother, and then met with the boy to present his rationale and his plan. The problem, according to the therapist, was that masturbation was not giving him enough pleasure. Therefore, he was to determine when it was most pleasurable and increase it at those times. The family was to not interfere or react. Asked to observe, not change the behavior during the next week, the boy determined that Sunday was the best day. Therefore, he was directed to limit his masturbation to Sunday—and when he came back admitting that he had slipped, masturbating on Monday as well, he was directed to spend more time masturbating the next Sunday. Within a few weeks, the masturbation had totally stopped and the boy had become involved again in his favorite activities. The family, meanwhile, had been reorganized in its ways of responding.

Playing Sick

Cloe Madanes (1981) injects a playful spirit into the family therapy literature, especially valuable with children. One of her most memorable interventions involves a child in the role of caretaker for a parent who is depressed or alcoholic. Such a child caretaker is often fearful of leaving the parent unsupervised, despite signs that the parent is improving. Madanes works out a contract with the two together: the parent is asked to pretend relapse, randomly and without announcement, and the child caretaker is forbidden to ask whether the symptoms are real. The child must determine whether any relapse will be taken seriously. Madanes reports that the stalemate rarely lasts through more than a couple of "relapses" before the caretaker tires of it and moves on.

Divided Experts

Todd (1984) described some approaches a clinician might choose when a couple seems to be stuck part way through a divorce process, unable to complete the divorce but unable or unwilling to work on the relationship. One of his options was the use of a co-therapist or consulting team, allowing the presentation of a "split vote" on what the couple should do. The clients were presented with two expert opinions; one opinion that they have a relationship worth saving and should work on it, the other opinion that they are hurting themselves and their children and should complete the divorce. He reported that couples typically became frustrated and angry at the experts and decided to take action on their own.

Assessing Effectiveness

With any couple or family intervention, one measure of success is the status of the presenting problem(s) that led to the intervention; often, the only source of information about the presenting problem comes from the clients themselves. Compared with the assessment-driven behavioral approaches, organizational approaches tend to not provide much structure for determining progress. With this lack of structure, self-reports may be either overoptimistic or overly negative and counselors will generally seek other supporting information. Fortunately, organizational interventions nearly always result in observable changes in client interactions. An enactment or a homework assignment is useful at any point when the counselor is seeking information about progress.

Closure

Organizational problems often disappear rather quickly once a pattern is identified and changed; therefore, long-term interventions are rare when using these perspectives. Follow-up sessions, 6 months or even a year after the end of the active intervention period, are often helpful. In the follow-up session, the professional can assess the success of the work, possibly fine-tuning something that continues to be a problem. More important, follow-up visits give clients a chance to receive the validation of returning to a situation that has been associated with a difficult time in their lives, coming in—and walking out again—with feelings of achievement and satisfaction based on the professional's recognition of their changes.

Cautions and Concerns

Organizational perspectives, with their tendency to leap from observing a presenting problem to inferring an underlying problem in the relational system, were revolutionary when they first appeared in the family therapy of the 1950s and 1960s. They attracted professional and public attention because relational interventions often eliminated a symptom when a more direct approach had failed. In short, these system-level interventions were powerful. But such power sometimes is associated with high risk. Any intervention can be associated with negative outcomes, but interventions that are focused on relational patterns—not observable, verifiable single behaviors—are based on professional judgments. The professional's conceptualization of the case, as well as the intervention itself, should be carefully monitored (through supervision) until a high level of expertise has been acquired.

Given that these perspectives often call for changing something that is hypothetical, something that cannot be directly linked to the presenting problem, there is a high probability that some organizational interventions will not achieve their goals—the presenting problem will not disappear, despite the clients' compliance with directives. It is important that a counselor be flexible, continually assessing progress and ready to try something different if a plan does not produce the intended results. With developing professional judgment, a family counselor is more likely to succeed with the first approach that is tried, but clients should be informed of the speculative nature of organizational intervention.

As mentioned in Chapter 3, critics in the 1980s and 1990s raised serious questions concerning both direct and indirect intervention into people's lives. The strongest criticisms have been reserved for the paradoxical interventions that made Strategic Family Therapy famous. I remember a couple who came to me in the early 1980s—a young couple with a history of serious fights in which one or the other had been injured. In the first appointment, they announced that they were imposing one condition on our work together. "Whatever you do," they said, "you must not tell us that we're not fighting enough, that we need to do more of it. That is what the last counselor told us. We followed her instructions. We nearly killed each other."

Suggested Individual and Group Activities

Your understanding of concepts and issues presented in this chapter may be enhanced by the following activities:

- *Examine triangles*. Dangerous triangles can occur when personal relationships compete with other attractions for time, money, and emotional involvement. Observe the people around you to see how they manage these tensions—and how they sometimes fail in their attempts.

- *Describe repetitive sequences*. Many relational patterns appear scripted. Given one action or statement, an observer can predict the next event. Can you recall any relationships in which this rigid sequence occurred? Try to reconstruct the sequence and include as many elements as possible.

- *Map key transition points*. Family developmental theorists generally agree that periods of relative stability can be seen, separated by periods when the existing organization is changing. Draw a time line for one of your relationships and see if you can locate one or more points when patterns changed.

Suggested Readings

Bateson, G. (1979). *Mind in nature: A necessary unity.* New York: Bantam Books.

Minuchin, S. (1974). *Families and family therapy.* Cambridge, MA: Harvard University Press.

Walsh, F. (Ed.). (2003). *Normal family processes.* New York: Guilford Press.

White, J. M. (1991). *Dynamics of family development.* New York: Guilford Press.

Narrative: Language, Culture, and Identity

The problems presented by a couple or family are inextricably interwoven with their ways of talking about themselves.

Objectives

In this chapter, you learn to:

1. Recognize stories as a core element in relationships.
2. Identify ways in which narratives are part of positive and negative relational experiences.
3. Differentiate among ways of describing language in relationships.
4. Use language-oriented concepts to understand couple and family issues.
5. Describe and explain several language-based interventions.
6. Recognize language-based components in popular family counseling approaches.

6

Chapter

The third dimension in the BONES taxonomy emphasizes language in people's lives, their relationships, their cultures, and their communities. According to Maturana and Varela (1992), it is language that distinguishes humans from other species; language is as much a biological part of the species as upright posture and the opposable thumb.

This language element is featured in many approaches to human behavior. Terms vary widely and it is sometimes hard to clarify the distinctions among related concepts such as *cognition* (Dattilio, 1998), *meaning* (Frankl, 1984), *discourse* (Hare-Mustin, 1998), *language games* (Wittgenstein, 1976), and *language systems* (H. Anderson, 1997). All of these related perspectives, in one way or another, suggest that human experience and behavior are shaped by the representation of reality through shared symbols. Related ideas appear under terms such as philosophy, cognitive and attributional psychology, metaphor, symbolism, communication,[1] hypnosis, discourse, identity, constructivism, and social construction. The perspectives we examine in this chapter range from modernist science—a belief in fact and objective reality—to postmodernist rejection of all claims of certainty.

---

[1] Communication is one of the more troublesome words in our field. Clearly everything we are talking about here is somehow communicative, but in this chapter, where the choice of words is especially critical, I differentiate among ways of "helping people communicate."

This chapter focuses particularly on language as it appears in human relationships—including the development and resolution of relationship problems. I have chosen the word Narrative as a summary term because of its interactional quality. The language activities we are most concerned about involve representing ourselves and others in life stories, code words, myths, attributions, and cultural scripts. These narrative activities have special relevance for issues related to gender, ethnicity, race, class, and social change.

But our discussion is not limited to works that use the word "narrative." Like the Behavior and Organization chapters, this chapter brings together many traditional and newer counseling approaches. Some of the ideas, theories, and methods may wander across the rather weak fences that contain the narrative category and socialize with some of their neighbors.[2] For example, we discuss the ways people understand their emotions—a language activity that relates to the Emotion theme of Chapter 7. The centrality of language in human life makes it hard to have any conversation about people without incorporating a linguistic component.

Language-based approaches, like those based on the behavioral and organizational themes, are optimistic. Some theories seem to promise magic; the late Steve deShazer, one of the pioneers of narrative ideas in family therapy, titled a book *Words Were Originally Magic* (1994). Published case studies do describe remarkable changes that have occurred as people told their stories differently. But there's another meaning to deShazer's assertion as well; there is a deep linkage between language and spirituality, a connection explored more thoroughly in Chapter 8.

A Case Illustration: Bruce and Jessica Watson

The Watsons, a married couple in their late 20s, came into Michelle Jackson's office in a way that signaled some of their relationship issues: looking at each other for approval, uneasy, and sitting down so close on the couch that they might have been on their honeymoon. She welcomed them, let them know that the first few sessions would be a discovery period in which she reserved the right to see things differently from either of their perspectives, and invited them to tell her why they were coming for counseling.

Bruce was quick to say that he was the problem. He had recently started to cut himself, he said. This cutting apparently was not suicidal, as he only used paper clips and ballpoint pens to break his skin and draw a little blood. It was an old problem, but something he had not done for many years—since he was in high school—and he was ashamed of it. Because he had prior history with the behavior he had told Jessica about the cutting soon after it first reappeared. He was pretty sure it would stop eventually, but he knew he couldn't hide it from her. His posture and his tone of voice were consistent with his summary statement, "I feel like such a loser."

Michelle, hearing this as an identity statement that was deeply implicated in the problem, began to shape her response based on this assumption. The conversation went something like this:

MICHELLE: *Yes, you look as if you feel like a loser. I can see it in your face. Is this a familiar feeling?*
BRUCE: *It's pretty much constant.*
MICHELLE: *Is this something that you and Jessica have talked about?*
JESSICA: *He's said it before, but I guess I haven't really taken it seriously until now. It's just so hard for me to believe, he's so smart and all. I've always thought I was the one who was the loser, dropped out of college, and grabbed the first job I could get.*
BRUCE: *I think it's what attracted us to each other, she looks at me like I'm better than I am and she puts herself down so much, it's like we go along holding each other up. Both wounded, you know.[3]*
MICHELLE: *So, this wounded feeling,[4] it's something you've been living with for a while, has it changed recently?*

---

[2] This is an example of *metaphor*, a special use of language we discuss later in the chapter. What does this metaphor imply about issues, theories, and methods?

[3] Note that Bruce and Jessica are describing their experience using language from the self-help literature.
[4] Michelle subtly changed the description from "we're wounded" to "we're living with a wounded feeling."

BRUCE: *I think that it only goes away when I'm feeling on top of the world, and I had a pretty good job for a while—selling mortgages—where I was a dealer, you know, people came to me and I made miracles happen, but then the interest rates changed and the company bottomed out. Now, I'm just a drudge in another company, I feel like people just look right through me.*

MICHELLE: *Does the cutting change it?*

BRUCE: *For a few minutes. I do it when I feel like I'm disappearing down a hole and it's the only thing that will stop the slide. It takes me a while to work up to it, but then it starts to occupy my mind and I don't know any way to stop it. Sometimes it's a couple of times in a day.*

JESSICA: *I feel so bad for him, I wish I could help, but I feel like I'm watching him on television or something. I really don't know what to say to make a difference.*

BRUCE: *You do make me feel better, but it doesn't last.*

Michelle assessed Bruce's behavior as not life threatening and therefore she could safely take a "not-knowing" stance (Anderson, 1993) and continue to explore the couple's shared reality. At her invitation, the couple described a relationship in which they both experienced low self-esteem and each of them thought the other one was exceptional. She heard about their remarkably similar childhood experiences—each of them having been the caretaker for a parent who was hypercritical and yet apparently incompetent. As the first session moved toward an end, she tested some new descriptions that might provide a positive sense of direction for the couple:

MICHELLE: *It sounds like the thing that has made your marriage work is that neither of you makes any demands . . . you give each other total acceptance, and it feels wonderful to get that acceptance.*

BRUCE: *That sounds right. Yeah, I'd say that's it, no pressure, a refuge in the storm, just come home and be held. She's good at that.*

JESSICA: *He is too. Sometimes we spend a whole weekend in bed, and I'm not talking about sex, just hiding under the covers together.*

MICHELLE: *But somehow, Bruce, even with this refuge to go to you still don't feel safe the rest of the time. . . . This reminds me of a movie, the Nev-*

erending Story. *The world is being slowly consumed by a mysterious force, "The Nothing." And most of the people sit in fear, hoping it won't get them, but they see the people around them disappear. It seems like that's what's happening to the two of you, you're sitting around paralyzed by fear.*

JESSICA: *Okay. . . .*

MICHELLE: *The hero of the story is a boy who—something like each of you as a child—becomes more grown up than the grownups, performs astounding feats of bravery, but the entire time doesn't think of himself as capable, just keeps being the only person left who can possibly save the world.*

JESSICA: *But we're not those kids anymore.*

MICHELLE: *I think each of you knew how to be a hero alone, when the worst that could happen was that you would be destroyed. But now you're taking care of each other, and you don't want to put the other one at risk. Bruce, your cutting feels like action but it's carefully chosen to make sure that you take all the suffering and you protect Jessica.*

BRUCE: *So are you saying that we just have to get brave and tough and all this will go away? People have been telling me that for 27 years. Snap out of it, be a man. You should hear my father!*

MICHELLE: *No, I really don't know how you're going to make this come out differently. In the movie, they used special effects; they had magic. All I know is that your refuge isn't protecting you the way it used to.*

Michelle asked Bruce and Jessica to see if they could rent the film during the week and come back the next week prepared to talk about it. In this session, she had already used the following interventions:

- She acknowledged the clients' individual and shared realities, including themes of cutting, personal inadequacy, over-responsibility, mutual dependency, and dread.
- She described the problem as something outside Bruce.
- She defined the problem in terms that called for shared energy and action.

Jessica and Bruce arrived for the next appointment looking like a different couple—relaxed, making small jokes. The cutting hadn't stopped yet, Bruce reported, but they were feeling less afraid of it. The film had been somewhat frightening at first, when they thought that maybe their struggle was going to be as long and strenuous as the one faced by the boy hero. But then they started feeling empowered. He was just a kid and up against supernatural powers, while they were adults and up against the mundane problems of living. They were ready, they said.

Michelle asked them to help her to rewrite their story. To do that, they would need to fill in some details of their early years together and the growth of the wounded feeling, and they would then explore some possible next chapters. Bruce was eager to do this; he had taken some undergraduate psychology courses. But Michelle asked him to try and avoid theory, just to describe events and attempt to recall how they made sense at the time. She noted that she would be stopping occasionally to write down a key word, because she didn't want to get things mixed up.

The story that came out in the second and third sessions started off as a happier one, a story of a young couple who met in college after both having dated partners who dominated them. In the early years, they played, studied, and began careers—Jessica deciding to put her law school dreams on hold so that they could get Bruce's degree finished. The Wounded Feeling (now known by its initials, "WF") didn't start to show up in their lives until Bruce started working 12-hour days, coming home exhausted, and falling asleep by 9 P.M. Jessica remembered feeling rejected and Bruce remembered feeling criticized for not being a better partner. Both agreed that WF had started to increase in strength, gaining power as each of them found sympathy from others. Bruce's family seemed more attentive and supportive than ever before, and Jessica's family told her to get a divorce. WF was starting to build a wall between them, and they didn't realize it until it was up to their necks.

By the fourth session, Bruce and Jessica were ready for a fight with WF—and they reported that the cutting had not occurred in the past week. With Michelle, they made plans to go back to where they "lost their way" and regain their forward momentum. They began to reduce expenses so that Jessica could finish school, and they

started discussing her new goals; law school didn't really have the appeal it had when she was younger. Bruce's bleak job situation was showing promise for change; he had been invited to a meeting about a new project, and he too started thinking about long-term goals. Most important, they agreed to start standing up to their families. Bruce's mother called 11 times with various crises the first week of this new program, but he was consistent in his message: "Mom, Jessica needs me at home right now. I hope you'll be able to get my sisters to help out."

Four months later, after meeting only once in the previous month, Bruce and Jessica told Michelle that they were ready to say goodbye for a while, but they would be back in a flash if WF ever appeared again.

Theory and Research

The entire history of counseling could be placed in this chapter, because counseling is essentially a language activity. And you may have noticed that you are already using language concepts in your personal life: Ideas such as "telling a convincing story" and "using different words but meaning the same thing" are not limited to use by professionals.

Many scholarly and practice traditions have examined ways in which people express themselves and seek to understand each other through language. Language includes not just verbal activity but all the symbols or gestures that accomplish the goal of communicating with self or others. This chapter could be expanded to include music, art, dance, poetry, fiction, religion, and anthropology. All are rich areas of study for the family counselor. But there isn't space so we will focus on a few questions:

- How do people organize their experiences and their perceptions into meaningful patterns?
- How do they work with others to reduce disagreements and misunderstandings that occur because of differences in those meanings?
- How do they resist and reject meanings that weaken and disempower them?

The scholarship we review fits into two broad traditions. The first examines language from the more person-based scientific perspectives of *cognition* and *constructivism,* emphasizing an individual who observes, classifies, and explains objective phenomena. A second moves into group-level understandings of language separated from its individual users, describing interactive language in terms of *social construction, narrative,* and *language systems.*

Internal and Interpersonal Language

The first body of theory and research can be illustrated with a sequence that starts as a single-person event. An individual—let's call her Diane—has a real, objective, indisputable experience—let's say she is hit on the head by a box falling off a shelf—and then she has one or more thoughts. The thoughts she might have after the impact could focus on the physical sensation, "That hurts!" followed by damage assessment, "I wonder if I'm bleeding," and reconstructions of the event to assess the cause of the fall. Diane might *sort through* sensations and memories, *form a logical conclusion* about the cause of the accident, *evaluate* damage, and *anticipate* the work of putting things back onto the shelf. All of these mental activities may be classified as individual-level cognitive activities.

From the perspective of working with people in their relationship contexts, these terms don't describe the entire event; Diane's cognitions take place in interpersonal contexts (Sampson, 1993). For example, before the accident, Diane most likely had heard stories of shelves and the tendency of things to fall off onto people. She may have *anticipated* being hit on the head and thought about the best way to prevent such an event. Her thoughts as she opened the door may have taken the form of an *internalized conversation* with an imaginary other: "I know, I shouldn't pull things out from under the stack like this, but I don't have time to take the whole shelf apart." And as the event unfolded, Diane may have been *rehearsing* the story as she was going to tell it to others. She'd have *imagined* her audience—their sympathies

and their criticisms—and her memory would have been enhanced by practicing parts of the story that would get her the response she wanted. Once she actually shared the story with other people, the story would have gained co-authors who would have further changed the narrative.

If Diane is functioning rather well in her life, this incident might not have special meaning for her. But it is possible that Diane's identity stories—her understandings and meanings about herself (Josselson, 1987) are negative. She may expect failure, and her interactions with other people may perpetuate this *negative identity.* Her sister, for example, may respond to this story with comments like, "You know what the doctor said, you just don't have good judgment and you should move back in with Mom and Dad until you grow up some more." Mom and Dad may say, "There you go again, being impatient and slap-dash about things. We really think you should be taking some medication to help you slow down." Her co-authors are contributing to an identity narrative in which Diane is *marginalized* and *subjugated*—she is portrayed as a defective person in a world where everyone else is fully functioning.

If Diane arrives in a counselor's office following this event, the counselor may work with Diane to examine and modify her patterns of self-talk (Beck et al., 1979) that contribute to her anxiety and her avoidance of responsibility. If the counselor is family oriented, other people may be invited into the process—the people in Diane's life who have contributed to the internalized conversation. Diane's internal voice will be easier to understand in the context of her relationships, and as she seeks to revise her identity she will have partners in the process—family members who are also working to change their stories of Diane into stories of challenge, hope, and achievement.

In the following pages, we are going to be asking not only how an *individual* sorts through labels and forms logical conclusions but also how *people in relationship* fit experiences together in a language-mediated social world. Even though Diane was having "her own" thoughts, she did not create the concepts of shelf, fall, accident, negligence, or impatience. And the narrative representations of the incident involved others in a collaborative creation of meanings. In positive cases—as in the counseling relationship—such interactions seem to alter meanings in ways that reduce stress, confusion, anxiety, and self-blame. But in problematic relationships, people find that attempts to share their understandings are unsuccessful, uncomfortable, and frustrating. Conversations increase confusion and doubt and raise anxiety. The goal of a helping intervention/interaction, from a narrative perspective, is to address meaning-making processes at a level where the co-creation of meanings has interfered with people's lives. One starting point is the internal language of the individuals. This internal language, shared or not, is a mediating process that intervenes between perception and experience.

Cognition as Behavior

Internal language can be seen as behavior; perceptions, intentions, specific plans, and assessments of outcome are parts of a behavioral sequence that involves language. This approach to language events has been widely applied in Cognitive Behavioral Therapy (CBT) (Beck et al., 1979), including applications to couple and family counseling (Baucom, Epstein, & LaTaillade, 2002; Dattilio, 1998). The advantage of this view for the counselor is that it provides a seamless connection between language events and other kinds of events.

Theoretically, this view relies on the basic principles set forth in Chapter 4. If one wants to experience more of a certain kind of thought, the theory calls for using principles of social learning and reinforcement to strengthen the desired behavior. Some cognitive-behavioral strategies for family intervention are presented in Chapter 4; others are discussed later in this chapter.

Cognition as a Representation of Reality

Internal language can also be seen as a process of representing external reality, but this is not an easy goal to achieve. This theory of language activity depends heavily on assumptions that a single, verifiable reality exists and it can be described, whereas Platonic and Aristotelian philosophers have disagreed for many generations concerning the nature of reality. Seen as a relational phenomenon, this view of language calls for the individual to represent experience in ways that are interpreted "accurately" by others. This view corresponds with the sender-receiver model of communication that was presented, along with interventions based on that theory, in Chapter 5.

Constructivism

The process of constructing a personal, internal representation of the world—organizing repeated experiences into categories, linking those categories—seems to be a human universal that begins before speech develops. Contrary to many people's assumptions, language is not always verbal, auditory, and oral. Hearing-impaired toddlers are often not identified until speech fails to develop; yet, they make sense of their environments just as well as hearing toddlers. They sequence events, draw distinctions and associations between events and objects, and communicate their intentions to others without verbal techniques. The *constructivist* tradition (Kelly, 1963; von Foerster, 1984) teaches that no two humans inhabit the same reality because their ways of experiencing events are always different. Some authors (e.g. Keeney, 1991) say that people put their experiences into *frames* that then influence the way the experiences are handled.

Frames Part I: Distinctions and Associations. All human language seems to be made up of *distinctions* (Keeney, 1983). Every language has its own sets of distinctions that shape reality for users of that language. English, for example, emphasizes distinctions based on time, but that distinction is less important to speakers of Japanese. The flip side of distinctions is *associations*—the tendency for words and other symbols to form clusters around similar meanings. Sophisticated language users, talking about familiar events and issues, demonstrate a multilevel languaging ability to represent large, general, inclusive *sets* and then to break those sets down in to smaller and smaller *subsets*. "Animals" is a set that is constructed from the commonalities of a child's experiences with squirrels, dogs, and birds. They move, they make noise, they eat, and so on. That category is then broken down again to emphasize differences as they are learned.

One of the most powerful traditions for examining language is *Personal Construct Psychology* (PCP) described by George Kelly (1963). Kelly viewed people's lives as shaped by their distinctive language *maps* of reality—the ways in which they represent the key features of their world. His research, and the ongoing work of scholars in the PCP tradition, has documented that these internal maps vary widely in their complexity, especially as they pertain to social phenomena. For some people, conflict is a single entity; even though they may use a variety of words such as fight, argue, and disagree, careful examination shows that the words are used interchangeably. With such an oversimplified internal representation of interpersonal conflict, they are likely to overreact to a minor disagreement because to them it is "a fight," and their attempts to communicate about conflict experiences are unsuccessful. Alternatively, some people use such fine-grained sets of distinctions that they can't communicate effectively. Lacking words to communicate their important distinctions, they can be cut off from their language community.

At the relational level, disagreements about the nature of reality are a major cause of distress. Casual speech is quite redundant, and this redundancy carries people through times when one person refers to the other's truck as a car or mispronounces the other's name. But in close relationships, most people seek greater understanding. It can be troubling when a partner of 10 years doesn't understand why you like blues but don't listen to jazz. Issues of power and influence are tied up in such language discrepancies: Some people's meanings seem to dominate as they describe experience in their own terms or challenge others' descriptions of actions, events, and feelings. When people demand agreement or forbid conversations about controversial topics, relationships suffer.

Frames Part II: Attributions and Accounts. Attribution theorists (e.g., Harold Kelley, 1973) have demonstrated that people also organize their experiences in causal terms. They view events as sequences with later events having been caused by prior events—often by someone's intentions or actions. Such attributions don't occur randomly, they tend to follow fairly stable patterns including the familiar pattern of scapegoating—blaming things on someone who had little to do with the event but who is an easy "target" for blame. In a pattern known as *the fundamental attributional error* (Jones & Nisbett, 1971), people often attribute their own behavior to situational constraints—"the traffic was so bad I couldn't help driving aggressively"—while attributing others' behavior to stable personal characteristics—"he's always blowing up at things, it takes nothing to set him off." The term *accounts* is sometimes used to refer to fully formed attributions, including all the supporting details that justify interpreting events in a particular way.

Accounts are noticeably present in situations where people have experienced great tragedy or disappointment. Theorists such as Frankl (1984) have said that accounts help with people's processing of these experiences and with their ability to "close the books" regarding a particular experience (e.g., see Gibson's, 1999, account of his son's murder).

Frames Part III: Locus of Control. You may have encountered this term in an introductory course in child development or psychology. You would have learned that *locus of control* is an individual personality characteristic involving an attribution people typically make about the events in their lives. As the topic is taught in many undergraduate courses, the most effective people attribute events in their lives to something inside themselves—*internal* locus of control. This internalizing tendency can motivate people to try harder. What is often left out of these discussions is the observation that the majority of the research was done on undergraduate students—a special, privileged group who have clearly defined, structured individual opportunities to influence what happens in their lives. Notably absent from this research is the experience of people who have little choice and limited ability to affect their current life circumstances—for example, people with traumatic brain injury or chronic illness. However, it is often appropriate for people to take responsibility for their choices, and learning about choice and responsibility is helpful in counseling with many clients.[5] David Reiss (1981) used the term *configuration* to describe a shared family belief that the world makes sense and actions are related to consequences. His research found a positive correlation between this characteristic and effective family functioning.

Seeing a connection between actions and outcomes can be either adaptive or maladaptive depending on the circumstances, and sometimes the difference is not clear. When people in couple and family relationships find meaning by finding causal linkages, sometimes those meanings lead to blaming. White and Epston (1990) suggested that *blaming each other* reduces a group's effectiveness in coping, while *blaming something external* to the relationship brings people together in their united opposition to the threat. White and Epston's solution is a narrative process they refer to as *externalizing* (see Restorying in this chapter).

Frames Part IV: Concepts of Self and Other.   Among the cognitions that people form and use in their lives, internal representations of self and others are extremely important. The term *self-concept* is in common use, along with a variety of terms that describe characteristics and aspects of the self-concept: self-esteem, self-efficacy, self-confidence, self-respect, self-love, self-hatred, and self-loathing. *Object relations*, a specialized theory of cognitive-emotional concepts (Bowlby, 1988) is discussed in Chapter 7, and the concept of *identity* is examined in the next section.

Language Systems and Social Construction

Moving up a level from cognitions that individuals create and use in their daily lives, another body of theory and research examines language at larger system levels. In the work of Wittgenstein (1976), all language is found to be imperfect and problematic. Language is metaphorical, not precise. Words that are similar in their general meanings may also have differing additional meanings.

Therefore, the ways in which people frame their experiences in language—the verbal process in which experiences are displayed and the listener is told how to interpret them—can create or support entirely different interpretations.

While an individual can give meaning to experience through language and can try to share that meaning with others, it is impossible to know for sure how that language is being heard. Members of a language community—speakers of a dialect, workers in the same industry—may be likely to share meanings, and those who interact frequently—family members, neighbors, co-workers—may be expected to accurately interpret each other's internalized meanings. But subtle differences in internal distinctions and associations still make it hard for people to understand each other.

Humberto Maturana and Ferdinand Varela, in *The Tree of Knowledge* (1992), argued that language is such an important part of human experience that different language groups might be thought of as being different in a biological sense—members of each group behave consistently, give attention to some but not other events. This idea fits well with another theory, one that comes out of a less biological and more social scientific perspective—the theory that people collaborate in giving meaning to their experiences through a shared process of only acknowledging "things" that come into existence when they are labeled.

This *social constructionist* perspective (see Chapter 3) describes processes through which two or more people develop a shared reality. Within a relationship group, according to Berger and Luckmann (1966), people provide each other with concepts that define their shared version of reality. When concepts gain general use, they come to *institutionalize* reality making the participants relatively predictable to members of their own group and possibly incomprehensible to others.

Paradigms and Discourses

In Chapter 3, we briefly discussed the concept of *family paradigm*, a term used by researcher David Reiss (1981). Reiss asserted that a family group's functioning was connected to their

---

[5] This emphasis on choice and responsibility is central in existentialist approaches.

shared representation of the world. As he described the phenomenon, a new family paradigm started to take shape as a couple met and began to challenge and merge their understandings. As they shared experiences—job loss or the anxiety of waiting to hear if a relative had survived an earthquake—they would find times when their different interpretations created crises. Out of those times, they would resolve their differences and adopt joint interpretations. Eventually, the process resulted, as Reiss demonstrated in his research, in couple and family realities that are remarkably consistent.

Somewhat later, as part of the postmodern movement (see Chapter 3), the term *discourse* came into common use to include all kinds of language activities. For family counselors, discourse has a specialized meaning that refers to a group, culture, or society-level tradition—a socially constructed reality that shapes or *positions* the perceptions and responses of its participants (Davies & Harre, 1990). *Dominant discourses* (e.g., concerning gender, race, and class) are transmitted by media and conversations of a surrounding culture, and a family's meaning-making is performed in the midst of multiple sources of cultural imagery and assumptions.

In Chapter 2, I mentioned French cultural historian Michel Foucault and his research on the process through which European societies developed institutions of social control. The process started by classifying a group of individuals as different; then progressed through labeling the difference as dangerous or otherwise negative; and finally enlisted not only the majority population but the minorities themselves in a process of *marginalizing* and *subjugating* criminals, the mentally ill, and sexual minorities. The term *hegemony* has come into regular use to describe the subtle but near-total power exercised by a majority.

But no discourse has absolute power and application in a diverse society, and in the postmodern period there are few societies in the world where diversity does not exist. With access to electronic media and with members who interact with outsiders on a daily basis, people in contemporary societies live at the intersections of multiple streams of discourse. No single set of rules or understandings can exist for very long without being confronted with *alternative discourses*.

Identity Constructions

The Western cultural tradition is noted for its emphasis on the individual. In religious, psychological, and philosophical writings and also in folk stories and fiction, the message is clear; each person has a unique identity and happiness is achieved by living in accordance with that identity. Erik Erikson's (1968) theory of psychosocial development emphasized the benefits of a young person making choices rather than being controlled by others. Identity, in the Eriksonian view, was an individual construction.

But the social constructionist description of shared meaning processes offers a different view of identity. Contemporary theorists have concluded that identities exist at many levels—couples and families have identities as well as do larger groups (Abrams & Hogg, 2001). A family may have an identity of entitlement and privilege (you might hear them say, "Don't they realize who we are?") or a group may have an identity of hard work and sacrifice (they might say, "After all the speeches are over, we stay up all night and make it happen").

Gender Identity. Dominant discourses of gender have been virtually unchallenged in many societies. In countries like the United States, where a *binary* view of gender is prevalent, significant parts of a person's identity are *assigned* based on biological sex—for example, females are expected to be nurturing and cooperative, and males are expected to be confident, competitive, and even aggressive. Everyone is supposed to accept classification as either male or female. Counter-normative experiences are denied, ridiculed, or pathologized.[6] But society is changing; contemporary youth trends in

---

[6] In *Middlesex*, Jeffrey Eugenides (2002) fictionalizes the experiences of a man whose biological sex is ambiguous. He found family and professionals eager—once they recognized the ambiguity—to surgically "correct" his body to match his childhood upbringing as a girl.

the United States and other industrialized nations include considerable *gender-bending,* challenging the dominant discourse through manipulations of symbols such as hair, clothing, and body adornment. Not only young people but even some of their parents and grandparents are insisting that life choices need not be constrained by biology and they may alter those choices. In this alternative discourse, gender is diverse, fluid, and socially constructed (Blume & Blume, 2003).

Sexual Identity.   Closely associated with gender is the assumption of universal heterosexuality. Only in the past 30 years has the social and legal climate begun to change enough that the large population of gay, lesbian, bisexual, and transgender individuals can claim their place in society. Again, the dominant discourse is binary—people are seen as either heterosexual or homosexual (Oswald et al., 2005). This insistence on labeling people is especially problematic for youth, who often report that they have experienced both same-sex and opposite-sex attractions. Contemporary discourses of sexuality are beginning to recognize that sexual identities are not fixed but may vary over time.

Ethnicity, Race, and Class.   Ethnic identities in the United States often seem limited to "normal" and "other"—with northern European ancestries considered normal. We need only look at Hollywood movies from the 1940s and 1950s, with their English accents and their English surnames, to sense the negativism directed at any diverse cultural history in a family. The melting pot metaphor, applied to the family, meant that a Norwegian wife and a Korean husband both tried to pretend that they were generic Americans. Much of Monica McGoldrick's work on ethnicity in family therapy (e.g., McGoldrick et al., 1996) addresses this problem; marriages based on denial of ethnic identities run into difficulties when those identities manifest themselves in different understandings, preferences, behaviors, and emotions. But there is a new set of attitudes in the postmodern world. People around the world—especially the indigenous people of the Americas, the Pacific,

and Africa—are reclaiming their cultures. In a world that increasingly values diversity, families are beginning to find comfort and connection in their cultural identities.

This valuing of difference extends to race and class, which are different kinds of distinctions—based more on status difference than on cultural background. In the eighteenth and nineteenth centuries being White had legal implications in the United States—only White males could vote and own property. Not only have women and people of color gained legal rights in the past century, the current definitions of whiteness have become much broader (see Sacks, 1994). Fewer people suffer from direct discrimination—the signs saying, "Irish need not apply" have disappeared—yet, indirect discrimination is rampant. Family members who share experiences of oppression can either join with the oppressor or, in the spirit of postmodern feminists "speaking truth to power," they can speak openly about the stratification of society. Children growing up in a racist, class-divided society may benefit from having ways to identify and discuss their racial and class identities (e.g., Robinson, 1999).

Narrative

A narrative perspective differs from cognition and discourse perspectives in its emphasis on the dynamic nature of linguistic activity. Attending to narrative issues, such as plot and character, does not deny the significance of individual concepts and the discursive practices that give some concepts special power in people's lives; instead, it focuses the discussion on the daily storytelling where concepts, discourses, and identities can be observed. When we listen for narratives, we hear opportunities for assessment and intervention. There are many ways of making sense of narratives and there are many ways of using narrative understandings in practice; only a simple overview follows in this chapter.

Narrative Co-Telling
Narration is not a one-way process. Even if an audience sits and listens throughout a long story, the teller is influenced by the audience's responses—

their attentiveness, their shock and amazement, their joy and celebration in response to the story. And in most conversations, the positions of audience and teller are continuously exchanged. The response to a partial narrative is a question, an evaluative comment, or a partial narrative from the other person. In this way, people become co-tellers of each other's narratives by contributing to a story's shape and content, adding language or asking for clarification, challenging the story, or even suggesting the familiar story they want to hear (Norrick, 1997). You may have experienced a listener providing a lie or an excuse: "I suppose you had to stay late for a meeting" or "I guess your best friends were going there, too."

Relational Identity.   Narrative perspectives view personal identities as collaborative productions, ongoing rather than fixed, and including many people's contributions. Just as there are multi-

ple discourses, multiple narratives define people's identities as well. The social context of identity formation and fragmentation is something that William James discussed over 100 years ago (1892/1961), but narrative theory has contributed new descriptions. As opposed to James' internal process of self-labeling, we can now describe a process in which *identity bids* are met with *identity feedback* (see Box 6.1). Viewed from this perspective, every verbal and nonverbal exchange is about identities in interaction. Some people build consistent identity narratives—ones that have little variation and that incorporate multiple contributions that agree on essential elements. This consistency tends to be highly valued by others, but over time can lead to a situation in which even small deviations seem monumental. Wearing a new color shirt or changing brands of sneakers, for some people, are frightening.

BOX 6.1

Narrative Co-Construction

Conversations between or among individuals can be seen as co-produced identity narratives in which meanings are negotiated. This narrative negotiation of identity may involve others who are not physically present: individuals, but also groups, communities, and entire cultures. Narrative influence, in these identity negotiations, occurs through the identity options that are variously articulated and either supported or rejected.

- Shared experiences provide a basis for co-narration of identities.
- Identities are defined by narrative elements: the actions attended to, their interpretations, and the language used in the telling.
- No two separate narratives of the same experience are identical.

- As co-narrators tell or retell a story, they negotiate whose perspective and language dominates the account.
- Audiences participate in the co-narration process as they validate narrative elements or offer additional ones.
- Previously co-narrated stories tend to be repeated from the same perspective and therefore tend to stabilize identity.
- New audiences offer the potential for a different kind of co-narration and therefore have the potential to destabilize identity
- New experiences provide new narrative opportunities and therefore offer opportunities for identity change.

Adapted from *Narrative Identity Negotiations of an Adult Student Couple*, by T. W. Blume and D. Weinstein, 2001, poster presented at the Biennial Conference of the Society for Research in Identity Formation, London, Ontario, Canada.

Intimate relationships are especially challenging from a relational identity perspective because partners develop considerable power to define each other. When a partner contributes more negative than positive identity feedback, it can seem as if the only way to restore a positive self-narrative is to end the relationship. But challenges to preferred identity narratives are a part of every life, and identity maintenance skills—awareness, questioning, searching for alternative voices—are essential components of survival in relationship.

Negative Identities. The co-authorship of identity stories is both a challenge and an opportunity. When one member of a relationship has become stuck in a *problem-saturated* identity narrative (e.g., depressed, overweight, alcoholic, unemployed, divorced) virtually every question or comment may seem to confirm and perpetuate the narrative. But a recognition of co-authorship is also an opportunity because in every conversation, the words chosen, the events that are noted, and the attributions of causality and intent can contribute to an alternative story of opportunity and hope (see Box 6.2).

Narrative Analysis

Scholars in different intellectual traditions have developed tools for locating and describing significant aspects of a narrative. Gergen (1994) explores literary traditions for descriptions and explanations of narrative *form,* finding that there are standards in a culture or language group about how one goes about presenting a story and that those standards privilege the stories of those who follow the rules. He attributes great power to a well-formed narrative (a narrative that fits community standards): "By using these narrative conventions we generate a sense of coherence and direction in our lives. They acquire meaning, and what happens is suffused with significance" (pp. 1993–1994).

Much of Gergen's work has focused on the idea of *plot.* Narrative plots are the subtle, often unnoticed patterns in which a story's events and interpretations are organized to achieve an audience response. Listening to family members in a casual conversation or in a counseling session, one may hear events being interpreted in comments such as, "But wait! It gets worse." The consistent use of a particular plot can prevent alternative realities from being noticed. Gergen classifies stories into *stability narratives, progressive narratives,* and *regressive narratives,* and K. Weingarten (2001) applies this scheme along with others to examine *illness narratives.* She concludes that many illness experiences are hard to share with others; the audience likes progressive narratives in which everything is getting better, and that plot structure may not match experience. If one's illness story is not heard, the chaos and pain of the illness are compounded by isolation.

BOX 6.2

Alcoholics Anonymous, a Narrative Approach

The process of sharing each person's recovery stories, a primary element in the traditions of Alcoholics Anonymous (AA), is likely to be one of the most widely practiced forms of narrative intervention in the world. Since its founding, AA has pointed to the value of telling and retelling personal, unique stories of repeated problems with alcohol and eventual success in living without it. This storytelling tradition has much in common with White and Epston's (1991) technique of externalization. Alcohol is located outside the self, the story is essentially one of struggle against a relentless enemy, and the narrator is encouraged to identify his or her ways of resisting alcohol's attempts to restore the problematic relationship. Within the community of mutual storytellers, shared meanings of powerlessness, acceptance, reconciliation, and service are developed and enriched through repetition.

Another contribution of literary theory has to do with the idea of *deconstruction*. Jacques Derrida (1994) suggested that the apparent structure of a story is not its most important element, but instead there are hidden messages in stories (hidden from the author as well as from many readers). These are often political messages about societal expectations. What the narrative scholar is asked to do in this "poststructural" tradition is to create *alternative readings* of a story, giving voice to the wide variety of meanings that may lay concealed in words and plots.

In the hands of the family counselor, this tradition calls for looking behind the explicit story to detect *themes*. These themes may go undetected by many listeners, who are distracted by the fascinating events and the colorful descriptions. But family members and others who are familiar with a theme may pick up a recurring message of inequality and superiority such as "My family said I was destined for greatness, and if I hadn't been dragged down by marrying this creep I would be living in a palace somewhere." Themes may need extra attention if they are to be noticed; women's and children's stories of being verbally or physically abused, for example, are sometimes offered in a joking manner and may be casually dismissed by listeners.

A common theme in competitive societies such as the United States, particularly common among people who come in for counseling, is the theme of failure. The details may involve many aspects of life—finances, school, dog training, parenting, shopping, and weight management—but the theme can be stated as "No matter how hard I try, I am not good enough."[7] Johnella Bird (2000), a narrative therapist from New Zealand, notes that this theme is prevalent in many cultures. The family counselor is challenged to hear and identify, in the narratives of clients, cultural themes of negativity and failure so that they can be challenged and changed.

Social scientists have subjected narratives to analysis for their degree of internal consistency

---

[7] An important alternative to this theme is "I'm good enough, but I have a self-destructive streak that keeps me from succeeding." We talk about this story when we discuss shame in Chapter 7.

and consensual validation. Gergen puts it this way: "Rather than see our life as simply 'one damned thing after another,' we formulate a story in which life events are systematically related, rendered intelligible by their place in a sequence. . . . Our present identity is thus not a sudden and mysterious event but a sensible result of a life story" (1994, p. 187). This *narrative continuity* view suggests that a fragmented or conflicted narrative has the potential of leaving an individual, couple, or family in a constant state of disorientation, confusion, and internal conflict. The ideal identity narrative, according to Spence (1986) and others, integrates multiple and diverse experiences in a way that does not force any of those experiences to be denied. A narrative may need to incorporate decisions that later proved to be wrong; career and other identity changes; and experiences of abuse, torture, and rape, but this goal of *narrative smoothing* can be accomplished by a skillful narrator who weaves those experiences together. Canadian identity researchers (Lalonde, Chandler, Hallett, & Paul, 2001) studied this process among First Nation adolescents, asking them to analyze fictional stories and their own life histories with the goal of explaining, "How, at the end of the story, can you still say that this is the same person?" The majority of their subjects resolved both challenges by constructing narrative accounts and those accounts showed increasing sophistication over the 2 years of the study.

Dialogue and Dialectics

If we say that narratives are co-constructed and that audiences contribute to narratives, we should be able to describe that contribution. One descriptive term is *dialogue*, which Tom Andersen (1987) defined as follows: "When two or more persons share their views, each receives from the other different versions of 'reality.' These differences will give new perspectives to each person's picture, and the enriched pictures created from these ongoing differences can become . . . an ecology of ideas" (p. 416). For Andersen, the important questions have to do with how much difference can be assimilated into a dialogue; he notes that some differences are so small that they are unnoticed, whereas other differences might be so great that they have "a disorganizing effect."

He advocates approaching differences in a gradual way, hoping that the dialogue will move through three levels called the *picture* level, the *explanation* level, and the *alternatives* level. At each level, participants may offer different understandings; by the time they complete the third level, all may be transformed by the experience.

Dialectics is a conceptual approach that adds a significant element to the dialogical view; a belief that human experience is typically organized into *dialectical dimensions*. These dimensions are seen as incorporating pairs of opposing alternatives that remain in tension with each other—tension that cannot be resolved, despite the fact that every action is in some way an attempted resolution. Conville (1998) suggests that human relationships are always in a state of transition related to two interacting dialectical dimensions: *security-alienation* and *disintegration-resynthesis*. Over time, every relationship can be mapped as moving through many positions on the two dimensions. Rather than focus entirely on people's conversations, Conville also interprets their actions as communicative. A couple working on their relationship following a period of separation would be seen as constantly sending messages to each other and interpreting each other's actions to discover the meaning behind them. He represents the process of verbal communication in a hopeful but cautious light, as a partial and incomplete attempt to share temporary and ambiguous states of being.

The Process of Counseling with Couples and Families

The various language traditions are nearly unanimous regarding the relationship between the helper and his or her clients. Working with language requires that the helper listen to both literal and relational meanings, often noticing features of language that are generally overlooked. Lyle and Gehart (2000) describe this listening using Ricoeur's (1996) concept of *translation*. Because each person's language world is only partially shared with others, lis-

tening requires an attitude of reaching out—a *hospitality* that makes a sincere attempt to make the other feel welcomed. The process of communicating goes beyond receiving the other's meanings, it is *transforming* (Anderson, 1993).

Beyond their shared commitment to hearing self and others, language approaches differ in how they portray the conversation with couples and families. Some (first order) practitioners feel an obligation to either direct or at least lead the process of identifying and implementing the needed changes. It can be reassuring to clients when the helper announces that the situation makes sense, that there is a procedure to make the problems disappear, and that he or she is expert in the procedure. But many (second order) narrative and language systems practitioners view such certainty as not only misleading but also unhelpful because such a relationship reproduces the power dynamics that appear to be implicated in the problem.

Where the following goals and techniques seem appropriate for all language approaches, I try to indicate their general application. At the same time, I highlight goals and techniques that are especially relevant for one orientation or another.

Engaging I: Entering a Language World

Language approaches start from a common premise that the meanings of language are not universal or transparent. Because meanings of words are not immediately clear, the practitioner in every setting—whether a two-person "individual" conversation or a family session involving 10 people—faces the same need to achieve a contexualized understanding of what is being said. Readers familiar with the work of Carl Rogers will find this process of engagement similar to active listening, even though it is generated from a different theoretical stance.

Suspending Judgment
The first of the conditions for this engagement process is attitudinal. The helper may or may not mention this attitude to the clients, but in either case he or she tries to suspend conventional

processes of ascertaining meaning. I have found that the majority of families include at least one person who tells me in the first session that the problem is "communication." I can either take this to mean that they require training in communication skills, as described in Chapter 4, or I can remain open to other meanings and engage in a co-authoring process to help them find words that clarify their intent.

Harlene Anderson (1993, 2005) refers to entering a conversation from a "not knowing" position. Rather than assume that they know what a person means, practitioners using such an approach take extra time to explore meanings—even those that might seem obvious—to make sure they are not imposing their own views. The term *neutrality,* as used by Selvini Palazzoli, et al. (1980), referred to an attitude of not only avoiding alignment with any family member but also avoiding the appearance of aligning with any particular belief or understanding, trying to stay open to all possible ways of experiencing the clients and their issues. Michael White refers to a similar idea when he talks about *decentering* (see Kogan & Gale, 1997) as a process of distancing from dominant discourses that reproduce themselves in a couple or family narrative.

Hearing Their Language

Counselors who are new to a language perspective may have difficulty remembering and using the exact words they heard from the clients, but for this work precise words can be especially important—though a word has the same meaning for others, it cannot be assumed to have the same meaning for the speaker. A 14-year-old who says that his little brother is "out to get him" may consider that a very different statement from saying that he "has it out for him." Lois Shawver (1998) coined the term *generous listening* to refer to an active listener stance, one that demonstrates a commitment to understanding and utilizes questions, rephrasings, and requests for clarification so as to achieve shared meanings. Harlene Anderson (1993) speaks of taking the time to write words down, checking with a speaker to ensure that an unfamiliar or ambiguous word is spelled correctly. An alternative way of capturing precise language uses audio or video recording (with the clients' permission), to add nonverbal information to the verbal, and it is sometimes useful when played back to the client. One may also ask clients to write their concerns and observations in a diary or send them in electronic form.[8]

Entering Their Experiential World

Even when words receive careful attention, meanings may be obscured if a conversation stays at the level of abstractions. Narrative therapists use the term *thick description* to refer to a narrative that moves beyond abstract concepts and includes more specific and local information that will contribute to a relational, contextual view of the problem.

Take the following exchange, for example:

COUNSELOR: *I understood from our brief telephone conversation that you were concerned about feelings of depression. Can you tell me more?*

ELIJAH: *Well, it's like someone's sitting on you, you can't get up and do anything, you just feel blah.*

PETER (ELIJAH'S PARTNER): *He seems like he's just not there any more, it's just like when my dad was depressed, they both used to be so vigorous and so full of joy, and then it was like they were replaced by robots.*

At this point the counselor has some choices to make. The clients have introduced the concept of time: "used to be" versus "now." And they have provided a physical metaphor ("you can't get up"), for problem feelings, in addition to several key words such as "blah," "do," "vigorous" and "joy" that may help in exploring the creation of this depression and the possible alternatives. Especially helpful will be information about the context in which the problem is or has been noticed:

---

[8] The various uses of technology, especially the Internet, with clients are still being developed. Before engaging in any use of electronic communication with clients a counselor should be familiar with legal and ethical issues as well as technological options for protecting confidentiality.

- Has there been a death in the family, layoff from employment, or other identifiable event that might create an expectation for depression?
- Who else in Elijah's relational world has experienced something that was labeled as depression?
- How has Elijah interacted with Peter when he has appeared to be depressed?
- Are there others who have participated in these interactions?
- Have others contributed observations or explanations to the narrative of Elijah's "depression"?

Asking questions about these elements of the narrative alters the narrative and could therefore be deferred until the clients have told the story in their own way. The postmodern emphasis on power in relationships makes us aware that the couple may transform their story to match the counselor's expectations, and such a modification limits information about their prior ways of making sense of their different realities.

Engaging II: Entering a Unique Intersection of Discourses

One of the criticisms that has been leveled at some contemporary narrative and language approaches is that the work is not "family" because the emphasis is not on direct communication among the members. In Chapter 3 we read about Minuchin's (1998) discomfort as he watched demonstration sessions in which family members were interviewed in each other's presence. This was the opposite of the counseling technique of enactment, pioneered by Minuchin, which had emphasized the need for clients to interact in the session.

The historic preference for direct conversation among family members seems to be based on assumptions that: (1) people who are in couple and family relationships are all talking about the same experiential world, and (2) with a common base of experience, they compare their experiences and work toward shared perceptions, goals, and strategies. The first assumption is erroneous, however,

when viewed from the narrative and language systems perspectives. Every person occupies a unique location in the social fabric, even when there are many shared experiences. And coordinating with others is difficult in part because the degree of difference is not understood. The long-range goal of direct communication may not be inappropriate, but it may require an intermediate step of exploring and clarifying individual voices within the context of dominant family or larger group discourses.

For many people, it is a new idea to think of multiple narrative and discursive voices and to think that they all may have some validity. Harlene Anderson (1993) used the term *multipartiality* to refer to the goal of creating an experience in which every participant feels especially important. With different stories being told by different individuals in the room, Dickerson and Zimmerman (1993) say, "we ask each to tell her or his story without interruption from the others" (p. 227). Freedman and Combs (2002a) add more specificity: "We ask one member of the couple to tell his or her story while the other listens from a witnessing position. Then we ask the *witnesser* to reflect on what he or she has heard" (p. 313). For many clients, such listening is hard to do. The strategies and techniques that follow are based on a shared assumption that people need help recognizing the extent and nature of their different experiences.

Group Preparation for Couple Sessions
Heterosexual couples in treatment for domestic violence epitimize the challenge of achieving collaborative exchanges between couple and family members. In many cases, there are no observers of the abusive events and there are two conflicting stories. The female victim/accuser, feeling that complaints have been minimized or ignored, may approach a counseling session as yet another frustrating encounter. The male accused, at the same time, may seem to have few reasons to validate his partner's story; legal systems tend to support female victims, he may fear that the counselor will be subpoenaed to testify, and a story that minimizes the incident could result in a shorter period in jail. By the time the couple arrives in the counselor's

office their stories have been retold with many "co-authors." Dominant discourses of masculinity and femininity—and their intersectionality with race, class, culture, and sexual orientation—have lent support to the two different experiences. Under these circumstances, the stories seem unlikely to change.

Given the prediction that a couple conversation would repeat the past pattern of the couple's struggles with the story, Almeida and Durkin (1999) precede couple's work with men's groups that move the conversation from questions of violence to questions of power and emphasize accountability, socioeducation, and sponsorship. Men and women from the same cultural group are brought in as *cultural consultants* to explore ways of being loyal to culture without perpetrating violence, and men are connected with other men who model relationships of mutuality and caring. In a second group phase, men and women both enter *culture circles* where they become more conscious of issues of privilege and oppression. Finally, when a mutual, respectful conversation seems possible, couples are brought together in a setting where their interactions can continue to be monitored by representatives of the *culture of accountability.*

Internalized Other Questioning

David Epston (1993), taking a different approach to domestic violence, employed a procedure in which the partners were physically present with each other, but the questioning was carefully structured. Instead of asking each partner to give his or her own perspective on the history and the specific events, Epston asked them each to present the other's perspective. The premise was that each partner: (1) had heard the other's version well enough to repeat it with a fair amount of accuracy, and yet (2) had only heard the other's story with the goal of trying to defend against it. Given the opportunity to step into the partner's reality (and the responsibility to give the partner a fair hearing), Epston surmised, the narrator would become more personally invested in this alternative story and would feel less certain about the "truth." The procedure proved effective. Partners rated each other as extremely accurate in reporting their stories, and the telling of the two stories in this format achieved its goal—taking a narrative and enriching it by making it multivocal.

Reflecting Teams and Witnessing Groups

Tom Andersen (1991), as noted in Chapter 3, pioneered a specialized modification of the traditional family therapy consulting team—something he called a *reflecting team*—in the late 1980s. The approach is intended to counteract the clients' tendency to focus on the counselor's perspective, which has special power because of the nature of the relationship. Multiple perspectives in response to the clients' stories help to present clients with multiple ways to make sense of their reality, expanding their options for redefining the issues that brought them to counseling.

Unlike the consulting team popularized by strategic and structural authors and trainers (Chapter 2), reflecting teams talk directly to the clients and the counselor(s) together. A typical session with a reflecting team may start like a session with a consulting team. The primary therapist is in a room with the couple or family, and the team is in an adjoining room behind a one-way mirror. The session begins with an exploratory, decentered conversation focused on the clients' problem narrative, but the conversation is interrupted at the midpoint of the session and the positions are reversed. At this point, the clients and their therapist(s) become the listeners as the team engages in its own conversation.

Even before the session begins, there is a difference in the composition of a reflecting team when compared with the consulting team. Rather than consisting only of expert practitioners, the team may include members who represent the voices of significant reference groups: the surrounding community, a religious body, extended family, multiple socioeconomic, or racial or gender perspectives. The team's conversation explores different ways of making sense of the therapist-client conversation, especially how the client narrative connects with team members' unique knowledge and experience. Rather than trying to achieve a consensus, the team seeks to *trouble* dominant stories and make room for alternative meanings. The team typically provides clients with alternative views of themselves, views with more positive qualities and fewer negative qualities than they brought into counseling.

Disengaging from the Verbal

Language approaches risk getting stuck in the details of words and precise meanings, whereas communication theory points to the power of nonverbal language as well. Verbal techniques give unfair advantage to family members who are persuasive talkers or who have powerful relationship vocabularies. People also differ in their experience and comfort with movement, music, art, and mime, but those who are most skilled in these forms are often at the greatest disadvantage when talking. What is important about "action" tools is that they create a space in which something different can happen, something that may be shaped less by community discourses of "family."

The family therapy tradition known as symbolic-experiential, most notably Virginia Satir's work, is known for an inclusive understanding of language. One of the best-known Satir tools is the *sculpting* process (Satir, 1972), in which family members' bodies are used for both expressing and receiving nonverbal messages. In one form of this technique, family members take turns placing each other in physical arrangements that illustrate something about their relationships. The sculptor is invited to think about a real or imaginary scene that would "say" something meaningful and then is asked to arrange family members in the scene—complete with gestures and facial expressions, if desired (see Box 6.3). Once the "sculpt" is completed, the sculptor is asked to talk about the core messages and family members may be invited to report on their experiences of being in the scene (we return to this idea in Chapter 7). One scene can easily consume an entire session; therefore, the counselor should secure a commitment of several sessions for repeated sculpting episodes to give each family member an opportunity to contribute.

Other nonverbal techniques for communicating relationship meanings include using objects, songs, and pictures to represent relationships. Kozlowska and Hanney (1999) describe procedures for setting up a session in which family members interactively explore their individual and group symbol language. Such an activity can also yield important information about patterns of interaction (Chapter 5).

Beginning a Dynamic Assessment Process

Language-based family counseling activities don't always fit well with the idea of phases in counseling. Engaging and assessing typically overlap and merge with intervening. Even in the first moments of developing a relationship and opening up a space for multiple voices, the counselor cannot avoid making changes in the problem-determined system. An additional challenge, if one were to try to isolate an assessment phase in this work, is that many language theories (e.g., Maturana & Varela, 1992), assume that the counselor—as a participant—cannot be outside the conversation, so counselor objectivity would be seen, from this perspective, as a myth. Rather than identify an assessment and an action phase, the language-oriented helper may feel more comfortable thinking about the conversation as essentially without a beginning or an end, without goals, and without identifiable markers of "progress."

But there are language-based approaches that focus on assessment. Assessment may involve learning about the context, identifying internal and external attributions, examining story styles, identifying keywords and themes, describing problem-determined systems, and exploring unique outcomes.

Context

The narratives that people tell are partial expressions of reality, but they generally include information that can be helpful in crafting an alternative story that is healing, hopeful, energizing, and forgiving. When the counselor enters the client language system and steps into the various discursive streams that are implicated in the problem, it is a good time to collect information that contextualizes the problem according to factors such as time, language, culture, and economic conditions. For example, Gillian Walker charac-

BOX 6.3

My Mother, the Table

Klaus and Hilda had made considerable progress in their work with the counselor, reconciling their different viewpoints on parenting (punishment versus love and acceptance). The counselor had coached both parents in their attempts to be clear about expectations without making threats, and they adapted quickly. From a developmental/structural perspective, the counselor saw the counseling process as successful. The identified patient, 10-year-old Lisa—withdrawn and depressed at the time of the referral—was becoming more outgoing at home and school.

As Lisa became less of a concern, her 13-year-old sister Brigitte started attracting her parents' attention with new friends, new clothing styles, and an expressed interest in boys. The counselor decided that the time was right for a series of sculpting sessions. Lisa was given the opportunity to direct the first session, and everyone participated comfortably in a scene that did not seem to offer any news about the family, and Brigitte was next. Brigitte had the advantage of having seen how the process worked; and, when she walked in for her session, she went right to work. She pulled three chairs together in the center of the room, put her dad and Lisa in two of them, and then placed her mother on the floor on

her hands and knees with her head down. To complete the sculpture, she invited the others to sit with her around "the table."

Once the players had been in their positions for a few seconds, the counselor invited everyone to return to their regular positions and discuss the scene. Hilda's eyes immediately filled with tears as she said, "She's right, you know. I really do feel like I'm just a piece of furniture. Everyone's important except me, and they just walk by me without a word." Brigitte was invited to say whether that was the intended message, and she acknowledged that she was quite angry with her mother for having become such a nonperson. As the oldest child, she had fond memories of a young, dynamic mother who painted and showed an occasional painting in community galleries. Over the years, according to Brigitte, Hilda had withdrawn into the "Mom" role—make the lunches and dinners, drive two children to two different schools, and help with homework—while Klaus spent long hours working and pursuing his hobbies.

The session helped Brigitte to bring up a powerful gender theme in the family, one for which there had been no words that were safe to express. The nonverbal message was a first step in challenging the rigidly gendered family expectations.

---

terizes herself as an ethnographer, approaching sexual minority couples as a straight therapist:

> For example, I ask questions such as, Does this behavior have a different meaning in your experience than it might have in mine? Most often, partners are at different levels of resolution about sexual orientation issues. If I can keep the discourse open to the idea that there could be an emergent, different culture from the heteronormative, both the partners and I become collaborative inquirers about these new territories of sexuality. (Siegel & Walker, 1996, p. 32)

Parent-adolescent conflicts in industrialized societies have become normative to the extent that many parents, who admire and respect their high-school sons and daughters, say that they are reluctant to admit their positive feelings in public. I have found that the first session with the family of an adolescent takes on a different tone when I begin with an exploration of the parents' exposure to negative stories of the teen years. Asked, "When did you first get the idea that adolescents are hard to live with?" many parents identify media portrayals, family discussions about their siblings when they were children themselves, and comments from friends and relatives at the time of their child's birth. A frequent quote from friends and family is, "You just wait. She's cute right now, but she'll turn into a monster by the age of 14." Contextualizing the family struggle in this way helps parents to make special efforts to take note of their children's positive as well as negative behavior.

Identities, Roles, and Scripts

Making sense of people's interactions is made easier by knowing more of their identity narratives. Language-oriented family counselors know that nothing about a person's self-definition can be assumed. A large, muscular man can view himself as puny because his brother is even bigger, just as a successful politician may still carry around self-doubts based on having lost a high school election.

Because there is no single narrative that captures all truths, a professional may look for ways to get a "quick fix" on each member of a family group. Often family members can articulate each other's roles and identities easier than they can their own. Asked to tell one or two important things about each other, they usually deliver concise statements that capture essentials: "She's everybody's doormat" or "He's so caught up in his new job that nothing else exists right now."

Internal and External Attributions

Many counselors listen to problem narratives with an ear tuned for causal attributions offered by the participants. Parents and other caregivers rarely arrive in the counselor's office saying simply, "Marcus's grades are dropping." More often the mother comes in saying "Marcus's grades are dropping, and it's all the fault of my sister, who lets his cousins get away with anything, and my mother who keeps interfering when I try to enforce some standards in my house." Or the identified patient arrives saying, "My husband has lost interest in me because I am depressed." At the extreme level, people may lose confidence in their own perceptions because they believe they are being controlled by a "disease" (V. Jackson, 2002).

Language-based perspectives are less focused on verifiability or factual support for attributions than they are on the conclusions that follow from

those attributions. In the case of Marcus's grades, the mother's blaming problems on her extended family leads her to believe that she should keep him away from his grandmother, aunt, and cousins. The woman who blames her marital problems on depression may conclude that there is no hope of change, and she is unlikely to challenge her husband's Internet obsession and emotional unavailability. Developing alternatives to these attributions requires subtle appreciation of contexts and identities.

Story Styles and Types

Janine Roberts (1994) classified family stories by their styles of telling rather than their content, and said that a counselor's handling of the tellers' perspectives should be different for each style. She described *intertwined* stories that seemed to overlap both in their coverage and their telling; family members tell these stories as answers or extensions to each other's stories, making it hard to distinguish perspectives. *Distinct/separated* stories present seemingly parallel yet unconnected dilemmas, and *minimal/interrupted* stories do not present enough information to be related to other stories in any way. *Silenced/secret* stories present a special challenge, as they are only gradually inferred and never put into words. *Rigid* stories seem frozen and not open to interpretation and *evolving* stories seem to be used to make points at different times and show changes in family meanings.

Robert Sternberg (1999) also took a categorical approach in his approach to the love stories of couples, although his five categories focused on symbolic content rather than narration. *Asymmetrical* stories feature complementary differences in personal characteristics such as power, achievement, dependency, or confidence, and may feature caretaking or teaching interactions but also may include exploitation and degradation. Some versions of these stories involve the reciprocal partners trading positions, but the asymmetry continues. *Object* stories feature a partner who is valued not for herself/himself but for some goal that the partner serves (e.g., an "art story" based on physical appearance). *Coordination* stories feature partners working together;

they may be working toward a common goal, or they may be sharing a common activity. *Narrative* stories draw on some outside source for their relationship imagery: he mentions princes and princesses, scientific principles and formulas, and recipes as examples. And *genre* stories following the rules of a literary form—war stories, mysteries, and humor—call for different kinds of roles and performances.

Metaphor

In Chapter 5, I referred to Cloe Madanes and her contention that problems often contain important *metaphors* for the family system. Even though that concept was introduced in the context of communication theory, the discussion can be continued as we talk about assessing narratives. We can now consider the possibility that an important *alternative story*—possibly the story of the less powerful family members—may be seeking expression through the problem. What is called for in this assessment is a willingness to enter into the clients' language in a playful, creative, "analogic" way (Madanes, 1981) rather than assuming that the meanings of a story are limited to those that lie on the surface. Listening for the metaphorical referents of the clients' language, a counselor might inquire, "What do you suppose your daughter is trying to cure with these drugs?"

Keywords and Themes

One of the more popular ways of examining narratives has to do with paying attention to frequently used words and their apparent organization into themes—patterns of meaning that may be detected by a careful listener even though obscured by details. Locating and clarifying these themes may be an intervention in itself, or it may be a step toward developing a plan for making changes in those themes. The theme-oriented counselor may (1) identify themes according to a theory that classifies them in some way or (2) find themes through an ad-hoc process of watching for repeated words or phrases.

Binaries. Bird (2000) emphasizes themes that organize the perceptual world into binaries: good

or bad, success or failure, male or female, young or old, attractive or repulsive. Binaries, once identified, can be examined, challenged, and redefined to increase alternatives and options. Listening for a binary requires attention to more than just the individual words in clients' talk; the binary stands out because of an absence of subtle shades of difference. A binary view of an adolescent's sexual identity may not be apparent when the parent first mentions finding LGBT literature in the girl's room, but becomes obvious when the parent insists on knowing whether her daughter is attracted to boys or to girls.

Predetermined Themes. Freedman and Combs (2002a) approach couples with the intention of investigating a set of topics that they consider especially relevant for relationships. They say, "We are particularly interested in bringing forth partners' evaluations of power relations. This often involves asking questions that invite them to consider the effects of discourses, of gender, ethnicity, heterosexual dominance, class, corporate culture, patriarchy, age, or other sociocultural factors on their relationship" (p. 312). This orientation leads them to ask direct questions and continue with follow-up questions until they feel satisfied that they have properly evaluated these themes. In this effort to disengage from "restraining patterns and the relationship discourse that supports them" (Zimmerman & Dickerson, 1993), many authors suggest questions such as "Where do you think you got the idea that men are supposed to get whatever they want, while women are supposed to compromise?" Parker (1998), too, encourages special investigation of power themes. She says, "Power is often the 'dirty little secret' that both partners collude to deny" (p. 23). The respondents in her qualitative study, 15 leaders in feminist family therapy, identified a variety of readings, homework and questioning techniques that helped to bring these themes to the forefront.

Ad-Hoc. The ad-hoc perspective is represented in Keeney's (1991) *improvisational therapy.* Keeney offers the metaphor of *frames and galleries* as a way of noting the different modes of discourse that are experienced as counselor(s) and multiple family members co-create a story. Keeney is using the concept of frames in a conventional way, referring to ways of contextualizing a problem, while galleries are Keeney's contribution—a way of describing the relationships among related frames. In Keeney's example, a woman's history of struggling with her weight included several frames describing her strategies and others' efforts to help. These frames all were hung in a gallery titled "weight control," which characterized the first part of the counseling. Over the course of the work with this client, she gradually introduced frames that hung in a second gallery titled "handling jealousy," explaining that her husband was upset when other men noticed her. The frames in this second gallery then became the focus for a problem-resolving conversation that explored other ways of handling jealousy.

Unique Outcomes

White and Epston (1990), acknowledging the power of a dominant story to keep a problem alive, organize opposition to the dominant story. They do this by searching through the couple's or family's narratives to locate *unique outcomes*—times when the problem either did not seem to exist or it did not operate in the usual way. These unique outcomes become the data proving that the problem is not as pervasive or powerful as it was thought to be. Having located and then elaborated on small stories that include elements of resistance and hope, the counselor and the clients will *re-author* the narrative in a way that begins to describe the problem as something in the past. The same basic understanding underlies the solution-focused brief therapy approach (deShazer, 1994) as it organizes the assessment process to emphasize *exceptions* that prove the client(s) already have the resources to overcome their problems.

Intervening: Changing Representations

Language-based approaches share the assumption that people move closer to their relationship goals as they find new language for their individual and shared experiences. One set of intervention strategies shares an essentially modernist perspective, a view that sees the counselor as being in charge of the helping relationship, language as separate from relationships, and individuals having independent control over the language they use.

Rethinking

Baucom et al. (2002) identify five categories of cognitive variables that may need modification in family interactions: selective attention, attributions, expectancies, assumptions, and standards. They label their work "cognitive-behavioral" and their approach generally resembles the process that Beck et al. (1979) have referred to as *collaborative empiricism*—conducting a single-case study of how and when the cognitions occur and then evaluating the evidence supporting the cognitions. Baucom and his colleagues offer two broad strategies to help achieve these goals, saying that "Often the partner has explicitly blamed the individual for their relationship problems, frequently telling the individual that his or her thinking is distorted" (p. 48). The first strategy is *Socratic questioning*, which they contrast with more direct cognitive challenging used with an individual client. This strategy involves questions that are designed to be face-saving for the individual who "was thinking in an extreme or distorted way." Another strategy, *guided discovery* is directed more at the level of the couple, offering experiences—exercises and discussions—that help the partners to reflect on their thinking and develop new ways of organizing their experience. The overall approach is careful, gentle, and rational.

Dattilio (1998), while also describing his approach as cognitive-behavioral, demonstrated a more playful, directive, and challenging approach as he provided a client family with a handout listing 10 "cognitive distortions" associated with relationship problems. The following segment of dialogue illustrates his style:

DATTILIO: *Okay, so let's see if we can identify some of the distortions that each of you engage in.*
ROB: *Oh! I have one that Mom does big time.*
DATTILIO: *All right, let's hear it.*

Rob: *I'm not sure which one this is, but, like, if we're out past curfew, she freaks out and starts accusing us of being up to no good—like we're guilty until proven innocent.*

Dattilio: *That's an arbitrary inference, and one that you may perceive Mom as doing. Do any of the other family members engage in the same distortion? (p. 70)*

Reframing

The concept of frames appeared in Chapter 5, but we postponed a more detailed examination of the concept until this chapter because of its linguistic nature. The term refers to descriptions and explanations that have been part of a problem-maintaining system; *reframing* is the intentional substitution of new language to replace the clients' descriptions. A kind of Reframing called *positive connotation* (Selvini-Palazzoli et al., 1980) has become popular because of its usefulness when couple and family members are engaged in blaming. In this intervention, a problem behavior is attributed to benign intent. An adolescent daughter's failure to complete her homework, for example, might be described as her way of forcing the family to spend time together managing the crisis. The effectiveness of a reframe depends on how well it fits the social context (Coyne, 1985). It must be somehow credible but also discrepant, creating confusion and forcing the clients to reconsider their perceptions and actions. In a classic reframe, the parents of a troubled adolescent are told, "Marie is worried about your marriage, and she's noticed that you don't fight as much when you're worried about her. She's decided to sacrifice herself in order to give you something to agree about."

Many approaches, including Imago Therapy (Harville Hendrix, 1992), object relations, and attachment, offer theories that the counselor can use to connect couple problems with intergenerational family patterns. Like a positive connotation, a family-of-origin intervention helps to reduce blaming because the patterns are traced to a source outside the current relationship (Gerson, Hoffman, Sauls, & Ulrici, 1993). Rather than getting stuck on the history of the problem, the counselor shifts the clients' attention toward a future that never oc-

curred because they weren't aware of their patterns. Love and Robinson (1994) rely on scientific discourse, attributing couple differences in sexual desire to variations in testosterone. This description explains the existence of women who seem more sexually demanding than average and men who seem more sexually passive than expected. Few couples have the resources to measure their testosterone levels, so this new understanding can be adopted by a particular couple or it can be rejected as irrelevant.

Word Substitution

Less disruptive and more subtle is the gradual introduction of words that did not appear in the family's description. In Virginia Satir's early work, as transcribed in Jay Haley and Lynn Hoffman's *Techniques of Family Therapy* (1967), Satir can be seen substituting words into the family members' narrative in an intake session (see partial transcript in Chapter 2). The family, whose 19-year-old son has been hospitalized following a period of agitation, sleeplessness, and extreme sociability, seems to be reacting to a family problem discussing differences. Family members state their goals in terms of regaining "homogeneity" and "becoming a real family again." Satir introduces an ambiguous word, *hurt*, to describe the identified patient, and gradually she leads and prods the introduction of other words: *feelings, emotion, sadness, anger, disappointment, and frustration, approve, and disapprove*. These words, in the hands of people who have not had an acceptable way to discuss these concepts, seem to transform the interactions and produce a different reality.

Metaphor and Ritual

Finally, metaphoric communication is ideally suited to the project of subtly disrupting the ways in which people represent their realities. Messages that are indirect and hard to refute can help people to accept new and different meanings; some authors suggest that metaphoric communication somehow bypasses rational arguments—possibly by creating confusion. Metaphors introduced by the counselor can be drawn from the clients' language. A husband who recalls feeling more confident on the baseball field than in bed with his wife may be offered symbols in the baseball environment that help him clarify how he wants to be different at home: "Maybe sex is more like playing right field than second base. There's lots of time waiting, and nobody seems to notice that you're out there, but you just have to remember that when the ball comes in your direction you need to be alert and know what you're doing."

Milton Erickson is legendary for the stories that he created to capture his clients' dilemmas of wanting to change but fearing that change. Stephen Pearce (1996) presents many examples from Erickson's work as he offers guidelines and examples for the counselor who wants to be deliberate and intentional in creating metaphoric stories for clients. The folk tales of many cultures (e.g., Ross & Walker, 1979) are also rich with examples of real issues transformed into safe stories of beasts and birds. Roberts (1994) presents metaphoric communication as especially useful when working with children, whose receptive and expressive language is often not precise and who are sometimes less prepared than adults to engage directly in a collaborative process of mutual discovery. As a child creates a sand tray scene or illustrates a story about a character who faces his or her own life challenges, it is possible to explore alternatives and also rehearse ways of telling others about the issues. The safety of being indirect often gives a child the ability to tell the story with other family members in the room.

Metaphoric communication is not all done through conversation or storytelling. Metaphor is an important element in ritual (another concept that was introduced in Chapter 5), which appears frequently in the family therapy literature. The first wave of writings about therapeutic use of ritual, strongly influenced by Milton Erickson, described the counselor either designing or helping clients to design special rituals that can help them through a major life transformation. Price (1989) has written about his practice of guiding divorced former spouses through the process of planning and implementing a ritual that will give them a sense of closure with each other. Rings, readings, music, travel, and clothing are a few of the elements his clients have used to create new meanings between them. Quinn et al. (1985) focused on adolescence as a period of adjustment in fami-

lies, encouraging counselors to help people create personal substitutes for the rites of passage that may have been part of a lost cultural heritage.

Legowski and Brownlee (2001) distinguish the metaphoric options for the family counselor as including processes that are "counselor directed but client generated, such as art therapy, play therapy, letter writing, journaling, audio and video taping and psychodrama" and other processes that "carefully scrutinize and eschew dominance by the therapist, including how metaphors are generated and incorporated within therapy" (p. 20). Family sculpting, for example, introduced earlier as an assessment process, is also an extremely powerful intervention. The visual and kinesthetic messages that are exchanged in a sculpting experience, combined with peoples' attempts to put those messages into more familiar language, tend to challenge the routine meanings that people have accepted as their reality.

As Legowski and Brownlee (2001) point out, the relationship between the clients and the counselor is itself metaphoric and the messages should be consistent. One cannot say to clients "this is a collaborative process in which you are encouraged to find your own answers" and at the same time engage them in a process that represents them as passive recipients of expert help. A respectful way of working with metaphor does not demand or impose but rather observes, noting what may be metaphoric communication and offering that observation as a possibility.

Intervening: Collaborative Retelling

Even though the preceding interventions have demonstrated their effectiveness and they are based in language-based understandings of relationships, they can all be characterized as limited by a modernist tendency to talk about individuals without talking about their cultural context. The approaches developed under the umbrella of social constructionist ideas, alternatively, have been described as "a view that construes families and other client groupings as interpretive communities, or *storying cultures*" (Pare, 1995; emphasis in original). The following interventions demonstrate this newer trend, emerging in the late

1980s and early 1990s, in which the counselor is seen less as *acting on* the couple or family language and more as *working with* their language. It should be noted that the word "intervention" would be rejected by many of the people using these approaches, both for the reason that they doubt that they can know the outcome of what they do and because they mistrust the power attributed to their status as professionals.

One theme integrating these strategies and practices has to do with qualities of *transparency, collaboration, and respect* in the helping relationship. A second theme that runs throughout these techniques and practices is the concept of *diverse voices.* Rather than working toward an agreed-upon couple or family narrative, story, paradigm, or explanation, the helper seeks to expand the variety of language available to them. Reflecting teams, described earlier, may be used at any point in the intervention process to help expand the clients' ways of making meaning from their interactions. Video or audio recordings of sessions can be replayed with the clients, giving them a chance to reinterpret their experiences. And couple or family members can be invited to exchange poems, songs, photographs, or other creative efforts to extend beyond the limitations of words. Narrative practitioners may move back and forth among these techniques and strategies based on predetermined goals or—more consistent with the values of the narrative approach—based on perceived needs as assessed during sessions.

Conversation

Among the first authors to explicitly apply postmodern concepts of language and discourse in working with families were Harlene Anderson and Harry Goolishian, who understood problems as linguistically embedded in *problem-maintaining systems* (Anderson & Goolishian, 1988). This perspective, along with their rejection of therapeutic techniques that used language as a tool to change families, led them to adopt a radically nondirective posture initially called "Collaborative Language Systems Therapy," but also referred to as simply "conversation."

This approach is challenging for the learner because its creators have written more about goals than about methods. But even those who have had

the opportunity to see its practitioners in action or read transcripts of their work sometimes say they wondered what was going on. I remember watching Goolishian (on videotape) ask a client to explain Alcoholics Anonymous to him. Harry sounded so genuinely ignorant of it, I wondered how he could have not known anything about the program. Only later did I realize that his ignorance—his "not knowing"—was making a space for the client to describe AA in his own terms—to make his own meanings of the experience. The other obvious characteristic of this approach, its apparent lack of structure, is also intentional and is assumed to be an essential element in creating change. Harlene Anderson (1993) states that the goal of the counselor is to disrupt existing modes of organizing information and create an opportunity for "problem dis-solving."

Deconstructing Dominant Discourses

Power and its operation in dominant discourses has become one of the core concerns in narrative work (Hare-Mustin, 1998; Zimmerman & Dickerson, 1993). Monk and Gehart (2003) refer to this orientation as a "sociopolitical activist" position. A discourse or narrative may be labeled "dominant" because it tends to reappear throughout clients' storytelling and conversations, or it may receive the label for more obviously political reasons—because it seems to capture and transmit meanings that have the effect of dominating and subjugating couple or family members. In the latter case, the discourse is seen as having prevented clients from accessing other discourses that would have promoted growth, healing, and relief. The power of dominant discourses can be so great that counselors are inducted and have difficulty disengaging enough to access alternative perspectives (Hare-Mustin, 1994).

Because of the power of a dominant discourse—the family's story of their rise from poverty, or the culture's story of appropriate gender performance—the deconstruction process may need to extend over many sessions and may require a variety of discursive strategies. It may be necessary to conduct entire sessions in which a single person is interviewed, while the partner or family members sit silently and then process the listening experience from a *witnessing position*—attempting to receive and understand the other's communication without interpreting or challenging in any way.

Such an extended exploration of one person's unique experience can provide all involved with a thicker, more nuanced understanding of a dominant discourse and its effects, understandings that might have seemed adversarial if they had been offered by the counselor in the midst of an interchange between the partners. Freedman and Combs (2002a) demonstrated this use of the partner witnessing position with a couple whose relationship had incorporated many expectations and beliefs from the larger culture. The dominant discourse of sexuality, in which men were expected to be in control and women were expected to create excitement by having a particular body type, had been neither recognized nor challenged by either partner. Each partner, as the interviews showed, had experienced the discourse differently. The opportunity to hear each other's partial understandings of the discourse enabled them to develop a common goal of resisting its negative effects. If clients can hear such a retelling, as it is processed by others (the counselor or a reflecting team), integrating new or rediscovered viewpoints is possible.

Borwick (1991) applied the concept of deconstructing a dominant discourse in working with families in alcoholism treatment. After describing the "culture" of alcoholism treatment, including its inconsistent use of concepts derived from Alcoholics Anonymous, Borwick said that "A major dilemma for therapists has been to create a treatment context that preserves the positive aspects of AA and other forms of self-help while constructing a relationship driven by the individual's and family's meaning rather than the care provider's or organization's values" (p. 5). The program described by Borwick focused on attitudes and exercises for *creating a context of surprise.* Because family members had been living in a language community that emphasized knowledge and certainty, Borwick said, they were likely to overlook unique strengths and miss evidence of progress. Furthermore, the culture of alcoholism treatment was a culture of *men's* alcohol problems that did not support women the

same way it did men. Over the phases of the family's interaction with the program, they were invited to focus on their own memories and current experiences, distance themselves from the standard recovery story, and create their own unique multivocal story.

Restorying

Where the emphasis in the deconstruction tradition tends to focus on awareness of the dominant discourse and its effects, other traditions focus more on the process of developing alternative narratives.

Solutions.   Probably the best known of the restorying approaches is a mixture of theories and techniques known as Solution-Focused Therapy (Berg & deShazer, 1993; Hoyt, 2002; Sklare, 2000). The term "solution-oriented," used by Bill O'Hanlon (1993), is broader; he has sometimes referred to his work as "possibility therapy." What this literature (over 50 books in print) shares is a belief that people improve rapidly in a process that emphasizes their strengths, their potentials, and their possibilities. One of O'Hanlon's sessions, as transcribed and analyzed by Gale (1991), shows O'Hanlon taking control of the conversation to shift it away from a problem focus and toward a solution focus. Gale catalogs nine different techniques that facilitate this "pursuit of a class of solution-oriented responses" (Gale, p. 95) with the result that the clients conclude they can make changes in their lives without professional help.

Starting from the same core assumption, but operating out of a different body of language theory, Berg and deShazer (1993) documented several specific strategies. They distinguished between "problem talk" and "solution talk," for example. Saying that most professional helpers focus on getting a detailed history of "the problem" during the first contact with clients, they suggested that that first conversation should focus on strengths and accomplishments, leading to a relationship based on respect. They encouraged the counselor to look for evidence of success; pointing out, for example, that calling for an appointment was proof that something different had started to happen. They also recommended teaching clients to use a numerical scale in comparing the current state of things with their ideal. The following transcript shows deShazer conducting a demonstration session, a consultation with clients of a German therapist:

SDES: *My first question is: Let's say that "10" stands for what you hoped to get out of therapy and "0" stands for how things were before you started therapy. Where would you say you are between "0" and "10" today?*

MRS. K: *"5"*

MR. K: *"8"*

SDES: *"8," you've gone from "0" to "8" (pointing to Mr. K.) and you from "0" to "5."*

MR. K./MRS. K: *Yeah.*

SDES: *How did you do that?*

Note that the questioning not only emphasizes change but also implies that the change happened because of something that the client(s) "did" (1994, p. 98).

Probably the best-known strategy developed by Berg and deShazer for creating an alternative reality and helping clients to believe in change is the *miracle question*. Clients are often asked the question in the first session, setting up expectations of change and providing a mechanism for negotiating the length and nature of the counseling process. The question is simple, yet elegant in its ability to invite people to step outside their problem stories. As presented in deShazer (1994), it goes like this:

> Suppose that tonight after you go to sleep a miracle happens and the problems that brought you to therapy are solved immediately. But since you were sleeping at the time you cannot know that this miracle has happened. Once you wake up tomorrow morning, how will you discover that a miracle has happened? (p. 95)

The miracle question is not an accident, it was carefully crafted based on assumptions about people's ways of organizing their realities. Asking for a fantasy rather than a prediction disrupts the personal and shared storytelling through which people protect themselves from

disappointment. Asked "How would your relationship look if it were better?" too often produces a response, "It can't get better because we hate each other" or some such rejection of hope. And the fantasy invites a complete picture, not just a description of a single aspect of the new reality. deShazer referred to the importance of asking not only about what others would be doing, but also something like, "And how would you be acting differently?" so that the preferred future is not only one in which other people have changed.

Even when clients resist the idea, saying things such as "it couldn't happen," deShazer said that a persistent counselor can usually get them to "pretend." Their suspension of disbelief and imaginary impressions of a future in which the problem no longer exists, enables them to identify the kinds of interpersonal as well as intrapersonal changes that would be part of a successful transformation. Once the future has been imagined, solution-focused counselors like to praise the clients for their performance, talk to them about how to move toward the ideal future they have imagined, and collaboratively plan for homework to help them with their goals (Hoyt, 2002).

Externalizing Problems. White and Epston (1990) popularized a much different approach to the creation of alternative stories in their classic book *Narrative Means to Therapeutic Ends*—creating stories that *externalize* problems. This strategy is based on the idea that clients are weakened and discouraged by their identification with their problems. They *have* ADHD or anorexia or they *are* depressed or addicted. From White and Epston's perspective, this narrative pattern makes change sound quite unlikely, and they offer the option of characterizing the client (or client family) as *victims of* ADHD or anorexia. The switch in use of words may be small as the counselor asking about "when ADHD first showed up in your life," but clients generally respond well to talking about the problem as something separate from themselves. They are typically encouraged to give a name to the problem and to construct a problem narrative in which they have been engaged with a crafty and determined opponent.[9] As we discussed earlier, clients are encouraged to find events or periods of time ("unique outcomes") when they succeeded in resisting the influence of the problem. Retelling the story over and over, they embellish these success stories until they become at least as powerful as the dominant stories of failure. White and Epston make extensive use of written documents—handwritten books, carefully executed certificates—that help to focus the work and serve as records of how much things change through the course of counseling.

Johnella Bird, a colleague of Epston's in New Zealand, developed a different approach to externalizing, focusing not on the problem but on the relational decision-making strategies that have gone into creating and maintaining problems. This *relational externalizing* attitude "acts to shift the focus, from that of an individual self to a self always in relationship" (2000, p. 7). She refers to *investigating* a word or a set of meanings or *re-searching* the client's experience with desire, insensitivity, touch, success, guilt, or gender. She recommends:

- *Listening to the emotions that support the words*
- *Negotiating the meaning of words rather than taking the meaning of words for granted*
- *Remaining alert to the contextual environment. (p. 74)*

Re-Membering. Among the creative restorying processes popularized by Michael White is one that focuses on the shared nature of narratives, a sharing that includes "members" who "belong" to a storytelling group (S. Russell & Carey, 2002; White, 1997) and are part of each other's identity stories. Viewed from this perspective, a story may be impoverished and incomplete because some voices are missing from its telling, and clients may be suffering from what is essentially a memory loss. It is helpful to bring together those who hold

the pieces of a story. In this "re-remembering"— provided that the sharing is done in a spirit of generous listening or hospitality—all members of the group are enriched by hearing each other.

The same concept can be applied to working with the stories that *would have been told* if an absent person or persons could have been present, and Hedtke and Winslade (2004) apply this view to the bereavement process. Such conversations reject the idea of knowledge, a way of talking that assumes a single body of wisdom, and instead speak of *knowledges,* a way of talking that credits many different sources and kinds of wisdom or expertise.

Stories That Reassure. Emily Brown (1999) focuses on couples who are having trust and commitment problems after the discovery of an affair, even when it is clear that the affair has ended. She has found that their stories of possible future improvement are typically thin and unconvincing; the negative expectations they hear from friends and relatives tend to dominate. She provides the partners with a standardized set of affair stories, all of which offer varying levels of explanation and prediction regarding possible recurrence. When both have read the same set of alternative stories, they can seek to reconcile the attributions and assumptions that are embedded in their different meanings of the affair (see Box 6.4).

Anne Bernstein (1999) discusses another negative story, the pervasive depiction of stepfamilies as love starved, hostile, painful, and frustrating. Rather than offer a predigested set of alternative stories, Bernstein instead challenges the narrative tradition of foreshadowing—attempting to anticipate the future. As an alternative, she teaches a concept of *sideshadowing*—imagining all the possible ways in which things may turn out for better or for worse.

Collaborative Ritual. In the preceding discussion of ritual, the professional was portrayed as the social engineer using ritual in ways that tended to be prescriptive. Laird's (1988) work is an example of a second approach, with the counselor serving less as a creator of ritual and more as an anthropologist studying the family culture. Her work

---

[9] This use of adversarial language is itself a source of controversy. Critics have pointed to the cultural assumptions embedded in such language and to the idea that many clients might not feel comfortable using images of fighting, enemies, and victory.

BOX 6.4

Narratives of Infidelity

According to Emily Brown (1999), infidelities occur for different reasons. Couples can recover from many affairs, and the recovery is easier when they are able to talk together and make sense of what happened. When the story makes sense, they can work on the underlying issues and prevent a recurrence.

Brown classifies affairs into five groups:

1. *Conflict avoiders:* The couple relationship is tentative. The affair is brief, generally one-sided, and serves as a substitute while the couple relationship has been taking a back seat to the rest of life.

2. *Intimacy avoiders:* The couple relationship is intense and conflictual, becoming fragile when the partners become close. Affairs are frequent, intense, often open and competitive, but not long lasting.

3. *Sexual addiction:* The addict has brief, meaningless affairs as a mood-altering tool. The partner is overfunctioning, trying to keep life stable in the midst of chaos.

4. *Split selves:* One or both partners find excitement when they connect with someone outside their rigid, predictable, unfulfilling, depressing marriage.

5. *Exit:* The affair is a bridge, providing one partner with confidence to leave the other. Both parties gain a face-saving way out of an unsuccessful relationship.

---

was based on a concern with women's special needs in light of cultural messages that devalued and denied their experiences. She said,

> *Ritual permeates family life and thus provides the therapist and family together with rich sources for understanding issues of gender as they affect women, as well as powerful sources for change. The family therapist should develop skill in understanding and interpreting the meanings and prescriptions embedded in existing family rituals, in assisting women and families in preserving rituals important to individual identity and family coherence, in reclaiming those that may have been passed over or now exist in truncated, outdated, or destructive forms, and in sharing in the construction of new rituals. (pp. 341–342)*

Assessing Effectiveness

Assessing outcomes in language-based intervention is integrated into the intervention process.

People's use of particular language in describing their experiences and in immediate communications of goals, feelings, and relationship assessments is assumed to be intimately connected with the problems they are experiencing and the ways in which they relate. Just as initial assessment tends to overlap with intervention in these approaches, intervention tends to overlap with assessment. Because the storytelling that is central to these strategies involves a constant flow of language, either that language is demonstrating progress or the progress is not occurring.

At the same time, most of the approaches described in this chapter attribute a great deal of significance to the clients' own perceptions of change. The counselor using a collaborative approach would be unwilling to judge that clients' lives were better based on the appearance of improvement. The principle of transparency that characterizes the initial phases of this work must extend through the middle and late phases as well. Using the solution-focused tradition as a clear example, clients are asked on a regular basis whether they perceive movement toward their goals. If clients report a sense of lost momentum, the counselor uses that information to make further changes in the process. The *witnessing effect* must not be discounted as a part of this perceived change. Clients are more likely to perceive change if they hear trusted others saying that the change appears to be happening. Periodic use of a reflecting team may be helpful for putting changes into perspective and remembering the way the clients were handling issues when they first arrived for help.

Closure

The approaches described in this chapter are generally in agreement that clients, not professionals, should decide when the counseling process is ready to be suspended. The process empowers clients to take charge of their life stories; it is to be expected that such a change may include finding other people to talk to besides the professional. Long-term intervention processes are generally not necessary, and a single conversation or performance of a ritual can bring the relief people were seeking. Therefore, the professional begins preparing for the possibility that this is the last session, even from the first conversation. This preparation emphasizes the clients' right to make choices and the professional's willingness to suspend or continue work at the clients' pace. It is not uncommon for clients in a narrative model to leave and return several times, staying for one or two sessions to work new observations, events, and concerns into their story.

Cautions and Concerns

Narrative perspectives have appeared in many forms over the years. Most of the intervention strategies we examined are rather gentle, indirect, and low risk, in comparison with those described in Chapters 4 and 5. Nevertheless, the broad umbrella of language-based models includes a wide range of interventions, and they share a tendency to destabilize relationships.

Being indirect, narrative interventions can lead to unanticipated change; it is fair to say that they predict unanticipated change. Therefore, there is a certain amount of risk, but the risks are probably as minimal with this group of approaches as with any helping orientation. One of the risks is that no change will occur; narrative practice clearly does not promise specific results.

The greatest challenge in this narrative arena may be keeping a professional center in the midst of a dizzying array of new concepts, techniques, and professional discourses. The Behavioral and Organizational themes have been explored for decades, and new discoveries are added to a strong, established knowledge base. The professional who depends on skill training or altering hierarchies in families can find extensive literature discussing the subtleties of this work. The same is not true in many of the emerging narrative traditions; a charismatic author's ideas may not have been challenged or re-examined in readily accessible journals. Therefore, a practitioner working in this exciting, rapidly moving arena must make special efforts to connect with other professionals at conferences, in peer learning groups, or in training programs where current ideas are examined and processed.

Suggested Individual and Group Activities

Your understanding of concepts and issues presented in this chapter may be enhanced by the following activities:

- *Family paradigms.* The next time you are around a couple or family, listen for evidence that they share some ways of understanding their world and don't share others. Are there particular strengths in their shared understandings? Are there also ways in which their shared meanings might create problems for them?
- *Discourses of sexuality.* Listen carefully to the lyrics of current popular music and, if possi-

ble, watch the videos that go along with the songs (you can often find the lyrics posted on the web). What are the messages that children and adolescents are getting about sexual behavior, feelings, and expectations? Are these messages the same as you remember from 5 or 10 years ago?

- *Mechanistic metaphors.* Try to refrain from using metaphors of physical science (elements, explosions, stone wall) when describing human relationships and communication. Do you have alternative language that captures your meanings but does not imply objective, observable reality?

Suggested Readings

Anderson, H. (1997). *Conversation, language, and possibilities: A postmodern approach to therapy.* New York: Basic Books.

Dattilio, F. M., & Padesky, C. A. (1990). *Cognitive therapy with couples.* Sarasota, FL: Professional Resource Exchange.

Parry, A., & Doan, R. E. (1994). *Story re-visions: Narrative therapy in the postmodern world.* New York: Guilford.

Reiss, D. (1981). *The family's construction of reality.* Cambridge, MA: Harvard University Press.

White, M., & Epston, D. (1990). *Narrative means to therapeutic ends.* New York: W. W. Norton.

Emotion: Regulation, Relationship, and Motivation

The problems presented by a couple or family are intertwined with their emotional interactions.

Objectives

In this chapter, you learn to:

1. Recognize and identify emotional components of relationship processes.
2. Differentiate among multiple traditions that describe emotion in relationships.
3. Distinguish between positive and problematic emotional patterns according to theory and research.
4. Describe and explain commonly accepted emotion-oriented interventions.
5. Select, plan, and implement emotional couple and family interventions appropriate to treatment goals.

7

Chapter

The fourth of the BONES dimensions focuses on what some people say is the only component that matters in couple and family relationships—Emotion. This chapter views human relationships as the interaction of people's feelings—interpreting their actions, systemic patterns, stories, and spiritual experiences as either leading to or caused by feelings. Close relationships are understood as special because of the intensity of feelings (even though virtually every human interaction somehow includes feelings).

Emotion is a central theme in the psychoanalytic tradition that dominated the mental health field for so many years; to this day, many people assume that therapists say little except, "How does that make you feel?" Feeling words are central in people's descriptions of good relationships—joy, excitement, satisfaction, comfort, trust—and in their descriptions of problem relationships—pain, loneliness, fear, disappointment, anxiety. When people say, "We're here because of a communication problem," it's not because their lives have been focused on achieving high scores on an empathy measure. They are complaining about communication problems (or money, sex, or children) because they aren't having the feelings they hoped for. They feel too much pain and anxiety, or they feel too little trust and joy.

Emotion has assumed its prominence in the fields of mental health and human services not only because it is a goal but also because it is the ultimate fallback theory. When we are confused by our own behavior, arriving late to a meeting because we gave in to a sudden impulse to shop for greeting cards, we can say, "I felt like doing it." And when logic seems useless to explain a child's lack of follow-through or his or her repeated involvement in self-destructive activities, it is hard to refute the proposition that the problem behavior is the result of frustration in early childhood or anger about her best friend moving away.

This perspective is somewhat less optimistic than the behavioral, organizational, and narrative perspectives. After all, emotions are neither easily assessed nor readily modified; some theories suggest that emotional patterns are established by age 3, and after that all people can do is learn to accept them. Nevertheless, the hope of emotional connection and fulfillment is what brings people to relationship counseling. Many popular self-help authors have achieved success by promising "the love you want" (H. Hendrix, 1992). This chapter shows that such promises are not totally unrealistic; feelings can be brought into the counseling process in many ways, and some emotional approaches lead to dramatic and long-lasting changes.

A Case Illustration: Frank and Anita

Frank, a 50-year-old Latino instructor at the police academy, and his Anglo wife Anita showed up at their first appointment for couple counseling looking extremely uncomfortable. Anita, who had made the appointment, explained the situation to Rosalie. Her sister-in-law Sandra had recently given her a brochure on domestic violence; Sandra had said, simply, "Read this." Anita said she could tell from Sandra's tone of voice that it was important, so she did what was asked and the experience changed her life. In the brochure was a list of indicators that promised to "tell whether or not you are in an abusive relationship." The list, she said, "read like my life story." She immediately passed the brochure to Frank. He did not immedi-

ately see himself described in the brochure, but he responded with a sense of urgency. "If this is how you see our marriage," he said, "we need help."

Frank had never hit or physically threatened Anita, they both wanted Rosalie to know. For that matter, they agreed that Frank had never raised his voice. But Anita's behavior fit the image of an abuse victim; easygoing and open with Rosalie—and, she said, with other people—she became almost silent when she turned toward her husband. She reported that Frank had become increasingly controlling in the relationship ever since they lost their first child to crib death. From that time on, Anita hadn't been allowed to have a car; she waited to be driven to stores, doctors' appointments, and even to their child's school to meet with teachers. If she took a bus instead, she was accused of sneaking around and meeting a man. When she saw a male doctor, Frank interrogated her about what happened in the office and implied that Anita was excited at being seen partially undressed. At one point, when she had been told to come back for a series of treatments, Frank insisted she change doctors because he believed that she and the doctor were planning an affair. She was not trusted with more than a few dollars cash at any one time, she said, and she was not allowed to have visitors other than Frank's family when she was home alone. Things had loosened up somewhat when their only daughter, Julia, earned her driver's license; Julia had been happy at first to drive her mother around and her father didn't oppose the two of them being out together. But now Julia was too busy to be her mother's driver, and Anita had been feeling like a prisoner at home.

When Rosalie asked for Frank's version of this story, Frank confirmed that he had been extremely jealous and extremely vigilant regarding Anita. But his jealousy was not totally unfounded, he said, because of a fact missing from Anita's story. Anita had failed to mention the fact that she disappeared for a week after their infant son William's death and she still, 20 years later, refused to tell him where she went. He was certain that there was a secret lover somewhere, and he was determined—with all the power of the police force behind him—to make sure that she didn't succeed in reconnecting. Did he realize that she was feeling confined and isolated? Yes. He thought it was an appropriate price for abandoning him in a time of need and for keeping him guessing for all those years. And he was sure, he said, that his vigilance had not been adequate. There were times when she was unexpectedly happy, and he was sure that those were times when she had somehow met with "her boyfriend."

In the next session, Rosalie gathered more history. Anita's family-of-origin experiences, she admitted, had been "horrible—worse than you can imagine." Her older siblings had dropped out of high school to get away from the family as early as possible, and she—the youngest—had only been allowed to leave home when she married Frank. Her parents were alcoholic, often violent with each other and neglectful of their children, and there were times Anita had to borrow money from relatives to have shoes or school supplies. Frank, whom she met at church, had seemed like an answer to her prayers. He had been stable, calm, sure of himself, and protective of her. He hadn't even lost his temper when he had conversations with her drunken, explosively angry parents. He had promised to take care of her, and he had done so for the first 2 years. They had bought a house, planted a garden, put up pictures on the walls, set up a nursery, and had a baby. She had thought she was in heaven, until it all crashed with William's death.

Frank's own history, he said, was pretty uneventful. He had been the oldest of three sons, had known since the age of 10 that he wanted to be a police officer, had gotten good grades, and had gone to college and majored in criminal justice. He had never known anyone like Anita's family. When he felt betrayed, he blamed it on her family background. "I should have known," he said, "that she wasn't brought up for a decent family life." He said that his parents, still married and living in the same city, had been supportive of his marriage, but his two brothers, both happily married, had never trusted Anita.

The counseling process started off slowly so long as Anita retained control over the one thing she "owned"—the secret of where she was for the week following William's death—even though

Frank tried to change his emotional interactions with her. He couldn't justify his behavior, now that he recognized its abusive quality, but he was less than comfortable when he tried to express affection or act supportive. Nevertheless, he recognized that she responded to him as if he had beaten her, and he wanted to see her frightened look go away.

After three meetings with the couple, Rosalie asked for an individual session with each partner, starting with Anita. Reassured that her confidentiality would be respected, Anita shared her secret. She had gone to a motel and for 3 days she had drunk herself into oblivion, leaving the room only to buy another bottle at a nearby convenience store. On the fourth day, she looked in the mirror and realized that she was following in her parents' footsteps, and she threw out the remaining vodka. It took her another few days to feel ready to go back home. She had thought, at first, that she would tell Frank, despite her feelings of shame, but then his reaction had seemed so hostile that she withdrew. She was now sure that telling him would end the relationship.

Frank, in his session, agreed to focus on his part in the problem. He admitted that his family history wasn't as uneventful as he liked to think. Pressed for details, he shared the memory of a time when his parents separated for a short time. He had been only 5 or 6 years old. No one told him what was happening; his mother just didn't come home, his father claimed to not know where she was, and when she returned home after a few weeks there was no discussion of the incident. Frank was beginning to think that his reactions had been irrational and that he had destroyed Anita's spirit with his anger.

In the next couple session, with support from Rosalie, each partner shared some of these thoughts and feelings, and the session ended with them both in tears. After a few more weekly sessions with further emotional sharing, they started coming in less frequently. Their last 6-month checkup, 3 years later, showed a remarkably close "empty nest" couple who were making the most of their time together, and Anita was so confident and direct as to be nearly unrecognizable.

Theory and Research

Emotion is central to the experience of being human. Spiritual traditions have included emotional concepts such as joy, serenity, and surrender, and the U.S. Declaration of Independence addressed the "pursuit of happiness." Among the most commonly used diagnostic categories in the current *DSM* are the mood disorders, and many counseling traditions have given emotion a central role in the helping process. Depression has become a topic discussed openly with friends and family, thrill rides and Halloween events boast of creating excitement and fear, and the mental health field has a long history of focusing on anxiety. Your own ways of understanding the world probably include some emotion concepts.

In the previous chapter, I introduced the concept of multiple discourses—linguistic conventions that shape how people experience reality. Even when the same events are observed, different discourses can shape how they are described. At this time in the helping professions, there are at least three major discourses on emotion—psychodynamic, social science, and biological explanations. These discourses explain emotion differently and they have different implications for conceptualizing the needs of couples and families.

Psychodynamic Discourse— Emotion as Struggle

The first discourse ties together various approaches that have evolved out of the psychoanalytic tradition. If we include all its branches, such as Emotionally Focused Therapy (EFT) (Johnson, 2003), Schnarch's (1991) *Sexual Crucible,* Imago Therapy (Hendrix, 1992), and other attachment-related work (e.g., Byng-Hall, 1995; Lopez, 1995), the psychodynamic perspective is probably the dominant discourse regarding feelings in relationship counseling.

Psychodynamic discussions of emotion, revolving around Freud's clinical observations and theorizing, start with the assumption that early experiences have special, powerful, lifelong effects on people's lives. This special significance is as-

sumed to arise from the intensity of interactions with caregivers. In the Freudian model, humans are born into a world as unsocialized animals whose biological drives bring them into intense conflict with caretakers. Later theorists such as Fairbairn cast parent-infant relationships in a more positive light, seeing the infant as driven to find love. In either view, these early relationships are not relationships among equals. Infants are helpless at birth, and early caregivers have tremendous importance in creating the first intimate relationships—through these interactions, we get to know ourselves. Early passions and handling of emotions build a foundation for emotional life, and future relationships will have emotional qualities that replicate infantile experience. Problems in adulthood, according to these theories, can be traced to a time when a dysfunctional emotional "lesson" was learned—when both experience and coping abilities were limited.

Psychodynamic authors also tend to agree that many emotional and relational processes are hidden from awareness. Freud, who thought that the hidden material was a threat to the conscious self, believed that mental health was achieved by learning to accept primitive feelings that lay hidden beneath the socially appropriate exterior. Perls described emotions in terms of polarities— each acceptable part of the self was assumed to have a rejected opposite. And Jung referred to the "shadow," a part of the self where feared aspects were kept hidden. When people's emotions are hidden, according to these theorists, they are handicapped in their attempts to make sense of their own and their family members' behavior.

Despite this consensus, an examination of two dominant perspectives shows many differences.

Drive Theory

Freud saw the early years as a struggle between children's biological drives and their need for acceptance. In infancy, he believed, existence is organized around pleasure and that undisguised pursuit of pleasure is embarrassing to the adult world. Caregivers, representatives of the adult world, create an emotional climate as they either meet or frustrate the infant's drive for oral gratification. As the child becomes more sophisticated, the source of pleasure shifts from the mouth to, in turn, the anal and eventually the genital areas—leading to more conflicts. The anal period is especially frustrating, and during that period the young child often begins to demonstrate another primary drive—an aggressive urge, which is unacceptable when it appears in undisguised form but proves to be acceptable when sublimated into competitive games. People are important primarily as tools for—and barriers to—gratification of drives.

As the child becomes older and achieves object permanence, memories and symbolic gratifications come to be important. A turning point occurs in the Oedipal period, a time when the opposite-sex parent—the mother, in Freud's original formulation—starts to become a fantasy lover. Unable to gratify this fantasy, the child learns to seek comfort in symbolic representations and substitutions. Having redirected selfish pleasure seeking and aggressive urges into social interaction, the adult eventually is ready to enter into mutually satisfying, responsible relationships but carries unresolved internal conflicts dating from earlier developmental stages.

These transformations are achieved by developing and using *defense mechanisms* that block forbidden urges and protect the ego—the conscious, decision-making part of the self—from being aware of the threatening impulses. Unfortunately, many of these defense mechanisms can be destructive if they are overused. Defense mechanisms that are especially relevant for the family counselor are repression, projection, and reaction formation. When *repressed urges* threaten to emerge, people typically try to distance themselves from the impulses. They *project* their own fantasy images onto others, who are assumed to have the same urges, and then *react* by punishing these others. This explanation has been used to explain violence of all kinds, especially violence involving differences of race, gender, culture, and class.

This framework seems to explain a tragic problem that seems to occur in many U.S. families as a result of parents' confusion about sexuality, cultural fascination with youth and their emerging sexual interest, and paternalistic attitudes to-

ward women. The problem typically shows up in adolescence as a painful sense of distance between father and daughter.[1] When this distance is mentioned by the counselor, family members recall that it was not always present; until the daughter reached puberty, the father was attentive and openly affectionate. Daughters mention how confused they were when their fathers withdrew. And the physical and emotional withdrawal does not, in some cases, end the painful sequence. Further scenarios include (1) fathers becoming increasingly angry, especially with the "wild youth of today"; and (2) fathers being openly hostile toward daughters' dates and—in extreme cases— their committed partners. This story makes sense in psychoanalytic terms as the father experiences (at a level below awareness) threatening sexual impulses in the presence of his daughter's maturing body. He defends against this response by avoiding her and denying her presence, projects his own sexual obsession onto a class of people who seem to be doing what he has fantasized about, and eventually is upset by being confronted with someone who is free to act out those forbidden urges.

Psychoanalytic theories have inspired many different approaches to individual and relational functioning. A common thread has to do with repressed parts of self and others. In intimate relationships, partners typically *project* onto each other the rejected parts of themselves; Bob accuses Joe of having become fat and repulsive, and Joe counters by saying that Bob's looks are his only redeeming quality. And in parent-child relationships, parents seem obsessed with the ways in which their children have failed to match family ideals. These relationship problems require not only facing and accepting the self but also facing and accepting one's own flaws in others.

No discussion of Freud's legacy is complete without examining the notion of transference and

---

[1] The stereotypical depiction of this as a father-daughter issue should not be interpreted to mean that parallel processes do not occur in other parent-adolescent relationships. Mother-son attraction and same-sex attraction might be expected to lead to the same kinds of distancing and reactive parenting.

its operation in any helping encounter—even non-professional encounters when one person attempts to engage with another's concerns. Freud believed that perceptions in all interpersonal encounters are colored by the unmet and unresolved issues of the participants. This means that helpers will not be perceived accurately, nor will we accurately perceive those we attempt to help. He encouraged helpers to know their own typical distortions so that they could sort them out from those of the clients, thereby leaving the clients' distortions highlighted for easy study and intervention. We return to this notion when we talk about intervention.

Object Relations and Attachment

Object relations thinkers, though also building on a Freudian base, took the opposite position—that people aren't merely driven by simple drives but instead have a deep, undeniable need for *connection* with others. Scharff and Bagnini (2002) summarize Fairbairn's position in the 1940s as ". . . the infant is not the inchoate conglomerate of drives that Freud described. The infant is born with a whole self through which it regulates affect and executes behaviors that secure the necessary relatedness. . . . The infant is looking for attachment, not discharge" (p. 60). This formulation was the starting point for research and theory using the concept of *attachment*.

Bowlby (1979, 1988) proposed his attachment theory to explain the behavior of infants whose access to their familiar caregivers had been disrupted during World War II. Working from a tradition of ethology rather than psychoanalysis, Bowlby asserted that human infants have an *attachment behavioral control system* that monitors the proximity and availability of a caregiver. When the attachment system signals that the bond with the caregiver is being disrupted, an infant is overwhelmed with anxiety and then protests, assumes a posture of despair, and after several days withdraws into detachment. In the presence of an emotionally available caregiver, alternatively, "attachment and the emotions that organize attachment behaviors are adaptive and serve to form a secure base . . . from which the individual can confront the world" (Johnson & Greenberg, 1994, p. 4).

In the first year of life, the dependency on others is as much physical as emotional—without

a caregiver[2] who both provides and soothes, an infant has a difficult time learning to use the body's built-in capabilities. A successful early *secure attachment* to one or more trusted caregivers results when an infant is fed and protected and learns to expect caring and constancy from others. A less stable and less supportive caregiver leads to a different attachment—one that is *insecure*. The attachment process is mutual; Bell and Richard (2000) postulated a *caregiving behavioral control system* that parallels the infant's. Early experiences of secure or insecure attachment, according to Bowlby, are retained in primitive memory forms he called *internal working models* that record movement, sensory/perceptual data, and moods.

Bowlby's internal working model is essentially what object relations theorists call *internalized objects*—representations of self and others—which record the dramas of infant life. Because every caregiver is imperfect, internalized caregiver representations include both rewarding (good) and rejecting or punishing (bad) images. In the extreme case, referred to as *splitting*, perceptions of self and other become rigidly organized into opposites of good self/bad self and good caregiver/bad caregiver. For the child (and eventually for the adult) who has undergone such a split, experiences organize themselves into a cycle of looking for the good (a new friend, counselor, or wife) but being disappointed by finding the bad. When things go well, I am "good me" and I deserve to be rewarded, but eventually disappointments and failures transform me into "bad me" and then I deserve to be punished.[3] This cycle describes, to a greater or lesser degree, many people's relationship histories with parents, siblings, friends, co-workers, partners, and children.

---

[2] I recognize that the term "mother" and the assumption that infant and mother relate through a "breast" appear throughout the psychodynamic literature. This appears anachronistic in contemporary society. Not only is it sexist—fathers and others are emotionally significant to the extent that they are caregivers—but even a biological mother does not always breast feed. Therefore, I am ignoring these elements of the theory.

[3] This object-splitting is hypothesized to be the early origin of Borderline Personality Disorder.

The infant's fragile state extends beyond depending on others for the basic requirements for survival. At a time when he or she is just learning about the human body, what feels good or bad, an infant can be caught up in others' own pursuit of pleasure or their expressions of destructive rage, presenting the young child with experiences of trauma. Extremely painful early memories may not only inhibit the ability to trust and accept relationships with others but also lead the infant—and later the adult—to suppress all feelings and adopt a strategy of emotional suppression.

Mary Ainsworth and her colleagues (e.g., Ainsworth, Blehar, Waters, & Wall, 1978) devised a *strange situation* experiment to assess young children's attachments to their mothers. In their laboratory, when the mother left the room and then returned, the child's responses to her departure and return showed that the largest group appeared *securely attached*; others appeared *anxious and ambivalent,* showing extreme feelings on separation and reunion; and a third group appeared *avoidant,* showing little emotion or interest when the mother left and when she returned. More recent work has redefined these categories, and researchers have added the concept of a *disorganized* attachment style with few fixed characteristics (Solomon & George, 1999).

Ainsworth's model has been extended in recent years into a concept of *adult attachment style,* with advocates demonstrating that there is considerable consistency in observed behavior and in apparent emotional experience across an individual's various relationships (Hazan & Shaver, 1987). Adult attachment styles, it is assumed, become especially relevant in situations that somehow activate the schemas that have survived from infancy. When those schemas predict disappointment and rejection, according to this theory, an adult may—even in the performance of basic parenting tasks with a child—revert to primitive responses of protecting the self by withdrawing into an emotional "shell." Likewise, an adult partner may respond to the other's sudden illness with rage and withdrawal. Theory predicts, and clinical experience seems to confirm, that such primitive responses often occur without warning and seem totally out of character.

The attachment perspective has been used to help make sense of one of the most powerful, pervasive, and confusing aspects of adult relationships—romantic love. Shaver, Hazan, and Bradshaw (1988) created and tested a detailed three-category model based on Ainsworth (see Table 7.1). As anticipated, student and community

Table 7.1 Adult Attachment Types and Their Frequencies

Question: Which of the following best describes your feelings?		
Answers and Percentages:	Newspaper Sample	University Sample
Secure: I find it relatively easy to get close to others and am comfortable depending on them and having them depend on me. I don't often worry about being abandoned or about someone getting too close to me.	56%	56%
Avoidant: I am somewhat uncomfortable being close to others; I find it difficult to trust them completely, difficult to allow myself to depend on them. I am nervous when anyone gets too close, and often, love partners want me to be more intimate than I feel comfortable being.	25%	23%
Anxious/Ambivalent: I find that others are reluctant to get as close as I would like. I often worry that my partner doesn't really love me or won't want to stay with me. I want to merge completely with another person, and this desire sometimes scares people away.	19%	20%

Source: From "Love as Attachment: The Integration of Three Behavioral Systems" (pp. 68–99), by P. Shaver, C. Hazan, and D. Bradshaw, in *The Psychology of Love,* R. J. Sternberg and M. L. Barnes (Eds.), 1988, New Haven, CT: Yale. Reprinted with permission.

survey respondents described their love experiences in ways that paralleled their self-ratings on attachment. *Secure* lovers reported comfort and trust, accepting partners' faults; *avoidant* lovers reported being fearful and jealous, suspicious of love; and *anxious/ambivalent* lovers reported obsession, frequent love experiences, and extreme sexual attraction. The researchers concluded that romantic love is "a complex dynamic system involving cognitions, emotions, and behaviors" that has "biological bases and functions" and "takes on somewhat different forms depending on a person's attachment history." While acknowledging that sexuality was one of the major differences between romantic love and experiences of parent-child attachment, they did not explore the sexual aspect in detail. Their theory does suggest that for the avoidant individual, sexual attraction and sexual pleasure might represent a threat—not because of a Freudian fear of repressed impulses but because sexual desire has always led to emotional pain.

Other researchers (Rothbaum, Rosen, Uhie, & Uchida, 2002) caution against applying attachment theory to any particular set of relationships, considering that cultures have different standards for defining appropriate emotional bonds in parent-child and mate relationships. Attachment theory is a social construction and the research supporting the theory has been done mostly in Western cultures that share certain assumptions about healthy and unhealthy relationships. These researchers note that Japanese mothers seek to maintain a level of dependence and security that is inconsistent with Western expectations that children explore and become self-sufficient. At the same time, marital relationships in Japan place less emphasis on gaining primary emotional fulfillment from one's partner.

Separation and Individuation

Object relations and attachment theories are in agreement on the young child's need to engage with caretakers and on the reciprocal nature of that engagement. But how are infantile attachment and its extreme dependency replaced by increasing levels of independence in the relationships of young children and their parents? The theme of *separation and individuation* was a key element in Bowlby's theory.

It is not enough that parents and children attach, they must also negotiate their growing separation in ways that do not seem like rejection. Margaret Mahler's (Mahler, Pine, & Bergman, 1975) observations of mother-child dyads provided dramatic examples of negotiations being handled badly; often it appeared as if the parent's attachment issues were disturbing the relationship.

In positive relationships, caregiver(s) and child(ren) gradually move apart and disengage from a symbiotic oneness. This typically begins around 9 months of age when the infant distinguishes familiar from unfamiliar people (a crisis in many families, when visiting grandparents or friends are greeted with cries of panic). The separation gains speed when the child develops the ability to move independently of the caregiver, first by crawling and then by walking and running. Successfully negotiated individuation processes, according to Mahler and colleagues, go through stages of *symbiosis, differentiation, practicing* (moving away, risking loss of the attachment), *rapprochement* (coming back and restoring the attachment), and eventually *mutual interdependence*. But the researchers also observed many unsuccessful processes, including the following:

- The caregiver appears threatened by the child's efforts to pull away, and responds by *restricting* the child. The child may abandon attempts to individuate, postponing the crisis and limiting emotional development, or may continue pulling away and individuation will be conflictual.

- The caregiver appears threatened by the child's efforts to pull away and responds by *rejecting* the child. The child may abandon attempts to individuate, postponing the crisis and limiting emotional development, or may continue pulling away and feel guilty.

These extreme responses predict relationship problems for the child who does not somehow find support and corrective emotional experiences with others. This is not only an early childhood concern; the separation-individuation process is, according to Blos (1985), repeated in adolescence. Mackey (1996) has documented the complexities of parent-adolescent separation and individuation, concluding that many adolescents do not get the nurturance they need to manage the emotional challenges of movement into young adulthood.

Bader and Pearson (1988) postulated that committed couple relationships follow a developmental path not unlike that of parents and their young children. Couple relationships begin in a symbiotic fusion, but their progression toward differentiation often leaves the two partners unmatched. Rather than attribute this mismatch to an inner limitation on the part of one partner or the other, Bader and Pearson point to the difficulty of the renegotiation. Couples must learn to manage feelings of betrayal and abandonment that are common when conflictual issues arise, and manage them in such a way that neither person is disadvantaged. Applying the attachment perspective to family level developmental processes, Lopez (1995) and Dankoski (2001) point out its salience during transitional periods when family composition is changing. Differing comfort levels with either increased closeness (marriage, birth, early childhood) or increased distance (adolescence, young adulthood) would be expected based on family members' attachment styles.

Loss, Grief, and Attachment Injury

Experiences of attachment and separation are not limited to childhood and adolescence, and adult life may seem to be a roller coaster ride on which the thrills of growing closer are mixed with periods of anxious waiting and the stomach-churning panic of feeling abandoned.

Death is the most predictable loss. The death of a close family member may occur during one's early years, but some people pass the age of 30 before their first such experience. People who describe the loss of a parent figure, sibling, partner, or child struggle to put their experiences into words. They refer to such losses as "feeling a hole where she used to be" or "losing my purpose for living." Where a secure attachment existed and it was suddenly broken, the resulting emotional distress suggests that there has been a merging of selves, an emotional interdependence that provided something beyond comfort and security. The period following such a loss is quite often a time when life seems to change. Clients describe starting to feel like they're moving through quicksand or looking through a dirty windowpane, unable to feel anything, make connections with others, or say the name of the lost loved one without sobbing.

Positive mourning processes seem to lead to a state where the loss is manageable, a distant memory of sadness along with a calm acceptance of life's joy and pain. In Chapter 8, we discuss spiritual traditions that seem to help people achieve a state of acceptance. But many people do not resolve their losses well, and a profound grief reaction can lead to serious disturbances in other relationships (Jordan, Kraus, & Ware, 1993). Children may not remember the death of a grandparent when they were 3 or 4, but years later the family may still be affected by a parent's grief. Grieving family members are especially prone to handle new attachments differently (see Box 7.1).

The other attachment injury that is a part of many people's lives is the experience of being rejected by a friend, lover, partner, or child. Many of us can remember such a rejection in elementary school when a former best friend suddenly found someone new to play with, and if a person has not experienced such a loss by the age of 30, we may wonder if he or she has been resisting attachments. As in the case of death, such an experience can leave the individual with the feeling that a part of the self is gone. But there is a different quality to these losses—the other is not really gone, the other is still out there in the world having a great time. Just as in the case of death, these attachment disturbances tend to interfere with other relationships and may produce a long-term avoidance of any further emotional connections (as well as advice to one's children, "don't let yourself get hurt").

Mate Choice, Intergenerational Patterns

The foregoing discussion partially explains how people create new relationships that replicate familiar patterns—even patterns that are uncomfortable. Several theorists have described the ways two partners can contribute to each other's emotional growth or add to their distress. According to Scharff and Scharff (2003), mates are selected in part because each person detects in the other hidden aspects (e.g., creativity, sexuality) that have been denied or rejected in the self. This *projective*

BOX 7.1

Saying Goodbye and Saying Hello

The cycle of family life is somewhat like the tides. People come in and people go out. The movement is predictable, but every time it happens it's a new event somehow. In the case of family arrivals and departures, we can't publish a family events table that says "first child at 16, first grandchild at age 32" but there is such a thing as "on-time events" for a particular family. Events that are anticipated are somehow easier to manage emotionally than ones that are a surprise, but even so, emotional pushes and pulls can get in the way of effective functioning.

Tyrone and Alya knew from the day they met that they both wanted children, but they did not start trying to have a family until they had established themselves financially in their early 30s. After about a year, they started worrying about the fact that they had not conceived and they sought a fertility consultation, which resulted in the opinion, "It doesn't look like you're going to get pregnant without some help." The next 3 years were exhausting and full of mixed joys and pains. First, they found out that there were physical problems that would make conception difficult, and they had the options of continuing to hope or beginning to intervene. They chose the intervention route, and their lives became regulated by various medical experts who prescribed drugs that changed their moods; demanded changes in their eating and sleeping habits; and told them when and how to engage in intercourse. During those 3 years, they wondered if it was going to be worth it, and then finally they were pregnant!

The doctors told them to be ready for disappointment, but at first they were having trouble feeling anything at all because of their anxiety. They started planning the nursery, watching other people's children, and imagining their own, trying to imagine the ways their lives were about to change. And then Alya miscarried. The miscarriage was a horrible experience, not so much physically as emotionally. Even the close friends and family who knew about the pregnancy didn't seem to share their feeling of loss. People were kind, but they also seemed to think that there was no need for mourning, and the couple had a hard time connecting with each other's feelings. After the years of emotional ups and downs, they were stuck in a down period. Routine was easy. Emotional crises could be avoided by not getting excited. And then shutting down became even easier when Alya's mother died.

As sometimes happens with fertility problems, it was only after they stopped trying—3 years later—that another pregnancy occurred. It was clearly different this time. Alya considered keeping the information from Tyrone, because she thought she could protect him from the disappointment she expected. But she overcame her reluctance and told him, and he responded with a lukewarm smile and hug. There were no discussions of setting up a nursery this time, and no fond looks at babies in the mall. They walked around in a fog, just waiting for the cruel joke to play itself out. But there was no miscarriage. After 5 months, they started to realize that they were not getting ready for a baby, but the baby was likely to arrive. They tried to get excited, but it wasn't working. Alya's sister said to the two of them, "You need to get some help or your baby's going to grow up without parents." Fortunately, the hospital had a program that provided prenatal groups, in-hospital visits from a "coach," and follow-up visits to discuss the emotional and practical issues of building a good relationship with a baby. As soon as they joined the prenatal group, the leader recognized that Tyrone and Alya were not emotionally engaging with their unborn child and referred them for couple counseling where the counselor helped them with their unresolved grief issues.

With the help of professionals and family members, the mourning process began to be addressed in the short time before Justin was born. He arrived, on time, into a home where he was welcomed and loved. But the shadow of loss did not disappear quickly.

identification, in its positive forms, can lead to a deep sense of joy and emotional bonding when the lost aspects are regained. In its negative forms, it creates rejection and even hatred when the hidden (and rejected) qualities begin to be apparent. This theory explains the common pattern in which a quality once prized in a partner eventually becomes the quality that is complained about the most. The husband who, as a dating partner and even during the childless early years following marriage, "could always make me laugh" eventually is rejected because "I can't get him to be serious about anything."

Napier (1971) explored the intergenerational nature of relationship patterns in a qualitative study of young couples and their parents. From his exploratory study, he hypothesized that people are attracted to partners who appear to come from a healthier family than their own. However, they eventually find that they have joined a family with similar dynamics, which merely displayed them differently. Napier's research couples seemed to fit a pattern of *complementarity,* with the partners' different strengths and needs fitting together so that each contributed some of the skills and aptitudes needed for a successful relationship.

Some couples seem to demonstrate intergenerational patterns of emotional dependency or conflicted and blocked relationship aptitudes (see Box 7.2). In such a situation, often described as involving partners with *weak ego boundaries* (Scharff & Scharff, 1987), partners have a hard time maintaining a healthy balance. This issue is described by Murray Bowen (1978) as involving a struggle over *self:*

> *The dynamics between the new husband and wife are determined by the way they fight, or share, the ego strength available to them. They go into the marriage with equal levels of "self," but they quickly fuse into a common self . . . and thereafter one spouse usually functions with more than an equal share of the available ego strength. (p. 110–111)*

Harville Hendrix (1992) describes such intergenerational patterns as resulting from a process in which individuals are programmed at an early age to feel comfortable in relationships that reproduce familiar emotional experiences. Expecting rejection and criticism, an individual finds them and chooses certainty over uncertainty.

BOX 7.2

Interacting Emotional Styles

Psychiatrist Peter Martin (1976) described four typical patterns from his practice with couples. It is not clear that the same patterns are being seen 30 years later, but these examples illustrate the ways in which partners' emotional styles can interact:

1. *The love sick wife and the cold sick husband:* The wife described feeling chronically unfulfilled and criticized in the relationship, while the high-functioning husband remained distant and complained of her emotionality.

2. *The in-search-of-a-mother marriage:* A passive man, having found one competent and independent woman to take care of him in marriage, then searched for other less powerful women to provide nurturance.

3. *The double parasite marriage:* These relationships involved "two people who cannot swim, clutching each other desperately and drowning together." These couples were typically in economic crisis unless supported by their families.

4. *The paranoid marriage:* A dysfunctional worldview—for example, an addiction—united the pair until one disengaged and sought help in trying to rescue the partner.

What these situations had in common, according to Martin, was an apparent limitation in one or both partners' ability to function as a separate person.

Another approach to partner choice, described by Lopez (1995), links partner choice to attachment styles and then predicts the dynamics of these pairings. A variety of studies have found that secure individuals choose other secure individuals, while anxious-anxious or avoidant-avoidant combinations are rare. The more common match is an anxious partner with an avoidant partner. Lopez notes, "As one partner attempts to manage personal distress by reducing interpersonal distance, the other is likely to be stressed by this partner's demand for greater closeness and disposed to respond to this change by increasing distance in various ways" (p. 14).

Emotional Self-Other Knowledge, Intimacy

In the safety of positive early relationships, a well-cared-for infant learns his or her own limits and learns about the reality of others. Pain, joy, sadness, and excitement are shared experiences that enlarge the infant's ability to enter into intense and satisfying relationships with others throughout life. For those who are less fortunate, early deprivation or distorted relationships may limit the child (and eventually the adult) by inhibiting the development of confidence and skills needed to engage in intimate encounters with others.

Daniel Wile's (1994) "ego-analytic" approach defines problems in relationships as problems of emotional understanding. In Chapter 4, we spoke of knowing self and other (e.g., "I have learned that my husband requires extra time to form his impressions of new people, whereas I immediately know whether I like someone."), and Wile's theory addresses such limitations in people's ability to accept the complexity of their reactions and desires, contradictory thoughts, and behaviors. He says that problems in relationships often result from partners' attempts to cover up their true feelings, expressing a "safe" and supposedly acceptable pseudo-feeling rather than an authentic response. Feeling unentitled to their emotions or fearing that they may hurt each other, they develop reactions that Wile calls "symptoms," which then interfere with relationships. They have *feelings about their feelings*—they feel depressed about being depressed, for example—and then hide from each other rather than connect on an emotional level.

Wile's work parallels other formulations that define intimacy in terms of the ability to connect without controlling—to express emotion without first processing it to take the rough edges off. Johnson and Greenberg (1994), basing their EFT model on attachment theory, assert that authentic emotional connection is a human necessity throughout the life span, but the need is often frustrated. Rather than connect at the level of *primary emotions* such as surprise, happiness, anger, sadness, and fear, people often communicate instead about *secondary emotions* such as embarrassment or shame that combine deeper feeling with more surface-level judgment and evaluation.

Terence Real (2002) also points to a lack of emotional authenticity in many couples and families. He writes, *"We enter life whole and connected, and we operate best when richly attached. Intimacy is our natural state as a species, our birthright."* But he says, "we teach boys and girls, in complementary ways, to bury their deepest selves, to stop speaking, or attending to, the truth, to hold in mistrust, or even in disdain, the state of closeness we all, by our natures, most crave. *We live in an antirelational, vulnerability-despising culture, one that not only fails to nurture the skills of connection but actively fears them*" (p. 21, emphases in the original).

The "Imago" approach of H. Hendrix (1992) refers to the situational nature of emotional responses and predicts that dating couples often will not find out about their intimacy limitations until they are called upon to handle intense interactions. A committed couple relationship, according to Hendrix, is the place where true self-knowledge begins. In this mutual encounter with others' unreasonable but unavoidable demands, partners who have the necessary skills can gradually work toward risk-taking and genuine awareness.

Emotion Management and Regulation

An attachment or object relations perspective seems to define mental health as the open expression of emotion, but there is an opposite view more consistent with Western cultural norms for men (Hare-Mustin, 1987; Real, 2002). This view places a high value on resisting emotions so as to achieve stability and predictability in relationships (see Box 7.3). Emotion, from this perspective, is something that is important but also threatens effective functioning. People who are excited, overjoyed, or starry-eyed, and those who are upset, depressed, tense, agitated, worried, anxious, or angry, are people whose judgment can't be trusted. Excessive expression of emotion is a "problem," and one of the essentials of successful family functioning is finding ways to control emotions.

A variety of theoretical constructs have been used to portray emotion negatively, and many have appeared in family counseling theories.[4] Bowen, for example, wrote about emotionality as *reactivity,* contrasting this unrestrained and irrational response with *differentiation*—emotional independence in the presence of other people's emotional fields. When a group of reactive people interacts, Bowen's concepts of *fusion* and *undifferentiated family ego mass* describe the quality of emotional interconnectedness that prevents them from having individual, rational thoughts. This view of the emotionally overconnected family has also been shared by others. Minuchin (1974) referred to *enmeshment,* characterized by weak intrafamilial boundaries, and more recently Leff and Vaughan (1985), among others, have described high levels of *expressed emotion* as a problem in families of psychiatric patients. The concept of *codependency* can be another such negative portrayal. Some authors (e.g., Schaef, 1986) are more careful in their presentations, but readers of other popular literature could easily conclude that any degree of caring about others was a sign of pathology.

Bowen's portrayal of emotion as dangerous and inherently uncontrollable was criticized by Knudson-Martin (1994, 1995) who claimed that Bowen's theory privileged thinking over feeling. Horne and Hicks (2002) responded with assertions that the theory describes a balanced emotional process in which both emotionality and rationality are seen as having inherent risks. They

noted that Kerr and Bowen (1988) specifically rejected efforts to suppress emotion and express an appreciation for the ability to experience feelings and, in fact, Bowen had called attention to the dangers of emotional *cutoff* in his theory, calling for family members to work toward emotionally engaging each other rather than risk making an emotional impasse permanent.

A neo-Bowenian position more closely resembles the way that David Schnarch (1991; Thorgren & Christensen, 1999) uses the concepts of differentiation and emotion. Schnarch refers to couple partners who over time lose their loving, attachment-maintaining emotions behind a façade of apparent disinterest or find themselves locked into negativity. Some protective behavior should be considered a positive sign: It demonstrates that the emotional intensity of the relationship has reached the heat of a *crucible,* a container in which molten metals are combined. At such a level, the partners are capable of wounding each other emotionally, but therapeutic improvement will come from (1) reducing the pathways by which the partners escape their emotional "crucible," and (2) helping them to differentiate—to develop insulation, as it were—so that they can individually experience intense emotion without fear for each other.

Social Science Discourse— Emotion as a Variable

A second discourse about emotion, featuring social, cognitive, and behavioral language, is somewhat newer. Within this discourse, nothing about human responses is innate, automatic, or biologically driven. Every individual is seen instead as beginning life as a learner in a social setting. The infant learns, in the preverbal years, what behavior is recognized and reinforced. As developing mental capacities support a more elaborate representational system, the infant begins to discriminate among stimuli, to compare the expressions and actions of caregivers, to construct an internal set of symbols that provide a sense of mastery, and, eventually, to use one or more languages to organize and share internalized symbolic representations. Emotional experiences throughout

---

[4] It should be remembered, of course, that many MFT theories were developed in efforts to eradicate schizophrenia—which was characterized by irrationality.

BOX 7.3

Where's the Emotion?

It is amazing to think that love, fear, and other emotions were ever left out of discussions of couples and families, but that has been the case in family counseling literature—much of which makes relationships sound about as emotional as changing a tire. This is particularly striking considering that Satir and Ackerman, two of the best-known family therapy pioneers, were not only known for their emotional style with families but also talked openly about emotion. How could such an omission have occurred? Aren't people essentially emotional? Isn't love a universal element in couple and family relationships?

I offer three hypotheses to explain the apparent absence of emotion in so many approaches to relationships. First, some authors may have excluded emotion from their work because their theories and practices seemed valid and complete without this "unnecessary" element; the master theory-building principle known as "Occam's Razor" demands that explanations be simplified as much as possible. The only rationale for including emotion in a theory would be that the theory didn't work without it, and theories such as classical conditioning describe behavior without emotion being involved.

A second possibility relates to the confusing nature of human emotion. Many different theories and research methodologies have been applied to questions about the nature of emotion and its functions in human relationships. The picture that emerges is fuzzy at best. We know that people in most, if not all, cultures have language for emotions, and we can observe what we agree seem to be indications of emotion, but there is little agreement about how emotions occur, whether emotions are viewed as more helpful or more problematic in human functioning, and what can be done when emotions seem to be problematic. Family counselors might avoid emotion because of an inadequate knowledge base.

But there is a third possibility. An honest observer of the family counseling field must acknowledge that theorizing was dominated, during the consensus years (see Chapter 3), by men who might

have been uncomfortable with the topic of emotion. Rationalist, patriarchal Western culture has a prejudice against emotion—one that has served to marginalize and pathologize women (Schwartz & Johnson, 2000). From the time of Freud's early work, the typical (female) psychiatric patient was labeled "hysteric" and her problems were attributed to emotional dysregulation. Ackerman (1958) described the Freudian heritage as follows:

> It discloses with remarkable brilliance how man perceives and falsifies his image of family, but it does not elucidate with equal clarity how man assimilates and uses the more correctly perceived experiences, the "realities" of family life. The Freudian image of love as a positive, healthy force in family relations is incomplete. (p. 27)

Building on this tradition, later theorists may have ignored emotion as something that cannot be addressed rationally. Eve Lipchik (2002) criticized the mainstream of Solution-Focused Therapy for continuing this omission. She wrote, "it may be in the clients' best interest to talk with them in their language, even if that is emotion, rather than risk that they do not feel understood." Other theorists have included emotion but cast it in a negative light (see the discussion of *emotion management* in this chapter). For better or for worse, suppressing or managing emotion has become more achievable than ever with recent advances in psychopharmacology (Prosky & Keith, 2003).

But a different attitude is noticeable among contemporary practitioners. There has been a resurgence in activity related to emotional experiencing and expression, and emotion-oriented interventions have been among the fastest-growing segment of the family counseling field. Emotion-oriented approaches connect with people's realities not only because these approaches often match the clients' own language and are widely applicable—nearly every presenting problem can be somehow related to emotion—but also because they deliver the changes people want. New developments are integrating findings from brain research, and emotion is exciting again.

life add to—or challenge and eventually modify—the internalized map of emotional experience.

The following categorization of theories and research traditions is a partial sampling of the social science literature on emotion, selected to highlight the concepts and findings that have contributed to current practice with couples and families.

Social Construction of Emotion

The first group of theories emphasizes the extent to which emotion is socially produced through the processes of selective attention and labeling (Staske, 1996; G. M. White, 2000). Without denying the physical sensations involved in many emotional phenomena, these approaches say that emotional events are collaboratively created through language in social situations. Nearly all of these theories acknowledge something like "primary" emotions that are closely tied to physiological states, and "secondary" emotions that are more the result of meaning-making.

Every language emphasizes some kinds of emotional experience, providing many words to distinguish among subtly different experiences while giving less attention to others. And within a language group, certain kinds of emotional experiences are considered appropriate while others are discouraged. This differential attention produces clusters of emotion labels. Vocabulary not only gives reality to emotional experiences, it also gives them shape and suggests something about their resolution. Cultures, families, and individuals differ in their available vocabulary for emotional experience. One family mocked a child's sad, tearful face: "If it's so awful, why don't you go out to the garden and eat worms?"

At the level of individual labeling, Schachter and Singer (1962) took the position that emotional experience is relatively undifferentiated at the physiological level. According to this theory, people experience some physiological arousal—"I am feeling something"—and they draw on their learnings to tell them what the feeling might be. Once a label has been applied, experiences that fit the label are selectively noticed and those that do not fit the label are ignored. Depression, for example, is a label that has become more common since selective serotonin reuptake inhibitor (SSRI) medications appeared. Counselors are now

accustomed to clients saying, "I'm here because my sister said I'm depressed, and after she said that, I read about depression, and now I am starting to notice that I'm tired all the time, lack energy, and feel worthless."

This view does not deny the complexity of the human emotional system, but it says that direct experience can be subordinated to external sources of knowledge when people are not sensitive to their internal states. For example, clinicians report that men in the United States and other Northern European cultures often identify only one feeling: anger. Anger is valued, for men, more than emotions that imply vulnerability. There are essentially two ways of analyzing emotional descriptions: multidimensional and discrete emotional clusters. A multivariate approach looks for dimensions that appear across many different emotional terms and concepts. Russell (1983), for example, identified two dimensions that appeared in many cultures: evaluation/pleasure and activity/arousal. Emotional experiences can be ranked on these dimensions from high pleasure (joy) to low pleasure (sadness) and from high arousal (rage) to low arousal (depression).

At the relational level, a social constructionist view of emotion predicts misunderstandings and experiences of isolation when people's emotional expressions are either not acknowledged or are reinterpreted by others. People often arrive for counseling with complaints such as, "I've been telling him for years now that I'm lonely and depressed, but he keeps saying that I'm just out of shape and I should go to the gym with him." Families during the period of adolescence often experience such emotional disconnects. Parents seem to often underestimate their child's emotional distress or label it as "normal," whereas to the adolescent it may seem intolerable. Such a parent seems to be operating from a behavioral theory of emotion—"If I reinforce those tears, she'll cry more often."

Emotions and Health

A global distinction between positive and negative emotions dominates social science approaches to the topic. In research environments, moods and emotions are studied multidimensionally by recording verbal expression of emotions, facial expressions and other nonverbal indicators, physiological changes such as skin conductance, and subjective self-reports. Emotion is a term more often used for states that are more situational and transient, as opposed to mood states that have a more stable and pervasive quality to them.

"Positive" emotions are ones that people want to experience and they seek in others—for example, love and happiness. "Negative" emotions are ones that (in a given culture) people don't want to experience and find uncomfortable in others—such as anger and fear. Positive emotions are generally assumed to be empowering and life-giving—sources of healthy energy in people's lives. Research has demonstrated a strong connection between positive emotions and various aspects of physical and emotional health (Schwartz & Johnson, 2000). The correlations between emotions and physical health were summarized by McGuire and Kiecolt-Glaser (2000). Seeking support for Sullivan's (1938) theory-based assertions that good relationships lead to emotional and physical well-being, they found studies that showed hormonal changes and improved health for people who had "supportive personal relationships" as opposed to "acrimonious interpersonal interactions."

McGuire and Kiecolt-Glaser's (2000) summary spoke even more strongly about negative emotions than positive ones; in both newlyweds and long-time couples, negative health indicators were positively correlated with negative or hostile marital interactions. The authors concluded that negative emotions themselves were a risk factor, but negative emotions such as fear and depression were less destructive for those whose primary relationships were supportive enough for them to process and resolve their thoughts and feelings.

Love.   Love is a complex topic, partially because this single English word has to carry the weight of so many related concepts. As a characteristic of couple relationships, love can be defined as "a deep emotional bond, mutual caring and attraction, trust and closeness" (Reihl-Emde, Thomas, & Willi, 2003). This definition may also be applied to feelings toward siblings, parents, and children. Gottman et al. (2002) more often speaks of *positive affect,* or *positive sentiment,* when he describes the caring that he considers essential in couple relationships, but he also refers to *love maps,* which he defines as an understanding of the partner, and a *fondness and admiration system.* All of these positive emotional elements serve as an *emotional bank account* that helps couples to remain connected through times when negative feelings occur.

Love may be the core of what Terrence Real (2002) has labeled *relational esteem.* Observing widespread agreement on self-esteem as a goal, Real counters with this relationship-level goal. This appears to be the same concept for which Virginia Satir used her homey metaphor, "pot," as in the statement "their pot was almost empty." With relational esteem, the group as a whole is strengthened by their interactions; alternatively, self-esteem may be achieved by some individuals, while others are sacrificed or left out of the positive developments.

Many times, however, when English-speaking people use the word love, they are referring to what Grunebaum (1997) categorized as romantic/erotic love. Grunebaum, acknowledging the difficulty of his task, attempted to sort through the variety of ways in which this special feeling has been understood. Identifying some of its features, and noting the many times when love is credited for being the cause of people's destructive acts, he offered guidelines for professionals to use when they believe romantic/erotic love to be an element in relationships. He encouraged the counselor to (1) try to assess the degree and nature of the feelings, (2) to treat the feelings as "rare and therefore precious," (3) to help people realize that "romantic/erotic love is not easily found and may be worth saving," (4) to believe that conflicts between a new love and loyalty to a previous love may be valid personal struggles, and (5) to promote people's understanding of their relationship as "different from and more than either of the partners" (p. 305).

Negativity.   Negative emotions seem to appear more often in the literature on couple and family relationship patterns, and these discussions often use the term "negative" in a very inclusive way.

Susan Johnson and Wayne Denton (2002), for example, used the summary term "relationship distress" to refer to feelings of anger, despair, depression, and detachment along with behavioral patterns that contribute to those emotions. John Gottman and his colleagues (Gottman et al, 2002) sometimes use "negative" in this kind of general way, citing research findings that show a need for both negativity and positivity (they say that the ratio should be 1:5). But they also identify four particular kinds of negativity that are particularly destructive in couple relationships. The negative emotional patterns they call the "four horsemen of the Apocalypse"—criticism, defensiveness, contempt, and stonewalling—seem to have destructive effects. These patterns contribute to the difference between two types of "negative affect reciprocity," one in which the negativity is returned *in kind* and another in which the response is an *escalation* from the partner's expression. The latter is destructive, whereas some satisfied, successful relationships are characterized by frequent negative exchanges. It appears that these negative interactions are somehow consistent with expectations (consistent with family and cultural definitions of what is acceptable?) and therefore not threatening.

When specific negative emotions are discussed in relationships, the most often mentioned are shame, guilt, anger, anxiety, and depression, and these often coexist in complex ways.

Shame.   Shame is a pervasive feeling of anxious depression, apparently related to self-assessments of unworthiness. Identified by Erik Erikson (1964) as developing early in life, it was presumed to result from unsupportive interactions with caregivers. Other authors have also identified the pattern as multigenerational: Shame-bound adults, say Merle Fossum and Marilyn Mason (1986), tend to pass on negative self-assessments to children and grandchildren. The shame-bound individual is unable to take credit for any positive achievements and lives in constant fear that others will discover his or her inadequacy; constant vigilance and control is necessary to prevent disaster.

Within social groups that are heavily shame influenced, two extreme lifestyles are common.

Some members strive to overcome the shame through obsessive overachievement, careful choices, and meticulous habits. Others consider failure to be inevitable and act in self-destructive ways (e.g., alcoholism) that guarantee that they will be criticized and rejected. Intimacy presents a challenge, as the dread of being discovered—especially when an event heightens awareness of the shame—leads people to a variety of negative strategies to maintain emotional distance (Balcom, Lee, & Tager, 1995). Negative strategies of rage, overcontrol, withdrawal, and contempt disempower both partners in a couple. And emotional distance, along with obsessiveness in basic caregiving, virtually guarantees that children will lack positive validation as they go through the period Erikson identified with the alternative outcomes of shame and autonomy (the "toddler" years).

Guilt.   Guilt is distinguished from shame by the presence of high expectations. Like shame, guilt is established early in life (Erikson, 1964). But Erikson theorized that guilt is a more advanced cognitive-emotional phenomenon, dating from the preschool years. The guilt-ridden individual views every situation as involving the potential for failure but believes—in a way that the shame-bound individual does not—that he or she has the ability to succeed. The guilt-establishing parenting message is, "you could have done better." Guilt, like shame, is often associated with compensatory overachievement. But because of its more optimistic basis it generally leads to a more balanced, successful performance in any task—including parenting. The emotional stress of anticipating failure is a constant in guilt-influenced families, but the underlying feeling is more anxiety than depression.

Anger.   Anger may appear early in life in response to various kinds of threat, but for many individuals it becomes an emotional theme maintained by patterns of externalizing attributions. Like guilt and shame, pervasive anger often seems connected to patterns of parenting. Whereas the guilt-oriented family tells a child that he or she should have "tried harder," the anger-oriented family says, "you tried, but the deck was stacked against you." The message need not come from the family—it may also be encountered later in life. To the angry person, life appears unfair and favors other individuals or other groups. The imbalance often seems to be based on diversities such as race, economic level, or sexual orientation.

These perceptions of unfair or abusive treatment may be correct. Minority youth, for example, are likely to have observed numerous occasions when privilege protected members of the dominant group who exploited their status (Hardy, 1996). Alternatively, perceptions can misrepresent reality. In recent years, the status of White boys (as a group) is diminishing as girls and minority boys have become more competitive in academic and athletic arenas. The White supremacist movement has capitalized on this shift, portraying it as the result of discrimination.

Anger is more widely discussed than shame and guilt, most likely because of its connection with violence. Angry young children create problems in schools and at home, but angry adolescents and adults also threaten their communities. A culture of angry, dangerous adolescent women has become more visible in recent years, but society's greater fears are still associated with men (Holtzworth-Munroe, Meehan, Rehman, & Marshall, 2002). The socialization of males often includes participation in hunting and violent sports, leading to advanced skills for managing pain and inflicting pain onto others. Furthermore, men's generally larger bodies often give them a physical advantage over women and children.

Primary-level anger is something that has been observed in early development (Lemerise & Dodge, 2000); infants are capable of responding to pain and frustration with an instantaneous vocal and muscular performance that leaves little doubt that they are angry. But in later years, as people learn about "display rules" and they develop strategies for control, anger may be chosen as the preferred emotional display (secondary-level anger). Many people, when they fell overwhelmed by shame, doubt, fear, and anxiety, find that anger seems safer than these "soft" feelings—it keeps people at a distance, and it serves as a motivating force for action. Others, who interpret every interaction as a struggle for dominance, learn that such a contest is won by the person who most convincingly becomes angry.

Anxiety.   Anxiety is a core concept in many theories of individual and relational pathology. It was a central theme in Freud's writing, and it was explored by existentialist philosophers such as Kierkegaard. Freud clearly viewed anxiety as negative, whereas existentialist authors such as Rollo May (1969) were more likely to see anxiety as a necessary by-product of modern life. Cultural and individual differences come into play when trying to sort through questions of appropriate versus inappropriate anxiety.

Whether it is labeled as anxiety or dread, this emotional state is one that has both adaptive qualities and problematic ones. Anxiety helps keep people alert for specific signs of danger, and it keeps their attention focused on salient aspects of the environment. In a refugee camp or on the streets of a busy city, the most anxious may be the one who survives. An anxious mother may protect her children by carefully observing who looks at them in public places. She may respond effectively by removing them from a park when she thinks a potential sexual predator has noticed them.

Alternatively, anxiety often leads to negative consequences. When it distracts people from other tasks—our fictional mother could have a traffic accident in her panic—it is a destructive force. Severe anxiety disorders, particularly those associated with trauma, interfere with social functioning as well as limit daily life through obsessive routines and phobic restrictions on activity. In relationships, anxiety affects others as well. Children of anxious parents may suffer from social deprivation caused by hypervigilance, in extreme cases not being allowed outside their homes. Children may also learn to be anxious themselves, just as the romantic partner of an anxious adult may find the emotion to be contagious. While anxiety is one of the most often treated psychiatric complaints, Rosen (1996) suggests that researchers and treatment professionals have given too little attention to the challenges of living with a family member's anxiety.

Depression. Depression may refer to transient, relatively harmless emotions, but in recent years the term more often describes patterns designated as mental disorders. Depression has been studied extensively in relationship systems, particularly marriage, and is generally viewed as destructive to relationships. At the same time, Kung (2000) concludes: "Depression does not occur in a vacuum. It occurs in an interpersonal context." Kung finds four themes in studies of depression and marriage: marital stress, support, role expectations, and interactional dynamics. The literature reviewed by Kung describes a bidirectional process in which relationship problems in these four areas exacerbate depression, which in turn creates further relationship problems. Gollan et al. (2002) also report studies that find depression and relationship distress to be highly correlated. Some studies show depression leading to later relationship problems and others show relationship problems existing prior to depression. Possible explanations include:

- The depressed person tends to overlook positive experiences and remember only negative ones, exacerbating the depression.

- Depressed individuals are relatively unrewarding to interact with, and therefore create stress for their relational partners.

- Depression is a result of living with hostility and tension.

Expressiveness, Emotional Intelligence, and Empathy

A limited range of emotional expression has been cited as contributing to health problems (McGuire & Kiecolt-Glaser, 2000). Researchers have focused on two major sets of variables, expressive range and accuracy. Expressive range varies throughout the life span, with low expressiveness in infancy being associated with attachment disturbances. Gender may influence emotions in infancy, as research has shown that infant-care patterns are influenced by the perceived gender of the child, but gender also gains power as a variable once children learn more about gender norms. Brody and Hall (2000) report that researchers have found few cultures that did not represent women as more

emotionally expressive than men, and by most measures, nonverbal as well as verbal, women as a group are more expressive. Physiological arousal is not clearly greater for either sex, but men are more often found to *internalize* anger, showing a negative correlation between facial expressiveness and physiological measures.

Accuracy of emotional expression refers to the correspondence between felt emotions and emotional displays. To the extent that an individual's emotions are expressed accurately, others can validate those expressed emotions and respond appropriately. Confusing emotional displays lead to frustration as Eva might say, "What's the matter, I thought you would like the present?" and Lonnie responds without visible enthusiasm, "Oh, I thought it was the most wonderful present I ever received." Eva is left not knowing what to believe. Lonnie may not be very expressive, but he might also be attempting to disguise his feelings. People's feelings are often difficult to interpret if they have learned to suppress nonverbal signs of emotion, and this is common among men. The one exception is men's facial displays of anger, which have been found to be more easily interpreted than women's.

Emotional Intelligence. The concept of *emotional intelligence* has become popular over the past few years, covering the study of emotional expression, facilitation, interpretation, and regulation (Salovey, Bedell, Detweiler, & Mayer, 2000). Representing a rejection of cultural values that emphasize reason, this movement is leading to increased knowledge about emotion as a motivational force and as a source of information. At this point, it is clear that people differ on several dimensions (see Table 7.2), and that measurable differences are often related to performance on real-life tasks. It is not yet clear how easily modified these skill sets may be.

Moving from the individual to the group level, it is possible to distinguish *feeling rules* and *expression rules* (Kemper, 2000). Feeling rules define what we should feel and how intense those feelings should be, and expression rules define appropriate ways of expressing those feelings. Complying with these rules requires attending to

Table 7.2   Emotional Intelligence

Perception, Appraisal, and Expression of Emotion

Ability to identify emotion in one's physical and psychological states

Ability to identify emotion in other people and objects

Ability to express emotions accurately and to express needs related to those feelings

Ability to discriminate between accurate and inaccurate, or honest and dishonest, expressions of feelings

Emotional Facilitation of Thinking

Ability to redirect and prioritize one's thinking based on the feelings associated with objects, events, and other people

Ability to generate or emulate vivid emotions to facilitate judgments and memories concerning feelings

Ability to capitalize on mood swings to take multiple points of view; ability to integrate these mood-induced perspectives

Ability to use emotional states to facilitate problem solving and creativity

Understanding and Analyzing Emotional Information; Employing Emotional Knowledge

Ability to understand how different emotions are related

Ability to perceive the causes and consequences of feelings

Ability to interpret complex feelings, such as emotional blends and contradictory feeling states

Ability to understand and predict likely transitions between emotions

Regulation of Emotion

Ability to be open to feelings, both those that are pleasant and those that are unpleasant

Ability to monitor and reflect on emotions

Ability to engage, prolong, or detach from an emotional state, depending upon its judged informativeness of utility

Ability to manage emotion in oneself and others

Source: From "Current Directions in Emotional Intelligence Research" (pp. 504–520), by P. Salovey, B. T. Bedell, J. B. Detweiler, and J. D. Mayer, in *Handbook of Emotions*, second edition, M. Lewis & J. M. Haviland-Jones (Eds.), 2000, New York: Guilford Press. Reprinted with permission.

one's emotional states and expressions and then modifying either or both so as to not violate expectations. The ability to impose and enforce such rules is a demonstration of relative power in relationships. Hochschild (1979) coined the term *emotion work* to describe this process of emotional management, finding that women were far more likely than men to be employed in occupations that required setting aside one's feelings in service of the group. Erickson (1993), studying emotion work in families, found that the same gender breakdown was typical in homes.

Empathy is a common theme in discussions of relationships (Giblin, 1996a), and it appears to be closely associated with issues of experiencing and expressing emotion—the more empathic one's parent or partner, the less precisely one needs to express feelings. Ginsberg (2004) summarizes the role of empathy in couple and family relationships:

> . . .*people learn to become more honest and compassionate when they understand their own needs, desires, preferences, aspirations, and values, and those of others. In such an empathic relationship, people can see and express issues and emotions more openly, without a great deal of defensiveness, guilt, and blame. When each person is more sensitive and aware of his or her own values, needs, and feelings regarding a relationship, the person engages in fewer psychological defense ploys. We relate to one another more clearly and directly so as to lessen the other's emotional pain and the common tendency to respond with defensiveness or to counterattack. (p. 11)*

Empathy, in this description, is dependent on the willingness and ability to engage with feelings—one's own feelings and those of others. Increasing clients' (and counselors' !!!) empathy is a multifaceted challenge that includes teaching specific skills but also includes expanding awareness and tolerance for emotion. At the same time, empathy seems to be situation specific; having the ability does not mean that in the current situation one is ready to face the emotions of another person. It is unfortunate, but many couple counselors have been frustrated when working with couples and families that included helping professionals. The skills were there, but appeared to be blocked when the otherwise sensitive person dealt with a son, daughter, partner, or sibling.

Biological Discourse—Emotion as Neurological Activity

The newest and probably the fastest-changing emotion discourse ties emotional experience to specific activity in the brain. Neurobiological research has been experiencing an upsurge in popularity based in part on the findings from such methods as positron emission tomography (PET) scans and magnetic resonance imaging (MRI). These new tools have permitted researchers to identify areas of the brain that show differential levels of blood flow during emotional states, enabling inferences about emotional brain structures.

Evolutionary Perspectives

This progress in brain research is fitting well with long-standing discussions about the human body and its evolutionary heritage, and progress in gene-mapping may soon contribute to a long-standing debate about human emotions—are they genetically encoded and not subject to significant modification? Edward O. Wilson (1988) coined the term *sociobiology* in the 1970s to describe the science of studying a species to derive its unique rules for behavior—rules that he assumed were genetically coded, not responsive to environmental changes. He advanced the notion that contemporary human behavior is organized by parts of the brain that have not changed substantially since human ancestors lived in trees and hunted and gathered. Our bodies, then, are operating by genetic rules that evolved for a completely different set of demands. This basic idea gained wide popularity, with most professionals accepting the premise that the demands of civilization, such as walking on flat surfaces and sitting for long periods of time, run counter to what our bodies are designed for. But Wilson's ideas went beyond the individual level. He believed that the social organization of a species is also "hard-wired." That idea has led to decades of debates about what the true, natural organization of humans might be. Fuentes (1998), as an example, examines the evidence for monogamy's supposed universality and finds considerable basis for doubt.

All emotions, from this perspective, exist for evolutionary reasons. Sociologist Jonathan Turner (2000) proposed that the naked, upright apelike creatures who developed our genetic code had special needs to coordinate their efforts in social systems. They needed to instantly tune into each other's moods and intentions—essentially, take a vote on any major decision—and they needed to do it silently if possible so that they wouldn't attract predators. The human emotional spectrum, he concluded, would be far more varied than those of other species, and human perceptual-motor-emotional linkages would be so advanced that looking at a face could transmit tremendous amounts of information.

Sloman, Atkinson, Milligan, and Liotti (2002), working from a similar assumption, developed a more focused proposal that emphasized human abilities to regulate affect. They contended that two social interactive processes, attachment and the negotiation of dominance hierarchies, depend on rapidly coordinating responses of multiple individuals, involve learning, and have implications for humans when the programmed responses are disrupted. They also mentioned something they call the involuntary defeat strategy (IDS). When it works, the IDS ends a contest by rapidly draining energy when winning is impossible; when learned "settings" are incorrect, that energy drain might be activated constantly. (This is a theory of depression as having an adaptive function.) The authors conclude that affect regulation problems are best treated at the level of relationships where they are learned and maintained.

Brain Research

The state of current research on brain activity and emotion allows a few strong statements and many inferences. Jaak Panksepp (2000), a widely published researcher and interpreter of this research, states, "Most certainly, the driving forces behind the fundamental feeling tones and autonomic/behavioral/cognitive tendencies that we commonly recognize as distinct types of emotional arousal. . . arise primarily from the neurodynamics of specific types of subcortical circuits" (p. 137). He further states that there appear to be a few *emotional systems,* shared in part with other mammals, that clearly and reliably "orchestrate coherent behavioral, physiological, cognitive, and affective consequences" (p. 143). He finds evidence for the emotional systems in Table 7.3, which are not coherent structures that can be seen but rather coordinated areas of activity that work together under some circumstances.

These systems are in the early stages of being described and tested, and there are many reasons—including ethics—why researchers are limited in their ability to experimentally study this topic. Panksepp is conservative in his predictions for the field, saying that even if brain systems can be accurately mapped they will not replace attention to the social and cognitive processes that

Table 7.3   Emotional Systems

Basic Emotional Systems	Key Brain Areas	Key Neuromodulators
General + motivation seeking/expectancy	Nucleus accumbens—VTA Mesolimbic mesocortical outputs Lateral hypothalamus—PAG	DA (+), Glutamate (+), many neuropeptides, opioids (+), neurotensin (+)
Rage/anger	Medial amygdala to BNST Medial and perifornical hypothalamus to dorsal PAG	Substance P (+), ACh (+), glutamate (+)
Fear/anxiety	Central and lateral amygdala to medial hypothalamus and dorsal PAG	Glutamate (+), many neuropeptides, DBI, CRF, CCK, alpha-MSH, NPY
Lust/sexuality	Corticomedial amygdala BNST Preoptic and ventromedial hypothalamus Lateral and ventral PAG	Steroids (+), vasopressin and oxytocin, LH-RH, CCk
Care/nurturance	Anterior cingulate, BNST Preoptic area, VTA PAG	Oxytocin (+), prolactin (+), DA (+), opioids (±)
Panic/separation	Anterior cingulate BNST and preoptic area Dorsomedial thalamus Dorsal PAG	Opioids (−), oxytocin (−), prolactin −), CFR (+), glutamate (+)
Play/joy	Dorsomedial diencephalon Parafascicular area Ventral PAG	Opioids (±), glutamate (+), Ach (+); any agent that promotes negative emotions reduces play

Note: The monoamines serotonin and norepinephrine are not indicated since they participate in nonspecific ways in all emotions. The higher cortical zones devoted to emotionality, mostly in frontal and temporal areas are not indicated. ACh, Acetylcholine; BNST, bed nucleus of stria terminalis; CCK, cholecystokinin; CRF, corticotropin-releasing factor; DA, dopamine; DBI, diazepam-binding inhibitor; LH-RH, luteinizing hormone-releasing hormone; MSH, melanocyte-stimulating hormone; NPY, neuropeptide Y; PAG, periaqueductal gray; VTA, ventral tegmental area; −, inhibits prototype; +, activates prototype. Data from Panksepp (1998a) and Watt (1998).

Source: From "Emotions as Natural Kinds within the Mammalian Brain" (pp. 137–156), by J. Panksepp, in *Handbook of Emotions,* second edition, M. Lewis and J. M. Haviland-Jones (Eds.), New York: Guilford Press. Reprinted with permission.

continually modify the ways in which the systems are activated.

Implications of a Biological View

Evolutionary and neurobiological data seem to be pointing toward a picture of humans as having, at some level, response systems or *motivational systems* that operate whether or not we are tuned into their activity. What impact might knowledge of such systems have on the future of family counseling? Combining this information with what is known about the social construction of emotion may help people to more effectively use the chemical signals that are being passed around in their nervous and endocrine systems. At the same time, knowing what kinds of preprogrammed signals might lead to socially undesirable responses—rage, for instance—may eventually help humans to design physical and social environments that are less inclined to activate those responses. Clearly, this is a topic that cannot be ignored, and over the next 20 years we may expect dramatic innovations.

The Process of Counseling with Couples and Families

When relationships are viewed primarily in terms of their emotional processes, the distinction between assessment and intervention is even less clear than in other kinds of couple and family counseling. Some theories assume that people are out of touch with some of their own emotional processes, while other orientations suggest that they are not only out of touch but also dedicated to fooling themselves and others. Therefore, client narratives—the stories told at the time of intake—must be considered flawed and possibly distorted. Even if intervention could wait for a complete assessment, this may not be possible; instead, assessment is part of the intervention, and every step yields more information.

The counseling alliance is important in every approach to relationship work, but it assumes special importance when emotions are concerned. Access to emotions is easier when people feel safe. If they have not trusted other relationships, they are only likely to open up to a professional who they believe is impartial but caring, emotionally strong but not dominating, emotionally resilient, and capable. Snyder and Schneider (2002) say that a collaborative alliance for couple counseling requires the ability to limit partners' negative exchanges in the session; this "holding" position is typical in emotion-oriented work. Johnson and Greenberg (1995) also discuss issues involved in establishing—and maintaining—an effective working alliance with a couple. They say that the counselor is constantly challenged to maintain balance, so as not to engage more with one partner than with the other, and needs to maintain a focus on emotional presence with the couple—"*being* skillfully" rather than "being skillful."

Considering how much importance is attached to the early years in emotion theories, one might expect the family counselor to pay special attention to emotional issues when working with children and adolescents. But the literature focusing on children and adolescents is more systemic and behavioral, and the largest part of the emotional literature refers to couples work. Nevertheless, nearly every technique discussed in this chapter can be applied in working with a variety of family forms.

Engaging: Creating an Emotion-Friendly Context

The typical office visit is not an experience that invites emotionally authentic interactions. First interviews often focus on a series of fact-oriented questions—communicating that facts are more important than feelings. To compensate, an emotion-oriented counselor may want to find ways to separate the "business" aspects of the meeting from the meaningful part. For example, counselors who function in institutional settings may have support staff who can manage the paperwork before they meet with the clients.

Physical settings also communicate expectations, and an emotion-friendly office says, "This is a personal space where real people interact with real people." Alternatively, the goal of being real could create other problems if offices have such strong identities—with ruffled pillows and flowered wallpaper, or with leather chairs and mounted deer heads—that some visitors feel out of place. Children, by the way, are very sensitive to the presence or absence of child-sized furniture and playthings.

However, the context is most clearly defined by the professional's style of interaction. If a professional seems distant and formal, clients will respond in kind. Videos of Virginia Satir, Carl Whitaker, and Salvador Minuchin show a disarming quality of emotional presence coexisting with an authoritative "holding" quality that reassures people of their safety. John Byng-Hall (1995), using attachment theory, calls for the family therapist to "provide a temporarily secure base for the whole family during therapy" (p. 54).

Acceptance

People often arrive in a counselor's office expecting criticism and judgment, in part because of responses they have received when they disclosed their relationship concerns to friends or relatives The first few exchanges with clients set a tone, and a helper who demonstrates acceptance and suspension of judgment can expect to bring out a more emotionally authentic version of the clients.

De-Triangling

With two or more clients in a professional's office, it is easy for individuals to get disproportionate levels of attention and validation: In a replay of what happens for the same group when they are in other settings, conversations are often dominated by a more verbal family member or the one who seems more helpless. But the family counselor wants to avoid reproducing triangles. One of the cardinal rules for an emotionally oriented counselor is to be aware of expectations but to resist them.

Assessment and Intervention: Early Stages

Even when a professional is open to emotion, feelings may not surface because the setting is not activating emotion. There are two basic approaches to dealing with this challenge. One group of strategies accepts the emotional distance and uses early ses-

sions to collect a history of emotional patterns and emotional events. It is also possible to set up tasks or ask questions in such a way that the couple or family reproduces some of their typical interactions in the office (compare the discussion of enactment in Chapter 5). Both approaches can yield information, leading to the selection of further interventions.

Retrospective Reports of Interactions

Nearly every couple or family arrive in a counselor's office expecting to tell about their problem(s), and emotionally oriented work can begin with this process—providing the focus is shifted from complaints about a single individual toward an emphasis on the couple or family's emotional impasses.

Identifying Problem Interactions. Emotions tend to vary in association with situations; therefore, most authors agree that a more emotional story comes out if people are encouraged to focus on specific situations and events. This story can be time-consuming; often, there are multiple interaction sequences that are problematic, and each has its own issues and feelings. Johnson and Denton (2002) start their emotionally focused approach by taking time for the partners' separate views of relational problems, hoping for commonality, and if they don't hear agreement they take separate complaints and "weave" them into a shared concern. Vatcher and Bogo (2001), conversely, express some doubts about waiting for the clients to pick an area of focus. Because they believe that many contemporary couples are distressed by conflicting gender expectations, their feminist and emotionally focused therapy integration actively seeks to address gender-related emotions.

Greene and Bogo (2002) emphasize the need to assess a couple's history for indications of violence, noting that "The history of family therapy is tarnished by our inability to detect and adequately respond to women who were being brutalized by their male partners" (p. 464). They note that professionals have failed to protect some clients, but have prevented other couples from receiving treatment because of rigid assumptions regarding the appropriateness of couple counseling. They suggest following procedures outlined by Bograd and

Mederos (1999) and assessing the indicators of either relational conflict or a pattern of male dominance that M. P. Johnson (1995) called "patriarchal terrorism":

- Range of control tactics
- Motivation for the use of violence
- Impact from the physical aggression
- Partner's subjective experience

Where patriarchal terrorism is identified, couple counseling is likely to lead to further violence. For couples with relational violence, it is possible to alter the relational pattern and learn nonviolent ways to interact. (See Anger Management Strategies in this chapter.) Case-by-case assessment is necessary to prevent overgeneralization and misassignment to treatment.

Exploring Interactional Patterns of Emotion.   Once the couple or family have begun to focus on particular interaction sequences or cycles, emotion-oriented approaches focus less on the content of an interaction than on the ways in which people activate each others' emotions (Snyder & Schneider, 2002). Wile (1993) conceptualizes emotional interactions as "an uninterrupted series of states of mind over which we have little control." He tries to focus on those times when someone is experiencing a *leading edge feeling* that is intense, confusing, and difficult to articulate. He provides an example from a fictional client, Marie, talking with her husband:

> I really enjoyed the way we were talking, too—I felt closer to you than I have in a long time—but that just makes me aware of all the ways we're not close (emphasis in the original). And suddenly I feel furious—because at the moment I blame you for it. (p. 3)

Gottman et al. (2002) try to identify "positions" taken by the participants, so the symbolic meaning of those positions can be identified and their interactional dynamics can be altered. Similarly, Johnson and Greenberg (1995) write about the concept of positions:

> *In close adult relationships, powerful emotional responses such as fear-mistrust, and associated prototypical models of self and other learned in past attachment contexts (e.g., "I am defective and unlovable, so others will leave me") are evoked, particularly when conflict arises. This inner experience orients one partner to the other and helps to organize interactional responses. These responses then become the basis of the habitual positions that the partners take with each other, particularly around issues of affiliation-closeness and control-dependence. (p. 122)*

In the "emotionally focused therapy" (EFT) model, conversations designed to increase emotional awareness begin with recalling and "replaying" interaction cycles that have taken place elsewhere; over time, the focus shifts to processing interactions that are taking place in the office. Johnson and Denton (2002) describe gaining access to unacknowledged emotions by reflecting a partner's story, validating his or her experience, and heightening awareness through empathic conjecture. They point out that with the stereotypical male, who has denied his attachment needs, the counselor may also model the expression of vulnerability. In Stage I of EFT, previously hidden emotions are not only identified but also reframed and restructured, contextualized in terms of the relationship and its unique cycle of needs, emotions, and interactions.

Carlson and Sperry's (2000) Adlerian approach to couple work emphasizes a *lifestyle analysis* exploring historical issues such as birth order. Similarly, Scharff and de Varela (2000) seek information about historical rather than current influences on interaction. History is clearly relevant in couple and family counseling, and emotional history is particularly so.

The most widely used structure for emotional intervention is the genogram (McGoldrick et al., 1999). As an assessment tool, the genogram organizes emotional information about relationships and facilitates the identification of troublesome emotional patterns in an extended family system: It can be coded in many ways to provide information beyond the simple facts of biological inheritance, birth order, marriage, and death. Figure 7.1 shows a segment of a genogram with symbols added to show closeness and distance.

In-Session Encounters

Rather than sort through participants' accounts for emotional process information, it is also possible to reproduce emotional interactions in the office. Several strategies are helpful in structuring sessions so that they focus more on the present and less on the past.

Seating Positions.   Without any direction from the counselor, people nearly always enter an office and move into seating positions that reflect and continue their emotional patterns. The males may sit on one side and the females on another, or the "good kids" may sit with the parent while the "bad kids" are left out. In these familiar positions, events may unfold in familiar ways. Minuchin and Satir used people's bodies to communicate that something new was expected to occur, redirecting people from their self-assigned seats or moving chairs around to challenge familiar patterns.

Enactment.   In Chapter 5, we discussed creating and making use of enactments. In the structural tradition, these enactments are generally analyzed

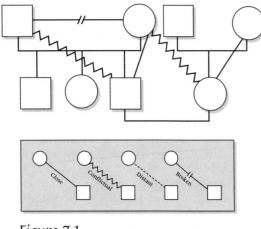

Figure 7.1

Emotional Coding of a Genogram

and discussed without explicit discussion of feelings. The following example shows a different way to conduct an enactment with an emotional focus:

Roberto and Ann arrived in the counselor's office a few days after a particularly frightening argument in which Ann threatened to leave. The couple reported that her complaint—his parents were constantly demanding attention and intruding on their couple time—was one that Roberto had repeatedly dismissed. He was proud of his family's closeness, and said that Ann had to learn how to become one of them. It seemed that the issue became a crisis when Ann announced that Roberto had to make a choice, "them or me."

The counselor, Tanisha, said, "Since you seem to get stuck whenever you talk about this, I would like you to repeat the conversation here. That way I can see how it goes, and maybe I can help you reach a resolution."

Within minutes, the couple's interactional pattern had been demonstrated. As Ann began talking about her concern, Roberto's body became more rigid and he turned away slightly. His responses were slow and imprecise, while her demands were forceful and clear. As he withdrew, she became more and more upset.

Tanisha interrupted: "Thank you, both, I now have a much better idea how this happens. Roberto, will you switch places with me? I'd like to show you how you were sitting. . . ."

With this short interaction, Tanisha gained access to key information about the couple's emotional system and helped them become aware of ways in which each of them contributed to the other's anxiety and defensiveness. Newly aware of their nonverbal signals and verbal styles, they resumed the conversation in a new way.

Sculpting and Psychodrama.   In Chapter 6, we looked at Virginia Satir's technique of family sculpting. Influenced by Jacob Moreno's (1945) *psychodrama*, sculpting combines historical and present-oriented emotional concerns. Where verbal approaches often involve discussing emotional events or interactions in the recent or distant past, sculpting attempts to bring their full emotional intensity into the office. Participants in a sculpting session may look like passive objects being posed, but they are interacting at an emotional level throughout the process. The dramatic license given to the sculptor makes it possible for Mom to experience being treated as the youngest child, or for the identified patient (IP) to represent the Angel of Death. Grandparents and great-grandparents can be brought into the room, as can future generations. Once placed in these roles, participants discover feelings and thoughts that challenge their assumptions—sometimes ending up in tears. The present-oriented aspect of this work involves processing the feelings from a scene and helping couple or family members incorporate their discoveries into new ways of sharing and responding to each other's feelings.

Psychodrama is not often used in a couple or family session because of the number of participants required, but it is an outstanding tool in multiple-family groups. Moreno's model called for casting people in roles that would be acted out, with the *director* setting up the scene and even providing actors with key lines. The director might even play one of the roles. Actors were backed up by *doubles* who helped them to conceptualize their roles. In a multiple family session, a critical father might be asked to be the double for an adolescent girl who is playing his daughter; in that position, his empathic abilities could be unblocked and he would then find himself explaining her feelings and motivations to someone else. With multiple levels of interaction and observation, the family group counselor using psychodrama can both reproduce painful experiences and experiment with new kinds of interaction.

Challenging. There are times in family sessions when a story is being told by one person and the teller's assumptions are clearly dominating the story; it is evident that the longer the story continues, the more the others disengage from the process. Under these circumstances, the counselor may act on behalf of the more silent parties, pointing out inflammatory language or calling attention to the one-sidedness of the presentation. A single challenge may change the monologue into an encounter with the counselor—thereby illustrating something about tolerance for different viewpoints. If challenges are accepted, their success may inspire family members to join in and change the monologue into a discussion.

Speaking For. Similarly, it is often possible to see a participant who appears uncomfortable and whose behavior and statements don't match. As a long-term goal, this person might be helped to become more vocal, but at the beginning of intervention the demand that emotions be expressed verbally is essentially unfair. It represents a value system that empowers those who verbalize their feelings. Consider the following encounter:

JOEY: *"I just don't understand how she can treat me like this. She knows what I want from a wife, and I take good care of her, she doesn't want anything, all I expect is that when I get home from work she is there. It's not like she has anything she has to do, she is just out playing with her single friends. Why can't you be there? Is that too much to ask?"*

MARIA: *"I . . . I just lose track of time, and I don't see my friends very often, I'm sorry."*

JUAN (COUNSELOR): *Maria, as Joey was talking I was watching your face, and it looked to me as if you were angry. And it is possible to believe that you might be punishing him, in a way, when you stay away from home. But then you spoke in that frightened voice, like he might leave you if you stood up for yourself. I'm wondering if that happens often. Is there a part of you that is angry about something, but doesn't like to fight about it?*

Maria is being given some words she may want to use if she chooses to follow Juan's lead and express anger toward Joey, but at the same time she is being given the option of denial. Either way, the assessment of the situation is advanced as the counselor is demonstrating a desire to understand her motivations and emotions.

Empathizing with the Group

In the same situation, Juan might have taken a slightly safer approach. Rather than attribute the feeling to Maria, essentially being empathic to her, he might have instead put himself into a position of empathizing with both participants. Empathizing with multiple perspectives is especially challenging, as it requires constructing a position that captures something they share. Here's an example:

JUAN: *"I can see that this is difficult for both of you. Joey, what you are asking for seems so simple to you, and Maria, you seem to care about his feelings and you're apologetic after you disappoint him, and yet this keeps happening? Is this a pattern? Joey asks, you say yes, then you come back later and apologize for not doing it? It must be very hard to live this way."*

In this brief summary, the counselor has captured the emotional bind that the couple is experiencing, without clearly identifying either one as the cause of the crisis.

Kempler (1981, pp. 232–233) provides an example of such a group-empathic response. In a case transcript, he shows a mother and adolescent son stuck in communication impasse while the husband/father remains uninvolved. The son and the mother take turns appealing to Kempler, who is apparently expected to rescue them by either translating their messages or telling them how they can overcome their difficulty. Instead, Kempler acknowledges to each in turn that he hears their desire for help, and then he suggests that the mother "talk with your husband about it. That's what spouses are for." He ends with the explanation that his strategy is this session is designed to "redirect the focus toward the family operation and at the same time encourage an interaction." He does not rescue the family from their dilemma or deny their pain.

Intervention— Regulating Emotions

As the emotional landscape of the clients begins to be clear, some situations may seem to be volatile. This first group of interventions shares the assumption that emotions can, and should, be regulated in some way—either modified in intensity or somehow transformed from one emotion to another. Excluded from this section are simple cognitive and behavioral techniques that may be used for mood management—see Chapters 4 and 6.

Anger Management Strategies

Relationships characterized by *patriarchal terrorism*—that is, ones in which an aggressive male conducts a one-sided campaign of emotional and physical intimidation (Johnson, 1995)—are generally considered to be inappropriate for any couple-level counseling. Holtzworth-Munroe et al. (2002), who work with couple relationships that have included violence, urge caution and careful assessment (see earlier discussion in this chapter) before intervening in ways that might increase emotional expressiveness.

Holtzworth-Munroe and colleagues find a significant number of couples who have experienced episodes of what Johnson calls *common couple violence*, characterized by verbal and physical exchanges in which both partners' anger becomes extreme. These couples, say the authors, can modify their relationship patterns. The first step in such work is to help both partners avoid reaching such extreme levels of anger. Partners are helped to become aware of their anger at low levels and are guided through negotiating a mutual agreement to use "time out" so that their physiological anger responses can subside.

A similar approach to anger is used in Integrative Behavioral Couple Therapy (IBCT) (Jacobson & Christensen, 1996). Partners are taught "unified detachment" as a strategy to limit emotional involvement in problems. Interventions consist of modeling and leading the couple in intellectualized analyses of emotional events, working toward behavioral descriptions of event sequences and also externalizing problems—describing problems as separate from the participants (this is essentially a narrative intervention described in Chapter 6) (Jones, Christensen, & Jacobson, 2000).

Meeting with Subsystems

When counselors are concerned that emotional regulation is an issue, it is often because sessions have been either volatile and unproductive or else lopsided, with some individuals seeming to be left out of the process. Under those circumstances, the counselor can meet with subsystems—including individuals—that need special attention; for example, to address internal issues such as a conflict between adult siblings as they address caregiving issues for their parents, or it can address ways in which the subsystem functions in relations with others.

Even when early conversations are productive, it is often helpful to meet separately with each family or couple member to provide a safe environment for exploring emotional concerns in more depth (Johnson & Denton, 2002).

Genograms

As family background information is being gathered, a genogram serves another important function besides recording information—to externalize emotions and store them in a safe place. As people sit with the visual representation of their relationships in front of them, the process and the clear, unambiguous product reassures participants that nothing escapes the attention of the counselor. Contrasted with a focus on understanding the presenting problem in the first session, the genogram emphasizes a patient, step-by-step attitude. This may be especially helpful in situations involving people at very different levels of emotional expression.

Coaching

A Bowen technique, *coaching* (McGoldrick & Carter, 2001), was designed for use with an individual but may be modified for use with any subsystem once a problem emotional pattern has been identified. The counselor, as coach, seeks to prepare the subsystem for a relationship-changing opportunity, a time when it will be possible to revise emotional history by doing something differently. The following vignette illustrates the role of the coach:

Sarah, mother of 15-year-old Jessica, and her husband Larry had brought Jessica to Sam's office despite her protests. Jessica denied having a problem. The problem, she said, was her school. The school was strictly enforcing class tardiness rules, and she had been sent home for late arrival eleven times since the beginning of the marking period. When

her mother and stepfather tried to discuss the rules and her reasons for being late to class, she reacted with rage. No one else, she said, got treated the way she did. The principal had been "on her case" since she transferred into the school at the beginning of the year, and she was angry with her mom and Larry for failing to defend her. In Sam's office, Larry reacted by yelling and threatening Jessica with punishments, while Sarah cried and pleaded for him to stop. Jessica ran out of the session saying she couldn't wait to be 18 so she could leave home.

Sam excused Jessica from the next session while he worked with Sarah and Larry, preparing them to break the cycle of angry outbursts by taking a more differentiated position with Jessica—recognizing that the emotional scenes were activating their own conflicted emotions about their marriage, their recent move, and their opposition to the school's discipline policies. The session focused on emotional triangles—how to recognize them and how to resist being pulled into an alignment with one side of a triangle or another.

As a result of the coaching, Sarah and Larry became more aware of their family emotional cycles, committed to work on their couple issues, and developed plans to handle parenting conversations in less volatile ways. When Jessica rejoined them in counseling, the interactions were more consistent and supportive.

Redefining Shame

Shame is an intergenerational pattern, a vague sense of dread that is learned early in life and often remains hidden from awareness, destroying intimate relationships. The direct manifestations of shame are often subtle and include low self-esteem, interpersonal hesitancy, and alienation from one's body. The indirect manifestations of shame are defenses used by people who lack appropriate boundaries (Fossum & Mason, 1986) as they try to keep others from gaining access to their true feelings—rage, contempt, and blame are only a few. In couple relationship systems, a shame cycle often develops, and even though only one partner may show direct manifestations, both are disabled by the systemic effects (Balcom et al., 1995).

Authorities recommend an active and direct approach to shame in relationship systems, beginning with naming it and teaching participants to recognize its effects. Because people feel ashamed of their shame, normalizing the emotion and making it a daily part of life takes away much of its power. Balcom et al. (1995) refer to "teaching couples to tolerate rather than eradicate shame." Instead of reducing the primary sense of shame, their approach works by reducing the secondary, reactive emotion and removing the need for maintaining distance from one another.

Interventions—Experiencing, Expressing, and Sharing Emotion

Many authors insist that family members must become more comfortable with their own primary, authentic, vulnerable emotions before they will be able to empathically hear each other in ways that will bring them closer.

The Imago approach (Hendrix, 1992; Luquet, 2000) focuses on making emotional expression easier and safer. Partners are taught the "couples dialogue process," a structured technique requiring careful attention to the speaker and listener roles. Within that environment, participants are expected to gradually open up their emotional wounds and learn to support each other. Wile (2002) also sees emotional awareness, expression, and empathy gradually increasing as couples abandon adversarial and withdrawn cycles through small discoveries he refers to as "solving the moment not the problem."

The contemporary helper has a wide range of theory-driven techniques to choose from in building what the Relationship Enhancement approach (Ginsberg, 2000) refers to as the skills of "owning of one's own motivation" and "empathic responding." In Stage II of EFT, once threatening emotions have been relabeled and normalized, partners are helped through a process of *self-reunification*—incorporating the denied parts of themselves, especially their attachment needs. Susan Johnson (2003) says that this is a more intense phase of the process. To protect against emotional injuries, the more withdrawn spouse may be invited to move through the development

of empathy for the critical partner and the creation of new, more realistic ways of expressing wants and needs. Having reached the point where the withdrawn spouse is self-aware and comfortable with a new level of honesty, the process moves to addressing the blaming, critical spouse.

Mackey (1996) provides examples of this type of emotion-oriented work with adolescents and their parents. Assuming that emotionally distancing parents can only provide nurturance for their adolescents to the extent that they are aware of their own emotional wounds, she guides parents through re-examination of their family-of-origin experiences. Recognizing how they were hurt as children by parental behavior, they can then see how they might be unwittingly hurting their own children. Mackey's approach is notable for its use of homework exercises—behavioral tasks and rituals designed to create new emotional experiences, which she refers to as "experiments."

Johnson and Greenberg (1995) describe one of the last steps in this process as something they call softening. "A *softening* is defined as a previously hostile/critical spouse asking, from a position of vulnerability, a newly accessible partner for what he or she needs." The following exchange is taken from a longer transcript that illustrated this process. The wife, Prue, long accustomed to feeling ignored, has been holding back from asking her husband for attention; he has been offered a new job, and she expects to be abandoned as he spends long hours in his basement office. (Note the amount of coaching that the therapist is doing, even though the couple is nearing the end of this middle phase of their work.) In this transcript, italicized words represent observable "facts" about what is happening, and bracketed statements represent interpretations of the interactions. The dialogue follows:

MARK: *I feel sad you can't come and say you need me. If you did, I'd be there in a flash—I would.*

THERAPIST: *Are you asking her to give you a chance? You'd like to be there? [The therapist heightens his accessibility to facilitate restructuring the interaction.]*

MARK: *Absolutely. I want to be needed (leaning toward her). I'm not going to turn you away.*

THERAPIST *[to Prue]: Do you hear him talking to that tiny afraid person inside you and he's saying, "Try me out. Risk it—reach for me—let me be there for you. Let go. I'll catch you—come and be close." He's inviting you [The therapist replays and heightens interaction event].*

PRUE: *Yes* (sobs).

MARK: *It's the issue. If I could just find a way round—solve the . . . why this happens (looks off into the distance).*

THERAPIST *[focusing, blocking, Mark's distancing]: Mark, I'd like you to just see that she's afraid and just stay with her—never mind the solution. Can you see she's afraid? I want you to meet your wife. Will you please come out of your head, come and meet your wife—like you took your business suit off to meet her—and now here she is (Prue bursts into tears.) [The therapist directs interaction toward engagement].*

THERAPIST *[to Prue]: What's happening, Prue?*

PRUE: *He probably doesn't want to meet me. I don't want him to meet me—I don't want anyone to ever meet this person [The therapist moves closer, hands Prue a tissue as she sobs, puts her hand on Prue's arm, long pause].*

THERAPIST: *You don't want anyone to see that needy scared part of you—no one could like her, right? [Empathic reflection; core model of self is enacted here.]*

PRUE: *I don't like her. I won't show anymore—*

THERAPIST: *Hmmm—you don't see that part of you as lovable. Mark certainly wouldn't want to put his arms around her and hold her—he couldn't possibly feel that. [The therapist evokes her longing/fear of rejection.]*

PRUE: *He'd feel disappointed.*

THERAPIST: *Disappointed?*

PRUE: *She's weak, she's needy . . .*

THERAPIST: *Ah, ha! What do you want, Prue, right now? Need, right now?*

PRUE: *I want Mark to hold me.*

THERAPIST: *Ask him. [Directs interaction.]*

PRUE: *Please hold me. I'm scared. [Mark holds her; the therapist looks out window. Prue cries.] (pp. 134–135, emphasis and bracketed explanations in the original)*

Intervention—Connecting

In the final stages of emotion-oriented couple and family counseling, as participants develop what the Relationship Enhancement approach refers to as *conversive skills,* they move past their previous emotional barriers and achieve genuine, supportive, intimate bonds. The parents in Mackey's case, for example, were coached in this phase of the work so that they could listen to their adolescent's feelings.

For participants in the Imago process, it is assumed that the couple will have opened up genuine dialogue on emotional issues and this permits them to effectively engage in joint problem solving. Similarly, couples in the later stages of Snyder and Schneider's (2002) process make changes in a broad range of issues: "Affective reconstruction of maladaptive schemas promotes resolution of persistent dysfunctional relationship patterns through redirected cognitive and behavioral strategies" (p. 168). And Gottman et al.'s (2002) couples are given problems to solve in the office, ensuring that they have moved beyond their negative interaction cycles.

Johnson and Denton (2002) say that the last stage of the EFT process includes working out new solutions to old problems, but the ultimate goal is to "consolidate new positions and cycles of attachment behavior." For Gottman, the process is not complete until couples have worked together to rebuild the positivity in their relationships by setting up rituals of connection.

Assessing Effectiveness

Assessment is ongoing in the various emotionally oriented approaches; whether through reports of out-of-session interactions or through observations of in-session behavior, the counselor typically knows how relationships are functioning at their best and at their worst. Many professionals prefer that clients move from an active intervention process into a stage of follow-up interviews before finally concluding that their work is complete. One-month or longer intervals provide clients relatively uncomplicated opportunities to bring their concerns into the office, and repeated sessions with no further problems support a view of the counseling as a success. When crises can be anticipated (the finalization of a divorce, a long-awaited birth to a couple with fertility problems), the counselor is advised to delay the last session until the need for special support is over.

Closure

Compared with the work described in Chapters 4, 5, and 6, the Emotional perspective is more likely to lead to extended intervention—and therefore to clients' dependence on the helping process. This likelihood is greater because the theories do not generally predict rapid change—or they say that rapid change is not to be trusted, and clients should be encouraged to remain in counseling until changes are stabilized. (Longer-lasting cases are also likely because the clients who self-select a professional who works in these ways tend to be people who themselves are suspicious of rapid change.) With clients who experience severe emotional symptoms, it is possible that a behavioral, organizational, or narrative approach would have been ineffective. At the same time, it is also possible that some people who select a longer-term orientation do not actually need "depth" approaches and find their problems resolved in a short time.

Several kinds of professional-client struggle tend to appear as the counseling process extends over weeks, months, even years. In the first scenario, one or more of the family/couple members feels that the process has met its goals and should be ended while other members of the couple/family feel a need for continued sessions. These situations are common, and they can appear as early as the second or third session. The professional is generally called on to take one position or the other, and in many cases a good argument can be made for both. Because those who want to continue are, to some extent, dependent on the cooperation of other family members, in most cases those who want to end couple or family counseling will succeed in leaving—especially if they have been expected to carry all or even part of the financial responsibility (in some of these cases, the departing individual will file for divorce or move away).

When someone drops out of couple or family counseling, the more connected member(s) may stay for individual work, as frequently occurs in couple cases, and this change in the contract has serious implications. Given the fact that we are discussing emotion-oriented approaches, it is not surprising if the remaining member(s) seem to feel that they now deserve the professional's allegiance—and then withdraw if they find that they are not receiving unconditional positivity. It is also possible that eventually the less connected member(s) may return. If the boundaries of the process are allowed to stay open, a family may continue counseling over a period of years without any individual remaining active throughout the process.

The opposite scenario involves a couple or family in which there is no individual sufficiently committed to remain in counseling as others are ready to quit. The professional is not able to compel anyone to continue; therefore, the process is reaching a fairly clear end. The primary question under such circumstances has to do with the idea of a closing session, which seems to be appropriate in many cases. The last session provides an opportunity for the professional to summarize what has been done, reiterate the message that the couple or family is welcome to return, demonstrate caring for all members of the group, and send people away with thoughts for the future. It is not uncommon for families to reappear in the counselor's office several years later, and at those times they often mention the messages they took away from the prior counseling.

Cautions and Concerns

Emotional issues lie at the heart of many helping approaches, and orientations toward emotions have ranged from respect, even awe, to disrespect and rejection. The theories in this chapter have offered ways of living with one's own emotions and those of others, and in some cases have suggested that it is possible to change emotions that are not desired. People may be drawn to these theories in hopes that they can change each other.

The latter agenda is frightening in the hands of the couple and family counselor or therapist—especially if the intervention can deliver such changes. When a client agrees to a process that may result in significant personal changes, and that consent is properly given, that individual can be said to have accepted the consequences of the intervention. But there are cases in which an individual is coerced into treatment, and there are cases when an individual's consent is based on incorrect information. These cases are of concern to every mental health or other professional, and couple and family work creates the risk that one person will threaten, bribe, or cajole others into participating in a process that has not been freely chosen. The people who are most vulnerable at such times are those whose current ways of handling their emotions and behavior have not been judged successful.

For the most part, the processes we have been describing in this chapter are respectful processes that are unlikely to create significant risk of emotional breakdown, and they are unlikely to radically transform clients unless the clients themselves invest heavily in the counseling. But there is potential for abuse, and it is inversely proportional to the client's existing level of functionality. Because they are so often applied in cases that involve differences in emotional competence, emotion-oriented approaches must be used with great care. The professional who would use these approaches has a special responsibility to not only learn them well and use them with skill but to also monitor emotional responses through continuous supervision or peer consultation.

Suggested Individual and Group Activities

Your understanding of concepts and issues presented in this chapter may be enhanced by the following activities:

- *Self-examination.* Rate yourself and your closest friends on adult attachment style. Do you seem to be more comfortable with people who are pretty much like yourself? Or are you more comfortable with people who are different?
- *Relationship interview.* Interview a couple about the emotional "temperature" of their relationship over time, beginning with the time when they met. Do they seem to remember the same ups and downs?
- *Film.* Many popular films portray family emotional issues in a compelling way, but *Ordinary People* is especially clear in its tracking of the interacting patterns in a nuclear family that has experienced a significant loss. You should watch the film with other people so that you can compare reactions to the characters.

Suggested Readings

Bowen, M. (1978). *Family therapy in clinical practice.* New York: Aronson.

Johnson, S. M., & Greenberg, L. S. (Eds.). (1994). *The heart of the matter: Perspectives on emotion in marital therapy.* New York: Brunner/Mazel.

Wile, D. (1993). *After the fight: A night in the life of a couple.* New York: Guilford.

Spirituality: Purpose, Acceptance, and Meaning

The problems presented by a couple or family are an indication of disturbances in their spiritual life.

Objectives

In this chapter, you learn to:

1. Recognize spirituality as an element in human experience.
2. Describe relational manifestations of spirituality.
3. Explain the relationship impact of spiritual experiences, beliefs, and practices.
4. Describe and explain commonly accepted spiritual practices and beliefs.
5. Select, plan, and implement spirituality-oriented couple and family interventions appropriate to treatment goals.

8

CHAPTER

The fifth and final BONES dimension emphasizes the spiritual life of a couple or family—the connections among their spiritual experiences, beliefs, and practices, on one hand, and their intimate relationships, emotional well-being, and effective functioning, on the other. Family life, religion, and spirituality are deeply intertwined in many people's lives.

The distinction between religion and spirituality is mentioned throughout this chapter. Even though we emphasize the term spirituality, many of the discussions apply to beliefs and practices that are typically viewed as religion. This usage is consistent with a social constructionist, multicultural orientation (e.g., Carlson & Erickson, 2002; West, 2000) that values diversity and seeks to honor both the unique characteristics of different traditions and the common threads that unite human existence.

A spiritual perspective on family functioning is nothing new; spiritual traditions have focused on family life for thousands of years. The first helping professionals concerned with families were spiritual leaders of some kind; before emotional and behavioral problems were addressed through the medical metaphor of "treatment," they were addressed through the spiritual metaphor of "healing" (Walsh, 1999a). But spiritual orientations and issues were moved toward the margins of the helping professions during the twentieth century, as science became the dominant metaphor (West, 2000). A spiritual orientation was present in the work of some family counseling pioneers (e.g., Satir, 1972), and pastoral counselors were among the groups who most enthusiastically embraced the emerging field. During the consolidation years, however, family therapy turned its back on such a nonscientific topic. Only since the 1990s, with cultural change and widespread demand for spiritual resources, has there been a rebirth of spiritual interest among the helping professions (Carlson & Erickson, 2002; Frame, 2002).

During the past decade, the mental health community rediscovered spirituality with such enthusiasm that some religious leaders expressed concern. Richard Wendel (2003), for example, accused the mental health field of relabeling religion as spirituality so that they would be permitted to talk about it. He argued that only specially trained clinicians, those with extensive backgrounds in the historical religions that underlie "lived religion," should attempt to discuss the complicated issues in people's spiritual lives. In a response (Doherty, 2003), family therapist William Doherty—whose credentials for addressing issues of religion and spirituality are impressive (see Doherty, 1999)—seconded Wendel's concern about professionals who apparently deny the complexity of spiritual issues. At the same time, though, Doherty brought up two different concerns. First, he expressed dismay that many people have been getting divided help, unable to integrate professional emotional and relationship guidance with the viewpoints they hear from their spiritual guides. Second, observing that families include mixtures of spiritual orientations and their issues often do not require advanced spiritual understandings, he suggested that a generalist—not a specialist—could be extremely helpful. From being almost invisible in family counseling discussions, spiritual issues have become the center of a new controversy about the appropriate scope of concern for professionals who operate from counseling and religious perspectives.

As we examine the many ways in which spirituality and religion manifest themselves in couple and family relationships, it will become clear that this theme overlaps with all of the other four relationship dimensions. This chapter emphasizes the special contributions of theorists, researchers, and clinicians whose viewpoint or content is explicitly spiritual.

A Case Illustration: The Aldrich Family

Melissa Aldrich made the first appointment to see Dr. Selena Walker alone. Melissa explained that she was there because of her family, but she wasn't sure she wanted them in the same room even if they would come. She was confused.

She had been married 25 years to Bill, the owner of a small construction company. He was "rough and tough," and his workmen were, too, so she had tried to accept the fact that he came home and acted the same way. When their two boys had been young, he had been gruff and demanding, but he had reserved his pushing and slapping for her, and she had put up with it. But then it got worse—the boys got older, and he started being abusive with them.

The oldest, Sam, never fought back. He worked for his dad during high school and gave up a college scholarship to help out with the company. But the second son, Willie, began to stand up to Bill when he was 15. Though Willie stayed at home, mostly keeping to himself, until he finished high school, he then left—that had been 3 years ago—and he hadn't set foot in the house since. Melissa could talk to him on the telephone, but Willie said he hated his dad and would never speak to him again. Willie and Sam kept up a cool, restrained relationship.

Melissa had been ready, about a year ago, to leave Bill. But then Bill made a complete turnaround at a weekend men's retreat in a stadium, where a Christian minister preached that men were God's representatives, called to show women and children that He was steadfast and loving. Most men, said the minister, didn't take their responsibilities seriously. Their wives and children had become disrespectful and they in turn had become angry and abusive. Bill heard the message directly aimed at him, and he came home determined to repair his life and his family relationships.

A year later, he now prayed, read the Bible daily, and attended church three times a week. Melissa's present dilemma was that Bill wanted to have the whole family together for Thanksgiving dinner, now 3 weeks away, and Willie refused to come. She asked Dr. Walker, "Do you think that it might work if we brought them in here together?" Dr. Walker said that she was optimistic.

The next meeting included all three men as well as Dr. Walker and Melissa. Sam and Bill came from work together and Willie arrived looking tense and upset. Bill asked if they could start the session with a prayer. Everyone agreed (although Willie seemed skeptical) and Bill led the prayer. He told God what he had done wrong, how bad he felt about the way he had treated everyone, and asked God to help everyone to forgive him so that he could be the kind of husband and father they needed. After the prayer, Dr. Walker explored the various hopes and dreams in the group and asked to be educated about Bill's new beliefs. That session was successful in that everyone agreed to come back.

The second meeting began the same way; Bill asked if he could pray. This time, he said that he felt God wanted some proof from him, so the family's wounds could be healed. He asked God for a clear sign of what he should do. Before the end of the session, the sign seemed to come; Willie mentioned that he had been laid off from his retail job and Bill offered him work. Things seemed to be coming together as Thanksgiving approached; they all agreed to be at the dinner, including Sam's girl friend. Melissa left a telephone message afterward to let Dr. Walker know that the celebration was the best they'd ever had.

Over the next year, meeting once or twice a month, the family oscillated back and forth between good news and bad news. Dr. Walker focused on the changes that were taking place in their relationships, which were increasingly connected through the church as Bill invited them to all join him there. Willie now worked in the company office, but that created stress; he had ended up with a better job than his brother who had been patient and loyal to their dad. Once again the family came together and prayed for an answer, this time with everyone contributing a few words. Within a week, Bill announced a plan: He would retire and devote his time to the church, putting Sam in charge of the company.

Through the next year, continuing to meet every few months with Dr. Walker, the family continued their progress in overcoming a history of verbal abuse, threats, and emotional distance. Bill worked with his spiritual director sorting out issues of power, control, authority, and obedience. He began volunteering in a violence prevention program for young men, but was forced to quit when he was diagnosed with colon cancer.

The family stopped coming for counseling, and Melissa withdrew from her active role in the company as she began spending more time focusing on Bill's care. Bill said on the phone with Dr. Walker that he saw his spiritual journey as a blessing; if the cancer had occurred 3 years before, he would have been bitter, angry, abusive, and alone in his suffering.

Bill did, in fact, struggle with feelings of anger and resentment, and his declining health was accompanied by mood changes. But he remained committed to his goal of showing God's love to others. He died at home approximately a year later, with his family—including a new daughter-in-law—around him. The family was prepared for economic survival and was emotionally connected. For Bill, his most important goals had been met and the forgiveness he wanted seemed to have arrived.

Theory and Research

Spirituality has become, in the past 20 years, the preferred term for referring to a broad domain of human existence that includes religion. Roof (2003) explains, "Spirituality is now less contained by traditional religious structures and Americans—whether we like it or not—are increasingly aware of alternatives for nurturing their souls" (p. 137). Less easily defined than religion because it is independent of cultures and institutions, spirituality has many aspects and therefore appears in many different forms.

The spirituality theme is often referred to in terms of *transcendence*. Giblin (1996b) finds two uses of this term in spirituality. First, humans are universally called on to be *self-transcendent*—to reject self-interest and find higher levels of interest. Second, in many traditions they are also oriented to be *aware of a transcendent dimension*, one involving spirit presences or beings. There may be times and places, events and practices, institutions and relationships associated with an altered experience in which individuals and their personal concerns are somehow incorporated into a more inclusive understanding of human life. A transcendent experience might include encounters with a supreme power, universal laws, a spirit world, or the primacy of nature. It might involve a new view of the past or future, it might be a private or shared experience, and it might be a one-time experience or a part of daily spiritual practice.

It is likely that your view of the world already acknowledges some such phenomena. Like the majority of Americans, you may subscribe to Christian, Jewish, or Islamic beliefs. With or without a belief in a specific creator, during a walk in the woods you may give thanks for the beauty of the natural world. Your spirituality may be quietly and unobtrusively present in your life; instead of observing nature as an outsider, you may attempt to live in harmony with all of creation. Or you may find that spirituality only enters your life when you think of others, and you try to be respectful of their beliefs.

The study of this amorphous and all-inclusive theme is distributed through many disciplines, using a variety of terms. For the purposes of this chapter, we focus on specific ways in which spirituality appears in relationships.

Contexts of Religion and Spirituality

To many family practitioners, working from a perspective of relational spirituality is not news; they are comfortable with the ways in which their spirituality and their other assets fit together in the helping process. But it seems that many other family professionals have not made spiritual concepts or practices a significant part of their approach. Even though Harris (1998) found spiritual themes "hidden" in some classic works, spirituality was not prominently featured in family counseling literature until the past few years.

Prest and Keller (1993) attributed this avoidance of explicit spiritual issues to several factors. For example, the family therapy field sought credibility in its early years through association with objective science. Religion and spirituality were associated with subjectivity, bias, and value-laden judgments, and they threatened to embarrass the new "science." Practitioners also may have avoided spiritual issues because they thought such issues would lead to dogmatic and competitive discussions. Stander et al. (1994) pointed to the value that Americans place on religious freedom, which might imply freedom from discussing religion anywhere outside one's faith community. Prest and Keller compared religious discussions with discussions of sex; they said that practitioners might consider themselves unqualified to discuss people's personal, private relationships with their deity.

This history is not unique to family-oriented practitioners; religion and spirituality were viewed negatively by the modernist social and behavioral sciences through most of the twentieth century (Frame, 2002; West, 2000). Sigmund Freud was only one of many public intellectuals in the early twentieth century who criticized and rejected religion. In the modern era, religion was associated with extremism, on one hand, and exploitation of the masses, on the other; the new sciences of mental health were intended to free humanity from the grip of primitive magic and to teach people that their poverty was not sent by God. Freud's scientific posture lent extra credibility to the rationalist, anti-spiritual perspective, and behaviorism further influenced theorists and practitioners to reject phenomena that couldn't be measured or counted, had no fixed meaning, and whose influence in human lives was unpredictable. This campaign to discredit religion resulted in many religious conservatives expressing negative attitudes toward mental health services.

By the last part of the twentieth century, researchers and professional helpers in the United States typically ignored spirituality. At the same time, they may have thought they knew about their research subjects' or clients' spirituality—after all, widely published survey results in the 1990s said that 40% of Americans attended religious services weekly (Walsh, 1999b). Other studies have led to lower estimates of religious activity but still find that "Fifty percent of Americans said '10' when asked to rate the importance of God in their lives on a scale of 1 to 10" (Chaves & Stephens, 2003, p. 90).

What is hard to grasp, for many Americans, is the degree to which the United States is no longer a Christian country. At the time of the American Revolution, nearly all of the White settlers were European Christians—and slaves were expected to adopt the religion of the slaveholders. The meaning of "freedom of religion" was essentially, "freedom to be any kind of Christian." Through the middle of the twentieth century, immigration policies severely restricted the number of non-Christians to immigrate and establish citizenship.

As Diana Eck (2001) documents, since U.S. immigration policies were liberalized in 1965 the country has seen dramatic changes in its religious landscape. At the same time, diversity was always present: As Trujillo (2000) points out, the 542 Native American tribes are quite diverse in their beliefs. In the past 20 years, all of the world's major religions have taken root in U.S. soil. Eck describes observing that her Harvard classes in comparative religion were including increasing numbers of Hindu, Buddhist, and Muslim students. Eventually, she began to leave the university for field research, and without leaving the Boston area, she visited Hindu communities, mosques and Islamic centers, Buddhist communities, and Sikh communities. From that beginning, she sent teams around the country, finding religious diversity not only in cities but also in small towns. Eventually, she had found many strong faith communities and a rich array of interfaith groups dedicated to peace and justice.

Positive and Negative Views of Religion

As a focus of counseling, religion has appeared in two roles. First, religion has been shown to be an important element in the lives of successful individuals and families. Richards and Bergin (2000b) summarized research showing religious commitment and involvement to be positively associated with a variety of desirable outcomes such as school success, longer life, and better recovery from illness and surgery, and negatively correlated with divorce, anxiety, depression, delinquency, and suicide. Pargament (1997), assessing the role of religion in people's ability to cope with life's challenges, found it to be a positive factor—especially in helping people to overcome feelings of defeat and consider themselves strong enough to utilize their existing resources.

Second, religion has been seen as either creating or exacerbating problems in some people's lives. Pargament pointed to negative outcomes when, for example, people believed in divine intervention and did not seek medical care or otherwise take effective action to help themselves. Overall, he suggested, religion is likely to cause problems to the extent that it oversimplifies the challenges of life. Another concern was expressed by Thurston (2000), as he warned that a dualistic belief in absolute right and wrong behavior could lead people to suicide, believing that they have permanently alienated God and therefore death is the only solution.

It may be that any belief can become distorted and part of a destructive and exploitative pattern. Negative experiences seem to result not so much from a belief system as from the way it is applied in a particular religious community or by a particular individual. For example, exploitive cult leaders have constructed belief systems that provided them tremendous control over the lives of their dependent followers. Even when a religious tradition seems to be free of exploitive intent, and its leaders are sincere, caring people, demands for obedience and submission to authority can easily become the basis for relationships in which sexual abuse and other kinds of exploitive behavior are accepted. Counselors must be prepared to rigorously follow up on any indications that adults or children have become involved in abuse of any kind.

It is important to point out the error of viewing spiritual traditions and religions as being either totally beneficial or totally an impediment in people's lives. Traditions differ in what they offer and how those offerings can be applied in particular circumstances. Counselors, according to Faiver, Ingersoll, O'Brien, and McNally (2001), cannot ignore their clients' spirituality any more than they can ignore any other aspect of their identities. Working with clients in a way that includes their religion, the practitioner gains important information on many aspects of the client's life. And in situations where beliefs and practices are creating problems, conversations about spirituality offer an opportunity to provide support, to question, and to refer to a spiritual advisor for more sophisticated help if necessary.

Social Climate and Spirituality

In the past 20 years, a new professional movement has become visible, seeking the integration of spirituality with family counseling and other mental health disciplines (Becvar, 1997; Weaver et al., 2002). Many factors have influenced this movement, but there seem to be two overlapping trends: increasing attention to diversity and renewed public interest in spirituality.

The United States has been characterized by racial and cultural tensions since its founding, but the dominant attitude during most of its first 200 years was one of assimilation. The values captured in the "melting pot" metaphor called for avoiding or minimizing any mention of difference. To the extent that spiritual and religious differences were acknowledged, the dominant discourse was one of *tolerance*. Most people avoided interfaith activities; the less one group knew about another group, it seemed, the easier it was to maintain a positive attitude. But, in the past 50 years, rapid social change has increased geographical and economic mobility, awareness of injustice, and political action by minority groups. A global economy has high-speed communication. Values have been shifting in the direction of celebrating and validating differences.

At the same time, the spiritual and religious diversity of the United States has become far greater, with declining membership in many traditional religious groups and growing numbers of people seeking spiritual alternatives (Christiano, 2000; Eck, 2001). During the 1960s and the 1970s, a time of worldwide political unrest, spiritual alternatives in the United States multiplied (Flowers, 1984). Many of the world's religions gained new visibility, and the climate was receptive to the development of new religions and revivals of ancient ones. Christianity became more internally diverse as well. The Roman Catholic Church, for example, revised many of its policies and practices to allow greater variety in spiritual expression, and

evangelical and charismatic denominations became larger and more powerful.

Spirituality and religion are central to the lives of many American families (Marks, 2004) and offer temporary stability and support for others whose lives are feeling out of control (Walsh, 1999b). Griffith and Rotter (1999) wrote:

> *As important as religion and spirituality appear to be for both the general public and practicing counselors, there needs to be a greater emphasis on this topic in the literature. Overlooking or ignoring religion and spirituality in working with families diminishes the significance of this influential piece of family life. If therapists are not aware of the benefits as well as the harm that certain beliefs can bring, then they are functioning in a vacuum and may, in fact, be practicing unethically. (p. 163)*

But, spirituality presents many challenges to traditional scholarly inquiry. Different traditions and language practices make it nearly impossible to agree on what is being discussed. Is there such a thing as atheist spirituality? Does the label "Christian" or "Muslim" define a spiritual identity, or can each of these terms sometimes refer only to cultural identity? If a person participates in the rituals of a religious tradition but doesn't believe in that tradition, is this a spiritual practice? There may be even greater confusion in the case of spiritual issues and families: When we refer to spirituality in the life of a couple or family, are we talking about something shared at the group level? Or are we talking about the varieties of spiritual experience that they manifest, individually and together?

Religion, Spirituality, and Diversity

Religion can be described from many perspectives. Viewed as sociological entities, religions have been an organized part of human life since the beginning of recorded history. Shared beliefs have served as powerful bonds, helping people to live in harmony with their neighbors as they followed the same rules for living and made the same attributions about their successes and their failures. Religious practices have also served as a significant tool in passing valuable knowledge from one generation to the next; for example, dietary laws have promoted healthful practices for the times and places of their origin.

Religions may be seen as cultures—systems of texts and discourses, practices, and identities that have spiritual issues at their core (Wendel, 2003). As discourse communities, religions have tremendous influence in the lives of followers who organize much of their experience around shared themes and constructs. Within families, use of religious symbols and terms not only leads to a strong sense of cohesion but also coordinates activity. This coordinating function is stronger when there is a complex vocabulary with special meanings, and, within a religious tradition such as Judaism, Christianity, or Islam, there are often subgroups each with its own preferred texts and special practices.

Religious groups also have operated as political institutions that advocated for the values they considered important, even to the extent of supporting or opposing revolutions. In contemporary times, the Roman Catholic opposition to abortion serves as an example of political activity by a religious group. As many religions advocate for opposing lifestyles and display symbols of their uniqueness, believers or followers of different faiths have often clashed with each other. A group's power can be used internally as well as externally: Youth in particular have been a focus of many religious rules, as adolescence is a time when lifelong habits can be formed. Intermarriage among religious groups has often been discouraged, and children may be discouraged from having friends outside their traditions. Those who break religious laws may be expelled from a group or may be required to accept punishment to maintain their standing.

The contemporary focus on spirituality—including the proliferation of religious options—has gained energy from a larger multicultural movement and from the postmodern trend. These movements recognize that people cannot be separated from their diversities. A professional cannot engage fully with an individual, couple, or family group when identity aspects including spirituality

are denied or misunderstood. Therefore, we briefly review some of the ways in which people's diversities and their commonalities appear in their ways of addressing spiritual issues of meaning and connectedness.

Spirituality and Culture. Most of the world's cultures include spirituality as a core element. In the past few years, representatives of the indigenous people of Australia, New Zealand, North America, South America, and Africa have been connecting through the organizing efforts of the Just Therapy Project, a group from New Zealand (Waldegrave, Tamasese, Tuhuka, & Campbell, 2003). These representatives are coming together to share their multiple and distinctive perspectives on human existence—including their common experiences as victims of genocide and exploitation. A common spiritual theme is the relationship of people to their land. The land is not a lifeless backdrop or a repository of resources that can be used; it has a presence. Aboriginal peoples still feel a connection—a relationship—with the places where their ancestors lived, and they attempt to connect with the land wherever they are. Another common theme is the intertwining of language and spirituality. Languages are not merely vehicles for the delivery of spiritual conversations; they are spiritual vessels that are an essential part of such conversations. Translating prayers, creation stories, and other "artifacts" of a spiritual culture not only distorts meanings but also takes away some of their power (Waldegrave et al., 2003).

Every culture—when assimilated, translated, and intermixed with others—may retain some of its original spiritual force. For example, Islam and Christianity have become dominant in countries far from the Middle East, and converts have learned words and concepts that connect them with the cultural sources of those traditions. Daneshpour (1998), writing about the rapid growth of Islam, acknowledges that the ethnicity of local groups of believers creates differences, but says that "Islamic ideology creates a fundamental link between cultures and establishes a common framework for understanding family life" (p. 356). And the common framework may include the land. Each year approximately 2 million Muslims from around the world gather for an annual pilgrimage to Mecca.

Belief Systems. Many people's spiritualities are organized around shared understandings. It is these shared belief systems that most people refer to when they speak of religion, and they may be most comfortable discussing their beliefs with another person who reads the same texts and espouses the same principles. This assumption leads many people to believe that a counselor should only attempt to address spiritual issues if he or she shares the same religion with the clients. But the notion of religious homogeneity is challenged by the research of Melissa Elliott Griffith and James Griffith. Their studies of Christian "conversations with a personal God" (e.g., Elliott Griffith, 1999) show amazing diversity of "god concepts" among subjects who describe themselves, in the early phase of these interviews, as conforming to a generic, standardized set of Christian beliefs.

While contemporary Americans describe themselves as overwhelmingly Christian (Chaves & Stephens, 2003), many who identify as Christian say that they also believe other things that are not part of that tradition (Beyer, 2003; Miller & Miller, 2000). There is a growing trend to seek alternative spiritualities and value people's unique integrations of spiritual experience and received spiritual teachings (Bloch, 1998).

Many belief systems are *theistic,* based on the existence of one or more supreme beings, but three of the major religions in the contemporary world—Christianity, Islam, and Judaism—are also *monotheistic.* Each declares loyalty to the "one creator and giver of all things." A skeptic might attribute the popularity of monotheistic religions to the comforting nature of such a belief—the creator of all things must be extremely powerful. If one could live in a way that pleased the creator, then one would clearly gain tremendously from acting with—not against—the creator of the universe. In the Hindu religion, God appears in many human forms (*incarnations* or *avatars*) as needed to provide for human needs, and Christianity includes a belief in a Trinity—God appearing in three different forms.

In some monotheistic belief systems, a believer can expect miracles from a responsive, protective deity who intervenes on behalf of the faithful and observant. Such belief systems sometimes create problems for those who have lived "a good life" and nevertheless experience tragedies such as earthquakes, floods, and chronic illness. Rabbi Harold Kushner's book, *Why Bad Things Happen to Good People* (1983) arose out of the need to find a way of making sense when religion hasn't "worked." The existence of evil is a further challenge for those who see God intervening in human life. Are murderers acting for God? Does murder somehow fit into God's plan, or do murderers prove that God is not powerful? Many believers have resolved these issues, but others seek assistance in finding ways to come to grips with tragedy and violence without rejecting their beliefs.

Polytheistic traditions may be, in some ways, more compatible with a world in which things don't always seem to be organized according to a single plan. These belief systems typically describe multiple spiritual beings—each with specialized domains of interest and partial influence in human affairs. A believer might have a special relationship with one or two gods, or might give honor to whichever god has dominion over a particular area of concern—human fertility or success in agriculture. A common variant on the polytheistic theme is one in which animals, plants, and even apparently inanimate objects have spirits and may act upon the world. With multiple spirits to be appeased, believers are obligated to be aware and to always follow local customs so as to not create trouble. Many Native American religions identify an infant's *totem* animal spirit, and the child grows up in both a physical family and a totem family—contributing to interconnectedness and caring.

Finally, many spiritual traditions do not identify any spiritual entity that is independent of humans. Those who have grown up in theistic traditions may have a hard time imagining spirituality without some object of worship. But there are at least two such broad categories of belief.

Transcendent belief systems acknowledge the existence of a spiritual realm, but one without any spirit that has godlike properties or powers. For some, for example, the spirit world is populated by human spirits living in a disembodied hereafter—possibly in a universal spiritual dimension where spirits from other planets and other times coexist. These belief systems do not necessarily reject the mystical aspect of spirituality. Visits from spirits may be as common as other people's conversations with God.

Rationalist belief systems such as Buddhism, Confucianism, and Taoism, alternatively, do not so much describe a separate spiritual world as a unified natural/spiritual world, which is organized in knowable ways.[1] Spiritual growth, in these traditions, consists of learning how to navigate in the world of reality. The Mahayana branch of Buddhism refers to an Absolute principle called *Dharmakaya,* but Buddhist scholars stop short of personifying this principle as God (Y. O. Kim, 1976). Likewise, the Tao is described as an absolute, as a force in the world, but not as a being.

Spirituality and Relational Well-Being

Having sampled the diverse, fluid nature of spirituality and religion in the contemporary world, we can now turn to the question of how spirituality operates in families. Our discussion begins with a rather global observation; it seems that people have sought relationship help, for thousands of years, from their religious and spiritual leaders. The pattern continues to this day, so we can assume that spiritual beliefs and practices are somehow supportive or facilitative of relational functioning. Unfortunately, the nature of this help is unclear. There is little research or theory that addresses spirituality at the level of a couple or a family; research on families and spirituality has generally focused on the perceptions of individual respondents. We know more about the re-

lationship between the individual and the transcendent than we do about ways in which the spiritual dimension enters into relationships.

An example of such individual findings, despite a relational topic, is Brotherson and Soderquist's (2002) study of families coping with a child's death. The research clearly indicates that the family members—as individuals—were helped by their spiritual traditions. The subjects in the study described, for example, the calming effect of believing that the untimely death was part of a larger plan that they could not hope to comprehend. However, the language of coping was individual because the coping narratives were collected individually. S. Kim's (2003) study of Korean parenting in light of Christian influences, likewise, focused on the subjects' values and beliefs rather than on relational processes.

Another link between individual findings and relational phenomena can be found in beliefs that specifically apply to relationships. A prime example is *forgiveness* (see Box 8.1). As a core concept in many, but not all, spiritual traditions, forgiveness is an essentially relational idea. Only through relationships with others can a person demonstrate the ability to set aside personal feelings in support of a larger good.

Shared Beliefs

Christiano (2000) found many studies demonstrating a positive correlation between *religious homogamy* and relational success. Couples who shared a spiritual orientation appeared to be more likely to pray together and attend church together—two other correlates of positive marital relationships. And active participation in religious activities seemed to be correlated with shared parenting attitudes and practices. Walsh (1998) also reported finding strong research support for the value of shared belief systems.

C. E. Bailey (2002) used qualitative methods and a combination of group and individual interviews to assemble a case study of a Christian family who were identified in their community as having "close, healthy relationships." His analysis identified five overlapping themes describing ways in which spirituality, religion, and family

---

[1] Family therapy pioneers Bateson and Satir, pioneers in promoting modern systemic understandings of human phenomena, each became active in spiritual movements featuring this ecosystemic view.

BOX 8.1

Forgiveness

Nearly every relationship, if it lasts more than a couple of minutes, struggles with issues of forgiveness. If we just met and you mistakenly call me by the wrong name, can I forgive you? Maybe we spent several hours together and you forgot to send me the recipe we discussed. Or worse, we may be longtime friends and I find out that you told someone else about my childhood sexual abuse history. In family and couple relationships, there are many real and perceived violations of trust, some of them seemingly unforgivable; a recent television drama portrayed a couple in which the husband had apparently left their infant son in a hot car, leading to the child's death. Such cases highlight the issue of self-forgiveness. To the extent that I feel my behavior has been unforgivable, I am likely to reject your forgiveness of me.

Forgiveness can be approached in many ways. As a behavioral issue, it may be seen as simply part of one's behavioral repertoire, learned, cued, and reinforced like any other behavior. If I want to be more forgiving, I must practice. Alternatively, a behavioral view could create concerns that forgiving you is somehow reinforcing your behavior. As a Narrative issue, some resolve it by finding an acceptable definition of forgiveness; if I think I am condoning your actions, I am unlikely to forgive (Butler, Dahlin, & Fife, 2002). Others resolve it by finding a story that makes the other's behavior forgivable, as Emily Brown has done with couples' possible explanations of an affair (Brown, 1999).

But for many people, forgiveness is a spiritual issue. For Christians, forgiveness is a central teaching that appears throughout their scriptures. Jesus taught that God always forgives human frailties and wants people to do the same; therefore, forgiveness is an essential step in growing closer to God. Tibetan Buddhism (e.g., Dalai Lama, 2001) emphasizes the negative effect of living with hatred and anger, and arrives at the conclusion that forgiving another is preferable. Such beliefs, when shared by couple and family members, help them pull together during difficult times. In the case of an affair, for example, both the offending partner and the victim believe that they have no choice but to forgive.

---

functioning were related. *Beliefs,* in one of his examples, operated through the family's shared understanding of life from an "eternal perspective" that focused decision making away from immediate rewards toward ultimate goals of following Jesus as a model for living and pleasing God. *Consistency* was expressed as the parents' desire to apply the same standards to themselves that they applied to their children. *Respect and trust* related to the ways in which family members viewed each other, positively, yet with acceptance of flaws. *Discipline and authority,* in light of the other themes, were defined not in terms of control but rather in terms of accepting the need to live harmoniously with each other and in accordance with God's will. And *commitment* described the parents' shared priority of children and family over all other demands.

Semans and Stone Fish (2000) created a larger system picture by interviewing 48 families in a small Jewish community in New York, seeking information about how Jewish ethnic and religious identities influenced their family life. The core conceptualization expressed by these families was one of having a shared viewpoint, one that was grounded in teachings, stories, and rituals. The authors identified 11 overlapping themes in the transcripts, many of which were clearly more spiritual than cultural. *Responsibility toward others,* for example, "teaches you how you should live your life not just for yourself, but also for the community." *Ethics* was defined as "a core mission that these families believe in, to act in a way that will improve the world." *Family* was expressed as a belief that "All members of the family are connected to each other and thrive within this intricate web of relationships." And *question and debate* referred to their conclusion that "The way these Jewish families make meaning out of conflict or disagreement is more of a connecting rather than a disconnecting process" (pp. 127–135).

There are also a few theorists who have attempted to map out the connections linking spirituality with relationships. Fowler (1981) has theorized that love, mutual trust, and loyalty in relationships are fragile unless they are anchored in a mutual commitment to one or more *shared centers of value and power*. He wrote, "We invest or devote ourselves because the other to which we commit has, for us, an intrinsic excellence or worth. . . .The centers of value and power that have god value for us, therefore, are those that confer meaning and worth on us and promise to sustain us in a dangerous world of power" (p. 18). He further referred to people as parts of many triads, and asked, ". . . can we authentically claim faith in an infinite source and center of value and power, in relation to which we are established in identities flexible and integrative enough to unify the selves we are in the various roles and relations we have?"

Fowler (1981) assumed that people who share an understanding of the divine, the transcendent, or a higher power of some kind will stay more connected with each other (see Figure 8.1). Such a conceptualization matches the research findings of Bailey and those of Semans and Stone Fish, mentioned earlier. This idea offers an intriguing alternative to the classic Bowen description of triangles. Murray Bowen (1978) also doubted the stability of a two-person relationship, but Bowen's theory did not envision that the entity occupying the third point in the triangle might be divine.

Douglas Anderson (1994) describes another way in which spirituality may function in rela-

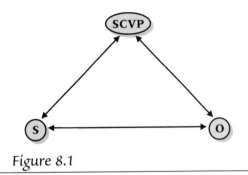

Figure 8.1

Relationship Triangle with a Higher Power

Along the base line of the triad we see the two-way flow between the self (s) and others (o) of love, mutual trust and loyalty that make selfhood possible. Above the base line, at the point of the triad, we see a representation of the family's shared center(s) of value and power (scpv). This includes the family's "story," its recognized and unrecognized collection of formative myths. Both self and others invest trust and loyalty in ("rest their hearts upon") this center or these centers. It is never quite that simple. Family members' degrees of awareness of the central myths and values they serve will vary greatly. Each member of a family probably participates in other, nonfamilial faith associations, including the family, are dynamic. The members change and their personal and corporate center(s) of value and power must evolve and be renewed. Nonetheless, the Triad, with its depiction of the structure of mutual trusts and loyalties, discloses the essential covenantal pattern of faith as relational.

Source: From *Stages of Faith: The Psychology of Human Development and the Quest for Meaning*, p. 17, by J. W. Fowler, 1981, San Francisco: Harper & Row. Reprinted with permission.

tionships. His couple counseling clients, he says, have often reported something he refers to as "the sudden appearance of change-inducing influence from beyond the partners." He says that "these experiences represent a human capacity to be aware of a source of power and meaning that lies beyond ourselves and yet that acts on us and within our concrete lives. When this transcendent force acts on us, personal and relational change is initiated, often in directions we have not intended or planned" (p. 38).

Individual and Family Experiences of Transcendence

Many authors address the topic of spirituality in terms of beliefs and practices—its cultural heritage. But the central experience of spirituality is far more difficult to describe. Since William James's book, *The Varieties of Religious Experience* (1902/1982), was published, authors have struggled to achieve some common language for addressing religious and spiritual phenomena. James and others (e.g., Carl Jung) have described cognitive, physical, and emotional experiences in which people have felt content and complete; connected with invisible forces; calmed by a new, deeper understanding of life; overjoyed with the splendor of creation; or pained by the unmet needs of humanity. The literature on spirituality tends to focus on the individual and his or her relationship with what James called "the divine." But our mission is different; we are trying to make sense of religion and spirituality as they: (1) contribute to relational well-being, and (2) are enhanced by couple and family relationships.

Spirituality can be present in the bricklayer's involvement with raw materials, seasons, and weather; in the daily abstinence-oriented routines and relationships of mutual support among alcoholics; or in the touches and prayers of family members surrounding a hospital bed. It may be conscious and organized, as in the case of a monk who structures his day around his prayers, or it may be unconscious and diffused for emergency room nurses and soup-kitchen workers who provide caring as well as direct services. Some people's spiritual lives are central to their existence—they meditate, they attend services, they read spiritual texts whenever possible. For others, spirituality is not a relevant idea and it has no presence in their lives.

The variety of spiritual experiences makes it hard to create a summary description that distinguishes spiritual from other aspects of existence. Every religion or spiritual tradition seems to describe certain kinds of activities that enhance the likelihood of achieving a state of transcendence, and each also offers a unique set of concepts for believers to use in making sense of transcendent experiences. Table 8.1 illustrates multiple ways in which spirituality has been described.

Spirituality, in its many forms, can be seen in this table as extremely diverse. But many spiritual traditions, in different ways, agree that spiritual growth involves giving up one's separateness and joining in the unity of creation. Albert Einstein is quoted by Walsh (1999a) as saying: "The religion of the future will be a cosmic religion. It should transcend a personal God and avoid dogma and theology. . . . [I]t should be based on a religious sense arising from the experience of all things natural and spiritual as a meaningful unity" (p. 32).

Individual Spiritual Development

The lifelong experience of having discrete spiritual experiences and incorporating them into the rest of life has been represented, in many religious and spiritual traditions, as a developmental process. The process of becoming more enlightened, holy, or pure is often represented as a journey (John Bunyan's fictional *The Pilgrim's Progress,* 1678/2003, comes to mind, as does Siddhartha Gautama's story of transformation into the Buddha, Mitchell, 2002).

Possibly the most widely accepted framework for understanding spiritual development is James Fowler's (1981) description in *Stages of Faith.* Fowler makes no claim that his discussion of faith describes all spiritual experiences, but he does suggest that it is broadly applicable. His model was based on work with adults in a spiritual retreat center and from immersion in the work of Jean Piaget and Erik Erikson and refined through research interviews with 359 individuals who were "overwhelmingly white, Christian, evenly divided by sex and distributed throughout the age categories."

Fowler describes six stages, the last of which he observed in only a handful of individuals. At the earliest stage, *intuitive-projective,* the young child typically shows an awareness of god concepts and a powerful ability to fantasize, but is typically not a serious student of beliefs. In the *mythic-literal* stage, the child learns the stories and incorporates the beliefs of a spiritual community, applying them

Table 8.1   **Spiritual Themes**

Concept	
Absolute love	The Buddhist Ultimate or Absolute, according to Kim (1976), is an all-embracing love that is dedicated to the goal of helping humans to reach Nirvana. Just as all are welcomed into this Absolute love, followers are invited to see the best in others and to extend love to them.
Connectedness	According to Becvar (1997) and Giblin (1996b), connectedness is one of the universal spiritual themes. People are implored to pay attention to their connections with each other, individually and in communities; with their immediate ecology, with nature at a global level, and with the spirit world.
Cyclical change, harmony, and fluidity	Jordan (1985) describes the Taoist belief in an endless, continuous cycling between the polarities of Yin and Yang such that an overemphasis on one will eventually result in a compensatory rise in the other. This belief predicts that any attempt to create unchanging order and stability will fail.
The divine	The divine (the ultimate Other, the One, the Great Spirit, the Absolute) is sometimes personified and sometimes described in more abstract terms, but most spiritual traditions incorporate a "vertical" dimension in which humans are dependent on a Higher Power.
Morality, virtue, ethics	Spiritual traditions are rarely value-free. Judaism is founded on the principle of living a moral and pious life, and Confucianism, according to Kim (1976), calls for practitioners, in their personal as well as their public lives, to act according to moral principles including piety.
Pain and suffering	According to Wright (1999) and Becvar (1997), human life involves suffering. Avoidance of suffering is avoidance of spiritual growth. Wolin, Muller, Taylor, & Wolin (1999), alternatively, cite Buddhist teaching that all must experience pain, but suffering is a choice.
Purpose	What are we here for, and how can we tell whether we are doing it right? The lack of purpose, according to Frankl (1984), is the ultimate spiritual crisis.
Relinquishment and acceptance	D. A. Anderson (1994) says that relationships suffer from "Willful attempts to make ourselves lovable or to get others to love us . . . " because we cannot "face the essential aloneness and helplessness that characterize the human condition" (p. 39).
Soul and spirit	Soul and spirit refer to the part of humans that is not physical or psychological. The soul may join God in an afterlife, join the spirits of the departed in providing guidance and support for the living, or return to Earth in another earthly form to continue working toward Nirvana.

literally (this stage also may be seen in adulthood, particularly when traumatic life experiences have occurred). The *synthetic-conventional* stage follows, a stage in which the individual—often in adolescence, but in other cases much later in life—begins to reflect on beliefs and to consolidate multiple meanings that incorporate a variety of experiences. By the age of 21, nearly all of Fowler's sample were in the *individuative-reflective* stage, a stage in which received knowledge is questioned and the individual begins to "take seriously the burden of responsibility for his or her own commitments, lifestyle, beliefs and attitudes." This stage fits with many people's adult spiritual practice, and the *conjunctive* stage appears for a smaller group of individuals who find that their experience is not readily assimilated into logically organized, rational abstract concepts. In this midlife stage, people grapple with contradictions and open themselves to the symbols, myths, and rituals of others. Finally, the *universalizing* stage—extremely rare—requires pushing past the contradictions and paradoxes of life to choose a vision that will organize reality. This last stage, Fowler acknowledged, is one that can produce both saints and fanatics.

Spiritual Practice

Spiritual development can be pursued through a variety of practices. The variety of religious and spiritual practice seems to be infinite, but the options seem to fall into a small number of categories.

Teaching, Studying, and Learning.   Some kind of learning is a nearly universal aspect of spiritual traditions. Typically there are individuals who are designated as *spiritual guides.* Whether they are known as rabbis, pastors, monks, or shamans, they are entrusted with others' spiritual lives. Oral and written texts known as *scriptures* often provide the background for spiritual learning. Stories of wars, births, political upheavals, sexual affairs, illness, family conflicts, and other elements of human life, ancient texts such as the Hindu Bhagavad Gita or the Jewish Torah often embed messages in a poetic form that is not easily understood. Such sacred stories are often interpreted by other texts that provide guidelines, rules, and procedures for examining one's own life. The texts of some traditions, such as Confucianism, consist primarily of specific instructions in living according to natural law.

Meditation, Altered States, and Dreamwork.   Many spiritual traditions include practices that help searchers to hear internal voices or voices that come from a spirit dimension. These practices often involve taking time to retreat from the daily cares of the world into a state of contemplation or ecstasy. Many Buddhists, for example, block out distractions through *meditation,* thereby becoming more able to reflect on their progress toward en-

lightenment. Other traditions use dancing or mind-altering substances to help people withdraw from the mundane world and be open to spiritual messages. Dreams may be encouraged and may be carefully examined for their spiritual content.

Prayer.   Prayer is more actively directed outward. Praying can be a one-way communication process in which an individual or group recites or spontaneously creates a message for one or more deities or spirits, messages of supplication—requesting support or assistance—or ones of honor or praise. But some spiritual/religious traditions also describe prayer that is interactive. Such prayers ask for guidance, help in understanding, clarification, or possibly for signs that indicate the correct decision. For those who pray in this manner, prayer is sometimes described as a conversation.

Worship.   Many religions involve organized prayer activity that is referred to as *worship.* It can involve the elevation of a deity (or a symbol of the deity) through praise, ritual sacrifice, and physical gestures of subjugation such as kneeling. In many traditions, the deity is publicly honored by the building of ornate houses of worship and by ceremonial worship that requires hundreds of participants to create music, dance, and ritual. At the opposite extreme are traditions that define worship as a private matter, performed at home with the family.

Rituals and Celebrations.   Rituals and celebrations are extremely important in many people's religious and spiritual lives (Bellah, 2003). As discussed in Chapter 6, rituals communicate meaning at a symbolic level that bypasses the rational/categorical language system. Rituals are often characterized by body involvement through singing and dance, transformation of identity with costumes, large-group cooperation, and repetition, and are often credited with magical properties.

Discipline and Obedience.   Many religious or spiritual traditions expect sacrifice or self-denial of some kind. The discipline may be silence during certain hours, or a dietary rule that does not interfere with adequate nutrition. Or the discipline may be more severe, such as Ghandi's disavowal of worldly goods, shelter, and regular meals. Buddhism and the Alcoholics Anonymous fellowship (see Table 8.2) require their followers to work on a rigorous program of self-analysis and self-improvement.

Caring and Action. Many religions and spiritual traditions call upon their followers to be concerned with the world around them—not only in the abstract but also in direct action. Spiritual leaders have created or supported major political movements, which include liberating people from slavery and starvation, ending war, and ending the exploitation of women and children. Religious communities often supply food, shelter, and medical care; operate schools, hospitals, day care centers, homeless shelters, and food banks; or sponsor social service agencies.[2]

Relational Spirituality

When these diverse spiritual and religious practices are viewed in families, the core issue seems to be one of coordination. Multiple spiritualities exist, even within a couple, and one person's beliefs and practices can conflict with those of another. Walsh (1999a) discusses the common experiences of religious conversion and intermarriage, both of which present extended families with the need to accommodate multiple perspectives and practices in their lives.

Even when people are on what seems to be the same spiritual path, they are likely to be in different "places" at different times. Relationships require flexibility and accommodation. Couples and families can strive to coordinate their spiritual development and build a shared spiritual life. I conceptualize the options as moving through levels of increasing spiritual intimacy (as illustrated in Figure 8.2).

Shared Preparation. Study and learning may seem to demand isolation, but learners often benefit from collaborative effort. In formal education settings, teachers have known for years that diffi-

Table 8.2 Twelve Steps of Alcoholics Anonymous

1. We admitted we were powerless over alcohol—that our lives had become unmanageable.
2. Came to believe that a Power greater than ourselves could restore us to sanity.
3. Made a decision to turn our will and our lives over to the care of God *as we understood Him.*
4. Made a searching and fearless moral inventory of ourselves.
5. Admitted to God, to ourselves, and to another human being the exact nature of our wrongs.
6. Were entirely ready to have God remove all these defects of character.
7. Humbly asked Him to remove our shortcomings.
8. Made a list of all persons we had harmed, and became willing to make amends to them all.
9. Made direct amends to such people wherever possible, except when to do so would injure them or others.
10. Continued to take personal inventory and when we were wrong promptly admitted it.
11. Sought through prayer and meditation to improve our conscious contact with God *as we understood Him,* praying only for knowledge of His will for us and the power to carry that out.
12. Having had a spiritual awakening as the result of these Steps, we tried to carry this message to others, and to practice these principles in all our affairs.

Source: A Brief Guide to Alcoholics Anonymous, by Alcoholics Anonymous, 2005, New York: Author. The Twelve Steps are reprinted with permission of Alcoholics Anonymous World Services, Inc. (A.A.W.S.) Permission to reprint the Twelve Steps does not mean that A.A.W.S. has reviewed or approved the contents of this publication, or that A.A.W.S. necessarily agrees with the views expressed herein. AA is a program of recovery from alcoholism *only*—use of the Twelve Steps in connection with programs and activities which are patterned after AA, but which address other problems, or in any other non-AA context, does not imply otherwise.

cult concepts are best learned in teams with assignments requiring them to put new material into practice. In the case of spiritual teachings, some spiritual themes are difficult to learn: Absolute love, for example, is a concept that is extremely hard to put into operation. However, couple and family relationships present ideal

---

[2] At the same time, spiritually led movements create suffering through their support for wars among groups who subscribe to different visions of an ideal world.

Figure 8.2

Spirituality and Relationships

learning environments; in intimate relationships, we get to know others in their full complexity—their good moods and their bad. In our closest relationships, we struggle with issues of cyclical change, harmony, ethics, and suffering. The relational unit that works together to study and apply its spiritual traditions should make consistent progress toward its spiritual goals for all members.

Shared Meditation and Prayer. These activities are common in spiritual retreat centers and houses of worship; therefore, there must be something about sharing that contributes to the spiritual experience. Butler, Gardner, and Bird (1998) concluded that praying together—especially in times of tension and conflict—was extremely helpful to the Christian couples they studied. Their subjects reported that praying together increased their empathy for each other and reduced their anxiety. Christian prayer has a unique function; God is expected to respond to requests, and a couple requesting guidance expects new insights from divine intervention.

Even without a personal God who answers prayers, couples and families may expect to come closer through the experience of entering a receptive, meditative state together. Prayers, whether they are ritualized or spontaneous, can contain messages that share individuals' concerns, frame those concerns in a collaborative way, and coordinate meanings into a shared perspective.

Shared Experiences of Spiritual Connection. Faiver et al. (2001) distinguish between exoteric and esoteric forms of spirituality. *Exoteric* forms are outward and public, the kind of visible shared activities described previously. *Esoteric* spiritual experiences are inward, subjective states that may be transformative in their impact. These experiences may occur during participation in exoteric activities, but may also occur unexpectedly through encounters with nature and intimate moments with loved ones.

While such a transforming experience is at one level internal and individual, partners and family members who communicate about their spiritual lives—even if their spiritual lives are, in some ways, different—can share such a transformation.

Shared Sense-Making. Spiritual traditions offer language tools that help their followers to achieve a sense of order in relationship to their lives. This is true even for followers who—like J. P. Bloch's (1998) "new agers"—creatively combine elements from many different traditions. Every discourse of spirituality includes multiple concepts that can radically transform an experience when used appropriately. Ideas of relinquishment and acceptance can be invoked at times when situations are uncontrollable and apparently unacceptable. Members of 12-step fellowships help each other with this challenge on a regular basis; when confronted with a friend's anxiety or anger, they need only say the key words from Step 3—"turn it over" to the Higher Power. When people support each other's uses of spiritual concepts, the effect unites them in their mutual desire for growth and personal effectiveness.

Shared Commitment and Renewal. Among the most powerful images of shared spiritual life are those of committed religious communities—groups whose renunciation of worldly alternatives is part of a dedication to their shared spiritual growth. Some groups live among the general public but make public statements—at least some of the time—through distinctive styles of dress and personal appearance (e.g., Native Americans, some Buddhist monks, Muslim women, Hasidic Jews, traditional Amish). Others withdraw from the secular world and live with a primary focus on their shared religious life (cloistered nuns, monks in monasteries). What these groups—and many families—share is *commitment,* which Scott Stanley (1998) describes as "making the choice to give up some choices." It is both a practice and an aspiration. At the daily level, the committed keep themselves and each other focused on questions and practices of their spiritual tradition. At another level, as the commitment is declared and renewed in daily or weekly gatherings, they remind each other of their ideals, values, and beliefs.

The Process of Counseling with Couples and Families

It should be clear by this point that the basic idea of family counselors becoming involved in people's spiritual lives is one that (1) has received mixed responses and (2) puts the practitioner in touch with a confusing variety of beliefs and practices that people bring to their spiritual quests. Furthermore, I hope that I have made the case that identifying religious and spiritual issues in couple and family terms can be a challenge. Unlike the other four themes in the BONES taxonomy, this one is still at the early stages of being articulated in the family therapy literature.

The following discussion uses the same general outline as the other themes, beginning with the process of engaging with clients and following the counseling process chronologically as much as possible. But I have also borrowed from Rivett and Street (2001) a framework for organizing the various combined spiritual/counseling options. This framework focuses not only on the spirituality of the clients but also on the spirituality of the professional. Rivett and Street separate counseling options into those that *do not assume* anything about the counselor's own spirituality and those that *rely on assumptions* that the counselor is inte-

grating his or her own beliefs into the process. The former position is termed *instrumental,* and the latter is termed *metaphysical.*

Engaging: Making Space for the Spirit

The same conditions that make a counseling relationship supportive for emotional work (Chapter 7) and open to discovery of clients' preferred narratives (Chapter 6) are helpful in creating an environment where people can share their spiritual lives. But many people experience special kinds of discomfort related to spiritual discussions, as noted earlier in this chapter.

Professionals who seek to hear about their clients' spiritual lives are encouraged to look at multicultural counseling work such as that of Paul Pedersen (2000). Pedersen says that people are so embedded in their own cultural histories that it is hard to recognize the times when clients' messages are being heard in a distorted way. In the case of spirituality, a counselor who has had only cursory contact with Paganism or Catholicism may be influenced by lurid news stories about these traditions. A client's comment, "A group of us used to gather for Pagan services, but I just couldn't stay with it" might be heard as rejection of beliefs and practices rather than problems with scheduling. Or perhaps a counselor who is a former Catholic might be more likely to hear Catholic references in a negative light and to respond with a comment such as "Yeah, I couldn't stand all that stuff either." Pedersen suggests that counselors need to develop an *internal supervisor* who listens to their conversations and notices when they are in danger of imposing their cultural perspectives on others.

Aponte (1999) points to the special relevance of spirituality for poor, marginalized minority clients who may have experienced:

- Loss of a sense of identity and self-worth
- Diminished power over everyday living and their future destiny
- Separateness from the larger society, and a loss of stable relationships in their personal lives and communities

For these clients, spiritual roots may have been lost as well. Boyd-Franklin (2003) discusses the challenge of assessing African American clients' belief systems and their relationships with those beliefs in such a way that the counselor neither imposes beliefs on clients nor faces client frustration because beliefs were not addressed.

A spiritually safe counseling environment needs to not only accept clients' statements about spirituality in an accepting and nonjudgmental manner but also recognize tentative expressions of spiritual concerns and actively invite spiritual issues into the room. Helmeke and Bischof (2002) offer specific "guidelines for the timid" that can help a counselor to find ways of being inviting but not threatening.

Conducting a Dynamic Assessment

Spirituality often is not mentioned in people's presenting issues, and depending on the setting—a counselor working in a religious setting would obviously have more freedom to be direct in exploring spiritual issues—assessment of spirituality is not likely to take place until a sensitive exploration has established the clients' willingness to view their relationship issues as having spiritual elements. Assessment may have many different goals, depending on the counselor's orientation and the particular spiritual situations that present themselves. In some cases, the focus may be on spirituality as a source of relationship conflict and misunderstanding, while in other cases the focus may be on the family or couple's movement toward spiritual goals. Given the potential for spirituality to be part of problem patterns as well as a solution to those patterns, the counselor should be alert for indications that an individual or the relationship system is being disabled by misused, misunderstood, or destructive spiritual involvements.

Spiritual Genogram

The classic genogram, with its advantages of facilitating a multigenerational view and sensitively portraying multiple intersections of history and context, has been adapted for spiritual use by Frame (2000). In this use, just as in other adaptations, the genogram helps in identifying relational

tensions and alliances—the emotional/political "structure" of a relational network. Frame retains the essential structure set forth in McGoldrick et al. (1999), but the arrows and jagged lines that typically represent emotional closeness and distance are appropriated to represent spiritual affinity or conflict. Most significantly, color-coding of individual symbols indicates spiritual orientations and religious affiliations—including changes over time. The visual representation itself, once complete, can be an aid in analyzing patterns in family systems. But the genogram's greater value may lie in its function of focusing conversations and recording the key items of information that were discussed.

Spiritual Ecomap

In an adaptation of another classic assessment technique, Hodge (2000) created an ecomapping technique based on the work of Hartman. He cites advantages over genograms for some purposes—the ecomap can be created more efficiently and it emphasizes current environmental factors rather than family history. Relational issues can be shown in some cases to be more related to extrafamilial than intrafamilial forces. Hodge's work offers not only a representational system but also an organizational framework and a detailed, culturally sensitive list of questions for use in a spiritually focused interview. In his anthropologically informed depiction of spiritual experience, experiences and institutions are given equal status with persons and transcendent beings. God can be a participant in relationships (Box 8.2), but angels or extraterrestrials can also influence relationships—as can rituals, traumatic experiences, a faith community, and a spiritual leader. As in the case of the genogram, the ecomap shares the advantage of involving participants in a process, which may be more important than the product that results.

Spiritual Narratives

Elliott Griffith and Griffith (2002) used a narrative approach to assess the presence and the nature of spiritual themes in the lives of persons struggling with major mental illnesses and their families. They focused on the ways in which such narratives can help in differentiating between

God Is on My Side

When people believe in a personified Higher Power who is intimately involved in personal relationships, it introduces a unique aspect into families. Butler and Harper (1994) say that many religious Christian families include God in their relationship systems; therefore, God is as likely as any other family member to become part of relationship triangles. This potential to claim that "God is on my side" is particularly meaningful when we consider that, as Stewart and Gale (1994) point out, different family members may choose different aspects of the scriptural God—judgmental versus forgiving, for instance—to support their positions. The "spiritually one-up" family member often expects that the therapist will agree with his or her perceptions and goals (Rotz, Russell, & Wright, 1993).

helpful and hurtful spiritual experiences—a particular concern where emotional and cognitive impairments pose particular vulnerabilities. In this kind of assessment, multiple voices are useful—clients may bring friends or extended family members whose perspectives help in understanding relationship history. And the presence of these extra informants can contribute verbal and nonverbal information about people's ways of being.

Spirituality Questionnaires

A variety of paper-and-pencil measures have been created that can be helpful in articulating the complexities of a couple's or a family's internal spiritual diversity and also in identifying goals for further spiritual development.

The Transformative Experience Questionnaire (TEQ; Mansager & Eckstein, 2002) is a 20-item measure designed to facilitate couple discussions of the role of spirituality in their relationship. Intentionally inclusive of atheistic and theistic views, it is organized into Adlerian dimensions of striving, integration, self-transcendence, and ultimate value.

The Spiritual Experience Index (Genia, 1991) is a 38-item, single-factor measure organized around a developmental faith model. Designed for use with spiritually diverse individuals, its detailed breakdown of spiritual beliefs is helpful in highlighting areas of couple and family difference.

The Spiritual Orientation Inventory (Elkins, Hedstrom, Hughes, Leaf, & Saunders, 1988) is an 85-item measure designed to be inclusive of broad aspects of spirituality. Its 9 subscales assess the transcendent dimension, meaning and purpose, mission in life, sacredness of life, material values, altruism, idealism, awareness of the tragic, and fruits of spirituality.

The Spiritual Wellness Inventory is published, along with scoring information, in Faiver et al. (2001), *Explorations in Counseling and Spirituality: Philosophical, Practical, and Personal Reflections.* The 55-item questionnaire yields scores on 10 subscales: conception of the absolute/divine, meaning, connectedness, mystery, spiritual freedom, experience/ritual, forgiveness, hope, knowledge/learning, present-centeredness, and spiritual freedom.

Nonverbal Assessment

Assessment does not have to be limited to verbal sources of information. A home visit can be a tremendous source of information on any kind of relational dynamics, but with a spiritual focus the home visit offers the opportunity for people to share objects—pictures, religious relics, souvenirs from pilgrimages, to cite a few possibilities—to enhance their verbal sharing. Art activities can also give a special communication opportunity to a family member who is not as verbally comfortable.

Intervening: Instrumental, Ethnosensitivity

Our first class of counseling responses includes those which are instrumental—they do not imply that the counselor and the client are sharing a spiritual experience—but are distinctive for their effort to be culturally sensitive and make the counseling process congruent with clients' beliefs and practices.

Falicov (1999) provides information to assist in such an approach to spiritual issues in Latino families. Referring to folk beliefs regarding physical and mental problems, Falicov writes, "I consider the folk approaches as having their own wisdom, effectiveness, and spiritual meaning and as playing a complementary part alongside conventional methods" (p. 105). She educates the counselor about culturally unique illnesses such as *susto* (fright), and the varieties of magic that may be part of clients' lives. Beliefs in magic are not likely to be shared publicly, according to Falicov, but believers consult both "black" and "white" witches to arrange for spells that will bring back a former lover or revenge an evil hex. *Curandismo,* or the use of native healers is more socially acceptable and may be integrated with modern medical treatment. Overall, Falicov represents Latino families as heirs to multiple spiritual traditions that are often incompatible in their assumptions. She encourages the practitioner to learn directly from families about their particular beliefs and adopt a collaborative attitude with "complementary" beliefs.

Stewart and Gale (1994) present a different cross-cultural challenge—providing services to evangelical and fundamentalist Protestant couples. The U.S. population includes approximately 77 million evangelical and fundamentalist Christians (Thurston, 2000), but they are underrepresented in the ranks of service providers. Just as Falicov provides information about the historical and cultural forces that influence Latino family spirituality, these authors offer understandings of ways in which "the religious right" differs from other Christian traditions and ways in which beliefs may differ within this apparently homogeneous population. The commonalities include a belief in the Bible as God's Word, a belief in being born again into a life of holiness and a personal relationship with God, and a determination to resist secular trends that would undermine their traditional values.

Stewart and Gale advise the professional to pay careful attention to the language that clients use in their descriptions of God and their descriptions of marriage. They write, "Biblical writings support a host of metaphors to describe the deity, ranging from the more traditional, patriarchal root-metaphors for Yahweh, such as father, lord, judge, warrior, king, to less traditional, but no less powerful, metaphors such as friend . . ." and they refer to four different marital metaphors—sacrament, vocation, covenant, and communion. These metaphors provide information about clients' perceived relationships and suggest ways in which a substitute metaphor (one that has Biblical authority) might provide support for relationship changes. They caution, however: "Therapists who contradict biblical teachings with evangelical clients do so at peril of sacrificing their therapeutic effectiveness and even being dismissed as ungodly or worse. . . ." Stewart and Gale recommend becoming familiar with biblical passages that pertain to marriage, but choosing a posture of learner rather than teacher, asking partners to bring scripture to sessions to inform the process. Applicable to other religions besides Christianity, as well, this strategy should provide a basis for exploring options and shared values.

Searching for Spiritual Connections
The professional who holds an open, inquiring attitude toward client spirituality is in a position to help families whose spiritual traditions have been disrupted or lost. In many cases, assessment of couple and family spirituality taps into a sense that an important part of the clients' cultural history has been sacrificed because they have "fallen away" and stopped being active members of the spiritual/religious communities of their childhood. This experience is especially common among couples and families who merge different spiritual backgrounds. They may have concluded that no single tradition can represent the multiple spiritualities in their family. The search for a spiritual home is also common among new stepfamilies, and when families relocate—the factors that made them comfortable in their prior religious or spiritual community may not be easy to locate in a new community or a new country. And family

changes may disrupt a family's experience of spiritual community; a death in the family or the arrival of a new child may change the feeling of support into one of anxiety.

With such a "spiritually searching" family, an ethnosensitive professional can provide a setting in which clients are able to discuss the missing elements in their lives and prepare to take action. Once they reach a level of some clarity about what they are seeking, they can plan a search for a spiritual community or a spiritual tradition that meets their needs. Many search by "shopping around," visiting services and renewal weekends and interviewing spiritual leaders. Others search by reading and sharing spiritual texts. Some will find a compatible new spiritual home, one that fits for all family members. Many, however, will conclude that they should not be confined by the goal of finding a single tradition that meets all needs. Such an intentionally polyspiritual family may choose to study and practice separately, or they may choose to join each other in simultaneously honoring the beliefs and practices of multiple traditions. In either case, they will find it useful to discuss the challenges of living with beliefs and practices that may conflict.

Intervening: Instrumental, Beliefs/Themes

The next class of counseling responses is similar, in that they are also instrumental, but in this case they are focused on making *direct use* of client beliefs. Doherty's (1999) concept of "graduated levels of intensity" (see Table 8.3) is especially relevant. Doherty says that he developed this model in working with nonspiritual definitions of morality, but then came to believe that it had relevance for practitioners who would like to incorporate explicit spiritual discussions into their work. He recommends, for the counselor who is just beginning work in a spiritual dimension, attempting to stay in the "low-intensity zone of affirming and asking questions." In this way, the counselor avoids statements that might be interpreted as either promoting or opposing clients' ways of engaging with spirituality. Words are especially important, he says, and the professional

Table 8.3   Levels of Spiritual Discussion

Degrees of Intensity of Spiritual Consultation in Therapy (from lowest to highest)

1. Acknowledge the client's spontaneous statements of spiritual belief.
2. Inquire about the client's spiritual beliefs and practices.
3. Inquire about how the client connects the spiritual, clinical, and moral dimensions of his or her life or problems.
4. Express agreement with the client's spiritual beliefs or sensibilities when such self-disclosure could be therapeutic.
5. Articulate the client's dilemma without giving your own position.
6. Point out the contradictions between the client's spiritual beliefs, or between spiritual beliefs and clinical realities or moral issues.
7. Challenge the client's way of handling spiritual beliefs on the basis of your own spiritual beliefs, your moral beliefs, or your clinical beliefs.

Source: From "Morality and Spirituality in Therapy (pp. 189–191), by W. J. Doherty, in *Spiritual Resources in Family Therapy,* F. Walsh (Ed.), 1999, New York: Guilford Press. Reprinted with permission.

must take care not to use words that the client(s) have not used.

Doherty's first and second levels correspond to a Beliefs/Themes focus—they are ways of *learning about* the belief system.

Studying Together
Spiritual traditions differ widely in the complexity and subtlety of their core beliefs. When couple and family members are attempting to share a spiritual journey, it is not uncommon for them to find differences in their ways of understanding their spiritual heritage or their experiences of spiritual development. The same words may be understood differently or may have changed in meaning over time, and in many cases the writings and teachings in a single tradition may seem to be in conflict. In many cases these conflicts surface during times when spiritual resources are

needed to strengthen resilience during experiences of suffering and loss (Walsh, 1999a). It cannot be assumed that resolving one family spiritual crisis will prevent future crises, as different issues call upon different beliefs.

Von Denffer (1994) offers an eloquent illustration of such conflicts in an analysis of the Qur'ān, which shows that Islam, as many other faiths, incorporates texts and oral teachings—some considered divine, others clearly the products of human thought—from different historical periods. An individual follower, and especially a couple or family, may find times when spiritual guidance seems to be confusing. Under such circumstances, it may be appropriate for the family counselor to support the family as they engage in a shared process of inquiry.

Doherty's remaining levels involve specifically exploring the ways in which the client(s) make use of beliefs. Joellyn Ross (1994), for example, illustrates moving from learning about beliefs to discussing those beliefs and their implications in people's lives. Referring to a case involving a Jehovah's Witnesses couple, in which the wife had experienced panic symptoms throughout their marriage, she wrote:

> My strategy in working with Helen was to tell her and her husband that I knew very little about the Witnesses and that I needed them to educate me so that I might understand them better. As proselytizing is a major component of being a Witness ("Faith without works is dead," Helen told me.), they were eager to teach me anything I wanted to know about their religion. Helen later told me that she believed Witnesses are misunderstood, and that she was pleased I was interested in learning the facts. (p. 10)

As the process moved forward and Ross had gathered information about both of the partners and their beliefs, she said, "I was able to determine that helping Helen to be able to tune into herself and to comfort herself would not be in conflict with her religious beliefs or practices. I explained to her that in order to be able to be giving to others, as Witnesses are expected to be, one first needs to feel as strong as possible" (p. 11).

As Helen became stronger, she expressed sadness that she and her husband saw so little of each other. "Frank was busy helping other people, she said, and she questioned the legitimacy of her complaint. 'I shouldn't be so selfish.' I confirmed with her that Witnesses value couples having a good relationship, and therefore it was good for her to want to feel closer to him" (p. 12). At the time the article was written, Ross said that the case was continuing, with Helen no longer experiencing panic attacks but worried about "limited emotional resources and energy to give to others." Her sensitivity to client beliefs, and her sensitive use of those beliefs to help organize the changes they sought, exemplifies this class of responses.

Another example of working with beliefs (Chang & Ng, 2000) applied the teachings from the I Ching in solution-focused therapy (SFT) with Chinese families. Chang and Ng had found their Chinese clients to be suspicious of Western therapists and therapeutic practices, and they concluded that they needed to work within their culture and their belief systems. Change, according to Chang and Ng's summary of Confucian and Taoist teachings, is constant but is continually balanced in a harmonization of Yin and Yang. Human disruption of these forces is discouraged. The SFT expectation that clients build on small exceptions and create larger changes was a threat to these beliefs.

Chang and Ng provided, in this article, sufficient background in the I Ching for their readers to understand why and how they selected key passages from that sacred text to meet their clients' needs. They located passages that communicated about creativity, urgency, readiness, and unfinished change so that their clients would understand that the therapists' techniques and theories were consistent with Chinese spiritual beliefs. They demonstrated that SFT emphases on exceptions and coping skills were merely new ways of expressing ideas that were thousands of years old.

Coordinating Lives

When family members hold strong spiritual beliefs concerning actions that are central in people's daily lives, shared study may provide guidance but still leave room for interpretation and/or influence processes. Family responses to a crisis, for example, may be quite different. The death of a young child or the destruction of a city in an earthquake is likely to cause some people to doubt their faith. In times when decisions are needed, some family members may insist, "It's God's will, we should leave our fate in His hands," while others assert, "God acts through us—we are His instruments, and we are being called to use the resources He has provided." Rather than proposing to resolve such issues, the family professional can remain in the position of spiritual ethnographer by asking questions, facilitating discussion, and avoiding the temptation either to act as a spiritual expert or to introduce solutions that come from outside the family's traditions.

Intervening: Instrumental, Religious/Spiritual Practices

Rivett and Street (2001) identified a third class of instrumental connections with spirituality, in which the helper makes use of practices from the spiritual tradition. The case at the beginning of this chapter is an example of such work, with the counselor participating in the family's prayers at the beginning of sessions. The family initiated this use of the family's practices, so there was no question of the counselor having made inappropriate use of the tradition. This example also involved practices that took place in the counselor's office, avoiding questions of privacy violations.

An invitation for the counselor to participate in a funeral, a wedding, or an ecstatic dancing workshop, would clearly raise additional issues beyond those of spirituality. But the unique spiritual practices of a particular tradition may include ones that are adaptable to use in office-based or home-based counseling. Reading daily inspirational reflections together, for example, could be an appropriate way to support a client's use of those materials. And it is not uncommon for individuals following the Twelve Steps of the Alcoholics Anonymous recovery program to choose a counselor for the sharing called for in Step 5 (see Table 8.2).

Rituals and Celebrations

Rituals and celebrations are extremely important in the religious and spiritual lives of many couples, families, and communities. As discussed in Chapter 6, rituals communicate meaning at a symbolic level that can bypass the rational/categorical language system. Imber-Black and Roberts (1992) noted that rituals vary according to their frequency and their degree of significance, with significant rituals having tremendous effects in people's lives. The family rituals in a spiritual tradition can invest people with their identities; heal their physical and emotional suffering; and connect them with lost loved ones, with the source of all being, or with an eternal love partner. At times of pain, joy, anxiety, and triumph, spiritual rituals overcome isolation and offer sources of shared power. Parker and Horton (1996) classified rituals into three groups: liberation rituals, transformation rituals, and celebration or commemoration rituals. Finding examples of each category in religious systems, they—like Imber-Black and Roberts—encouraged both the maintenance of traditional rituals and the creation of new rituals as clients' special needs become clear.

Intervening: Metaphysical

The shift from an instrumental to a metaphysical connection of spirituality and counseling is more about the person of the counselor than it is about the procedures and activities of counseling. Many authors have written about the transformative possibilities when counselors step outside their science-based training and engage with their clients at a level of spiritual presence.

Anderson and Worthen (1997) write: "To share his or her spirituality continually, the therapist brings to bear upon the process . . . assumptions about the fourth dimension of experience, that a transcendent Being exists, that humankind yearns for connection with this Being, and that this Being may actively influence the lives of human beings to promote beneficial change" (p. 6). Application of this different level of being can be seen in how the therapist listens and how the therapist responds—verbally and nonverbally. Walsh (1999a) concurs on the goal of the professional being more attuned to spirituality in self and others, suggesting that "exploring our own spiritual roots and branches" is an important element in spiritually sensitive work.

Dorothy Becvar (1997) has written eloquently about the spiritual journey of helping professionals (Box 8.3).

Assessing Effectiveness

Assessing the impact of spiritually oriented couple and family counseling is a process that incorporates nearly all other assessment discussed in this book; it is integrated into the process of intervention, and it relies heavily on the clients' subjective reports of improvement. It is likely that the counselor will directly question each

member's satisfaction or comfort with his or her spirituality because of the core belief that spirituality itself is of value and has significance in people's lives. A spiritually oriented counselor may also assess clients' spiritual wellness in other ways, through direct experience of various interactions as well as through their stories. Progress toward greater family spiritual wellness may be slow and it may not be consistent; new discoveries and new spiritual efforts can have destabilizing effects on other aspects of functioning, and life experiences can seem to negate the positive effects of spiritual change.

BOX 8.3

Spiritual Healing

Spiritual healers, notes Dorothy Becvar (1997), were the members of traditional cultures who were primarily concerned with physical and emotional well-being until the modern professions of medicine and psychology claimed them as belonging to the realm of science. These shamanic healers, who still exist in some cultures (e.g., Keeney, 1994), typically communicate with a spirit world as they also utilize herbs and other active interventions. Becvar has defined her inclusive spirituality—a blend of her childhood experience of Lutheran Christianity, her adult studies of modern and shamanic spiritualities, and quantum physics, her studies and experience in family therapy, and her lifetime experiences of tragedy and sense-making, in terms of the following principles:

1. There is a continuous interplay between our thoughts, emotions, and our physical and emotional state of health and well-being.
2. Each of us has primary responsibility for our life and thus for our health.
3. Since the mind and the emotions play a large part in the creation of disease, they also can be employed in the healing process.
4. The body/mind has an intelligence of its own. Each cell has the wisdom and inclination to

carry out its particular function, which may be negatively or positively influenced consistent with the messages received.

5. The body/mind speaks to us and can be our teacher if we are willing to learn. Pain, discomfort, and disease provide information about conflict and disharmony.
6. It is important to consider the symptoms of illness at a variety of levels, including the mental, the physical, the emotional and the spiritual/soul levels.
7. The inner self, or the self at the spiritual/soul level, is always seeking to grow.
8. Harmony and the reduction or elimination of conflict are facilitated by desire, by a willingness actively to pursue these states, and by self-awareness.
9. What appears to be an illness may actually be the necessary byproduct of a deeper level of healing. As we heal holistically, we go through periods of detoxification that may be experienced as temporary discomfort.
10. Each of us knows his or her body/mind better than anyone else. By learning to listen within, we also become our own greatest healers (adapted from p. 20).

Source: From *Soul Healing: A Spiritual Orientation in Counseling and Therapy*, by D. S. Becvar, 1997, New York: Basic Books. Reprinted with permission.

Therefore, it is important that the professional who operates from a spiritually oriented framework also attend to other aspects of the clients' lives, whether or not those are explicitly raised as client concerns. A spiritual agenda in counseling can, and often will, combine with other agendas and should lead to significant improvements in family relational functioning and members' performance of many "real world" functions.

Closure

The process of ending couple or family intervention in a spiritually oriented process has much in common with the process discussed in Chapter 7. Participation in the later stages of the process may be different for some family members than for others. Significant relationship-oriented work can take place even if only one person remains in counseling, but other family members may join midway through counseling, and the process may continue for a year or more as people come and go. A clear sense of completion may be hard to achieve, because the immediate concerns that led to family counseling often become less of a focus and other, longer-term concerns assume greater importance. When asked, "How will we know when we're finished with what you came here to do?" clients may express doubt that they will ever feel ready to leave.

When the clients' goals shift in this direction, three main options exist for the counselor. The first option is to keep the counseling process going, but on an increasingly spread-out schedule that gradually moves from monthly to bimonthly and eventually stops. The advantage of this plan is that it doesn't force the family members to immediately decide whether they feel finished; they can try a month, then try 2 months, and if at any point they feel a need they can pick up the pace. Such a plan may not fit well with many institutional/legal systems, because the couple or family members might all—for the purposes of legal liability—be considered to be "in treatment" for years without much professional contact.

Second, you may schedule a series of follow-up sessions. They may be set up semiannually or even annually. It may be possible even in this situation to have a clear expectation that the follow-up visit will be set up as an assessment of possible relapse, and in the meantime a "discharge summary" is entered into the file. Such a follow-up structure can be useful as it brings family members together from time to time with the goal of reviewing progress toward long-term goals. Even if a child is away at school or in military service, it may be possible to plan for a meeting on a yearly basis.

Third, we can assume that eventually the prescheduled visits will end and the couple and/or family will choose to face life on their own without professional assistance. This may be the hardest time for the counselor, who has "joined" the family and who may have a hard time believing that they will function on their own. Fortunately, a spiritually oriented professional should be prepared to "turn it over" and accept that control is neither possible nor desirable.

Cautions, Concerns, and New Directions

Of the five orientations featured in this section of the book, the spiritual theme is the one that is most likely to face opposition from funding sources, other professionals, and even from clients themselves. The history of professional helping is, as I pointed out early in this chapter, closely tied to science and mainstream science has not been comfortable with spirituality. It is possible that colleagues in nonreligious settings will accuse the spiritually oriented family counselor of unprofessional activity—even of having impaired judgment. But the tide is turning; of the references cited in this chapter, many are less than 10 years old. Special issues of journals and edited books have been appearing on a regular basis. For the couple and family counselor who is exploring the spiritual theme, it's 1960 again! A small number of committed, creative people are eagerly sharing their work with each other while the larger community of professionals is only starting to notice.

There are other concerns besides professional support and client acceptance. One is that clients with strong spiritual orientations are likely also to have strong value systems that could clash with a professional's deeply held beliefs. Child discipline is one of the topics on which some spiritual traditions have established positions that are at odds with some science. The professional who tries to bridge the gap between "spare the rod and spoil the child" and "hitting teaches violence" will need to be expert helping others to live with contradictions. The "spiritually one up" family member may resist.

The spiritually oriented couple or family counselor can also expect that clients bring their own (internal, as well as interpersonal) value and belief conflicts to sessions. A midlife woman who has been a fulltime home manager and parent, for example, may have received strong support from a traditional religious background but may begin questioning the meaning of her life as her children move into adulthood. Here, too, the spiritually adept professional will call upon a tolerance for ambiguity—but will also find uses for the conflict management and decision-making skills discussed in Chapter 4 and the restorying approaches from Chapter 6. Progress in our own spiritual growth can help us to resist being caught up in the struggles of our clients.

Suggested Individual and Group Activities

Your understanding of concepts and issues presented in this chapter may be enhanced by the following activities:

- *Library and Internet research.* Browse and/or search for books, articles, and web sites related to religion and spirituality. Read about a tradition with which you are not familiar (try to find sources with an "insider" perspective rather than comparative or critical works).

- *Spiritual ecomap or genogram.* Create a map of your spiritual influences, not limited to family. How might you represent your relationship(s) with the infinite/divine/higher power?

Suggested Readings

Becvar, D. S. (1997). *Soul healing: A spiritual orientation in counseling and therapy.* New York: Basic Books.

Faiver, C., Ingersoll, R. E., O'Brien, E., & McNally, C. (2001). *Explorations in counseling and spirituality: Philosophical, practical, and personal reflections.* Belmont, CA: Brooks/Cole.

Nowinski, J. K. (1999). *Family recovery and substance abuse: A twelve-step guide for treatment.* Thousand Oaks, CA: Sage.

Patterson, J., Hayworth, M., Turner, C., & Raskin, M. (2000). Spiritual issues in family therapy: A graduate-level course. *Journal of Marital and Family Therapy, 26,* 199–210.

Walsh, F. (Ed.) (1999) *Spiritual resources in family therapy.* New York: Guilford Press.

JUDGMENT, ACTION, AND PERSONAL DEVELOPMENT IN FAMILY COUNSELING

One of the questions that I keep asking my colleagues is, "Why don't *more* counselors do family counseling?" This book has grown out of my efforts to answer that question, and the various parts in this book represent multiple answers. This section is based on one answer: "Counseling with families is challenging on a personal level—maybe much more challenging than seeing individuals."

I can see it in people's faces when I tell them what I do. Some even say it: "How can you stand to be with people who hate each other and listen to all those horrible stories?" Even though I consider those reactions to be exaggerated, my challengers are asking an important question: "How do we do it?" Family counseling does require more than simply knowing theories and techniques. The work involves constant personal change, including new skills, new attitudes, and self-discovery.

Every helping professional has to face many of the same demons (Kottler, 1993). Professors and students joke that studying human problems leads to seeing many of the problems in ourselves, but the joke is based on a simple truth: There are some common frailties that most humans share. Walt Kelly's popular *Pogo* comic strip in the 1950s captured this reality perfectly with the statement, "We have met the enemy and he is us." It is hard to listen to some of the stories people share with us, and it may be because those stories bring the counselor into contact with painful realities.

No matter how much a professional wants to believe in people's innate goodness and ability to change, the counselor often works with people who challenge that belief. An easy, comfortable helping relationship doesn't happen automatically. We don't always achieve the results we seek. People come into our lives in distress and some of them discontinue contact while they are still in distress—their suffering may even seem worse than before they came for help. We get emotionally involved with the people we attempt to help, and they go on with their lives and it feels like they take parts of us with them.

Am I saying that on top of all these challenges—which face everyone who gets involved in a helping relationship—the family counselor faces even more challenges? No. There are special experiences that accompany the process of entering someone else's relationship system, but the experiences of family counseling are as emotionally rewarding as they are draining. Carl Whitaker was fond of saying, "When you work with a couple you're not doing therapy, you're supervising therapy." He was referring to his belief that the people we work with are trying to cure each other, and that the process is not limited to the one hour they are together in a counselor's office. It is reassuring to me that many of my clients have found someone to love them and I have often helped that love to survive.

In Chapter 9, you get an in-depth example of the intellectual and emotional struggle of working with a couple and their children. This fictional family, the Morgan-Thompsons, is loosely based on families from my 25 years of practice; therefore, they may be the typical American family of our times. Their early relationship included a period of living together before marriage. Both were married before and each has a child from those marriages, so each adult must coordinate with their child's other parent. Stepfamily researchers (e.g., Whiteside, 1989) speak of significant and predictable differences among family types, based on the history and structure of the household, and this case incorporates some research-based assumptions. The family also struggles with addictive behavior, another typical issue faced in contemporary practice.

But you also see other issues besides the family's history and structure in Chapter 9. One is how each family presents the professional with a learning experience. Effective family counseling demands that the counselor gradually enter the clients' world. This learning is complex whether the family are owners or employees in a business, recipients of disability or welfare services, law enforcement professionals or drug producers and dealers, or patients and caregivers surviving after cancer. In the Morgan-Thompson case, we encounter new issues at several points; each time their world becomes clearer and our work has the potential for becoming more effective. In the end, we depart from the family with a sense of accomplishment, but without knowing exactly how the interventions affect their future life. The chapter ends with a discussion of how professionals can maintain our own stability when we are engaged in interactions with people who sometimes present unrealistic demands, faulty communication and logic, and immature responses.

In Chapter 10, we discuss the ethics and pragmatics of working with families. Family work involves many choices, and the basis for those choices is not always clear. Ignorance is not an excuse; when we take on the challenge of working with families, we must either dedicate ourselves to performing at a high level or else refer them to someone who lives up to that standard. We examine, in this chapter, some of the most challenging issues we face. And we may miss issues because our awareness is often blocked by our discourses. Effective family counseling also demands that we work within service delivery systems, and such systems are often designed to handle unrelated individuals rather than couples and families. The family counselor must plan ways to address the family's needs, and he or she must effectively communicate the rationale and plan to the people paying for the work. Often the bill goes to a third party who needs to be educated about why a family approach is appropriate. In this chapter, I provide guidelines and outline a process that improves your success in fitting family practice into an individually oriented environment.

Finally, Chapter 11 steps back from the present content of family counseling—the families, their lives, the service delivery systems—to examine the future of family counselors as individuals and as a profession. Family counselors, in our various cultures, are participating in an ongoing experiment in living. Contemporary families are facing circumstances that challenge their relationships, and their professional support systems are going to be challenged to help them meet the functional requirements we discussed in Chapter 5. At the same time, each professional who becomes part of any family system over time is altered by every couple and family; I discuss some of the ways in which family counselors have learned to recognize and manage the times when their multiple system membership creates problems. These unique couple and family counseling challenges are examined as part of a larger set of existential realities facing all counselors: being open to ourselves and others, experiencing the dilemmas of choice and responsibility that are the core of humanness.

Joining, Struggling Together, and Saying Goodbye

Working with couples and families can involve multiple issues and different approaches over time.

Objectives

In this chapter, you learn to:

1. Conceptualize a couple or family case according to multiple perspectives.
2. Develop an intervention plan based on intake information.
3. View a case in long-term perspective.
4. Revise a family intervention plan based on new information.
5. Assess a family's readiness to end counseling.

9

Chapter

In the previous chapters you have been introduced to a variety of concepts and practices that belong to the tradition of family therapy and counseling. The chapters in Section II presented an organizational scheme (BONES) designed to improve your comfort with multiple perspectives on working with a couple or family.

I have emphasized the multifaceted nature of couple and family relationships throughout this book. Relationships are complicated, and any helping process—conceptualizing issues, planning for intervention, and implementing an action plan—is always a partial response to the many issues that could be a focus for help. A helping process is also an interaction in which counselor and clients mutually influence what is done.

This chapter uses an in-depth case study, a fictional account based on work with many different families, to illustrate this interaction. As we follow this family's progress from the first session through successful termination, I emphasize choice points, alternatives, multiple strategies, client empowerment, and professional self-care.

The Morgan-Thompsons: A Family in Crisis

Before we begin to observe the session-by-session progress of this case, it may be helpful to introduce the two main characters.

Rick

Rick Thompson, a 43-year-old White divorced father, was referred for outpatient substance abuse counseling. He was coming out of a 3-day hospitalization after a 10-day cocaine binge. Unemployed, living with his widowed mother, he probably would not have followed through with the referral without the support and company of the new woman in his life, Alice Morgan. Rick was addicted and, like many who suffer from addictions, went through periods in which he had little confidence in himself and didn't feel that he deserved help from anyone.

Rick had begun getting high with alcohol and marijuana during his late adolescence. He had wanted to go to college, but eventually dropped out of school, married, had a daughter, and settled into working at a club where he handled sound equipment for bands. There he was exposed to other drugs, and in the mid-1980s he discovered the newly marketed super drug: crack cocaine. Every available dollar went into buying crack. It pushed his wife and his child out of the way, destroying his ability to manage his moods and meet his responsibilities. He sold drugs to support his use, but still created a trail of debts. He sought treatment for the first time when he felt he was at "the bottom," out of work and abandoned by his wife and daughter. Once clean he worked his way up to a management position in a fast food restaurant, away from the clubs and the dealers. Within a year or so, he gradually began to spend time with his old buddies in the nightclubs and his life spiraled down again. Like many other addicts, he felt that his first treatment program had "failed."[1]

What was different this time was his relationship with Alice, whom he had begun dating during the months prior to the relapse. Unlike his ex-wife, who had been naïve regarding drugs—and who quickly became discouraged over his cocaine use—Alice was a child of an alcoholic parent and she wasn't a quitter. Rick had been trying to keep his crack use hidden, and his effort to hide it had slowed his relapse, but he called Alice when the money ran out, he was fired from his job, and he was thinking of suicide. Alice was an ally for his better side. She believed in a version of Rick that he didn't believe in.

Alice

Alice, a 38-year-old White divorced mother, was Rick's primary support person. They had been ro-

---

[1] This view of relapse is outdated, but it still dominates both the professional and lay views of addiction. The landmark Institute of Medicine report (1990), a rigorous survey of alcohol treatment research, concluded that most alcoholics are treated successfully, but success comes with repeated treatment rather than a single episode. Therefore, the "failed" treatment episode is actually part of a successful—but incomplete—course of treatment.

mantically involved, but since his relapse she had pulled back to protect herself and her son. Alice was a *caregiver,* with all of the best and worst meanings that that word can convey. She was a nurse having worked her way up to a management position. She performed in an impressive way as single parent of an adolescent, working long hours to provide her son with all the material goods expected in their upper middle-class suburb. Her life had been through its ups and downs, but her perfectionist style had driven her to achieve a position of self-sufficiency and leadership.

Rick was the latest in a series of men who had entered Alice's life in apparent physical, emotional, and financial health and whose lives had then apparently deteriorated. She was starting to think that her influence was negative—maybe she couldn't have a relationship with a man without destroying him. Furthermore, Rick had borrowed money when his problem had surfaced; she had dipped into her savings to help him. Worse yet, she had just found out that he had used her credit cards. She was accompanying Rick for his first appointment with a counselor, but she was prepared to let him go to save him and herself as well.

Phase 1: Separation and Rapprochement

In their early relationship struggle, we can see the addicted couple's issues fitting the concepts of extreme dependency and insecure attachment, as suggested by Peele and Brodsky (1975). Having developed a pattern in which Rick's dependency on Alice rapidly came to threaten her survival, both of them seem afraid of separation. As they face and work through this fear, they will develop greater strength and competence.

Engaging and Assessing

When people walk into an office together, they often provide early indications of what is coming. Rick was smiling and chatting in the hallway, but as the door closed his face shifted into a knot of clenched muscles and a forced smile. Alice's expression changed in the opposite direction. She hardly made eye contact in the waiting room, but coming into my office she seemed to straighten up and relax. It was clear that counseling was her idea, not his.

I try to get as many perspectives as possible in a first session, so it doesn't matter who goes first. Leaving the decision up to the clients provides me with an opportunity to gather more impressions. I opened the conversation:

Том: *So, who would like to start letting me know why you're here?*

"Why you're here" is an open-ended question that leaves much room for different perspectives. It doesn't say what the problem is; it doesn't even say that there is a problem.

RICK: *I think you got a call from the hospital, they gave me your name.*

Rick appeared to be hoping that he could avoid talking about behavior and events that he saw as shameful.

Том: *Yes, I did. I prefer to not get too much information on the phone, though, so I'd like you to just start wherever you like and tell me what you think I need to know.*

I wanted him to struggle with telling the story. I preempted Alice's possible "editing" of the story by emphasizing that he should choose what to tell me.

RICK: *I've just . . . destroyed my whole life. Alice was the first decent person who ever cared about me, and I've been . . . lying to her and stealing money from her to buy drugs.*

Having concluded that he couldn't avoid telling the story, he started with an appeal for mercy. His disaster script had worked in the past to elicit sympathy—people jumped overboard to save him.

Том: *Mmmm*

I like to position myself as neutral during the information-gathering phase. I want to tell him "It'll be okay." But if I'm too sympathetic to him I'll not only lose Alice's trust, I'll leave him wondering whether or not I can handle pain and suffering.

ALICE: *He's addicted to cocaine, and I knew it, but I thought he was in recovery and I can't believe that I put myself and my son at risk by letting this con artist into my life!*

Alice appears to be somewhat familiar with the language of drug abuse and recovery. She rejected Rick's sympathy ploy by immediately making sure I know she was hurt, angry, and frightened.

Том: *I see. Rick . . . this wasn't exactly a new kind of experience for you, then.*

I empathized with the hopelessness that people feel when they see an old problem recurring in their lives.

RICK (tearing): *No . . . I've hurt everybody who ever got involved with me. But I thought it was different this time. Alice is such a positive person, you know? And she was so pleased with me being straight and turning my life around, I just couldn't stand bursting the bubble by telling her it wasn't real.*

Rick continued to elaborate on the narrative theme "Bad Rick took advantage of poor, sweet Alice." At the same time, he tried blaming her for his behavior pattern—he lied to her because she preferred the lies to the truth.

The session continued with Rick and Alice both contributing to the story. I had begun the session with the assumption that the purpose of our meeting was to help Rick, and therefore most of the conversation focused on his newly reestablished recovery. He needed to take responsibility for his own actions, and Alice was encouraged to stay in the background.

Alice had her own issues that soon became central in the story: a need to become more comfortable with independence. As a person whose relationship history seemed to fit the concept of *codependency*,[2] she was in a position that paralleled Rick's—both of them were in recovery, trying to stop doing things that got them into trouble. He needed to get away from his drug use and his exploitation of others. She needed to get away from people whose out-of-control lives created emotional and financial chaos for her. She suggested that they stop spending time together for the immediate future.

Making Sense of the Clients' Needs

In this glimpse into my first hour with this couple, we can already see some of the issues that became a focus of the counseling I provided over the next 2 years. A quick scan of the five BONES themes and some subthemes of each (Table 9.1) shows many perspectives that might be helpful in working with Rick and Alice's ambivalent relationship and their interlocking problem histories. Within each of the five themes, I had at least one way of making sense of this case and there were many rather clear directions that could be taken.

But this listing of so many alternatives does not mean that one should think of a case in so many ways at once; too much complexity can paralyze a professional, and the most important function of a theory is to help you decide where to direct your attention. In this case, several of the themes fit into my integrative theory of Identity Renegotiation Counseling (IRC; Box 9.1). The IRC theory would guide my initial choices and shape the ways in which further information was integrated into my approach.

---

[2] This term has been overused, as mentioned in Chapter 7, but as a narrative device it helps some people make sense of their relationship histories. Codependency is interactive; it involves a covert contract between an underfunctioner and an overfunctioner (Bowen, 1978). In this pattern, the overfunctioning person loses his or her balance, pulled down by the other's persistent self-destructive behavior.

Tentative Treatment Plan

At the beginning of the process, I chose to focus on Behavioral issues—specifically, on a cluster of needs for internal knowledge and external knowledge (IRC Cluster 1). I assumed that Rick and Alice were confused, surrounded by conflicting ideas about appropriate behavior and decision-making processes. With friends, family, and various experts trying to influence their behavior (IRC Cluster 2), they were having a hard time coordinating their efforts. I would focus on helping them reduce the confusion that resulted from their multiple and conflicting information and opinion sources.

It was clear that Rick and Alice's relationship had rather quickly turned destructive for them both, despite the tentative nature of their commitment. If they had talked about continuing the relationship, I would have raised questions about the advisability of that plan. But they were not announcing any such intent; they were both upset and they didn't trust themselves with each other. Alice had suggested that they stop seeing each other for a while, and this course of action seemed to be safe. Working on relationship issues directly would be difficult unless the two of them could first restabilize their lives.

At the conclusion of this initial visit, Rick was my client; he would work on getting his life back on track, staying sober with outpatient counseling from me together with involvement in Narcotics Anonymous (NA). Alice offered to pay for his counseling and give him money to keep up his health insurance until he was employed again, but she was not making a commitment beyond the financial one. To address her vulnerability to relationships such as this one with Rick, she would involve herself in Nar-Anon (Box 9.2). Alice said she would consider resuming the relationship once Rick could show her 6 months of "clean time."

Intervention

The plan started off well. Rick came in for two sessions by himself. He said that he was applying for jobs and we worked on a *relapse prevention* program that required him to review his

Table 9.1   **Theme Analysis at Time of Intake**

Theme	Ideas and Issues
Behavior	*Skills:* Decision-making and basic communication skills are limited.
	External knowledge: The partners need information on recovery processes and relationships.
	Internal knowledge: The new couple are learning about self and other.
	Cued responses: Environmental cues predictably lead to negative patterns.
	Contingent responding: Reinforcements help to sustain negative patterns.
Organization	*Function:* Rick's alcoholism and Alice's rescuing are the basis of their relationship.
	Conflict: It is easy to resolve conflicts at this point because Rick accepts the losing position in any negotiations.
	Development: As parents of adolescents, Rick and Alice are both seeking "post-parental" intimacy.
	Intergenerational patterns: It will eventually be discovered that Rick and Alice are both children of alcoholic parents.
	Direct communication: Rick and Alice seem uncomfortable with dependency, and Rick's relapse provides a safe avenue for these feelings.
	Indirect communication: Both partners express the same message: I want to be closer but if you get too close I'll hurt you.
	Structure: Their shared crisis helps to create a bond between Rick and Alice.
	Systemic patterns: The complementary pattern (Bateson) describes a system that could get continually worse over time.
	Evolution of system: Because a traumatic disruption has already transformed the system, counseling should promote stability and healing.
Narrative	*Identity:* Both Alice and Rick are living with negative identity stories.
	Cognitive complexity: Focusing on addictions is important, but this relationship also involved other issues that interfere with recovery.
	Dominant discourse: Both the addict discourse and the codependent discourse emphasize a sense of hopelessness and powerlessness.
Emotion	*Connection:* Closeness may have become uncomfortable for one or both partners.
	Internal experiencing: Shame issues on both sides make intense feelings a threat.
	Emotional expression: Neither partner was identifying and expressing emotions in a clear, open, nonmanipulative manner.
	Empathy: Alice's stable relationship with her son helps her to maintain balance.
	Emotion management: In an attempt to escape from strong emotions, Rick used cocaine as an emotional buffer.
Spirituality	*Ethnosensitivity:* Both Rick and Alice were estranged from their religious backgrounds.
	Beliefs and themes: AA and Al-Anon seemed to offer reasonable replacements.
	Instrumental practices: Neither was practicing any spiritual or religious discipline or studying spiritual teachings.
	Metaphysics: Both Alice and Rick had become isolated from larger forces beyond themselves.

previous successes and the events surrounding his failures (Box 9.3). The relapse prevention aspect of our work seemed to go well; Rick was receptive to information about addictive processes and recovery, and he was a good student. Observant of his own behavior and able to recall his relapse history, he was able to talk in an abstract way about the situations and the behaviors that would make him vulnerable to relapse.

Identity Renegotiation Counseling

Identity Renegotiation Counseling is a way of thinking about counseling focused on aspects of postmodern life that may create problems in people's personal, relational, educational, and career experiences. Emphasizing the isolation and rapid social change that characterize life in the early twenty-first century, this approach is intended to help people manage multiple demands and influences that compete for their attention and loyalty. Rather than focusing on the losses of the past, Identity Renegotiation Counseling provides an optimistic focus on opportunities in the present and near future.

At the core of Identity Renegotiation Counseling is an idea of *relational identity.* This view sees identity as the product of interaction; others tell us who we are, and we work toward the goal of being comfortable with the feedback we receive. This comfort is achieved through negotiation: If a child doesn't want to be described as a slob, she can clean her room or she can try to convince her parent that she's being compared to unrealistic standards. With changing relationships, needs, and personal characteristics, life consists of a constant process of identity renegotiation.

This idea stands in contrast with the popular Western view of the individual as the "captain of my soul" whose success depends on struggling against outside influence. The concept of *control* is a good way of describing the difference. Spiritual traditions and social science have challenged the illusion that people are in control of their lives. Nevertheless, thought control, behavior control, and mood control remain at the center of many counseling approaches.

The Process

There are many ways to help clients with identity renegotiation. I have identified four clusters of understandings, goals, and counseling techniques that fit with the goal of helping people to participate in the identity renegotiations that are a daily part of their lives.

I view these four clusters of conversations and activities as being organized in a circular process. As a counselor, I may step into a client's life at any point in the process and our work together will be characterized by returning many times to focus on each point on the circle. There is a general sense of movement around the circle in the clockwise direction, but all points on the circle remain available at all times.

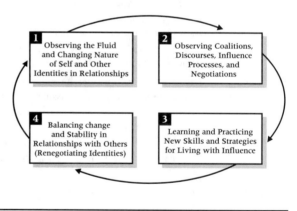

1 Observing the Fluid and Changing Nature of Self and Other Identities in Relationships

2 Observing Coalitions, Discourses, Influence Processes, and Negotiations

3 Learning and Practicing New Skills and Strategies for Living with Influence

4 Balancing change and Stability in Relationships with Others (Renegotiating Identities)

However, he continued to have limited self-knowledge regarding his emotions, and he was resisting the NA involvement that would have helped him develop that awareness. He said he was a person who was easily influenced by others, and he preferred to stay away from anyone who tried to change him (this avoidance of influence was similar to what might be expected with adolescents). He considered me safe, but didn't trust NA. He visited two different meetings and came back each time reporting a negative experience. As defined in the IRC model, we

Twelve Steps of Nar-Anon

1. We admitted we were powerless over the Addict—that our lives have become unmanageable.
2. Came to believe that a Power greater than ourselves could restore us to sanity.
3. Made a decision to turn our will and our lives over to the care of God as we understood Him.
4. Made a searching and fearless moral inventory of ourselves.
5. Admitted to God, to ourselves, and to another human being the exact nature of our wrongs.
6. Were entirely ready to have God remove all these defects of character.
7. Humbly asked Him to remove our shortcomings.
8. Made a list of all persons we had harmed and became willing to make amends to them all.
9. Made direct amends to such people whenever possible except when to do so would injure them or others.
10. Continued to take personal inventory and when we were wrong promptly admitted it.
11. Sought through prayer and meditation to improve our conscious contact with God as we understood Him, praying only for knowledge of His will for us and the power to carry that out.
12. Having had a spiritual awakening as a result of these steps, we tried to carry this message to others and to practice these principles in all our affairs.

Source: From http://nar-anon.org/aboutnaranon.htm. Represented with permission.

were facing a need to work on the Narrative process of accepting influence from others and expressing one's own intentions (Cluster 3). Alice appeared to be following through on her intentions of keeping her distance.

Crisis #1

Rick and Alice arrived together for the third session, and the tension was obvious in both of their faces when I met them in the waiting room. Alice had received bills for her credit cards and had found recent charges that she recognized as Rick's. That had led her to examine her online banking records, and she found cash withdrawals as well. She was frantic as she described her feeling that she was "chained to a sinking ship." Rick was contrite and admitted that he'd had some "slips." He had run into some old friends, and one thing had led to another because the old friends were also his old drug connections. He had made

some cocaine purchases—just a few, not like the old days, but he did recognize that it was illegal and self-destructive and a violation of the agreement he'd made with Alice. He was prepared for the consequences.

We discussed those consequences. Alice would cancel and reopen all her accounts to prevent any further unauthorized use, and Rick would have a harder time getting back together with her. She would talk with a lawyer about legal options she could hold in reserve, things that might help him think twice before taking advantage of her again. He would have to rebuild his life without her.

It seemed that this experience frightened Rick into working on a recovery program more seriously. He decided that he wouldn't wait for a comfortable, secure job because he needed money and he needed to have his time occupied. The timing was right for seasonal employment in the construction business. He hadn't been a very

Relapse Prevention

Alan Marlatt (1985) and his colleagues have developed a multifaceted approach to relapse that seeks to reduce the client's vulnerabilities and increase his or her strengths. One of the greatest vulnerabilities, they believe, comes from loss of confidence when a relapse seems to have occurred. As a way of challenging this "abstinence violation effect," they distinguish between a relapse—a full-blown return to addictive use—and a "lapse," which is less threatening. Lapses are good, because people learn from them.

Marlatt and colleagues explain relapse processes from a cognitive-behavioral perspective that emphasizes their sequential nature. Professionals using their approach encourage addicts to recall prior experiences when they did not intend to use but used anyway (lapses). From these partial memories, adding new information each time there is another lapse, the addict learns the steps that make using more likely (events that provide the environmental cues for the behavior). This knowledge allows the addict and his or her support system to: (a) find ways to avoid situations that have served as cues, and (b) take effective action to disrupt the behavior chain when one of the steps has occurred.

---

fit person, so the physical demands were a challenge, but he was determined. He was hired and quickly proved to be one of the more reliable and sensible people on the crew, and he was given responsibilities and overtime opportunities. He avoided his old friends, worked 12-hour days as much as possible, and committed himself to physical fitness and emotional well-being. He was still suspicious of NA, attending meetings occasionally but expressing negative attitudes about being dependent on a group. He did begin reading the "Big Book" (Narcotics Anonymous, 1991), and his behavior during this period was consistent with the principle of "one day at a time." Rather than focus on long-range goals, Rick was able to focus on living in ways that worked for the moment. Within a few months, Rick was looking and sounding like a different person. Alice began to meet Rick for lunch occasionally and the couple found that their mutual attraction had not waned. Alice was impressed with the changes Rick had accomplished, and her guard was starting to drop. She asked to see me.

After Alice discussed her new attitudes and feelings in an individual session, I convened a couple session to discuss the risks as well as the potential benefits if they became more closely involved in each other's lives. Not only would both of them face the danger of relapse, with all its physical and financial consequences, the two of them needed to assess their life goals and how their children would fit into their plans. In that couple session, I began to focus on basic relationship skills. They both had problems expressing themselves and hearing each other, especially when identity issues were involved. Rick showed a tendency to change the subject when he felt criticized, and Alice quickly became frustrated and withdrew at those times. They agreed to a goal of improving their ability to remain connected during periods of stress.

Looking Back

The decision to work with this quasi-family case was risky. Many professionals would have insisted on separating the recovery issues and the relationship issues, probably ending up with three cases and three professionals—one focused on addiction, a second focused on codependency, and a third focused on early relationship issues. Each of the three professionals would have been working with partial information. My acceptance of this boundary-stretching case was based on the belief that I had the three kinds of expertise that were needed—and I could combine the information to the benefit of both parties whether or not they stayed in each other's lives.

The risk seemed to have been justified. Both parties were somewhat motivated (remember Prochaska's levels from Chapter 1), and the individual recovery work fit together in the ways I had anticipated. The IRC model predicted that increased knowledge of self and other would make their experiences less confusing, and that seemed to be the case.

Phase 2: Building a Stepfamily

The next phase of our work took me by surprise. Rick was still living with his mother and the arrangement had created stresses on both sides. I found out, in a routine session with Rick, that he had just accepted Alice's invitation to move in with her and her son. Issues we had discussed in the abstract became immediately real. The arrangement exacerbated and institutionalized the shame cycle (Chapter 7) often seen in recovery stories. The addict becomes partnered with someone whose tendency to maintain control—in this case, through careful management of resources—compensates for the addict's tendency to abandon control. Each hopes that somehow the other's best qualities will "rub off." A flawed relationship contract at this early stage predicted later disaster, and I saw a need for planning.

As a careful planner and a stable professional, Alice had the resources to be able to make this offer, but there was an inherent flaw in the relationship contract. Its timing was a response to Rick's shaky circumstances, and he was in no position to make guarantees. In addition, residing in the house with Alice was her son, Bill. Rick was not only on probation with Alice, he was also facing all of the issues of being a new stepparent. And Rick's 17-year-old daughter Teresa, currently living out of state, was expecting to spend the summer with her father.

The updated cast of characters, as we began to discuss larger family interactions, included:

Bill

Bill, 15, had been the undisputed king of Alice's household. He not only had the privileged status of the only child, he benefited from his divorced parents competing for his attention. His father, who lived nearby, paid for a roomful of computer equipment and other toys (Bill occupied the entire upper floor of the small house), and Bill had a standing invitation to come live with his dad if he ever felt that things weren't going his way. He was a star high school athlete, attractive, socially active, earning his own spending money, and not answering to anyone. He had mixed feelings about Rick. He thought Rick was taking advantage of his mother, and therefore he wanted him to be sent away. On the other hand, like many boys in their mothers' custody, he had felt overly responsible for his mother. He was happy to think that Rick would take his place when he went away to school in a couple more years.

Teresa

Rick's daughter Teresa, 16, who lived with her mother in another state, had much in common with her father. She was bright, but she had been in constant trouble at home and at school, and much of her trouble was related to alcohol and other drugs. It had been some time since she had been around her dad because of a combination of factors—conflict between the parents, Rick's chaotic lifestyle, and money problems all contributed to a history of inconsistent contact. It seemed likely that the upcoming visit would be cancelled, like many visits before.

Making Sense of the Clients' Needs

The needs identified at the beginning of the case still required attention. Addiction professionals know that it generally takes years rather than months for recovery to become truly stabilized—for the addict to become able to survive emotional demands, and for lifestyle changes to settle down. Recovery groups warn their members that they should try to let the changes in their lives occur gradually rather than force them. Not only

Rick and Alice were at risk in this new situation. Bill, on the surface a well-adjusted adolescent, appeared to be likely to weather any changes. Teresa, though, had never done well in any situation and it seemed likely that this one as well would challenge her coping abilities.

When relationship changes cannot be avoided or delayed, despite the advice of friends and professionals, people in recovery need specific relationship skills and understandings. In this case, the family needed to resolve destructive triangles that involved issues of resource management and trust.

Triangles

Stepfamilies are inherently triangulated, as we discussed in Chapters 5 and 7. Relationship triangles shift constantly, and one member (or a subsystem that gets treated as a unit) is always on the weaker side. This new household had elements that made these triangles very powerful. Rick's status was shaky—he had a history of problems, he was being brought into the household without Bill's support, and he seemed to be contributing minimally to the household. And because Alice had been a doting mother, who had defended Bill in many disputes with his father, Bill expected his mother to respond quickly if he complained. Alice, however, like many parents of adolescents (see Chapter 5), was starting to see a future beyond the immediate present. She recognized that she had only a few years left until she might be left alone in her house. Having found someone with whom she wanted to build a future, she had made her choice and she was prepared to handle some complaints.

Triangles are not all equal in their effects, but a triangle in which an adolescent can overpower an adult is especially problematic. Rick and Alice recognized that Bill was going to have to give up some of his control and accept his new status as a child. Neither Bill nor Teresa would receive adequate parenting if the two parents in this new household were disabled by politics.

Competition for Time and Other Resources

The merging of any two households creates resource management issues. Time, space, and money are always in short supply, but a merged household typically involves rapid, poorly planned redistributions that feel unfair. In her single-parent household, Alice had often made decisions that sacrificed her own comfort and lifestyle for her son's comfort and well-being. She was about to revise that pattern. Fortunately, this plan had a chance of working; she also had learned how to say no to some of Bill's requests because their economic well-being depended on her working long hours.

Bill might have viewed the changes as positive ones. Time and money had been stretched rather thin during the brief period in which Alice and Rick had been dating. Comparing that period with the new arrangement, Bill could have found that he was going to see more of his mother now that Rick was living in their house. And he could have seen that his mom was spending less money going out, thereby leaving more money for Bill's athletic shoes and summer camps. But this was not the comparison he was making; instead, he was comparing "Life With Rick," in global terms, with "Life Before Rick." Rick's moving into the house was proof that his mom was prepared to sacrifice Bill's happiness for her own. If someone got gifts, it would now be Rick. If someone's vacation preferences were honored, it would now be Rick's. Bill was prepared for the worst . . . and he hadn't even begun thinking about what might happen if Teresa came to live with her dad.

Rick was thrilled with his improved living circumstances. Alice's house was comfortable, and he and Alice now had much more couple time than ever before. He, like Alice, could see ahead to the time when Bill would be leaving home. But he also had his own fantasy future, one in which he would be able to get Teresa to come live with him. This house would be large enough, and he would get his old earning power back so that Alice wasn't carrying so much of the financial load.

Trust

Resource distributions aside, the main relationship triangle was tilted in Bill's favor because of trust issues. Alice had already suffered from Rick's financial mismanagement and his brief relapse, and his history included a variety of illegal and unwise activities. If Bill was patient and observant, it seemed only a matter of time before Rick would do something to get ejected from their life, and the sooner it happened, the better. Rick's old car sitting in the driveway was an embarrassment.

Bill was quick to raise questions. If Rick arrived 15 minutes after he was expected home from work, Bill would wonder aloud if he'd gone to visit his dealer. And Bill repeatedly raised questions about the family finances. Didn't it seem that there was money mysteriously disappearing? Had someone taken money out of his dresser drawer? And hadn't a friend seen Rick on the other side of town when he was supposedly at work? If Alice had been sure of Rick's recovery and he had totally earned her trust, these questions would have been offensive and she would have responded with anger. But she had her doubts, and she had a difficult time rejecting these allegations.

Rick felt a sense of panic when he realized how easily his record could be challenged. When he and Bill had seen little of each other, Bill knew only what his mother told him. But under Bill's constant gaze, Rick's lifestyle lent itself to speculation. After all, he worked irregular hours and his pay fluctuated dramatically. He would arrive after a hard day of physical labor in a state that might appear drug-induced, and his dashing immediately into the bathroom made it seem that he had something to hide. He really wanted to put all of his negative past behind him and live like others. Instead, he was on probation and he was reporting to an adolescent.

Intervention

The new household needed a solid parental coalition. Even if their love relationship was not yet solid, Alice and Rick's parenting partnership had to become strong. Therefore, couple sessions became more frequent and we attempted to focus on plans, rules, and decisions—and to continue working on IRC Cluster 3 issues of influence, intentionality, and acceptance. Alice reported feeling silenced at home regarding Rick's recovery—she could no longer express her own doubts, because they fed into Bill's strategy of "divide and con-

quer." Now, couple sessions also performed an important function of monitoring the recovery process. Keeping these multiple agendas going was stressful, and sessions often felt incomplete.

I talked with Alice and Rick about bringing Bill into our sessions, and we concluded that the best strategy—unless he asked to come in—was to tell him that we were working on adult issues but he should talk with them about his concerns. I assured them that he was always welcome, if they felt it was time to bring him into a session. Referring back to the BONES model, the Behavioral and Narrative themes had broadened into Organizational work.

Crisis #2

The following winter was a challenging period for Rick and Alice. Rick's seasonal work had fallen off, so he looked for employment in a more stable arena but had no success. He began to explore self-employment possibilities, and he became involved in buying and selling sports memorabilia on the Internet.

It seemed like a self-fulfilling prophecy. After a month or two of negotiating the details of family life, as everyone was watching for signs of relapse, those signs started to appear. Rather than returning to cocaine, Rick had started to "reward himself" with Internet pornography when he was alone at home. Alice had found credit card charges, had searched the computer, and had found evidence that it had been going on for weeks. When Rick was confronted with the facts, in a couple's session in my office, he was angry rather than repentant. He admitted that he had been lying to me as well as to Alice, but he said that he was "tired of living a boring life." He accepted that he was an addict who couldn't use cocaine any more, but he wanted the freedom to live "like other people."

This announcement challenged the relationship. It was not that Alice felt she had to agree; I was on her side, saying that Rick's newfound source of enjoyment was not acceptable. As the mother of a teenage son, she had the right to keep pornography out of her house. Rick was advised against ever visiting another porn site on the Internet. But the relationship contract, building toward a future in which the two partners had a shared vision of life, was now in question.

Rick continued with criticism of Alice; he had resentments and complaints about his treatment since he had moved into the house. Not only did he challenge the idea of being labeled an addict and committing himself to a drug-free future, he also challenged the idea that Alice's motivations were honorable. She was, he now said, obsessed with other people's behavior. Alice was the one with a problem, and her obsession was going to create problems between her and her son. He even said that not all of the pornography on the computer was his, and he was sure Bill had been indulging his own curiosity. Unless Alice could do something about her problems, Rick didn't know whether she could have a relationship with him or anyone else.

Struggles over Control

Even though his way of bringing up his concern was unacceptable, Rick had brought the focus back to an important pattern that now came to dominate couple sessions. Alice really did have issues with control. In a perfect illustration of a principle expressed by Bateson (1972) and other observers of addictive problems, Alice's life seemed to have an organizing theme—people should control all aspects of their lives. This theme, according to Fossum and Mason (1986), is an intergenerational pattern based on inherited or learned shame. The inherited tendency was, in Alice's case, exacerbated by a lifetime of disasters. She disclosed something that Rick had heard vaguely mentioned but hadn't quite understood: While she had avoided ever using drugs, and had generally distanced herself from those who used them, she had gone through a period when gambling had nearly destroyed her life. This loss of control had resulted in a rebound into the careful, well-defended, comfortable, and stable lifestyle that she had when Rick met her.

Family counseling now focused on several different but interrelated dynamics. Rick was, reluctantly, accepting the challenges of learning how to live a clean and stable life; he recognized that there were coping skills he'd never acquired, and he could see that many self-medicating behaviors, including sex, could serve as a substitute for internal resources. He decided to make a serious attempt to engage with a support group; even though he continued to resist NA, he began attending meetings of an alternative recovery group.

He now understood that Alice's reactions to his negative behavior were part of something bigger, a personal struggle of her own. This belief encouraged him to think that someday she would be able to relax and credit him with having put his life together. Alice, for her part, was now facing a new view of herself. She was suspecting that her judgmental attitude toward herself and others—a major part of her professional success—was covering up basic insecurities that had led her into destructive relationships with men and an overcontrolling style of parenting. If Rick's allegations were true, she needed to change to keep Rick in her life, but she also needed to change because of her son.

The couple relationship was now struggling openly with a theme of control—control of self, control of one another (Cluster 4 in the IRC model). Several painful and intimacy-promoting conversations followed, in their home and in my office. Having become dependent on one another in many ways, both partners were finding that personal change was necessary to maintain the relationship. Alice continued to relapse into searching the computer for evidence of pornography and monitoring the bank and credit card statements for unexplained charges, but she recognized that Rick felt better about his recovery when he felt personally responsible. Rick flirted with pornography a couple more times, but concluded that the benefit was far outweighed by the resulting guilt, shame, and anxiety.

Looking back

The sudden emergence of emotional issues at this stage in the process is something that may have been inevitable. At the same time, the way that they emerged threatened everything we had been working on. Even though the couple and family issues were being addressed in relatively unemotional terms, both new emotional challenges and old emotional patterns were swirling around the rational conversations in my office. It seems in retrospect that it would have been better to have given more attention to issues of shame and mood management during the earlier phase. Such an effort might have run into roadblocks, of course, and other progress might have been slower.

Phase 3: Enlarging the Family

In the spring, with his fledgling Internet auction business expanding its scope but still producing little income, Rick returned to the construction business but this time with a different employer and a more stable position. He was able to replace his broken-down car with something more reliable, come home at a more predictable time, and otherwise live a more respectable lifestyle than he had during the previous summer. The couple relationship was becoming more balanced. Although Alice still brought home ¾ of the monthly income, there was hope that Rick would become successful in self-employment. And the household was relatively stable; Bill was finishing his junior year with good grades and a short list of universities that interested him. Rick was unhappy about his continuing lack of access to his daughter, but he was able to communicate with her on the Internet and he was confident that during the summer he could pay for her to come for a visit.

Marriage and Economic Partnership

Just as the decision to move in together had been sudden, Alice and Rick's decision to get married was also swift, and they made the decision without discussing it in counseling. They would get married during the summer at home, in the backyard, in a small ceremony. The two children would be there, along with some family members and friends from both sides. They explained that it would accomplish many things on their joint agenda—send a positive message to the

children, reassure the other relatives, and symbolize the commitment that was becoming more real every day.

One of the things that had made the decision seem wise was Alice's increasing involvement in Rick's Internet business. They had opportunities to begin traveling to national trade shows, and they felt that it would be better to be a married couple if they wanted to take either of the children on these business trips. Counseling for the next few sessions was focused on positives—clarifying expectations as a married couple, creating visions for a life together, and making plans.

The wedding went smoothly, although the contact between the two families stirred up some defensiveness on both sides. Teresa was able to attend, although the arrangements were delayed until the last minute because her mother—Rick's ex-wife Pat—had resisted the idea. By the end of summer, Rick was once again looking for a salaried position that was not seasonal.

Making Sense of the Clients' Needs

Even though a couple may appear to have made a commitment when they have been living together, sharing assets and expenses, and co-parenting, many couples nevertheless report that getting married changes their relationship with each other and with friends and family. It seemed as if many people—possibly including Alice and Rick—had been expecting their relationship to fail and had not planned for its continuance. Their decision to marry was an announcement that failure was no longer expected. This decision meant that everyone in the family could start making plans for a future in which Alice and Rick would be a couple, and this new commitment would precipitate a review of virtually every aspect of their life together.

One of the most important changes would be occurring in the arena of identity. Alice had not introduced Rick to many of her work colleagues when he had no legal status, but as her husband he would be expected to conform to the social norms of an extremely controlling group. He was both intrigued and repelled by the idea that he could fit into a group of nurses and hospital administrators.

And Alice, in a culture where married women's status is often linked to that of their husbands, was facing the possibility that her career would suffer unless Rick was stable and successful.

Intervention

The plan for this phase was focused on understanding and resolving differences between Rick and Alice and on managing change, including identity change. With their lives more tightly linked, emotional tensions were increasing. As this emotional volatility threatened the recovery of both Rick and Alice, Alice was tempted to return to an overcontrolling stance, and Rick was tempted to act like a rebellious child. Discussing those tendencies and recognizing the dangers involved, they worked well together and enjoyed their new couplehood.

Crisis #3

The new school year had not yet begun when Rick received a call from Teresa. She was refusing to go back to school, using the reason that she was too far behind to graduate with her class anyway, and Pat said that Teresa would have to find another place to live if she wasn't in school. This time, Rick and Alice brought a pending decision to a counseling session; Rick wanted to offer Teresa a place to live, but it wasn't a decision he could make without Alice's commitment. Alice saw the situation as more complicated than it seemed to Rick. Teresa had been in legal trouble, and Alice feared a negative influence on Bill.

In the end, they agreed to give Teresa a chance. They would develop clear rules and work together to communicate the rules to Teresa and enforce them. In preparation, I would work with Rick to ensure that he was realistic about his expectations.

When Teresa arrived she was brought to a counseling session within a few days to make sure that she understood the rules and didn't have questions. As it turned out, she did have questions and those questions continued for a few weeks. She didn't like the household rules regarding drinking, smoking, curfew, and studying; un-

fortunately, she wasn't in a good bargaining position, having accepted the rules in writing before Rick mailed her an airline ticket, but now she was hoping that people would take pity on her. Rick found it hard to be the tough parent, but he came for individual counseling sessions to get help in being tough. He stood his ground, and soon Teresa went to school without complaints. At the same time, Rick found a new job, a retail position that required him to work evening hours a few days a week, so Alice stepped into being Teresa's parent despite her reservations.

More Triangles

Teresa's presence in the house added possibilities for new triangles and she seemed to be quite skilled at stirring up constant turmoil. She upset Alice with her rebellious behavior, and she came to Rick with complaints about Alice's meanness. She badgered Bill to join her in challenging parental rules.

Teresa was attending the same school as Bill and he was influenced by her growing reputation—which she manipulated with her wardrobe of drug-themed t-shirts and with her immediate affiliation with the school's most notorious druggies. Bill came to his mother with his complaints: He was pretty sure that Teresa was drinking and using illegal drugs. Teresa, in turn, claimed that Bill had been offering her drugs, and she insisted that she was being framed.

As this conflict raged, only 3 months into Teresa's presence in the home, Teresa disappeared. Over the next few days, a series of telephone calls established that her new best friend had also disappeared; they had told some friends about their plan to run away together.

Looking Back

The agenda at this point in the process could not have been more appropriate, considering the demands that were going to be put on the relationship. Rick and Alice were able to resist the pushes and pulls that Teresa's arrival brought into the home because they had been working through their differences. They performed well as a team, balancing each other's limitations and presenting a united front to the world. Even though Teresa had tried to blame her misery on everyone around her, and her disappearance could have been cause for mutual finger-pointing, Alice and Rick stood together and felt good about their handling of the crisis.

Phase 4: Pulling Together

The household rebounded fairly quickly. Teresa's tactics had created unintended effects; Rick, Alice, and Bill were now united as victims of Teresa's unreasonable behavior. It was Bill's senior year, and conversations about college were becoming more serious. He was likely to go away to school, which would leave Alice and Rick alone together (especially challenging for couples who were never childless together).

Making Sense of the Clients' Needs

Bill now became the family focus. Even though his grades and his sports performances continued to be exceptional, he was starting to cause concern because of his increasing hours spent at work and his relationship with an older girl he met at work. The increased work hours were needed because he was saving up for a car. His mother had promised him a car for high school graduation, but she had started to express doubts after spending so much money on Rick's debts and the wedding. Bill not only announced that he would now have to buy the car himself but also that he now saw no reason to pay attention to his mother's wishes concerning any aspect of his life. He intended to leave home at 18 and never return. His father, he said, would be happy to have him live there if his mother didn't want him around.

Alice was guilt-ridden but also baffled by this focus on immediate gratification at a time when she thought Bill should have been focused on preparing for college. As Alice felt increasingly powerless to influence Bill's behavior, Rick stepped into more of a parenting role. Alice's parent-child relationship with Bill was something that she had always taken for granted. The two of them had

lived alone for several years following her divorce, and it had never occurred to Alice that Bill would have trouble separating. But that seemed to be what was going on. Unable to just walk out the door and go on with his life, Bill had created a conflict so that he could leave. He and his mother needed an intensive focus on their relationship, but it was going to be a challenge because Bill said that the relationship was over.

Crisis #4

Things came to a head one evening when Bill and Rick were arguing about curfew. Rick tried to be firm, Bill began to belittle him and accuse him of ruining his life, Rick picked up the car keys and threatened to ground Bill, and Bill hit him and tried to grab the keys. Alice called the police; Bill was taken to the police station, booked on assault charges, and the next day released on bail.

Since Rick first moved into the house, Alice had repeatedly made her priorities clear. She would risk frustrating Bill and invest in the long-term potential of her new marriage. And this incident symbolized that choice. If Bill had any doubt about where he stood in the family, the doubts were resolved. He would either have to fit in or he would be stuck following through with his threat to leave permanently. When Bill's trial date arrived, he was placed on probation and ordered into treatment for anger management. The probation office accepted Alice's suggestion that I provide the anger management therapy, and Bill and I began a 10-session program of exploring his rage and building effective coping skills.

Intervention

To some extent my individual work with Bill was generic—every person has sources of anger and frustration, and many of the cognitive and behavioral skills that help with the management of anger work regardless of the issue. But this counseling opportunity provided Bill with more than skills, it offered him a place to explore his thoughts and feelings about the changes in his life beginning with his parents' divorce when he was 3 years old. He had lived the past 14 years as if he were living in a border town—changing language and customs when he crossed the border, loving both of his nationalities but unable to fully engage with either of them. His stronger attachment had been to his father, who had been nonjudgmental and playful, but in recent years that attachment had become weaker as his mom provided guidance his dad couldn't provide. His relationship with his mother, historically strained, had then lost its appeal when Rick came along and got the kind of love and acceptance Bill had always wanted. This counseling provided an opportunity to not only examine this history and make sense of it but also to make plans on how it could become better. We gradually moved from individual sessions into mother-son sessions that addressed the long-standing alienation both had felt.

The theme of these sessions was clearly emotional—attachment issues were front and center, and the tone of the sessions quickly moved from the abstract into the personal. Bill was initially aloof and disdainful, talking about his mother as a liar and a cheat, and Alice responded with self-righteous anger. Using a strategy from couples work, in the second session I shifted the focus from the present to the past and asked about the times when they were close. Bill softened by the end of the session, and they wept together over the financial and emotional struggles they had been through. We scheduled a third session to talk about finding ways to stay connected once Bill went away to school. Alice and Bill still had their differences, but they were now working together.

Rebuilding

The remainder of Bill's senior year was a period of consolidation and restoration of damaged relationships. As Bill was able to shift from being reactive and resistant to being thoughtful and strategic, he made the decision to accept Rick and learn to live with him. Rick had learned the stepparent lesson—when you try to be the disciplinarian for your partner's children, you're stepping into a danger zone—so he settled into a stable pattern of providing emotional support for Alice. And Alice began the serious work of connecting with her son, an agenda she had postponed until the

last minute. The three of them planned and took some trips together. Bill did buy his car but with advice and assistance from Rick in addition to financial help from his father, and he accepted family limits on how many hours he could work.

As the crises appeared to be resolved, Rick and Alice turned their energies to addressing another aspect of their lives. Both had in their youth been active and committed Christians, but they had each dropped out of participation in any kind of religious community. They now wanted to go together to a church where they could reconnect with this source of strength and support, but they had some decisions to make—should they go back to a place where one of them had connections and a past, or start fresh in a place where they could present themselves as they wanted to be seen? They opted for rejoining a church where Alice had, years earlier, been active in the leadership but then left during a political conflict. This decision was based on their conclusion that their joint recovery—Rick's recovery from cocaine addiction and Alice's recovery from perfectionism and over-control—was inconsistent with dishonesty and avoidance. They had to go back and face their past, and the church was a place where this kind of reconnecting was possible.

Looking Back

Many families face such periods without having professional help available. Conflicts between stepparents and stepchildren are not uncommon, and adolescents often discover their own strength just as their parents are at a vulnerable stage in their own lives. When police become involved, the family's normal separation and individuation struggles have the potential to be transformed into tensions that last a lifetime.

The interventions that turned this crisis around focused on two aspects of Bill's *emotional* interactions with others. First, Bill made significant progress in facing his family's shame-based insecurity and accepting his lack of control over others. Fossum and Mason (1986) suggest that the effects of shame persist for generations, and this confrontation with his legacy prepared Bill to take emotional risks in his sessions with his mother. With her, he was able to acknowledge the impossibility of ever getting the parenting he had wanted—and he was able to give her some level of forgiveness for being imperfect. That exchange might not have taken place without Alice's preparation during prior year as she worked through intimacy issues with Rick.

Phase 5: Moving On

Bill completed his high school career stronger than ever, and he was accepted to two of the universities in his most-preferred category. Teresa's allegations of Bill's drug use might have been correct, but no further evidence had been found and he seemed to be on a positive track. Rick and Alice's new business partnership was succeeding, and they began to look forward to the phase when Bill would be out of the house.

Making Sense of the Clients' Needs

This would be a different kind of stressful period for Alice and Rick, learning to be together without the stabilizing influence of a triangled child. Nearly every couple in the nuclear family situation finds this transition to be challenging because the change in the emotional climate of the household is sudden—almost like the traditional wedding night, the first time a couple are allowed to be alone together. Given the partners' complicated relationship histories, it was possible that this would be the time when the new marriage would feel like a trap and one of them would try to escape. They would need to practice everything they had learned about emotional awareness and self-management, acceptance, communication, and coordination of goals and actions.

Intervention

Sessions during this period were quite varied. Sometimes the couple came in together, sometimes Bill and his mother came in together, and a few times either Rick or Alice seemed to need an individual session. The circular path of the IRC model suggests that the basic elements of rela-

tional success can be revisited over and over. In this case, each cluster of issues was reviewed several times. Individually, and in groups, we talked about being aware of self and other, paying attention to coalitions and discourses through which influence occurs, developing better skills for handling coalitions and discourses, and focusing those skills on one issue at a time.

I envisioned the time as one in which the family was trying to stay afloat through dangerous rapids of relational identity negotiation; and they had to stay focused on one specific section of the rapids at a time. Changes were occurring rapidly, and one person's movement in their little raft would create the need for all parties to shift their balance. Individual coaching was sometimes necessary, but everyone needed to understand what the others were trying to do.

Launching

In this planning phase, Bill proved to be more like his mother than he had ever admitted—he was anxious about going away, he didn't like being alone, and he was worried about failing at his goal of independence. With a girlfriend at home, he was strongly tempted to give up on the universities that had accepted him and instead go to a nearby school where he could continue to see the girlfriend every weekend. This safe alternative would also be a place where he could be a star student and athlete, whereas going away would mean a higher level of competition.

The process of working through these anxieties brought Alice and her son together. They spent a week together traveling to make the school decision; they explored the communities, toured the campuses, and explored housing options. Alice had never talked much about her own college years; now, she admitted that she had been a socially isolated, fearful student whose good grades, she felt, were attributable to her obsessive behavior rather than brilliance. She realized that she had spent the next 25 years learning to overcome those obsessive habits and achieve balance in her life, and she wanted Bill to have a better experience. When they returned from the trip the two of them came to talk with me about choices and goals. They developed a plan for the next year that would give Bill a balance of support and freedom. His mother would drive him to school at the end of the summer, stay for a week in case she was needed, and then return home. Bill would be welcomed home for every vacation.

Alice and Rick, at the same time, were exploring who they might be if they were not defined so much by the demands of parenting. While they did not want to abandon Bill too quickly, he was often out with his girlfriend and they were able to plan an evening or weekend day when they would focus on each other. Alice had many ways of hiding in her work and she needed to be reminded that she was setting priorities and had to choose between investing more in her work or in her personal life. Rick was not accustomed to being the demanding member of the couple, but he found a new side of himself as he took over primary responsibility for their relational life. It had not been easy for him to compete with Bill, whose needs seemed to be so great, but he now decided to take the risk of asking for what he wanted, and Alice seemed to accept the new behavior.

When I last met with Rick and Alice, Bill was away at school and the transition had been a positive experience; in ways she never thought possible, Alice now felt she had a meaningful relationship with her young adult son. Teresa had come back to visit—she and her friend were now admitting they were lovers, and they were struggling but fiercely independent. And Rick and Alice's marriage was settling into a new period of developing intimacy. They had experienced some tense moments, but they were clear about their goal of staying together and making things work.

Reviewing the Case

This fictionalized case shows several of the realities I see as central in working with couples and families. My primary goal was to show the complexity of relationship counseling. In 2 years of working with Rick and Alice and their children, the focus of my work shifted several times in re-

sponse to new circumstances and newly disclosed but pre-existing issues. Successful intervention in one domain often seemed to uncover needs in another domain, and different individuals occupied the position of identified patient during the different phases.

In creating this case, I often simplified the issues for clarity (a complete inventory of all the likely issues and characters would fill a book); even so, starting with a complex list of possible issues, I chose issues that were high priorities for the various members of the family. At the same time, I influenced those choices with my tendency or ability to notice and make sense of specific parts of the stories that came into my office.

At the beginning of this chapter, I examined the case as it appeared before intervention using the various lenses of the five BONES themes and some of their subthemes. Now, looking back at the case that we created together, the list of what happened (Table 9.2) looks both similar and different. Once again, my listing all of these alternatives is not intended to suggest that a professional should be able to think of a case in so many ways. This description could only have been created after the fact, not during the work.

Choice Points and Alternatives

There were many significant choice points in the 2-year span covered by this case—choices of structure, theme, theory, and strategy. Initially, my clients identified their goals as building separate lives, and I chose to see Rick as an individual client, while Alice was seen in a supportive role. The structure became more complex as Rick and Alice changed their goals and their children's issues became more of a focus.

The five BONES themes, in many variants, were interwoven—partially because of my intentionality and partially because of circumstances. The spiritual and emotional themes were the last to show resolution, but they were no less important. The IRC model guided the selection of themes and strategies, despite many new sources of information, because it was one that had been developed and tested with such issues—addictive behaviors and remarriage/stepfamily formation. Finally, the strategies themselves were simple

Table 9.2   **Theme Analysis at Closure**

Theme	Areas of Concern, Intervention, and Change
Behavior	*Skills:* Skill development included self-disclosure, assertiveness, and contingency contracting.
	External knowledge: Learning about their parallel needs helped Rick and Alice to bond, even though the patterns continued to present challenges.
	Internal knowledge: As Alice and Rick learned to be honest, they became more committed and more able to provide appropriate support.
	Cued responses: Rick and Alice learned to avoid conditions that made relapses more likely and they developed alternative responses.
	Contingent responding: Family members learned to accept realistic limits on enjoyment and satisfaction.
Organization	*Function:* As Alice and Rick learned to achieve intimacy, there was less need for manipulation.
	Conflict: The family developed skills for handling conflicts in a productive way.
	Development: From being ignored, the developmental needs of adolescents became central to the counseling.
	Intergenerational: Rick and Alice broke free of patterned ways of dealing with others, making life easier for their children.
	Direct communication: Alice, Rick, and Bill all challenged each other to be more direct about their desires and their discomforts.
	Indirect communication: Family members learned to examine behavior for its underlying messages, then neutralize them or express them directly.
	Structure: Alice and Rick developed shared concerns focused on their children. Teresa remained in an ambiguous status, but Bill received appropriate support for moving into adulthood.
	Systemic patterns: The complementarity in Alice and Rick's relationship was reduced.
	Evolution of system: Crises and transformations left the family in a healthier position.
Narrative	*Identity:* Caught between a familiar story and a new reality, each family member took some risks.
	Complexity: A complete and healing story of this family integrated the parents' intimacy problems and their search for approval and security.
	Dominant discourse: Rick and Alice resisted recovery discourse but found a discourse of small business owners to help organize forward movement.
Emotion	*Connection:* Closeness and distance became less problematic because the potential of rejection was reduced.
	Internal experiencing: Shame led to frequent misunderstanding. Progress included facing fears instead of hiding from them.
	Emotional expression: Direct expression of feelings and thoughts allowed the couple and family members to know "where they stood" with each other.
	Empathy: All members of the family made progress toward understanding each other's feelings and feeling understood.
	Emotion management: Rick's withdrawal into drugs and Alice's withdrawal into control each became less necessary.
Spirituality	*Ethnosensitivity:* Rick and Alice recalled young adult values and beliefs that had come from religious involvement.
	Beliefs and themes: Alice and Rick learned to fit the beliefs of NA, Nar-Anon, and their church into an integrated whole.
	Instrumental practices: Returning to regular participation in religious services felt comforting to both Alice and Rick.
	Metaphysics: Having tried to control their life together, each eventually found ways to fit into a larger system of meaning and purpose.

ones—teaching and listening, facilitating conversations, confronting discrepancies, and seeking alternative meanings. Many times I went into a session with a plan, only to see the planned session pushed aside by newly discovered or resurfaced issues.

One of the choices I demonstrated with this case had to do with a willingness to continue seeing these people as a family case after I had initially established the treatment under a framework of individual counseling. Some authors have expressed a view that such a decision is unethical—if a case is opened as an individual case, then it must be referred to another professional for family work, and if it's a family case it must be referred for individual work. This perspective, which is explored in Chapter 10, views individual counseling as a separate and different kind of work that depends on assumptions of confidentiality. It is hard to offer a guarantee that "what is said in this room stays in this room," when a counselor working with multiple family members might lose track of individual conversations. My own perspective is close to that of Leslie (2003), who has published a *nonconfidentiality* contract for family members to sign. Confidentiality for the individual, from this perspective, is only one value among many, and people who want help for their relationships must accept that sometimes the good of a relationship comes at the expense of some individual discomfort.

Multiple Strategies

Many authors have suggested that the multiple approaches taken with a family or an individual can be organized into a sequence based on immediacy of need, a readiness for change, or both (Pinsof, 1995; Prochaska, 1999). This case demonstrates such a sequencing of strategies.

In the early work with Rick and Alice, my emphasis was on Behavioral and Narrative themes of achieving and maintaining abstinence, modifying both decision processes and coping behaviors, and retelling both the problem and recovery stories. The Behavioral and Narrative approaches adapt well to situations in which clients have limited commitment to the counseling process—such counseling does not require a high level of trust

and self-disclosure, it tends to stabilize rather than destabilize relationships, and it offers relatively rapid indications of change. These strategies are combined in the NA program as well, where storytelling is paired with emphasis on behavior change. NA also emphasizes spirituality, but the 12 Steps of NA create very low expectations for the beginner's involvement in spiritual life.

As behaviors and identities began to change, Rick and Alice began to alter the Organizational aspects of their relationship by moving in together. Whether a couple is living together, I find that behavioral and narrative change typically results in organizational shifts—the old patterns no longer work the same way and new, alternative patterns start to appear. But in this case, with the children either present or expected to appear, the shift of emphasis to Organizational issues was especially critical.

Next, all these changes created situations in which family members' old emotion management strategies would no longer work: Feelings of anxiety, depression, and anger began to disrupt interactions. Therefore, Emotional themes came into increasing prominence, and changing views of self and other then led to work on identities.

Spirituality, in this case, was the last area of emphasis to receive major attention; Organizational changes had created discomfort with the couple's lack of a spiritual center and spiritual practice seemed to offer a setting where the new marriage could be supported. When spiritual practice extended into spiritual awareness and changing experiences, family members were empowered to face each other more directly and engage in serious emotional work.

Like many family cases, this one did not go through a carefully planned process of closure. Instead, the family cancelled one appointment and never agreed on a time for another one. Follow-up telephone contact indicated that they knew they were welcome to come back but they didn't feel a need.

Client Empowerment

Overall, this case seems to me to demonstrate an attitude toward clients in which expert authority is tempered by a desire to "tread lightly" in the arena of the family's relationships. From the first session, Alice and Rick presented as two people who needed direction. At many points during our work together, I was tempted to tell them how to handle things differently. Of course, their repeated pattern of not discussing decisions in our sessions until the decisions had been implemented showed that they were not entirely open to my opinions.

Rather than attempt to take control over their lives and create new dependencies, I attempted to use my presence to strengthen and refine their own decision-making processes. That choice required accepting the decisions that they made, and sometimes it required that I help them recover from apparent errors. But the result was a strengthening of emotional connections among these people who would still have each other for support when my work was done.

Personal Challenges of Family Counseling

Kottler (1993, 2000) has written about the joys and pains of engaging with people in helping relationships. In his writings, as in the work of Guggenbuhl-Craig (1986), professionals can be seen struggling with their humanness. This case is intended to show what it is like working with people who are at the same time charming and frustrating, brilliant and unaware, selfless and selfish, and impulsive but paralyzed with fear. I have tried, by portraying myself in this position, to highlight the analysis and decision-making aspect of the work. What I have not described adequately is the rapid play of feelings that the counselor experiences in this kind of work. Some weeks are exhilarating; people do wonderful things for which the professional can take some credit. Other weeks are depressing, and the professional feels responsible for every mistake. David Treadway (2004) is remarkably successful in bringing the professional's personal experience to life through a mixture of fiction and analysis.

Every couple or family case offers opportunities as well as challenges. The people who come into a professional's office bring multidimensional humanity, and the professional responds with his or her own humanity. We learn about the clients through our responses, but we also learn about ourselves—the ways in which we share their feelings and their motivations, their dreams and their self-doubt. When we leave the office, we can't help carrying these people with us. And when we are with friends and family we may have a hard time taking off the uniform and being real. Our loved ones sometimes express jealousy because the clients seem to get a better version of us than the one we show at home.

As the story of the Morgan-Thompsons is intended to show, the rewards of relational work are at least equal to the challenges. We learn every day from people who take us into their unique places in the world, and we repay them by giving them new ways of handling their uniqueness.

Suggested Individual and Group Activities

Your understanding of concepts and issues presented in this chapter may be enhanced by the following activities:

- *12-Step meeting.* The various self-help fellowships such as AA and NA typically conduct "open meetings" at which professionals and the public are welcome as observers. Locate a schedule for one of your local fellowships (call a coordinating office or conduct a web search) and attend a meeting. Does your experience at this meeting match what you expected?
- *Film.* Many films have featured portrayals of alcohol and other drug issues in relationships. A powerful film that gets credit for realism in some of its family scenes is *When a Man Loves a Woman.*

Suggested Readings

Kottler, J. A. (1993). *On being a therapist.* San Francisco: Jossey-Bass.

Fossum, M. A., & Mason, M. (1986). *Facing shame: Families in recovery.* New York: Norton.

Treadway, D. C. (2004). *Intimacy, change, and other therapeutic mysteries.* New York; Guilford Press.

The Ethical
Family Counselor

*Family-oriented professionals are creating new
definitions of ethical practice.*

Objective

In this chapter, you learn to:

1. Appreciate the complexity of ethical decision making and behavior when working with couples and families.
2. Understand the functions of context, values, ethics codes, and law in guiding decision making.
3. Recognize and improve your ways of making ethical choices.
4. Identify common ethical issues in work with couples and families.
5. Apply values in creating an ethical stance for your own practice.

10

Chapter

A mong the signs of maturation is a shift in perspective. One's own needs and concerns become less urgent and others' needs and concerns become more important. One of the ways of describing this kind of mature orientation is "ethical." This chapter demonstrates that family counseling has made tremendous strides toward becoming a mature profession whose commonality is defined by its ethical commitment. In the process, we explore the various perspectives that have been advanced regarding ethics, particularly in the context of work with couples and families, using illustrations from the ethics codes of various professions.

Couple and family practice is particularly complex in terms of ethics (Doherty & Boss, 1991; Vesper, 1991). Extending the ethically complex professional/client relationship by adding more people further complicates many of the decisions that counselors make. Before discussing ethical issues faced by the family counselor, we first discuss ethical decision making as a process.

Ethical Decision-Making Processes

Ethical behavior is often challenging. Decision-making situations are complex, and even when a situation appears simple there can be conflicts among ways of determining the most ethical response. Even laws and professional ethics codes often differ from one another. Therefore, scholars of professional ethics such as Kitchener (1984) have tended to focus on the *process* of ethical decision making as much as on the *content* of ethical standards (Tarvydas, Cottone, & Claus, 2001).

The process described in the Integrative Decision-Making Model of Ethical Behavior (Tarvydas et al., 2003) begins with four themes or attitudes: reflection, balance of parties and issues, attention to contexts, and collaboration. The process moves through the following stages, each of which has several components:

- Interpreting the situation through awareness and fact finding
- Formulating an ethical decision
- Selecting an action by weighing competing, nonmoral values, personal blind spots, or prejudices
- Planning and executing the selected course of action

Cottone's (2001) social constructionist approach to ethical decision making, which emphasizes the location of the decision maker in a social context, gives special attention to values and principles that guide the identification of issues and the search for ethically supportable ways of acting (Cottone & Tarvydas, 2003). A professional is able to be most effective in day-to-day ethical behavior when there has been time spent exploring and clarifying core principles and values. For those who work from a couple and family perspective, the basic definition of what matters generally includes some beliefs about relationships and their importance in human life, which shape the priorities that guide efforts to be a helper.

However, having core values and principles is not enough, when one may not necessarily see how to apply those values in a particular situation. The awareness of a "situation" is, in itself, an important step in ethical performance. Ethics codes are intended to help people identify ethical dilemmas that might not be obvious, or to reflect on these dilemmas and find out what other professionals consider to be the most ethically and legally defensible alternatives. Codes are updated on a regular basis to more accurately identify current issues in practice and to reflect current thinking. Throughout this chapter we refer to a few codes to help us explore issues.

Ethics codes are integrally connected with legal guidelines that also highlight ethically challenging situations and provide guidance for practitioners. The legal climate includes case law—the history of judicial decisions—as well as licensing laws and criminal statutes. The legal and legislative community often depends on ethics codes to define current practice, but laws and decisions often include specific language that puts limits on individual choice. In the end, ethics codes, along with legal precedents and legal statutes, do not resolve questions of ethics and only partially resolve questions of legality. The professional must fall back on values in resolving questions about ethical behavior. We examine situations in which decision making is difficult because of multiple definitions of a situation. An ethical response according to one perspective is in many cases an ethical error from another perspective.

Principles and Values

Ethics are not universal; rather, they are determined by the social context. Decisions and actions are judged unethical when they appear to violate the principles and values of those who are doing the judging. Conflicts over ethics often revolve around culturally defined principles and values, or around the question of whether agreed-on principles and values were enacted in a particular case. Conflicts of both kinds are present in couple and family counseling because especially sensitive principles and value differences regarding marriage, divorce, sexual orientation, roles and responsibilities, child rearing, and affairs are intense, widespread, and often unacknowledged (Corey, Corey, & Callanan, 2003).

Principles, in this usage, are broader and less precise than values. Western authors in the field of human services have identified five basic principles for ethical decision making: autonomy, beneficence, nonmaleficence, justice, and fidelity (Cottone & Tarvydas, 2003; Kitchener, 1984; Zygmond & Boorhem, 1989). The first principle, *autonomy*, asserts that individuals and groups have the right to make decisions regarding their own welfare. The second principle, *beneficence*, emphasizes the professional's commitment to being a force for positive change in the lives of individuals, their families, and their communities. The third principle, *nonmaleficence*, emphasizes the contrasting concern that achieving good outcomes is not enough—the goal is to also avoid bad outcomes. The fourth principle, *justice*, suggests that a professional's resources should not be used to advantage one individual or group over another or to otherwise violate the basic values of a democratic, capitalistic society: equal access, equal opportunity, and equal treatment. The fifth and final principle, *fidelity*, summarizes the expectation that professionals are honest, loyal, and reliable.

These five principles often leave doubts about the correct course of action because people's actual values—the ways in which they define and prioritize different kinds of behavior as more or less desirable—differ widely. Furthermore, people encounter differences in language regarding the meanings of words such as "advantage," "equal," and "positive." As seen in this chapter, the particular values held by professionals lead to differences in understandings of ethics. The following examples illustrate such values:

- Best-selling author Michelle Weiner-Davis (1992) states that she is guided by a value of preserving marriages. She rejects the idea that some marriages should end.
- Jerome Price (1996) expresses a value of parents maintaining authority over their children. He believes that children should accept the hierarchical organization of society and wait for adulthood, when it will be their turn to be decision makers.
- In the Chapter 9 case (Morgan-Thompsons), I prioritized a value of recovery from chemical dependency and other addictions.
- Representing an even more distinctive principle, Bradford Keeney said in a recent interview (Englar-Carlson, 2003) that he values challenging, emotional, theatrical encounters with clients.

To further complicate ethical decision making, not only may professionals working with the same case hold different values, a professional may hold values that do not match those of clients. Within couples and families, there is also diversity of values. At all levels, discussions may be difficult because the language being used does not clarify value differences, and even sincere attempts to achieve the same goals may lead to working at cross-purposes.

Social Construction of Values

Values are generally learned at an early age and are refined and altered by personal experience and study, and often attached to family, religious, and other traditions. Whether a professional is able to identify the source of values or not, we can assume that values result from a social construction process in which events get noticed, categorized, and labeled. Values are not individually created, they are transmitted and co-created in discourse. (See Rabin, 2005 for examples).

For example, we can look at marriage preservation values such as those held by Weiner-Davis and assume that she does not hold them in isolation; the content of those values is likely to include contributions from many conversations with family, professionals, clients, and possibly with political and religious figures. She has expressed the belief that too many people are committed to their relationships only for the good times, and any disruption in life causes them to abandon their commitments. She has said that she thinks commitment itself is a good thing, and she thinks that married couples should honor their obligations to others besides themselves. These are statements that have widespread support from groups that would define the issues as children's well-being, morality in society, maturity and responsibility, and effective management of public resources. Each of these different discourses, even though it agrees with the others on one common goal, has its own emphases.

Competing Values

In some situations, two sets of principles and values seem to be in conflict, even when people agree on their interpretation. The principle of justice, with values of equal opportunity and fairness, often conflicts with values of excellence and achievement. Let us look, for example, at the distribution of resources in the family of Ken and Sue Lee, where the parents—both employed in stable careers—are considering adoption of Karina, a 3-year-old who has been living in an orphanage and has been blind since birth. The adoption, which is being encouraged by Sue, seems likely to benefit Karina; she will have access to resources she could never have hoped to receive in the institutional setting because of the Lees' residence in a major city and their adequate income. However, there is already another child in the family, 8-year-old Nancy, and Ken is worried about the impact on her. As an only child, Nancy would have had family support toward any goal she chose. Ken has heard stories of families paying for college, even medical school, and he had dreamed of such a life for Nancy. With Karina's adoption, the family goal would not be so focused. Their increased justice commitment would mean dramatic improvements in Karina's options, but probably those would come at the expense of Nancy's.

When values are in conflict, as in this example, people may benefit from examining them at the personal, group, and societal levels. At the individual level, self-reflection activities such as meditation, prayer, journaling, and personal counseling can help to sort through competing discourses and achieve some resolution of the conflicts. Even when competing values cannot be entirely resolved, it is possible to find strategies that permit decisions to be made. Couples, families, and work groups can participate in group values clarification exercises that help them sort through the discursive influences on their values and work toward ways of making decisions despite competing values.

From Values to Action

The movement from values to action is a daily challenge as a professional decides what she or he stands for, what needs to be done, and how to act in the immediate present. For people who enter the specialty area of family counseling, we can assume that a primary value is the preservation and enhancement of human relationships, which leads to an exploration of ways to work with couples and families and a choice among those that have been studied. But values may also demand creativity. The same core value can motivate a professional to create new ways of being a helper, much as the pioneers of family counseling did in the 1930s, 1940s, and 1950s

when they received little attention and had little in the way of theory to guide them. For example, a contemporary movement involves shifting attention away from individuals and working with schools, workplaces, communities, and other *larger systems* (e.g., Waldegrave et al., 2003). For innovators, the highest form of ethical practice requires doing what seems right, even when it goes against the traditions of mental health practice.

Identifying Ethical Issues

Beyond clarifying one's location within multiple value discourses, ethical decision making also involves identifying times when the clear ethical choice is not apparent. This is a challenge because what presents itself may seem to be a clear, problem-free opportunity. Let's say, for example, that your clients Jude and Rose Ellington mention that their weekend plans are a mess because their regular babysitter is sick. And you remember that your son Kevin has begun babysitting for some of the neighbors, seeming to do a good job, and you're pretty sure his weekend is free. It might seem natural to put these circumstances together and help everyone out by connecting the Ellingtons with Kevin. It might seem that the unethical act would be to *not* connect them with each other; especially, if you have been encouraging Jude and Rose to spend time together without their children. But an informed professional knows that situations involving multiple relationships are often ethical quicksand, and this idea will be quickly rejected. It may not be apparent how such multiple relationships will become problematic, but even when they seem innocent they can lead to struggles around loyalty and judgment. Ethical dilemmas occur when your values, or those of groups to which you are obligated, conflict—when you are simultaneously guided by multiple values that seem incompatible.

In this case, you have already noted that the clients' relational well-being is one of your values. But you may, on reflection, see that many other values could influence your decisions. If your values are consistent with those of a democratic society, you are likely to value your clients' autonomy and seek to intervene as little as possible in their lives. You also value their privacy and want them to feel that your sources of information are limited; you know only those things they chose to share with you. Having Kevin in their home, even just once, might compromise these values. But depending on your political, ethnic, religious, and generational identity your values might instead put more emphasis on connectedness and interdependence, on breaking down the walls of privacy that keep people from experiencing a spiritual oneness. This alternative set of values might lead you to believe that autonomy is a flawed idea that eventually leads people to isolation, anxiety, and risk of emotional and physical illness.

Generally speaking, professional helpers face some issues over and over, and the multiple relationships issue is only one; we examine a series of these frequently encountered issues later in this chapter. Those issues that come up most often are generally discussed in the various ethics codes of professional organizations. The encoding of these discussions in written form serves multiple functions. For the person who comes to look for guidance, a code provides something of a consensus about what a group of peers would say. In the case of the Ellingtons, a group of peers is likely to say, "The potential problems associated with this referral outweigh the expected benefits." But even more important, the fact that a code has identified this kind of issue serves an educational function—it helps the professional become aware of potential problems. Given that awareness, a reflective practitioner hesitates before acting, and pulls out one or more relevant codes, thinks about principles and values, consults with respected colleagues, and then makes a considered decision. I think of this event-driven process as *reactive ethics*.

But ethical awareness goes beyond focusing on individual decisions. Issues arise continually. *Proactively ethical practitioners* pay close attention to their motivations, so as to avoid taking actions that might sacrifice the interests of others for personal gain. They carefully observe influence attempts from others, individuals, and groups, to better avoid distortions of judgment based on influence. But even more, they seek to adopt a sensitivity to multiple perspectives because the greatest risk of unethical behavior results from seeing a decision out of context.

Consultations, Codes, and Laws

When faced with dilemmas, there are two essential strategies that help with decision making. The first is to consult with a supervisor, trusted colleague, legal counsel, or a combination of these. A supervisor is an especially important person to involve in any decisions that are ethically challenging. Your supervisor will be held legally responsible for your decisions if there is any negative outcome, and should be eager to evaluate the choices you are making and give clear guidance. Your supervisor is also the natural person to consult because this is a person who knows you, knows your caseload, and can put the situation in context. In contrast, some colleagues may be more likely to answer in a casual manner, failing to take all factors into consideration. Finally, the supervisor is able to put the individual decision onto the supervision agenda so that these issues are considered in future discussions, reading assignments, and assignment of cases or other duties. When there is no one supervising your work or you are interested in a broader perspective, then you can select trusted colleagues who have the experience and the perspective to provide sensitive, authoritative input. And legal advice provides a somewhat different perspective, one that acknowledges professional standards but focuses on the unique legal setting where you are practicing.

When you take an ethics question to your supervisor or your colleagues, they will rely to a great extent on relevant ethics codes and standards and to legal authority, looking for specific guidelines related to your situation. When such guidelines are clearly stated, decision making is easier. If you follow written guidelines, your decisions will be defended by your peers, professional organizations, licensing body, and liability insurance provider. For example, many counselors have been charged with ethical violations for becoming sexually involved with former clients. We may understand some of the reasons these relationships tend to occur, but they are clearly an illegitimate exercise of power. Professional ethics codes have responded to this common issue with similar rules: If a client has been actively involved in receiving services from the professional within 2 years (ACA specifies 5 years) of the beginning of the sexual relationship, it is inappropriate and unethical.

If, going back to the Ellingtons' need for a babysitter and your thoughts about Kevin, you felt conflicted, then you and your supervisor might sit down and look at the ethics codes of the American Association for Marriage and Family Therapy (AAMFT) and the International Association for Marriage and Family Counseling (IAMFC). Because IAMFC's code is a supplement to the code of the American Counseling Association (ACA) and is not intended to address all ethical issues, you should review that code as well.

The 2001 AAMFT code, in standard 1.7, states a basic concern: Professionals do not further their own interests at the expense of their clients. In this case, the same behavior could further both interests—you are trying to benefit the clients, but Kevin's benefit would extend to you. So this standard has not provided much guidance.

Looking through the ethics codes for something more specific, we find AAMFT (standard 1.3), IAMFC (standard A.9), and ACA (article A.5.c), respectively, speaking about multiple relationships (AAMFT and IAMFC); or nonprofessional interactions or relationships (ACA). All, in some way, express caution about the influential position held by the professional and the danger that multiple relationships could impair judgment or increase the risk of exploiting the clients' dependency. The groups address such risks in quite different ways:

- AAMFT states that "Therapists, therefore, make every effort to avoid conditions and multiple relationships with clients that could impair professional judgment or increase the risk of exploitation." and "When the risk of impairment or exploitation exists due to conditions or multiple roles,

therapists take appropriate precautions" (standard 1.3).

- IAMFC states, "Couple and family counselors avoid whenever possible multiple relationships, such as business, social, or sexual contacts with any current clients or their family members." They are "responsible for demonstrating there is no harm from any relationship with a client or family member." (guideline A.9).

- ACA, in the most explicit statement of the three, says, "Counselor-client nonprofessional relationships with clients, former clients, or their family members should be avoided, except when the interaction is potentially beneficial to the client" (A.5.c). Then, in article A.5.d, the code articulates a mandatory procedure of documenting any expected benefits before any discussion with the client. It states that any such interactions should be "initiated with appropriate client written consent. Where unintentional harm occurs to the client or former client, or to an individual significantly involved with the client or former client, due to the nonprofessional interaction, the counselor must show evidence of an attempt to remedy such harm."

In conclusion, these three codes appear to strongly advise against the kind of multiple relationship that would arise from sending Kevin to babysit for the clients. They all include some allowance for "conditions" where such relationships are "unavoidable," but it is hard to argue that this is such a case. If this were a situation that could not be avoided, then the ethical professional would be obligated to carefully document the reasons for considering the exception, discuss the situation with the clients so that they are informed of risks, get their written consent, and then assess possible negative consequences and address any negative consequences that are detected. Clearly, ethical handling of this situation would create stresses for the Ellingtons that do not seem to be justified by the potential benefit.

It is possible that, following this research, you still want to examine the legal climate surrounding this decision. Your attorney will refer to the ethics codes that cover you as a licensed or certified professional and also examine federal, state, and local statutes and court decisions. You will find out that you have no legal liability if you ignore your clients' need for a babysitter, whereas if you give them Kevin's name, you could be held responsible for any mishap. The clients could claim that they accepted Kevin's assistance under duress, and you could not only lose them as clients but also be liable for damages.

Ethics Themes in Couple and Family Counseling

Professionals face ethical challenges in any kind of helping relationship. But working with groups, couples, and families is especially challenging because of the complexities involved in considering the needs of more than a single client, possibly even conceptualizing the group, family, or couple as "the client." Any unethical behavior could have long-term consequences, as the counselor is intimately involved in the conversations, decisions, and interactions of the clients.

Fifty years of couple and family therapy literature has produced consensus on several themes that represent unique challenges in this specialized arena. For each of these themes, the field has changed over the years in how issues are defined, principles are applied, and ethical practice is conceptualized.

Competence

Among the universally supported expectations of the ethical professional is competence (Doherty & Boss, 1991; Magee, 1997). According to the ACA Code of Ethics, for example, "Counselors practice only within the boundaries of their competence, based on their education, training, supervised experience, state and national professional credentials, and appropriate professional experience" (standard C.2.a); and "Counselors practice in specialty areas new to them only after appropriate education, training, and supervised experience" (standard C.2.b). These statements clearly indicate that a professional is expected to recognize his or

her limitations and take appropriate action when knowledge and skills seem insufficient for handling the issues presented in a case. The IAMFC code goes further in Guideline C.1, stating that marriage and family counselors, "have the responsibility to develop and maintain basic skills in marriage and family counseling through graduate training, supervision, and consultation"; and in standard C.5: "do not attempt to diagnose or treat problems beyond the scope of their training and abilities." Returning to the ACA standard C.2.a, every case calls for a review of one's competence. This standard states, "Counselors gain knowledge, personal awareness, sensitivity, and skills pertinent to working with a diverse client population."

These are daunting expectations, considering the complexities of the problems that couples and families can bring into the counseling session. For example, the intricacies of human development can make the behavior of a normal, healthy child or adolescent difficult to understand. A counselor is likely to encounter a wide variety of exceptional cases—children with handicapping conditions or terminal illnesses, twins or other multiple births, infants or adolescents with severe attachment disturbances. Sexuality—performance, identity, desire, fulfillment—is a complex aspect of human interaction, one that involves subtle and confusing symbolic as well as biological elements. Further, family economic issues, including careers and spending/saving patterns, are extremely powerful regulators of well-being. And couples or families who are divorcing, living in a second or subsequent marriage, and creating and maintaining stepfamily households have all the issues faced by other families, yet their special family characteristics have unique developmental patterns.

By now you may be asking yourself, "How much preparation will I need before I am able to ethically provide services to couples and families?" This is quite a different question from "What preparation is required for *independent* work with couples and families?" It is also quite different from asking, "Once I have the necessary credentials for independent practice, will I be able to ethically provide service to *all* couples and families?" Each of these three questions is important not only for the individual practitioner but also for the availability of couple and family counseling services in the community.

The first question covers a wide range of contexts, and is therefore difficult to answer. With close, effective supervision by a highly qualified couple and family specialist, a student or postgraduate professional in a training clinic will be practicing ethically after a basic introduction to family counseling theories and skills. Lacking those conditions, the counselor with only generalized skills is likely to feel ethically bound to avoid taking these cases and refer them to qualified practitioners. Fortunately, increasing numbers of clinics are hiring couple and family specialists to meet these needs. In many communities, however, there is no qualified referral available and the ethical dilemma has no clear answer. Clients may be offered individual services as a substitute for the relational services they need, but it is possible to argue that they would be disadvantaged by this attempt to live up to an ethical standard. As an alternative, counselors who lack specialized training can engage in self-directed study to develop the knowledge and skills of family counseling (Kaplan and Associates, 2003). A counselor who follows such a path would still be expected to find a qualified supervisor who can direct further study and training so as to "ensure the competence of their work and . . . protect others from possible harm" (ACA standard C.2.b).

The second question has clearer answers. As we discussed in Chapter 1, standards for competence in Marriage and Family Therapy (or Counseling) have been developed at several levels. State licensing laws are one place to look for these standards. Achieving full licensure or certification in Marriage and Family Therapy, in the 47 states and the District of Columbia where such a credential has been established, requires extensive study and supervised practice and reassures the community that a practitioner is qualified beyond the minimal level of competence. A similar statement of competence is made when a professional completes the training and testing to earn certification or credentialing from a nongovernmental body. Clinical Membership in AAMFT is widely accepted as a standard, and an alternative credentialing procedure is available through the National Academy for Certified Family Therapists (NACFT).

But these standards ensure only that a professional is prepared to work with the most commonly seen issues and levels of severity. Doherty (2002) has pointed out that in many professions it is common for people to refer their most difficult cases to the most qualified practitioners, but in couple counseling such referrals seem to be rare. ACA standards say that the counselor should seek support from others with appropriate expertise when knowingly faced with new issues. How can this be done when the family is simultaneously struggling with medical, sexual, economic, and developmental issues that the counselor has not had the opportunity to study in detail? Must every session include a team behind the mirror including an accountant, a speech pathologist, a sex therapist, and a dietician? Such a treatment team might be ideal but it is not an achievable solution in every setting.

What every family counselor may aspire to, instead, is to follow a three-step plan that will provide appropriate support for couple and family clients who present varied demands for specialized knowledge and skills:

1. *Actively seek to develop a network including a variety of qualified professionals.* Such networks help counselors to recognize their own limitations and to identify sources of expertise before they are needed. Recognizing their own limitations, counselors do not misrepresent themselves by claiming specialized competencies.

2. *Confer and consult with other professionals whenever there are doubts about a case.* These other professionals can help in locating advanced training and supervision, when needed, to upgrade and update knowledge.

3. *Present the situation to the clients and help them to make an informed decision.* If the counselor believes a referral is indicated, the client(s) should be told as quickly as possible. If the counselor believes that he or she can effectively manage the case with appropriate supervision, the clients should be informed of the arrangement (and the identity of the su-

pervisor). In the end, it is the clients who must choose to start with a new professional.

Finally, in addition to acquiring the specialized knowledge required for effectiveness with particular clients, it is important to periodically step back and question whether *any* professional is providing appropriate help for couples and families. As discussed in Chapter 3, Hare-Mustin (1978, 1980) issued such a challenge. She said that the practice of family therapy, as it existed at the time, was inherently damaging to its female members, and she called for a re-examination so that the family counselor of the future would be able to claim competence.

Systemic versus Individual Ethics

The systems metaphor was criticized, in the 1970s, for being value-free. But there was a core value. Whatever served the survival needs of the system was essentially good, and a system was assumed to have something like "mind"—a kind of wisdom that promoted things that were good for all of its members (Bateson, 1979). There is an inherent conflict between an ethical perspective that emphasizes the good of the group with one that emphasizes the good of the individual, and the ethics of individuality are deeply engrained in Western traditions.

It can be argued that the marriage and family counseling movement was a reaction to a cultural overemphasis on the individual. During the 100 years following the emergence of the industrial age, industrial employment, new educational systems, changing cultural values, and the new mental health field seemed to create a climate in which families were viewed as unnecessary baggage. Families, according to this individualistic perspective, held individuals back in their pursuit of happiness and prosperity. Family therapy in its early days was not value-free, it was a political movement that opposed the abuses of an individually oriented society.

How did this value shape the emerging field? The most zealous of the family systems advocates seemed to believe that the individual did not exist, but was instead merely a piece of a system.

When some suggested that families were characterized by power and control efforts and might not be able to balance the abuses of powerful members, systemic purists quoted Bateson's (1972) pronouncements that power was an epistemological error that existed only if one believed in it. There actually was a time when systemic perspectives as practiced stood in opposition to the values of individual freedom, dignity, and equality.

Hare-Mustin's (1978) challenge to the new field focused on the ways in which these new ideas were defending and preserving ancient patterns of domination and oppression of women. She, and eventually other feminist family therapists (e.g., Walters, Carter, Papp, & Silverstein, 1988), said that the new movement seemed to be unaware of the economic and physical power that men exercised in relationships with women. They further suggested that the oppression was not so much a result of individual behavior as it was a systemic pattern. Individual men did not need to assert their dominance in order to benefit from it; the force of the dominant culture would guarantee that most women suppressed their goals and their needs and honored those of their male partners. And feminist authors cited the recent history of the women's consciousness-raising movement. It had shown that progress required helping the oppressed to recognize and resist subtle pressures to conform—the system only changed when individuals were empowered to disrupt its effects.

This challenge based on gender inequality and abuse of women occurred at a time when other questioning voices were also being raised in the MFT literature. One group of voices challenged the commonplace treatment of children and adolescents as "system elements" that were not understood in their proper developmental context (Keith, 1986; Madanes, 1986; Wachtel, 1990). Another group of voices challenged the widespread refusal to consider individual-level motivations, feelings, memories, and habits (Nichols, 1987). Individuals in all their gendered, developing, personal-historical reality were on their way back to being a focus of couple and family counseling.

Other revolutionary voices focused on larger systems as oppressors, again challenging the systems paradigm and its tendency to stabilize one system level by promoting change at another level. Challenging what Hardy (1989) referred to as the "myth of sameness," professionals of color demanded a politically sensitive and activist approach to the experiences of minority families (Boyd-Franklin, 1993; Falicov, 1998). And professionals serving gay, lesbian, and transgendered couples and families called for increasing understanding of sexual diversities and more effective work with those whose family experiences were denied or even suppressed by the larger society (Laird & Green, 1996).

The ethical pendulum has begun to shift toward the good of the individual rather than the system. Since the 1990s, with the increasing influence of postmodern theory and the heritage of Foucault's and Baudrillard's sensitivity to the experience of marginalized people, it is no longer accurate to say that family counselors are united in trying to preserve systems, regardless of their negative effects on individuals.

Gender and Sexuality

Gender, meaning the individual expression of characteristics that are culturally defined as constituting maleness or femaleness, has been regulated by religious and secular traditions since the beginning of recorded history. But the topic has been a hotly contended issue in couple and family life for at least the past two centuries; in Europe, for example, English and French novels from the early 1800s show women and men challenging the expectations of their times and creating new kinds of relationships where men could be sensitive and women could assert themselves in business or farming. Rather than being a creation of the late twentieth century, the movement toward gender flexibility has a long history including the cross-cultural scholarship of Margaret Mead, the theorizing and clinical work of figures such as Alfred Adler and Karen Horney, the political activism of suffragists, and a few documented cases of individual women who assumed male identities and lived their lives as husbands and fathers.

Not only did activists challenge gender norms, but economic and social conditions also opened up opportunities for change; for example, women in the United States were transformed by their experiences on wagon trains and in World War II factories. Mead was especially important in this history; her anthropological studies of family life suggested that societies could organize themselves in such a way that people's family and community responsibilities were determined not by biological sex but rather by other personal characteristics (Mead, 1935/2001). In various places around the world, Mead's vision is being implemented to the extent that more women are bankers, lawyers, and engineers while increasing numbers of men stay at home with children.

Sexuality, a closely related topic, has been contested longer than has gender. The control of reproductive activity has been viewed by many cultures as a mark of civilization or religious obedience. Early Christian writings glorified abstinence and lectured followers on the importance of restricting sexual activity to the formal structure of marriage; other cultures and times organized their expectations differently but enforced various kinds of sexual norms. And the conflicts between these expectations and people's actual behavior are well documented in poetry, drama, paintings, and novels. Over the past 200 years, discussions of sexuality have become more open and sexual norms have come under greater scrutiny. Utopian leaders have organized communities in which monogamy was outlawed, celebrities have described their group sexual activities in diaries, and casual sex has proliferated since oral and other contraceptives created a climate of "sex without consequences." Moreover, same-sex relationships have become increasingly visible, recently gaining the legal status of marriage in some jurisdictions.

Gender and sexuality are ethical issues in couple and family therapy because clients struggle to reconcile discourses that call for gender flexibility and authentic sexual expression, on one hand, with discourses that call for a rededication to traditional norms, on the other. Conservative groups in the United States and other societies, many of them using religious teachings and texts to support their demands, view the changes of the past 200 years as negative—as evidence of the disintegration of society, the result of acquiescing to the whims of individuals and rejecting authority of all kinds. For the couple or family who are at the crossroads of these discourses, the family counselor's responses to their conflict have deep ethical implications. Parents who threaten to withdraw financial support from a gay son, husbands who threaten to divorce wives if they take college classes, and relatives who refuse to have contact with an unmarried couple are only a few examples of the cases that appear with increasing frequency in a couple and family practice.

Race and Class

It may seem strange, considering that one of the classic texts of family therapy is *Families of the Slums* (Minuchin et al., 1967), that race and class have often been ignored in family therapy (Hardy, 1989). This may also seem hard to understand considering that there has been 20 years for the field to develop since McGoldrick and her coauthors published the first edition of their *Ethnicity and Family Therapy* (McGoldrick, Pearce, & Giordano, 1982), and that their enormously popular book led to a massive literature on ways in which ethnic identities presented themselves in couple and family problems. How can it be that ethnicity (and multiculturalism, another popular topic) are openly discussed without talking about race and class?

Part of the answer to this riddle comes from the multiplicity of issues that are referenced by the different terms *ethnicity, race, class,* and *culture*. The essential concept that differentiates the widespread discussions of ethnicity from the marginalized discussions of race and class is *privilege*. Discussions of ethnicity tend to focus on cultural assumptions and traditions while not discussing how those assumptions and traditions interact with oppression. Race and class are social realities. Where prejudices are strong a person can be racially categorized based on a single ancestor of minority heritage several generations in the past. Race, as opposed to ethnicity, specif-

ically calls attention to the unequal distribution of access to education and employment and the various benefits—adequate nutrition and medical care, for example—that are considered to be the equal right of all citizens in a free society. Issues of race and class are often emotional, both for those who identify with the oppressed and for those who identify with the oppressor, leading to what Stevenson (1994) refers to as a "fear of dialogue" (p. 191). Conversation about race and class seems to have the potential of increasing, rather than decreasing, the tension between groups if it does not achieve the quality of dialogue—genuine exchange of perspectives. It is especially important that counselors have the knowledge and skills necessary to participate in and facilitate such processes. Many experts on racial issues suggest that genuine dialogue can begin among professionals, and that such dialogue paves the way for cross-racial interactions with clients (Laszloffy & Hardy, 2000).

For minority groups who have experienced generations of oppression in the United States— for example, Asians, African Americans, Native Americans, and Hispanics—racial identity is a primary factor in daily life (Abrams & Hogg, 2001; Robinson, 1999). Where positive racial identity has been promoted, this primary identification can be a source of pride and joy despite experiences of overt and covert discrimination (Stevenson, 1994). Where group identities are negative, as in the case of Black males (Hardy, 1996; Hardy & Laszloffy, 2005), ethical practice calls for clear recognition and challenging of negative discourses that limit opportunities and foster self-doubt.

Power and Deception

When systems theories became widespread in the 1960s and 1970s, popular beliefs characterized families as resistant to change. The concept of homeostasis seemed to justify drastic measures in the name of change. Given that attitude, it is not surprising that some therapists valued inequalities of power in the consulting room. Attitudes toward power became a divisive issue in the family therapy field. On one hand were theorists and practitioners who believed that rapid change was essential, clients were ambivalent about change, and people came to therapy to be manipulated (Haley, 1963; Selvini-Palazzoli et al., 1978). On the other hand were theorists and practitioners such as Bateson (1972) and Boszormenyi-Nagy and Spark (1973) who emphasized values of respect and ecological awareness.

For the strategic family therapist, deception was an important source of therapeutic power, to a great extent because of a belief that people always resist authority. In one of the typical "paradoxical interventions" that grew out of the work of Milton Erickson (Haley, 1973b), a mother might be told that her son's school failure was too complicated for the therapist to understand without further information, and she would be told to encourage him to fail more dramatically so that the pattern would be easier to understand. Bedwetting was treated by prescribing how many times during the night it should occur, parents were told that their child's school failure was a necessary sacrifice to keep their marriage together, and clients were cautioned to not begin changing because they were not ready to handle life without their symptoms. Many family therapists were troubled by such manipulations, but strategic practitioners proudly pointed to the success of these tactics. With the most extreme cases, such as families with schizophrenic or anorexic members, they claimed success where others were unsuccessful.

The ethical backlash against these tactics gained power when the use of paradox moved out of verbal and into written modalities in the work of Mara Selvini-Palazzoli and her colleagues in Milan (Selvini-Palazzoli et al., 1978). The Milan team (see Chapters 3 and 6) developed a technique of writing letters to their clients in which they embedded various paradoxical messages such as telling a family that their adult son's schizophrenia was a necessary part of the family's carefully evolved, delicate emotional balance. In the United States, this technique became popular for a brief time, but practitioners began—rightly or wrongly—to fear legal reprisals. By the time Doherty and Boss (1991) published their landmark review of ethical issues in the field, they observed that "No area of family therapy has witnessed

more disputatious ethical debate than that of deceptive practices by therapists" and expressed fear that the public's trust in the emerging field would be "seriously undermined" unless such activities were curtailed.

Diagnosis

The use of *diagnosis,* a word that has traditionally been used in referring to a disease entity that needs treatment, was rejected 30 years ago by many professionals in the emerging family therapy movement. Individual-level problems were considered by systemic purists to be distractions from the real problems in the couple or family system. An individual patient, if one were identified, was referred to as an *identified patient*—a useful fiction that facilitated payment and helped bring in other family members to fix the person who had a problem. From this perspective, the ethical provider was obligated to the patient—the system that needed help—and was justified in saying anything that enabled the patient to receive treatment. Researchers, meanwhile, worked toward creating classifications of family dysfunctions consistent with a view of family level problems and family level intervention.

This lax attitude toward individual-level diagnosis presented few ethical challenges within reimbursement systems that authorized unlimited treatment—entitlement systems. In the 1970s and 1980s, a reimbursement request under many mental health insurance policies consisted of name, birth date, membership number, diagnosis, and dates of sessions. But the managed care revolution of the 1990s, driven by a concern that mental health expenditures were rising, radically changed this picture. In the interest of cost containment, companies implemented accountability mechanisms to shift expenditures toward the most serious and responsive cases and reduce expenditures for cases that seemed mild or untreatable. Diagnosis suddenly became extremely relevant, and the insurance companies started requiring backup data to verify that a correct diagnosis had been provided. Rather than just putting a number into a block on a form, the practitioner might be required to participate in a detailed interview with a case manager who would review the criteria from the current *DSM* before accepting the diagnosis.

By the time *DSM-IV* was in preparation in the early 1990s, a movement was underway to promote the idea of family level diagnosis (Kaslow, 1993), and a task force was created. The result was a small advance toward helping the practitioner to include family level information in assessment and diagnosis; the new *DSM* included the newly created Global Assessment of Relational Functioning (GARF) scale, with which it was possible to quantify the extent of relationship dysfunction. The work of the task force was published in the *Handbook of Relational Diagnosis and Dysfunctional Family Patterns* (Kaslow, 1996). The issue was not resolved. The American Psychiatric Association announced in 2003 that a new proposal had been submitted, asking for a Relational Disorder category to be included in the next edition. The issue continues to be studied; in the near future, it may be possible to identify the primary problem in a mental health case as *relational dysfunction*.

At present, the ethical climate has clearly rejected the attitude that treated diagnosis either as irrelevant or as a tool that could be ethically manipulated to serve the ends of the family. The couple and family counselor is expected to perform careful and accurate diagnosis and treatment planning, as outlined later in this chapter.

Consent

Professional ethics codes universally demand that clients be willing participants in any kind of intervention and that they know what will occur—they give their *informed consent*. This concern has become increasingly strong over the past 25 years; the community mental health movement has defined clients as "consumers" and service delivery systems of all kinds have strengthened their client/patient rights procedures.

With an individual client, this part of the process can be clear. When the client enters the office, or even earlier when the appointment is made, the counselor or administrative staff member explains the process and provides written materials that detail counselor qualifications, confidentiality, and payment policies, and client expectations and responsibilities and risks. Even with such a well-informed individual client there are potential problems—the client may not have been paying attention, written materials may be lost following the orientation, and the full meaning of a policy may not be clear until the client says, "Oh, that's what you meant when you said I had to call or I would be charged."

But couple and family practice introduces additional challenges. It is often the case that one individual makes an appointment—in an informed manner, understanding what is likely to take place—and others are invited or coerced into attending. In the case of children and adolescents, involuntary counseling is commonplace. The child or adolescent who is mandated into counseling generally does not have a choice of counselor or the ability to demand family involvement in the process. In individual counseling, just as in family counseling, it is only by developing a relationship with the professional that the child or adolescent begins to have a significant voice in further decisions about the nature and the length of the process. The parent or guardian is legally empowered to consent on behalf of the minor.

From an ethical perspective, family counselors seem to be obligated to acknowledge each new participant individually, regardless of how many sessions have elapsed with other family members, and to ensure that the new person understands the expectations. Especially in the case of confidentiality issues, people must make decisions about what they feel safe saying to the counselor, both when others are in the room and when there seems to be a private conversation taking place. These decisions cannot be made properly without adequate information.

Confidentiality

Confidentiality is among the most complicated aspects of working with couples and families (Brendel & Nelson, 1999; D. H. Hendrix, 1991). In addition to the universal professional concerns about disclosing client information to "outside parties" such as insurance companies, the family counselor must attend to handling disclosures *within* the "client"—the couple or family. Therefore, confidentiality is one of the topics universally addressed in specialized family ethics codes such as those of AAMFT and IAMFC. There is no simple, completely satisfactory way to ensure the confidentiality that some clients desire while also achieving the facilitation of relationships that other clients want. Furthermore, the confidentiality issues differ from one kind of case to the next; the expectations of a couple in counseling together may be quite different from those of a family with a 12-year-old child, and those are likely to be different from what would be encountered with a 25-year-old heroin addict and her parents.

Confidentiality as a Value

We can start with acknowledging a societal discourse, in the United States at least, that values privacy of thoughts, feelings, and behavior. Some people are exempted from these privacy values, either by statute or by custom—young children, patients in nursing homes, adults with severe emotional problems, and individuals convicted of sex crimes against minors. These special groups expect that their actions are being observed and they are accustomed to others asking probing questions. They may even be subject to severe punishment if they refuse to answer such questions. And there are cultural variations such that some families and cultures encourage a more privacy-oriented lifestyle and others encourage a "let it all hang out" way of living. But the average American is somewhat uncomfortable with the idea of anyone else knowing the details of his or her life. Threats to this privacy assumption, whether they result from governmental actions or the marketing efforts of corporations, create outrage (even as people revel in the misdeeds of celebrities).

The value for privacy conflicts with the valuing of cooperative effort with those who help with medical, legal, educational, emotional, or other kinds of problems. We assume that the doctor, the lawyer, and the counselor will be treated differently from the society at large be-

cause their education and experience enable them to be responsible with extremely private information, and they are legally mandated to keep other people's secrets. Those who handle the most volatile secrets—drug testing and treatment facilities, for example—must collaborate with each other even though they face extreme penalties if they even disclose to "outsiders" that they recognize the name of someone who was once a patient or client.

Confidentiality in Practice

It is under this umbrella of professional privilege that people approach the couple and family counselor. They assume, unless told otherwise, that they should be able to tell their counselor about affairs, drug habits, cosmetic surgery, and bankruptcy, and the information will not be shared with anyone. Many professionals believe that this expectation is inviolable. Such an attitude is especially common among those whose training and early professional experience has been only with adults in individual counseling. Even with such an expectation, many participants in individual as well as family counseling are reluctant to share information that might prejudice the counselor against them. Those who work with adults on an individual basis are accustomed to waiting weeks, even years, while a client gradually builds up to a major disclosure.

One of the greatest advantages of couple and family counseling, in my opinion, is that people have a harder time keeping their secrets from a professional who is conversing with other family members or is visiting the home. But many people recognize this potential as they schedule appointments and come to our offices—they know that someone may disclose a *family secret*. And family secrets are often at the core of presenting problems (Imber-Black, 1998; Karpel, 1980). In a rather frequent scenario in the couple counselor's office, one partner is sure that the other has been having an affair. Participants in family counseling hope that they will finally—in the counseling process—get answers to their questions about each other's sexual orientations or activities, family histories, job prospects, and divorce plans. Given these concerns, participants who share a counselor—

even if they have some individual sessions with that counselor—may be even less forthcoming than they would be if they had the counselor's absolute loyalty.

This brings the family counselor up against another value, one that is central to most approaches to working with couples and families—disrupting and disabling relationship triangles (Brendel & Nelson, 1999). If a secret is disclosed and the counselor holds information that is not being shared with other family members, "The therapist hereafter must participate in the intricate dance around the family secret" (Brendel & Nelson, p. 112). How does the counselor avoid being caught in a triangle? Karpel (1980) differentiates among reparative and preventive situations. In the reparative situation, the professional is dragged into the triangled position of *secret holder* without warning. In that situation, Karpel announces to the sharer of the secret that keeping secrets will not be supported. He discusses his intention of breaking the secrecy, offering the client the opportunity to prepare for that event and to be the one who does the talking.

But a preventive stance may limit the number of occasions when such a tactic is necessary. Some professionals announce at the outset of counseling that there will be a "I don't keep secrets, but if you don't tell me I won't ask" policy (e.g., Leslie, 2003). If participants disclose, they are giving permission for the counselor to make carefully considered decisions about sharing; the policy often results in less sharing with the counselor.

The IAMFC Ethics code (guideline B.7) endorses the opposite position, stating that "statements made by a family member to the counselor during an individual counseling, consultation, or collateral contact are to be treated as confidential." This policy reproduces family triangles. Knowledge may be power, but knowledge of unethical behavior makes the counselor a conspirator and thereby reduces his or her ethical power. Given the choice between these two extremes, it is hard to justify either one as a solution for all cases, but the lack of a policy creates anxiety and prepares the way for charges of malpractice. Brendel and Nelson (1999) suggest

giving thought to one's goals and then creating a policy that allows for some flexibility in response to changing circumstances.

Finally, it is important to note that confidentiality in family counseling extends to handling of information that is property of the "client," and information cannot therefore be released without the individual permission of *every participant*. A complete disclosure policy must address this issue as well, informing clients that the counselor will be unable to testify in court or release records on behalf of any couple or family member without agreement from the others.

Multiple Relationships

Issues related to multiple relationships are not unique to couple and family counseling; an individual counselor, too, is likely to find that the categories of "clients" and "nonclients" do not stay neatly divided. If the professional is a parent, clients and former clients often appear at school functions, and if the professional gets sick then the orderly, nurse, or surgeon may be a client. These multiple relationship realities are especially likely for those who practice in small communities such as rural towns, close-knit urban neighborhoods, religious orders and places of worship, and patients who are being treated for the same rare disease. Certain kinds of practice bring their own multiple relationship challenges as well; referrals from courts, employee assistance programs (EAPs), and protective services programs often involve conflicting loyalties to both the client and the referral source.

The two major challenges, in these classic multiple relationships, involve compartmentalization of knowledge and the potential of abusing the power differential that is inherent in the professional role. Imagine that my daughter invites Gloria, the daughter of my client, to go to the beach with our family. I may have heard many things about Gloria from the client (e.g., she has an eating disorder, she can't make friends, she is allergic to bee stings), and I may know things about the client (e.g., the parent is a drug dealer). Any request I might have made of another parent in this situation (e.g., bring Gloria to my house, let her stay overnight so we don't have to drive back the same day) may be heard as demands that cannot be refused. The fact that I am not thinking in terms of my professional power does not mean that the power is not present—it means that I am missing out on a significant aspect of the interaction and failing to address potential disturbances in the counseling process. Any time there are multiple interests there is a potential for those interests to be in conflict, and whenever interests are in conflict there is a potential for abuse of power. Ethics codes until recent years prohibited "dual relationships" and might have led me, in this example, to say that this beach trip was unprofessional. More recent ethics codes have softened their language, calling for awareness, discussion, and management of such situations.

For the couple and family counselor, multiple relationships are the norm (Gladding, Remley, & Huber, 2001). Every session that includes more than one client is a situation involving multiple relationships combining issues of information and power, and many professionals are uncomfortable in such a situation. The family counselor hears people discuss medical information that is not common knowledge, plans that have not been disclosed, perceptions that have not been shared, and family secrets such as a parent's history of affairs, imprisonment, and addiction. The professional is called upon to be aware of what is known and by whom. In many cases, a member of a family is behaving badly—stealing money, having affairs—and yet ethical codes seem to prohibit breaking confidentiality unless someone's life is endangered.

Like the beach trip with Gloria, some of these multiple relationship conflicts can be avoided by setting limits. Some counselors refuse to see family members alone, for example, even for a few minutes. Such a rule makes it much less likely that the counselor will be the participant in secrets, although this choice leaves the counselor with less information and also may prevent a family member from taking the first steps toward disclosure. Applying the concepts of awareness, discussion, and management, on the other hand, may enable a counselor to responsibly handle the relationship challenges of serving the multiple

and sometimes conflicting interests of several individuals, the couple/family as a system, and possibly also the referral source/funding source that had a particular outcome in mind when the referral was made.

Psychotropic Medications

It is impossible to write about contemporary practice in the field of family counseling without acknowledging the impact of psychotropic medications. In the early 1990s a new generation of psychotropic drugs began to be available, especially for people whose problems fit into a general description of depression. These drugs, beginning with Prozac, were less threatening than previous antidepressant drugs, and the marketing practices of the drug industry made consumers instantly aware of their availability. Many family practitioners began to work in collaborative relationships with psychiatrists so that their clients could have the advantage of both medical and contextual approaches, and many of these collaborations have been respectful of and productive for the clients. When a prescribing physician recognizes the power of a client's relational contexts, the simultaneous use of medication and relational therapy can break negative cycles of interaction and help to restore trust, hope, and positive experiences.

Unfortunately, the economic power of the pharmaceutical industry makes such collaborations difficult to sustain, and the family counselor who refers clients for medication sometimes finds the family work displaced. Drugs seem to promise immediate and permanent change, and these expectations can lead to impatience with approaches that require gradual improvement and offer no guarantee. Prosky and Keith (2003) have called on family professionals to carefully examine the evidence supporting drug therapy and to educate their clients in its limitations.

Records and Reimbursement

Ethical practice requires not only that a practitioner provide effective services to clients but also that the services conform to the laws and rules that prevail in a clinical setting. Unfortunately, many professionals have the impression that they cannot ethically provide family therapy or counseling in their clinics or other settings. They may have been told by other professionals, "You can't be reimbursed for couple and family counseling; therefore, you have to see everyone separately."

Such beliefs have a legitimate history; they have grown out of experiences with record keeping and reimbursement systems structured around the assumption that a "case" consists of a single, autonomous individual patient or client. This history is increasingly irrelevant, however, as family therapy has become a regular part of the service delivery menu. Most clinics and reimbursement systems have begun to recognize the need for new procedures at the family level. The following examples are only a small sample of organizations and institutions that have developed policies that support couple and family services:

- Blue Cross/Blue Shield of Michigan, in its guidelines for outpatient clinics, encourages family therapy and provides guidelines for appropriately documenting cases.
- New Directions Behavioral Health notifies providers that parents are expected to be involved in children's treatment. In their managed care system, they automatically provide authorization for at least one family session in every case serving a child.
- The American Academy of Child and Adolescent Psychiatry approved a *Policy Statement on Family Psychotherapy* for members to use to convince third-party payers to reimburse for this important service.
- APS Healthcare has set up a monitoring system to increase the number of child and adolescent cases treated with family sessions.

Record keeping and reimbursement systems in the human services and mental health fields generally follow a medical model, assuming that services are being delivered to individuals. In such a setting, the reasons for a family approach may not be clear to some supervisors and management personnel, who may prefer the idea of five individual cases in a family and resist a single case in which the shared problems are treated.

Managed care systems, in which services are carefully rationed according to guidelines that assume standardized client needs, subject documentation to careful scrutiny and may deny treatment if a case manager has doubts about its appropriateness or effectiveness. Therefore, a family-oriented provider needs to be intentional, knowledgeable, and articulate in documentation. The process may be conceptualized as involving several different steps, each of which involves decision making and documentation.

Identifying an Individual with Appropriate Needs

When reimbursement systems pay only for services that focus on an individual client or patient, a case cannot be opened unless one or more members of the couple or family suffers from an eligible condition. In one of the most common systems, outpatient mental health coverage under a health insurance plan, coverage pays only for treatment—not for preventive services—and treatment must be prescribed for a *diagnosed individual*. Eligibility is limited to individuals who suffer from "mental disorders" as described in the American Psychiatric Association's *Diagnostic and Statistical Manual of Mental Disorders*, fourth edition, text revision (*DSM-IV-TR*). *Procedure codes* specify what kind of service is provided, and the procedure must be considered appropriate for the diagnosed condition. Individual and family sessions have different procedure codes.

It is possible that a couple or family may include *multiple* individuals who are eligible for services; for example, one may suffer from a Depressive Disorder, while another shows signs of a Reactive Attachment Disorder. For the purposes of eligibility, only one diagnosed individual is needed to open a case. Generally, clinic staff will discern from an intake telephone contact that there is a person who is covered under a policy and qualifies for treatment, but diagnosis will not be attempted until the first session. It is normal practice for an intake session to include multiple family members; however, many times a single family member will arrive for this first session. The outcome of this session is the identification of the patient(s) and planning for appropriate intervention, possibly including involvement of other family members.

Assessing the Appropriateness of Couple or Family Treatment

A properly completed case file at the end of the intake process will identify the patient/client; document the attendance and participation of any family members at the time of intake; describe the presenting problem(s) along with relevant history and context, including relationships; tentatively diagnose the problem, pending further assessment; and outline a course of treatment. A file that justifies family therapy documents family level issues and provides a clear rationale for including the partner or family in the treatment. Not every case will be appropriate for family level intervention.

One of the situations that is easiest to document in this way is one in which one or more members exhibit an Adjustment Disorder—a category which is further subdivided into categories that show anxious mood, depressed mood, mixed emotional features, or a disturbance of behavior. This diagnosis assumes that (1) there has been an identifiable stressor that required effective coping, and (2) the patient's response has been problematic. This situation makes sense as a family case if the patient's anxiety, depression, or behavioral problem is linked to situational or environmental factors in couple or family relationships, and improving the situation promises to reduce the patient's symptom(s). However, the case file needs to specify the relationship factors that seem to have contributed to the adjustment disorder and to explain how the proposed treatment will alleviate the situational or environmental stresses. In many cases, reducing the original stressors will not totally remove symptoms because of behavioral, organizational, narrative, emotional, and spiritual processes that tend to be self-perpetuating. These self-maintaining processes will also need to be addressed with plans for their disruption.

The rationale for family treatment of Adjustment Disorders seems relatively simple, but many other conditions have been examined for the presence of special family level factors in their onset or maintenance. Kaslow's (1996) *Handbook of Relational Diagnosis and Dysfunctional Family Patterns* includes several excellent examples of such analysis. To date, the best-documented diagnostic category from a family perspective may be depression, a disorder for which couple treatment has been shown to be logical and effective (Gollan, Friedman, & Miller, 2002). There is a continuing need for further research that helps practitioners document the interrelatedness of relationships with emotional and behavioral problems.

Conducting Focused, Theory-Driven Treatment

A treatment plan at the early stage of intervention may not always specify all the aspects of the proposed program; the concept of dynamic assessment, as presented in Chapters 4 through 8, suggests that it would be premature to assume that all issues are clearly identified at the beginning of the process. Treatment planning, in most mental health systems, is a dynamic process in which new issues can be added and previously identified issues can be removed from the agenda as they are resolved; therefore, a practitioner has some flexibility to modify the plan.

The need for changes will be less if one uses theories to identify the issues that are most likely to be addressed. A defensible, logically consistent, relatively complete treatment plan is easier to create if the practitioner is able to connect treatment planning to a clearly defined body of clinical theory such as Bowen Family Systems Theory, Emotion Focused Therapy, or Integrative Couple Behavior Therapy. It should be possible to make a clear argument for seeking changes in family/couple patterns such as:

- Discomfort with closeness, intimacy, and expressions of affection
- Difficulty achieving appropriate levels of autonomy or privacy

- Unclear or inconsistent rules for family members' behavior
- Acceptance of negative discourses regarding sexual identity, race, or gender
- Parental rigidity and overcontrol
- "Randomness" in family life—a lack of security or predictability
- Disagreement among significant adults about the best way of handling a problem
- Violence—physical or verbal
- "Coercive cycles," with one family member punishing another for being punishing
- Use of threats and/or bribes, with resulting breakdowns in trust and caring
- Inappropriate expectations for child or adult development
- Negative comments about each other's spiritual beliefs and practices
- Poor communication, misunderstanding, and lack of support
- Family cognitive patterns such as pervasive shame and/or negative expectations

Having made the argument for change is not sufficient, of course and the treatment plan should further indicate specific treatment elements that will be used to achieve the identified goals.

Maintaining Family Oriented Progress Notes

Even when the treatment plan is specific and clearly links couple and family intervention to the patient's problems, there is a risk that payment will be denied if progress notes are vague or seem unrelated to the diagnosis. Session notes for conjoint and family therapy might include:

- The date of the therapy session and its duration
- The number of participants and their relationships to the patient
- The patient's symptom levels
- Major issues addressed
- Major interventions attempted

- Responses and interventions, with emphasis on the patient and the problematic family dynamics
- Summary of the session's contribution to working toward treatment goals

When there are multiple diagnosed individuals in the same session, it may not be necessary to keep notes of every session in every chart. Instead, some institutional guidelines permit the case note for a session to be put in the file of the family member whose symptoms or disorders were most likely to have been implicated in the particular session; that would be the individual under whose coverage the session was billed. Individual case files of related family members could then be maintained in a "superfile" or "family file" so that auditors and/or supervisors can read the files together as a group to get an integrated impression of the ways in which individual members' issues and family issues are intertwined.

Assessing Change

Just as with a case that is being treated with individual sessions, continuing treatment is only justified to the extent that (1) the patient continues to experience the same or new symptoms (or symptomatic relief has occurred and relapse is likely), and (2) the treatment is showing some signs of working. These two themes—need for treatment and evidence of change—should be addressed throughout progress notes. Problematic family interactions, by themselves, do not justify further treatment if the patient is no longer symptomatic. Statements about progress toward treatment goals may be appropriate less often than each therapy session. However, the record should include documentation that each therapy session was an active, directed process and that the therapist regularly took stock of this important issue.

When describing changes in family level dimensions, it may be helpful to use some of the wide variety of assessment methods that have been developed for documenting family functioning. Conoley and Werth (1995) and Sperry (2004) provide summaries and references for many measures and the research literature that supports their use.

Even when the patient no longer is symptomatic, some additional work *may* be justified as "relapse prevention" with an argument such as "the changes in the support system do not yet appear to be stable." Many insurance companies would rather pay for three more sessions if it will prevent another 20-session episode from occurring.

Suggested Individual and Group Activities

Your understanding of concepts and issues presented in this chapter may be enhanced by the following activities:

- *Self-examination.* An ethical dilemma is a situation in which two different definitions of "good" are in conflict with each other. Try to recall a time when you were challenged by competing beliefs or feelings about what would be the most appropriate action. How did you resolve the situation?

- *Observation.* Values are often unspoken, but can be detected by observing oneself and oth-

ers. For 48 hours, keep a diary of your own (or someone else's) statements and actions (including actions that were NOT taken). What values seem to be influencing this person?

- *Media.* Organizers of entertainment have long used the suffering of one group of people to amuse another group. At the time of this writing, a powerful trend in television programming involves recruiting volunteers who are observed as they compete in painful and/or humiliating tasks. Familiarize yourself with one of these programs and write an ethics code for participants.

Suggested Readings

Dalai Lama (1999). *Ethics for the new millennium.* New York: Riverhead Press.

Gladding, S. T., Remley, T. P., & Huber, C. H. (2001). *Ethical, legal, and professional issues in the practice of marriage and family therapy.* Upper Saddle River, NJ: Merrill-Prentice Hall.

Guggenbuhl-Craig, A. (1986). *Power in the helping professions.* London: Karnac Books.

White, M. (1997). *Narratives of therapists' lives.* Adelaide, Australia: Dulwich Centre.

Future Directions for Family Counseling

The story of couple and family counseling is still being written.

Objectives

In this chapter, you learn to:

1. Reflect on family counseling in a historical and global context.
2. Theorize about connections between societal forces and relationship issues.
3. Observe local and global trends that may influence relationship needs.
4. Be part of systemic responses to emerging problems.
5. Recognize new trends in couple and family counseling.

11

Chapter

In only 50 years, family counseling and therapy has grown from an esoteric specialty with a few dozen practitioners to a large, well-organized movement that is recognized in the United States as an independent profession and is seeking similar status in other countries (Northey, 2004). Much of that growth can be attributed to a climate of intense competition and the creativity and hard work of many talented, committed people. But the growth of family counseling also may reflect social change. Societies around the world, with new problems and new definitions of problems, seem to have special needs for family-oriented practitioners who can provide understanding, hope, skills, and focused attention (Gorell Barnes, 1998). These changes in family and society may signal a need for radical changes in the structure and content of helping systems.

A statement from the classic GAP (Group for the Advancement of Psychiatry, 1970) report, one of the first overviews of family therapy, seems remarkably prescient. The authors said:

> In the future, the most important field of practical application of family theory may not be family therapy but large-scale social planning and the prevention of disorders. . . . Ultimately, the full utilization of family process principles will require the integration of knowledge about the dynamic processes of subcultures and conflict among groups in society as a whole." (p. 567)

Indeed, this focus on conflicts among groups is one of the emerging trends in the field. In country after country, the framework of society seems to need help. Families are struggling against larger forces that create distress.

Furthermore, as the family counseling field becomes increasingly global in its practice, professionals are working with conditions—and resources—that are different from those in the

United States. John Bell (1970), in an address on "The future of family therapy" said, ". . . family therapy is, in one form or another, being practiced in an increasing number of the developing countries. Wait until we are quiet enough to listen and humble enough to learn from them—how our eyes will be opened by the secrets of family living they will share with us" (p. 129). Fortunately, the field now draws upon perspectives from Asia and the Pacific Rim, Africa, Europe, the Middle East, and the Americas. Practices and theories are being shaped by multiple cultures, geographies, and political and economic systems (Ng, 2005).

The future of this rapidly changing field is hard to predict. Nevertheless, in this chapter I draw upon a variety of sources to attempt such a prediction and discuss its implications.

The Successes and Failures of Modernity

Family counseling was born in a period dominated by modernist ideals of professionalism, social improvement, and rational analysis (Cheal, 1993; Parry, 1993). By the early twentieth century, industrialization and economic revolution had contributed to changes in the ways in which people lived, and these changes were blamed for social ills. The family sociology of the 1930s, 1940s, and 1950s was focused on describing the "new family" in industrialized nations. Once this new family form was understood, experts said, it would be possible to tell people how to make it function in an optimal way. The new society was made up of individuals, responsible for their own actions but obedient to social rules. To function in this new society, families needed to be portable, emotionally autonomous, and achievement oriented. The nuclear family—the form that fit these criteria—succeeded in these goals to the extent that it had strong internal authority; parents could then loosen their bonds to tradition and live without extended relationship networks. The modern family also needed to release its young adults into the workforce at the earliest age possible, and any extended period of emotional or financial dependency was discouraged.

The scientific terminology of the family therapy movement was reassuring. "The apparent chaos of your lives makes sense," the experts of the 1960s and 1970s seemed to say, "You don't have the kind of formal structures that provided security for prior generations, but you can learn to make effective use of the new options you have been given." And the relationship expertise of the new family professionals was impressive; in a few sessions, they helped people approximate the family ideals of the time. The modernist agenda worked, to some extent, but there were other forces operating that would limit its success.

From Idealism to Realism

The modernist agenda of improving public safety, health, and well-being struggled with internal divisions; its advocates, leaders, and practitioners espoused two dialectically opposed views of humanity.

One view emphasized a *social control* agenda, which initially focused on juvenile delinquents who disrupted the lives of the law-abiding majority. An agenda of strengthening families promised to not only reduce delinquency but also improve the career and relationship performance of all youth. Social service agencies were established to end multigenerational patterns of poverty, child abuse, and dependence on public funding. The social control agenda later became focused on disease and disability. Schizophrenia and anorexia, for example, were destroying people's lives, and family intervention offered the possibility that these pervasive disorders would be eliminated. Divorce was becoming an increasingly prevalent and disruptive phenomenon, and relationship counseling offered the hope that people could achieve more stable marriages.

At the same time, some of the same family counseling pioneers were motivated by the contrasting but equally modernist *social liberation* agenda. It may seem like a long time in U.S. history since slavery was abolished, women gained the right to vote, racial segregation of public facilities was outlawed, and voting rights were extended to members of all races. But all of these events occurred in only 100 years, and they were part of a worldwide movement that also led to the end of apartheid in South Africa; access to land ownership and self-government for the people of many countries; as well as access to higher education, jobs, and property rights for women who previously lived as virtual servants in their own homes. The common theme in these movements had to do with liberation from ownership, domination, exploitation, and restricted opportunity. Each of these struggles seemed at times to be impossible, yet in each case a powerful group eventually yielded. The human potential movement of the 1960s and 1970s challenged abuses of power. Applied to families, it encouraged counselors to confront inequalities based on economic power, gender, age, and race.

The approaches to family work that became prominent in the 1970s typically accentuated one or the other side of this authority dialectic. But the social control agenda was the more popular one. While Satir and Ackerman were helping families become more egalitarian, Haley and Minuchin were helping parents to re-establish their authority. On both sides, theorists and practitioners subscribed to a belief in change. Scott Johnson (2001) has described this as a "messianic" theme in the field, a belief that family therapists could eliminate all human problems. Consumers and professionals alike rejected notions of passive coping or adjustment to unhappiness and agreed on goals of individual happiness, personal growth, and individual achievement. Professional helpers were preferred to family members and other natural helpers (who might resist change). And cultural diversity was generally dismissed as an unnecessary complication in people's lives, a holdover from "the old country" that was expected to have little relevance in a homogenized, economically integrated new society.

Some time in the 1980s, these early patterns in family therapy began to encounter resistance and to discover their limitations. The social control agenda suffered from association with patriarchy and oppression. Patriarchal and parent-dominated families were viewed as being like totalitarian governments, which—in the case of Italy's Fascist regime—made the trains run on time but did so at the expense of

individual rights and civil rights. Rather than taking pride in their ability to exact obedience from their children, a new generation of parents was rejecting authority of any kind. Seeking to give their children the opportunity to become self-directed rather than other-directed, baby-boomer parents wanted to achieve a democratic ideal by not imposing their values on their children.

The social liberation agenda likewise began to confront its limits. The civil rights movement in the United States achieved dramatic successes in some places, but the overall record showed that efforts directed at liberating the oppressed also threatened the privilege that others enjoyed. Conflict came to be more widely acknowledged as an essential element in social systems, along with differentials in the power that opposing groups could exercise. A growing feminist movement was joined by other movements demanding recognition of sexual minorities, people with disabilities, and other oppressed people. Family counselors found themselves at the center of open, hostile conflicts as couples and families struggled with a new awareness of power, control, and inequality. Furthermore, larger social forces were not always dedicated to democratic ideals, and many families found that their children did not share their values. Lacking strong messages at home, they were responding to strong messages from religious and political groups as well as marketing campaigns seeking to train them as consumers.

At the same time, the agenda of change was increasingly questioned. Challengers said that such a goal was relevant only in industrialized societies—ones that had already lost their connections to traditional knowledge. In the United States and around the world, voices of tradition were demanding recognition. Indigenous populations supported each other in their efforts to preserve ancient wisdom, and conservative religious groups—despite significant differences in their beliefs—also supported each other in their efforts to resist being subsumed into the dominant culture. Both the social control and liberation perspectives were shown to hold a negative view of diversity. The modernist view of a homogenized world, a brave new world of technologically enhanced life and freedom from cultural and linguistic barriers, was anachronistic in an increasingly interconnected global society.

It is not surprising that many of the family counseling approaches described in Chapter 2 have fallen on hard times in a postmodern era, and that the approaches we have seen developing in the past 25 years have been less dogmatic in their messages. Some scholars have raised doubts about what constitutes a healthy family in any particular social, cultural, geographic, political, and economic location. Others have totally rejected the goal of defining family well-being or have challenged efforts to define "family." Families in all of their complexity are difficult to address in an abstract way, and what is true of one form is not true of others. It is possible that the diverse families of the twenty-first century will choose to organize themselves around a few clearly defined models, but it is equally possible that they will become even more creative and dynamic in their ways of staying connected (Stacey,

1996). Therefore, family counselors will need to demonstrate creativity and dynamism in their efforts to help those who experience frustration and pain in their relationships. I briefly sketch some "postmodern family" issues and speculate on some possibilities for addressing those issues.

Moving Forward without a Map

It is hard to imagine what family professionals will be doing in 25 years. Much of what we can expect in the next few decades may be predictable, such as more diversity in family forms. At the same time, a look back at the past few decades shows us how hard it may be to look ahead with any confidence. A time-traveler from 1985 would be amazed to see some of the changes, such as people driving while supervising the activities of their children by mobile phone (see Box 11.1). That same visitor would also be amazed at things that have not changed. In 1980, the Civil Rights Act was still rather new

---

BOX 11.1

Mobile Phone Life

Among the contemporary features of family life that were not predicted 20 years ago, one of the most dramatic is the presence of mobile phones. Portable communications devices were predicted as long ago as the 1950s, when Batman and Dick Tracy had constant contact with police headquarters. But it seems that no one imagined, until recently, a society in which high school students (and even some elementary school students) could carry powerful communications devices that would allow them to send notes to their friends in class, take pictures in the bathroom and post them on international bulletin boards, call their friends for help when they are in trouble at home, and track their friends' as well as their parents' movements.

Family scholars are observing ways in which mobile phones have changed societies where they have been introduced (e.g., see the index published at http://socio.ch/mobile/index_mobile.htm). Questions and findings vary. Those who are looking for decline in society find it in affairs and other violations of family boundaries. They also express concern about the loss of immediacy in people's lives and possible long-term effects on intimacy. Optimists are discovering improved parent-adolescent relationships and increased confidence among previously shy and isolated youth. Clearly, these omnipresent devices are changing the ways in which people relate to each other.

in the United States and it seemed that busing and other policy innovations would put an end to unequal education in public schools. The gender revolution in the United States seemed to be moving rapidly toward women having career options and rejecting the trappings of patriarchy. Instead, children of poor minority families have returned to segregated schools, and middle school girls are rejecting academic success to attract boys (Pipher, 1994).

Life in a postmodern world is characterized by a high level of discontinuity. People around the world are experiencing what Alvin Toffler (1984) referred to as "future shock." It may have always been true that each generation of parents confronts conditions that seem unique. I grew up hearing stories of my father and his brothers "sitting around the living room fussing with that radio, so nobody could talk." But the kinds of social change people face in the contemporary world create a situation in which families and couples have few guidelines for effective relationships.

Social Change

Some claim that family life has deteriorated in the United States and other postindustrial countries, saying families need to return to a time when standards were clear and those who conformed to those standards were happy (see, for example, Popenoe, 1989). Others (e.g., Coontz, 1992) assert that the diversity of family forms and ideals is not new, we have just become more aware of that diversity. But there are clearly societal trends around the world related to families, both within the typical home and in the surrounding environment.

Political Change in Families

Probably the most significant change for many families is the extension of liberation politics into family life. The worldwide movement to extend equal rights for women has deep roots and counts queens as well as slave women among its pioneers. The women's movement in the United States became particularly visible as women successfully fought for the right to vote in the early

twentieth century, and it then went into a period of relative decline until it was revived in the 1950s and 1960s. The revival appears to have been stimulated by World War II experiences in which women had opportunities to display their leadership, dedication, and energy in civilian as well as military roles. It is also likely that the civil rights movements in India and the United States gave encouragement to women. There was a receptive climate for Germaine Greer's (1971) *The Female Eunuch* and other feminist books of the time. But the revolution was not happening only in the United States; it also changed people's lives in other countries around the world (Inglehart & Norris, 2003; W. Lee, 2004).

In addition to gender, family political issues have included sexual orientation, disability, marital status, immigration status, culture, race, and class. According to Foucault (1979), in prior generations members of minority groups protected the status quo by silently accepting oppression. In the new era, public activism and personal risk taking have made the larger public aware of injustice. As a result, increasing numbers of people have been able to bring their family lives into the social mainstream. Others, unfortunately, remain either excluded or fearful of the majority or both. And even this amount of progress is fragile; some have predicted a backlash (see Faludi, 1992) that will reverse the process and replace diversity with conformity.

Even if large numbers of people return to denying their differences, it seems likely that issues of power can never return to being invisible and universally accepted. Couples and families will, in all likelihood, continue to struggle with external and internal conflicts related to equity, conformity, and values. Family professionals will need advanced understandings and skills to facilitate the redistribution of resources and help to create a society in which no one is exploited.

Structural Change in Families

Families also seem to have been experiencing other kinds of change, less clearly related to political movements, as many factors contribute to diversity in family structures. For example, improved nutrition and medical care have led to longer life spans and the expense of keeping patients alive for many years in nursing facilities. The period of active workforce participation is also increasing, with the result that many younger workers are finding it hard to become meaningfully employed.

During the period of modernity, relationships became less linked to social norms and more based on consent and voluntary participation. The ideal of the companionate marriage was promoted in novels of the nineteenth century, but the image of romantic bliss only began to dominate family decision making in the United States following World War II, when the divorce rate rose sharply and the size of families began to drop. Legal processes were eventually modified to reduce the economic and emotional damage caused by the adversarial system. The streamlined divorce system seems to have contributed to further escalation in the rate of divorce, reaching a peak in 1980. Many feared that marriage had became more of a temporary arrangement. Divorce lost much of its stigma, and specialized services were created to provide support for adults and children in divorce transition. With the increased prevalence of divorce, a large percentage of those entering new marriages have been married before and large numbers of children are spending a portion of their childhood in blended or stepfamily situations—which have been described in earlier chapters.

Not only have more people elected to divorce after marriage, many now delay marriage until their late twenties or early thirties and others choose not to marry at all. Unmarried adults (over age 15) now make up approximately 28% of the U.S. population, up from 23% in 1950 (U.S. Bureau of the Census, 2004), and the figure is higher in some other countries. Some of these unmarried adults are in committed relationships but are prohibited from marrying because they are same-sex partners. Others are coupled but choose to remain unmarried because they fear that the institutionalized status of marriage will destroy the companionate relationship they enjoy. In prior generations, these couples would have been denied the opportunity for parenthood

because of social pressure as well as legal penalties, but medical technology, as well as legal and social reforms, now makes it possible for many unmarried couples to successfully bear children or adopt. Legal statuses in an unmarried family are not as clear as those in a married family, however, and these differences become most obvious if a couple relationship ends and one or both parents form new families.

A parallel change involves a decline in expectations that all adults will become part of a couple. A high divorce rate, along with the sexual revolution—now spreading through many countries around the world—has encouraged many people to remain single rather than participate in the cycle of *serial monogamy* that they see around them. A single lifestyle no longer implies sexual abstinence, in postindustrial nations, and it offers exceptional opportunities to participate in consumer cultures such as travel, recreation, decorating, gourmet cooking, and video games. At the same time, single parenthood—both biological and adoptive—has become more socially accepted and has been facilitated by legal changes.

Finally, family life in the United States and other postindustrial nations is changing in the opposite direction. Particularly in recent immigrant families, who may bring different expectations from their countries of origin, three-generation and four-generation households are becoming more numerous and more socially acceptable. Multigenerational households are attractive to many people because they permit grandparents to be more closely involved in children's lives at the same time that they provide a safe, supportive environment for the later years when the older generation is no longer capable of independent living. The trend is also being fueled by economic changes. With more of the workforce engaged in service jobs or telecommuting, freed from the mobility demands of the industrial economy, households with more workers—including part-time workers—are economically stronger and more resilient. Like farm families, many urban families now involve their children in activities that make an economic contribution to their households.

It is likely that many, if not most, of these diverse structures are meeting the needs of their members and the larger society. Why should family professionals pay attention to the changes? Even if problems are occurring at rates that are no greater than those experienced by prior generations whose lives seemed more conventional, there will be a need for appropriate assistance. The diversity of family forms will require that professionals understand unique relational and change processes within each of these structural options.

Shrinking World

Human relationships over the centuries have been altered by many discoveries and inventions—written languages, gunpowder, and medicine are only a few examples. In the past 50 years, it is likely that the most dramatic changes have involved the interconnectedness of the world's people. For example, intercontinental travel and communication until the 1950s was expensive and limited. At the time family therapy was being developed, people used telegrams to contact their relatives in other parts of the world (if they could afford the fees) and returning to one's birthplace might require weeks of travel. During the next 30 years, air travel became easier and more affordable, airmail became cheaper, international telephone calls became easier and cheaper, mailing of audio and video tapes became commonplace, and fax machines made documents instantly accessible. In the past 2 decades, the process has accelerated for residents of the most technologically advanced countries. Distances seem to have disappeared as mobile phones and computerized communication have become widespread in much of the world. And the speed of communication and travel has contributed to a more rapid pace of life. People seem to have little time for relationships in this speeded-up world.

A positive result of this shrinking world phenomenon is that people are able to maintain communication with those who share their concerns, language, culture, and personal and group history. We might say that they have an easier time preserving their *cultural identities;* however, the effects of cultural reconnection have not always

been positive. In the past, physical distance and geographical barriers ensured that groups who settled on opposite sides of a mountain—even opposite sides of a river or in different parts of a metropolitan area—remained somewhat independent of each other in language and customs. People's lives were contained by their local, homogenous environments where they had intense interactions and in-depth knowledge regarding their social worlds. They may have often portrayed outsiders in negative terms, but physical distance protected them from constantly clashing with traditions that might confuse or offend.

In the postmodern world, new patterns of migration and communication have broken down the geographic barriers that divided people into homogeneous groups and provided a sense of comfort to those who feared difference. The U. S. population absorbed over nine million new immigrants between 1993 and 2003 (U.S. Office of Immigration Statistics, 2004), and predictions vary but generally agree that by 2050 the White, non-Hispanic population will drop to approximately 50% of the total. Not only in large cities, but now in small towns and suburbs as well, white Americans have neighbors who speak different languages, dress in distinctive clothing, engage in different spiritual and religious practices, and relate to each other in distinctly non-European ways.

In addition to these direct contacts with cultural difference, satellite-based global television systems confront viewers with images of people whose values, lifestyles, and traditions may be sources of distress. In the United States, the most common views of other countries come in television news shows with portrayals of violence. But for many viewers around the world the disturbing images on television are those of (fictionalized and perhaps exaggerated) "typical" family life in the United States and other wealthy countries. This portrayal of dominant cultures not only shows economic privilege, it shows family relationships lacking basic respect, violence as a daily occurrence, maltreatment of minority groups, and commercialization of sexuality. It should come as no surprise that a backlash seems to be occurring, one focused on values and cultural difference. And the backlash is occurring within the

United States as well as elsewhere—families and communities are becoming militant in their efforts to resist the values of popular culture. Family professionals are being challenged to help families preserve their values.

Mediated Societies

Life in contemporary societies is distinctive in part because people live in a mediated world—an existence in which direct experiences such as relationships are somehow secondary to experiences that are scripted, edited, and produced in multimedia intensity—what Baudrillard (1975) refers to as *simulacra*. In this media-driven society, many experiences are computer enhanced and today's new product is replaced by tomorrow's newer one. Video games have supplanted board games and games of physical challenge (see Box 11.2). Even the word "reality" has lost its meaning as television producers manipulate people's lives to create distress. In this world of manufactured realities, prevailing values do not serve relationships well. If there are five people living in a house, there may be at least five entertainment systems running and five different meals being served. There is no need to compromise or accommodate to others' needs because each individual has the right to "have it your way," as one advertising slogan expressed the cultural message. And games, television shows, and films carry consistent messages: "Get them before they get you," "Success comes through luck and speed," "Good looks outweigh all other attributes," and "What you see is not real."

The agenda of advertisers and the entertainment industry may have always been one of fostering discontent—discontent with one's body, with one's partner, with one's community, and with one's family. But contemporary technology gives special power to these agents of dissatisfaction. In response to this mediated existence, many people—most notably children and adolescents—are developing an unprecedented level of skepticism. These members of a new, media-savvy culture are adept at recognizing the signs of manipulation; they know that they are being sold cigarettes, thin bodies, fast cars, and an illusion of ecological responsibility. They understand that sound and video files can be altered, they know that filmmakers and authors have agendas, and they assume that they are being misled unless they have absolute proof otherwise. Recognizing the tools of influence—juxtaposition of images, assertions of causality, word substitutions—they

---

BOX 11.2

Video Games and Music Videos

Generational differences have divided people in the past, and such divisions seem impossible to prevent. A generation gap existed when horse-and-buggy parents watched their kids drive around in flivvers and wondered what they would do without a horse to keep them safe. Parents of the television generation worried about their children becoming lazy and passive.

Many parents of the computer generation have been upset by violent, sexist imagery in video games and music videos. Censorship of video games and popular music is, for many contemporary parents and children, an issue that stirs up feelings as

intense as those associated with abortion and drug abuse. Some observers note that the fascination with violent games and music appears greatest among young men who are suspected of having real feelings of aggression and hatred toward women. It appears, however, that many of the critics have not watched the videos or played the games.

Advocates claim that themes of violence and sexual domination are play, a safe way to externalize negative thoughts and see their negative effects. And video games are being praised for their contribution to players' problem-solving and memory skills.

can distance themselves from many of the influence attempts they encounter in a day. The connection between physical location and experience has begun to change, both at the family and the larger group levels. It is now possible to listen to radio programs and watch television from the other side of the globe and to spend more time in conversations with distant friends than with near-by relatives, co-workers, and neighbors.

In personal relationships, these trends seem to have negative effects. Many people do not trust perceptions and they question the possibility of knowing reality. The adolescent, manipulated by the sexual programming of popular music and clothing ads, finds it difficult to trust something as apparently real as a sexual response. If knowing the external world is a challenge, knowing one's internal world is even more difficult because one's internal world is a complex, constantly changing product of external influence (Gergen, 1991). In a culture that both celebrates and mocks influence processes, youth recognize—and resist—social programming to grow up and become producing members of society.

Possibly the most dramatic and troubling aspect of technologically enhanced life is the extent to which family and community boundaries are open to messages from outsiders, including political and commercial goals. Television is only one medium; homes and schools have Internet access, and telemarketers can reach children through their mobile phones. Families who abstain from gambling, smoking, and alcohol use are unable to protect their children from cigarette, beer, and casino ads. Social justice activists find that their children are being recruited on the Internet by White supremacist groups, and children as well as adults receive unsolicited pornography through e-mail. Family professionals need the knowledge and skills to help people maneuver within this dangerous and powerful "jungle."

Fragmentation and Isolation
It is ironic that many current social trends arose from an Enlightenment-era desire to explore and celebrate the oneness or sameness of all humanity. Instead, it seems as if people are experiencing less and less connection to each other, feeling less

a part of the same human experience. Parry (1993) explains how the rejection and gradual dismantling of institutional and governmental controls led, over time, to a situation in which people seem overwhelmed with the need to define themselves, make choices, and compete for scarce resources.

Relating to the "other," according to Parry (1993), is an essential part of learning about the self. The cultural ideal of "You can have it your way" has turned all others into threats, and as a result people have become more uncomfortable with each other and more uncomfortable being alone as well. Family professionals are called on to help couples and families overcome their fears, so they can find love and support from each other.

Political and Economic Instability

The family level and the personal level are not the only dimensions of life that have changed in the past 50 years. At community, national, and international levels, political and economic realities have also changed. These larger society conditions are strongly influencing couple and family relationships.

In the early modern period, industrialization was advancing and rural life was retreating in a few parts of the world. That advance has not ended, but has rather increased in its pace and its impact as a globalized economy has made it easier to move goods and materials. A new factory is now built and a workforce is trained in only a few months, at the same time that a workforce on the other side of the globe loses jobs and an obsolete factory is left to disintegrate. With the movement of industry into rural areas around the globe, more of the world's people are experiencing the environmental impacts of modernist society. In the United States, with all its wealth, obesity is being recognized as a legitimate health concern, reproductive failure is on the rise, and infant mortality continues to exceed that in most other economically developed countries. Family-oriented professionals are challenged to help people to live in ways that promote physical as well as emotional well-being.

As the world economy changes, some people are more disadvantaged than others. Over the past 20 years, a series of political, medical, and natural disasters such as the civil war in Sudan and the devastation of New Orleans have brought attention to the vast differences between the privileged and those who struggle for survival—or die from lack of resources. Families of previous generations relocated for safety and greater opportunity, but media coverage was more limited and refugees' desperate living conditions were more easily concealed. Decreasing distances in the postmodern world are raising awareness of the need for family professionals to address people's life circumstances—which may require shifting some of our attention to political and economic activity.

Emerging Ideas and Movements

Partially as a result of these challenges, new family therapy theories and techniques have proliferated. Nevertheless, the family counseling field remains in a position of playing catch-up. Given that contemporary social trends are creating challenges for innovation, it seems reasonable that we should look both inside and outside the family counseling literature for intellectual and cultural trends that may have implications for our work. What research, practice, and theory trends show the greatest promise for helping family counselors to make a difference? I see the greatest hope in themes of reconnection.

In many ways, the dream of working with human issues in a truly contextual manner remains to be fulfilled because so many people have lived in such disconnected ways—cut off from themselves and each other. When clients arrive in our offices in such a cut-off state, our efforts may seem to represent a threat to their well-being. Fortunately, there are several movements that echo the ideal Bateson (1979) referred to in his book, *Mind and Nature: A Necessary Unity.*

Reconnecting with Each Other

Postmodern and social constructionist authors offer not only encouragement but also specific ideas about how people can work toward ending

their isolation and finding a kind of emotional connection that gives them increased strength and joy. Mona Fishbane (1998, 2001), for example, applies a social constructionist perspective in her exploration of interconnectedness, focusing on the extent to which people are co-creators of each other's lives. At the same time, a postmodern frame is not necessary to see and value people's complex and emotionally enriching presences in each other. Framo et al. (2003) using an Object Relations perspective, demonstrated the possibilities when adult family members reach beyond their comfort zones to find out more about who they were at earlier times in their lives and who they have become.

Reconnecting with the Embodied Nature of Humanness

As we discussed in Chapter 7, human emotion is increasingly viewed as a physical process resulting from the actions of specific neurological structures. At the same time, cultural or cognitive phenomena such as gender and identity are being viewed as having physical components; body experiences are essential in the social experience of co-creating identity (Blume & Blume, 2003). Many of these ideas are not new; holistic therapists have been speaking for decades about the connection between emotional and physical well-being, and Maturana and Varela's (1992) work provides a biological systems perspective on the connections between our physical natures and our ways of living.

In recent years, these ideas have received increased attention in the mental health professions. Family counseling approaches that attend to the embodiment of emotion are beginning to be described in the literature (e.g., Atkinson, 2005), and Weingarten (2001) talks about the human connections that come from accepting and living with illness. With our access to information about people's lives and our opportunity to provide input into their lifestyle choices, family counselors are positioned to collaborate with experts in nutrition, fitness, and other health-related disciplines whenever possible. Furthermore, as people rely on drugs to create and enhance sexual responses, relational sexuality is in danger. Sexual technique—a behaviorist's view of sexuality—may become less of a focus in coming decades as family counselors explore the total experience of sexuality and desire in couples and families.

Reconnecting with the Natural World

Even more radical than a reconnection with the human body is the idea that people may be naturally connected to places—to the land where we have lived. This idea is not new for many of the world's people, especially for those who maintain connections with their indigenous cultures. Family counselors such as Australia's Michael White and New Zealand's David Epston have been working with tribal peoples locally and on other continents, and the significance of the land is one of their most powerful learnings.

Even for urban dwellers who have lost connections with their animal nature, it is possible to find reconnection with others and experience a spiritual connection to nature through shared experiences. Sam Keen (1994) and Jackie Gerstein (1999) offer different but complementary images of family members acknowledging their embodied nature, enjoying sensory experiences and physical challenge as they set out to heal themselves and find something larger than themselves. For Keen, physical contact with others is part of a reconnection with being human. He says, "We are a tactophobic culture, accustomed to 'reach out and touch somebody' by phone but inhibited about the communion of flesh." He encourages his readers to experiment with touching others, and he recognizes that his message will be troubling to many people: ". . . we have so sexualized the sense of touch that we are uncomfortable with bodily contact. Touch itself has become suspect" (p. 141).

Gerstein's physicality is of a different kind. Rather than telling people about the need to be physical, she works directly with families in adventure-type activities where they confront challenges together and learn about their own and each other's strengths and limitations. She observes that alienation and misunderstanding often yield to nonverbal communication when talk has failed. If we connect her work to Bate-

son's ideas, we may also think that reconnecting with the physical world is an important healing process for many adults and children whose daily lives are spent immobilized inside concrete, glass, and steel boxes.

Reconnecting with Culture

In the United States of the 1950s, recalled one of my colleagues, her parents' Polish accents and "foreign" household furnishings were such an embarrassment that she avoided letting her friends meet her family, and she moved away at the earliest possible age to become a person without a culture. Only in midlife did she come to realize that she had lost the possibility of carrying forward a rich family history of language and traditional activities.

Hardy and Laszloffy (1995), Arnold (2002), and others have suggested that professionals and clients alike can benefit from concerted efforts to recover such lost parts of our identities. The recovery process can include language learning, travel to ancestral lands, reading traditional folk stories, and learning traditional folk dances. Cultural centers, common in urban areas, are helping many current immigrants to maintain and even strengthen their ties to their cultural roots. When economically feasible, counselors may help plan family vacations to meet relatives and absorb culture; an investment in the next generation's diversity and understanding.

Accepting Contradiction and Complexity

Truly accepting people's connections with their own bodies, with the natural environment, and with the social setting including culture(s) would require that people recognize and accept the contradictory nature of existence. Fortunately, attention to conflicts between physical and social realities is not new to the mental health community. Freud's theories identified such a conflict as the central theme in human emotion. He suggested that the emotionally healthy person was one who acknowledged both the drives associated with being a living creature and the rules associated with being part of human society. Contemporary family counselors could do worse than to seek the same goals with their clients.

Continued Evolution of the Profession

In addition to seeking new issues and themes to organize our work, it is likely that there will also be changes in the way couple and family counselors organize our activities in the next several years. Some of these changes can already be seen taking shape, but there will undoubtedly be others that are harder to predict. The following are some of the more likely:

Further Integration

The theme of theoretical integration has been emphasized throughout this book. At this point, the goal of integration is only partially accepted in the field of family counseling and in the larger fields of mental health and human services. Market forces may inhibit the free exchange and sharing of ideas, but consumer demand can gradually shape a generation of practitioners who value freedom to incorporate new ideas into their work and adapt to the needs of particular clients. Therefore, I expect to see boundaries among different (but similar) professions, as well as different theories, begin to disappear. Crossover effects among theories and technologies may, in turn, revise ways in which people are understood and helping is organized (e.g., Boczkowski, 1996).

Diversification in Service Delivery

At the same time, it does not make sense that the psychotherapy model of a 50-minute hour in a professional office continues to dominate the work that is done with couples and families. The "session" is only one way in which professionals can interact with those they serve, and its limitations may outweigh its advantages. Many potential clients are unable to get appropriate help for their personal and relationship problems because they would have to overcome financial, physical,

and social barriers to place themselves in our offices. Fortunately, new options may help us reach a larger audience.

Larger Systems Approaches

As I have attempted to demonstrate, our theories draw connections between people's problems and their social, economic, and geographic environments. With this awareness, professionals can make significant contributions by joining the leadership of such larger systems as community groups, religious institutions, schools, athletic leagues, and arts organizations. Elected office likewise offers the family professional an opportunity to work toward change in the circumstances that create and maintain problems in people's lives. More achievable, and more widespread, is the option of working as a consultant to an organization or a community as they work to reduce or eliminate racism, inadequate support for education, sexual exploitation of youth, deceptive labeling of food, contamination of water supplies, and other systemic patterns that are hurting current and future generations.

The skills and understandings required to provide direct services to families may also appear in new, as-yet-unknown forms of intervention. The Public Conversations Project is an example of a radical experiment that worked. Organizers SallyAnn Roth and Laura Chasin (Denborough, 2001) developed their community-level intervention model to address bitter, violent conflicts over abortion. Providing structure and personal support for participants, they invited representatives of the pro-abortion and anti-abortion movements to a series of meetings where they learned about each other and developed appreciation for each other's values, concerns, and connections with the topic. As a result, participants found it hard to continue engaging in the antagonistic debates that had characterized their history. Since that beginning, the project has continued to sponsor meetings between groups who are polarized in opposition to each other.

Technologically Enhanced Services

As increasing numbers of people have ready access to computers, hand-held computing devices, and mobile phones, a small group of pioneers is exploring the options that technology offers to the practitioner (Bischoff, 2004).

If the counseling session remains the model for service delivery, technology offers ways to extend the session beyond the physical boundaries of an office. Using text-based technology, family members can log on to a chat room where the counselor can monitor their interactions as well as provide input to help them make their communications more effective. This option may be available on mobile phones in the near future, if it is not available already. As hardware and software for live video exchanges becomes more reliable and available in clients' homes, another option involves virtual counseling sessions in which the professional and the family can see as well as hear each other from a distance. Telephones have been available for counseling use as long as the family counseling field has existed, but possibly they have been underutilized. Innovations in speaker-phone technology, along with the ability to reach multiple family members through their mobile phones, may lead to innovations in this distance counseling methodology as well.

Leaving behind the counseling session as the service delivery model, many other possibilities exist and more can be expected. For example, the tradition of letter writing has a long history in individual and family counseling, and one option involves translating this history into various forms of text-based contact with clients. Jedicka and Jennings (2001), for example, instructed couples to exchange e-mail messages with each other and responded online to those direct communications between the clients. The same model holds promise for parent-adolescent communication, communication with emerging adults, and parenting discussions among separate households in the postdivorce family. Information sharing and skill training are activities that have been performed in counselors' offices, and these functions may be performed through interaction with web sites or other electronic media. Multiple-family groups, which are extremely difficult to organize in real time, may be simulated by creating e-mail lists or discussion boards. And the reflecting team or consultation team may be re-created in virtual space—involving international experts, possibly with live computer-facilitated translation.

Meeting the Clients Where They Are

A less exciting change, possibly, but one that is already underway, is the movement toward home-based (or neighborhood-based) services (Reiter, 2000). The in-home provider of family counseling services has tremendous access to information, and it is harder for family members to make the claim "you just don't understand what we're dealing with." When case loads are small and adequate time is available the in-home provider can work with issues when they are most easily resolved rather than waiting for an appointment. Furthermore, extended family and household members who consider themselves to be "not family" are more readily involved in work that takes place in the home.

Given these advantages, why have home-based and neighborhood-based services received so little attention from practitioners, theorists, and researchers? A key reason is efficiency. Travel time is a major barrier; in-home service delivery and research seem to work best when professionals and clients/participants live and work in a small area—a small town or an urban neighborhood. Another reason is client resistance. Many people are reluctant to have professionals enter their home, fearing judgment for their failure to live according to social norms. Safety issues are often mentioned; in-home providers are probably more vulnerable than they would be in offices where they would be surrounded by co-workers. And professionals may seek to maximize their comfort and convenience, preferring to let the clients drive through the snow while they sit in their heated offices.

It is likely that the next 20 years will see many of these, as well as other changes to the service delivery patterns that people think of when they say "family counseling." People may readily check into the "Family Wellness Lodge" for a 10-day stay or embark on a weeklong "relationship cruise." Schools may set up family counseling centers and offer financial incentives for families who use those services. Family assessment centers (Box 11.3) may become as numerous as dental offices. Fitness clubs may include relationship fitness in their goals and provide couples groups, just as workplaces may increase their investment in employee assistance programs and provide on-site family counseling. The discount store where

BOX 11.3

A Family Assessment Center?

When couples and families come to a professional for help, assessment is typically limited to self-report questionnaires and observations of their behavior in the office. With the exception of child custody evaluations, it seems that no family parallel of the psychological report exists. Custody evaluations, for that matter, are typically focused on the parents as individuals rather than on the relationship system. What if it were possible to send a family for a full relationship report before beginning intervention? Such a service appears to be rare, if it exists at all.

There are some clues in the research literature that suggest what such a center might look like. It would need to provide a variety of activities in which the couple or family could be observed. For families with preschool children, for example, a block play area and a housekeeping area would seem essential. Adventure-type activities would challenge families to solve problems and work toward a common goal, and art activities would offer opportunities for observing interactions that are less task oriented. A video game corner would seem essential, as would a simulated home office where computer tasks could be assigned. Couples could be asked to balance a checkbook together, parents and their high school children could be asked to look at college catalogs, families could plan vacations online . . . the possibilities are endless. At the end of the day, video records would be coded and combined with the results on standardized instruments to produce a report summarizing strengths, concerns, coalitions, and conflicts.

---

families have to choose between tires and baby food may offer professional help in making that choice. The day may come when the concept of going to a "clinic" for relationship help is very hard to imagine.

Suggested Individual and Group Activities

Your understanding of concepts and issues presented in this chapter may be enhanced by the following activities:

- *Library and Internet research.* When authors write about the future of the family, quite often they are positioned within a discourse that promotes particular changes. Search for a title that implies a look into the future and examine its references and/or links to other information. Is there a pattern in the citations? Does the work represent a discourse community that you can readily identify?

- *Film.* Films and television programs have attempted to portray relationships in a future time. Choose a futuristic film (or an episode of a television series) from 20 years ago that has relationships as a central theme. Can you identify aspects of relationship change that have occurred faster than the screenwriters predicted?

- *Board/video game.* Design a game that captures an alternative future you can imagine for family relationships. How do players score points? What strategies/options do they have? What can they win? Can they start over? When is the game finished?

Suggested Readings

Gergen, K. J. (1991). *The saturated self: Dilemmas of identity in contemporary life.* New York: Basic.

Moynihan, D. P., Smeeding, T. M., & Rainwater, L. (2004). *The future of the family.* New York: Russell Sage Foundation.

Stacey, J. (1996). *In the name of the family: Rethinking family values in the postmodern age.* Boston: Beacon Press.

ACA Code of Ethics

As approved by the ACA Governing Council, 2005

A

Appendix

Mission

The mission of the American Counseling Association is to enhance the quality of life in society by promoting the development of professional counselors, advancing the counseling profession, and using the profession and practice of counseling to promote respect for human dignity and diversity.

Contents

ACA Code of Ethics Preamble

The American Counseling Association is an educational, scientific, and professional organization whose members work in a variety of settings and serve in multiple capacities. ACA members are dedicated to the enhancement of human development throughout the life span. Association members recognize diversity and embrace a cross-cultural approach in support of the worth, dignity, potential, and uniqueness of people within their social and cultural contexts.

Professional values are an important way of living out an ethical commitment. Values inform principles. Inherently held values that guide our behaviors or exceed prescribed behaviors are deeply ingrained in the counselor and developed out of personal dedication, rather than the mandatory requirement of an external organization.

ACA Code of Ethics Purpose

The *ACA Code of Ethics* serves five main purposes:

1. The *Code* enables the association to clarify to current and future members, and to those served by members, the nature of the ethical responsibilities held in common by its members.
2. The *Code* helps support the mission of the association.

3. The *Code* establishes principles that define ethical behavior and best practices of association members.
4. The *Code* serves as an ethical guide designed to assist members in constructing a professional course of action that best serves those utilizing counseling services and best promotes the values of the counseling profession.
5. The *Code* serves as the basis for processing of ethical complaints and inquiries initiated against members of the association.

The *ACA Code of Ethics* contains eight main sections that address the following areas:

Section A: The Counseling Relationship
Section B: Confidentiality, Privileged Communication, and Privacy
Section C: Professional Responsibility
Section D: Relationships with Other Professionals
Section E: Evaluation, Assessment, and Interpretation
Section F: Supervision, Training, and Teaching
Section G: Research and Publication
Section H: Resolving Ethical Issues

Each section of the *ACA Code of Ethics* begins with an Introduction. The introductions to each section discuss what counselors should aspire to with regard to ethical behavior and responsibility. The Introduction helps set the tone for that particular section and provides a starting point that invites reflection on the ethical mandates contained in each part of the *ACA Code of Ethics*.

When counselors are faced with ethical dilemmas that are difficult to resolve, they are expected to engage in a carefully considered ethical decision-making process. Reasonable differences of opinion can and do exist among counselors with respect to the ways in which values, ethical principles, and ethical standards would be applied when they conflict. While there is no specific ethical decision-making model that is most effective, counselors are expected to be familiar with a credible model of decision making that can bear public scrutiny and its application.

Through a chosen ethical decision-making process and evaluation of the context of the situation, counselors are empowered to make decisions that help expand the capacity of people to grow and develop.

A brief glossary is given to provide readers with a concise description of some of the terms used in the *ACA Code of Ethics*.

Section A: The Counseling Relationship

Introduction

Counselors encourage client growth and development in ways that foster the interest and welfare of clients and promote formation of healthy relationships. Counselors

actively attempt to understand the diverse cultural backgrounds of the clients they serve. Counselors also explore their own cultural identities and how these affect their values and beliefs about the counseling process.

Counselors are encouraged to contribute to society by devoting a portion of their professional activity to services for which there is little or no financial return (pro bono publico).

A.1. Welfare of Those Served by Counselors
  a. *Primary Responsibility.* The primary responsibility of counselors is to respect the dignity and to promote the welfare of clients.
  b. *Records.* Counselors maintain records necessary for rendering professional services to their clients and as required by laws, regulations, or agency or institution procedures. Counselors include sufficient and timely documentation in their client records to facilitate the delivery and continuity of needed services. Counselors take reasonable steps to ensure that documentation in records accurately reflects client progress and services provided. If errors are made in client records, counselors take steps to properly note the correction of such errors according to agency or institutional policies. (See A.12.g.7., B.6., B.6.g., G.2.j.)
  c. *Counseling Plans.* Counselors and their clients work jointly in devising integrated counseling plans that offer reasonable promise of success and are consistent with abilities and circumstances of clients. Counselors and clients regularly review counseling plans to assess their continued viability and effectiveness, respecting the freedom of choice of clients. (See A.2.a., A.2.d., A.12.g.)
  d. *Support Network Involvement.* Counselors recognize that support networks hold various meanings in the lives of clients and consider enlisting the support, understanding, and involvement of others (e.g., religious/spiritual/community leaders, family members, friends) as positive resources, when appropriate, with client consent.
  e. *Employment Needs.* Counselors work with their clients considering employment in jobs that are consistent with the overall abilities, vocational limitations, physical restrictions, general temperament, interest and aptitude patterns, social skills, education, general qualifications, and other relevant characteristics and needs of clients. When appropriate, counselors appropriately trained in career development will assist

in the placement of clients in positions that are consistent with the interest, culture, and the welfare of clients, employers, and/or the public.

A.2. Informed Consent in the Counseling Relationship (See A.12.g., B.5., B.6.b., E.3., E.13.b., F.1.c., G.2.a.)

   a. *Informed Consent.* Clients have the freedom to choose whether to enter into or remain in a counseling relationship and need adequate information about the counseling process and the counselor. Counselors have an obligation to review in writing and verbally with clients the rights and responsibilities of both the counselor and the client. Informed consent is an ongoing part of the counseling process, and counselors appropriately document discussions of informed consent throughout the counseling relationship.

   b. *Types of Information Needed.* Counselors explicitly explain to clients the nature of all services provided. They inform clients about issues such as, but not limited to, the following: the purposes, goals, techniques, procedures, imitations, potential risks, and benefits of services; the counselor's qualifications, credentials, and relevant experience; continuation of services upon the incapacitation or death of a counselor; and other pertinent information. Counselors take steps to ensure that clients understand the implications of diagnosis, the intended use of tests and reports, fees, and billing arrangements. Clients have the right to confidentiality and to be provided with an explanation of its limitations (including how supervisors and/or treatment team professionals are involved); to obtain clear information about their records; to participate in the ongoing counseling plans; and to refuse any services or modality change and to be advised of the consequences of such refusal.

   c. *Developmental and Cultural.* Sensitivity Counselors communicate information in ways that are both developmentally and culturally appropriate. Counselors use clear and understandable language when discussing issues related to informed consent. When clients have difficulty understanding the language used by counselors, they provide necessary services (e.g., arranging for a qualified interpreter or translator) to ensure comprehension by clients. In collaboration with clients, counselors consider cultural implications of informed consent procedures and, where possible, counselors adjust their practices accordingly.

   d. *Inability to Give Consent.* When counseling minors or persons unable to give voluntary consent, counselors seek the assent of clients to services, and include them in decision making as appropriate. Counselors recognize the need to balance the ethical rights of clients to make choices, their capacity to give consent or assent to receive services, and parental or familial legal rights and responsibilities to protect these clients and make decisions on their behalf.

A.3. Clients Served by Others

   When counselors learn that their clients are in a professional relationship with another mental health professional, they request release from clients to inform the other professionals and strive to establish positive and collaborative professional relationships.

A.4. Avoiding Harm and Imposing Values

   a. *Avoiding Harm.* Counselors act to avoid harming their clients, trainees, and research participants and to minimize or to remedy unavoidable or unanticipated harm.

   b. *Personal Values.* Counselors are aware of their own values, attitudes, beliefs, and behaviors and avoid imposing values that are inconsistent with counseling goals. Counselors respect the diversity of clients, trainees, and research participants.

A.5. Roles and Relationships with Clients (See F.3., F.10., G.3.)

   a. *Current Clients.* Sexual or romantic counselor–client interactions or relationships with current clients, their romantic partners, or their family members are prohibited.

   b. *Former Clients.* Sexual or romantic counselor–client interactions or relationships with former clients, their romantic partners, or their family members are prohibited for a period of 5 years following the last professional contact. Counselors, before engaging in sexual or romantic interactions or relationships with clients, their romantic partners, or client family members after 5 years following the last professional contact, demonstrate forethought and document (in written form) whether the interactions or relationship can be viewed as exploitive in some way and/or whether there is still potential to harm the former client; in cases of potential exploitation and/or harm, the counselor avoids entering such an interaction or relationship.

   c. *Nonprofessional Interactions or Relationships (Other Than Sexual or Romantic Interactions or*

Relationships). Counselor–client nonprofessional relationships with clients, former clients, their romantic partners, or their family members should be avoided, except when the interaction is potentially beneficial to the client. (See A.5.d.)

d. *Potentially Beneficial Interactions.* When a counselor–client nonprofessional interaction with a client or former client may be potentially beneficial to the client or former client, the counselor must document in case records, prior to the interaction (when feasible), the rationale for such an interaction, the potential benefit, and anticipated consequences for the client or former client and other individuals significantly involved with the client or former client. Such interactions should be initiated with appropriate client consent. Where unintentional harm occurs to the client or former client, or to an individual significantly involved with the client or former client, due to the nonprofessional interaction, the counselor must show evidence of an attempt to remedy such harm. Examples of potentially beneficial interactions include, but are not limited to, attending a formal ceremony (e.g., a wedding/commitment ceremony or graduation); purchasing a service or product provided by a client or former client (excepting unrestricted bartering); hospital visits to an ill family member; mutual membership in a professional association, organization, or community. (See A.5.c.)

e. *Role Changes in the Professional Relationship.* When a counselor changes a role from the original or most recent contracted relationship, he or she obtains informed consent from the client and explains the right of the client to refuse services related to the change. Examples of role changes include

1. changing from individual to relationship or family counseling, or vice versa;
2. changing from a nonforensic evaluative role to a therapeutic role, or vice versa;
3. changing from a counselor to a researcher role (i.e., enlisting clients as research participants), or vice versa; and
4. changing from a counselor to a mediator role, or vice versa.

Clients must be fully informed of any anticipated consequences (e.g., financial, legal, personal, or therapeutic) of counselor role changes.

A.6. Roles and Relationships at Individual, Group, Institutional, and Societal Levels

a. *Advocacy.* When appropriate, counselors advocate at individual, group, institutional, and societal levels to examine potential barriers and obstacles that inhibit access and/or the growth and development of clients.

b. *Confidentiality and Advocacy.* Counselors obtain client consent prior to engaging in advocacy efforts on behalf of an identifiable client to improve the provision of services and to work toward removal of systemic barriers or obstacles that inhibit client access, growth, and development.

A.7. Multiple Clients

When a counselor agrees to provide counseling services to two or more persons who have a relationship, the counselor clarifies at the outset which person or persons are clients and the nature of the relationships the counselor will have with each involved person. If it becomes apparent that the counselor may be called upon to perform potentially conflicting roles, the counselor will clarify, adjust, or withdraw from roles appropriately. (See A.8.a., B.4.)

A.8. Group Work
(See B.4.a.)

a. *Screening.* Counselors screen prospective group counseling/therapy participants. To the extent possible, counselors select members whose needs and goals are compatible with goals of the group, who will not impede the group process, and whose well-being will not be jeopardized by the group experience.

b. *Protecting Clients.* In a group setting, counselors take reasonable precautions to protect clients from physical, emotional, or psychological trauma.

A.9. End-of-Life Care for Terminally Ill Clients

a. *Quality of Care.* Counselors strive to take measures that enable clients

1. to obtain high quality end-of-life care for their physical, emotional, social, and spiritual needs;
2. to exercise the highest degree of self-determination possible;
3. to be given every opportunity possible to engage in informed decision making regarding their end-of-life care; and
4. to receive complete and adequate assessment regarding their ability to make competent, rational decisions on their own behalf from a mental health professional

who is experienced in end-of-life care practice.

b. *Counselor Competence, Choice, and Referral.* Recognizing the personal, moral, and competence issues related to end-of-life decisions, counselors may choose to work or not work with terminally ill clients who wish to explore their end-of-life options. Counselors provide appropriate referral information to ensure that clients receive the necessary help.

c. *Confidentiality.* Counselors who provide services to terminally ill individuals who are considering hastening their own deaths have the option of breaking or not breaking confidentiality, depending on applicable laws and the specific circumstances of the situation and after seeking consultation or supervision from appropriate professional and legal parties. (See B.5.c., B.7.c.)

A.10. Fees and Bartering

a. *Accepting Fees from Agency Clients.* Counselors refuse a private fee or other remuneration for rendering services to persons who are entitled to such services through the counselor's employing agency or institution. The policies of a particular agency may make explicit provisions for agency clients to receive counseling services from members of its staff in private practice. In such instances, the clients must be informed of other options open to them should they seek private counseling services.

b. *Establishing Fees.* In establishing fees for professional counseling services, counselors consider the financial status of clients and locality. In the event that the established fee structure is inappropriate for a client, counselors assist clients in attempting to find comparable services of acceptable cost.

c. *Nonpayment of Fees.* If counselors intend to use collection agencies or take legal measures to collect fees from clients who do not pay for services as agreed upon, they first inform clients of intended actions and offer clients the opportunity to make payment.

d. *Bartering.* Counselors may barter only if the relationship is not exploitive or harmful and does not place the counselor in an unfair advantage, if the client requests it, and if such arrangements are an accepted practice among professionals in the community. Counselors consider the cultural implications of bartering and discuss relevant concerns with clients

and document such agreements in a clear written contract.

e. *Receiving Gifts.* Counselors understand the challenges of accepting gifts from clients and recognize that in some cultures, small gifts are a token of respect and showing gratitude. When determining whether or not to accept a gift from clients, counselors take into account the therapeutic relationship, the monetary value of the gift, a client's motivation for giving the gift, and the counselor's motivation for wanting or declining the gift.

A.11. Termination and Referral

a. *Abandonment Prohibited.* Counselors do not abandon or neglect clients in counseling. Counselors assist in making appropriate arrangements for the continuation of treatment, when necessary, during interruptions such as vacations, illness, and following termination.

b. *Inability to Assist Clients.* If counselors determine an inability to be of professional assistance to clients, they avoid entering or continuing counseling relationships. Counselors are knowledgeable about culturally and clinically appropriate referral resources and suggest these alternatives. If clients decline the suggested referrals, counselors should discontinue the relationship.

c. *Appropriate Termination.* Counselors terminate a counseling relationship when it becomes reasonably apparent that the client no longer needs assistance, is not likely to benefit, or is being harmed by continued counseling. Counselors may terminate counseling when in jeopardy of harm by the client, or another person with whom the client has a relationship, or when clients do not pay fees as agreed upon. Counselors provide pretermination counseling and recommend other service providers when necessary.

d. *Appropriate Transfer of Services.* When counselors transfer or refer clients to other practitioners, they ensure that appropriate clinical and administrative processes are completed and open communication is maintained with both clients and practitioners.

A.12. Technology Applications

a. *Benefits and Limitations.* Counselors inform clients of the benefits and limitations of using information technology applications in the counseling process and in business/billing procedures. Such technologies include but are not limited to computer hardware and software, telephones, the World Wide Web, the Internet, online assessment instruments and other communication devices.

b. *Technology-Assisted Services.* When providing technology-assisted distance counseling services, counselors determine that clients are intellectually, emotionally, and physically capable of using the application and that the application is appropriate for the needs of clients.

c. *Inappropriate Services.* When technology-assisted distance counseling services are deemed inappropriate by the counselor or client, counselors consider delivering services face to face.

d. *Access.* Counselors provide reasonable access to computer applications when providing technology-assisted distance counseling services.

e. *Laws and Statutes.* Counselors ensure that the use of technology does not violate the laws of any local, state, national, or international entity and observe all relevant statutes.

f. *Assistance.* Counselors seek business, legal, and technical assistance when using technology applications, particularly when the use of such applications crosses state or national boundaries.

g. *Technology and Informed Consent.* As part of the process of establishing informed consent, counselors do the following:

1. Address issues related to the difficulty of maintaining the confidentiality of electronically transmitted communications.

2. Inform clients of all colleagues, supervisors, and employees, such as Informational Technology (IT) administrators, who might have authorized or unauthorized access to electronic transmissions.

3. Urge clients to be aware of all authorized or unauthorized users including family members and fellow employees who have access to any technology clients may use in the counseling process.

4. Inform clients of pertinent legal rights and limitations governing the practice of a profession over state lines or international boundaries.

5. Use encrypted Web sites and e-mail communications to help ensure confidentiality when possible.

6. When the use of encryption is not possible, counselors notify clients of this fact and limit electronic transmissions to general communications that are not client specific.

7. Inform clients if and for how long archival storage of transaction records are maintained.

8. Discuss the possibility of technology failure and alternate methods of service delivery.

9. Inform clients of emergency procedures, such as calling 911 or a local crisis hotline, when the counselor is not available.

10. Discuss time zone differences, local customs, and cultural or language differences that might impact service delivery.

11. Inform clients when technologyassisted distance counseling services are not covered by insurance. (See A.2.)

h. *Sites on the World Wide Web.* Counselors maintaining sites on the World Wide Web (the Internet) do the following:

1. Regularly check that electronic links are working and professionally appropriate.

2. Establish ways clients can contact the counselor in case of technology failure.

3. Provide electronic links to relevant state licensure and professional certification boards to protect consumer rights and facilitate addressing ethical concerns.

4. Establish a method for verifying client identity.

5. Obtain the written consent of the legal guardian or other authorized legal representative prior to rendering services in the event the client is a minor child, an adult who is legally incompetent, or an adult incapable of giving informed consent.

6. Strive to provide a site that is accessible to persons with disabilities.

7. Strive to provide translation capabilities for clients who have a different primary language while also addressing the imperfect nature of such translations.

8. Assist clients in determining the validity and reliability of information found on the World Wide Web and other technology applications.

Section B: Confidentiality, Privileged Communication, and Privacy

Introduction

Counselors recognize that trust is a cornerstone of the counseling relationship. Counselors aspire to earn the trust of clients by creating an ongoing partnership, establishing and upholding appropriate boundaries, and maintaining confidentiality. Counselors communicate the parameters of confidentiality in a culturally competent manner.

B.1. Respecting Client Rights

a. *Multicultural/Diversity Considerations.* Counselors maintain awareness and sensitivity regarding cultural meanings of confidentiality and privacy. Counselors respect differing views toward disclosure of information. Counselors hold ongoing discussions with clients as to how, when, and with whom information is to be shared.

b. *Respect for Privacy.* Counselors respect client rights to privacy. Counselors solicit private information from clients only when it is beneficial to the counseling process.

c. *Respect for Confidentiality.* Counselors do not share confidential information without client consent or without sound legal or ethical justification.

d. *Explanation of Limitations.* At initiation and throughout the counseling process, counselors inform clients of the limitations of confidentiality and seek to identify foreseeable situations in which confidentiality must be breached. (See A.2.b.)

B.2. Exceptions

a. *Danger and Legal Requirements.* The general requirement that counselors keep information confidential does not apply when disclosure is required to protect clients or identified others from serious and foreseeable harm or when legal requirements demand that confidential information must be revealed. Counselors consult with other professionals when in doubt as to the validity of an exception. Additional considerations apply when addressing end-of-life issues. (See A.9.c.)

b. *Contagious, Life-Threatening Diseases.* When clients disclose that they have a disease commonly known to be both communicable and life threatening, counselors may be justified in disclosing information to identifiable third parties, if they are known to be at demonstrable and high risk of contracting the disease. Prior to making a disclosure, counselors confirm that there is such a diagnosis and assess the intent of clients to inform the third parties about their disease or to engage in any behaviors that may be harmful to an identifiable third party.

c. *Court-Ordered Disclosure.* When subpoenaed to release confidential or privileged information without a client's permission, counselors obtain written, informed consent from the client or take steps to prohibit the disclosure or have it limited as narrowly as possible due to potential harm to the client or counseling relationship.

d. *Minimal Disclosure.* To the extent possible, clients are informed before confidential information is disclosed and are involved in the disclosure decision-making process. When circumstances require the disclosure of confidential information, only essential information is revealed.

B.3. Information Shared with Others

a. *Subordinates.* Counselors make every effort to ensure that privacy and confidentiality of clients are maintained by subordinates, including employees, supervisees, students, clerical assistants, and volunteers. (See F.1.c.)

b. *Treatment Teams.* When client treatment involves a continued review or participation by a treatment team, the client will be informed of the team's existence and composition, information being shared, and the purposes of sharing such information.

c. *Confidential Settings.* Counselors discuss confidential information only in settings in which they can reasonably ensure client privacy.

d. *Third-Party Payers.* Counselors disclose information to third-party payers only when clients have authorized such disclosure.

e. *Transmitting Confidential Information.* Counselors take precautions to ensure the confidentiality of information transmitted through the use of computers, electronic mail, facsimile machines, telephones, voicemail, answering machines, and other electronic or computer technology. (See A.12.g.)

f. *Deceased Clients.* Counselors protect the confidentiality of deceased clients, consistent with legal requirements and agency or setting policies.

B.4. Groups and Families

a. *Group Work.* In group work, counselors clearly explain the importance and parameters of confidentiality for the specific group being entered.

b. *Couples and Family Counseling.* In couples and family counseling, counselors clearly define who is considered "the client" and discuss expectations and limitations of confidentiality.

Counselors seek agreement and document in writing such agreement among all involved parties having capacity to give consent concerning each individual's right to confidentiality and any obligation to preserve the confidentiality of information known.

B.5. Clients Lacking Capacity to Give Informed Consent

a. *Responsibility to Clients.* When counseling minor clients or adult clients who lack the capacity to give voluntary, informed consent, counselors protect the confidentiality of information received in the counseling relationship as specified by federal and state laws, written policies, and applicable ethical standards.

b. *Responsibility to Parents and Legal Guardians.* Counselors inform parents and legal guardians about the role of counselors and the confidential nature of the counseling relationship. Counselors are sensitive to the cultural diversity of families and respect the inherent rights and responsibilities of parents/guardians over the welfare of their children/charges according to law. Counselors work to establish, as appropriate, collaborative relationships with parents/guardians to best serve clients.

c. *Release of Confidential Information.* When counseling minor clients or adult clients who lack the capacity to give voluntary consent to release confidential information, counselors seek permission from an appropriate third party to disclose information. In such instances, counselors inform clients consistent with their level of understanding and take culturally appropriate measures to safeguard client confidentiality.

B.6. Records

a. *Confidentiality of Records.* Counselors ensure that records are kept in a secure location and that only authorized persons have access to records.

b. *Permission to Record.* Counselors obtain permission from clients prior to recording sessions through electronic or other means.

c. *Permission to Observe.* Counselors obtain permission from clients prior to observing counseling sessions, reviewing session transcripts, or viewing recordings of sessions with supervisors, faculty, peers, or others within the training environment.

d. *Client Access.* Counselors provide reasonable access to records and copies of records when requested by competent clients. Counselors limit the access of clients to their records, or portions of their records, only when there is compelling evidence that such access would cause harm to the client. Counselors document the request of clients and the rationale for withholding some or all of the record in the files of clients. In situations involving multiple clients, counselors provide individual clients with only those parts of records that related directly to them and do not include confidential information related to any other client.

e. *Assistance with Records.* When clients request access to their records, counselors provide assistance and consultation in interpreting counseling records.

f. *Disclosure or Transfer.* Unless exceptions to confidentiality exist, counselors obtain written permission from clients to disclose or transfer records to legitimate third parties. Steps are taken to ensure that receivers of counseling records are sensitive to their confidential nature. (See A.3., E.4.)

g. *Storage and Disposal After Termination.* Counselors store records following termination of services to ensure reasonable future access, maintain records in accordance with state and federal statutes governing records, and dispose of client records and other sensitive materials in a manner that protects client confidentiality. When records are of an artistic nature, counselors obtain client (or guardian) consent with regards to handling of such records or documents. (See A.1.b.)

h. *Reasonable Precautions.* Counselors take reasonable precautions to protect client confidentiality in the event of the counselor's termination of practice, incapacity, or death. (See C.2.h.)

B.7. Research and Training

a. *Institutional Approval.* When institutional approval is required, counselors provide accurate information about their research proposals and obtain approval prior to conducting their research. They conduct research in accordance with the approved research protocol.

b. *Adherence to Guidelines.* Counselors are responsible for understanding and adhering to state, federal, agency, or institutional policies or applicable guidelines regarding confidentiality in their research practices.

c. *Confidentiality of Information Obtained in Research.* Violations of participant privacy and confidentiality are risks of participation in research involving human participants. Investigators maintain all research records in a secure manner. They explain to participants the risks of violations of privacy and confidentiality and disclose to participants any limits of confidentiality that reasonably can be expected. Regardless of the degree to which confidentiality will be maintained, investigators must disclose to participants any limits of confidentiality that reasonably can be expected. (See G.2.e.)

d. *Disclosure of Research Information.* Counselors do not disclose confidential information that reasonably could lead to the identification of a research participant unless they have obtained the prior consent of the person. Use of data derived from counseling relationships for purposes of training, research, or publication is confined to content that is disguised to ensure the anonymity of the individuals involved. (See G.2.a., G.2.d.)

e. *Agreement for Identification.* Identification of clients, students, or supervisees in a presentation or publication is permissible only when they have reviewed the material and agreed to its presentation or publication. (See G.4.d.)

B.8. Consultation

a. *Agreements.* When acting as consultants, counselors seek agreements among all parties involved concerning each individual's rights to confidentiality, the obligation of each individual to preserve confidential information, and the limits of confidentiality of information shared by others.

b. *Respect for Privacy.* Information obtained in a consulting relationship is discussed for professional purposes only with persons directly involved with the case. Written and oral reports present only data germane to the purposes of the consultation, and every effort is made to protect client identity and to avoid undue invasion of privacy.

c. *Disclosure of Confidential Information.* When consulting with colleagues, counselors do not disclose confidential information that reasonably could lead to the identification of a client or other person or organization with whom they have a confidential relationship unless they have obtained the prior consent of the person or organization or the disclosure can-

not be avoided. They disclose information only to the extent necessary to achieve the purposes of the consultation. (See D.2.d.)

Section C: Professional Responsibility

Introduction

Counselors aspire to open, honest, and accurate communication in dealing with the public and other professionals. They practice in a nondiscriminatory manner within the boundaries of professional and personal competence and have a responsibility to abide by the *ACA Code of Ethics.* Counselors actively participate in local, state, and national associations that foster the development and improvement of counseling. Counselors advocate to promote change at the individual, group, institutional, and societal levels that improve the quality of life for individuals and groups and remove potential barriers to the provision or access of appropriate services being offered. Counselors have a responsibility to the public to engage in counseling practices that are based on rigorous research methodologies. In addition, counselors engage in self-care activities to maintain and promote their emotional, physical, mental, and spiritual well-being to best meet their professional responsibilities.

C.1. Knowledge of Standards

Counselors have a responsibility to read, understand, and follow the *ACA Code of Ethics* and adhere to applicable laws and regulations.

C.2. Professional Competence

a. *Boundaries of Competence.* Counselors practice only within the boundaries of their competence, based on their education, training, supervised experience, state and national professional credentials, and appropriate professional experience. Counselors gain knowledge, personal awareness, sensitivity, and skills pertinent to working with a diverse client population. (See A.9.b., C.4.e., E.2., F.2., F.11.b.)

b. *New Specialty Areas of Practice.* Counselors practice in specialty areas new to them only after appropriate education, training, and supervised experience. While developing skills in new specialty areas, counselors take steps to ensure the competence of their work and to protect others from possible harm. (See F.6.f.)

c. *Qualified for Employment.* Counselors accept employment only for positions for which they are qualified by education, training, supervised experience, state and national professional credentials, and appropriate professional experience. Counselors hire for professional counseling positions only individuals who are qualified and competent for those positions.

d. *Monitor Effectiveness.* Counselors continually monitor their effectiveness as professionals and take steps to improve when necessary. Counselors in private practice take reasonable steps to seek peer supervision as needed to evaluate their efficacy as counselors.

e. *Consultation on Ethical Obligations.* Counselors take reasonable steps to consult with other counselors or related professionals when they have questions regarding their ethical obligations or professional practice.

f. *Continuing Education.* Counselors recognize the need for continuing education to acquire and maintain a reasonable level of awareness of current scientific and professional information in their fields of activity. They take steps to maintain competence in the skills they use, are open to new procedures, and keep current with the diverse populations and specific populations with whom they work.

g. *Impairment.* Counselors are alert to the signs of impairment from their own physical, mental, or emotional problems and refrain from offering or providing professional services when such impairment is likely to harm a client or others. They seek assistance for problems that reach the level of professional impairment, and, if necessary, they limit, suspend, or terminate their professional responsibilities until such time it is determined that they may safely resume their work. Counselors assist colleagues or supervisors in recognizing their own professional impairment and provide consultation and assistance when warranted with colleagues or supervisors showing signs of impairment and intervene as appropriate to prevent imminent harm to clients. (See A.11.b., F.8.b.)

h. *Counselor Incapacitation or Termination of Practice.* When counselors leave a practice, they follow a prepared plan for transfer of clients and files. Counselors prepare and disseminate to an identified colleague or "records custodian" a plan for the transfer of clients and files in the case of their incapacitation, death, or termination of practice.

C.3. Advertising and Soliciting Clients

a. *Accurate Advertising.* When advertising or otherwise representing their services to the public, counselors identify their credentials in an accurate manner that is not false, misleading, deceptive, or fraudulent.

b. *Testimonials.* Counselors who use testimonials do not solicit them from current clients nor former clients nor any other persons who may be vulnerable to undue influence.

c. *Statements by Others.* Counselors make reasonable efforts to ensure that statements made by others about them or the profession of counseling are accurate.

d. *Recruiting Through Employment.* Counselors do not use their places of employment or institutional affiliation to recruit or gain clients, supervisees, or consultees for their private practices.

e. *Products and Training Advertisements.* Counselors who develop products related to their profession or conduct workshops or training events ensure that the advertisements concerning these products or events are accurate and disclose adequate information for consumers to make informed choices. (See C.6.d.)

f. *Promoting to Those Served.* Counselors do not use counseling, teaching, training, or supervisory relationships to promote their products or training events in a manner that is deceptive or would exert undue influence on individuals who may be vulnerable. However, counselor educators may adopt textbooks they have authored for instructional purposes.

C.4. Professional Qualifications

a. *Accurate Representation.* Counselors claim or imply only professional qualifications actually completed and correct any known misrepresentations of their qualifications by others. Counselors truthfully represent the qualifications of their professional colleagues. Counselors clearly distinguish between paid and volunteer work experience and accurately describe their continuing education and specialized training. (See C.2.a.)

b. *Credentials.* Counselors claim only licenses or certifications that are current and in good standing.

c. *Educational Degrees.* Counselors clearly differentiate between earned and honorary degrees.

d. *Implying Doctoral-Level Competence.* Counselors clearly state their highest earned degree in counseling or closely related field. Counselors do not imply doctoral-level competence when only possessing a master's degree in counseling or a related field by referring to themselves as "Dr." in a counseling context when their doctorate is not in counseling or related field.

e. *Program Accreditation Status.* Counselors clearly state the accreditation status of their degree programs at the time the degree was earned.

f. *Professional Membership.* Counselors clearly differentiate between current, active memberships and former memberships in associations. Members of the American Counseling Association must clearly differentiate between professional membership, which implies the possession of at least a master's degree in counseling, and regular membership, which is open to individuals whose interests and activities are consistent with those of ACA but are not qualified for professional membership.

C.5. Nondiscrimination

Counselors do not condone or engage in discrimination based on age, culture, disability, ethnicity, race, religion/spirituality, gender, gender identity, sexual orientation, marital status/partnership, language preference, socioeconomic status, or any basis proscribed by law. Counselors do not discriminate against clients, students, employees, supervisees, or research participants in a manner that has a negative impact on these persons.

C.6. Public Responsibility

a. *Sexual Harassment.* Counselors do not engage in or condone sexual harassment. Sexual harassment is defined as sexual solicitation, physical advances, or verbal or nonverbal conduct that is sexual in nature, that occurs in connection with professional activities or roles, and that either

  1. is unwelcome, is offensive, or creates a hostile workplace or learning environment, and counselors know or are told this; or

  2. is sufficiently severe or intense to be perceived as harassment to a reasonable person in the context in which the behavior occurred.

Sexual harassment can consist of a single intense or severe act or multiple persistent or pervasive acts.

b. *Reports to Third Parties.* Counselors are accurate, honest, and objective in reporting their professional activities and judgments to appropriate third parties, including courts, health insurance companies, those who are the recipients of evaluation reports, and others. (See B.3., E.4.)

c. *Media Presentations.* When counselors provide advice or comment by means of public lectures, demonstrations, radio or television programs, prerecorded tapes, technology-based applications, printed articles, mailed material, or other media, they take reasonable precautions to ensure that

  1. the statements are based on appropriate professional counseling literature and practice,

  2. the statements are otherwise consistent with the *ACA Code of Ethics,* and

  3. the recipients of the information are not encouraged to infer that a professional counseling relationship has been established.

d. *Exploitation of Others.* Counselors do not exploit others in their professional relationships. (See C.3.e.)

e. *Scientific Bases for Treatment Modalities.* Counselors use techniques/procedures/modalities that are grounded in theory and/or have an empirical or scientific foundation. Counselors who do not must define the techniques/procedures as "unproven" or "developing" and explain the potential risks and ethical considerations of using such techniques/procedures and take steps to protect clients from possible harm. (See A.4.a., E.5.c., E.5.d.)

C.7. Responsibility to Other Professionals

a. *Personal Public Statements.* When making personal statements in a public context, counselors clarify that they are speaking from their personal perspectives and that they are not speaking on behalf of all counselors or the profession.

Section D: Relationships with Other Professionals

Introduction

Professional counselors recognize that the quality of their interactions with colleagues can influence the quality of services provided to clients. They work to become knowledgeable about colleagues within and outside the field of counseling. Counselors develop positive working relationships and systems of communication with colleagues to enhance services to clients.

D.1. Relationships with Colleagues, Employers, and Employees

a. *Different Approaches.* Counselors are respectful of approaches to counseling services that differ from their own. Counselors are respectful of traditions and practices of other professional groups with which they work.

b. *Forming Relationships.* Counselors work to develop and strengthen interdisciplinary relations with colleagues from other disciplines to best serve clients.

c. *Interdisciplinary Teamwork.* Counselors who are members of interdisciplinary teams delivering multifaceted services to clients, keep the focus on how to best serve the clients. They participate in and contribute to decisions that affect the well-being of clients by drawing on the perspectives, values, and experiences of the counseling profession and those of colleagues from other disciplines. (See A.1.a.)

d. *Confidentiality.* When counselors are required by law, institutional policy, or extraordinary circumstances to serve in more than one role in judicial or administrative proceedings, they clarify role expectations and the parameters of confidentiality with their colleagues. (See B.1.c., B.1.d., B.2.c., B.2.d., B.3.b.)

e. *Establishing Professional and Ethical Obligations.* Counselors who are members of interdisciplinary teams clarify professional and ethical obligations of the team as a whole and of its individual members. When a team decision raises ethical concerns, counselors first attempt to resolve the concern within the team. If they cannot reach resolution among team members, counselors pursue other avenues to address their concerns consistent with client well-being.

f. *Personnel Selection and Assignment.* Counselors select competent staff and assign responsibilities compatible with their skills and experiences.

g. *Employer Policies.* The acceptance of employment in an agency or institution implies that counselors are in agreement with its general policies and principles. Counselors strive to reach agreement with employers as to acceptable standards of conduct that allow for changes in institutional policy conducive to the growth and development of clients.

h. *Negative Conditions.* Counselors alert their employers of inappropriate policies and practices. They attempt to effect changes in such policies or procedures through constructive action within the organization. When such policies are potentially disruptive or damaging to clients or may limit the effectiveness of services provided and change cannot be effected, counselors take appropriate further action. Such action may include referral to appropriate certification, accreditation, or state licensure organizations, or voluntary termination of employment.

i. *Protection from Punitive Action.* Counselors take care not to harass or dismiss an employee who has acted in a responsible and ethical manner to expose inappropriate employer policies or practices.

D.2. Consultation

a. *Consultant Competency.* Counselors take reasonable steps to ensure that they have the appropriate resources and competencies when providing consultation services. Counselors provide appropriate referral resources when requested or needed. (See C.2.a.)

b. *Understanding Consultees.* When providing consultation, counselors attempt to develop with their consultees a clear understanding of problem definition, goals for change, and predicted consequences of interventions selected.

c. *Consultant Goals.* The consulting relationship is one in which consultee adaptability and growth toward self-direction are consistently encouraged and cultivated.

d. *Informed Consent in Consultation.* When providing consultation, counselors have an obligation to review, in writing and verbally, the rights and responsibilities of both counselors and consultees. Counselors use clear and understandable language to inform all parties involved about the purpose of the services to be provided, relevant costs, potential risks and benefits, and the limits of confidentiality. Working in conjunction with the consultee, counselors attempt to develop a clear definition of the problem, goals for change, and predicted consequences of interventions that are culturally responsive and appropriate to the needs of consultees. (See A.2.a., A.2.b.)

Section E: Evaluation, Assessment, and Interpretation

Introduction

Counselors use assessment instruments as one component of the counseling process, taking into account the client personal and cultural context. Counselors promote the well-being of individual clients or groups of clients by developing and using appropriate educational, psychological, and career assessment instruments.

E.1. General
  a. *Assessment.* The primary purpose of educational, psychological, and career assessment is to provide measurements that are valid and reliable in either comparative or absolute terms. These include, but are not limited to, measurements of ability, personality, interest, intelligence, achievement, and performance. Counselors recognize the need to interpret the statements in this section as applying to both quantitative and qualitative assessments.
  b. *Client Welfare.* Counselors do not misuse assessment results and interpretations, and they take reasonable steps to prevent others from misusing the information these techniques provide. They respect the client's right to know the results, the interpretations made, and the bases for counselors' conclusions and recommendations.

E.2. Competence to Use and Interpret Assessment Instruments
  a. *Limits of Competence.* Counselors utilize only those testing and assessment services for which they have been trained and are competent. Counselors using technology assisted test interpretations are trained in the construct being measured and the specific instrument being used prior to using its technology based application. Counselors take reasonable measures to ensure the proper use of psychological and career assessment techniques by persons under their supervision. (See A.12.)
  b. *Appropriate Use.* Counselors are responsible for the appropriate application, scoring, interpretation, and use of assessment instruments relevant to the needs of the client, whether they score and interpret such assessments themselves or use technology or other services.
  c. *Decisions Based on Results.* Counselors responsible for decisions involving individuals or policies that are based on assessment results have a thorough understanding of educational, psychological, and career measurement, including validation criteria, assessment research, and guidelines for assessment development and use.

E.3. Informed Consent in Assessment
  a. *Explanation to Clients.* Prior to assessment, counselors explain the nature and purposes of assessment and the specific use of results by potential recipients. The explanation will be given in the language of the client (or other legally authorized person on behalf of the client), unless an explicit exception has been agreed upon in advance. Counselors consider the client's personal or cultural context, the level of the client's understanding of the results, and the impact of the results on the client. (See A.2., A.12.g., F.1.c.)
  b. *Recipients of Results.* Counselors consider the examinee's welfare, explicit understandings, and prior agreements in determining who receives the assessment results. Counselors include accurate and appropriate interpretations with any release of individual or group assessment results. (See B.2.c., B.5.)

E.4. Release of Data to Qualified Professionals
Counselors release assessment data in which the client is identified only with the consent of the client or the client's legal representative. Such data are released only to persons recognized by counselors as qualified to interpret the data. (See B.1., B.3., B.6.b.)

E.5. Diagnosis of Mental Disorders
  a. *Proper Diagnosis.* Counselors take special care to provide proper diagnosis of mental disorders. Assessment techniques (including personal interview) used to determine client care (e.g., locus of treatment, type of treatment, or recommended follow-up) are carefully selected and appropriately used.
  b. *Cultural Sensitivity.* Counselors recognize that culture affects the manner in which clients' problems are defined. Clients' socioeconomic and cultural experiences are considered when diagnosing mental disorders. (See A.2.c.)
  c. *Historical and Social Prejudices in the Diagnosis of Pathology.* Counselors recognize historical and social prejudices in the misdiagnosis and pathologizing of certain individuals and groups and the role of mental health professionals in perpetuating these prejudices through diagnosis and treatment.
  d. *Refraining From Diagnosis.* Counselors may refrain from making and/or reporting a diagnosis if they believe it would cause harm to the client or others.

E.6. Instrument Selection
  a. *Appropriateness of Instruments.* Counselors carefully consider the validity, reliability, psychometric limitations, and appropriateness of instruments when selecting assessments.
  b. *Referral Information.* If a client is referred to a third party for assessment, the counselor provides specific referral questions and sufficient objective data about the client to ensure that

appropriate assessment instruments are utilized. (See A.9.b., B.3.)

c. *Culturally Diverse Populations.* Counselors are
cautious when selecting assessments for culturally diverse populations to avoid the use of
instruments that lack appropriate psychometric properties for the client population. (See
A.2.c., E.5.b.)

E.7. Conditions of Assessment Administration
(See A.12.b., A.12.d.)

a. *Administration Conditions.* Counselors administer assessments under the same conditions that
were established in their standardization.
When assessments are not administered under
standard conditions, as may be necessary to accommodate clients with disabilities, or when
unusual behavior or irregularities occur during
the administration, those conditions are noted
in interpretation, and the results may be designated as invalid or of questionable validity.

b. *Technological Administration.* Counselors ensure
that administration programs function properly and provide clients with accurate results
when technological or other electronic methods are used for assessment administration.

c. *Unsupervised Assessments.* Unless the assessment
instrument is designed, intended, and validated for self-administration and/or scoring,
counselors do not permit inadequately supervised use.

d. *Disclosure of Favorable Conditions.* Prior to administration of assessments, conditions that
produce most favorable assessment results
are made known to the examinee.

E.8. Multicultural Issues/Diversity in Assessment
Counselors use with caution assessment techniques that were normed on populations other
than that of the client. Counselors recognize the
effects of age, color, culture, disability, ethnic
group, gender, race, language preference, religion,
spirituality, sexual orientation, and socioeconomic
status on test administration and interpretation,
and place test results in proper perspective with
other relevant factors. (See A.2.c., E.5.b.)

E.9. Scoring and Interpretation of Assessments

a. *Reporting.* In reporting assessment results,
counselors indicate reservations that exist
regarding validity or reliability due to circumstances of the assessment or the inappropri-
ateness of the norms for the person tested.

b. *Research Instruments.* Counselors exercise caution when interpreting the results of research
instruments not having sufficient technical

data to support respondent results. The specific purposes for the use of such instruments
are stated explicitly to the examinee.

c. *Assessment Services.* Counselors who provide assessment scoring and interpretation services to
support the assessment process confirm the
validity of such interpretations. They accurately describe the purpose, norms, validity,
reliability, and applications of the procedures
and any special qualifications applicable to
their use. The public offering of an automated
test interpretations service is considered a
professional-to-professional consultation. The
formal responsibility of the consultant is to the
consultee, but the ultimate and overriding responsibility is to the client. (See D.2.)

E.10. Assessment Security
Counselors maintain the integrity and security of tests and other assessment techniques
consistent with legal and contractual obligations. Counselors do not appropriate, reproduce, or modify published assessments or
parts thereof without acknowledgment and
permission from the publisher.

E.11. Obsolete Assessments and Outdated Results
Counselors do not use data or results from assessments that are obsolete or outdated for
the current purpose. Counselors make every
effort to prevent the misuse of obsolete measures and assessment data by others.

E.12. Assessment Construction
Counselors use established scientific procedures, relevant standards, and current professional knowledge for assessment design in the
development, publication, and utilization of
educational and psychological assessment
techniques.

E.13. Forensic Evaluation: Evaluation for Legal
Proceedings

a. *Primary Obligations.* When providing forensic
evaluations, the primary obligation of counselors is to produce objective findings that
can be substantiated based on information
and techniques appropriate to the evaluation,
which may include examination of the individual and/or review of records. Counselors
are entitled to form professional opinions
based on their professional knowledge and
expertise that can be supported by the data
gathered in evaluations. Counselors will define the limits of their reports or testimony,
especially when an examination of the individual has not been conducted.

b. *Consent for Evaluation.* Individuals being evaluated are informed in writing that the relationship is for the purposes of an evaluation and is not counseling in nature, and entities or individuals who will receive the evaluation report are identified. Written consent to be evaluated is obtained from those being evaluated unless a court orders evaluations to be conducted without the written consent of individuals being evaluated. When children or vulnerable adults are being evaluated, informed written consent is obtained from a parent or guardian.

c. *Client Evaluation Prohibited.* Counselors do not evaluate individuals for forensic purposes they currently counsel or individuals they have counseled in the past. Counselors do not accept as counseling clients individuals they are evaluating or individuals they have evaluated in the past for forensic purposes.

d. *Avoid Potentially Harmful Relationships.* Counselors who provide forensic evaluations avoid potentially harmful professional or personal relationships with family members, romantic partners, and close friends of individuals they are evaluating or have evaluated in the past.

Section F: Supervision, Training, and Teaching

Introduction

Counselors aspire to foster meaningful and respectful professional relationships and to maintain appropriate boundaries with supervisees and students. Counselors have theoretical and pedagogical foundations for their work and aim to be fair, accurate, and honest in their assessments of counselors-in-training.

F.1. Counselor Supervision and Client Welfare
   a. *Client Welfare.* A primary obligation of counseling supervisors is to monitor the services provided by other counselors or counselors-in-training. Counseling supervisors monitor client welfare and supervisee clinical performance and professional development. To fulfill these obligations, supervisors meet regularly with supervisees to review case notes, samples of clinical work, or live observations. Supervisees have a responsibility to understand and follow the *ACA Code of Ethics.*
   b. *Counselor Credentials.* Counseling supervisors work to ensure that clients are aware of the qualifications of the supervisees who render services to the clients. (See A.2.b.)

c. *Informed Consent and Client Rights.* Supervisors make supervisees aware of client rights including the protection of client privacy and confidentiality in the counseling relationship. Supervisees provide clients with professional disclosure information and inform them of how the supervision process influences the limits of confidentiality. Supervisees make clients aware of who will have access to records of the counseling relationship and how these records will be used. (See A.2.b., B.1.d.)

F.2. Counselor Supervision Competence
   a. *Supervisor Preparation.* Prior to offering clinical supervision services, counselors are trained in supervision methods and techniques. Counselors who offer clinical supervision services regularly pursue continuing education activities including both counseling and supervision topics and skills. (See C.2.a., C.2.f.)
   b. *Multicultural Issues/Diversity in Supervision.* Counseling supervisors are aware of and address the role of multiculturalism/diversity in the supervisory relationship.

F.3. Supervisory Relationships
   a. *Relationship Boundaries with Supervisees.* Counseling supervisors clearly define and maintain ethical professional, personal, and social relationships with their supervisees. Counseling supervisors avoid nonprofessional relationships with current supervisees. If supervisors must assume other professional roles (e.g., clinical and administrative supervisor, instructor) with supervisees, they work to minimize potential conflicts and explain to supervisees the expectations and responsibilities associated with each role. They do not engage in any form of nonprofessional interaction that may compromise the supervisory relationship.
   b. *Sexual Relationships.* Sexual or romantic interactions or relationships with current supervisees are prohibited.
   c. *Sexual Harassment.* Counseling supervisors do not condone or subject supervisees to sexual harassment. (See C.6.a.)
   d. *Close Relatives and Friends.* Counseling supervisors avoid accepting close relatives, romantic partners, or friends as supervisees.
   e. *Potentially Beneficial Relationships.* Counseling supervisors are aware of the power differential in their relationships with supervisees. If they believe nonprofessional relationships

with a supervisee may be potentially beneficial to the supervisee, they take precautions similar to those taken by counselors when working with clients. Examples of potentially beneficial interactions or relationships include attending a formal ceremony; hospital visits; providing support during a stressful event; or mutual membership in a professional association, organization, or community. Counseling supervisors engage in open discussions with supervisees when they consider entering into relationships with them outside of their roles as clinical and/or administrative supervisors. Before engaging in nonprofessional relationships, supervisors discuss with supervisees and document the rationale for such interactions, potential benefits or drawbacks, and anticipated consequences for the supervisee. Supervisors clarify the specific nature and limitations of the additional role(s) they will have with the supervisee.

F.4. Supervisor Responsibilities

a. *Informed Consent for Supervision.* Supervisors are responsible for incorporating into their supervision the principles of informed consent and participation. Supervisors inform supervisees of the policies and procedures to which they are to adhere and the mechanisms for due process appeal of individual supervisory actions.

b. *Emergencies and Absences.* Supervisors establish and communicate to supervisees procedures for contacting them or, in their absence, alternative on-call supervisors to assist in handling crises.

c. *Standards for Supervisees.* Supervisors make their supervisees aware of professional and ethical standards and legal responsibilities. Supervisors of postdegree counselors encourage these counselors to adhere to professional standards of practice. (See C.1.)

d. *Termination of the Supervisory Relationship.* Supervisors or supervisees have the right to terminate the supervisory relationship with adequate notice. Reasons for withdrawal are provided to the other party. When cultural, clinical, or professional issues are crucial to the viability of the supervisory relationship, both parties make efforts to resolve differences. When termination is warranted, supervisors make appropriate referrals to possible alternative supervisors.

F.5. Counseling Supervision Evaluation, Remediation, and Endorsement

a. *Evaluation.* Supervisors document and provide supervisees with ongoing performance appraisal and evaluation feedback and schedule periodic formal evaluative sessions throughout the supervisory relationship.

b. *Limitations.* Through ongoing evaluation and appraisal, supervisors are aware of the limitations of supervisees that might impede performance. Supervisors assist supervisees in securing remedial assistance when needed. They recommend dismissal from training programs, applied counseling settings, or state or voluntary professional credentialing processes when those supervisees are unable to provide competent professional services. Supervisors seek consultation and document their decisions to dismiss or refer supervisees for assistance. They ensure that supervisees are aware of options available to them to address such decisions. (See C.2.g.)

c. *Counseling for Supervisees.* If supervisees request counseling, supervisors provide them with acceptable referrals. Counselors do not provide counseling services to supervisees. Supervisors address interpersonal competencies in terms of the impact of these issues on clients, the supervisory relationship, and professional functioning. (See F.3.a.)

d. *Endorsement.* Supervisors endorse supervisees for certification, licensure, employment, or completion of an academic or training program only when they believe supervisees are qualified for the endorsement. Regardless of qualifications, supervisors do not endorse supervisees whom they believe to be impaired in any way that would interfere with the performance of the duties associated with the endorsement.

F.6. Responsibilities of Counselor Educators

a. *Counselor Educators.* Counselor educators who are responsible for developing, implementing, and supervising educational programs are skilled as teachers and practitioners. They are knowledgeable regarding the ethical, legal, and regulatory aspects of the profession, are skilled in applying that knowledge, and make students and supervisees aware of their responsibilities. Counselor educators conduct counselor education and training programs in an ethical manner and serve as role models for professional behavior. (See C.1., C.2.a., C.2.c.)

b. *Infusing Multicultural Issues/Diversity.* Counselor educators infuse material related to multicultluralism/diversity into all courses and workshops for the development of professional counselors.

c. *Integration of Study and Practice.* Counselor educators establish education and training programs that integrate academic study and supervised practice.

d. *Teaching Ethics.* Counselor educators make students and supervisees aware of the ethical responsibilities and standards of the profession and the ethical responsibilities of students to the profession. Counselor educators infuse ethical considerations throughout the curriculum. (See C.1.)

e. *Peer Relationships.* Counselor educators make every effort to ensure that the rights of peers are not compromised when students or supervisees lead counseling groups or provide clinical supervision. Counselor educators take steps to ensure that students and supervisees understand they have the same ethical obligations as counselor educators, trainers, and supervisors.

f. *Innovative Theories and Techniques.* When counselor educators teach counseling techniques/ procedures that are innovative, without an empirical foundation, or without a well-grounded theoretical foundation, they define the counseling techniques/procedures as "unproven" or "developing" and explain to students the potential risks and ethical considerations of using such techniques/procedures.

g. *Field Placements.* Counselor educators develop clear policies within their training programs regarding field placement and other clinical experiences. Counselor educators provide clearly stated roles and responsibilities for the student or supervisee, the site supervisor, and the program supervisor. They confirm that site supervisors are qualified to provide supervision and inform site supervisors of their professional and ethical responsibilities in this role.

h. *Professional Disclosure.* Before initiating counseling services, counselors-in-training disclose their status as students and explain how this status affects the limits of confidentiality. Counselor educators ensure that the clients at field placements are aware of the services rendered and the qualifications of the students and supervisees rendering those services. Stu-

dents and supervisees obtain client permission before they use any information concerning the counseling relationship in the training process. (See A.2.b.)

F.7. Student Welfare

a. *Orientation.* Counselor educators recognize that orientation is a developmental process that continues throughout the educational and clinical training of students. Counseling faculty provide prospective students with information about the counselor education program's expectations:

1. the type and level of skill and knowledge acquisition required for successful completion of the training;

2. program training goals, objectives, and mission, and subject matter to be covered;

3. bases for evaluation;

4. training components that encourage self-growth or self-disclosure as part of the training process;

5. the type of supervision settings and requirements of the sites for required clinical field experiences;

6. student and supervisee evaluation and dismissal policies and procedures; and

7. up-to-date employment prospects for graduates.

b. *Self-Growth Experiences.* Counselor education programs delineate requirements for self-disclosure or self-growth experiences in their admission and program materials. Counselor educators use professional judgment when designing training experiences they conduct that require student and supervisee selfgrowth or self-disclosure. Students and supervisees are made aware of the ramifications their self-disclosure may have when counselors whose primary role as teacher, trainer, or supervisor requires acting on ethical obligations to the profession. Evaluative components of experiential training experiences explicitly delineate predetermined academic standards that are separate and do not depend on the student's level of selfdisclosure. Counselor educators may require trainees to seek professional help to address any personal concerns that may be affecting their competency.

F.8. Student Responsibilities

a. *Standards for Students.* Counselors-in-training have a responsibility to understand and follow the *ACA Code of Ethics* and adhere to applicable laws, regulatory policies, and rules and policies governing professional staff behavior at the agency or placement setting. Students have the same obligation to clients as those required of professional counselors. (See C.1., H.1.)

b. *Impairment.* Counselors-in-training refrain from offering or providing counseling services when their physical, mental, or emotional problems are likely to harm a client or others. They are alert to the signs of impairment, seek assistance for problems, and notify their program supervisors when they are aware that they are unable to effectively provide services. In addition, they seek appropriate professional services for themselves to remediate the problems that are interfering with their ability to provide services to others. (See A.1., C.2.d., C.2.g.)

F.9. Evaluation and Remediation of Students

a. *Evaluation.* Counselors clearly state to students, prior to and throughout the training program, the levels of competency expected, appraisal methods, and timing of evaluations for both didactic and clinical competencies. Counselor educators provide students with ongoing performance appraisal and evaluation feedback throughout the training program.

b. *Limitations.* Counselor educators, throughout ongoing evaluation and appraisal, are aware of and address the inability of some students to achieve counseling competencies that might impede performance. Counselor educators

   1. assist students in securing remedial assistance when needed,
   2. seek professional consultation and document their decision to dismiss or refer students for assistance, and
   3. ensure that students have recourse in a timely manner to address decisions to require them to seek assistance or to dismiss them and provide students with due process according to institutional policies and procedures. (See C.2.g.)

c. *Counseling for Students.* If students request counseling or if counseling services are required as part of a remediation process, counselor educators provide acceptable referrals.

F. 10. Roles and Relationships Between Counselor Educators and Students

a. *Sexual or Romantic Relationships.* Sexual or romantic interactions or relationships with current students are prohibited.

b. *Sexual Harassment.* Counselor educators do not condone or subject students to sexual harassment. (See C.6.a.)

c. *Relationships with Former Students.* Counselor educators are aware of the power differential in the relationship between faculty and students. Faculty members foster open discussions with former students when considering engaging in a social, sexual, or other intimate relationship. Faculty members discuss with the former student how their former relationship may affect the change in relationship.

d. *Nonprofessional Relationships.* Counselor educators avoid nonprofessional or ongoing professional relationships with students in which there is a risk of potential harm to the student or that may compromise the training experience or grades assigned. In addition, counselor educators do not accept any form of professional services, fees, commissions, reimbursement, or remuneration from a site for student or supervisee placement.

e. *Counseling Services.* Counselor educators do not serve as counselors to current students unless this is a brief role associated with a training experience.

f. *Potentially Beneficial Relationships.* Counselor educators are aware of the power differential in the relationship between faculty and students. If they believe a nonprofessional relationship with a student may be potentially beneficial to the student, they take precautions similar to those taken by counselors when working with clients. Examples of potentially beneficial interactions or relationships include, but are not limited to, attending a formal ceremony; hospital visits; providing support during a stressful event; or mutual membership in a professional association, organization, or community. Counselor educators engage in open discussions with students when they consider entering into relationships with students outside of their roles as teachers and supervisors. They discuss with students the rationale for such interactions, the potential benefits and drawbacks, and the anticipated consequences for the student. Educators clarify the specific nature and limitations of the additional role(s) they will have with the student prior to engaging in a nonprofessional relationship. Nonprofessional relationships with students should be time-limited and initiated with student consent.

F.11. Multicultural/Diversity Competence in Counselor Education and Training Programs

    a. *Faculty Diversity.* Counselor educators are committed to recruiting and retaining a diverse faculty.

    b. *Student Diversity.* Counselor educators actively attempt to recruit and retain a diverse student body. Counselor educators demonstrate commitment to multicultural/diversity competence by recognizing and valuing diverse cultures and types of abilities students bring to the training experience. Counselor educators provide appropriate accommodations that enhance and support diverse student well-being and academic performance.

    c. *Multicultural/Diversity Competence.* Counselor educators actively infuse multicultural/diversity competency in their training and supervision practices. They actively train students to gain awareness, knowledge, and skills in the competencies of multicultural practice. Counselor educators include case examples, role-plays, discussion questions, and other classroom activities that promote and represent various cultural perspectives.

Section G: Research and Publication

Introduction

Counselors who conduct research are encouraged to contribute to the knowledge base of the profession and promote a clearer understanding of the conditions that lead to a healthy and more just society. Counselors support efforts of researchers by participating fully and willingly whenever possible. Counselors minimize bias and respect diversity in designing and implementing research programs.

G.1. Research Responsibilities

    a. *Use of Human Research Participants.* Counselors plan, design, conduct, and report research in a manner that is consistent with pertinent ethical principles, federal and state laws, host institutional regulations, and scientific standards governing research with human research participants.

    b. *Deviation From Standard Practice.* Counselors seek consultation and observe stringent safeguards to protect the rights of research participants when a research problem suggests a deviation from standard or acceptable practices.

    c. *Independent Researchers.* When independent researchers do not have access to an Institutional Review Board (IRB), they should consult with researchers who are familiar with IRB procedures to provide appropriate safeguards.

    d. *Precautions to Avoid Injury.* Counselors who conduct research with human participants are responsible for the welfare of participants throughout the research process and should take reasonable precautions to avoid causing injurious psychological, emotional, physical, or social effects to participants.

    e. *Principal Researcher Responsibility.* The ultimate responsibility for ethical research practice lies with the principal researcher. All others involved in the research activities share ethical obligations and responsibility for their own actions.

    f. *Minimal Interference.* Counselors take reasonable precautions to avoid causing disruptions in the lives of research participants that could be caused by their involvement in research.

    g. *Multicultural/Diversity Considerations in Research.* When appropriate to research goals, counselors are sensitive to incorporating research procedures that take into account cultural considerations. They seek consultation when appropriate.

G.2. Rights of Research Participants

    (See A.2, A.7.)

    a. *Informed Consent in Research.* Individuals have the right to consent to become research participants. In seeking consent, counselors use language that

       1. accurately explains the purpose and procedures to be followed,

       2. identifies any procedures that are experimental or relatively untried,

       3. describes any attendant discomforts and risks,

       4. describes any benefits or changes in individuals or organizations that might be reasonably expected,

       5. discloses appropriate alternative procedures that would be advantageous for participants,

       6. offers to answer any inquiries concerning the procedures,

       7. describes any limitations on confidentiality,

       8. describes the format and potential target audiences for the dissemination of research findings, and

       9. instructs participants that they are free to withdraw their consent and to discontinue

participation in the project at any time without penalty.

b. *Deception.* Counselors do not conduct research involving deception unless alternative procedures are not feasible and the prospective value of the research justifies the deception. If such deception has the potential to cause physical or emotional harm to research participants, the research is not conducted, regardless of prospective value. When the methodological requirements of a study necessitate concealment or deception, the investigator explains the reasons for this action as soon as possible during the debriefing.

c. *Student/Supervisee Participation.* Researchers who involve students or supervisees in research make clear to them that the decision regarding whether or not to participate in research activities does not affect one's academic standing or supervisory relationship. Students or supervisees who choose not to participate in educational research are provided with an appropriate alternative to fulfill their academic or clinical requirements.

d. *Client Participation.* Counselors conducting research involving clients make clear in the informed consent process that clients are free to choose whether or not to participate in research activities. Counselors take necessary precautions to protect clients from adverse consequences of declining or withdrawing from participation.

e. *Confidentiality of Information.* Information obtained about research participants during the course of an investigation is confidential. When the possibility exists that others may obtain access to such information, ethical research practice requires that the possibility, together with the plans for protecting confidentiality, be explained to participants as a part of the procedure for obtaining informed consent.

f. *Persons Not Capable of Giving Informed Consent.* When a person is not capable of giving informed consent, counselors provide an appropriate explanation to, obtain agreement for participation from, and obtain the appropriate consent of a legally authorized person.

g. *Commitments to Participants.* Counselors take reasonable measures to honor all commitments to research participants. (See A.2.c.)

h. *Explanations After Data Collection.* After data are collected, counselors provide participants with full clarification of the nature of the study to remove any misconceptions participants might have regarding the research. Where scientific or human values justify delaying or withholding information, counselors take reasonable measures to avoid causing harm.

i. *Informing Sponsors.* Counselors inform sponsors, institutions, and publication channels regarding research procedures and outcomes. Counselors ensure that appropriate bodies and authorities are given pertinent information and acknowledgement.

j. *Disposal of Research Documents and Records.* Within a reasonable period of time following the completion of a research project or study, counselors take steps to destroy records or documents (audio, video, digital, and written) containing confidential data or information that identifies research participants. When records are of an artistic nature, researchers obtain participant consent with regard to handling of such records or documents. (See B.4.a, B.4.g.)

G.3. Relationships with Research Participants (When Research Involves Intensive or Extended Interactions)

a. *Nonprofessional Relationships.* Nonprofessional relationships with research participants should be avoided.

b. *Relationships with Research Participants.* Sexual or romantic counselor–research participant interactions or relationships with current research participants are prohibited.

c. *Sexual Harassment and Research Participants.* Researchers do not condone or subject research participants to sexual harassment.

d. *Potentially Beneficial Interactions.* When a nonprofessional interaction between the researcher and the research participant may be potentially beneficial, the researcher must document, prior to the interaction (when feasible), the rationale for such an interaction, the potential benefit, and anticipated consequences for the research participant. Such interactions should be initiated with appropriate consent of the research participant. Where unintentional harm occurs to the research participant due to the nonprofessional interaction, the researcher must show evidence of an attempt to remedy such harm.

G.4. Reporting Results

a. *Accurate Results.* Counselors plan, conduct, and report research accurately. They provide thorough discussions of the limitations of their data and alternative hypotheses. Counselors do not engage in misleading or fraudulent research, distort data, misrepresent data, or deliberately bias their results. They explicitly mention all variables and conditions known to the investigator that may have affected the outcome of a study or the interpretation of data. They describe the extent to which results are applicable for diverse populations.

b. *Obligation to Report Unfavorable Results.* Counselors report the results of any research of professional value. Results that reflect unfavorably on institutions, programs, services, prevailing opinions, or vested interests are not withheld.

c. *Reporting Errors.* If counselors discover significant errors in their published research, they take reasonable steps to correct such errors in a correction erratum, or through other appropriate publication means.

d. *Identity of Participants.* Counselors who supply data, aid in the research of another person, report research results, or make original data available take due care to disguise the identity of respective participants in the absence of specific authorization from the participants to do otherwise. In situations where participants self-identify their involvement in research studies, researchers take active steps to ensure that data is adapted/changed to protect the identity and welfare of all parties and that discussion of results does not cause harm to participants.

e. *Replication Studies.* Counselors are obligated to make available sufficient original research data to qualified professionals who may wish to replicate the study.

G.5. Publication

a. *Recognizing Contributions.* When conducting and reporting research, counselors are familiar with and give recognition to previous work on the topic, observe copyright laws, and give full credit to those to whom credit is due.

b. *Plagiarism.* Counselors do not plagiarize, that is, they do not present another person's work as their own work.

c. *Review/Republication of Data or Ideas.* Counselors fully acknowledge and make editorial reviewers aware of prior publication of ideas or data where such ideas or data are submitted for review or publication.

d. *Contributors.* Counselors give credit through joint authorship, acknowledgment, footnote statements, or other appropriate means to those who have contributed significantly to research or concept development in accordance with such contributions. The principal contributor is listed first and minor technical or professional contributions are acknowledged in notes or introductory statements.

e. *Agreement of Contributors.* Counselors who conduct joint research with colleagues or students/supervisees establish agreements in advance regarding allocation of tasks, publication credit, and types of acknowledgement that will be received.

f. *Student Research.* For articles that are substantially based on students course papers, projects, dissertations or theses, and on which students have been the primary contributors, they are listed as principal authors.

g. *Duplicate Submission.* Counselors submit manuscripts for consideration to only one journal at a time. Manuscripts that are published in whole or in substantial part in another journal or published work are not submitted for publication without acknowledgment and permission from the previous publication.

h. *Professional Review.* Counselors who review material submitted for publication, research, or other scholarly purposes respect the confidentiality and proprietary rights of those who submitted it. Counselors use care to make publication decisions based on valid and defensible standards. Counselors review article submissions in a timely manner and based on their scope and competency in research methodologies. Counselors who serve as reviewers at the request of editors or publishers make every effort to only review materials that are within their scope of competency and use care to avoid personal biases.

Section H: Resolving Ethical Issues

Introduction

Counselors behave in a legal, ethical, and moral manner in the conduct of their professional work. They are aware that client protection and trust in the profession depend on a high level of professional conduct. They hold other counselors to the same standards and are willing to take appropriate action to ensure that these standards are upheld. Counselors strive to resolve ethical dilemmas with direct and open communication among all parties involved and seek consultation with colleagues and supervisors when necessary. Counselors incorporate ethical practice into their daily professional work. They engage in ongoing professional development regarding current topics in ethical and legal issues in counseling.

H.1. Standards and the Law
(See F.9.a.)
a. *Knowledge.* Counselors understand the *ACA Code of Ethics* and other applicable ethics codes from other professional organizations or from certification and licensure bodies of which they are members. Lack of knowledge or misunderstanding of an ethical responsibility is not a defense against a charge of unethical conduct.
b. *Conflicts Between Ethics and Laws.* If ethical responsibilities conflict with law, regulations, or other governing legal authority, counselors make known their commitment to the *ACA Code of Ethics* and take steps to resolve the conflict. If the conflict cannot be resolved by such means, counselors may adhere to the requirements of law, regulations, or other governing legal authority.

H.2. Suspected Violations
a. *Ethical Behavior Expected.* Counselors expect colleagues to adhere to the *ACA Code of Ethics.* When counselors possess knowledge that raises doubts as to whether another counselor is acting in an ethical manner, they take appropriate action. (See H.2.b., H.2.c.)
b. *Informal Resolution.* When counselors have reason to believe that another counselor is violating or has violated an ethical standard, they attempt first to resolve the issue informally with the other counselor if feasible, provided such action does not violate confidentiality rights that may be involved.
c. *Reporting Ethical Violations.* If an apparent violation has substantially harmed, or is likely to substantially harm a person or organization and is not appropriate for informal resolution or is not resolved properly, counselors take further action appropriate to the situation. Such action might include referral to state or national committees on professional ethics, voluntary national certification bodies, state licensing boards, or to the appropriate institutional authorities. This standard does not apply when an intervention would violate confidentiality rights or when coun-

selors have been retained to review the work of another counselor whose professional conduct is in question.
d. *Consultation.* When uncertain as to whether a particular situation or course of action may be in violation of the *ACA Code of Ethics,* counselors consult with other counselors who are knowledgeable about ethics and the *ACA Code of Ethics,* with colleagues, or with appropriate authorities.
e. *Organizational Conflicts.* If the demands of an organization with which counselors are affiliated pose a conflict with the *ACA Code of Ethics,* counselors specify the nature of such conflicts and express to their supervisors or other responsible officials their commitment to the *ACA Code of Ethics.* When possible, counselors work toward change within the organization to allow full adherence to the *ACA Code of Ethics.* In doing so, they address any confidentiality issues.
f. *Unwarranted Complaints.* Counselors do not initiate, participate in, or encourage the filing of ethics complaints that are made with reckless disregard or willful ignorance of facts that would disprove the allegation.
g. *Unfair Discrimination Against Complainants and Respondents.* Counselors do not deny persons employment, advancement, admission to academic or other programs, tenure, or promotion based solely upon their having made or their being the subject of an ethics complaint. This does not preclude taking action based upon the outcome of such proceedings or considering other appropriate information.

H.3. Cooperation with Ethics Committees
Counselors assist in the process of enforcing the *ACA Code of Ethics.* Counselors cooperate with investigations, proceedings, and requirements of the ACA Ethics Committee or ethics committees of other duly constituted associations or boards having jurisdiction over those charged with a violation. Counselors are familiar with the *ACA Policy and Procedures for Processing Complains of Ethical Violations* and use it as a reference for assisting in the enforcement of the *ACA Code of Ethics.*

Glossary of Terms

Advocacy—promotion of the well-being of individuals and groups, and the counseling profession within systems and organizations. Advocacy seeks to remove barriers and obstacles that inhibit access, growth, and development.

Assent—to demonstrate agreement, when a person is otherwise not capable or competent to give formal consent (e.g., informed consent) to a counseling service or plan.

Client—an individual seeking or referred to the professional services of a counselor for help with problem resolution or decision making.

Counselor—a professional (or a student who is a counselor-in-training) engaged in a counseling practice or other counseling-related services. Counselors fulfill many roles and responsibilities such as counselor educators, researchers, supervisors, practitioners, and consultants.

Counselor Educator—a professional counselor engaged primarily in developing, implementing, and supervising the educational preparation of counselors-in-training.

Counselor Supervisor—a professional counselor who engages in a formal relationship with a practicing counselor or counselor-in-training for the purpose of overseeing that individual's counseling work or clinical skill development.

Culture—membership in a socially constructed way of living, which incorporates collective values, beliefs, norms, boundaries, and lifestyles that are cocreated with others who share similar worldviews comprising biological, psychosocial, historical, psychological, and other factors.

Diversity—the similarities and differences that occur within and across cultures, and the intersection of cultural and social identities.

Documents—any written, digital, audio, visual, or artistic recording of the work within the counseling relationship between counselor and client.

Examinee—a recipient of any professional counseling service that includes educational, psychological, and career appraisal utilizing qualitative or quantitative techniques.

Forensic Evaluation—any formal assessment conducted for court or other legal proceedings.

Multicultural/Diversity Competence—a capacity whereby counselors possess cultural and diversity awareness and knowledge about self and others, and how this awareness and knowledge is applied effectively in practice with clients and client groups.

Multicultural/Diversity Counseling—counseling that recognizes diversity and embraces approaches that support the worth, dignity, potential, and uniqueness of individuals within their historical, cultural, economic, political, and psychosocial contexts.

Student—an individual engaged in formal educational preparation as a counselor-in-training.

Supervisee—a professional counselor or counselor-in-training whose counseling work or clinical skill development is being overseen in a formal supervisory relationship by a qualified trained professional.

Supervisor—counselors who are trained to oversee the professional clinical work of counselors and counselors-in-training.

Teaching—all activities engaged in as part of a formal educational program designed to lead to a graduate degree in counseling.

Training—the instruction and practice of skills related to the counseling profession. Training contributes to the ongoing proficiency of students and professional counselors.

AAMFT Code of Ethics

Effective July 1, 2001

$\mathcal{B}$

Appendix

Preamble

The Board of Directors of the American Association for Marriage and Family Therapy (AAMFT) hereby promulgates, pursuant to Article 2, Section 2.013 of the Association's Bylaws, the Revised AAMFT Code of Ethics, effective July 1, 2001.

The AAMFT strives to honor the public trust in marriage and family therapists by setting standards for ethical practice as described in this Code. The ethical standards define professional expectations and are enforced by the AAMFT Ethics Committee. The absence of an explicit reference to a specific behavior or situation in the Code does not mean that the behavior is ethical or unethical. The standards are not exhaustive. Marriage and family therapists who are uncertain about the ethics of a particular course of action are encouraged to seek counsel from consultants, attorneys, supervisors, colleagues, or other appropriate authorities.

Both law and ethics govern the practice of marriage and family therapy. When making decisions regarding professional behavior, marriage and family therapists must consider the AAMFT Code of Ethics and applicable laws and regulations. If the AAMFT Code of Ethics prescribes a standard higher than that required by law, marriage and family therapists must meet the higher standard of the AAMFT Code of Ethics. Marriage and family therapists comply with the mandates of law, but make known their commitment to the AAMFT Code of Ethics and take steps to resolve the conflict in a responsible manner. The AAMFT supports legal mandates for reporting of alleged unethical conduct.

The AAMFT Code of Ethics is binding on Members of AAMFT in all membership categories, AAMFT-Ap-

This Code is published by:
American Association for Marriage and Family Therapy
112 South Alfred Street, Alexandria, VA 22314
Phone: (703) 838-9808; Fax: (703) 838-9805
www.aamft.org

© Copyright 2001 by the AAMFT. All rights reserved. Printed in the United States of America. No part of this publication may be reproduced, stored in a retrieval system, or transmitted, in any form or by any means, electronic, mechanical photocopying recording, or otherwise, without the prior written permission of the publisher.

Violations of this Code should be brought in writing to the attention of:

AAMFT Ethics Committee
112 South Alfred Street, Alexandria, VA 22314
Phone: (703) 838-9808; Fax: (703) 838-9805;
e-mail: ethics@aamft.org

proved Supervisors, and applicants for membership and the Approved Supervisor designation (hereafter, AAMFT Member). AAMFT members have an obligation to be familiar with the AAMFT Code of Ethics and its application to their professional services. Lack of awareness or misunderstanding of an ethical standard is not a defense to a charge of unethical conduct.

The process for filing, investigating, and resolving complaints of unethical conduct is described in the current Procedures for Handling Ethical Matters of the AAMFT Ethics Committee. Persons accused are considered innocent by the Ethics Committee until proven guilty, except as otherwise provided, and are entitled to due process. If an AAMFT Member resigns in anticipation of, or during the course of, an ethics investigation, the Ethics Committee will complete its investigation. Any publication of action taken by the Association will include the fact that the Member attempted to resign during the investigation.

Contents

Principle I: Responsibility to Clients

Marriage and family therapists advance the welfare of families and individuals. They respect the rights of those persons seeking their assistance, and make reasonable efforts to ensure that their services are used appropriately.

1.1. Marriage and family therapists provide professional assistance to persons without discrimination on the basis of race, age, ethnicity, socioeconomic status, disability, gender, health status, religion, national origin, or sexual orientation.

1.2 Marriage and family therapists obtain appropriate informed consent to therapy or related procedures as early as feasible in the therapeutic relationship, and use language that is reasonably understandable to clients. The content of informed consent may vary depending upon the client and treatment plan; however, informed consent generally necessitates that the client: (a) has the capacity to consent; (b) has been adequately informed of significant information concerning treatment

processes and procedures; (c) has been adequately informed of potential risks and benefits of treatments for which generally recognized standards do not yet exist; (d) has freely and without undue influence expressed consent; and (e) has provided consent that is appropriately documented. When persons, due to age or mental status, are legally incapable of giving informed consent, marriage and family therapists obtain informed permission from a legally authorized person, if such substitute consent is legally permissible.

1.3 Marriage and family therapists are aware of their influential positions with respect to clients, and they avoid exploiting the trust and dependency of such persons. Therapists, therefore, make every effort to avoid conditions and multiple relationships with clients that could impair professional judgment or increase the risk of exploitation. Such relationships include, but are not limited to, business or close personal relationships with a client or the client's immediate family. When the risk of impairment or exploitation exists due to conditions or multiple roles, therapists take appropriate precautions.

1.4 Sexual intimacy with clients is prohibited.

1.5 Sexual intimacy with former clients is likely to be harmful and is therefore prohibited for two years following the termination of therapy or last professional contact. In an effort to avoid exploiting the trust and dependency of clients, marriage and family therapists should not engage in sexual intimacy with former clients after the two years following termination or last professional contact. Should therapists engage in sexual intimacy with former clients following two years after termination or last professional contact, the burden shifts to the therapist to demonstrate that there has been no exploitation or injury to the former client or to the client's immediate family.

1.6 Marriage and family therapists comply with applicable laws regarding the reporting of alleged unethical conduct.

1.7 Marriage and family therapists do not use their professional relationships with clients to further their own interests.

1.8 Marriage and family therapists respect the rights of clients to make decisions and help them to understand the consequences of these decisions. Therapists clearly advise the clients that they have the responsibility to make decisions regarding relationships such as cohabitation, marriage, divorce, separation, reconciliation, custody, and visitation.

1.9   Marriage and family therapists continue therapeutic relationships only so long as it is reasonably clear that clients are benefiting from the relationship.

1.10 Marriage and family therapists assist persons in obtaining other therapeutic services if the therapist is unable or unwilling, for appropriate reasons, to provide professional help.

1.11 Marriage and family therapists do not abandon or neglect clients in treatment without making reasonable arrangements for the continuation of such treatment.

1.12 Marriage and family therapists obtain written informed consent from clients before videotaping, audio recording, or permitting third-party observation.

1.13 Marriage and family therapists, upon agreeing to provide services to a person or entity at the request of a third party, clarify, to the extent feasible and at the outset of the service, the nature of the relationship with each party and the limits of confidentiality.

Principle II: Confidentiality

Marriage and family therapists have unique confidentiality concerns because the client in a therapeutic relationship may be more than one person. Therapists respect and guard the confidences of each individual client.

2.1   Marriage and family therapists disclose to clients and other interested parties, as early as feasible in their professional contacts, the nature of confidentiality and possible limitations of the clients' right to confidentiality. Therapists review with clients the circumstances where confidential information may be requested and where disclosure of confidential information may be legally required. Circumstances may necessitate repeated disclosures.

2.2   Marriage and family therapists do not disclose client confidences except by written authorization or waiver, or where mandated or permitted by law. Verbal authorization will not be sufficient except in emergency situations, unless prohibited by law. When providing couple, family or group treatment, the therapist does not disclose information outside the treatment context without a written authorization from each individual competent to execute a waiver. In the context of couple, family or group treatment, the therapist may not reveal any individual's confidences to others in the client unit without the prior written permission of that individual.

2.3   Marriage and family therapists use client and/or clinical materials in teaching, writing, consulting, research, and public presentations only if a written waiver has been obtained in accordance with Subprinciple 2.2, or when appropriate steps have been taken to protect client identity and confidentiality.

2.4   Marriage and family therapists store, safeguard, and dispose of client records in ways that maintain confidentiality and in accord with applicable laws and professional standards.

2.5   Subsequent to the therapist moving from the area, closing the practice, or upon the death of the therapist, a marriage and family therapist arranges for the storage, transfer, or disposal of client records in ways that maintain confidentiality and safeguard the welfare of clients.

2.6   Marriage and family therapists, when consulting with colleagues or referral sources, do not share confidential information that could reasonably lead to the identification of a client, research participant, supervisee, or other person with whom they have a confidential relationship unless they have obtained the prior written consent of the client, research participant, supervisee, or other person with whom they have a confidential relationship. Information may be shared only to the extent necessary to achieve the purposes of the consultation.

Principle III: Professional Competence and Integrity

Marriage and family therapists maintain high standards of professional competence and integrity.

3.1   Marriage and family therapists pursue knowledge of new developments and maintain competence in marriage and family therapy through education, training, or supervised experience.

3.2   Marriage and family therapists maintain adequate knowledge of and adhere to applicable laws, ethics, and professional standards.

3.3   Marriage and family therapists seek appropriate professional assistance for their personal problems or conflicts that may impair work performance or clinical judgment.

3.4   Marriage and family therapists do not provide services that create a conflict of interest that may impair work performance or clinical judgment.

3.5   Marriage and family therapists, as presenters, teachers, supervisors, consultants and researchers, are dedicated to high standards of scholarship, present accurate information, and disclose potential conflicts of interest.

3.6 Marriage and family therapists maintain accurate and adequate clinical and financial records.

3.7 While developing new skills in specialty areas, marriage and family therapists take steps to ensure the competence of their work and to protect clients from possible harm. Marriage and family therapists practice in specialty areas new to them only after appropriate education, training, or supervised experience.

3.8 Marriage and family therapists do not engage in sexual or other forms of harassment of clients, students, trainees, supervisees, employees, colleagues, or research subjects.

3.9 Marriage and family therapists do not engage in the exploitation of clients, students, trainees, supervisees, employees, colleagues, or research subjects.

3.10 Marriage and family therapists do not give to or receive from clients (a) gifts of substantial value or (b) gifts that impair the integrity or efficacy of the therapeutic relationship.

3.11 Marriage and family therapists do not diagnose, treat, or advise on problems outside the recognized boundaries of their competencies.

3.12 Marriage and family therapists make efforts to prevent the distortion or misuse of their clinical and research findings.

3.13 Marriage and family therapists, because of their ability to influence and alter the lives of others, exercise special care when making public their professional recommendations and opinions through testimony or other public statements.

3.14 To avoid a conflict of interests, marriage and family therapists who treat minors or adults involved in custody or visitation actions may not also perform forensic evaluations for custody, residence, or visitation of the minor. The marriage and family therapist who treats the minor may provide the court or mental health professional performing the evaluation with information about the minor from the marriage and family therapist's perspective as a treating marriage and family therapist, so long as the marriage and family therapist does not violate confidentiality.

3.15 Marriage and family therapists are in violation of this Code and subject to termination of membership or other appropriate action if they: (a) are convicted of any felony; (b) are convicted of a misdemeanor related to their qualifications or functions; (c) engage in conduct which could lead to conviction of a felony, or a misdemeanor related to their qualifications or functions; (d) are expelled from or disciplined by other professional organizations; (e) have their licenses or certificates suspended or revoked or are otherwise disciplined by regulatory bodies; (f) continue to practice marriage and family therapy while no longer competent to do so because they are impaired by physical or mental causes or the abuse of alcohol or other substances; or (g) fail to cooperate with the Association at any point from the inception of an ethical complaint through the completion of all proceedings regarding that complaint.

Principle IV: Responsibility to Students and Supervisees

Marriage and family therapists do not exploit the trust and dependency of students and supervisees.

4.1 Marriage and family therapists are aware of their influential positions with respect to students and supervisees, and they avoid exploiting the trust and dependency of such persons. Therapists, therefore, make every effort to avoid conditions and multiple relationships that could impair professional objectivity or increase the risk of exploitation. When the risk of impairment or exploitation exists due to conditions or multiple roles, therapists take appropriate precautions.

4.2 Marriage and family therapists do not provide therapy to current students or supervisees.

4.3 Marriage and family therapists do not engage in sexual intimacy with students or supervisees during the evaluative or training relationship between the therapist and student or supervisee. Should a supervisor engage in sexual activity with a former supervisee, the burden of proof shifts to the supervisor to demonstrate that there has been no exploitation or injury to the supervisee.

4.4 Marriage and family therapists do not permit students or supervisees to perform or to hold themselves out as competent to perform professional services beyond their training, level of experience, and competence.

4.5 Marriage and family therapists take reasonable measures to ensure that services provided by supervisees are professional.

4.6 Marriage and family therapists avoid accepting as supervisees or students those individuals with whom a prior or existing relationship could compromise the therapist's objectivity. When such situations cannot be avoided, therapists take appropriate precautions to maintain objectivity. Examples of such relationships include, but are not limited to, those individuals with whom the therapist has a current or prior sexual, close personal, immediate familial, or therapeutic relationship.

4.7 Marriage and family therapists do not disclose supervisee confidences except by written authorization or waiver, or when mandated or permitted by law. In educational or training settings where there are multiple supervisors, disclosures are permitted only to other professional colleagues, administrators, or employers who share responsibility for training of the supervisee. Verbal authorization will not be sufficient except in emergency situations, unless prohibited by law.

Principle V: Responsibility to Research Participants

Investigators respect the dignity and protect the welfare of research participants, and are aware of applicable laws and regulations and professional standards governing the conduct of research.

5.1 Investigators are responsible for making careful examinations of ethical acceptability in planning studies. To the extent that services to research participants may be compromised by participation in research, investigators seek the ethical advice of qualified professionals not directly involved in the investigation and observe safeguards to protect the rights of research participants.

5.2 Investigators requesting participant involvement in research inform participants of the aspects of the research that might reasonably be expected to influence willingness to participate. Investigators are especially sensitive to the possibility of diminished consent when participants are also receiving clinical services, or have impairments which limit understanding and/or communication, or when participants are children.

5.3 Investigators respect each participant's freedom to decline participation in or to withdraw from a research study at any time. This obligation requires special thought and consideration when investigators or other members of the research team are in positions of authority or influence over participants. Marriage and family therapists, therefore, make every effort to avoid multiple relationships with research participants that could impair professional judgment or increase the risk of exploitation.

5.4 Information obtained about a research participant during the course of an investigation is confidential unless there is a waiver previously obtained in writing. When the possibility exists that others, including family members, may obtain access to such information, this possibility, together with the plan for protecting confidentiality, is explained as part of the procedure for obtaining informed consent.

Principle VI: Responsibility to the Profession

Marriage and family therapists respect the rights and responsibilities of professional colleagues and participate in activities that advance the goals of the profession.

6.1 Marriage and family therapists remain accountable to the standards of the profession when acting as members or employees of organizations. If the mandates of an organization with which a marriage and family therapist is affiliated, through employment, contract or otherwise, conflict with the AAMFT Code of Ethics, marriage and family therapists make known to the organization their commitment to the AAMFT Code of Ethics and attempt to resolve the conflict in a way that allows the fullest adherence to the Code of Ethics.

6.2 Marriage and family therapists assign publication credit to those who have contributed to a publication in proportion to their contributions and in accordance with customary professional publication practices.

6.3 Marriage and family therapists do not accept or require authorship credit for a publication based on research from a student's program, unless the therapist made a substantial contribution beyond being a faculty advisor or research committee member. Coauthorship on a student thesis, dissertation, or project should be determined in accordance with principles of fairness and justice.

6.4 Marriage and family therapists who are the authors of books or other materials that are published or distributed do not plagiarize or fail to cite persons to whom credit for original ideas or work is due.

6.5 Marriage and family therapists who are the authors of books or other materials published or distributed by an organization take reasonable precautions to ensure that the organization promotes and advertises the materials accurately and factually.

6.6 Marriage and family therapists participate in activities that contribute to a better community and society, including devoting a portion of their professional activity to services for which there is little or no financial return.

6.7 Marriage and family therapists are concerned with developing laws and regulations pertaining to marriage and family therapy that serve the public interest, and with altering such laws and regulations that are not in the public interest.

6.8 Marriage and family therapists encourage public participation in the design and delivery of professional services and in the regulation of practitioners.

Principle VII: Financial Arrangements

Marriage and family therapists make financial arrangements with clients, third-party payors, and supervisees that are reasonably understandable and conform to accepted professional practices.

7.1 Marriage and family therapists do not offer or accept kickbacks, rebates, bonuses, or other remuneration for referrals; fee-for-service arrangements are not prohibited.

7.2 Prior to entering into the therapeutic or supervisory relationship, marriage and family therapists clearly disclose and explain to clients and supervisees: (a) all financial arrangements and fees related to professional services, including charges for canceled or missed appointments; (b) the use of collection agencies or legal measures for nonpayment; and (c) the procedure for obtaining payment from the client, to the extent allowed by law, if payment is denied by the third-party payor. Once services have begun, therapists provide reasonable notice of any changes in fees or other charges.

7.3 Marriage and family therapists give reasonable notice to clients with unpaid balances of their intent to seek collection by agency or legal recourse. When such action is taken, therapists will not disclose clinical information.

7.4 Marriage and family therapists represent facts truthfully to clients, third-party payors, and supervisees regarding services rendered.

7.5 Marriage and family therapists ordinarily refrain from accepting goods and services from clients in return for services rendered. Bartering for professional services may be conducted only if: (a) the supervisee or client requests it, (b) the relationship is not exploitative, (c) the professional relationship is not distorted, and (d) a clear written contract is established.

7.6 Marriage and family therapists may not withhold records under their immediate control that are requested and needed for a client's treatment solely because payment has not been received for past services, except as otherwise provided by law.

Principle VIII: Advertising

Marriage and family therapists engage in appropriate informational activities, including those that enable the public, referral sources, or others to choose professional services on an informed basis.

8.1 Marriage and family therapists accurately represent their competencies, education, training, and experience relevant to their practice of marriage and family therapy.

8.2 Marriage and family therapists ensure that advertisements and publications in any media (such as directories, announcements, business cards, newspapers, radio, television, Internet, and facsimiles) convey information that is necessary for the public to make an appropriate selection of professional services. Information could include: (a) office information, such as name, address, telephone number, credit card acceptability, fees, languages spoken, and office hours; (b) qualifying clinical degree (see subprinciple 8.5); (c) other earned degrees (see subprinciple 8.5) and state or provincial licensures and/or certifications; (d) AAMFT clinical member status; and (e) description of practice.

8.3 Marriage and family therapists do not use names that could mislead the public concerning the identity, responsibility, source, and status of those practicing under that name, and do not hold themselves out as being partners or associates of a firm if they are not.

8.4 Marriage and family therapists do not use any professional identification (such as a business card, office sign, letterhead, Internet, or telephone or association directory listing) if it includes a statement or claim that is false, fraudulent, misleading, or deceptive.

8.5 In representing their educational qualifications, marriage and family therapists list and claim as evidence only those earned degrees: (a) from institutions accredited by regional accreditation sources recognized by the United States Department of Education, (b) from institutions recognized by states or provinces that license or certify marriage and family therapists, or (c) from equivalent foreign institutions.

8.6 Marriage and family therapists correct, wherever possible, false, misleading, or inaccurate information and representations made by others concerning the therapist's qualifications, services, or products.

8.7 Marriage and family therapists make certain that the qualifications of their employees or supervisees are represented in a manner that is not false, misleading, or deceptive.

8.8 Marriage and family therapists do not represent themselves as providing specialized services unless they have the appropriate education, training, or supervised experience.

Ethical Code of the International Association of Marriage and Family Counselors

Approved by the Board of IAMFC, 2005

C
Appendix

Preamble

The International Association of Marriage and Family Counselors (IAMFC) is an organization dedicated to advancing practice, training, and research in couple and family counseling.* Members may specialize in areas such as premarital counseling, marriage counseling, family counseling, sex counseling, intergenerational counseling, separation and divorce counseling, relocation counseling, custody evaluation, and parenting training. Marriage and family counselors may work with special populations including stepfamilies, nontraditional couples and family systems, multicultural couples and families, disadvantaged families, and dual career couples. In conducting their professional activities, members commit themselves to protect family relationships and advocate for the healthy growth and development of the family as a whole and each member's unique needs. The IAMFC member recognizes that the relationship between the provider and consumer of services is characterized as professional. However, the IAMFC member should remain informed of social and cultural trends, as well as scientific and tech-

nological changes affecting the foundation of the professional counseling relationship.

This code of ethics provides a framework for ethical practices by IAMFC members and other professionals engaged in couple and family counseling. It is divided into eight sections: the counseling relationship and client well-being; confidentiality and privacy; competence and professional responsibilities; collaboration and professional relationships; assessment and evaluation; counselor education and supervision; research and publication; and ethical decision making and resolution. The observations and recommendations presented within these eight areas are meant to supplement the current ethical standards of the American Counseling Association. Although an ethical code cannot anticipate every possible situation or dilemma, the IAMFC ethical guidelines can assist members in ensuring the welfare and dignity of the couples and families who seek services.

The ethical code of the IAMFC incorporates the ethics of principles and virtues. The code of ethics articulates some specific principles and guidelines, protecting consumers from potentially harmful practices

*The 2005 Ethical Code of the International Association of Marriage and Family Counselors (IAMFC) was written for the Ethics Committee and approved by the Board of IAMFC.

    Stephen Southern, Chair of the Ethics Committee, and Marvarene Oliver, Department of Counseling and Educational Psychology, Texas A & M University-Corpus Christi.

    Loretta J. Bradley, Department of Counselor Education, Texas Tech University.

    Bobbie Birdsall, Counselor Education Department, Boise State University.

and encouraging professionals to maintain high standards for effective practice. The ethical code also addresses the character of the professional couple and family counselor. Ethics of character or virtue contribute to professional aspirations and values. Each of the eight sections includes aspirations and principles.

Section A: The Counseling Relationship and Client Well-Being

Marriage and family counselors contribute to the healthy development and evolution of family systems. They are committed to understanding problems and learning needs from multiple contexts. Couple and family counselors, in particular, embrace models of practice based on family dynamics and systems. Professional counselors realize their perspectives influence the conceptualization of problems, identification of clients, and implementation of possible solutions. Couple and family counselors examine personal biases and values. They actively attempt to understand and serve couples and families from diverse cultural backgrounds. Professional marriage and family counselors are willing to remove barriers to the counseling relationship, act as responsible public servants, and become involved in advocacy in the best interests of couples and families.

1. Marriage and family counselors demonstrate caring, empathy, and respect for client well-being. They promote safety, security, and sense of community for couples and families. Due to potential risks involved, couple and family counselors should not use intrusive interventions without sound theoretical rationale, research support, and clinical consultation or supervision.

2. Marriage and family counselors recognize that each family is unique. Couple and family counselors do not promote bias and stereotyping regarding family roles and functions.

3. Marriage and family counselors respect the autonomy of the families with whom they work. They do not make decisions that rightfully belong to family members. When indicated and possible, couple and family counselors share with clients clinical impressions and recommendations, decision-making processes, problem-solving strategies, and intervention outcomes.

4. Marriage and family counselors respect cultural diversity. They do not discriminate on the basis of race, gender, disability, religion, age, sexual orientation, cultural background, national origin, marital status, or political affiliation.

5. Marriage and family counselors promote open, honest and direct relationships with consumers of professional services. Couple and family counselors inform clients about the goals of counseling, qualifications of the counselor(s), limits of confidentiality, potential risks and benefits associated with specific techniques, duration of treatment, costs of services, appropriate alternatives to marriage and family counseling, and reasonable expectations for outcomes.

6. Marriage and family counselors promote primary prevention. They advocate for the development of clients' cognitive, moral, social, emotional, spiritual, physical, educational, relational, and vocational skills. Couple and family counselors promote effective marital and family communication and problem solving skills needed to prevent future problems.

7. Marriage and family counselors have an obligation to determine and inform counseling participants who is identified as the primary client. The marriage and family counselor should make clear when there are obligations to an individual, a couple, a family, a third party, or an institution.

8. Marriage and family counselors who are IAMFC members have a professional duty to monitor their places of employment to make recommendations so the environment is conducive to the positive growth and development of clients. When there is a conflict of interest between the needs of the client and counselor's employing institution, the IAMFC member works to clarify his or her commitment to all parties. IAMFC members recognize that the acceptance of employment implies agreement with the policies and practices of the agency or institution.

9. Marriage and family counselors do not harass, exploit, coerce, or manipulate clients for personal gain. Couple and family counselors avoid whenever possible multiple relationships, such as business, social or sexual contacts with any current clients or their family members. Marriage and family counselors should refrain generally from nonprofessional relationships with former clients and their family members because termination of counseling is a complex process. Couple and family counselors are responsible for demonstrating there is no harm from any relationship with a client or family member. The key element in this ethical principle is the avoidance of exploitation of vulnerable clients.

10. Marriage and family counselors have an obligation to withdraw from a counseling relationship if the continuation of services would not be in the best interest of the client or would result in a vio-

lation of ethical standards. If the counseling relationship is no longer helpful or productive, couple and family counselors have an obligation to assist in locating alternative services and making referrals as needed. Marriage and family counselors do not abandon clients. They arrange for appropriate termination of counseling relationships and transfer of services as indicated.

11. Marriage and family counselors maintain accurate and up-to-date records. They make all file information available to clients unless there is compelling evidence that such access would be harmful to the client. In situations involving multiple clients, couple and family counselors provide individual clients with parts of records related directly to them, protecting confidential information related to other clients who have not authorized release. Marriage and family counselors include sufficient and timely documentation in client records to facilitate delivery of services and referral to other professionals as needed.

12. Marriage and family counselors establish fees that are reasonable and customary depending upon the scope and location of their practices. Couple and family counselors in community agencies, schools, and other public settings do not solicit gifts or charge fees for services that are available in the counselor's employing agency or institution. Culturally sensitive counselors recognize that gifts are tokens of respect and gratitude in some cultures. Marriage and family counselors may receive gifts or participate in family rituals that promote healthy interaction and do not exploit clients.

13. Marriage and family counselors maintain ethical and effective practices as they address the benefits and limitations of technological innovations and cultural changes. Counseling may be conducted or assisted by telephones, computer hardware and software, and other communication technologies. Technology-assisted distance counseling services may expand the scope and influence of marriage and family counseling. However, counselors are responsible for developing competencies in the use of new technologies and safeguarding private and confidential information.

Section B: Confidentiality and Privacy

Marriage and family counselors recognize that trust is the foundation of an effective counseling relationship. Professional counselors maintain appropriate boundaries so that clients reasonably expect that information shared will not be disclosed to others without prior written consent. Due to the nature of couple and family counseling, safeguards must be established in the counseling process to insure privacy of client disclosures without contributing to dysfunctional family secrets. Clients have the right to know the limits of confidentiality, privacy, and privileged communication.

1. Marriage and family counselors may disclose private information to others under specific circumstances known to the individual client or client family members. Ideally, the client consents to disclosure by signing an authorization to release information. Each person receiving counseling who is legally competent to sign a waiver of right to confidentiality should execute an authorization. The authorization should clearly indicate to whom information will be disclosed under which specific circumstances. The authorization should be time-limited, consistent with legal statutes, and limited to the scope agreed by the counselor and client. The client may rescind or withdraw the authorization.

2. Marriage and family counselors inform parents and legal guardians about the confidential nature of the counseling relationship. When working with minor or juvenile clients, as well as adult clients who lack the capacity to authorize release of confidential information, couple and family counselors seek consent from the appropriate custodial parent or guardian to disclose information.

3. Marriage and family counselors inform clients of exceptions to the general principle that information will be kept confidential or released only upon written client authorization. Disclosure of private information may be mandated by state law. For example, states require reporting of suspected abuse of children or other vulnerable populations. Couple and family counselors may have sound legal or ethical justification for disclosing information if someone is in imminent danger. A court may have jurisdiction to order release of confidential information without a client's permission. However, all releases of information not authorized by clients should be minimal or narrow as possible to limit potential harm to the counseling relationship.

4. Marriage and family counselors inform clients who may have access to their counseling records, as well as any information that may be released for third-party payment or insurance reimbursement. State and Federal laws may affect record-keeping and release of information from client records.

5. Marriage and family counselors store records in a way that protects confidentiality. Written records should be kept in a locked file drawer or cabinet

and computerized record systems should have appropriate passwords and safeguards to prevent unauthorized entry.

6. Marriage and family counselors inform clients if sessions are to be recorded on tape or digital media and obtain written consent authorizing recording for particular purposes. When more than one person is receiving counseling, all persons who are legally competent must give informed consent in writing for the recording.

7. Marriage and family counselors inform clients that statements made by a family member to the counselor during an individual counseling, consultation, or collateral contact are to be treated as confidential. Such statements are not disclosed to other family members without the individual's permission. However, the marriage and family counselor should clearly identify the client of counseling, which may be the couple or family system. Couple and family counselors do not maintain family secrets, collude with some family members against others, or otherwise contribute to dysfunctional family system dynamics. If a client's refusal to share information from individual contacts interferes with the agreed goals of counseling, the counselor may terminate treatment and refer the clients to another counselor. Some marriage and family counselors choose to not meet with individuals, preferring to serve family systems.

8. Marriage and family counselors provide reasonable access to counseling records when requested by competent clients. In situations involving multiple clients, counselors provide only the records directly related to a particular individual, protecting confidential information related to any other client.

9. Marriage and family counselors provide reasonable access to counseling records of minor children when requested by parents or guardians having legal rights to custody and health decision-making. However, counselors do not become embroiled in custody disputes or parent-child conflicts occasioned by records release. Professional counselors attempt to protect the counseling relationship with children by suggesting limits to disclosure appropriate to the particular situation.

10. Marriage and family counselors maintain privacy and confidentiality in research, publication, case consultation, teaching, supervision, and other professional activities. Ideally, counselors secure informed consent and authorization to release information in all professional activities.

Section C: Competence and Professional Responsibilities

Marriage and family counselors aspire to maintain competency through initial training, ongoing supervision and consultation, and continuing education. They have responsibilities to abide by this ethical code, as well as other professional codes related to professional identity and group membership. In particular, couple and family counselors should become active in professional associations such as the International Association of Marriage and Family Counselors and the American Counseling Association to encourage beneficial changes in professionals and the counseling profession.

1. Marriage and family counselors have the responsibility to develop and maintain basic skills in marriage and family counseling through graduate training, supervision, and consultation. An outline of these skills is provided by the current Council for Accreditation of Counseling and Related Educational Programs (CACREP) *Standards for Marital, Couple, and Family Counseling/Therapy Programs*. The minimal level of training shall be considered a master's degree in a helping profession.

2. Marriage and family counselors recognize the need for familiarizing oneself with new developments in the field of marriage and family counseling. They pursue continuing education afforded by books, journals, courses, workshops, conferences, and conventions.

3. Marriage and family counselors accurately represent their education, expertise, training, and experience. Professional counselors objectively represent their professional qualifications, skills, and specialties to the public. Membership in a professional organization, including IAMFC, is not used to suggest competency.

4. Marriage and family counselors insure that announcements or advertisements of professional services focus on objective information that enables the client to make an informed decision. Providing information, such as highest relevant academic degree, licenses or certifications, office hours, types of services offered, fee structure, and languages spoken, can help clients select marriage and family counselors.

5. Marriage and family counselors do not attempt to diagnose or treat problems beyond the scope of their training and abilities. They do not engage in specialized counseling interventions or techniques unless they have received appropriate training and preparation in the methods.

6. Marriage and family counselors do not undertake any professional activity in which their personal problems might adversely affect their performance. Instead, they focus on obtaining appropriate professional assistance to help them resolve the problem.

7. Marriage and family counselors do not engage in actions that violate the legal standards of their community. They do not encourage clients or others to engage in unlawful activities.

8. Marriage and family counselors have the responsibility to provide public information that enhances marriage and family life. Such statements should be based on sound, scientifically acceptable theories, techniques, and approaches. Due to the inability to complete a comprehensive assessment and provide follow-up, members should not give specific advice to an individual through the media.

9. Marriage and family counselors produce advertisements about workshops or seminars that contain descriptions of the audiences for which the programs are intended. Due to their subjective nature, statements either from clients or from the counselor about the uniqueness, effectiveness, or efficiency of services should be avoided. Announcements and advertisements should never contain false, misleading, or fraudulent statements.

10. Marriage and family counselors promoting tapes, books, or other products for commercial sale make every effort to insure that announcements and advertisements are presented in a professional and factual manner.

Section D: Collaboration and Professional Relationships

Marriage and family counselors work to maintain good relationships with professional peers within and outside the field of counseling. Consultation and collaboration represent means by which couple and family counselors can remove barriers to underserved populations. Interdisciplinary teamwork may be required to best serve clients.

1. Marriage and family counselors are knowledgeable about the roles and functions of other disciplines, especially in the helping professions such as psychiatry, psychology, social work, and mental health counseling. Counselors work to strengthen interdisciplinary relations with colleagues.

2. Marriage and family counselors enter into professional partnerships in which each partner adheres to the ethical standards of their professions. Couple and family counselors should not charge a fee for offering or accepting referrals.

3. Marriage and family counselors do not engage in harmful relationships with individuals over whom they have supervisory, evaluative, or instructional control. They do not engage in harassment or other abuses of power or authority.

4. Marriage and family counselors work to insure the ethical delivery of effective services in any agency or institution in which they are employed. Couple and family counselors engaging in consultation and collaboration take responsibility for the well-being and ethical treatment of clients. Counselors alert administrators about inappropriate policies and practices in institutions they serve.

5. Marriage and family counselors working as subcontractors for counseling services for a third party have a duty to inform clients of limitations that the organization may place on the counseling or consulting relationship.

6. Marriage and family counselors maintain good working relationships with team members and collaborators. They promote healthy boundaries and organizational climate. Couple and family counselors refrain from becoming involved in splitting, triangulation, and indirect forms of communication which could be harmful to colleagues or the organization they share.

7. Marriage and family counselors do not offer services to clients served by other professionals without securing a referral or release. The counselor should be authorized by the client to contact the other professional to coordinate or transfer care. There may be special considerations regarding transfer of care in the termination of an abusive counseling relationship.

Section E: Assessment and Evaluation

Marriage and family counselors are highly skilled in relational and interpersonal assessment. They recognize the potential values to clients from appropriate educational, psychological, and vocational evaluation. However, marriage and family counselors are sensitive to misuse and abuse of assessment results. Counselors avoid whenever possible evaluation, assessment, or diagnosis that restricts the overall development and freedom of choice of individuals, couples, and families. Recognizing the origins of marriage and family counseling in systems thinking, they avoid whenever possible assigning problems to individuals. Instead, professional counselors aspire to identify solutions that promote the well-being of family systems.

1. Marriage and family counselors use assessment procedures to promote the best interests and well-being of the client in clarifying concerns, establishing treatment goals, evaluating therapeutic progress, and promoting objective decision making.

2. Marriage and family counselors recognize that clients have the right to know the results, interpretations, and conclusions drawn from assessment interviews and instruments, as well as how this information will be used. Couple and family counselors safeguard assessment data and maintain the confidentiality of evaluation records and reports.

3. Marriage and family counselors use assessment methods that are reliable, valid, and relevant to the goals of the client. Couple and family counselors using tests or inventories should have a thorough understanding of measurement concepts, including relevant psychometric and normative data. When using computer-assisted scoring, counselors obtain empirical evidence for the reliability and validity of the methods and procedures.

4. Marriage and family counselors do not use inventories and tests that have outdated items or normative data. They refrain from using assessment instruments and techniques likely to be biased or prejudiced.

5. Marriage and family counselors do not use assessment methods that are outside the scope of their qualifications, training, or statutory limitations. They consult with psychologists, mental health counselors, or other professional colleagues in interpreting and understanding particular test results.

6. Marriage and family counselors conducting custody evaluations recognize the potential impact that their reports can have on family members. They are committed to a thorough assessment of both parents. Therefore, custody recommendations should not be made on the basis of information from only one parent. Couple and family counselors only use instruments that have demonstrated reliability, validity, and utility in custody evaluations. They do not make recommendations based solely on test and inventory scores.

7. Members strive to follow current guidelines and standards for testing published or disseminated by the American Counseling Association, American Educational Research Association, American Psychological Association, Association for Assessment in Counseling and Education, National Council on Measurement in Evaluation, and other groups dedicated to professional expertise in assessment.

Section F: Counselor Education and Supervision

Marriage and family counselors are likely to engage in some training and supervision activities, including peer consultation and supervision. Couple and family counselors recognize potential power imbalances in teacher-student, supervisor-supervisee, and consultant-consultee relationships. They do not abuse power or influence and work to protect students, supervisees, and consultees from exploitation. Marriage and family counselors maintain appropriate boundaries that promote growth and development for all parties. They recognize and respect cultural differences, adjusting their professional efforts to fit the learning needs of trainees.

1. Marriage and family counselors who provide supervision acquire and maintain skills pertaining to the supervision process. They are able to demonstrate for supervisees the application of counseling theory and process to client issues. Supervisors are knowledgeable about different methods and conceptual approaches to supervision.

2. Marriage and family counselors who provide supervision respect the inherent imbalance of power in the supervisory relationship. They do not use their potentially influential positions to exploit students, supervisees, or employees. Supervisors do not ask supervisees to engage in behaviors not directly related to the supervision process, and they clearly separate supervision and evaluation. Supervisors also avoid multiple relationships that might impair their professional judgment or increase the possibility of exploitation. Sexual intimacy with students or supervisees is prohibited.

3. Marriage and family counselors who provide supervision are responsible for both the promotion of supervisee learning and development and the advancement of marriage and family counseling. Supervisors recruit students into professional organizations, educate students about professional ethics and standards, provide service to professional organizations, strive to educate new professionals, and work to improve professional practices.

4. Marriage and family counselors who provide supervision have the responsibility to inform students of the specific expectations regarding skill building, knowledge acquisition, and development of competencies. Supervisors also provide ongoing and timely feedback to their supervisees.

5. Marriage and family counselors who provide supervision are responsible for protecting the rights and well-being of their supervisees' clients. They monitor their supervisees' counseling on an ongoing basis, and maintain policies and procedures to protect the confidentiality of clients whose sessions have been electronically recorded.

6. Marriage and family counselors who provide supervision maintain ethical standards for counselor supervision. Counselor educators and supervisors may consult publications of the Association for Counselor Education and Supervision to clarify ethical issues in supervisory relationships.

7. Marriage and family counselors who are counselor educators encourage their programs to maintain the current guidelines provided in the CACREP *Standards for Marital, Couple, and Family Counseling/Therapy Programs*. They also encourage training programs to offer coursework and supervision indicated by particular accreditation boards.

8. Marriage and family counselors involved in training and supervision, especially educators and students, should explore ethical principles as well as aspirational goals. Counselor educators should infuse ethical studies throughout the curriculum.

9. Marriage and family counselors refer to the current American Counseling Association *Code of Ethics* as a source document for training and supervision in professional counseling.

Section G: Research and Publication

Marriage and family counselors should engage in research and publication that advances the profession of marriage and family counseling. They act to prevent harm to research participants and produce results that are beneficial to couples and families. Couple and family counselors maintain high ethical standards for informed consent and protection of confidentiality when conducting research projects or producing publications. They solicit input from peers, institutional review boards, and other stakeholders to minimize risks and enhance outcomes.

1. Marriage and family counselors shall be fully responsible for their choice of research topics and the methods used for investigation, analysis, and reporting. They must be particularly careful that findings do not appear misleading, that the research is planned to allow for the inclusion of alternative hypotheses, and that provision is made for discussion of the limitations of the study.

2. Marriage and family counselors safeguard the privacy of their research participants. Data about an individual participant are not released unless the individual is informed about the exact nature of the information to be released and gives written permission for disclosure.

3. Marriage and family counselors protect the safety of their research participants. Researchers follow guidelines of a peer review committee or institutional research board. Prospective participants are informed, in writing about any potential risk associated with a study and are notified that they can withdraw at any time.

4. Marriage and family counselors make their original data available to other researchers. They contribute to the advancement of the field by encouraging the research and publication efforts of colleagues.

5. Marriage and family counselors only take credit for research in which they make a substantial contribution, and give credit to all contributors. Authors are listed from greatest to least amount of contribution.

6. Marriage and family counselors do not plagiarize. Ideas or data that did not originate with the author and are not common knowledge are clearly credited to the original source.

7. Marriage and family counselors are aware of their obligation to be role models for graduate students and other future researchers and act in accordance with the highest standards possible while engaged in research and publication.

8. Marriage and family counselors review materials submitted for research, publication, and other scholarly purposes. They respect the confidentiality and proprietary rights of those who submit their products for review. Counselors engaged in reviews of manuscripts and presentation proposals use valid and defensible standards, act within the limits of their competencies, and refrain from personal biases. In this manner, authors and researchers are supported and the field of marriage and family counseling is advanced.

Section H: Ethical Decision-Making and Resolution

Marriage and family counselors incorporate ethical practices in their daily work. They discuss ethical dilemmas with colleagues and engage in ethical decision-making in all aspects of marriage and family counseling. They hold other counselors to sound ethical principles and encourage professional virtues and aspirations. Couple and family counselors work with other professionals to resolve ethical issues.

1. Marriage and family counselors are responsible for understanding the American Counseling Association *Code of Ethics*, the *Ethical Code of the International Association of Marriage and Family Counselors*, and other applicable ethics codes from professional associations, certification and licensure boards, and other credentialing organizations by which they are regulated.

2. Marriage and family counselors have the responsibility to confront unethical behavior of other counselors or therapists, particularly members of the International Association of Marriage and Family Counselors (IAMFC). The first step should be discussing the violation directly with the caregiver. If the problem continues, the marriage and family counselor may contact the professional organization or licensure board of the counselor or therapist in question. IAMFC members may contact the executive director, president, executive board members, or chair of the ethics committee at any time for consultation on identifying or resolving ethical violations.

3. Marriage and family counselors specify the nature of conflicts between work requirements and other demands of an employing organization and the relevant codes of ethics. Employment and consultation of couple and family counselors should not compromise ethical standards. They work toward beneficial changes in the organizations of which they are members.

4. Marriage and family counselors do not engage in unwarranted or invalid complaints. Ethics violations are reported when informal attempts at resolution have failed or violations are likely to substantially harm an individual or organization. Couple and family counselors should follow the reporting requirements specified by laws and regulations in their jurisdictions.

5. Marriage and family counselors cooperate with ethics committees and other duly constituted organizations having jurisdiction over the professional charged with an ethics violation. Counselors assist professional associations in promoting ethical behavior and professional conduct.

References

Abrams, D., & Hogg, M. A. (2001). Collective identity: Group membership and self-conception. In M. A. Hogg & S. Tindale (Eds.), *Blackwell handbook of social psychology: Vol. 3. Group processes* (pp. 425–461). Oxford, England: Blackwell.

Ackerman, N. W. (1958). *The psychodynamics of family life.* New York: Basic Books.

Ackerman, N. W., & Franklin, P. F. (1965). Family dynamics and the reversibility of delusional formation: A case study in family therapy. In I. Boszormenyi-Nagy & J. L. Framo (Eds.), *Intensive family therapy* (pp. 245–287). Hagerstown, MD: Harper & Row.

Ahrons, C. (1994). *The good divorce: Keeping your family together when your marriage comes apart.* New York: HarperCollins.

Ainsworth, M. D. S., Blehar, M. C., Waters, E., & Wall, S. (1978). *Patterns of attachment: A psychological study of the strange situation.* Hillsdale, NJ: Lawrence Erlbaum.

Alexander, J. F., Barton, C., Schiavo, R. S., & Parsons, B. V. (1977). Systems-behavioral intervention with families of delinquents: Therapist characteristics, family behavior, and outcome. *Journal of Consulting and Clinical Psychology, 44,* 656–664.

Almeida, R. V., & Durkin, T. (1999). The cultural context model: Therapy for couples with domestic violence. *Journal of Marital and Family Therapy, 25,* 313–324.

American Association for Marriage and Family Therapy. (2001). *Code of ethics.* Retrieved December 7, 2005, from http://www.aamft.org/resources/LRMPlan/Ethics/ethicscode2001.asp.

American Counseling Association. (2005). *Code of ethics and standards of practice.* Retrieved December 7, 2005., from http://www.counseling.org/Resources/CodeOfEthics/TP/Home/CT2.aspx.

American Psychiatric Association. (1994). *Diagnostic and statistical manual of mental disorders* (4th ed.). Washington, DC: Author.

Anderson, C. (2003). The diversity, strengths, and challenges of single-parent households. In F. Welsh (Ed.), *Normal family processes: Growing diversity and complexity* (3rd ed., pp. 121–152). New York: Guilford Press.

Anderson, D. A. (1994). Transcendence and relinquishment in couple therapy. *Journal of Systemic Therapies, 13*(3), 36–41.

Anderson, D. A., & Worthen, D. (1997). Exploring a fourth dimension: Spirituality as a resource for the couple therapist. *Journal of Marital and Family Therapy, 23,* 3–12.

Anderson, H. (1993). On a roller coaster: A collaborative language systems approach to therapy. In S. Friedman (Ed.), *The new language of change: Constructive collaboration in psychotherapy* (pp. 323–344). New York: Guilford Press.

Anderson, H. (1997). *Conversation, language, and possibilities: A postmodern approach to therapy.* New York: Basic Books.

Anderson, H. (2005). Myths about "not-knowing." *Family Process, 44,* 497–504.

Anderson, H., & Goolishian, H. A. (1990). Beyond cybernetics: Comments on Atkinson and Heath's "further thoughts on second-order family therapy." *Family Process, 29,* 157–167.

Anderson, H., & Goolishian, H. A. (1988). Human systems as linguistic systems: Preliminary and evolving ideas about the implications for clinical theory. *Family Process, 27,* 371–393.

Anderson, H., Goolishian, H., & Winderman, L. (1986). Problem determined systems: Toward transformation in family therapy. *Journal of Strategic and Systemic Therapies, 5*(4), 1–13.

Anderson, S. A., Rigazio-DiGilio, S. A., & Kunkler, K. P. (1995). Training and supervision in family therapy: Current issues and future directions. *Family Relations, 44,* 489–500.

Andersen, T. (1987). The reflecting team: Dialogue and meta-dialogue in clinical work. *Family Process, 26,* 415–428.

Andersen, T. (Ed.). (1991). *The reflecting team: Dialogues and dialogues about the dialogues.* New York: Norton.

Andolfi, M., & Angelo, C. (1981). The therapist as director of the family drama. *Journal of Marital and Family Therapy, 7,* 255–264.

Aponte, J. H. (1976). The family-school interview: An eco-structural approach. *Family Process, 15,* 303–311.

Aponte, H. J. (1999). The stresses of poverty and the comfort of spirituality. In F. Walsh (Ed.), *Spiritual resources in family therapy* (pp. 76–89). New York: Guilford Press.

Aries, P. (1962). *Centuries of childhood: A social history of family life.* New York: Vintage Books.

Arnett, J. J. (2004). *Emerging adulthood: The winding road from the late teens through the twenties.* Oxford, England: Oxford University Press.

Arnold, M. S. (2002). Culture-sensitive family therapy. In J. Carlson & D. Kjos (Eds.), *Theories and strategies of family therapy* (pp. 19–40). Boston: Allyn & Bacon.

Atkinson, B. J. (2005). *Emotional intelligence in couples therapy: Advances in neurobiology and the science of intimate relationships.* New York: Norton.

Atkinson, B. J., & Heath, A. W. (1990). Further thoughts on second-order family therapy—This time it's personal. *Family Process, 29,* 145–155.

Auel, J. M. (1984). *The clan of the cave bear.* New York: Bantam Books.

Auerswald, E. H. (1987). Epistemological confusion in family therapy and research. *Family Process, 26,* 317–330.

Azrin, N. H., Besalel, A., Bechtel, R., Michalicek, A., Mancera, M., Carroll, D., et al. (1980). Comparison of reciprocity and discussion-type counseling for marital problems. *American Journal of Family Therapy, 8,* 22–28.

Azrin, N. H., Naster, B. J., & Jones, R. (1973). Reciprocity counseling: A rapid learning-based procedure for marital counseling. *Behavioral Research and Therapy, 11,* 365–382.

Bachelor, A., & Horvath, A. (1999). The therapeutic relationship. In M. A. Hubble, B. L. Duncan, & S. D. Miller (Eds.), *The heart and soul of change: What works in therapy* (pp. 133–178). Washington, DC: American Psychological Association.

Bacigalupe, G. (1998). Cross-cultural systemic therapy training and consultation: A postcolonial view. *Journal of Systemic Therapies, 17*(1), 31–44.

Bader, E., & Pearson, P. T. (1988). *In quest of the mythical mate: A developmental approach to diagnosis and treatment in couples therapy.* New York: Brunner/Mazel.

Bagarozzi, D. A. (1996). *The couple and family in managed care: Assessment, evaluation, and treatment.* New York: Brunner/Mazel.

Bailey, B. (1999). *Sex in the heartland.* Cambridge, MA: Harvard University Press.

Bailey, C. E. (2002). The effect of spiritual beliefs and practices on family functioning: A qualitative study. In T. D. Carlson & M. J. Erickson (Eds.), *Spirituality and family therapy* (pp. 127–144). New York: Haworth Press.

Balcom, D., Lee, R. G., & Tager, J. (1995). The systemic treatment of shame in couples. *Journal of Marital and Family Therapy, 21,* 55–65.

Baltimore, M. L. (2000). Ethical considerations in the use of technology for marriage and family counselors. *Family Journal: Counseling and Therapy for Couples and Families, 8,* 390–393.

Bandler, R., Grinder, J., & Satir, V. (1976). *Changing with families: A book about further education for being human.* Palo Alto, CA: Science and Behavior Books.

Bandura, A., & Walters, R. (1963). *Social learning and personality development.* New York: Holt, Rinehart and Winston.

Baptiste, D. A. (2002). *Clinical epiphanies in marital and family therapy: A practitioner's casebook of therapeutic insights, perceptions, and breakthroughs.* New York: Haworth Press.

Bardill, D. R. (1976). The simulated family as an aid to learning family group treatment. *Child Welfare, 55,* 703–709.

Barnhill, L. R. (1979). Healthy family systems. *Family Coordinator, 28,* 94–100.

Bartholomew, K., & Horowitz, L. (1991). Attachment styles among young adults: A test of a four category model. *Journal of Personality and Social Psychology, 61,* 226–244.

Bateson, G. (1951). The convergence of science and psychiatry. In J. Reusch & G. Bateson (Eds.), *Communication: The social matrix of psychiatry* (pp. 257–301). New York: Norton.

Bateson, G. (1972). *Steps to an ecology of mind.* New York: Ballantine Books.

Bateson, G. (1979). *Mind in nature: A necessary unity.* New York: Bantam Books.

Bateson, G., Jackson, D. D., Haley, J., & Weakland, J. H. (1963). A note on the double bind—1962. *Family Process, 2,* 154–161.

Baucom, D. H., Epstein, N., & LaTaillade, J. J. (2002). Cognitive-behavioral couple therapy. In A. S. Gurman & N. S. Jacobson (Eds.), *Clinical handbook of couple therapy* (3rd ed., pp. 26–58). New York: Guilford Press.

Baudrillard, J. (1975). *The mirror of production.* St. Louis, MO: Telos Press.

Baumrind, D. (1991). The influence of parenting style on adolescent competence and substance use. *Journal of Early Adolescence, 11,* 56–95.

Beamish, P. M., Navin, S. L., & Davidson, P. (1994). Ethical dilemmas in marriage and family therapy: A constructivist/ecosystem view. *Journal of Mental Health Counseling, 16,* 129–142.

Bean, R. A., Perry, B. J., & Bedell, T. M. (2002). Developing culturally competent marriage and family therapists: Treatment guidelines for non-African American therapists working with African American families. *Journal of Marital and Family Therapy, 28,* 153–164.

Beavers, W. R., & Hampson, R. B. (2003). Measuring competence: The Beavers Systems Model. In F. Walsh (Ed.), *Normal family processes* (3rd ed., pp. 549–580). New York: Guilford Press.

Beck, A. T., Rush, A. J., Shaw, B. F., & Emery, G. (1979). *Cognitive therapy of depression.* New York: Guilford Press.

Becvar, D. S. (1997). *Soul healing: A spiritual orientation in counseling and therapy.* New York: Basic Books.

Beels, C. C. (2002). Notes for a cultural history of family therapy. *Family Process, 41,* 67–82.

Bell, D. C., & Richard, A. J. (2000). Caregiving: The forgotten element in attachment. *Psychological Inquiry, 11*(2), 69–83.

Bell, J. E. (1970). The future of family therapy. *Family Process, 9,* 127–141.

Bell, J. E. (1975). *Family therapy.* New York: Aronson.

Bellah, R. N. (2003). The ritual roots of society and culture. In M. Dillon (Ed.), *Handbook of the sociology of religion* (pp. 31–44). Cambridge, England: Cambridge University Press.

Belson, R. (1993). "You wouldn't even say hello" or My three joining principles. *Journal of Systemic Therapies, 12*(4), 66–68.

Berg, I. K., & deShazer, S. (1993). Making numbers talk: Language in therapy. In S. Freidman (Ed.), *The new language of change* (pp. 5–24). New York: Guilford Press.

Berg, I. K., & Jaya, A. (1993). Different and same: Family therapy with Asian American families. *Journal of Marital and Family Therapy, 19,* 31–38.

Berger, P., & Luckmann, T. (1966). *The social construction of reality.* Garden City, NY: Doubleday.

Bernardes, J. (1993). Responsibilities in studying postmodern families. *Journal of Family Issues, 14,* 35–49.

Bernstein, A. C. (1999). Reconstructing the Brothers Grimm: New tales of stepfamily life. *Family Process, 38,* 415–429.

Beyer, P. (2003). Social forms of religion and religions in contemporary global society. In M. Dillon (Ed.), *Handbook of the sociology of religion* (pp. 45–60). Cambridge, England: Cambridge University Press.

Bird, J. (2000). *The heart's narrative: Therapy and navigating life's contradictions.* Auckland, New Zealand: Edge Press.

Birdwhistell, R. (1952). *An introduction to kinesic: An annotation system for analysis of body motion and gesture.* Louisville, KY: University of Louisville Press.

Bischoff, R. J. (2004). Considerations in the use of telecommunications as a primary treatment medium: The application of behavioral telehealth to marriage and family therapy. *American Journal of Family Therapy, 32,* 173–187.

Bischoff, R. J., Barton, M., Thober, J., & Hawley, R. (2002). Events and experiences impacting the development of clinical self-confidence: A study of the first year of client contact. *Journal of Marital and Family Therapy, 28,* 371–382.

Bjork, D. W. (1993). *B. F. Skinner: A life.* New York: Basic Books.

Bloch, J. P. (1998). *New spirituality, self, and belonging: How new agers and neo-pagans talk about themselves.* Westport, CN: Praeger.

Bloch, D., & Simon, R. (Eds.). (1982). *The strength of family therapy: Selected papers of Nathan W. Ackerman.* New York: Brunner/Mazel.

Blos, P. (1985). *On adolescence.* New York: Free Press.

Blume, L. B., & Blume, T. W. (2003). Toward a dialectical model of family gender discourse: Body, identity, and sexuality. *Journal of Marriage and Family, 65,* 770–799.

Blume, T. W. (1996). Social perspectives on violence. *Michigan Family Review, 2*(1), 9–23. Retrieved October 24, 2005, from http://www.hti.umich.edu/m/mfr.

Blume, T. W. (1998). Couple intimacy and sexuality questionnaire. In L. L. Hecker & S. Deacon (Eds.), *The therapist's notebook: Homework, handouts, and activities* (pp. 197–200). New York: Haworth Press.

Blume, T. W. (2002). Negotiating couple sexuality. In L. Burlew & D. Capuzzi (Eds.), *Sexuality counseling* (pp. 89–109). Upper Saddle River, NJ: Merrill/Prentice-Hall.

Blume, T. W., & Weinstein, D. (2001, May). *Narrative identity negotiations of an adult student couple.* Poster presented at the Biennial Conference of the Society for Research in Identity Formation, London, Ontario, Canada.

Blumstein, P., & Schwartz, P. (1985). *American couples: Money-work-sex.* New York: Pocket Books.

Boczkowski, P. J. (1996). From text to hypertext: Technologies, metaphors, and the social construction of family therapy. *Journal of Systemic Therapies, 15*(4), 59–79.

Bograd, M., & Mederos, F. (1999). Battering and couples therapy: Universal screening and selection of treatment modality. *Journal of Marital and Family Therapy, 25,* 291–312.

Borwick, B. (1991). The co-created world of alcoholism. *Journal of Strategic and Systemic Therapies, 10*(1), 3–19.

Boszormenyi-Nagy, I., & Framo, J. (Eds.). (1965). *Intensive family therapy.* Hagerstown, MD: Harper & Row.

Boszormenyi-Nagy, I., & Spark, G. M. (1973). *Invisible loyalties: Reciprocity in intergenerational family therapy.* New York: Harper & Row.

Bowen, C. (2002). Parental accounts of blaming within the family: A dialectical model for understanding blame in systemic therapy. *Journal of Marital and Family Therapy, 28,* 129–144.

Bowen Family Center. (2004). *Family projection process.* Retrieved September 2, 2005, from http://www.thebowencenter.org/pages/conceptfpp.html.

Bowen, M. (1966). The use of family therapy in clinical practice. *Comprehensive Psychiatry, 7,* 345–374.

Bowen, M. (1978). *Family therapy in clinical practice.* New York: Aronson.

Bowlby, J. (1979). *The making and breaking of affectional bonds.* London: Tavistock.

Bowlby, J. (1988). *A secure base.* New York: Basic Books.

Boyd-Franklin, N. (1993). Race, class, and poverty. In F. Walsh (Ed.), *Normal family processes* (2nd ed., pp. 361–376). New York: Guilford Press.

Boyd-Franklin, N. (2003). *Black families in therapy: Understanding the African American experience* (2nd ed.). New York: Guilford Press.

Boyd-Franklin, N., & Lockwood, T. W. (1999). Spirituality and religion: Implications for psychotherapy with African American clients and families. In F. Walsh (Ed.), *Spiritual resources in family therapy* (pp. 90–103). New York: Guilford Press.

Bradley, C. R. (1998). Cultural interpretations of child discipline: Voices of African American scholars. *Family Journal: Counseling and Therapy for Couples and Families, 6,* 272–278.

Braverman, S. (2002). The use of genograms in supervision. In T. Todd & C. L. Storm (Eds.), *The complete systemic supervisor: Context, philosophy, and pragmatics* (pp. 349–362). New York: Authors Choice Press.

Brendel, J. M., & Nelson, K. W. (1999). The stream of family secrets: Navigating the islands of confidentiality and triangulation involving family therapists. *Family Journal: Counseling and Therapy for Couples and Families, 7,* 112–117.

Bristor, M. W., Wilson, A. L., & Helfer, R. E. (1985). Perinatal coaching: Program development. *Cinical Perinatology, 12,* 367–380.

Broderick, C. B., & Schrader, S. S. (1991). The history of professional marriage and family therapy. In A. S. Gurman & D. P. Kniskern (Eds.), *Handbook of family therapy* (Vol. 2, pp. 3–40). New York: Brunner/Mazel.

Brody, L. R., & Hall, J. A. (2000). Gender, emotion, and expression. In M. Lewis & J. M. Haviland-Jones (Eds.), *Handbook of emotions* (2nd ed., pp. 338–349). New York: Guilford Press.

Bronfenbrenner, U. (1979). *The ecology of human development: Experiments by nature and design.* Cambridge, MA: Harvard University Press.

Brotherson, S. E., & Soderquist, J. (2002). Coping with a child's death: Spiritual issues and therapeutic implications. In T. D. Carlson & M. J. Erickson (Eds.), *Spirituality and family therapy* (pp. 53–86). New York: Haworth Press.

Brown, E. M. (1999). *Affairs: A guide to working through the repercussions of infidelity.* San Francisco: Jossey-Bass.

Brown, S., & Lewis, L. (1999). *The alcoholic family in recovery: A developmental model.* New York: Guilford Press.

Buber, M. (1958). *I and thou* (R. G. Smith, Trans., 2nd ed.). New York: Scribner.

Buchanan, M., Dzelme, K., Harris, D., & Hecker, L. (2001). Challenges of being simultaneously gay or lesbian and spiritual and/or religious: A narrative perspective. *American Journal of Family Therapy, 29,* 435–449.

Buckley, W. F. (1967). *Sociology and modern systems theory.* Englewood Cliffs, NJ: Prentice-Hall.

Bumpass, L. L., Sweet, J. A., & Cherlin, A. J. (1991). The role of cohabitation in declining rates of marriage. *Journal of Marriage and the Family, 53,* 913–927.

Bunyan, J. (2003). *Pilgrim's progress.* Mineola, NY: Dover Publications. (Original work published 1678)

Burggraf, S. P. (1997). *The feminine economy and economic man: Reviving the role of the family in the postindustrial age.* Englewood Cliffs, NJ: Prentice-Hall.

Burton, L. A. (Ed.). (1992). *Religion and the family: When God helps.* Binghamton, NY: Haworth Pastoral Press.

Butler, M. H., Dahlin, S. K., & Fife, S. T. (2002). "Languaging" factors affecting clients' acceptance of forgiveness intervention in marital therapy. *Journal of Marital and Family Therapy, 28,* 285–298.

Butler, M. H., Gardner, B. C., & Bird, M. H. (1998). Not just a time-out: Change dynamics of prayer for religious couples in conflict situations. *Family Process, 37,* 451–478.

Butler, M. H., & Harper, J. M. (1994). The divine triangle: God in the marital system of religious couples. *Family Process, 33,* 277–286.

Buttny, R. (1993). *Social accountability in communication.* London: Sage.

Butz, M. R., Carlson, J. M., & Carlson, J. (1998). Chaos theory: Self-organization and symbolic representation in family systems. *Family Journal: Counseling and Therapy for Couples and Families, 6,* 106–115.

Byng-Hall, J. (1979). Re-editing family mythology during family therapy. *Journal of Family Therapy, 1,* 103–116.

Byng-Hall, J. (1995). Creating a secure family base: Some implications of attachment theory for family therapy. *Family Process, 34,* 45–58.

Capra, F. (1982). *The turning point: Science, society, and the rising culture.* New York: Bantam Books.

Carl, D. (1990). *Counseling same-sex couples.* New York: Norton.

Carlson, J., & Sperry, L. (2000). Adlerian therapy. In F. M. Dattilio & L. J Bevilacqua (Eds.), *Comparative treatments for relationship dysfunction* (pp. 102–115). New York: Springer.

Carlson, T. D., & Erickson, M. J. (Eds.). (2002). *Spirituality and family therapy.* New York: Haworth Press.

Carter, B., & McGoldrick, M. (Eds.). (2004). *The expanded family life cycle: Individual, family and social perspectives* (3rd ed.). Boston: Allyn & Bacon.

Cate, R. M., Huston, T. L., & Nesselroade, J. R. (1986). Premarital relationships: Toward the identification of alternative pathways to marriage. *Journal of Social and Clinical Psychology, 4,* 3–22.

Caputo, J. D. (Ed.). (1994). *Deconstruction in a nutshell: A conversation with Jacques Derrida* (Perspectives in Continental Philosophy No. 1). New York: Fordham University Press.

Chang, T. H., & Ng, K. S. (2000). I Ching, solution-focused therapy and change: A clinical integrative framework. *Family Therapy, 27,* 47–57.

Chaves, M., & Stephens, L. (2003). Church attendance in the United States. In M. Dillon (Ed.), *Handbook of the sociology of religion* (pp. 85–95). Cambridge, England: Cambridge University Press.

Cheal, D. (1993). Unity and difference in postmodern families. *Journal of Family Issues, 14,* 5–19.

Christensen, A., Jacobson, N. S., & Babcock, J. C. (1995). Integrative behavioral couple therapy. In N. S. Jacobson & A. S. Gurman (Eds.), *Clinical handbook of couple therapy* (pp. 31–64). New York: Guilford Press.

Christiano, K. J. (2000). Relition and the family in modern American culture. In S. K. Houseknecht & J. G. Pankhurst (Eds.), *Family, religion, and social change in diverse societies* (pp. 43–78). New York: Oxford University Press.

Clark, W. M., & Serovich, J. M. (1997). Twenty years and still in the dark? Content analysis of articles pertaining to gay, lesbian, and bisexual issues in marriage and family therapy journals. *Journal of Marital and Family Therapy, 23,* 239–253.

Coale, H. W. (1998). *The vulnerable therapist: Practicing psychotherapy in an age of anxiety.* New York: Haworth Press.

Colapinto, J. (1991). Structural family therapy. In A. S. Gurman & D. P. Kniskern (Eds.), *Handbook of family therapy* (Vol. 2, pp. 417–443). New York: Brunner/Mazel.

Combrinck-Graham, L. (1985). A developmental model for family systems. *Family Process, 24,* 139–150.

Combrinck-Graham, L. (1989). *Children in family contexts: Perspectives on treatment.* New York: Guilford Press.

Combs, G., & Freedman, J. (1990). *Symbol, story and ceremony: Using metaphor in individual and family therapy.* New York: Norton.

Combs, G., & Freedman, J. (1998). Tellings and retellings. *Journal of Marital and Family Therapy, 24,* 405–408.

Connell, G., Mitten, T., & Bumberry, W. (1999). *Reshaping family relationships: The symbolic therapy of Carl Whitaker.* Philadelphia: Brunner/Mazel.

Conoley, J. C., & Werth, E. B. (Eds.). (1995). *Family assessment.* Lincoln, NE: Buros Institute of Mental Measurements.

Constantine, L. L. (1986). *Family paradigms: The practice of theory in family therapy.* New York: Guilford Press.

Conville, R. L. (1998). Narrative, dialectic, and relationships. In R. L. Conville & L. E. Rogers (Eds.), *The meaning of "relationship" in interpersonal communication* (pp. 133–148.). Westport, CN: Praeger.

Cook, D. R. (1991). Shame, attachment, and addictions: Implications for family therapists. *Contemporary Family Therapy, 13,* 405–419.

Cooklin, A. (2001). Eliciting children's thinking in families and family therapy. *Family Process, 40,* 293–312.

Coontz, S. (1992). *The way we never were: American families and the nostalgia trip.* New York: Basic Books.

Cooper, C. R., Grotevant, H. D., & Condon, S. M. (1983). Individuality and connectedness in the family as a context for adolescent identity formation and role-taking skill. In H. D. Grotevant & C. R. Cooper (Eds.), *Adolescent development in the family* (pp. 43–59). San Francisco: Jossey-Bass.

Corey, G., Corey, M. S., & Callanan, P. (2003). *Issues and ethics in the helping professions.* Pacific Grove, CA: Brooks/Cole.

Cottone, R. R. (2001). A social constructivism model of ethical decision making in counseling. *Journal of Counseling and Development, 79,* 39–45.

Cottone, R. R., & Tarvydas, V. M. (2003). *Ethical and professional issues in counseling* (2nd ed.). Upper Saddle River, NJ: Merrill-Prentice Hall.

Covey, S. R. (1997). *The seven habits of highly effective families.* New York: Golden Books.

Coyne, J. C. (1985). Toward a theory of frames and reframing: The social nature of frames. *Journal of Marital and Family Therapy, 11,* 337–344.

Coyne, J. C., Denner, B., & Ransom, D. C. (1982). Undressing the fashionable mind. *Family Process, 21,* 391–396.

Crane, D. R., & Griffin, W. (1983). Personal space: An objective measure of marital quality. *Journal of Marital and Family Therapy, 9,* 325–327.

Cromwell, R., & Olson, D. E. (Eds.). (1975). *Power in families.* New York: Wiley.

Cron, E. (2000). Couple rating scales: Clarifying problem areas. *Family Journal: Counseling and Therapy for Couples and Families, 8,* 302–304.

Cuber, J. F., & Haroff, P. (1965). *The Significant Americans: A study of sexual behavior among the affluent.* New York: Appleton-Century-Crofts.

Cummings, E. M., & Davis, P. (1994). *Children and marital conflict: The impact of family dispute and resolution.* New York: Guilford Press.

Curtis, J. A., Blume, L. B., & Blume, T. W. (1998). Becoming a father: Marital perceptions and behaviors during pregnancy. *Michigan Family Review, 3*(1), 31–44.

Dalai Lama. (2001). *An open heart: Practicing compassion in everyday life.* New York: Little, Brown.

Daneshpour, M. (1998). Muslim families and family therapy. *Journal of Marital and Family Therapy, 24,* 355–390.

Dankoski, M. E. (2001). Pulling on the heart strings: An emotionally focused approach to family life cycle transitions. *Journal of Marital and Family Therapy, 27,* 177–187.

Dattilio, F. M. (1998). Cognitive-behavioral family therapy. In F. M. Dattilio (Ed.), *Case studies in couple and family therapy: Systemic and cognitive perspectives* (pp. 62–84). New York: Guilford Press.

Davies, B., & Harre, R. (1990). Positioning: The discursive production of selves. *Journal for the Theory of Social Behaviour, 20,* 43–63.

Davis, D. D., Berensen, P., Steinglass, P., & Davis, S. (1974). The adaptive consequences of drinking. *Psychiatry, 37,* 209–225.

Dell, P. F. (1982a). Beyond homeostasis: Toward a concept of coherence. *Family Process, 21,* 21–41.

Dell, P. F. (1982b). In search of truth: On the way to clinical epistemology. *Family Process, 21,* 407–414.

Denborough, D. (2001). The Public Conversations Project: An interview with Sallyann Roth. In D. Denborough (Ed.), *Family therapy: Exploring the field's past, present and possible futures* (pp. 107–115). Adelaide, S. Australia: Dulwich Centre Publications.

Derrida, J. (1998). *Of grammatology.* Baltimore: Johns Hopkins University Press. (Original work published 1967)

deShazer, S. (1994). *Words were originally magic.* New York: Norton.

Deutsch, M. (1969). Conflicts: Productive and destructive. *Journal of Social Issues, 25,* 7–41.

Deutsch, M. (1973). *The resolution of conflict: Constructive and destructive processes.* New Haven, CT: Yale.

Dickens, D. R., & Fontana, A. (Eds.). (1994). *Postmodernism and social inquiry.* New York: Guilford Press.

Dickerson, V. C., & Zimmerman, J. L. (1993). A narrative approach to families with adolescents. In S. Friedman (Ed.), *The new language of change: Construcitve collaboration in psychotherapy* (pp. 226–250). New York: Guilford Press.

Dindia, K. (1998). "Going into and coming out of the closet": The dialectics of stigma disclosure. In B. M. Montgomery & L. A. Baxter (Eds.), *Dialectical approaches to studying personal relationships* (pp. 83–108). Mahwah, NJ: Erlbaum.

Doherty, W. J. (1999). Morality and spirituality in therapy. In F. Walsh (Ed.), *Spiritual resources in family therapy* (pp. 179–192). New York: Guilford Press.

Doherty, W. J. (2002, November/December). Bad couples therapy. *Psychotherapy Networker,* 26–33.

Doherty, W. J., & Beaton, J. (2000). Family therapists, community, and civic renewal. *Family Process, 39,* 149–161.

Doherty, W. J., & Boss, P. G. (1991). Values and ethics in family therapy. In A. S. Gurman & D. P. Kniskern (Eds.), *Handbook of family therapy* (Vol. 2, pp. 606–637). New York: Brunner/Mazel.

Doherty, W. J., & Carlson, B. Z. (2002). *The intentional family: Simple rituals to strengthen family ties.* New York: Owl Books.

Dreikurs, R. (1976). *Children: The challenge.* New York: Hawthorn Books.

Doherty, W. J. (1999). Morality and spirituality in therapy. In F. Walsh (Ed.), *Spiritual resources in family therapy* (pp. 179–192). New York: Guilford Press.

Dunn, J., & Plomin, R. (1991). Why are siblings so different? The significance of differences in sibling experiences within the family. *Family Process, 30,* 271–284.

Duvall, E. M. (1957). *Family development.* Philadelphia: J. B. Lippincott.

Eck, D. L. (2001). *A new religious America: How a "Christian country" has become the world's most religiously diverse nation.* San Francisco: HarperCollins.

Efron, D. (1991). Special section: Reflecting on ourselves after 10 years—J. S. S. T. looks ahead to the next ten. *Journal of Strategic and Systemic Therapies, 10*(3/4), 104.

Efron, D. (1992). Reflections on strategic-systemic therapy. *Journal of Marital and Family Therapy, 18,* 3.

Elkins, D., Hedstrom, L., Hughes, L., Leaf, J., & Saunders, C. (1988). Toward a humanistic-phenomenological spirituality: Definitiion, description, and measurement. *Journal of Humanistic Psychology, 28,* 5–18.

Elliott Griffith, M., & Griffith, J. L. (2002). Addressing spirituality in its clinical complexities: Its potential for healing, its potential for harm. In T. D. Carlson & M. J. Erickson (Ed.), *Spirituality and family therapy* (pp. 167–194). New York: Haworth Press.

Ellis, K. M., & Eriksen, K. (2002). Transsexual and transgenderist experiences and treatment options. *Family Journal: Counseling and Therapy for Couples and Families, 10,* 289–299.

Emery, R. E. (1994). *Renegotiating family relationships: Divorce, child custody, and mediation.* New York: Guilford Press.

Ende, M. (1983). *The Neverending story.* Hammondsworth, England: Penguin Books. (Original work published 1976)

Englar-Carlson, M. (2003). Enough about models and abstractions, let your therapeutic soul be free: An interview with Bradford Keeney. *Family Journal: Counseling and Therapy for Couples and Families, 11,* 309–314.

Epstein, N. B., Ryan, C., Bishop, D., Miller, I., & Keitner, G. (2003). The McMaster Model: A view of healthy family functioning. In F. Walsh (Ed.), *Normal family processes* (3rd ed., pp. 581–607). New York: Guilford Press.

Epston, D. (1993). Internalised other questioning with couples: The New Zealand version. In S. Gilligan & R. Price (Eds.), *Therapeutic conversations* (pp. 183–189). New York: Norton.

Erickson, R. J. (1993). Reconceptualizing family work: The effect of emotion work on perceptions of marital quality. *Journal of Marriage and the Family, 55,* 888–900.

Erikson, E. E. (1964). *Childhood and society.* New York: Norton.

Erikson, E. E. (1968). *Identity: Youth and crisis.* New York: Norton.

Eugenides, J. (2002). *Middlesex.* New York: Farrar, Straus and Giraux.

Facundo, A. (1990). Social class issues in family therapy: A case-study of a Puerto Rican migrant family. *Journal of Strategic and Systemic Therapies, 9*(3), 14–34.

Faiver, C., Ingersoll, R. E., O'Brien, E., & McNally, C. (2001). *Explorations in counseling and spirituality: Philosophical, practical, and personal reflections.* Belmont, CA: Brooks/Cole.

Falicov, C. J. (1998). *Latino families in therapy: A guide to multicultural practice.* New York: Guilford Press.

Falicov, C. J. (1999). Religion and spiritual folk traditions in immigrant families: Therapeutic resources with Latinos. In F. Walsh (Ed.), *Spiritual resources in family therapy* (pp. 104–120). New York: Guilford Press.

Falloon, I. R. H. (1991). Behavioral family therapy. In A. S. Gurman & D. P. Kniskern (Eds.), *Handbook of family therapy* (Vol. 2, pp. 65–95). New York: Brunner/Mazel.

Faludi, S. (1992). *Backlash: The undeclared war against American women.* New York: Anchor Books.

Fisch, R., Weakland, J. H., & Segal, L. (1982). *The tactics of change: Doing therapy briefly.* San Francisco: Jossey-Bass.

Fishbane, M. D. (1998). I, thou, and we: A dialogical approach to couples therapy. *Journal of Marital and Family Therapy, 24,* 41–58.

Fishbane, M. D. (2001). Relational narratives of the self. *Family Process, 40,* 273–291.

Fisher, R., & Brown, S. (1988). *Getting together: Building relationships as we negotiate.* New York: Penguin.

Fisher, R., & Ury, W. (1981). *Getting to yes: Negotiating agreement without giving in.* New York: Penguin.

Fishman, H. C., & Rosman, B. L. (Eds.). (1986). *Evolving models for family change: A volume in honor of Salvador Minuchin.* New York: Guilford Press.

Fivaz-Depeursinge, E. (1991). Documenting a time-bound, circular view of hierarchies: A microanalysis of parent-infant dyadic interaction. *Family Process, 30,* 101–120.

Flowers, R. B. (1984). *Religion in strange times: The 1960s and 1970s.* Macon, GA: Mercer University Press.

Floyd, F. J., Markman, H. J., Kelly, S., Blumbert, S. L., & Stanley, S. M. (1995). Preventive intervention and relationship enhancement. In N. S. Jacobson & A. S. Gurman (Eds.), *Clinical handbook of couple therapy* (pp. 212–226). New York: Guilford Press.

Foley, V. D. (1974). *An introduction to family therapy.* New York: Grune & Stratton.

Fossum, M. A., & Mason, M. (1986). *Facing shame: Families in recovery.* New York: Norton.

Foucault, M. (1979). *Discipline and punish: The birth of the prison.* New York: Random House.

Foucault, M. (1980). *Power/knowledge: Selected interviews and other writings 1972–1977* (C. Gordon, Trans. & C. Gordon, L. Marshall, J. Mephan, & K. Soper, Eds.). Berkeley: University of California Press.

Fowler, J. W. (1981). *Stages of faith: The psychology of human development and the quest for meaning.* San Francisco: Harper & Row.

Fox, G. L. (1970). The woman graduate student in sociology. In Center for Continuing Education for Women (Ed.), *Women on campus: Proceedings of the symposium October 14, 1970* (pp. 32–35). Ann Arbor: University of Michigan.

Fraenkel, P. (2005, May/June). Whatever happened to family therapy? *Psychotherapy Networker, 30–70.*

Frame, M. W. (2000). Spiritual and religious issues in counseling: Ethical considerations. *Family Journal: Counseling and Therapy for Couples and Families, 8,* 72–74.

Frame, M. W. (2002). *Integrating religion and spirituality in counseling.* Pacific Grove, CA: Thomson Brooks/Cole.

Framo, J. L., Weber, T. T., & Levine, F. B. (2003). *Coming home again: A family-of-origin consultation.* New York: Brunner-Routledge.

Frankl, V. E. (1984). *Man's search for meaning: An introduction to logotherapy* (3rd ed.). New York: Touchstone.

Freedman, J., & Combs, G. (2002a). Narrative couple therapy. In N. S. Jacobson & A. S. Gurman (Eds.), *Clinical handbook of couple therapy* (3rd ed., pp. 308–334). New York: Guilford Press.

Freedman, J., & Combs, G. (2002b). *Narrative therapy with couples . . . and a whole lot more! A collection of papers, essays, and exercises.* Adelaide, South Australia: Dulwich Centre Publications.

French, M. (1988). *Women's room.* New York: Ballantine Books.

Friedlander, M. L., Ellis, M. V., Raymond, L., Siegel, S. M., & Milford, D. (1987). Convergence and divergence in the process of interviewing families. *Psychotherapy, 24,* 570–583.

Friedman, E. H. (1991). Bowen theory and therapy. In A. S. Gurman & D. P. Kniskern (Eds.), *Handbook of family therapy* (Vol. 2, pp. 134–170). New York: Brunner/Mazel.

Friedman, S. (1993). Does the "miracle question" always create miracles? *Journal of Systemic Therapies, 12,* 71–74.

Fuentes, A. (1998). Re-evaluating primate monogamy. *American Anthropologist, 100,* 890–907.

Gale, J. E. (1991). *Conversation analysis of therapeutic discourse: The pursuit of a therapeutic agenda.* Norwood, NJ: Ablex.

Garfield, S. L. (1992). Eclectic psychotherapy: A common factors approach. In J. C. Norcross & M. R. Goldried (Eds.), *Handbook of psychotherapy integration* (pp. 169–201). New York: Basic Books.

Gaylin, N. L. (2001). *Family, self, and psychotherapy: A person-centred perspective.* Langarron, England: PCCS Books.

Genia, V. (1991). The spiritual experience index: A measure of spiritual maturity. *Journal of Religion and Health, 30,* 337–345.

Gergen, K. J. (1991). *The saturated self: Dilemmas of identity in contemporary life.* New York: Basic Books.

Gergen, K. J. (1994). *Realities and relationships: Soundings in social construction.* Cambridge, MA: Harvard University Press.

Gerson, R. (1995). The family life cycle: Phases, stages, and crises. In R. H. Mikesell, D.-D. Lusterman, & S. H. McDaniel (Eds.), *Integrating family therapy: Handbook of family psychology and systems theory* (pp. 91–111). Washington, DC: American Psychological Association.

Gerson, R., Hoffman, S., Sauls, M., & Ulrici, D. (1993). Family-of-origin frames in couples therapy. *Journal of Marital and Family Therapy, 19,* 341–354.

Gerstein, J. S. (1999). *Sticking together: Experiential activities for family counseling.* Philadelphia: Accelerated Development.

Giblin, P. (1996a). Empathy: The essence of marriage and family therapy. *Family Journal: Counseling and Therapy for Couples and Families, 4,* 229–235.

Giblin, P. (1996b). Spirituality, marriage, and family. *Family Journal: Counseling and Therapy for Couples and Families, 4,* 46–52.

Gibson, G. (1999). *Gone boy: A walkabout.* New York: Kodansha International.

Ginsberg, B. G. (2000). Relationship enhancement couples therapy. In F. M. Dattilio & L. J Bevilacqua (Eds.), *Comparative treatments for relationship dysfunction* (pp. 273–298). New York: Springer.

Ginsberg, B. G. (2004). *Relationship enhancement family therapy.* Doylestown, PA: Relationship Enhancement Press.

Gladding, S. T., & Henderson, D. A. (2000). Creativity and family counseling: The SCAMPER model as a template for promoting creative processes. *The Family Journal: Counseling and Therapy for Couples and Families, 8,* 245–249.

Gladding, S. T., Remley, T. P., & Huber, C. H. (2001). *Ethical, legal, and professional issues in the practice of marriage and family therapy.* Upper Saddle River, NJ: Merrill-Prentice Hall.

Golann, S. (1988). On second-order family therapy. *Family Process, 27,* 51–71.

Goldberg-Arnold, J. S., Fristad, M. A., & Gavazzi, S. M. (1999). Family psychoeducation: Giving caregivers what they want and need. *Family Relations, 48,* 411–417.

Goldenberg, I., & Goldenberg, H. (1980). *Family therapy: An overview.* Monterey, CA: Brooks/Cole.

Goldner, V. (1989). Generation and gender: Normative and covert hierarchies. In M. McGoldrick, C. M. Anderson, & F. Walsh (Eds.), *Women in families: A framework for family therapy* (pp. 42–60). New York: Norton.

Gollan, J. K., Friedman, M. A., & Miller, I. W. (2002). Couple therapy in the treatment of major depression. In A. S. Gurman & N. S. Jacobson (Eds.), *Clinical handbook of couple therapy* (3rd ed., pp. 653–676). New York: Guilford Press.

Gordon, S., & Waldo, M. (1986). The effects of assertiveness training on couples' relationships. *American Journal of Family Therapy, 12,* 73–77.

Gorell Barnes, G. (1998). *Family therapy in changing times.* Houndsmills, England: Macmillan.

Gotlib, I. H., & Beach, S. R. H. (1995). A marital/family discord model of depression: Implications for therapeutic intervention. In N. S. Jacobson & A. S. Gurman (Eds.), *Clinical handbook of couple therapy* (pp. 411–436). New York: Guilford Press.

Gottman, J. M. (1994). *What predicts divorce? The relationship between marital processes and marital outcomes.* Hillsdale, NJ: Erlbaum.

Gottman, J. M., Coan, J., Carrere, S., & Swanson, C. (1998). Predicting marital happiness and stability from newlywed interactions. *Journal of Marriage and the Family, 60,* 5–22.

Gottman, J. M., Driver, J., & Tabares, A. (2002). Building the sound marital house: An empirically derived couple therapy. In A. S. Gurman & N. S. Jacobson (Eds.), *Clinical handbook of couple therapy* (3rd ed., pp. 373–399). New York: Guilford Press.

Gottman, J. M., & Krokoff, L. J. (1979). The relationship between marital interaction and marital satisfaction: A longitudinal view. *Journal of Consulting and Clinical Psychology, 57,* 47–52.

Gray, L. A., House, R. M., & Eicken, S. (1996). Human sexuality instruction: Implications for couple and family counselor educators. *Family Journal: Counseling and Therapy for Couples and Families, 4,* 208–216.

Green, R. J. (1988). Impasse and change: A systemic/strategic view of the therapeutic system. *Journal of Marital and Family Therapy, 14,* 383–395.

Greenan, D. E., & Tunnell, G. (2003). *Couple therapy with gay men.* New York: Guilford Press.

Greene, K., & Bogo, M. (2002). The different faces of intimate violence: Implications for assessment and treatment. *Journal of Marital and Family Therapy, 28,* 455–466.

Greer, G. (1971). *The female eunuch.* New York: McGraw-Hill.

Griffith, B. A., & Rotter, J. C. (1999). Families and spirituality: Therapists as facilitators. *Family Journal: Counseling and Therapy for Couples and Families, 7,* 161–164.

Griffith, M. E. (1999). Opening therapy to conversations with a personal God. In F. Walsh (Ed.), *Spiritual resources in family therapy* (pp. 209–222). New York: Guilford Press.

Griffith, M. E., & Griffith, J. L. (2002). Addressing spirituality in its clinical complexities: Its potential for healing, its potential for harm. In T. D. Carlson & M. J. Erickson (Ed.), *Spirituality and family therapy* (pp. 167–194). New York: Haworth Press.

Grodin, D., & Lindhof, T. R. (1996). *Constructing the self in a mediated world.* Thousand Oaks, CA: Sage.

Group for the Advancement of Psychiatry. (1970). *The field of family therapy.* New York: Author.

Grunebaum, H. (1997). Thinking about romantic/erotic love. *Journal of Marital and Family Therapy, 23,* 295–307.

Guerin, P. J., Fay, L. F., Burden, S. L., & Kautto, G. (1987). *The evaluation and treatment of marital conflict: A four-stage approach.* New York: Basic Books.

Guggenbuhl-Craig, A. (1986). *Power in the helping professions.* London: Karnac Books.

Gurman, A. S., & Kniskern, D. P. (1980). *Handbook of family therapy.* New York: Brunner/Mazel.

Gutsche, S. (1994). Voices of healing: Therapists and clients journey towards spirituality. *Journal of Systemic Therapies, 13*(3), 3–5.

Haley, J. (1963). *Strategies of psychotherapy.* New York: Grune & Stratton.

Haley, J. (Ed.). (1971). *Changing families: A family therapy reader.* New York: Grune & Stratton.

Haley, J. (1973a). Strategic therapy when a child is presented as the problem. *Journal of the American Academy of Child Psychiatry, 12*(4), 641–659.

Haley, J. (1973b). *Uncommon therapy.* New York: Norton.

Haley, J. (1976). *Problem-solving therapy.* New York: Harper Colophon.

Haley, J. (1986). *The power tactics of Jesus Christ and other essays.* New York: Norton.

Haley, J. (1997). *Leaving home: The therapy of disturbed young people* (2nd ed.). New York: Brunner/Mazel.

Haley, J., & Hoffman, L. (1967). *Techniques of family therapy.* New York: Basic Books.

Halford, W. K., & Moore, E. N. (2002). Relationship education and the prevention of couple relationship problems. In A. S. Gurman & N. S. Jacobson (Eds.), *Clinical handbook of couple therapy* (3rd ed., pp. 400–419). New York: Guilford Press.

Hardy, K. V. (1989). The theoretical myth of sameness: A critical issue in family therapy training and treatment. *Journal of Psychotherapy and the Family, 6(1/2),* 17–33.

Hardy, K. V. (1994). Marginalization or development? A response to Shields, Wynne, McDaniel, and Gawinski. *Journal of Marital and Family Therapy, 20,* 139–143.

Hardy, K. V. (1996, May/June). Breathing room: Creating a zone of safety and connection for angry Black teens. *Family Therapy Networker,* 53–39.

Hardy, K. V., & Laszloffy, T. A. (1995). The cultural genogram: Key to training culturally competent family therapists. *Journal of Marital and Family Therapy, 21,* 227–237.

Hardy, K. V., & Laszloffy, T. A. (2002). Couple therapy using a multicultural perspective. In A. S. Gurman & N. S. Jacobson (Eds.), *Clinical handbook of couple therapy* (3rd ed., pp. 569–593). New York: Guilford Press.

Hardy, K. V., & Laszloffy, T. A. (2005). *Teens who hurt: Clinical interventions for breaking the cycle of violence.* New York: Guilford Press.

Hare-Mustin, R. T. (1978). A feminist approach to family therapy. *Family Process, 17,* 181–194.

Hare-Mustin, R. T. (1980). Family therapy may be dangerous for your health. *Professional Psychology, 11,* 935–938.

Hare-Mustin, R. T. (1987). Discussions: Rejoinder—Theory and transformation. *Family Process, 26,* 32–33.

Hare-Mustin, R. T. (1994). Discourses in the mirrored room: A postmodern analysis of therapy. *Family Process, 33,* 19–35.

Hare-Mustin, R. T. (1998). Challenging traditional discourses in psychotherapy: Creating space for alternatives. *Journal of Feminist Family Therapy, 10(3),* 39–56.

Hargrave, T. D., & Hanna, S. M. (1997). *The aging family: New visions in theory, practice, and reality.* New York: Brunner/Mazel.

Harris, S. M. (1998). Finding a forest among trees: Spirituality hiding in family therapy theories. *Journal of Family Studies, 4,* 77–86.

Hartman, A. (1995). Diagrammatic assessment of family relationships. *Families in Society: Journal of Contemporary Human Services, 76,* 111–122.

Havas, E., & Bonnar, D. (1999). Therapy with adolescents and families: The limits of parenting. *American Journal of Family Therapy, 27,* 121–135.

Hazan, C., & Shaver, P. (1987). Romantic love conceptualized as an attachment process. *Journal of Personality and Social Psychology, 52(3),* 511–524.

Hedtke, L., & Winslade, J. (2004). *Re-membering lives: Conversations with the dying and the bereaved.* Amityville, NY: Baywood Publishing.

Held, B. S. (1990). What's in a name? Some confusions and concerns about constructivism. *Journal of Marital and Family Therapy, 16,* 179–186.

Helmeke, K. B., & Bischof, G. H. (2002). Recognizing and raising spiritual and religious issues in therapy: Guidelines for the timid. In T. D. Carlson & M. J. Erickson (Ed.), *Spirituality and family therapy* (pp. 195–214). New York: Haworth Press.

Hendrix, D. H. (1991). Ethics and intrafamily confidentiality in counseling with children. *Journal of Mental Health Counseling, 13(3),* 232–333.

Hendrix, H. (1992). *Getting the love you want: A guide for couples.* New York: Henry Holt.

Hochschild, A. R. (1979). Emotion work, feeling rules, and social structure. *American Journal of Sociology, 85,* 551–575.

Hodge, D. R. (2000). Spiritual ecomaps: A new diagrammatic tool for assessing marital and family spirituality. *Journal of Marital and Family Therapy, 26,* 217–228.

Hoffman, E. (1994). *The drive for self: Alfred Adler and the founding of individual psychology.* Reading, MA; Addison-Wesley.

Hoffman, L. (1981). *Foundations of family therapy: A framework for systems change.* New York: Basic Books.

Hoffman, L. (1983). A co-evolutionary framework for systemic family therapy. In B. P. Keeney (Ed.), *Diagnosis and assessment in family therapy* (pp. 37–61). Rockville, MD: Aspen.

Hoffman, L. (1985). Beyond power and control: Toward a "second-order" family systems therapy. *Family Systems Medicine, 3,* 381–396.

Hoffman, L. (2002). *Family therapy: An intimate history.* New York: Norton.

Holtzworth-Munroe, A., & Jacobson, N. S. (1991). Behavioral marital therapy. In A. S. Gutman & D. P. Kniskern (Eds.), *Handbook of family therapy* (Vol. 2, pp. 96–133). New York: Brunner/Mazel.

Holtzworth-Munroe, A., Meehan, J. C., Rehman, U., & Marshall, A. D. (2002). Intimate partner violence: An introduction for couple therapists. In A. S. Gurman & N. S. Jacobson (Eds.), *Clinical handbook of couple therapy* (3rd ed., pp. 441–465). New York: Guilford Press.

Hooks, B. (2000). *Feminism is for everybody: Passionate politics.* Cambridge, MA: South End Press.

Horne, K. B., & Hicks, M. W. (2002). All in the family: A belated response to Knudson-Martin's feminist revision of Bowen theory. *Journal of Marital and Family Therapy, 28,* 103–113.

Hoyt, M. F. (2002). Solution-focused couple therapy. In A. S. Gurman & N. S. Jacobson (Eds.), *Clinical handbook of couple therapy* (3rd ed., pp. 335–369). New York: Guilford Press.

Hubble, M. A., Duncan, B. L., & Miller, S. D. (1999). *The heart and soul of change: What works in therapy.* Washington, DC: American Psychological Association.

Imber-Black, E. (1998). *The secret life of families: Truth-telling, privacy, and reconciliation in a tell-all society.* New York: Bantam Doubleday Dell.

Imber-Black, E., & Roberts, J. (1992). *Rituals for our time.* New York: HarperCollins.

Inclan, J., & Ferran, E. (1990). Poverty, politics, and family therapy: A role for systems theory. In M. P. Mirkin (Ed.), *The social and political contexts of family therapy* (pp. 193–213). Needham Heights, MA: Allyn & Bacon.

Inglehart, R., & Norris, P. (2003). *Rising tide: Gender equality and cultural change around the world.* Cambridge, England: Cambridge University Press.

Institute of Medicine. (1990). *Broadening the base of treatment for alcohol problems.* Washington, DC: National Academy Press.

International Association of Marriage and Family Counselors. *Ethical Standards.* Retrieved October 24, 2005, from http://iamfc.com/ethical_codes.html.

Jackson, D. (1962). Family affairs. *Family Process, 1*(1), 153–155.

Jackson, V. (2002). In our own voice: African American stories of oppression, survival and recovery in mental health systems. *International Journal of Narrative Therapy and Community Work, 2002*(2), 11–31.

Jacobson, N. S., & Christensen, A. (1996). *Acceptance and change in couple therapy.* New York: Norton.

Jacobson, N. S., & Follette, W. C. (1985). Clinical significance of improvement resulting from two behavioral marital therapy components. *Behavior Therapy, 16,* 249–262.

Jacobson, N. S., & Margolin, G. (1979). *Marital therapy: Strategies based on social learning and behavior exchange principles.* New York: Brunner/Mazel.

Jacobson, N. S., Schmaling, K. B., & Holtzworth-Munroe, A. (1987). Component analysis of behavioral marital therapy: 2-year follow-up and prediction of relapse. *Journal of Marital and Family Therapy, 13,* 187–195.

James, W. (1892/1961). *Psychology: The briefer course* (G. Allport, Ed.). New York: Harper Torchbooks.

James, W. (1982). *The varieties of religious experience.* New York: Penguin Books.

Jedicka, D., & Jennings, G. (2001). Marital therapy on the internet. *Journal of Technology in Counseling, 2*(1). Retrieved October 27, 2005, from http://jtc.colstate.edu/vol2_1/Marital.htm.

Jencius, M. J., & Rotter, J. C. (1998). Bedtime rituals and their relationship to childhood sleep disturbance. *Family Journal: Counseling and Therapy for Couples and Families, 6,* 94–105.

Johnson, A. C. (1995). Resiliency mechanisms in culturally diverse families. *Family Journal: Counseling and Therapy for Couples and Families, 3,* 316–324.

Johnson, M. P. (1995). Partriarchal terrerism and common couple violence: Two forms of violence against women. *Journal of Marriage and the Family, 57,* 283–294.

Johnson, P., & Wilkinson, W. K. (1995). The "re-nesting" effect: Implications for family development. *Family Journal: Counseling and Therapy for Couples and Families, 3,* 126–131.

Johnson, S. (1993). Structural elements in Franz Kafka's "The Metamorphosis." *Journal of Marital and Family Therapy, 19,* 149–157.

Johnson, S. M. (2001). Family therapy saves the planet: Messianic tendencies in the family systems literature. *Family Process, 27,* 3–11.

Johnson, S. M. (2003). Emotionally focused couples therapy: Empiricism and art. In In T. L. Sexton, G. R. Weeks, & M. S. Robbins (Eds.), *Handbook of family therapy: The science and practice of working with families and couples* (pp. 263–280). New York: Brunner-Routledge.

Johnson, S. M., & Denton, W. (2002). Emotionally focused couple therapy: Creating secure connections. In A. S. Gurman & N. S. Jacobson (Eds.), *Clinical handbook of couple therapy* (3rd ed., pp. 221–250). New York: Guilford Press.

Johnson, S. M., & Greenberg, L. S. (1994). Emotion in intimate relationships: Theory and implications for therapy. In S. M. Johnson & L. S. Greenberg (Eds.), *The heart of the matter: Perspectives on emotion in marital therapy* (pp. 3–22). New York: Brunner/Mazel.

Johnson, S. M., & Greenberg, L. S. (1995). The emotionally focused approach to problems in adult attachment. In N. S. Jacobson & A. S. Gurman (Eds.), *Clinical handbook of couple therapy* (pp. 121–141). New York: Guilford Press.

Johnson, S. M., Makinen, J. A., & Millikin, J. W. (2001). Attachment injuries in couple relationships: A new perspective on impasses in couples therapy. *Journal of Marital and Family Therapy, 27,* 145–155.

Jones, E. E., & Nisbett, R. E. (1971). *The actor and the observer: Divergent perceptions of the causes of behavior.* Morristown, NJ: General Learning Press.

Jones, J., Christensen, A., & Jacobson, N. (2000). Integrative behavioral couple therapy. In F. M. Dattilio & L. J. Bevilacqua (Eds.), *Comparative treatments for relationship dysfunction* (pp. 186–209). New York: Springer.

Jordan, J. R. (1985). Paradox and polarity: The Tao of family therapy. *Family Process, 24,* 165–174.

Jordan, J. R., Kraus, D. R., & Ware, E. S. (1993). Observations on loss and family development. *Family Process, 32,* 425–440.

Josselson, R. (1987). *Finding herself: Pathways to identity development in women.* San Francisco: Jossey-Bass.

Kanfer, F. H., & Saslow, G. (1965). Behavioral analysis: An alternative to diagnostic classification. *Archives of General Psychiatry, 12,* 529–538.

Kaplan, D. M., & Associates (Eds.). (2003). *Family counseling for all counselors.* Alexandria, VA: American Counseling Association.

Karpel, M. A. (1980). Family secrets. *Family Process, 19,* 205–306.

Kaslow, F. (1995). *Projective genogramming.* Sarasota, FL: Professional Resource Press.

Kaslow, F. W. (1993). Relational diagnosis: An idea whose time has come. *Family Process, 32,* 255–259.

Kaslow, F. W. (1996). *Handbook of relational diagnosis and dysfunctional family patterns.* New York: Wiley.

Kaslow, F. W. (2000). History of family therapy: Evolution outside of the U.S. A. *Journal of Family Psychotherapy, 114,* 1–35.

Keen, S. (1994). Hymns to an unknown God: *Awakening the spirit in everyday life.* New York: Bantam Books.

Keeney, B. P. (1979). Ecosystemic epistemology: An alternative paradigm for diagnosis. *Family Process, 18,* 117–129.

Keeney, B. P. (1982). What is an epistemology of family therapy? *Family Process, 21,* 153–168.

Keeney, B. P. (1983). Ecological assessment. In B. P. Keeney (Ed.), *Diagnosis and assessment in family therapy* (pp. 157–169). Rockville, MD: Aspen.

Keeney, B. P. (1991). *Improvisational therapy: A practical guide for creative clinical strategies.* New York: Guilford Press.

Keeney, B. P. (1994). *Shaking out the spirits: A psychotherapist's entry into the healing mysteries of global shamanism.* Barrytown, NY: Station Hill Press.

Keeney, B. P., & Ross, J. M. (1983). Cybernetics of brief family therapy. *Journal of Marital and Family Therapy, 9,* 375–382.

Keeney, B. P., & Sprenkle, D. H. (1982). Ecosystemic epistemology: Critical implications for the aesthetics and pragmatics of family therapy. *Family Process, 21,* 1–19.

Keith, D. V. (1986). Are children necessary in family therapy. In L. Combrinck-Graham (Ed.), *Treating young children in family therapy* (pp. 1–10). Rockville, MD: Aspen.

Kelley, H. H. (1973). The processes of causal attribution. *American Psychologist, 28,* 107–128.

Kelly, E. W. (1992). Religion in family therapy journals: A review and analysis. In L. A. Burton (Ed.), *Religion and the family: When God helps* (pp. 185–208). Binghamton, NY: Haworth Pastoral Press.

Kelly, G. A. (1963). *A theory of personality: The psychology of personal constructs.* New York: Norton.

Kemper, T. D. (2000). Social models in the explanation of emotions. In M. Lewis & J. M. Haviland-Jones (Eds.), *Handbook of emotions* (2nd ed., pp. 45–58). New York: Guilford Press.

Kempler, W. (1981). *Experiential psychotherapy within families.* New York: Brunner/Mazel.

Kerby, A. P. (1991). *Narrative and the self.* New York: Indiana University Press.

Kerr, M. E., & Bowen, M. (1988). *Family evaluation: An approach based on Bowen theory.* New York: Norton.

Kiecolt-Glaser, J. K. (1999). Stress, personal relationships, and immune function: Health implications. *Brain, Behavior, and Immunity, 13,* 61–72.

Kim, S. (2003). The influence of Christianity on Korean parenting. *Michigan Family Review, 8*(1), 29–44.

Kim, Y. O. (1976). *World religions: Vol. 3. Faiths of the Far East.* New York: Golden Gate Publishing.

Kitchener, K. (1984). Intuition, critical evaluation and ethical principles: The foundation for ethical decisions in counseling psychology. *Counseling Psychologist, 12,* 43–55.

Kliman, J. (1998). Social class as a relationship: Implications for family therapy. In M. McGoldrick (Ed.), *Re-visioning family therapy: Race, culture, and gender in clinical practice* (pp. 50–61). New York: Guilford Press.

Knudson-Martin, C. (1994). The female voice: Applications to Bowen's family systems theory. *Journal of Marital and Family Therapy, 20,* 35–46.

Knudson-Martin, C. (1995). Constructing gender in marriage: Implications for counseling. *Family Journal: Counseling and Therapy for Couples and Families, 3,* 188–199.

Kogan, S. M., & Gale, J. E. (1997). Decentering therapy: Textual analysis of a narrative therapy session. *Family Process, 36,* 101–126.

Kogan, S. M., & Gale, J. E. (2000). Taking a narrative turn: Social constructionism and family therapy. In A. M. Horne (Ed.), *Family counseling and therapy* (3rd ed., pp. 208–242). Itasca, IL: Peacock Press.

Kottler, J. A. (1993). *On being a therapist.* San Francisco: Jossey-Bass.

Kottler, J. A. (1994). *Beyond blame: A new way of resolving conflicts in relationships.* San Francisco: Jossey-Bass.

Kottler, J. A. (2000). *Doing good: Passion and commitment for helping others.* Philadelphia: Brunner-Routledge.

Kozlowska, K., & Hanney, L. (1999). Family assessment and intervention using an interactive art exercise. *Family Therapy, 20,* 61–69.

Krishnakumar, A., & Buehler, C. (2000). Interparental conflict and parenting behaviors: A meta-analytic review. *Family Relations, 49,* 25–44.

Kuehl, B. P., Newfield, N. A., & Joanning, H. (1990). A client-based description of family therapy. *Journal of Family Psychology, 3,* 310–321.

Kuhn, T. S. (1970). *The structure of scientific revolutions* (2nd ed.). Chicago: University of Chicago Press.

Kung, W. W. (2000). The intertwined relationship between depression and marital distress: Elements of marital therapy conducive to effective treatment outcome. *Journal of Marital and Family Therapy, 26,* 51–63.

Kurdek, L. A. (2002). On being insecure about the assessment of attachment styles. *Journal of Social and Personal Relationships, 19,* 811–834.

Kushner, H. S. (1983). *When bad things happen to good people.* New York: Avon.

Kushner, H. S. (2004). *When bad things happen to good people.* New York: Anchor.

Lacan, J. (1968). *Speech and language in psychoanalysis* (A. Wilden, Trans.). Baltimore: Johns Hopkins Press.

Laird, J. (1988). Women and ritual in family therapy. In E. Imber-Black, J. Roberts, & R. Whiting (Eds.), *Rituals in families and family therapy* (pp. 331–362). New York: Norton.

Laird, J., & Green, R.-J. (Eds.). (1996). *Lesbians and gays in couples and families: A handbook for therapists.* San Francisco: Jossey-Bass.

Lalonde, C., Chandler, M. J., Hallett, D., & Paul, D. (2001, April). *A Longtitudinal Study of Identity Formation Processes in Native North American Youth.* Paper presented at the biennial meeting of the Society for Research in Child Development, Minneapolis, MN. Retrieved October 14, 2004 from http://web.uvic.ca/~lalonde/native/SRCD2001.html.

Lambert, M. J. (1992). Implications of outcome research for psychotherapy integration. In J. C. Norcross & M. R. Goldfried (Eds.), *Handbook of psychotherapy integration* (pp. 94–129). New York: Basic Books.

Laszlo, E. (1975). Foreword. In E. Taschdjian (Ed.), *Perspectives on general system theory: Scientific-philosophical studies by Ludwig von Bertalanffy* (pp. 8–13). New York: George Braziller.

Laszloffy, T. A., & Hardy, K. V. (2000). Uncommon strategies for a common problem: Addressing racism in family therapy. *Family Process, 39,* 35–50.

Lazarus, A. A., Beutler, L. E., & Norcross, J. C. (1992). The future of technical eclecticism. *Psychotherapy, 29,* 11–20.

Lebow, J. L. (1997). The integrative revolution in couple and family therapy. *Family Process, 36,* 1–17.

Lee, W. Y. (2004). Three "depressed families" in transitional Beijing. *Journal of Family Psycotherapy, 15*(4), 57–71.

Leff, J., & Vaughan, C. (1985). *Expressed emotion in families: Its significance for mental illness.* New York: Guilford Press.

Legowski, T., & Brownlee, K. (2001). Working with metaphor in narrative therapy. *Journal of Family Psychotherapy, 12*(1), 19–28.

Lemerise, E. A., & Dodge, K. A. (2000). The development of anger and hostile interactions. In M. Lewis & J. M. Haviland-Jones (Eds.), *Handbook of emotions* (2nd ed., pp. 594–606). New York: Guilford Press.

Leslie, R. S. (2003). Ethical and legal matters: Using a "no secrets" policy when treating a couple or family. *Family Therapy Magazine, 2*(3), 45–47.

Lewis, J. M. (1979). *How's your family? A guide to identifying your family's strengths and weaknesses.* New York: Brunner/Mazel.

Liddle, H. A. (1982). On the problems of eclecticism: A call for epistemologic clarification and human-scale theories. *Family Process, 21,* 243–250.

Lipchik, E. (2002). *Beyond technique in solution-focused therapy: Working with emotions and the therapeutic relationship.* New York: Guilford Press.

Lopez, F. G. (1995). Attachment theory as an integrative framework for family counseling. *Family Journal: Counseling and Therapy for Couples and Families, 3,* 11–17.

Love, P., & Robinson, J. (1994). *Hot monogamy: Essential steps to more passionate, intimate lovemaking.* New York: Dutton.

Lowe, R. (2004). *Family therapy: A constructive framework.* London: Sage.

Luborsky L., Singer, B., & Luborsky, L. (1975). Comparative studies of psychotherapies: Is it true that "everyone has won and all must have prizes?" *Archives of General Psychiatry, 32,* 995–1008.

Luquet, W. (2000). Imago relationship therapy. In F. M. Dattilio & L. J Bevilacqua (Eds.), *Comparative treatments for relationship dysfunction* (pp. 116–133). New York: Springer.

Lyle, R. R., & Gehart, D. R. (2000). The narrative of ethics and the ethics of narrative: The implications of Ricoeur's narrative model for family therapy. *Journal of Systemic Therapies, 19*(4), 73–89.

Lyotard, J. F. (1984). *Theory and history of literature: Vol. 10. The postmodern condition—A report on knowledge*

(G. Bennington & B. Massumi, Trans.). Minneapolis: University of Minnesota Press.

Mackey, S. K. (1996). Nurturance: A neglected dimension in family therapy with adolescents. *Journal of Marital and Family Therapy, 22,* 489–508.

Madanes, C. (1981). *Strategic family therapy.* San Francisco: Jossey-Bass.

Madanes, C. (1986). Integrating ideas in family therapy with children. In H. C. Fishman & B. L. Rosman (Eds.), *Evolving models of family change* (pp. 183–203). New York: Guilford Press.

Madanes, C. (1993). Strategic humanism. *Journal of Systemic Therapies, 12*(4), 69–75.

Magee, R. D. (1997). Ethical issues in couple therapy: Therapist competence and values. In D. T. Marsh & R. D. Magee (Eds.), *Ethical and legal issues in professional practice with families* (pp. 112–126). New York: Wiley.

Mahler, M., Pine, F., & Bergman, A. (1975). *The psychological birth of the human infant: Symbiosis and individuation.* New York: Basic Books.

Malcolm, J. (1978, May 15). Reporter at large: The one-way mirror. *New Yorker,* 39.

Malinen, T. (2002). *Practice is theory lived through: A conversation with Dr. Wendel Ray at the Brief Therapy Network Conference.* Retrieved September 21, 2004, from www.brieftherapynetwork.com/wendelrayii.htm.

Mansager, E., & Eckstein, D. (2002). The Transformative Experience Questionnaire (TEQ): Spirituality in a couples context. *Family Journal: Counseling and Therapy for Couples and Families, 10,* 227–233.

Marks, L. (2004). Sacred practices in highly religious families: Christian, Jewish, Mormon, and Muslim perspectives. *Family Process, 43,* 217–231.

Marlatt, G. A. (1985). Relapse prevention: Theoretical rationale and overview of the model. In G. A. Marlatt & J. R. Gordon (Eds.), *Relapse prevention: Maintenance strategies on the treatment of addictive behaviors* (pp. 3–70). New York: Guilford Press.

Martin, P. (1976). *A marital therapy manual.* New York: Brunner/Mazel.

Maruyama, M. (1963). The second order cybernetics: Deviation amplifying mutual causal processes. *American Scientist, 51,* 164–179.

Mash, E. J. (1997). Treatment of child and family disturbance: A behavioral-systems approach. In E. J. Mash & R. A. Barkley. *Treatment of childhood disorder* (pp. 3–36). New York: Guilford Press.

Masters, W. H., & Johnson, V. E. (1966). *Human sexual response.* Philadelphia: Lippincott, Williams, & Wilkins.

Maturana, H. R., & Varela, F. J. (1992). *The tree of knowledge: The biological roots of human understanding* (Rev. edition). Boston: Shambhala.

May, K. (2003). Family therapy theory: What is important in the training of today's family counselors? *Family Journal: Counseling and Therapy for Couples and Families, 11,* 42–44.

May, R. (1969). *Love and will.* New York: Norton.

McGoldrick, M., & Carter, B. (2001). Advances in coaching: Family therapy with one person. *Journal of Marital and Family Therapy, 27,* 281–300.

McGoldrick, M., Gerson, R., & Shellenberger, S. (1999). *Genograms: Assessment and intervention.* New York: Norton.

McGoldrick, M., Giordano, J., & Pearce, J. K. (Eds.). (1996). *Ethnicity and family therapy* (2nd ed.). New York: Guilford Press.

McGoldrick, M., Pearce, J. K., & Giordano, J. (Eds.). (1982). *Ethnicity and family therapy.* New York: Guilford Press.

McGuire, L., & Kiecolt-Glaser, J. K. (2000). Interpersonal pathways to health. *Psychiatry, 63,* 136–139.

Mead, D. E., & Vatcher, G. M. (2001). Comprehensive areas of change questionnaire. In B. F. Perlmutter, J. Touliatos, & G. W. Holden (Eds.), *Handbook of family measurement techniques* (Vol. 3, pp. 122–129). Thousand Oaks, CA: Sage.

Mead, M. (1999). *Continuities in cultural evolution.* New Brumswick, NJ: Transaction Press. (Original work published 1964)

Mead, M. (2001). *Sex and temperament in three primitive societies.* New York: Perennial Currents. (Original work published 1935)

Miller, D. E., & Miller, A. M. (2000). Introduction: Understanding generation X. In R. W. Flory & D. E. Miller (Eds.), *Gen X religion* (pp. 1–12). New York: Routledge.

Miller, I. W., Kabacoff, R. I., Epstein, N. B., Bishop, D. S., Keitner, G. I., Baldwin, L. M., et al. (1994). The development of a clinical rating scale for the McMaster Model of Family Functioning. *Family Process, 33,* 53–69.

Minuchin, S. (1974). *Families and family therapy.* Cambridge, MA: Harvard University Press.

Minuchin, S. (2004). Foreword. In M. P. Nichols & R. C. Schwartz. *Family therapy: Concepts and methods* (6th ed., pp. xvii–xix). Boston: Allyn & Bacon.

Minuchin, S. (1998). Where is the family in narrative family therapy? *Journal of Marital and Family Therapy, 24,* 397–403.

Minuchin, S., & Fishman, H. C. (1981). *Family therapy techniques.* Cambridge, MA: Harvard University Press.

Minuchin, S., Montalvo, B., Guerney, B., Rosman, B., & Schumer, F. (1967). *Families of the slums.* New York: Basic Books.

Minuchin, S., Rosman, B., & Baker, L. (1978). *Psychosomatic families: Anorexia nervosa in context.* Cambridge, MA: Harvard University Press.

Mitchell, D. W. (2002). *Buddhism: Introducing the Buddhist experience.* New York: Oxford University Press.

Moen, P., Kim, J. E., & Hofmeister, H. (2001). Couples' work/retirement transitions, gender, and marital quality. *Social Psychology Quarterly, 64,* 55–71.

Monastersky, R. (2001, November 2). Land mines in the world of mental maps. *Chronicle of Higher Education,* A-20, A-21.

Monk, G., & Gehart, D. R. (2003). Sociopolitical activist or conversational partner? Distinguishing the position of the therapist in narrative and collaborative therapies. *Family Process, 42,* 19–30.

Moreno, J. L. (1945). *Psychodrama and the psychopathology of inter-personal relations.* New York: Beacon House.

Morrow, C. (1999). Family values/valued families: Storytelling and community formation among LBG families with children. *Journal of Gay, Lesbian, and Bisexual Identity, 4*(4), 345–356.

Moynihan, D. P., Smeeding, T. M., & Rainwater, L. (2004). *The future of the family.* New York: Russell Sage Foundation.

Napier, A. Y. (1971). The marriage of families: Cross-generational complementarity. *Family Process, 10,* 373–395.

Napier, A. Y., & Whitaker, C. A. (1978). *The family crucible.* New York: Harper & Row.

Narcotics Anonymous. (1991). *Narcotics anonymous.* Minneapolis: Hazelden Publishing and Educational Services.

Ng, K. S. (2005). The development of family therapy around the world. *Family Journal: Counseling and Therapy for Couples and Families, 13,* 35–42.

Nichols, M. P. (1987). *The self in the system: Expanding the limits of family therapy.* New York: Brunner/Mazel.

Nichols, M. P. (1999). *Inside family therapy: A case study in family healing.* Boston: Allyn & Bacon.

Nichols, M. P., & Fellenberg, S. (2000). The effective use of enactments in family therapy: A discovery-oriented process study. *Journal of Marital and Family Therapy, 26,* 143–152.

Nichols, M. P., & Schwartz, R. C. (2004). *Family therapy: Concepts and methods* (6th ed.). Boston: Pearson Allyn & Bacon.

Nichols, W. C. (1992). *The AAMFT: Fifty years of marital and family therapy.* Washington, DC: American Association for Marriage and Family Therapy.

Norrick, N. R. (1997). Twice-told tales: Collaborative narration of familiar stories. *Language in Society, 26,* 199–220.

Northey, W. F. (2004, November/December). Who are marriage and family therapists? *Family Therapy Magazine,* pp. 10–13.

Nowinski, J. K. (1999). *Family recovery and substance abuse: A twelve-step guide for treatment.* Thousand Oaks, CA: Sage.

O'Hanlon, W. H. (1993). Take two people and call them in the morning: Brief solution-oriented therapy with depression. In S. Freidman (Ed.), *The new language of change* (pp. 50–84). New York: Guilford Press.

Olson, D. H., & Gorall, D. M. (2003). Circumplex model of marital and family systems. In F. Walsh (Ed.), *Normal family processes* (3rd ed., pp. 514–548). New York: Guilford Press.

Olson, D. H., Gorall, D. M., & Teisel, J. (2002). *Family inventories package.* Minneapolis, MN: Life Innovations.

Oswald, R. F., Blume, L. B., & Marks, S. R. (2005). Decentering heteronormativity: A model for family studies. In V. L. Bengtson, A. C. Acock, K. R. Allen, P. Dilworth-Anderson, & D. M. Klein (Eds.), *Sourcebook of family theory and research* (pp. 143–165). Thousand Oaks, CA: Sage.

Panksepp, J. (2000). Emotions as natural kinds within the mammalian brain. In M. Lewis & J. M. Haviland-Jones (Eds.), *Handbook of emotions* (2nd ed., pp. 137–156). New York: Guilford Press.

Papp, P. (1980). The Greek chorus and other techniques of paradoxical therapy. *Family Process, 19,* 45–57.

Pare, D. A. (1995). Of families and other cultures: The shifting paradigm of family therapy. *Family Process, 34,* 1–19.

Pargament, K. I. (1997). *The psychology of religion and coping: Theory, research, and practice.* New York: Guilford Press.

Parker, L. (1998). The unequal bargain: Power issues in couples therapy. *Journal of Feminist Family Therapy, 10*(3), 17–38.

Parker, R. J., & Horton, H. S., Jr. (1996). A typology of ritual: Paradigms for healing and empowerment. *Counseling and Values, 40,* 82–97.

Parry, T. A. (1993). Without a net: Preparations for postmodern living. In S. Friedman (Ed.), *The new language of change: Constructive collaboration in psychotherapy* (pp. 428–459). New York: Guilford Press.

Parsons, T. (1951). *The social system.* Glencoe, IL: Free Press.

Parsons, T., & Bales, R. (1955). *Family, socialization and interaction process.* Glencoe, IL: Free Press.

Patterson, G. R. (1971). *Families: Applications of social learning to family life.* Champaign, IL: Research Press.

Patterson, G. R. (1976). *Living with children: New methods for parents and teachers.* Champaign, IL: Research Press.

Patterson, G. R. (1982). *Coercive family process*. Eugene, OR: Castalia.

Patterson, J., Hayworth, M., Turner, C., & Raskin, M. (2000). Spiritual issues in family therapy: A graduate-level course. *Journal of Marital and Family Therapy, 26*, 199–210.

Patterson, J., Williams, L., Grauf-Grounds, C., & Chamow, L. (1998). *Essential skills in family therapy: From the first interview to termination*. New York: Guilford Press.

Patterson, T. (1997). Theoretical unity and technical eclecticism: Pathways to coherence in family therapy. *American Journal of Family Therapy, 25*, 97–109.

Pearce, S. S. (1996). *Flash of insight: Metaphor and narrative in therapy*. Boston: Allyn & Bacon.

Pedersen, P. (2000). *Hidden messages in culture-centered counseling: A triad training model*. Thousand Oaks, CA: Sage.

Peele, S., & Brodsky, A. (1975). *Love and addiction*. New York: Signet.

Perlmutter, B. F., Touliatos, J., & Holden, G. W. (2001). *Handbook of family measurement techniques: Vol. 3. Instruments and index*. Thousand Oaks, CA: Sage.

Peterson, C. M. (2001). Multiple relationships. In R. H. Woody & J. D. Woody (Eds.), *Ethics in marriage and family therapy* (pp. 43–60). Washington, DC: American Association for Marriage and Family Therapy.

Philpot, C. L., & Brooks, G. (1995). Intergender communication and gender-sensitive family therapy. In R. H. Mikesell, D.-D. Lusterman, & S. H. McDaniel (Eds.), *Integrating family therapy: Handbook of family psychology and systems theory* (pp. 303–325). Washington, DC: American Psychological Association.

Piercy, F. P., Laird, R. A., & Mohammed, Z. (1983). A family therapist rating scale. *Journal of Marital and Family Therapy, 9*, 49–60.

Pinderhughes, E. (1989). *Understanding race, ethnicity, and power: The key to efficacy in clinical practice*. New York: Free Press.

Pinderhughes, E. (1990). Legacy of slavery: The experience of Black families in America. In M. P. Mirkin (Ed.), *The social and political contexts of family therapy* (pp. 289–305). Needham Heights, MA: Allyn & Bacon.

Pinsof, W. M. (1979). The Family Therapist Behavior Scale (FTBS): Development and evaluation of a coding system. *Family Process, 18*, 451–461.

Pinsof, W. M. (1992). Commentary: Culture and psychotherapy integration. *Family Process, 31*, 116–118.

Pinsof, W. M. (1995). *Integrative problem-centered therapy: A synthesis of family, individual, and biological therapies*. New York: Basic Books.

Piotrkowski, C. S., & Hughes, D. (1993). Dual-earner families in context: Managing family and work systems. In F. Walsh (Ed.), *Normal family processes* (2nd ed., pp. 185–207). New York: Guilford Press.

Pipher, M. D. (1994). *Reviving Ophelia: Saving the selves of adolescent girls*. New York: Putnam.

Pittman, F. (1989, January/February). Commentary: In L. Gordon, B. S. Duhl, F. J. Duhl, M. McGoldrick, F. Pittman, & M. Baldwin (Eds.), Remembering Virginia. *Family Therapy Networker*, 34–35.

Plaud, J., & Eifert, G. (Eds.). (1998). *Behavior theory to behavior therapy*. Boston: Allyn & Bacon.

Popenoe, D. (1989). *Disturbing the nest: Family change and decline in modern societies*. New York: Aldine de Gruyter.

Prest, L. A., & Keller, J. F. (1993). Spirituality and family therapy: Spiritual beliefs, myths, and metaphors. *Journal of Marital and Family Therapy, 19*, 137–148.

Price, J. A. (1988). How to stabilize families: A therapist's guide to maintaining the status quo. *Journal of Strategic and Systemic Therapies, 7*(4), 21–27.

Price, J. A. (1989, July/August). New divorce rituals. *Family Therapy Networker*, 45.

Price, J. A. (1994). The Tao in family therapy. *Journal of Systemic Therapies, 13*(3), 53–63.

Price, J. A. (1996). *Power and compassion: Working with difficult adolescents and abused parents*. New York: Guilford Press.

Prochaska, J. O. (1999). How do people change, and how can we change to help many more people. In M. A. Hubble, B. L. Duncan, & S. D. Miller (Eds.), *The heart and soul of change: What works in therapy* (pp. 227–255). Washington, DC: American Psychological Association.

Prochaska, J. O., & Norcross, J. C. (2002). *Systems of psychotherapy: A transtheoretical analysis* (5th ed.). Pacific Grove, CA: Brooks/Cole.

Prosky, P. S., & Keith, D. V. (2003). *Family therapy as an alternative to medication: An appraisal of pharmland*. New York: Brunner-Routledge.

Quinn, W. H., & Davidson, B. (1984). Prevalence of family therapy models: A research note. *Journal of Marital and Family Therapy, 10*, 393–398.

Quinn, W. H., Newfield, N. A., & Protinsky, H. O. (1985). Rites of passage in families with adolescents. *Family Process, 24*, 101–111.

Rabin, C. L. (2005). Gender and culture in the helping process: A professional journey. In C. L. Rabin (Ed.), *Understanding gender and culture in the helping process: Practitioners' narratives from global perspectives* (pp. 9–30). Belmont, CA: Thomson Wadsworth.

Ravich, R. A. (1969). The use of an interpersonal game-test in conjoint marital psychotherapy. *American Journal of Psychotherapy, 23*, 217–229.

Ray, W. A. (1992). Our future in the past: Lessons from Don Jackson for the practice of family therapy with hospitalized adolescents. *Family Therapy, 19*, 61–71.

Real, T. (2002). *How can I get through to you? Reconnecting men and women.* New York: Scribner.

Reihl-Emde, A., Thomas, V., & Willi, J. (2003). Love: An important dimension in marital research and therapy. *Family Process, 42*, 253–267.

Reiss, D. (1981). *The family's construction of reality.* Cambridge, MA: Harvard University Press.

Reiss, D., Plomin, R., Neiderhiser, J. M., & Hetherington, E. M. (2000). *The relationship code: Deciphering genetic and social influences on adolescent development.* Cambridge, MA: Harvard University Press.

Reiter, M. D. (2000). Utilizing the home environment in home-based family therapy. *Journal of Family Psychotherapy, 11*(3), 27–39.

Richards, P. S., & Bergin, A. E. (2000a). *A spiritual strategy for counseling and psychotherapy.* Washington, DC: American Psychological Association.

Richards, P. S., & Bergin, A. E. (2000b). Toward religious and spiritual competency for mental health professionals. In P. S. Richards & A. E. Bergin (Eds.), *Handbook of psychotherapy and religious diversity* (pp. 3–26). Washington, DC: American Psychological Association.

Richmond, M. E. (1917). *Social diagnosis.* New York: Russell Sage Foundation.

Ricoeur, P. (1996). Reflections on a new ethos for Europe. In P. Kearney (Ed.), *Paul Ricoeur: The hermeneutics of action* (pp. 3–13). Thousand Oaks, CA: Sage.

Ridenour, T. A., Daley, J. G., & Reich, W. (1999). Factor analyses of the family assessment device. *Family Process, 4*, 497–510.

Riesman, D. (2001). *The lonely crowd: A study of the changing American character* (Rev. ed.). New Haven, CT: Yale University Press. (Original work published 1950)

Rivett, M., & Street, E. (2001). Connections and themes of spirituality in family therapy. *Family Process, 40*, 459–467.

Robbins, M. S., Mayorga, C. C., & Szapocznik, J. (2003). The ecosystemic "lens" to understanding family functioning. In T. L. Sexton, G. R. Weeks, & M. S. Robbins (Eds.), *Handbook of family therapy: The science and practice of working with families and couples* (pp. 21–36). New York: Brunner-Routledge.

Roberts, J. (1994). *Tales and transformations: Stories in families and family therapy.* New York: Norton.

Robin, A. L., & Foster, S. L. (1989). *Negotiating parent-adolescent conflict: A behavioral-family systems approach.* New York: Guilford Press.

Robinson, T. L. (1999). The intersections of dominant discourses across race, gender, and other identities. *Journal of Counseling and Development, 77*, 73–79.

Rogers, C. R. (1957). The necessary and sufficient conditions of therapeutic personality change. *Journal of Consulting Psychology, 21*, 95–103.

Rogers, C. R. (1961). *On becoming a person: A therapist's view of psychotherapy.* New York: Houghton Mifflin.

Rogers, C. R. (1972). *Becoming partners: Marriage and its alternatives.* New York: Delacorte Press.

Rolland, J. S. (1994). *Families, illness, and disability: An integrative treatment model.* New York: Basic Books.

Ronfeldt, H. M., Kimerling, R., & Arias, I. (1998). Satisfaction with relationship power and the perpetration of dating violence. *Journal of Marriage and the Family, 60*, 70–78.

Roof, W. C. (2003). Religion and spirituality: Toward an integrated analysis. In M. Dillon (Ed.), *Handbook of the sociology of religion* (pp. 137–148). Cambridge, England: Cambridge University Press.

Rosen, A. (1996). Anxiety disorders as they impact on couples and families. In F. W. Kaslow (Ed.), *Handbook of relational diagnosis and dysfunctional family patterns* (pp. 239–250). New York: Wiley.

Rosenblatt, P. C. (1994). *Metaphors of family systems theory: Toward new constructions.* New York: Guilford Press.

Rosman, B. L. (1986). Developmental perspectives in family therapy with children. In H. C. Fishman & B. L. Rosman (Eds.), *Evolving models of family change* (pp. 227–233). New York: Guilford Press.

Ross, J. L. (1994). Working with patients within their religious contexts: Religion, spirituality, and the secular therapist. *Journal of Systemic Therapies, 13*(3), 7–15.

Ross, M. H., & Walker, B. K. (1979). *"On another day . . .": Tales told among the Nkundo of Zaire.* Hamden, CN: Archon Books.

Rossi, A. S. (1968). Transition to parenthood. *Journal of Marriage and the Family, 30*, 26–39.

Rothbaum, F., Rosen, K., Uhie, T., & Uchida, N. (2002). Family systems theory, attachment theory, and culture. *Family Process, 41*, 328–350.

Rotz, E., Russell, C., & Wright, D. W. (1993). The therapist who is perceived as "spiritually correct": Strategies for avoiding collusion with the "spiritually one-up" spouse. *Journal of Marital and Family Therapy, 19*, 369–375.

Russell, J. A. (1983). Pancultural apects of the human conceptual organization of emotion. *Journal of Personallity and Social Psychology, 45*, 1281–1288.

Russell, S., & Carey, M. (2002). Re-membering: Responding to commonly asked questions.

International Journal of Narrative Therapy and Community Work, 3, 23–31.

Ryder, R. G., & Bartle, S. (1991). Boundaries as distance regulators in personal relationships. *Family Process, 30,* 393–406.

Sacks, K. B. (1994). How Jews became White. In S. Gregory & R. Sanjek (Eds.), *Race* (pp. 78–102). New Brunswick, NJ: Rutgers University Press.

Salovey, P., Bedell, B. T., Detweiler, J. B., & Mayer, J. D. (2000). Current directions in emotional intelligence research. In M. Lewis & J. M. Haviland-Jones (Eds.), *Handbook of emotions* (2nd ed., pp. 504–520). New York: Guilford Press.

Sampson, E. E. (1993). *Celebrating the other: A dialogic account of human nature.* San Francisco: Westview Press.

Sarbin, T. R. (Ed.). (1986). *Narrative psychology: The storied nature of human conduct.* New York: Praeger.

Satir, V. (1967). *Conjoint family therapy.* Palo Alto, CA: Science and Behavior Books.

Satir, V. (1972). *Peoplemaking.* Palo Alto, CA: Science and Behavior Books.

Satir, V., & Bitter, J. (2000). The therapist and family therapy: Satir's human validation process model. In A. M. Horne (Ed.), *Family counseling and therapy* (3rd ed., pp. 62–101). Itasca, IL: Peacock Press.

Sayger, T. V., & Horne, A. M. (2000). Common elements in family therapy theory and strategies. In A. M. Horne (Ed.), *Family counseling and therapy* (3rd ed., pp. 41–61). Itasca, IL: Peacock Press.

Schachter, S., & Singer, J. E. (1962). Cognitive, social and physiological determinants of emotional state. *Psychological Review, 69,* 379–399.

Schaef, A. W. (1986). *Codependence: Misunderstood—Mistreated.* San Francisco: Harper & Row.

Scharff, D. E., & Scharff, J. S. (1987). *Object relations family therapy.* Northvale, NJ: Aronson.

Scharff, J. S., & Bagnini, C. (2002). Object relations couple therapy. In N. S. Jacobson & A. S. Gurman (Eds.), *Clinical handbook of couple therapy* (3rd ed., pp. 59–85). New York: Guilford Press.

Scharff, J. S., & de Varela, Y. (2000). Object relations therapy. In F. M. Dattilio & L. J Bevilacqua (Eds.), *Comparative treatments for relationship dysfunction* (pp. 81–101). New York: Springer.

Scheflen, A. E. (1978). Susan smiled: On explanation in family therapy. *Family Process, 17,* 59–68.

Schnarch, D. M. (1991). *Constructing the sexual crucible: An integration of sexual and marital therapy.* New York: Norton.

Schneider, E. C. (1992). *In the web of class: Delinquents and reformers in Boston, 1810s–1930s.* New York: New York University Press.

Schulman, G. L. (1999). Siblings revisited: Old conflicts and new opportunities in later life. *Journal of Marital and Family Therapy, 25,* 517–524.

Schwartz, R. C., & Johnson, S. M. (2000). Commentary: Does couple and family therapy have emotional intelligence? *Family Process, 39,* 29–33.

Selman, R. L., & Demorest, A. P. (1984). Observing troubled children's interpersonal negotiation strategies: Implications of and for a developmental model. *Child Development, 55,* 288–304.

Selvini-Palazzoli, M., Boscolo, L., Cecchin, G., & Prata, G. (1978). *Paradox and counterparadox: A new model in the therapy of the family in schizophrenic transaction.* Northvale, NJ: Aronson.

Selvini-Palazzoli, M., Boscolo, L., Cecchin, G., & Prata, G. (1980). Hypothesizing-circularity-neutrality: Three guidelines for the conductor of the session. *Family Process, 19,* 3–12.

Semans, M. P. (2000). Dissecting life with a Jewish scalpel: A qualitative analysis of Jewish-centered family life. *Family Process, 39,* 121–139.

Semans, M. P., & Stone Fish, L. (2000). Dissecting life with a Jewish scalpel: A qualitative analysis of Jewish-centered family life. *Family Process, 39,* 121–139.

Sexton, T. L., Robbins, M. S., Hollimon, A. S., Mease, A. L., & Mayorga, C. C. (2003). Efficacy, effectiveness, and change mechanisms in couple and family therapy. In T. L. Sexton, G. R. Weeks, & M. S. Robbins (Eds.), *Handbook of family therapy: The science and practice of working with families and couples* (pp. 229–261). New York: Brunner-Routledge.

Shaver, P., Hazan, C., & Bradshaw, D. (1988). Love as attachment: The integration of three behavioral systems. In R. J. Sternberg & M. L. Barnes (Eds.), *The psychology of love* (pp. 68–99). New Haven, CT: Yale.

Shawver, L. (1998). Postmodernizing the unconscious. *American Journal of Psychoanalysis, 58*(4), 329–336.

Sheehy, G. (1976). *Passages: Predictable crises of adult life.* New York: Dutton.

Sheidow, A. J., Henggeler, S. W., & Schoenwald, S. K. (2003). Multisystemic therapy. In T. L. Sexton, G. R. Weeks, & M. S. Robbins (Eds.), *Handbook of family therapy: The science and practice of working with families and couples* (pp. 303–322). New York: Brunner-Routledge.

Shields, C. G. (1986). Critiquing the new epistemologies: Toward minimum requirements for a scientific theory of family therapy. *Journal of Marital and Family Therapy, 12,* 359–372.

Shoemaker, M. E., & Paulson, T. L. (1976). Group assertive training for mothers: A family intervention strategy. In E. J. Mash, L. C. Handy, & L. A. Hamerlynck (Eds.), *Behavior modification approaches to parenting.* New York: Brunner/Mazel.

Shreve, A. (1990). *Women together, women alone: The legacy of the consciousness-raising movement.* New York: Ballantine Books.

Siegel, S., & Walker, G. (1996). Connections: Conversations between a gay therapist and a straight therapist. In J. Laird & R.-J. Green (Eds.), *Lesbians and gays in couples and families: A handbook for therapists* (pp. 28–68). San Francisco: Jossey-Bass.

Simmel, G. (1955). *Conflict and the web of group affiliations.* New York: Free Press.

Simon, G. M. (1992). Having a second-order mind while doing first-order therapy. *Journal of Marital and Family Therapy, 18,* 377–387.

Simon, G. M. (1995). A revisionist rendering of structural family therapy. *Journal of Marital and Family Therapy, 21,* 17–26.

Skinner, B. F. (1953). *Science and human behavior.* New York: Appleton-Century-Crofts.

Skinner, B. F. (1971). *Beyond freedom and dignity.* New York: Vintage.

Skinner, B. F. (1976). *Walden Two.* Upper Saddle River, NJ: Prentice-Hall.

Sklare, G. (2000). Solution-focused brief counseling strategies. In J. Carlson & L. Sperry (Ed.), *Brief therapy with individuals and couples* (pp. 437–468). Phoenix, AZ: Zeig, Tucker and Theisen.

Sloman, L., Atkinson, L., Milligan, K., & Liotti, G. (2002). Attachment, social rank, and affect regulation: Speculations on an ethological approach to family interaction. *Family Process, 41,* 313–327.

Snyder, D. K., & Aikman, G. (1999). Marital satisfaction inventory (Rev. ed.). In M. Maruish (Ed.), *Use of psychological testing for treatment planning and outcome assessment* (2nd ed., pp. 1173–1210). Hillsdale, NJ: Erlbaum and Associates.

Snyder, D. K., & Schneider, W. J. (2002). Affective reconstruction: A pluralistic, developmental approach. In A. S. Gurman & N. S. Jacobson (Eds.), *Clinical handbook of couple therapy* (3rd ed., pp. 151–179). New York: Guilford Press.

Snyder, M. (2002). Applications of Carl Rogers' theory and practice to couple and family therapy: A response to Harlene Anderson and David Bott. *Journal of Family Therapy, 24,* 317–325.

Solomon, J., & George, C. (Eds.). (1999). *Attachment disorganization.* New York: Guilford Press.

Spence, D. P. (1986). Narrative smoothing and clinical wisdom. In T. R. Sarbin (Ed.), *Narrative psychology: The storied nature of human conduct* (pp. 211–232). New York: Praeger.

Sperry, L., & Carlson, J. (1991). *Marital therapy: Integrating theory and practice.* Denver, CO: Love.

Sperry, L. (Ed.). (2004). *Assessment of couples and families: Contemporary and cutting edge strategies.* New York: Brunner-Routledge.

Spock, B. (1945). *The common sense book of baby and child care.* New York: Duell, Sloan, & Pearce.

Sprenkle, D. H., Blow, A. J., & Dickey, M. H. (1999). Common factors and other nontechnique variables in marriage and family therapy. In M. A. Hubble, B. L. Duncan, & S. D. Miller (Eds.), *The heart and soul of change: What works in therapy* (pp. 329–359). Washington, DC: American Psychological Association.

Sprey, J. (1971). On the management of conflict in families. *Journal of Marriage and the Family, 33,* 722–731.

Sprey, J. (1969). The family as a system in conflict. *Journal of Marriage and the Family, 31,* 699–706.

Stacey, J. (1996). *In the name of the family: Rethinking family values in the postmodern age.* Boston: Beacon Press.

Stahmann, R. F., & Hiebert, W. J. (1997). *Premarital and remarital counseling: The professional's handbook.* San Francisco: Jossey-Bass.

Stander, V., Piercy, F. P., Mackinnon, D., & Helmeke, K. (1994). Spirituality, religion and family therapy: Competing or complementary worlds? *American Journal of Family Therapy, 22,* 27–41.

Stanley, S. (1998). *The heart of commitment.* Nashville, TN: Thomas Nelson.

Stanton, M. D. (1981). An integrated structural/strategic approach to family therapy. *Journal of Marital and Family Therapy, 7,* 427–439.

Stanton, M. D. (1992). The time line and the "why now?" question: A technique and rationale for therapy, training, organizational consultation and research. *Journal of Marital and Family Therapy, 18,* 333–343.

Stanton, M. D., Todd, T. C., & Associates. (1982). *The family therapy of drug abuse and addiction.* New York: Guilford Press.

Staske, S. A. (1996). Talking feelings: The collaborative construction of emotion in talk between close relational partners. *Symbolic Interaction, 19*(2), 111–135.

Steinglass, P. (1991). Editorial. *Family Process, 30,* 267–269.

Steinglass, P., Bennett, L., Wolin, S. J., & Reiss, D. (1987). *The alcoholic family.* New York: Basic Books.

Sternberg, R. J. (1999). *Love is a story: A new theory of relationships.* New York: Oxford University Press.

Stevenson, H. C. (1994). Racial socialization in African American families: The art of balancing intolerance and survival. *Family Journal: Counseling and Therapy for Couples and Families, 2,* 190–198.

Stewart, S. P., & Gale, J. E. (1994). On hallowed ground: Marital therapy with couples on the religious right. *Journal of Systemic Therapies, 13*(3), 16–25.

Stolk, Y., & Perlesz, A. J. (1990). Do better trainees make worse family therapists? A followup study of client families. *Family Process, 29,* 45–58.

Stone Fish, L. (2000). Hierarchical relationship development: Parents and children. *Journal of Marital and Family Therapy, 26,* 501–510.

Stone Fish, L., & Piercy, F. P. (1987). The theory and practice of structural and strategic family therapies: A delphi study. *Journal of Marital and Family Therapy, 13,* 113–125.

Stuart, R. B. (1980). *Helping couples change: A social learning approach to marital therapy.* New York: Guilford Press.

Sullivan, H. S. (1938). Psychiatry: Introduction to the Study of Interpersonal Relations. *Psychiatry, 1*(1), 121–134.

Swanson, G. E. (1993). The structuring of family decision-making: Personal and societal sources and some consequences for children. In P. A. Cowan, D. Fields, D. A. Hanson, A. Skolnick, & G. E. Swanson (Eds.), *Family, self, and society: Toward a new agenda for family research* (pp. 235–263). Hillsdale, NJ: Erlbaum.

Szapocznik, J., Foote, F. H., Perez-Vidal, A., Hervis, O., & Kurtines, W. M. (1989). One person family therapy: The Alfaro family. In J. Szapocznik & W. M. Kurtines (Eds.), *Breakthroughs in family therapy with drug abusing and problem youth* (pp. 130–158). New York: Springer.

Tannen, D. (1985). Cross-cultural communication. In T. A. Van Dijk (Ed.), *Handbook of discourse analysis: Vol. 4. Discourse analysis in society* (pp. 203–215). London: Academic Press.

Tannen, D. (1991). *You just don't understand: Women and men in conversation.* New York: Ballantine Books.

Tarvydas, V. M., Cottone, R. R., & Claus, R. E. (2003). Ethical decision-making processes. In R. R. Cotone & V. M. Tarvydas. *Ethical and professional issues in counseling* (2nd ed., pp. 82–108). Upper Saddle River, NJ: Merrill-Prentice Hall.

Thorgren, J. M., & Christensen, T. M. (1999). An interview with David Schnarch. *Family Journal: Counseling and Therapy for Couples and Families, 7,* 187–194.

Thomas, V., & Olson, D. H. (1993). Problem families and the circumplex model: Observational assessment using the Clinical Rating Scale (CRS). *Journal of Marital and Family Therapy, 19,* 159–175.

Thurston, N. S. (2000). Psychotherapy with evangelical and fundamentalist protestants. In P. S Richards &

A. E. Bergin (Eds.), *Handbook of psychotherapy and religious diversity* (pp. 131–153). Washington, DC: American Psychological Association.

Todd, T. C. (1984). Strategic approaches to marital stuckness. *Journal of Marital and Family Therapy, 10,* 373–379.

Toffler, A. (1984). *Future shock.* New York: Bantam Books.

Tomm, K. (1988). Interventive interviewing: Part 3. *Family Process, 27,* 1–15.

Treadway, D. (1989). *Before it's too late: Working with substance abuse in the family.* New York: Norton.

Treadway, D. C. (2004). *Intimacy, change, and other therapeutic mysteries.* New York: Guilford Press.

Trujullo, A. (2000). Psychotherapy with Native Americans: A view into the role of religion and spirituality. In P. S. Richards & A. E. Bergin (Eds.), *Handbook of psychotherapy and religious diversity* (pp. 445–466). Washington, DC: American Psychological Association.

Turner, J. H. (2000). *On the origins of human emotions.* Stanford, CA: Stanford University Press.

Updike, J. (1960). *Rabbit, run.* New York: Alfred Knopf.

U.S. Bureau of the Census. (2004). *Table MS–1: Marital status of the population 15 years old and over, by sex and race: 1950 to present.* Retrieved October 28, 2005, from http://www.census.gov/population/www/socdemo/hh-fam.html.

U.S. Office of Immigration Statistics. (2004). *2003 yearbook of immigration statistics.* Retrieved October 28, 2005, from http://uscis.gov/graphics/shared/statistics/yearbook/2003/2003Yearbook.pdf.

Van Amberg, S. M., Barber, C. E., & Zimmerman, T. S. (1996). Aging and family therapy: Prevalence of aging issues and later family life concerns in marital and family therapy literature (1986–1993). *Journal of Marital and Family Therapy, 22,* 195–203.

Varela, F. (1984). The creative circle: Sketches on the natural history of circularity. In P. Watzlawick (Ed.), *The invented reality* (pp. 309–323). New York: Norton.

Vatcher, C.-A., & Bogo, M. (2001). The feminist/emotionally focused therapy practice model: An integrated approach for couple therapy. *Journal of Marital and Family Therapy, 27,* 69–83.

Ventura, S. J., Abma, J. C., Mosher, W. D., & Henshaw, S. (2003). Revised pregnancy rates, 1990–1997, and new rates for 1998–1999: United States. *National Vital Statistics Reports, 52*(7), 1–16.

Vesper, J. H. (1991). *Ethics, legalities, and professional practice issues in marital and family therapy.* Boston: Allyn & Bacon.

Visher, E. B., & Visher, J. S. (1996). *Therapy with stepfamilies.* New York: Brunner/Mazel.

von Bertalanffy, L. (1967). *Robots, men, and minds: Psychology in the modern world.* New York: George Braziller.

von Bertalanffy, L. (1975). The history and development of general system theory. In E. Taschdjian (Ed.), *Perspectives on general system theory: Scientific-philosophical studies by Ludwig vom Bertalanffy* (pp. 149–169). New York: George Braziller.

Von Denffer, A. (1994). *Ulūm al-Qurʾān An introduction to the sciences of the Qurʾān*(Rev. ed.). Leicester, England: Millat Book Centre.

Von Foerster, H. (1984). On constructing a reality. In P. Watzlawick (Ed.), *The invented reality* (pp. 41–61). New York: Norton.

von Glasersfeld, E. (1984). An introduction to radical constructivism. In P. Watzlawick (Ed.), *The invented reality* (pp. 17–40). New York: Norton.

Wachtel, E. E. (1994). *Treating troubled children and their families.* New York: Guilford Press.

Waldegrave, C., Tamasese, K., Tuhuka, F., & Campbell, W. (2003). *Just therapy—A journey.* Adelaide, South Australia: Dulwich Centre Publications.

Walsh, F. (1998). *Strengthening family resilience.* New York: Guilford Press.

Walsh, F. (1999a). Opening family therapy to spirituality. In F. Walsh (Ed.), *Spiritual resources in family therapy* (pp. 28–58). New York: Guilford Press.

Walsh, F. (1999b). Religion and spirituality: Wellsprings for healing and resilience. In F. Walsh (Ed.), *Spiritual resources in family therapy* (pp. 3–27). New York: Guilford Press.

Walsh, F. (Ed.). (2003). *Normal family processes.* New York: Guilford Press.

Walters, M., Carter, B., Papp, P., & Silverstein, O. (1988). *The invisible web: Gender patterns in family relationships.* New York: Guilford Press.

Watson, J. B. (1928). *Psychological care of infant and child.* New York: Norton.

Watzlawick, P. (1982). *The tactics of change: Doing therapy briefly.* San Francisco: Jossey-Bass.

Watzlawick, P., Beavin, J. H., & Jackson, D. D. (1967). *Pragmatics of human communication: A study of interactional patterns, pathologies, and paradoxes.* New York: Norton.

Watzlawick, P., Weakland, J., & Fisch, R. (1974). *Change: Principles of problem formation and problem resolution.* New York: Norton.

Weakland, J., Johnson, L. D., & Morrissette, P. (1995). Brief strategic psychotherapy consultation: The Mental Research Institute Model. *Journal of Systemic Therapies, 14,* 46–60.

Weaver, A. J., Samford, J. A., Morgan, V. J., Larson, D. B., Koenig, H. G., & Flannelly, K. J. (2002). A systematic review of research on religion in six primary marriage and family journals 1995–1999. *American Journal of Family Therapy, 30,* 293–309.

Webster-Stratton, C., & Herbert, M. (1994). *Troubled families: Problem children.* New York: Wiley.

Wegscheider, S. (1981). *Another chance: Hope and health for the alcoholic family.* Palo Alto, CA: Science and Behavior Books.

Weigel, D. J., & Murray, C. (2000). The paradox of stability and change in relationships: What does chaos theory offer for the study of romantic relationships? *Journal of Social and Personal Relationships, 17,* 425–449.

Weiner-Davis, M. (1992). *Divorce busting: A revolutionary and rapid program for "staying together."* New York: Summit Books.

Weingarten, H., & Leas, S. (1987). Levels of marital conflict model: A guide to assessment and intervention in troubled marriages. *American Journal of Orthopsychiatry, 57,* 407–417.

Weingarten, K. (2001). *Making sense of illness narratives: Braiding theory, practice and the embodied life.* Retrieved October 17, 2004 from http://www.dulwichcentre.com.au/kaethearticle.html.

Wendel, R. D. (2003). Lived religion and family therapy: What does spirituality have to do with it? *Family Process, 42,* 164–180.

Wendt, R. N., & Ellenwood, A. E. (1994). From impotence to activation: Conjoint systemic change in the family and school. In M. Andolfi & R. Haber (Eds.), *Please help me with this family: Using consultants as resources in family therapy* (pp. 219–233). New York: Brunner/Mazel.

West, C., & Zimmerman, D. (1987). Doing gender. *Gender and Society, 1,* 125–151.

West, W. (2000). *Psychotherapy and spirituality: Crossing the line between therapy and religion.* London: Sage.

Whiffin, R., & Byng-Hall, J. (Eds.). (1982). *Family therapy supervision: Recent developments in practice.* New York: Grune & Stratton.

Whitaker, C. A., & Bumberry, W. M. (1988). *Dancing with the family: A symbolic-experiential approach.* New York: Brunner/Mazel.

White, G. M. (2000). Representing emotional meaning: Category, metaphor, schema, discourse. In M. Lewis & J. M. Haviland-Jones (Eds.), *Handbook of emotions* (2nd ed., pp. 30–44). New York: Guilford Press.

White, J. M. (1991). *Dynamics of family development.* New York: Guilford Press.

White, M. (1986). Negative explanation, restraint, and double description: A template for family therapy. *Family Process, 25,* 169–184.

White, M. (1995). Reflecting teamwork as definitional ceremony. In M. White (Ed.), *Re-authoring lives: Interviews and essays* (pp. 172–198). Adelaide, South Australia: Dulwich Centre Publications.

White, M. (1997). *Narratives of therapists' lives.* Adelaide, South Australia: Dulwich Centre Publications.

White, M. (2002). Addressing personal failure. *International Journal of Narrative and Community Work, 3,* 33–76.

White, M., & Epston, D. (1990). *Narrative means to therapeutic ends.* New York: Norton.

Whiteside, M. F. (1989). Remarried systems. In L. Combrinck-Graham (Ed.), *Children in family contexts: Perspectives on treatment* (pp. 135–160). New York: Guilford Press.

Wiener, N. (1961). *Cybernetics: Or control and communication in the animal and the machine.* Cambridge, MA: MIT Press.

Wile, D. (1993). *After the fight: A night in the life of a couple.* New York: Guilford Press.

Wile, D. B. (1994). The ego-analytic approach to emotion in couples therapy. In S. M. Johnson & L. S. Greenberg (Eds.), *The heart of the matter: Perspectives on emotion in marital therapy* (pp. 27–45). New York: Brunner/Mazel.

Wile, D. B. (2002). Collaborative couple therapy. In A. S. Gurman & N. S. Jacobson (Eds.), *Clinical handbook of couple therapy* (3rd ed., pp. 281–307). New York: Guilford Press.

Wilson, E. O. (1988). *On human nature.* Cambridge, MA: Harvard University Press.

Wittgenstein, L. (1976). *Philosophical investigations* (G. E. M. Anscombe, Trans., 3rd ed.). New York: Macmillan.

Wolin, S. J., Muller, W., Taylor, F., & Wolin, S. (1999). Three spiritual perspectives on resilience: Buddhism, Christianity, and Judaism. In F. Walsh (Ed.), *Spiritual resources in family therapy.* New York: Guilford.

Wolpe, J. (1970). *The practice of behavior therapy.* Des Moines, IA: Allyn & Bacon.

Woody, R. H., & Woody, J. D. (2001a). Ethics, professionalism, and decision making. In R. H. Woody & J. D. Woody (Eds.), *Ethics in marriage and family therapy* (pp. 1–11). Washington, DC: American Association for Marriage and Family Therapy.

Woody, R. H., & Woody, J. D. (2001b). The future of marriage and family therapy. In R. H. Woody & J. D. Woody (Eds.), *Ethics in marriage and family therapy* (pp. 197–217). Washington, DC: American Association for Marriage and Family Therapy.

Wozniak, R. H. (Ed.). (1994). *Reflex, habit and implicit response: The early elaboration of theoretical and methodological behaviourism 1915–1928.* London: Routledge/Thoemmes.

Wright, L. M. (1999). Spirituality, suffering, and beliefs: The soul of healing with families. In F. Walsh (Ed.), *Spiritual resources in family therapy* (pp. 61–75). New York: Guilford Press.

Wylie, P. (1942). *Generation of vipers.* New York: Rinehart.

Wynne, L. (1998). Foreword. In L. C. Yingling, W. E. Miller, A. L. McDonald, & S. T. Galewaler (Eds.), *GARF Assessment sourcebook: Using the DSM-IV Global Assessment of Relational Functioning* (pp. vii–viii). New York: Brunner/Mazel.

Yingling, L. C., Miller, W. E., McDonald, A. L., & Galewaler, S. T. (1998). *GARF Assessment sourcebook: Using the DSM-IV Global Assessment of Relational Functioning.* New York: Brunner/Mazel.

Zimmerman, J. L., & Dickerson, V. C. (1993). Separating couples from restraining patterns and the relationship discourse that supports them. *Journal of Marital and Family Therapy, 19,* 403–413.

Zygmond, M. J., & Boorhem, H. (1989). Ethical decision making in family therapy. *Family Process, 28,* 269–280.

Zuk, G. H. (1988). The conflict cycle in families and therapy. *Contemporary Family Therapy, 10,* 145–153.

Name Index

Subject Index

A

Abstinence, 256, 282, 294, 322
Acceptance, 90, 132, 166, 190
Accounts, 185, 191, 236, 281
Active listening, 9, 157, 192
Adolescents:
  communication with parents, 238, 240, 241
  culture, 151
  developmental transitions, 112, 143, 202, 225
  identities, 151–152, 199
  sexuality, pregnancy and parenthood, 159, 199
  social experience, 151
  stereotypes, 197
  unsupervised, 79
Adult attachment styles, 217, 243
African Americans, 98, 262, 307
Alcoholics Anonymous (AA), 190, 203, 204, 259, 267
Alcohol and other drugs, 20, 113, 162, 204, 227, 279
Alliance for the Mentally Ill, 26
Altered states, 258
Alternative:
  discourses, 187
  readings, 191
  spiritualities, 252
  stories, 205, 206
American Association for Marriage and Family
    Therapy (AAMFT), 25, 26, 28, 302, 304, 310
  Code of Ethics, 355
American Counseling Association (ACA), 25–27, 82,
    302–304
  Code of Ethics, 331
American Family Therapy Academy (AFTA), 26
American Orthopsychiatric Association, 26
Analog messages, 156
Anger, 115, 119, 225, 227, 235, 238
Anxious/ambivalent attachment style, 217
Areas of Change Questionnaire, 126
Assertiveness, 112, 132, 293
Assessment:
  dynamic, 170, 171, 262, 314
  effectiveness, 268

instruments, 338, 339, 349, 358
methods, 315, 349, 358
process, 101, 120, 122, 126, 171, 173, 196, 200, 202
Assumptions, 17, 58–59, 85, 200
Attachment:
  adult, 217, 243
  theory, 216, 218, 222, 234
Attachment behavioral control system, 216
Attention-Deficit/Hyperactivity Disorder (ADHD), 53,
    113, 114, 205
Attributions, 95, 123, 124, 180, 185, 190, 196, 198,
    200, 206, 227, 250
Autonomy, 16, 217, 227, 298, 300, 301, 314
Autopoesis, 85, 167
Avoidant attachment style, 217, 218

B

Baby boom, 54
Balanced empathy, 12
Baseline, 116, 119, 126, 137, 174
Basic communication skills, 112, 279
Behavior, 109–140
Behavioral:
  analysis, 113, 134
  approaches, 47, 90, 130, 138, 139
  assessment, 120, 123
  genetics, 91
  interventions, 109, 119, 126, 129, 130, 133, 136
  theory, 113
Belief systems, 12, 249, 252, 253, 262, 265, 266
Beliefs, attitudes, and discourses, 129
Beneficence, 298
Binaries, 187, 199
Binuclear family, 160
Blaming, 66
Blended families, 154
Blocking previous patterns, 175
BONES, 100, 101, 106, 109, 141, 142, 168, 179, 211,
    245, 261, 275, 278, 285, 292
Boundaries, 80, 166, 177